Handbook on Employment and the Elderly

HANDBOOK ON EMPLOYMENT AND THE ELDERLY

EDITED BY *William H. Crown*

Greenwood Press
Westport, Connecticut • London

Library of Congress Cataloging-in-Publication Data

Handbook on employment and the elderly / edited by William H. Crown.
    p.   cm.
    Includes bibliographical references and index.
    ISBN 0–313–28598–5 (alk. paper)
    1. Aged—Employment—Government policy—United States. 2. Aged—
Employment—United States—History. 3. Age discrimination in
employment—United States. 4. Employee fringe benefits—United
States—Costs. 5. Retirement—United States. 6. Social security—
United States. I. Crown, William H.
    HD6280.H36   1996
    331.3'98—dc20   95–42916

British Library Cataloguing in Publication Data is available.

Library of Congress Catalog Card Number: 95–42916
ISBN: 0–313–28598–5

First published in 1996

Greenwood Press, 88 Post Road West, Westport, CT 06881
An imprint of Greenwood Publishing Group, Inc.

Printed in the United States of America

The paper used in this book complies with the
Permanent Paper Standard issued by the National
Information Standards Organization (Z39.48–1984).

10 9 8 7 6 5 4 3 2 1

Contents

1. The Growing Interest in Older Worker Employment Policy   1
    William H. Crown, Yung-Ping Chen, and
    Richard W. McConaghy

2. Labor Force Characteristics of Older Americans   15
    Thomas Leavitt

3. Demographic Trends and the Future of Older Workers   57
    Eric R. Kingson

4. Historical Trends in the Employment and Labor Force
    Participation of Older Americans   81
    Christopher J. Ruhm

5. Older Women Workers   103
    Regina O'Grady-LeShane

6. Social Security, Pensions, Disability, and Retirement:
    An International Perspective   110
    Stuart Dorsey and John A. Turner

7. Retirement before Social Security   128
    W. Andrew Achenbaum

8. Social Security Wealth and Labor Supply Incentives   144
    Barry L. Friedman

9. Pensions and Retirement   165
    John A. Turner and Tabitha Doescher

10. Early Retirement Incentive Programs (ERIPs): Mechanisms for
    Encouraging Early Retirement   182
    Phyllis H. Mutschler

11. Age Discrimination in Employment: Economic and Legal
    Perspectives   194
    Steven H. Sandell and Marc Rosenblum

12. Economic Model of Work–Leisure Choice   213
    Michael V. Leonesio

13. Social Gerontological Models of Retirement and Employment
    of Older Persons   249
    Robert M. Whaples and Charles F. Longino, Jr.

14. Theoretical Perspectives on Productive Aging   262
    Scott A. Bass and Francis G. Caro

15. The Productivity and Functional Limitations of Older Adult
    Workers   276
    Anthony A. Sterns, Harvey L. Sterns, and Lisa A. Hollis

16. Investing in the Future: What Role for Older Worker Training? 304
    Sara E. Rix

17. The Costs and Benefits of Older Workers   324
    Michael C. Barth, William McNaught, and Philip Rizzi

18. The Economics of Occupational Labor Shortages   349
    Burt S. Barnow

19. Impacts of an Aging Workforce on Productivity and Economic
    Growth   374
    William J. Serow

20. The Political Context of Older Worker Employment Policy   391
    William H. Crown

References   405

Index   441

About the Contributors   447

*Handbook on Employment
and the Elderly*

The Growing Interest in Older Worker Employment Policy

William H. Crown, Yung-Ping Chen, and
Richard W. McConaghy

Many reasons explain the growing interest in employment policy for older persons; most of these reasons are economic in nature, stemming from population aging. Population aging has raised concerns about the ability of society to finance social security, private pensions, and health care for older Americans. In addition, projections of slower growth in the labor force resulting from population aging have led to concerns about labor force shortages in the future. Labor shortages have implications for future economic growth which, in turn, affects the ability of society to afford retirement benefits. Finally, researchers and policy makers have observed for many years that older persons who work are much less likely to be impoverished than those who do not.

Other concerns also explain the increased interest in policy on older workers. For decades, sociologists and psychologists have examined the noneconomic benefits of work to individuals, especially the continued opportunity for social interaction and feelings of self-worth that stem from being a "productive" member of society. More recently, researchers have begun to expand the definition of what it means to be a productive member of society beyond formal labor force participation. The broader definition of productive aging includes volunteer activities and caregiving roles in which older persons often participate.

It is critical that policy makers keep this broader definition of productive aging in mind when developing employment policies for older Americans because of the potential trade-offs involved in encouraging increased labor force participation on the part of older persons. In particular, policies to encourage increased labor force participation of the elderly may reduce their ability to fulfill other roles such as caring for their grandchildren or volunteering their services at community organizations.

Ironically, although we know a great deal about the determinants of retirement, we know remarkably little about older workers and what motivates them to remain in the labor force. Are these motivations necessarily the mirror image of those that induce older workers to retire? Probably they are not. We know that older workers tend to be healthier and better educated than those who chose to retire. People with higher educations are likely to have better, higher-paying jobs than people with poorer educations. It is well known that health status is positively correlated with economic status. Thus, it is not surprising that those who remain in the labor force tend to be healthier and better educated than those who leave.

Clearly, however, the picture is more complicated than this. We know that many healthy, highly educated older workers in well-paying jobs choose to retire. Perhaps this is because of complicated trade-offs between the gains from another year of earnings versus opting for pension benefits. However, workers do not always choose to retire at the point where their pension wealth is maximized—they also trade off the wealth effects of work and of retirement with other uses of their time. Moreover, some individuals may leave the labor force with the expectation to reenter it in another job. However, contrary to their expectations, they may find that the anticipated work opportunities do not exist (or they may have inadequate training for opportunities that are available). Others may simply prefer pursuing nonwork activities such as caring for grandchildren, volunteering, or pursuing "nonproductive" activities such as travel, golf, or fishing.

In short, there are many reasons why older persons choose to continue working or to retire. As a result, policies designed to influence economic incentives related to retirement, such as changes to social security and private pension provisions, might not have the intended effect of "encouraging" increased labor supply by older persons. Although most older workers choose to retire at least partly as a result of financial considerations, changes to social security and private pension provision may not change the economic implications of retirement enough to alter their retirement decisions. Moreover, a significant minority of older workers retire as a result of health limitations. Policies that "encourage" the increased labor force participation of older persons (such as raising the normal retirement age for social security benefits) may inflict financial penalties on those with health limitations even though the decision to leave work is beyond their control.

OBJECTIVES OF THE BOOK

This book presents a wide range of information relevant to the development of employment policies and programs for older persons. In contrast to the extensive literature on retirement, the literature on the employment of older persons is comparatively small—although growing rapidly. Nevertheless, there is no reference work that summarizes in one volume the available literature on employment policy for older workers. Recent research on the economics of aging has demonstrated that retirement patterns are much more complex than previously realized. For example, more than a third of all ''retired'' persons work at least part time for a period after they leave their longest job. This suggests that the concepts of employment and retirement need to be viewed as a continuum.

Summarizing the literature on employment policy for older persons is not an easy task. One reason for the difficulty is the need to take account of the various perspectives from which employment policy can be viewed. Three perspectives are represented in this book: the individual, the firm, and society. Nearly every topic discussed has elements of all three perspectives, but most place the emphasis on one more than the others. For example, the determinants of retirement are discussed at several points in the book. This topic has relevance for firms and society as a whole, but the literature has focused mainly on the perspective of the individual, as it is the individual who makes retirement decisions in response to various retirement incentives or work disincentives. On the other hand, employee benefit costs are primarily the concern of employers. Demographic trends are the concern of both employers and society as a whole. As a result of these different perspectives, it is anticipated that many readers will use this book as a reference volume. Some (we hope most) will read the book from cover to cover. For those who do not, and for those who would like an overview of what is to come, the remainder of this chapter provides a synopsis.

SYNOPSIS

Chapter 2 provides a descriptive profile of the older workforce. Information about older workers is reported on a routine basis in a number of government publications, newsletters of organizations on aging, and other publications. In isolation, however, these publications do not provide a complete picture of the characteristics of older workers. In Chapter 2, Thomas Leavitt has gathered information from a variety of sources to provide one of the few profiles of older workers available in the literature. Among the characteristics that he considers are (1) full-time versus part-time work status and work schedules, (2) employment type and occupation, (3) earnings, (4) unionization, (5) absenteeism, (6) training, and (7) job benefits. Many of these characteristics are further detailed by gender, age group, or race.

Leavitt also provides comparisons of older workers with the unemployed and nonworkers. Although much of what we know, or we think we know, about older workers has been inferred from *retirement* studies, the factors that cause older persons to participate in the labor force may not be the mirror images of those that cause them to leave. The success of policies to encourage increased labor force participation on the part of older persons will hinge, to a large degree, on this point.

In Chapter 3, Eric R. Kingson considers the implications of population aging for the future employment of older persons. He points out that while the numbers of persons in the shifting age structure of the population matter, the education level of the population, changing family and caregiving responsibilities, and changes in the health status of older persons are also important. All these factors will influence the quality and quantity of labor supplied by older persons. Moreover, they may be influenced in complex ways by immigration and shifts in the racial composition of the population.

Kingson comments on recent reports of a decrease in morbidity among members of the elderly population. However, he notes how uncertain such trends may be in predicting retirement behavior. Can we assume that each unit decrease in morbidity (especially in the critical age 60–70 range) results in a corresponding unit increase in employability? Moreover, will that decrease in morbidity postpone or accelerate retirement?

An especially interesting subject is that of dependency ratios and their influence on work and retirement. Kingson remarks that, although the elderly dependency ratio will surely increase, the total dependency ratio (both elders and children under 18) will remain relatively stable and below historic highs in the 1950s. However, dependency ratios are only the tip of the iceberg for assessing the implications of population aging. For example, how are the traditional dependency ratio results influenced by taking account of the relative costs of supporting dependent children and elders? (There is little influence, as it turns out.) More important, how will society choose to reallocate limited resources among the shifting segments of the population as it ages?

Even more important than dependency ratios are the composition and productivity of the future labor force. Only recently has the workforce begun to show high educational attainment in all worker age groups. Will that continue as minorities, who traditionally have had less education than whites, become an ever-increasing proportion of the population and the workforce?

Another important factor involves the dramatic changes in the American family. High divorce rates inevitably strain household budgets, and single parenthood creates powerful inducements to join the workforce. However, will divorcees and single parents be working beyond age 65? The only thing of which we are certain is that many older workers and retirees will have to care for aged, frail parents, both instrumentally and financially.

In Chapter 4, Christopher J. Ruhm considers the downward trend in labor force participation rates among older persons (especially older men). In contrast to Kingson's chapter, Ruhm's looks largely backward and includes a discussion of historical trends in labor force participation rates, determinants of retirement behavior, and transitions into retirement.

Ruhm notes that, not only have older Americans become less likely to hold jobs over time, those who are employed work fewer hours. He is also surprised that recent cohorts of older workers hold part-year jobs less often than their earlier counterparts—possibly reflecting labor market rigidities. Demand-side rigidities in the labor market may also help to explain the larger fraction of older workers who are now self-employed.

As to why men have been leaving the labor force at younger ages, Ruhm discusses various factors such as health status, availability of disability insurance and retiree health benefits, and financial incentives created by social security and employer pension programs. Corroborating Barry L. Friedman (Chapter 8), John A. Turner and Tabitha Doescher (Chapter 9), and Michael V. Leonesio (Chapter 12), Ruhm believes that early retirement has been heavily influenced by the financial incentives created by social security and employer pension programs.

Ruhm notes that studies have traditionally focused on the retirement behavior of men and have treated retirement as a discrete event. More recent research, however, has placed much more emphasis on the retirement behavior of women, joint retirement decision making by couples, and transitions into retirement by older workers. In contrast to the declining labor force participation rates of older men, which concern policy makers worried about social security financing, the labor force participation rates of older women have remained relatively stable. Perhaps more important, the labor force participation rates of younger women have increased dramatically since the 1950s.

In Chapter 5, Regina O'Grady-LeShane focuses on the sociological and economic determinants behind the trends in female labor force participation rates. Prior to the 1950s, most women left the labor force after becoming married. Often, this was not a matter of choice but was brought about by labor force discrimination against married women. In each decade since, however, the female labor force participation rates of successive birth cohorts have been steadily rising. Moreover, the likelihood that women will exit the labor force during the child-rearing years has declined over time. These trends would seem to bode well for the future social security and private pension coverage of older women.

On the other hand, there are several reasons to be concerned about the economic status of future cohorts of older women. Rising divorce rates may reduce spousal pension benefits. On average, women are paid less than men with equal work experience for the same jobs, thereby reducing their ability to save for retirement and implying that pensions based on earning histories will continue to be lower for women than for men. In addition, women are less likely to work in industries and occupations offering pension benefits. Finally, despite improvements in the continuity of their work histories, women are still society's caregivers and are more likely than men to have spells of no labor force participation.

The recent research on the retirement decisions of older women highlights a number of practical problems associated with attempts to design policy for older workers. For example, changes in social security provisions that are intended to encourage continued labor force participation on the part of older workers may not have the anticipated effects if retirement decisions are made jointly with a spouse. Moreover, contrary to popular perceptions, recent research indicates that only about 40 percent of older persons enter full retirement directly from their lifetime longest job.

Stuart Dorsey and John A. Turner (Chapter 6) cover many of the same topics as Ruhm, but from an international perspective. As in the United States, Dorsey and Turner find that labor force participation rates of older men in other industrialized countries have been declining since at least the 1970s. Nevertheless, they demonstrate that there is considerable variation in trends in labor force participation rates across countries, resulting from differences in public and private pension incentives. These pension incentives do not occur by accident. Rather, they reflect attempts to achieve specific policy objectives—particularly the reduction of unemployment by encouraging older workers to leave the labor force in order to create employment opportunities for younger workers.

The role of public pensions in managing unemployment, which is sometimes overlooked by policy makers concerned about the implications of population aging for pension costs, is illustrated by several European countries that already have age distributions similar to that which the United States will have when the baby boom generation retires. In countries such as France, Germany, and Sweden, persistently high unemployment has kept public pension retirement ages from rising despite the large public costs associated with providing these pensions.

Chapters 7 through 11 of the book explore the reasons behind declining labor force participation rates in more detail by examining retirement prior to the enactment of social security, the retirement incentives and disincentives in social security, retirement incentives in private pensions, the role of early retirement incentive programs (ERIPs), and age discrimination issues and legislation.

In Chapter 7, W. Andrew Achenbaum points out that the overriding motivation for social security, which was enacted in the depths of the Great Depression, was its role in encouraging the increased employment of younger persons by removing older workers from the labor force. However, as was to be true in the years that followed, social security accomplished a number of other policy objectives at the same time. Few older women worked, and in the absence of private or public pensions, most older men had no alternative but to work as long as possible. With age discrimination on the rise and aggravated by a variety of other prejudices such as racism, nativism, sexism, and class biases, the prospects for older workers were grim. Social security dealt with the policy objective of providing a basic floor of income protection for older persons at the same time that it pursued its primary objective—reducing unemployment.

Achenbaum's study of the history of retirement shows how recently this phenomenon has appeared and how closely related it is to technological change. Retirement as we know it arose when the U.S. economy made the transition from an agricultural to a manufacturing-based system. During the first part of the twentieth century, older industrial workers were said to be "inefficient," according to contemporary researchers cited by Achenbaum, and were "retired" (laid off). The assumptions were that older workers could not be retrained and that their productivity rates were lower than those of younger workers in the physically demanding, repetitive jobs of that era.

In the years since its initial passage in 1935, social security has continued to pursue multiple policy objectives simultaneously. In Chapter 8, Barry L. Friedman examines the complex interrelationships between the retirement incentives and disincentives in social security that have evolved over time. These include the early retirement penalty and delayed retirement credit, the recomputation of benefits when a person works beyond the date of initial eligibility (age 62), the earnings test, the taxation of benefits, and the payroll tax. By computing the social security wealth of individuals having particular sets of characteristics, Friedman demonstrates the financial implications of the retirement decision at different ages and under different interest rate assumptions. The results are instructive; rarely does delayed retirement or postretirement work increase social security wealth.

Higher monthly benefits for late retirement do not compensate fully for the loss of social security benefits one could have received had one retired in the earliest years of eligibility. The reason is that loss of the present year's benefit forms a very large part of the current value of the total lifetime benefit. Friedman finds that benefits to be received in the near future count much more heavily than do benefits to be received in the more distant future, for two reasons: (1) lower mortality makes the probability of receiving the near future's benefit more likely, and (2) postponement of its receipt means a permanent loss of the opportunity to enjoy the compound interest imputed to these funds by reason of their having been received now rather than later. In other words, the opportunity costs associated with later retirement are high, and the supposedly neutral adjustments are not actuarially fair because they do not reimburse the loss represented by these opportunity costs. Other incentives contained in social security— the earnings test and the recomputation of the Primary Insurance Amount for workers who retire after age 62—do not overcome the effect of this disincentive.

What effect do these work disincentives have on retirement behavior? According to findings of other researchers summarized by Friedman, they have next to none. However, these researchers face the difficult task of trying to determine what effect an increased work incentive would have on retirement behavior when, in fact, the incentive is operating in the opposite direction. Policy makers must understand that people's reactions to hypothetical changes are often far different than their reaction to real changes.

Of course, social security wealth is not the only factor influencing the retirement decisions of older workers. In Chapter 9, John A. Turner and Tabitha Doescher point out that there is now considerable evidence that, like social security, private pensions were developed (at least partly) as a labor force management tool. Turner and Doescher's chapter on pension plans (and on defined benefit plans in particular) shows clearly how the structure of pension plans encourages employee retirement behavior in the direction most suited to the employer's needs.

Turner and Doescher explain some of the actuarial mathematics necessary to determine whether, for any given employee at any given time, the alternative of "retiring on a pension" is more attractive than to "keep working for a salary." In a properly designed defined benefit plan, say the authors, pension accruals are most rapid in the period immediately preceding early retirement, encouraging workers to remain up to that age, and then taper off swiftly, encouraging workers to retire at that point.

Are defined benefit plans structured to suit the employer's needs or the employee's desires? We do not know the real answer because the motives of workers and employers seem congruent at present: employers want older workers out the door, which is where most older workers want to be, anyway. However, will employers and workers continue to think in the same way in the future? Turner and Doescher note the trend toward phased retirement marked by gradual withdrawal from the labor force through one or more part-time jobs. The almost complete failure of all industries except the low-paying, high-turnover, service industries to create part-time opportunities suggests that there is employer resistance to this concept. Perhaps only when the potential conflict between employer needs and employee desires is resolved will we know for sure whose agenda is reflected more clearly by the existing pension system.

With the shift from defined benefit plans to defined contribution plans, it is possible that we will witness a decline in firms' ability to influence worker retirement behavior. Firms are making this change to divest themselves of the economic risk associated with obligating themselves to pay lifetime pensions regardless of the longevity of the worker or the performance of the pension fund portfolio. Have employers decided that these financial risks are more serious than the risks of having an older, less well-educated, and stereotypically less-productive group of workers who, under federal law, cannot be forced to leave? Perhaps ERIPs, the temporary early retirement window plans offered by many firms and described in Phyllis Mutschler's chapter (Chapter 10), will replace the defined benefit plan as the primary source of controlling retirement behavior.

In contrast to social security, the retirement incentives and disincentives in private pension plans are tailored to the workforce needs of specific employers in specific industries. These needs vary widely; consequently, so do the characteristics of private pension plans. As with social security, the retirement incentives and disincentives in private pension plans affect pension wealth and thus influence the timing of the retirement decision.

Neither private pensions nor social security operate in a vacuum, however. As a consequence, attempts by policy makers to influence the labor force participation of older persons through changes to the incentives and disincentives in social security are likely to be frustrated by countervailing incentives and disincentives in private pension plans—especially in certain industries. The historical evidence makes it abundantly clear that in the future, firms will develop mechanisms to help manage the size and compositions of their workforces.

Phyllis H. Mutschler points out in Chapter 10 that the policy environment is complicated still further by the emergence of ERIPs, which developed in the late 1970s and early 1980s as firms searched for ways to reduce their personnel costs without exposing themselves to charges of age discrimination. ERIPs can take many forms but they usually involve cash payments, pension plan adjustments, or some other type of benefit. ERIPs highlight the complexity of the pension wealth calculations that individuals face when making retirement decisions. Often, individuals who retire under an ERIP will leave the labor force prior to initial eligibility for social security benefits (age 62). ERIPs often take the form of cash payments or unreduced pension benefits that make it economically feasible to retire before social security benefits begin. In deciding whether to accept an ERIP, individuals must consider the value of the ERIP itself as well as the influence of the retirement decision on their private pension wealth and social security wealth. Such calculations are enormously complex and will yield different decision rules for individuals with different characteristics (e.g., age, years of service, and wage level).

Theoretically, this suggests that it should be possible for firms to design ERIPs that will be financially attractive only to the subset of their labor force that they would like to have leave. However, this assumes that employees are able to perform an extremely complex financial computation and also have perfect information about the future. A worker who decides to accept an ERIP under a certain set of assumptions about future employment opportunities may be very unhappy if these opportunities fail to materialize.

In a competitive international economy, downsizing has been another imperative behind the ERIP, as American firms try to remain competitive with foreign firms using much cheaper labor. Reducing the American worker's pay is extremely difficult, and the ERIP serves the useful function of encouraging older workers (traditionally assumed to be the most expensive category, relative to their productivity) to retire early so that overall labor costs can be reduced.

As Mutschler points out, the actual success of an ERIP may be difficult to predict. This should make it primarily a tool of large employers, who are better able to statistically predict how many workers can be expected to depart. Smaller firms will find using ERIPs to be dangerously unpredictable. What mechanisms, aside from attrition or layoffs, can they use to reduce the workforce?

The future of the ERIP is cloudy for other reasons as well. Changing workforce demographics, the extent to which technological change will enable firms to substitute capital for labor, and continued economic expansion in third world countries with significantly cheaper labor costs exert pressures in many different directions.

When older workers decide to retire as a result of public or private pension incentives, they generally leave the labor force voluntarily. In Chapter 11, Steven H. Sandell and Marc Rosenblum consider *involuntary* dismissals from the labor force as well as other forms of age discrimination, including the failure to hire older job applicants, lower pay, and the denial of promotions due to age. Prior to the extensive research on retirement behavior by economists in the 1970s and 1980s, mandatory retirement, age discrimination, and health problems were thought to be major determinants of exit from the labor force by older persons. Sandell and Rosenblum's chapter describes the efforts of economists, legislators, and courts to identify and quantify age discrimination. This practice has existed throughout labor history, but it resists full exposure through the distorting effects of other closely related variables such as poor health or "voluntary" departure from the labor force after a futile job search. Statistics about education, job tenure and skills, earnings, unemployment, and retirement mask age discrimination, making it next to impossible to isolate as a causal factor. The necessity for frequent amendments to the Age Discrimination in Employment Act of 1967 (ADEA) are evidence of congressional frustration in attempting to eradicate the widespread prejudice against older workers.

Sandell and Rosenblum point out that the ADEA's greatest success has been in protecting older workers from being disproportionately singled out for layoff during tough economic times. Virtually no progress has been made, however, in eradicating age discrimination in *hiring*, a practice that might be justifiable for jobs requiring lengthy training but is otherwise due to age-based stereotypes. Ironically, because of the demonstrated importance of pension incentives in the research literature, age discrimination seems to have dropped off the economists' radar screen at the very time when the numbers of age discrimination cases filed with the federal Equal Employment Opportunity Commission are escalating rapidly.

Chapters 12 through 14 of the book consider alternative theoretical perspectives of retirement. In Chapter 12, Michael V. Leonesio discusses the economic model of work–leisure choice—the theoretical framework for the extensive research on retirement by economists in the 1970s and 1980s, as well as most of the other chapters in this volume. Leonesio describes the basic economic model of work–leisure choice and then reviews the major retirement studies of the 1970s and 1980s in the context of this model.

Leonesio points out that the economic model is much broader than noneconomists often assume. "Contrary to some popular misconceptions, economics does not claim that people are primarily money oriented or that their behavior is narrowly self-interested." Rather, economics focuses on how individuals and businesses make choices in the face of limited resources. The theoretical framework provided by economic theory is extremely general and opens up a wide range of areas for potential analysis—labor force participation and retirement among them.

Nevertheless, it is also true that noneconomic perspectives are invaluable for understanding retirement behavior and, consequently, for developing employment policy for older persons. Two alternatives to the economists' model of work–leisure choice are discussed in this volume. In Chapter 13, Robert M.

Whaples and Charles F. Longino, Jr., describe social gerontological models of retirement and employment of older persons. Whaples and Longino argue that the economist's view of retirement is too narrow because it fails to consider people's feelings about work, their jobs, their workplaces, and their expectations and attitudes about retirement. Many economists would disagree with this characterization, yet it is certainly true that social gerontologists see the world differently than economists. As Whaples and Longino put it, "While economists see retirement as a relationship between income and leisure, social gerontologists see it as a relationship between people and jobs."

In Chapter 14, Scott A. Bass and Francis G. Caro describe the perspective on retirement and employment of older persons offered by the relatively new area known as productive aging. Productive aging examines the broad range of socially valued activities in which older people engage. Because this is an evolving area of inquiry, the activities subsumed under productive aging vary somewhat from study to study. Most studies, however, include volunteering, labor force participation, and caregiving in the list of productive activities. As with social gerontological models of retirement and employment, the productive aging framework cuts across disciplinary lines and draws on psychology, economics, and sociology.

The productive aging perspective has interesting implications for older worker policy. In one way or another, all older worker policies are designed to encourage elderly persons to continue working in the paid labor force. Hours spent in the labor force, however, are hours that are unavailable for other activities such as caregiving and volunteering. Thus, the perspective provided by the productive aging framework highlights the potential opportunity costs associated with older worker policies.

Chapters 15, 16, and 17 deal with three topics that should be of great interest to employers—the productivity and functional limitations of older workers, the merits of older worker training programs, and the costs and benefits associated with older workers. In Chapter 15, Anthony A. Sterns, Harvey L. Sterns, and Lisa A. Hollis provide a comprehensive review of the literature that has assessed age-related functional and cognitive changes and limitations. They find that most individuals experience declines in physical, sensory and some facets of cognitive abilities over their lifetimes. The implications of these declines for productivity, however, are poorly understood, as are the effects of interventions to ameliorate these declines.

The lack of evidence on how age-related changes in functional, cognitive, and sensory abilities affect job performance does not provide employers with much guidance concerning the merits of training programs for older workers. Perhaps this is why Sara E. Rix notes, in Chapter 16, that employers are reluctant to provide older workers with training. The costs of training are easily determined by employers, but the benefits of training or, perhaps even more important, the costs of *not* training older workers are much more difficult to quantify.

Rix argues that employers will invest in the training of older workers only when it is in their financial best interest to do so or when younger workers are in short supply. Rix also notes that additional research on older worker training in the United States is badly needed. Research is needed on the characteristics of recipients of training by age, types of training provided, whether training is formal or provided on the job, and on the costs and benefits of training to workers and employers. She also notes that it is necessary to recognize that workers and employers may have different goals and objectives related to training.

An important factor in the unwillingness of employers to train older workers is the perception that older workers are more expensive than younger workers. The costs and benefits of older workers are discussed in Chapter 17 by Michael C. Barth, William McNaught, and Philip Rizzi, who find that the productivity of older workers frequently compares very favorably to younger workers. Moreover, in some instances where they do not, the shortcomings of older workers may be due to less access to training. Although employers are legally banned by the Age Discrimination in Employment Act from discriminating against training older workers on the basis of age, the available evidence indicates that they are much more likely to provide training to younger than to older workers. The reasons for the emphasis on training younger workers are clear. Although older workers are often as productive as younger ones, they also tend to be more expensive because of pension and health care costs. Moreover, employers have a longer time horizon with younger workers over which to recoup an investment in training.

It is interesting to speculate about how employer perceptions of older workers may affect the future demand for this group—particularly in light of the changes that have been taking place in the structure of private pensions in recent years. As described in Chapter 9, defined benefit plans have a strong influence on the timing of retirement through the effect of plan provisions on pension wealth. However, employers have been shifting from defined benefit plans to defined contribution plans, which have no such effects on the timing of the retirement decision. This suggests that employers may not be as concerned about holding onto younger workers and encouraging older ones to leave as they have been historically.

The declining interest in defined benefit plans as a tool for encouraging the retirement of older workers is understandable given the success of employers with ERIPs. However, the lack of interest in defined benefit plans as a tool for retaining younger workers is curious—especially in light of concerns about future labor shortfalls brought about by population aging. Perhaps employers are simply trying to reduce expenses; they may be reluctant to invest in pensions to retain younger workers until the much-discussed labor shortages actually materialize.

The economic theory of occupational labor shortages is discussed by Burt S. Barnow in Chapter 18. Barnow points out that the opportunities offered to older workers by occupational shortages depend on the cause of the shortage. Shortages can arise because of increases in demand, decreases in supply, or restrictions on wages. Barnow argues that changes in demand or supply will often lead to job opportunities for older workers. Although this is also true of restrictions on wages, the available jobs will tend to pay less than the market-clearing wage. Employment opportunities for older workers will also be influenced by whether employers believe the labor shortages to be permanent or temporary. In the latter case, employers may have their existing labor force work additional hours. Older workers will also generally find it difficult to take advantage of opportunities in occupations where they lack experience if employers are reluctant to provide training.

The final two chapters of the book return to the macro-perspective of the opening chapters. In Chapter 19, William J. Serow discusses the implications of an aging workforce for labor force productivity and economic growth. He concludes that the aging of the labor force should not have detrimental effects on labor force productivity and economic growth for two primary reasons. First, the educational level of the labor force will be the highest it has ever been. Second, the productivity of the labor force depends not only on the characteristics of the workers themselves, but also on the capital with which each employee works. Thus, the substitution of capital for labor can offset the influence of slower labor force growth as a result of population aging.

In Chapter 20, William H. Crown examines a wide variety of factors that influence the labor supply decisions of older workers. The complexity of the interactions between social security provisions, ERIPs, and private pension plan provisions, to name but a few, create an enormously difficult problem for policy makers. In such a complex environment, it is virtually impossible to predict how older workers will respond to any particular policy initiative. For example, it is entirely possible that attempts to encourage delayed retirement by raising the normal retirement age for social security may work at cross-purposes with private pension incentives encouraging early retirement. To make matters even more difficult, many policies may raise horizontal equity issues because they have differential impacts on alternative groups of older workers.

With these considerations as a backdrop, Crown examines the underlying motivations for the current interest in older worker policy. He argues that many policies—especially retirement disincentives in social security—are based on assumptions about future developments that may never materialize. These include concerns about the implications of population aging for social security financing and labor force shortages.

In addition, it is clear that several changes to social security provisions since the early 1980s have been designed to reduce perceived inequities between the economic gains of the elderly relative to members of the younger population and account for the improvements in average life expectancy that have taken place since the initial passage of the Social Security Act in 1935. However, a closer look indicates little evidence that the economic gains of the elderly have come at the expense of the younger population. Nor is it clear that improvements in life expectancy translate to improvements in morbidity that would enable people to work longer.

These considerations do not mean that policy makers should give up on the objective of encouraging increased labor force participation of older persons. However, older worker policy discussions *do* need to take account of a much broader set of factors than they have historically. Increased labor supply on the part of older persons can be achieved through policies that use the "carrot" (employment incentives) or the "stick" (retirement disincentives). The distributional consequences of the two approaches are likely to be quite different and are closely tied to the underlying motivations for pursuing older worker employment policies in the first place.

FINAL COMMENTS

This book is intended primarily as a reference volume, although, as is hopefully apparent from the foregoing description, there are many interconnections among the chapters. To help keep the length manageable, redundant material in certain chapters has been removed and appropriate cross-references have been inserted to guide readers to similar (and sometimes more detailed) discussions of particular topics in other chapters.

Of course, no handbook such as this can claim to be comprehensive. For a variety of reasons, some topics have had to be omitted from the book altogether. In addition, many readers will want to go beyond the discussions of particular topics that have been included. For these readers, it is hoped that the references will be a useful guide to the relevant literature.

2

Labor Force Characteristics of Older Americans

Thomas Leavitt

In 1993 there were more than 52 million Americans over the age of 55, 60 percent of whom were age 65 or older and 24 percent of whom were age 75 or over. Most of these older Americans are working or have had work experience. Many are retired; others are about to go through the transition from work to retirement. This chapter profiles the labor force characteristics of this population in four sections: (1) labor force participation, (2) data on the unemployed, (3) characteristics of the employed, and (4) comparisons between the working and nonworking populations.

LABOR FORCE PARTICIPATION

Labor force participants are individuals who make themselves available for work—they may be either currently working or unemployed. In 1993, the civilian labor force participation rate was 56.4 percent for the age 55–64 population and 11.3 percent for the age 65+ population. The labor force participation rates for these two age groups are substantially higher for males (66.5% and 15.6%) than for females (47.3% and 8.2%).

On dividing the older population into narrower age categories, it is clear that labor force participation rates are substantially lower for older age groups. For example, nearly 80 percent of persons age 50–54 are in the labor force, compared to just over 4 percent of those age 75 and older (Figure 2.1). The most

Figure 2.1
Percent of Civilian Noninstitutionalized Population in Labor Force, by Age and Sex, 1993

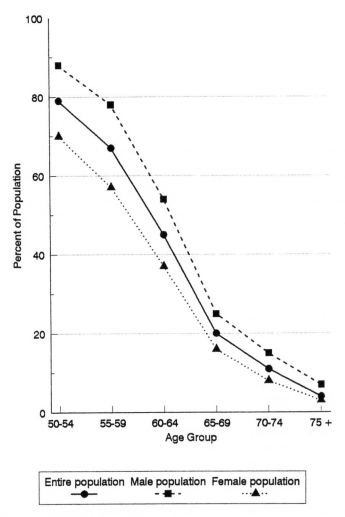

Source: U.S. Department of Labor (1994).

precipitous drop in labor force participation occurs during ages 55–64, but the decline continues after age 65.

Participation rates are higher for males than for females in each age category, but the difference between the sexes narrows considerably with age. The labor force participation rate for males is 18 percentage points higher than that for females at ages 50–54, 9 percentage points higher at ages 65–69, and 3 percentage points higher at age 75+.

Table 2.1
Labor Force Participation Rates, by Age, Race, and Gender: 1993

Age Group	Whites			Blacks		
	All	Males	Females	All	Males	Females
50-54	80	90	70	71	76	67
55-59	68	79	58	59	67	53
60-64	46	55	37	41	48	36
65-69	21	26	16	17	19	16
70-74	11	15	8	8	9	7
75+	4	7	3	4	5	3

Source: U.S. Department of Labor (1994).

Participation rates are higher for whites than for blacks at all ages, but again, the difference narrows with age (Table 2.1). Looking at both sexes together, the participation rate for whites is 9 percentage points higher than that for blacks at ages 50–54 (80% versus 71%) and ages 55–59 (68% versus 59%). However, this difference declines to 5 percentage points at ages 60–64 (46% versus 41%) and to less than 1 percentage point at age 75+ (4% for both).

Male–female participation rate differences are lower at all ages for blacks than for whites. For example, the participation rate of white males is 21 percentage points higher than that for white females at ages 55–59 (79% versus 58%) compared to a 14 percentage point gender difference for blacks (67% versus 53%). Similarly, the participation rate of white males is 10 percentage points higher than that for white females at ages 65–69 (26% versus 16%), compared to a 3 percentage point gender difference for blacks (19% versus 16%). The primary reason for smaller male–female labor force participation rate differences for blacks is that black males have considerably lower participation rates than white men, while black female participation rates are quite similar to those of white females.

There have been changes in participation rates since 1950 (Figure 2.2). Participation rates for the prime working age categories (25–34, 35–44, and 45–54) have moved upward over the last 30 years or more. Participation rates for the age 55–64 group have stayed within a narrow range, going down somewhat during the 1970–1985 period but up again after 1985. In contrast, participation rates for the age 65+ population have declined steadily since 1950, from 28 percent to 11 percent, reflecting the institutionalization of retirement during this period.

Figure 2.2
Civilian Labor Force Participation by Age, 1950–1993

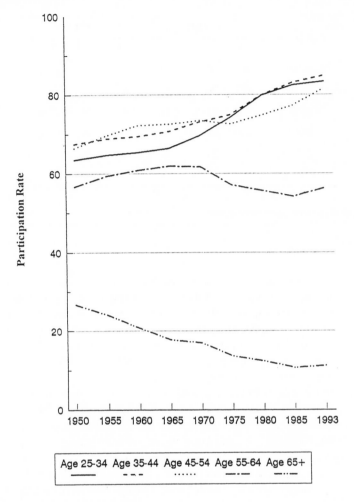

Source: U.S. Department of Labor (1994).

Looking at labor force participation trends for males and females (Figures 2.3 and 2.4), it is clear that the trend upward in prime working-age participation rates is due entirely to significant increases in female participation. Traditionally, nearly all males have made themselves available for work, and this has not changed markedly since 1950. However, participation rates for working-age females have nearly doubled during this period.

The more or less unchanged participation rate for persons in the 55–64 age

Figure 2.3
Male Civilian Labor Force Participation by Age, 1950–1993

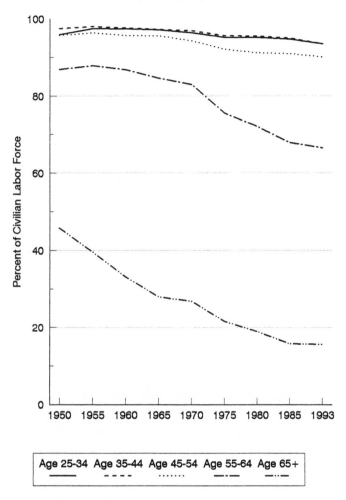

Source: U.S. Department of Labor (1994).

group is the result of substantial male declines in participation being offset by significant increases in female participation. Moreover, the decline in labor force participation among those 65 and over is due to steep declines in male participation. Male participation rates in 1993 are approximately one-third the 1950 rates. In contrast, female participation rates have remained close to 10 percent for the entire 1950–1993 period.

Figure 2.4
Female Civilian Labor Force Participation by Age, 1950–1993

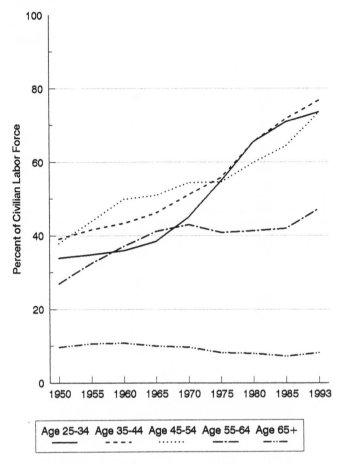

Source: U.S. Department of Labor (1994).

UNEMPLOYMENT

There are always individuals within the labor force who are available for work but are not working. Generally, the percentage of workers who are unemployed declines with age for both sexes (Figure 2.5). Several reasons have been suggested for the lower unemployment rate experienced by older workers. Older workers tend to have longer tenure in their jobs and are therefore not as susceptible to job loss as younger workers. Moreover, older workers have an alternative available to them—retirement—that is not generally a viable option for younger workers. In fact, as we will see in this section, older workers are

Figure 2.5
Unemployment Rate by Age and Sex For Civilian Noninstitutionalized Population,
1992

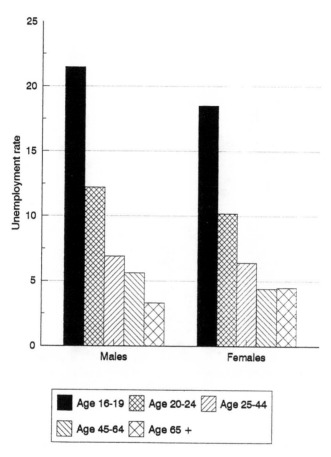

Source: U.S. Bureau of the Census (1994).

much more likely to experience a period of unemployment prior to withdrawing from the labor force (i.e., retiring). This suggests that some older workers retire in preference to spending a long period in unemployment.

The relative decline in unemployment can be seen clearly in Figure 2.6. The section of each bar that represents the unemployed becomes progressively smaller with age until it virtually disappears for those in the 70–74 and 75+ age groups.

The unemployment rate for whites is always lower than it is for blacks and Hispanics (Figure 2.7). However, Hispanic and (especially) black unemployment rates drop somewhat more quickly from the age 25–54 group to the age 55+

Figure 2.6
Employment Status of Civilian Noninstitutionalized Population by Age, 1993

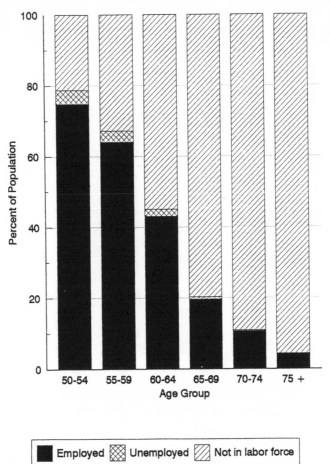

Source: Calculated from data in U.S. Department of Labor (1994).

group than white unemployment rates. This may reflect the fact that minority older workers are more likely to be discouraged and leave the labor force.

The propensity for older workers to become discouraged while unemployed has been mentioned as a possible reason for their lower unemployment rates. Recent attempts to gauge the number of discouraged workers in each age group tend to buttress the view that the underlying unemployment rate may be quite similar for all age groups. Estimates by the U.S. Department of Labor (1989c) indicate that when discouraged male workers are added to the official male unemployment rate, the "total" unemployment rate is similar for all age groups

Figure 2.7
Unemployment Rate, by Age, Race, and Hispanic Origin: 1993

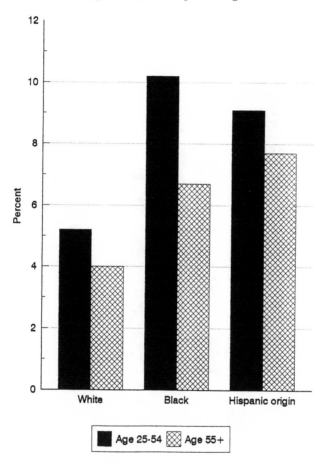

Source: U.S. Department of Labor (1994).

(Figure 2.8). Moreover, for females, it is estimated that the total unemployment rate for age 65+ is actually higher than for the age 25–54 group (Figure 2.9).

Evidence also indicates that older unemployed workers very quickly become discouraged by the search for other employment. The likelihood of withdrawing from the labor force following a spell of unemployment increases rapidly with age (Figures 2.10 and 2.11). Nearly half of both males and females age 65+ have left the labor force within a month of being listed as unemployed. This high level of discouragement is not hard to understand. Only 15 percent of women and 19 percent of men age 65 and over are working in the month after they are listed as unemployed.

Figure 2.8
Male Unemployment Rate and Modified Rate Including Discouraged Workers, by Age: 1987

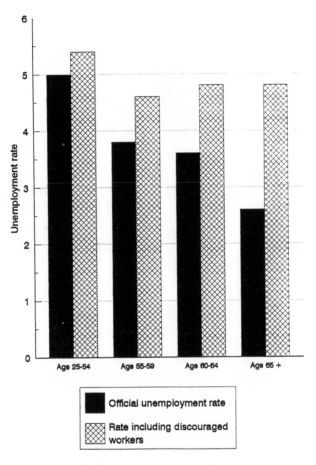

Source: U.S. Department of Labor (1989c).

For unemployed older workers, the wait for a new job is often very long (Table 2.2). Among unemployed workers in the age 55–64 group, more than 36 percent of males and 29 percent of females remain unemployed for more than half a year. Males tend to remain unemployed longer than females, which may be related to the fact that males are more apt to be searching for higher-level jobs or are less likely to exit from the labor force.

The pattern is very similar for unemployed workers who are age 65 and older. It is interesting to note that both males and females in this age group are more likely to find new jobs in less than five weeks than are their counterparts in the

Figure 2.9
Female Unemployment Rate and Modified Rate Including Discouraged Workers,
by Age: 1987

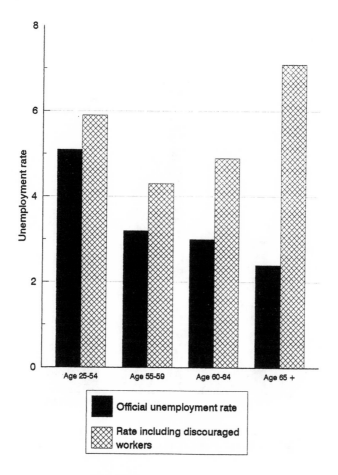

Source: U.S. Department of Labor (1989c).

age 55–64 group. This is probably because older unemployed workers are more likely to be looking for low-wage or part-time employment.

THE EMPLOYED POPULATION

Older workers are employed for a wide variety of reasons, and these reasons change as workers grow older. At ages 40–49, workers most often mention (in descending order) the need for money, their enjoyment of working, and the fact that work makes them feel useful. At ages 50–62, the most common reasons

Figure 2.10
Labor Force Status In Current Month of Males Unemployed in Previous Month,
by Age: 1987

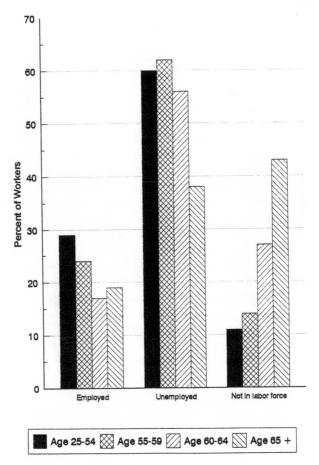

Source: U.S. Department of Labor (1989c).

are the enjoyment of working and the fact that work makes people feel useful, followed by the need to make money. At age 62+, however, the need for money is a major reason for working for a much smaller percentage of workers; in this group, the enjoyment of working is the most frequently cited reason.

Data are available on a large variety of older worker characteristics, including full-time/part-time status, worker type (wage and salary, self-employed, etc.), earnings, occupations, work schedules, benefit coverage, union status, access to and attitude toward job training, and absence rates. This section describes what is known about these characteristics.

Figure 2.11
Labor Force Status In Current Month of Females Unemployed in Previous Month, by Age: 1987

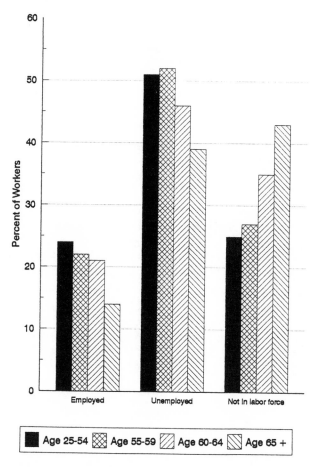

Source: U.S. Department of Labor (1989c).

Work Status

In 1993, 86 percent of workers ages 45–64 and 47 percent of workers ages 65+ were employed full-time (Figure 2.12). Among those working full-time, the majority of both age groups work 40 hours or less per week, but there are significant numbers who work more than 40 hours. Even among age 65+ workers, 13 percent work more than 40 hours per week.

Workers may be employed part-time voluntarily or because of economic reasons (insufficient work to support full-time employment). Nearly half of age

Table 2.2
Duration of Unemployment, by Age and Gender: 1993 (percent distribution)

Duration	Age 55-64		Age 65+	
	Males	Females	Males	Females
Less than 5 weeks	20.1	28.9	24.6	32.6
5-14 weeks	22.3	25.6	23.1	23.9
15-26 weeks	20.6	16.1	16.9	13.0
27+ weeks	36.2	28.9	35.4	26.1

Source: U.S. Department of Labor (1994).

65+ workers work part-time voluntarily, compared to less than 10 percent of those age 45–64. Approximately 5 percent of both age 65+ and age 45–64 workers work part-time for economic reasons.

Full-time work is significantly less common among females than males (Figures 2.13 and 2.14). In the 45–64 age group, 93 percent of males and 79 percent of females work full-time, while in the 65+ age group 52 percent of males and 39 percent of females work full-time. Female full-time workers are much less likely than male full-time workers to be working more than 40 hours per week. In the 65+ group, voluntary part-time work is common for both males (44%) and females (54%).

Employment Type

Most older workers are private wage and salary workers (Table 2.3). Two-thirds of workers age 55–64 and 61 percent of workers age 65+ fell into this category in 1993. Some shifts in employment types occur between the age 55–64 and age 65+ groups. Government workers are significantly less common in the older age group (12% versus 18%), reflecting the early retirement ages common in most government employment. Self-employment is more common in the older age group (18% versus 12%), both because self-employed persons tend to retire later and because retirees from other jobs often turn to some form of self-employment in their retirement years. Agricultural workers constitute a larger segment of the age 65+ working population than of the age 55–64 population (8% versus 3%).

A similar proportion of males and females in the age 55–64 group are private wage and salary workers. However, females in this age group are more likely than males to be government workers (22% versus 16%) and less likely to be self-employed (9% versus 13%). After age 65, males are significantly less likely

Figure 2.12
Work Status of Workers In Nonagricultural Industries, by Age: 1993

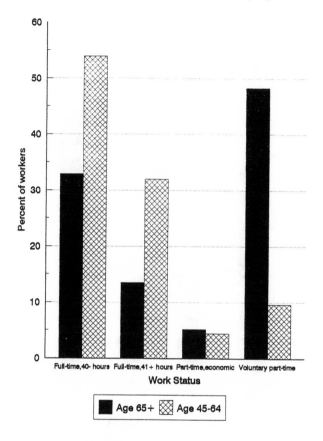

Source: U.S. Department of Labor (1994).

than females to be private wage and salary workers (55% versus 68%) and more likely to be self-employed (22% versus 13%).

Occupations

The distribution of occupations for the 55–64 age group is quite similar to the distribution for younger ages. However, there are major differences in the occupational distribution for the age 65+ population. The occupational distributions for various age groups are shown in Tables 2.4 (males) and 2.5 (females).

For males, the most common occupations prior to age 65 are executive, administrative, and managerial; precision production, craft, and repair; operators,

Figure 2.13
Work Status of Male Workers In Nonagricultural Industries, by Age: 1993

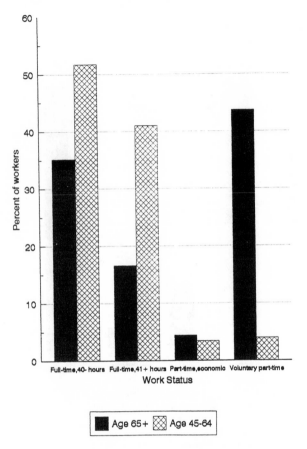

Source: U.S. Department of Labor (1994).

fabricators, and laborers; and professional specialties. The only major change in
this distribution for older age groups is that a larger proportion of workers fit
into the executive, administrative, and managerial category. This is probably
due to the fact that workers are more likely to be in these positions of responsibility as they grow older. The male occupational distribution for age 65+
workers is different than distributions for younger age groups in several respects.
The proportions of workers who are in the precision production, craft, and repair
and the operators, fabricators, and laborers categories are much smaller, while
the proportions in sales occupations and in farming, forestry, and fishing are
considerably higher. The proportions in executive, administrative, and managerial and in professional specialties remain similar to pre–age 65 levels.

Figure 2.14
Work Status of Female Workers In Nonagricultural Industries, by Age: 1993

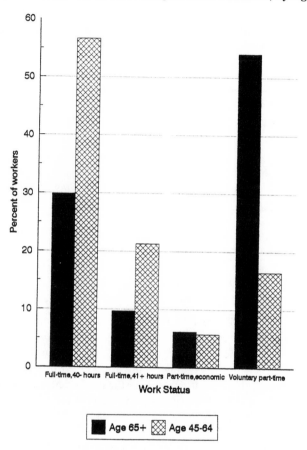

Source: U.S. Department of Labor (1994).

It is difficult to put an exact interpretation on these changes, since the distributions are affected by retirements, transitions to part-time employment (which may be in different occupations than full-time employment), the greater likelihood that workers in some occupations will continue to work longer, and the different levels of attraction that some occupations have for older workers. It seems clear, however, that the distribution of occupations for age 65+ workers is strongly affected by the fact that "rank-and-file" production workers (often unionized) in the precision production, craft, and repair and the operators, fabricators, and laborers categories tend to retire prior to age 65.

The female distribution of occupations is dominated by the administrative support and service categories, which together account for nearly half of female

Table 2.3
Employment Type, by Age and Gender: 1993 (percent distribution)

Employment Type	All Workers		Male Workers		Female Workers	
	Age 55-64	Age 65+	Age 55-64	Age 65+	Age 55-64	Age 65+
Private wage and salary	67	61	66	55	68	68
Government wage and salary	18	12	15	10	22	16
Self-employed	12	18	14	22	9	13
Agriculture	3	8	5	12	1	3
Total*	100	100	100	100	100	100

*Total may not add to 100 due to rounding.
Source: U.S. Department of Labor (1994).

workers in the age 55–64 category. Women are much less likely than men to be in the precision production, craft, and repair or the operators, fabricators, and laborers categories than men. They are also less likely to be in farming, forestry, and fishing. There is a far less dramatic shift for women from pre–age 65 occupations to post–age 65 occupations; the post age–65 occupational distribution continues to be dominated by the administrative support and service occupations.

There are marked differences in the occupational distributions of the different racial and ethnic groups (Tables 2.6, 2.7, 2.8, and 2.9). Whites are quite evenly distributed among the nine occupational categories. At age 55–64, seven of the nine occupational categories account for between 11 and 16 percent of the working population each. In contrast, workers in other racial/ethnic categories are more concentrated in a small number of occupations. For example, 56 percent of blacks and 48 percent of Hispanics in the age 55–64 group are in the service occupations or the operators, fabricators, and laborers categories.

Earnings

The age 45–49 group has higher median earnings than any other group. Earnings for many individuals continue to increase after these ages, but median earnings decline due to retirements and transitions from full-time to part-time work. Figures 2.15 and 2.16 show male and female median earnings for age categories ranging from 50–54 to 72+. For both sexes there is a gradual decline

Table 2.4

Male Persons by Occupation and Age: 1990 Annual Averages (percent distribution)

Occupation	Age 25-44	Age 45-54	Age 55-64	Age 65+
Executive, Administrative, Managerial	14.2	18.6	17.8	16.1
Professional Specialty	13.1	14.0	13.8	13.9
Technicians + Related Support	3.6	2.6	2.0	1.0
Sales Occupations	10.7	11.3	11.8	16.4
Administrative Support	5.5	5.1	5.4	6.3
Service Occupations	8.2	7.0	8.5	10.9
Precision Production, Craft + Repair	21.1	20.3	17.7	9.3
Operators, Fabricators, Laborers	20.0	17.7	17.5	12.3
Farming, Forestry, Fishing	3.6	3.5	5.5	13.8

Source: U.S. Congressional Research Service (1991).

in median earnings through age 61, reflecting the gradual increase in retirement rates. At age 62–64 there is a large decline in median earnings (nearly $6,000 for men and more than $3,000 for women), which coincides with the initial eligibility for social security benefits. An even larger decline in median earnings occurs at age 65, when workers are eligible for full (i.e., unreduced) social security benefits.

Unionization

In 1993 more than 20 percent of workers age 55–64 were unionized (Figure 2.17). Male workers in this age group were considerably more likely to be unionized than females. A slightly lower percentage of workers age 25–54 were unionized. The higher unionization rate for older workers is likely the result of recent declines in the influence of unions; in all likelihood, the extent of unionization for older workers will decline from this point on.

Unionization rates for workers age 65+ are much lower than for younger workers. The male unionization rate for age 65+ is approximately one third the rate for age 55–64 and the female rate for age 65+ is about half the rate for age 55–64. This sharp drop-off in unionization rate is due to the fact that unionized workplaces typically have strict rules about the retirement of their members at or before the age of 65.

Table 2.5
Female Persons by Occupation and Age: 1990 Annual Averages (percent distribution)

Occupation	Age 25-44	Age 45-54	Age 55-64	Age 65+
Executive, Administrative, Managerial	12.6	12.7	10.4	7.8
Professional Specialty	17.6	16.7	13.6	11.3
Technicians + Related Support	4.4	2.9	2.2	1.2
Sales Occupations	10.7	11.0	12.4	15.2
Administrative Support	27.9	27.8	27.5	26.9
Service Occupations	15.2	16.2	20.3	27.6
Precision Production, Craft + Repair	2.3	2.4	2.1	2.1
Operators, Fabricators, Laborers	8.4	9.4	9.9	5.6
Farming, Forestry, Fishing	0.9	1.0	1.5	2.2

Source: U.S. Congressional Research Service (1991).

Absence and Lost Worktime Rates

There is a widely held perception that older workers have lower work attendance rates and higher lost worktime rates than younger workers due to health problems and other factors. Data for men tend to bear out this perception, but it is not true for women. The absence rate (the ratio of worker absences to total full-time employment) for age 55+ is slightly more than 5.5 compared to approximately 4.7 for age 25–54 (Figure 2.18). The absence rate for older men is more than one and a half points higher than for younger men. The rates for older and younger women are very close. The data show that differences in absence rates between older and younger workers are entirely due to health-related absences (Figure 2.19). There is no difference in the absence rates due to other reasons.

The same pattern emerges when one looks at lost worktime rates (the ratio of hours absent to hours usually worked). Workers age 55+ lose a higher percentage of worktime than workers age 25–54 (Figure 2.20). The difference is entirely due to the male difference in lost worktime rates. Older workers have a higher lost worktime ratio because they have more health-related lost hours than younger workers (Figure 2.21).

Table 2.6
White Persons by Occupation and Age: 1990 Annual Averages (percent distribution)

Occupation	Age 25-44	Age 45-54	Age 55-64	Age 65+
Executive, Administrative, Managerial	14.2	17.8	15.5	13.4
Professional Specialty	15.6	16.5	14.1	13.4
Technicians + Related Support	4.0	2.8	2.1	1.1
Sales Occupations	11.3	12.5	13.0	17.0
Administrative Support	15.2	16.8	15.4	15.8
Service Occupations	10.3	4.0	11.4	15.0
Precision Production, Craft + Repair	13.1	13.2	11.3	6.3
Operators, Fabricators, Laborers	13.9	13.7	13.3	8.8
Farming, Forestry, Fishing	2.5	2.7	3.9	9.2

Source: U.S. Congressional Research Service (1991).

Work Schedules

Eighty-four percent of age 55–64 workers and 88 percent of age 65+ workers work regular daytime schedules. Nevertheless, there are substantial numbers of older workers—7 million in the 55–64 group and 1 million in the 65+ group—who work on other shifts. Figure 2.22 shows the percentages of workers in the two older age groups who work various types of shifts other than regular daytime shifts.

Approximately a quarter of the age 55–64 workers who do not work regular daytime hours work evening shifts. The second most common shift for this age group is the night shift, but there are also substantial numbers on rotating or irregular (i.e., employer-arranged) shifts. In the 65+ age group, the largest percentage are in an undefined "other" type of shift, but there are also significant percentages of this age group working on evening, night, and irregular shifts.

Approximately 15 percent of the American workforce works a flexible schedule which permits workers to vary the time they begin and end their workday. Workers age 55–64 are slightly below the national average (12%) and workers age 65+ are slightly above the national average (16%) for flexible schedules. Males are consistently more likely to work flexible schedules than females.

Table 2.7
Black Persons by Occupation and Age: 1990 Annual Averages (percent distribution)

Occupation	Age 25-44	Age 45-54	Age 55-64	Age 65+
Executive, Administrative, Managerial	7.9	8.4	6.9	4.2
Professional Specialty	9.8	10.7	9.7	6.1
Technicians + Related Support	3.5	2.9	1.6	1.1
Sales Occupations	6.5	5.3	3.8	3.8
Administrative Support	19.6	13.6	10.4	6.8
Service Occupations	19.4	23.4	33.0	49.8
Precision Production, Craft + Repair	9.6	10.4	9.2	5.7
Operators, Fabricators, Laborers	22.2	23.6	22.5	17.1
Farming, Forestry, Fishing	1.5	1.8	3.0	5.3

Source: U.S. Congressional Research Service (1991).

Training

Recent data indicate that a significant amount of older worker training is occurring; however, a lower percentage of older workers age 55 and over receive skills improvement training on their current job than workers age 25–54. In 1991, 37 percent of workers age 55–64 and 25 percent of workers age 65+ received skills improvement training (Table 2.10). This compares with 41 percent for age 25–34, 48 percent for age 35–44, and 46 percent for age 45–54. The incidence of skills improvement training increased for all age groups (except for those age 16–19) during the 1980s, but it increased most rapidly for age 65+ workers. Workers in the 65+ age group were 32 percent more likely to take training in 1991 than in 1983.

As to the type of training that workers prefer, there are significant changes as workers get older (Figure 2.23). Workers in their 40s prefer training that will get them a better job (43%) or update their job skills (37%). Less than 5 percent express no desire for training. In the age 50–62 group, the largest percentage of workers prefers training that will update their job skills (44%), but they are still likely to want training that will help them get a better job (33%). Ten percent prefer no training. In the 65+ group of workers, nearly one-third prefer no training. The most common training preferred in this age group is training that updates job skills (35%). A much lower percentage of the 65+ group express a desire for training that will get them a better job (19%).

Table 2.8
Hispanic Persons by Occupation and Age: 1990 Annual Averages (percent distribution)

Occupation	Age 25-44	Age 45-54	Age 55-64	Age 65+
Executive, Administrative, Managerial	7.3	8.4	8.4	9.1
Professional Specialty	6.7	7.8	8.3	7.1
Technicians + Related Support	2.2	1.7	1.4	1.0
Sales Occupations	7.4	6.9	6.6	9.1
Administrative Support	13.9	12.4	11.3	10.1
Service Occupations	18.7	20.2	22.3	29.3
Precision Production, Craft + Repair	14.5	13.7	10.1	10.1
Operators, Fabricators, Laborers	24.4	24.0	25.7	18.2
Farming, Forestry, Fishing	5.1	4.8	5.9	6.1

Source: U.S. Congressional Research Service (1991).

Job Benefits

The percentage of workers covered by retirement and health benefits generally declines as workers approach retirement age. The primary reason for this is that workers covered by retirement and health benefits tend to retire earlier than others, presumably because they can afford to do so. This leaves a higher percentage of workers without coverage in the workforce.

This pattern can be seen in the older worker pension coverage rates for private full-time wage and salary workers shown in Figure 2.24. Pension coverage approaches 60 percent for those age 55–59, but it declines to 56 percent for those age 60–64 and 46 percent for those 65+. Males are more likely than females to be in pension-covered employment at every age. Only slightly more than a third of women age 65+ with full-time private wage and salary jobs are covered by pensions.

In recent years, increasing numbers of employers have been offering 401K plans to employees. These plans have been designed to supplement or, in some case, to replace traditional pension plans. These plans permit workers to place a percentage of their pre-tax salaries (thereby reducing their current tax liabilities) in accounts that are invested for retirement income. Overall, only about two-thirds of employees who are offered 401K plans actually opt to participate.

The percentage of private full-time wage and salary workers covered by

Table 2.9
Asian Plus "Other" Persons by Occupation and Age: 1990 Annual Averages
(percent distribution)

Occupation	Age 25-44	Age 45-54	Age 55-64	Age 65+
Executive, Administrative, Managerial	12.6	5.7	11.7	7.6
Professional Specialty	19.0	8.3	15.0	12.1
Technicians + Related Support	5.5	2.0	2.7	1.5
Sales Occupations	9.6	4.3	9.3	9.1
Administrative Support	14.5	4.6	11.3	13.6
Service Occupations	13.4	65.3	22.3	30.3
Precision Production, Craft + Repair	9.9	4.0	8.7	6.1
Operators, Fabricators, Laborers	13.7	5.3	16.0	10.6
Farming, Forestry, Fishing	1.7	0.4	3.0	9.1

Source: U.S. Congressional Research Service (1991).

401Ks declines as workers approach retirement. In the 55–59 age group, 27 percent of workers were covered in 1993; this compares with 23 percent of workers age 60–64 and 12 percent of workers age 65+. Female workers are less likely in each age group to opt for 401K coverage.

Worker access to, and coverage by, 401K plans has grown explosively in the past decade. In 1983, only 7 percent of full-time private wage and salary workers in the age 55–59 group were offered 401K plans. Ten years later, 35 percent of employees in this group were offered coverage. For the age 65+ group, the percentage offered coverage rose from 6 percent to 28 percent in the same period.

Most wage and salary workers work in jobs where employers offer health insurance coverage. Slightly over 80 percent of private workers and approximately 95 percent of government workers below the age of 65 work for firms that have health plans. A lower, but still substantial, percentage of employees age 65+ (58% of private workers and 84% of public workers) work for employers that sponsor health insurance coverage.

Not all employees elect to participate in health plans that are offered to them. Some, for example, may be covered by a spouse's plan. Others may not want to pay the health insurance premiums required. In the case of the age 65+ wage and salary workers, employees may not feel the need for coverage because of

Figure 2.15
Median Annual Earnings for Men, by Age: 1990

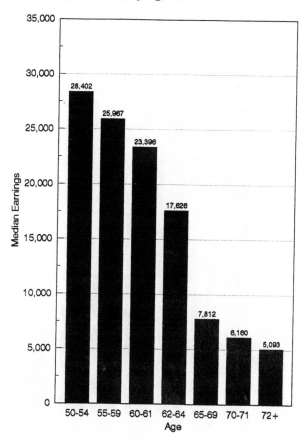

Source: U.S. Social Security Administration (1993).

medicare. Participation rates are significantly lower for 65+ wage and salary workers (63% of private workers and 57% of government workers) than for younger workers (over 80%).

The high health care costs associated with older workers have frequently been mentioned as a barrier to their employment. Data indicate that health care costs are higher for older men than for younger men but that health care costs for women remain quite stable through the working career. Older worker health care costs are discussed in more detail by Barth, McNaught, and Rizzi in Chapter 17.

Figure 2.16
Median Annual Earnings for Women, by Age: 1990

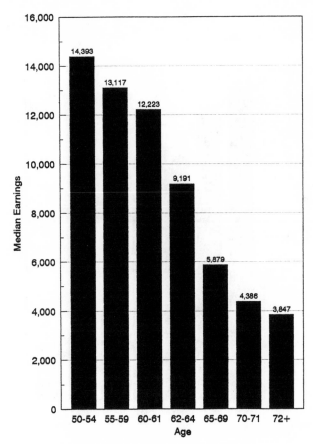

Source: U.S. Social Security Administration (1993).

COMPARISONS OF THE OLDER WORKING AND NONWORKING POPULATIONS

Income and Expenditures

There are large differences between the income of retired and nonretired persons (Figure 2.25). For married couples over age 50, the average income of retired persons in 1986–1987 was approximately $17,000 dollars less than for nonretired persons. For single men and women, the average income for retired persons was about half the income of nonretired persons. Expenditures were

Figure 2.17
Unionization Rate, by Age and Sex: 1993

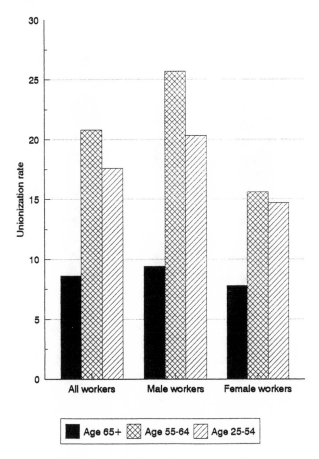

The unionization rate is the percent of workers in unions or employee associations.
Source: U.S. Department of Labor (1994).

also significantly less for retired persons, but there was not as big a difference in expenditures as there was in income (Figure 2.26). This indicates, not surprisingly, that retired persons, with their generally lower incomes, must use a larger portion of their income for living expenses than those who are not retired. Looking at the difference between income and expenditures (Figure 2.27), the average net income for retired married couples was less than $2,000, compared to almost $11,000 for nonretired couples. On average, retired single men and women had a negative net income, compared to significant positive net earnings for their nonretired counterparts.

Figure 2.18
Absence Rates for Full-Time Workers, by Age and Sex: 1993

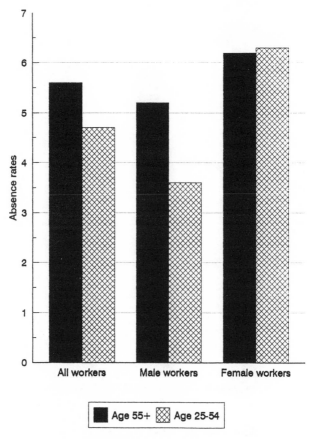

The absence rate is the ratio of worker absences to total full-time employment.
Source: U.S. Department of Labor (1994).

Educational Attainment

Those who are still in the labor force are much more likely to have higher educational levels than those who have retired (Figures 2.28, 2.29, and 2.30). For example, in married couples, 43 percent of respondents who were not retired had a college education or postgraduate education, compared to 26 percent of those who had retired. The percentage of married couples with only an elementary education was twice as high for retired persons as for nonretired persons.

The differences are even more noteworthy for single men and women. For

Figure 2.19
Absence Rates for Full-Time Workers, by Age and Reason for Absence: 1993

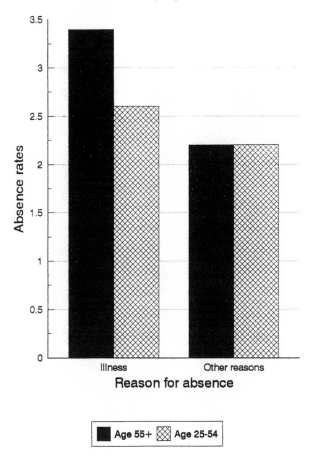

The absence rate is the ratio of worker absences to total full-time employment.
Source: U.S. Department of Labor (1994).

example, among single men, 40 percent of retired individuals had an elementary education or less, compared to 14 percent of the nonretired population.

Miscellaneous Comparisons

Measured by health expenditure levels (both covered and not covered by insurance), the working population is considerably more healthy than the retired population. For men, the average annual health expenditures of retirees is more than double the level of expenditures for workers of the same age, suggesting

Figure 2.20
Lost Worktime Rates for Full-Time Workers: 1993

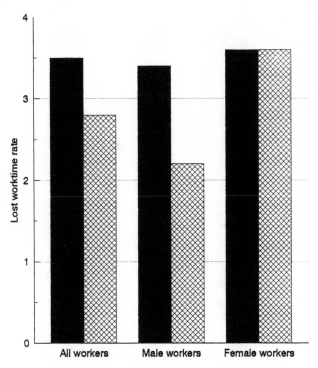

Age 55+ Age 25-54

The lost worktime rate is the ratio of hours absent to hours usually worked.
Source: U.S. Department of Labor (1994).

that poor health is a major motivator of retirement. The differences between working and nonworking women are not as large, but they are still substantial.

The differences between the health status of persons who are and are not working can also be seen in self-assessed health status percentages. In the 55–64 age group, 82 percent of those who were working said that they were in good or excellent health, compared to 60 percent of those who were not working. In the age 65–74 age group, 84 percent of those who were working said they were in good or excellent health, compared to 58 percent of those not working. Working individuals were also more likely to say they were very satisfied with life and were more likely to have professional or technical skills (Table 2.11).

Figure 2.21
Lost Worktime Rates for Full-Time Workers, by Age and Reason for Lost Worktime: 1993

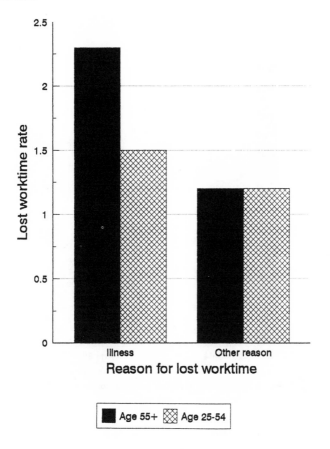

The lost worktime rate is the ratio of hours absent to hours usually worked.
Source: U.S. Department of Labor (1994).

CONCLUSION

This chapter has highlighted a number of labor force characteristics of older Americans. Labor force participation declines steadily after age 55, with the most precipitous declines occurring after initial eligibility for social security benefits at age 62. Moreover, labor force participation rates at older ages have been declining steadily over time, particularly for males. Nevertheless, significant portions of the older population continue to work.

Unemployment rates are somewhat lower for older labor force participants

Figure 2.22
Work Schedules of Those Not Working Regular Daytime Schedules, by Age: 1991

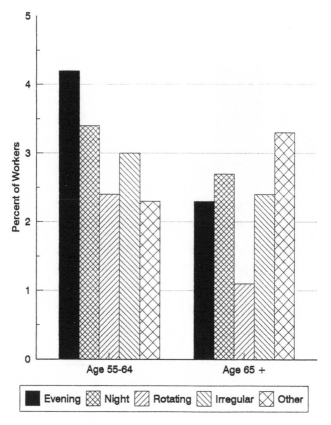

Source: U.S. Bureau of Census (1994).

than younger workers, but "real" unemployment rates for older labor force participants—those that include discouraged workers—are similar to those of younger labor force participants.

An occupational shift occurs starting with age 65. By this point, many older workers have left their full-time careers and are working part time in jobs that are different than those in prior careers.

Older male workers have higher absence and lost worktime rates than younger male workers. This difference is due entirely to differences in health-related absences and lost worktime. In contrast, the absence rates for older and younger female workers are very similar.

Table 2.10
Percentage of Workers Taking Skills Improvement Training on Current Job: 1983 and 1991

Age Group	1983	1991	Percent Change
16-19	18	18	--
20-24	28	31	11
25-34	39	41	5
35-44	41	48	17
45-54	37	46	24
55-64	31	37	19
65+	19	25	32

Source: U.S. Department of Labor (1992c).

Figure 2.23
Type of Training Preferred, by Age

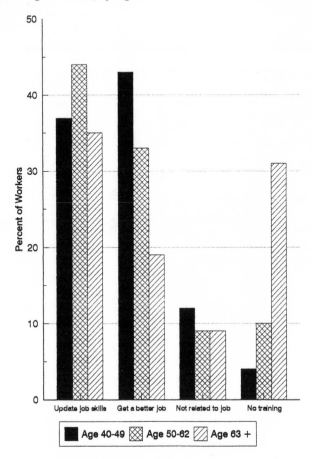

Source: U.S. Department of Labor (1989c).

Figure 2.24
Pension Coverage Rates for Private Full-Time Wage and Salary Workers, by Age and Sex: 1993

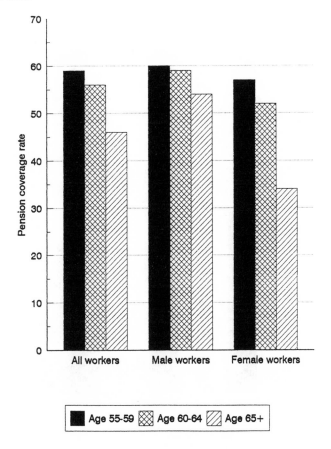

Source: U.S. Department of Labor, Social Security Administration, U.S. Small Business Administration, Pension Benefit Guarantee Corporation (1994).

Figure 2.25
Mean Income of Persons Age 50 and Over by Retirement and Marital Status:
1986–1987

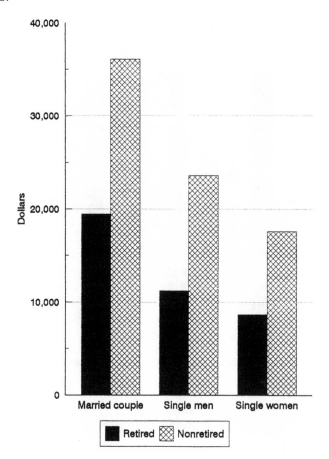

Source: Rubin and Nieswiadomy (1994).

Figure 2.26
Mean Expenditures of Persons Age 50 and Over, by Retirement and Marital Status: 1986–1987

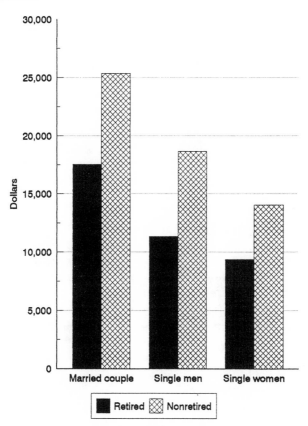

Source: Rubin and Nieswiadomy (1994).

Figure 2.27
Mean Income-Mean Expenditures for Persons Age 50 and Over, by Retirement and Marital Status: 1986–1987

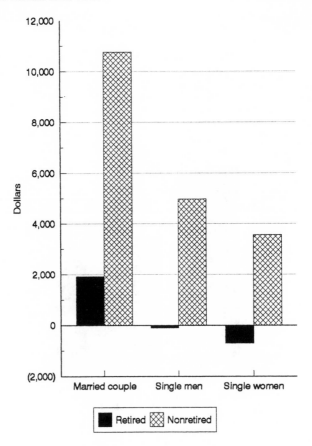

Source: Rubin and Nieswiadomy (1994).

Figure 2.28
Educational Attainment of Married Couples Age 50 and Over, by Retirement Status: 1986–1987

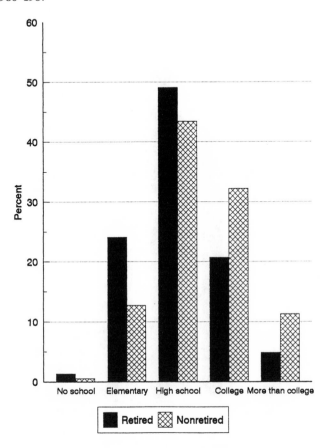

Source: Rubin and Nieswiadomy (1994).

Figure 2.29
Educational Attainment of Single Men Age 50 and Over, by Retirement Status:
1986–1987

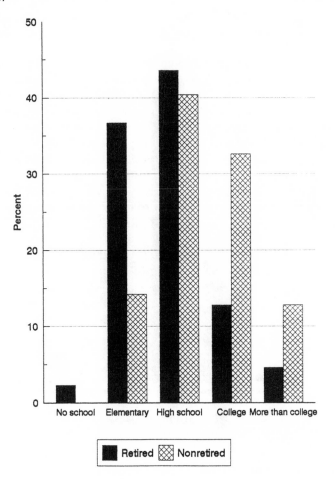

Source: Rubin and Nieswiadomy (1994).

Figure 2.30
Educational Attainment of Single Women Age 50 and Over, by Retirement Status: 1986–1987

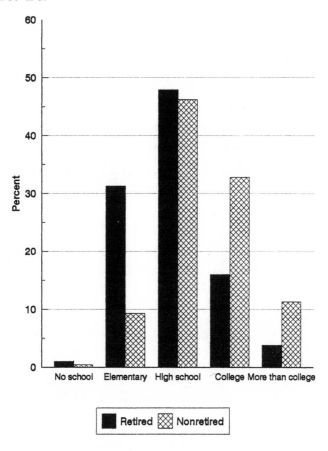

Source: Rubin and Nieswiadomy (1994).

Table 2.11
Characteristics of Those Working and Not Working

Characteristic	Age 55-64		Age 65-74	
	Working	Not Working	Working	Not Working
Percentage in good or excellent health	82	60	84	58
Percentage very satisfied with life	66	57	71	62
Percentage with some college or more	40	24	36	21
Percentage with professional or technical skills	52	38	51	31

Source: Louis Harris and Associates (1992).

Demographic Trends and the Future of Older Workers

Eric R. Kingson

For the next 40 years, newspaper stories about older worker trends and policies will be laced with numerous references to the aging of the post–World War II baby boom cohorts. Just as the baby boom cohorts were often reported as first straining hospital nurseries, then schools, and later the housing market, increasingly there will be stories about baby boomers blocking pathways to promotion for younger persons, accepting lucrative early retirement offers, and reentering the labor force in second and third careers. These will be followed by less frequent references to working boomers until, one day, perhaps 70 years from now, the "last working boomer"—an enterprising centenarian—will tell the "Charles Kerault" of her day about why and how she has worked for eighty years, only rarely missing a day.

There is no doubt that population aging is an important demographic trend with numerous labor force implications, but discussions of the effects of demographic change need to acknowledge many factors and trends that variously shape and constrain the opportunities and barriers before older workers. Consequently, this chapter reviews a number of important demographic and related

This chapter draws from a monograph prepared by the author for the American Association of Retired Persons (Eric R. Kingson, *The Diversity of the Baby Boom Generation: Implications for their Retirement Years*, American Association of Retired Persons, Forecasting and Environmental Scanning Division, April 1992). The chapter also draws on work in progress by Eric Kingson and John C. Cornman (*Social Security and the Baby Boom, forthcoming*), specifically a chapter drafted by Eric Kingson entitled, "The Challenge of Work."

labor force trends—most centrally, the aging of baby boomers—which provide the context for the employment of today's and tomorrow's older workers. It concludes by highlighting the importance of tempering speculation about older worker trends and policy with an understanding of two realities: (1) there is much uncertainty associated with economic, institutional, and demographic change, and (2) there is much diversity within cohorts transitioning through older worker status.

OVERVIEW OF THE TRENDS

The movement of new cohorts of older people into older worker status occurs within a social and demographic context. The population is continually growing, aging, and diversifying—presenting numerous opportunities and challenges for older workers and the nation. The interaction of long-term trends in fertility and mortality is contributing to a workforce profile which is becoming increasingly older. The nation is more racially and ethnically diverse, a result of differences in fertility between various groups and of changing patterns of immigration. Today's workforce is, on average, better educated than the cohorts of workers who preceded them, arguably facilitating a continuation of work at later ages. Changes in family structure have paralleled and interacted with labor force changes and with growing pressures associated with providing care to younger and older members. The powerful early retirement trend of the past 40 years has been partially offset by increased labor force participation among certain groups of women (see, e.g., Ruhm, Chapter 4). There is evidence that the aging of the workforce may swell disability rolls, but there are also indications that new cohorts of older workers may be healthier—on average—than those who preceded them. These trends are now reviewed as they relate to *older workers*, a term used in a variety of ways in popular and academic discourse, and also defined under the Age Discrimination in Employment Act as referring to people aged 40 and over. As the discussion progresses, distinctions will sometimes be made between "younger" older workers—early and late middle-aged persons ages 40 to 64—and "advanced" older workers—those ages 65 and over.

A GROWING AND CHANGING POPULATION

Recent census bureau projections tell the story of an America that is expected to grow from 249 million people in 1990 to about 323 million in 2020 and 383 million in 2050 (under the middle series projections), a 50 percent increase in the population over this 60-year period (Day, 1992). There are huge differences in the population projections based on different sets of assumptions. For example, census projections based on the lowest series estimate 276 million people in 2050, compared to 507 million people under the highest series. All three series, however, paint a picture of a nation that is simultaneously becoming older and far more diverse (Tables 3.1, 3.2, and 3.3).

The variation between estimates primarily reflects differences in assumptions about life expectancy, fertility, and immigration. The middle series projections build on the modest improvements in mortality experienced during the 1980s and assume that life expectancy at birth will "increase slowly from 75.8 years in 1992 to 82.1 years in 2050" (Day, 1992, xi). These projections also assume age-specific fertility rates for most of the population groups that are just below the 1990 levels for most groups, as well as a 10 percent fertility rate decline for persons of Hispanic origin and for non-Hispanic Asians and Pacific Islanders. Net annual immigration is expected to remain about the same as in 1990 (880,000 per year). In contrast, the lowest series projection assumes a slight drop in life expectancy and an average decline in age-specific fertility of 10 percent for non-Hispanic white groups and 20 percent for all other groups. This series also assumes a decrease in net yearly immigration to 350,000 persons. In contrast, the highest series assumes net yearly immigration of 1,370,000 people and large increases in life expectancy, which parallel the improvements occurring during the 1970–1980 period. It also assumes a 20 percent increase in the age-specific fertility rates of non-Hispanic whites and a 10 percent increase for all others (Day, 1992).

POPULATION AGING

The context surrounding older worker trends and policy is being shaped by a growing awareness of population aging, a phenomenon that some see as providing the opportunity, and perhaps the necessity, for longer worklives. Century-long public health, nutritional, and biomedical advances have combined with economic development to lower mortality rates at all ages. More people are reaching old age and, once doing so, living longer. As a result of birth and mortality trends and the aging of the baby boom cohorts, the population age 65 and over and, to an even greater extent, the population age 85 and over is expected to grow very rapidly over the next 60 years—both in absolute numbers and as a percentage of the entire population (Kingson, Hirshorn, and Cornman, 1986). Under the middle series projections, the U.S. Bureau of the Census (Day, 1992) estimates that there will be about 54 million people age 65 or over in 2020 (20.2 percent of the population) and 79 million in 2050 (20.6 percent of the population), compared to 31 million (12.5 percent) in 1990. Perhaps more significantly, the bureau projects that by 2050 almost 18 million people (4.6 percent) will be age 85 and over, compared to 3.1 million (1.3 percent) in 1990.

Not surprisingly, for most of this period a corresponding decline is projected in the proportion of the population in all age groups under age 45, although the number of persons in each age category is expected to increase in general (Tables 3.1, 3.2). The exceptions to this pattern are primarily a function of the aging of the cohorts of persons born since the early 1980s, variously termed the "baby boom echo" or "baby blippers," because many of their parents are baby boomers. These cohorts are generally numerically and proportionally larger than

Table 3.1
Population by Age: 1990 to 2050 (in thousands, as of July 1, resident population, consistent with the 1990 census, as enumerated)

Year	Total	Under 5 years	5 to 13 years	14 to 17 years	18 to 24 years	25 to 34 years	35 to 44 years	45 to 64 years	65 years and over	85 years and over	100 years and over
ESTIMATE											
1990	249,415	18,874	32,000	13,312	26,829	43,136	37,765	46,277	31,224	3,050	36
PROJECTIONS											
Lowest Series											
1995	260,715	19,165	34,185	14,644	24,623	40,469	42,296	51,998	33,335	3,575	51
2000	268,108	17,438	35,247	15,454	25,438	36,310	43,995	60,258	33,968	4,055	66
2005	273,605	16,531	33,436	16,587	27,123	34,697	40,978	69,678	34,575	4,442	89
2010	278,078	16,356	31,203	15,835	28,742	36,028	36,782	76,439	36,694	4,852	103
2020	285,200	16,709	30,566	14,096	25,901	39,579	36,486	74,680	47,182	4,820	130
2030	286,710	15,735	30,494	14,367	24,724	35,587	39,946	67,830	58,027	5,569	152
2040	282,286	15,336	28,841	13,900	25,081	34,670	35,986	70,911	57,560	7,933	167
2050	275,647	15,153	28,464	13,299	23,706	34,732	35,055	70,080	55,157	9,228	250

Middle Series

Year	Total	Under 5 years	5 to 13 years	14 to 17 years	18 to 24 years	25 to 34 years	35 to 44 years	45 to 64 years	65 years and over	85 years and over	100 years and over
1995	262,754	19,553	34,372	14,754	24,903	40,844	42,500	52,235	33,594	3,638	54
2000	274,815	18,908	36,051	15,734	26,117	37,416	44,662	61,042	34,886	4,289	77
2005	286,324	18,959	35,782	17,020	28,111	35,495	42,284	71,257	36,414	4,937	118
2010	298,109	19,730	35,425	16,908	30,007	38,367	38,853	79,115	39,705	5,702	160
2020	322,602	21,388	38,068	16,847	29,685	43,024	39,786	80,179	53,627	6,480	278
2030	344,951	21,961	40,368	18,449	31,275	42,629	44,364	76,069	69,839	8,381	435
2040	364,349	23,192	41,739	19,159	33,530	45,329	43,977	81,836	75,588	13,221	620
2050	382,674	24,411	44,223	19,999	34,482	48,020	46,626	86,038	78,876	17,652	1,170

Table 3.1 (continued)

Year	Total	Under 5 years	5 to 13 years	14 to 17 years	18 to 24 years	25 to 34 years	35 to 44 years	45 to 64 years	65 years and over	85 years and over	100 years and over
Highest Series											
1995	264,685	19,949	34,551	14,857	25,175	41,214	42,726	52,434	33,778	3,685	55
2000	281,306	20,448	36,846	15,999	26,773	38,524	45,461	61,722	35,534	4,484	82
2005	298,773	21,621	38,176	17,433	29,066	38,281	43,828	72,660	37,707	5,372	134
2010	317,895	23,640	39,904	17,971	31,231	40,655	41,191	81,513	41,790	6,473	196
2020	360,123	27,101	46,782	19,817	33,570	46,391	43,396	85,211	57,855	6,028	407
2030	405,130	30,104	52,439	23,206	38,690	49,906	49,228	83,826	77,731	11,083	746
2040	453,687	34,355	58,778	25,662	43,627	57,323	52,886	92,198	88,857	18,374	1,198
2050	506,740	38,645	66,797	29,009	48,381	63,826	60,428	101,728	97,926	26,160	2,491

Source: Day (1992), xiv.

Table 3.2

Percentage Distribution of the Population by Age: 1990 to 2050 (in thousands, as of July 1, resident population, consistent with the 1990 census, as enumerated)

Year	Total	Under 5 years	5 to 13 years	14 to 17 years	18 to 24 years	25 to 34 years	35 to 44 years	45 to 64 years	65 years and over	85 years and over	100 years and over
ESTIMATE											
1990	100.0	7.6	12.8	5.3	10.8	17.3	15.1	18.6	12.5	1.2	0.0
PROJECTIONS											
Lowest Series											
1995	100.0	7.4	13.1	5.6	9.4	15.5	16.2	19.9	12.8	1.4	0.0
2000	100.0	6.5	13.1	5.8	9.5	13.5	16.4	22.5	12.7	1.5	0.0
2005	100.0	6.0	12.2	6.1	9.9	12.7	15.0	25.5	12.6	1.6	0.0
2010	100.0	5.9	11.2	5.7	10.3	13.0	13.2	27.5	13.2	1.7	0.0
2020	100.0	5.9	10.7	4.9	9.1	13.9	12.8	26.2	16.5	1.7	0.0
2030	100.0	5.5	10.6	5.0	8.6	12.4	13.9	23.7	20.2	1.9	0.1
2040	100.0	5.4	10.2	4.9	8.9	12.3	12.7	25.1	20.4	2.8	0.1
2050	100.0	5.5	10.3	4.8	8.6	12.6	12.7	25.4	20.0	3.3	0.1

Table 3.2 (continued)

Year	Total	Under 5 years	5 to 13 years	14 to 17 years	18 to 24 years	25 to 34 years	35 to 44 years	45 to 64 years	65 years and over	85 years and over	100 years and over
Middle Series											
1995	100.0	7.4	13.1	5.6	9.5	15.5	16.2	19.9	12.8	1.4	0.0
2000	100.0	6.9	13.1	5.7	9.5	13.6	16.3	22.2	12.7	1.6	0.0
2005	100.0	6.6	12.5	5.9	9.8	12.7	14.8	24.9	12.7	1.7	0.0
2010	100.0	6.6	11.9	5.7	10.1	12.9	13.0	26.5	13.3	1.9	0.1
2020	100.0	6.6	11.8	5.2	9.2	13.3	12.3	24.9	16.6	2.0	0.1
2030	100.0	6.4	11.7	5.3	9.1	12.4	12.9	22.1	20.2	2.4	0.1
2040	100.0	6.4	11.5	5.3	9.2	12.4	12.1	22.5	20.7	3.6	0.2
2050	100.0	6.4	11.6	5.2	9.0	12.5	12.2	22.5	20.6	4.6	0.3

Highest Series

Year	Total	Under 5 years	5 to 13 years	14 to 17 years	18 to 24 years	25 to 34 years	35 to 44 years	45 to 64 years	65 years and over	85 years and over	100 years and over
1995	100.0	7.5	13.1	5.6	9.5	15.6	16.1	19.8	12.8	1.4	0.0
2000	100.0	7.3	13.1	5.7	9.5	13.7	16.2	21.9	12.6	1.6	0.0
2005	100.0	7.2	12.8	5.8	9.7	12.8	14.7	24.3	12.6	1.8	0.0
2010	100.0	7.4	12.6	5.7	9.8	12.8	13.0	25.6	13.1	2.0	0.1
2020	100.0	7.5	13.0	5.5	9.3	12.9	12.1	23.7	16.1	2.2	0.1
2030	100.0	7.4	12.9	5.7	9.6	12.3	12.2	20.7	19.2	2.7	0.2
2040	100.0	7.6	13.0	5.7	9.6	12.6	11.7	20.3	19.6	4.0	0.3
2050	100.0	7.6	13.2	5.7	9.5	12.6	11.9	20.1	19.3	5.2	0.5

Source: Day (1992), 15.

Table 3.3

Percentage Distribution of the Population, by Race and Hispanic Origin (in thousands, as of July 1, resident population, consistent with the 1990 census, as enumerated)

Year	Total	Race				Hispanic Origin[3]	Not of Hispanic origin, by race			
		White	Black	American Indian[1]	Asian[2]		White	Black	American Indian[1]	Asian[2]
ESTIMATE										
1990	100.0	83.9	12.3	0.8	3.0	9.0	75.7	11.8	0.7	2.8
PROJECTIONS										
1995	100.0	82.8	12.6	0.9	3.7	10.1	73.6	12.1	0.7	3.5
2000	100.0	81.7	12.9	0.9	4.5	11.1	71.6	12.3	0.8	4.2
2005	100.0	80.7	13.2	0.9	5.2	12.2	69.6	12.6	0.8	4.9
2010	100.0	79.6	13.6	0.9	5.9	13.2	67.6	12.8	0.8	5.5
2020	100.0	77.7	14.2	1.0	7.2	15.2	63.9	13.3	0.9	6.8
2030	100.0	75.8	14.8	1.0	8.4	17.2	60.2	13.8	0.9	7.9
2040	100.0	73.8	15.5	1.1	9.6	19.2	56.4	14.4	1.0	9.1
2050	100.0	71.8	16.2	1.2	10.7	21.1	52.7	15.0	1.1	10.1

**LOWEST
SERIES**

| 2050 | 100.0 | 74.3 | 15.1 | 1.3 | 9.3 | 18.4 | 57.4 | 14.1 | 1.1 | 8.9 |

**HIGHEST
SERIES**

| 2050 | 100.0 | 71.6 | 15.7 | 1.1 | 11.6 | 22.7 | 51.3 | 14.3 | 0.9 | 10.9 |

[1] American Indian represents American Indian, Eskimo, and Aleut.
[2] Asian represents Asian and Pacific Islander.
[3] Persons of Hispanic origin may be of any race.
Source: Day (1992), xviii.

cohorts born during the 1970s ("baby busters"), when total fertility rates plummeted to a historic low of an average of 1.7 births per woman (see Bouvier and DeVita, 1991) before increasing in the late 1980s to current levels of about 2.05 births per woman (Federal Old Age and Survivors Insurance, 1994). Thus, projections show the "echo" elevating both the numbers and the percentage of the population that fall into the age categories as they age.

CHANGING DEPENDENCY RATIOS

Anxiety over population aging is often expressed with reference to the changing old-age support ratios, commonly termed old-age dependency ratios. With the projected increase in the number and proportion of older persons during the next 60 years, the number of persons aged 18 through 64, the so-called working age population, is projected to decline as a proportion of the entire population. That is, the ratio of elderly persons (65 and over) to every 100 "working age" persons (18 to 64) has increased from about 15:100 persons in 1955 to roughly 21:100 today and is expected to increase to about 36:100 persons in 2030, the apex of the retirement of baby boomers. Consequently, some ask whether workers of the future will be able to afford to support a growing aged population and conclude that they cannot.

However, analysis based on the *overall dependency ratio* (also called the *total support ratio*)—which includes children under 18 and the elderly as "dependent" populations—leads to a different conclusion (Crown, 1985). During the next 65 years, the overall dependency ratio is not projected to exceed the levels it attained in 1964 (Torrey, 1982). This is because the proportion of the population under 18 is projected to decline. Even from 2030 through 2050, the total dependency ratio is projected to be well below (about 78:100) what it was during the 1960s (e.g., 83:100 in 1965) when most of the baby boomers were children. Although the composition of governmental and private spending for children and elderly persons is different, analysis that includes the expanded notion of dependency ratios does not lead to the automatic conclusion that changing demographics will overwhelm the nation's ability to respond to the retirement needs of future generations (Crown, 1985; Kingson and Berkowitz, 1993; Schulz, Borowski, and Crown, 1991). Neither does it suggest that the nation will necessarily be able to meet these needs. Much depends on the future productivity of the economy and on other economic factors such as the composition of the workforce. In fact, economic variables are considerably more important than demographic variables with regard to the nation's ability to adjust to an aging population (Crown, 1993). However, no matter whether one accepts or rejects frightening predictions about the implications of population aging and changing dependency ratios, an awareness of these demographic events should add force to efforts to encourage the labor force participation of healthy elderly Americans and other potential older workers.

GROWING NUMBERS OF OLDER WORKERS

The aging of the baby boom cohorts portends an increasing number (and proportion) of people entering the "younger" older worker age categories. The numbers in the age category that includes the great bulk of older workers, 45–64, are expected to swell dramatically during the next 25 years or so, from 52 million workers in 1995 to 79 million in 2010, and then level off as the baby boom cohorts age (Tables 3.1, 3.2). This demographic event strongly suggests that older worker policy will grow in importance on public and private employment policy agendas during the next 25 years, with increasing attention being brought to bear on such issues as retraining, retention and rehiring, and second careers. Similarly, as the baby boom cohorts move into more advanced older worker status (that is, past age 65), a trend that will occur after 2010 Tables 3.1, 3.2), interest in phased retirement, part-time employment, and self-employment is likely to grow.

AN INCREASINGLY DIVERSE SOCIETY

Population aging and workforce aging will be taking place in a more heterogeneous nation with respect to racial and ethnic minorities at risk, groups who, due to racial or ethnic status, often experience restrictions that limit economic and social mobility (African Americans, Asian and Pacific Islander populations, Native American populations, and Hispanic populations). Old populations will be more diverse; younger populations, even more so. By 2035, the various populations among minorities at risk will constitute more than half of the population under age 20 (Day, 1992).

Under the middle series projections, the non-Hispanic white population is projected to decline as a percent of the total population from 75.7 percent in 1990 to 67.6 percent in 2010 and 52.7 percent in 2050. Stated differently, the Hispanic populations are expected to more than double during this period as a percentage of the entire population, from 9.0 percent to 21.1 percent, and the Asian and Pacific Islander populations to more than triple, from 2.8 to 10.1 percent. The African-American population is projected to increase by 25 percent, from 11.8 to 15.0 percent, while the Native American population will increase by about 50 percent, from 0.7 to 1.1 percent (Table 3.3).

The changing racial and ethnic composition is a function of the interaction of race, Hispanic ethnicity, and age, with several demographic trends. The number and proportion of births is expected to vary across racial and ethnic groups because of factors such as the higher rates of fertility among Hispanic populations (who are also relatively younger than other racial and ethnic groups) and the lower rates of fertility among non-Hispanic white populations (who are also relatively older than other ethnic groups) (Day, 1992). The relative increase in immigration from Asia and Latin America is contributing to the growing diversity of the nation, especially among younger population groups. Immigration flows are expected to expand all cohorts, but especially those that are younger, either directly through the entrance of immigrants or indirectly, by giving birth once in the United States. Immigration is so important that the baby bust cohorts—sometimes defined as people born from 1970 through 1979—"will actually *increase* in size between 1990 and 2010. By 2010, when members of the baby-bust generation will be between 30 and 39 years old, close to 19 percent of this group will be foreign-born, in contrast to 5 percent of baby boomers at the same age" (Bouvier and DeVita, 1991, 12).

This growing diversity of the population has implications for policy development directed at older workers. Fernando Torres-Gil (1992) and Martha Ozawa (1985) have observed the potential for a large elderly population composed disproportionately of non-Hispanic whites competing with a growing young minority population for social resources. Similarly, it is conceivable that one of the subthemes of an aging workforce will be competition between younger, minority workers and older, nonminority workers. Thus, it may be important to anticipate the need for mechanisms to expand employment and promotion opportunities for younger workers, lest their mobility be blocked by virtue of the larger cohorts ahead of them. Similarly, though perhaps somewhat at odds with the goal of expanding mobility for the young, encouraging healthy elders to contribute to the economy through continued employment is likely to become increasingly important if they are not to be perceived as a burden to the young.

A BETTER EDUCATED POPULATION

Future cohorts of older workers will be better educated and therefore better positioned to work longer. Simultaneously, there will be much variance in education and skill development, leaving those with less education and limited skills at greater risk of becoming "obsolete" as they age.

Take the baby boom cohorts as an example. These cohorts have, on average, already progressed further with their education than previous groups (U.S. House of Representatives, 1987; Light, 1988; Russell, 1982). Twenty-two percent of baby boomers ages 25 to 29 in March 1985 had completed 4 years of college and 86 percent had completed high school. In contrast, in March 1965, 12 percent of persons in this age cohort had completed college and 70 percent had completed high school, and in March 1950, only 8 percent had completed college and 52 percent had completed high school (Siegel, 1989).

Educational progress, however, has been uneven across population subgroups. Although the proportion of Hispanic baby boomers ages 25 to 29 who completed four years of college increased from 8.8 percent in 1975 to 11.3 percent in 1988, the proportion of Hispanic college graduates was slightly less than one-half of that for the non-Hispanic population (U.S. Bureau of the Census, 1989). Similarly, although the proportion of African-Americans and whites receiving high school diplomas has greatly narrowed since 1950, substantial disparities remain.

Proportionately, twice as many whites (23.2 percent) as African Americans (11.5 percent) in the 25 to 29 age group had graduated from college by 1988 (Siegel, 1989).

Thus, although educational profiles have improved, in the aggregate, some members of all cohorts have very little preparation for employment settings requiring an increasingly skilled workforce. Of concern, the Joint Economic Committee reported in 1988 that approximately "13 percent of 17-year old Americans cannot read, write, or [count]" (U.S. Congress, Joint Economic Committee, 1989, 1); moreover, while "97 percent of high school seniors and 17-year olds can 'understand specific or sequentially related information' they read, only 40 percent of that group can comprehend the basic essence of that information" (U.S. Congress, Joint Economic Committee, 1989, 2). The committee also reports that an estimated "17 to 21 million adults cannot read" (U.S. Congress, Joint Economic Committee, 1989, 14).

What does the educational profile of today's youth and today's young and middle-aged workers imply for the future? Given that they will, in the aggregate, be more educated than the prior cohorts of older (and elderly) workers, it seems likely that a growing proportion will maintain links to lifelong learning (Moody, 1988). Given the current relationship between higher levels of educational attainment and the lower incidence of chronic illness, future older workers may experience lower rates of chronic illness. Higher socioeconomic status, healthier lifestyles (i.e., diet and exercise), and the less arduous demands of the workplace may combine to reduce the age-specific incidence of chronic illness and facilitate longer worklives (U.S. House of Representatives, 1987; Manton, 1993). These possibilities should not be overstated because, as discussed, there is much diversity of educational attainment within cohorts and, to the extent that a linkage exists between chronic illness and educational attainment, the relationship is complex.

CHANGING FAMILY AND CAREGIVING RESPONSIBILITIES

The American family life is characterized by (1) change, (2) a diversity of family types, (3) high likelihood of transitioning through several forms of family life, (4) fewer children than today's older cohorts, (5) changing patterns of caregiving to children, and (6) increasingly complex relationships with kin networks.

Much of the change in composition of households and families since 1960 is a function of changes that took place as the baby boom cohorts emerged into adulthood. Cohabitation increased, ninefold during the 1970s among young couples under age 25 (Jones, 1980). It is anticipated that a high proportion of baby boomers (about 10 percent compared to 5 percent of their parents' cohorts) will not marry (Committee on Ways and Means, 1987). As a group, members of the baby boom cohorts often postponed childbearing, had fewer children than their parents, divorced more frequently, and raised more children in single-parent households (Saluter, 1989). About half of their marriages are expected to result in divorce; but estimates indicate that ¾ will remarry (Cherlin and Furstenberg, 1982).

Andrew Cherlin and Frank Furstenberg (1982) suggest that by the millennium three types of ''families will dominate the personal lives of most Americans: families of first marriages, single-parent families, and families of remarriages.'' The ''traditional family'' of the 1950s—a mother with children under age 18 who is a full-time homemaker and a father who is employed—described 27.5 percent of married couples with a wife aged 18 through 44 in 1987 compared to 43.2 percent as recently as 1976. During this period, ''dual earner couples with children rose from 33 to 46 percent'' (U.S. Bureau of the Census, 1989, 18). Single parenthood has also grown dramatically, doubling since 1970 to include 27 percent of all families with children under age 18 in 1988, with women heading seven out of every eight of these families. Demographers estimate now that one-half of young children will spend some portion of their childhood in a single-parent family.

Changing family relationships and changing demographic trends are giving rise to a more complex kin network than in the past. Greater longevity and generally smaller family sizes result in more intergenerational relationships for most family members, while relationships within generations (i.e., cousins, siblings) decline. The typical married couple has more parents than children, a demographic change that can lead to increased parental caregiving responsibilities as adult children make the transition into early and late older worker ages. Moreover, divorce, single parenthood, and remarriage generally result in more complex family ties and often raise new issues of caregiving responsibility for former in-laws, for stepparents, and for parents (Hagestad, 1986).

The impact of these changes in the family on the labor force participation of today's and tomorrow's older and elderly workers is difficult to gauge. For many single parents, financial and family responsibilities often leave little room for retirement savings, a reality that may encourage longer worklives. Clearly, some older workers, particularly those in late middle age and early old age, will find themselves responsible for providing care to aged parents, sick spouses, or other family members. Such responsibilities, on the one hand, encourage income-generating activity and, on the other hand, encourage older workers to reduce their labor force efforts in order to provide care. Of course, faced with dual responsibilities as family caregiver and employee, some workers will choose to leave work, while others will maintain their labor force connection and simultaneously seek to provide care. Recognizing the pressures on employees and the potentially negative consequences for productivity, a growing number of employers are expanding benefit packages and employee assistance programs to provide such services as information and referral to long-term care services to assist employees with elder care responsibilities. As the workforce ages and assumes more responsibilities, the use of these services will likely expand.

A CHANGING LABOR FORCE

Today's early and late middle-age workers have been part of an economy that added large numbers of jobs during the past 20 years while also undergoing structural shifts that have seen the loss of many generally higher-paying manufacturing jobs and the growth in numbers of, often lower-paying, service sector jobs. The economy experienced a net increase of 31 million jobs between 1975 and 1990, increasing participation in the labor force by 12 million men and 19 million women (U.S. House of Representatives, 1992).

The entrance of many baby boomers into the labor market—beginning in the late 1960s—combined with the increased participation of women to drive this large expansion of jobs. Female labor force participation rose from 34 percent in 1950 to 46 percent in 1975 and 58 percent in 1990, while male labor force participation declined from 86 percent in 1950 to 78 percent in 1975 and 76 percent in 1990.

The 1.9 percent annual increase in the labor force during the 1975–1990 period is, however, expected to slow to a 1.3 percent annual increase from 1990–2005 (U.S. House of Representatives, 1992). This is partially a function of the narrowing of the gap between the labor force participation of men and women. Although women's involvement in the labor force is expected to continue to expand, the rate of increase is expected to be slower than in the past. The fact that the baby boom cohorts have now arrived at prime working ages is the other major factor that explains the anticipated slowdown in the rate of increase of the labor force. Late middle-age workers—the ranks of whom will soon be swelled by baby boomers—generally experience higher rates of labor force withdrawal due to disability and early retirements. Moreover, the number of annual entry-age workers who followed the baby boom was, and remains, smaller. It should be noted, however, that even though the baby busters and the baby blippers represent smaller portions of the population relative to the baby boomers, their numbers are still substantial (which explains, in large part, why the Bureau of Labor Statistics projects a net increase in the labor force of 26 million people from 1990 to 2005).

LONG-TERM TRENDS OF OLDER MEN

All observers agree that there has been a rapid decline in the labor force participation of male workers ages 45 and over since the late 1940s. There are, however, at least two stories about the trends preceding this decline (Quinn, Burkhauser, and Myers, 1990). The old and, until recently, generally accepted story is of a century-long decline in the labor force participation of older workers (Clague, Pahli, and Kramer, 1971), which is a function of economic growth, shifts from a largely agricultural to an industrial economy, and changing taste and opportunity for retirement leisure. Support for this view is found in U.S. government statistics showing male labor force participation dropping from over

80 percent in 1870 to just under 70 percent in 1890, less than 60 percent in 1930, 46 percent in 1950, and 16 percent in 1991 for persons aged 65 and over (see Clague, Pahli, and Kramer, 1971; U.S. House of Representatives, 1993; Quinn, Burkhauser, and Myers, 1990).

More recent research by Roger Ransom and Richard Sutch (1986, 1988) "indicates that there was virtually no change in retirement rates among American men from 1870 to 1937 and, therefore, that nearly all of the change in retirement patterns has occurred during the past fifty years" (Quinn, Burkhauser, and Myers, 1990, 15). After 1890, the Census Bureau no longer counted people as employed if they received rental income or interest or dividends from capital. Apparently, this change accounts for what is actually a statistical artifact showing a decline in the labor force participation of men ages 65 and over from 1870 to 1937 (Quinn, Burkhauser, and Myers, 1990, 15).

The Ransom and Sutch analysis provides support for the view that expansions of social security and pension incentives since 1937 have exerted a very powerful effect on older workers, substantially explaining early retirement trends since the late 1940s (Quinn, Burkhauser, and Myers, 1990). However, as with the question that addresses the ordering of the origins of "the chicken and the egg," another view is also possible. These incentives may be simply the vehicles used to engineer the labor force or respond to changing preferences for leisure. The acceptance of Ransom and Sutch's analyses and of the view that retirement income exerts the strongest influence over the retirement decision of most older workers does not necessarily lead to the conclusion that expanded social security and employer pension incentives are the primary *cause* of the declining labor force participation among men. We might find causal explanations elsewhere (e.g., in economic growth that allows for a greater consumption of leisure and in decisions to promote early retirement as an alternative to laying off workers).

DECLINING LABOR FORCE PARTICIPATION OF OLDER MEN SINCE 1950

No matter how one interprets the long-term statistics, a brief review of existing data since 1950 indicates the magnitude of the trend toward early labor force withdrawal among men and underlines the diversity of labor force participation patterns among older workers. The participation rates for men aged 65 and over dropped from about 46 percent in 1950 to 16 percent in 1993, almost all of which occurred prior to 1985 (Table 3.2). Participation among men aged 45 through 64 has declined substantially too, with the participation of men aged 55 through 64 going from roughly 87 percent in 1950 to 67 percent in 1993. Nearly all this decline occurred in the period prior to 1985. As Quinn observed:

Recent data suggest that the male early retirement trend may have stopped, since the participation rates of older men have been virtually constant since 1986. An alternative interpretation is that the trend continues, but in another guise—reduced hours, since the proportion of employed older Americans who work part-time continues to rise. (1993, p. 10)

LABOR FORCE PARTICIPATION TRENDS AMONG WOMEN

The participation rates for women aged 65 and over have been consistently low, but the overall trend has been for increased participation, especially during youth and early middle age. Arguably, the increased labor market involvement of women is the most significant labor force trend of the past 40 years. For example, women aged 45–54 increased their participation from about 38 percent in 1950 to 73 percent in 1992. In general, the trends for women aged 55–64 show an increase in participation rates of 27 percent in 1950 to 41 percent in 1965, and a slower rate of increase thereafter to about 47 percent in 1993. The labor force participation of elderly women, however, has fluctuated between 11 and 7 percent since 1950 (Table 3.4).

Overall, the data seem to suggest that at the older ages, the powerful trend of increased labor force participation of women has been modified somewhat by the similarly powerful early retirement trend—resulting in lower levels of labor force participation for these women than would otherwise be the case. Within subgroups of women aged 55–64 there are interesting variations. In rather dramatic contrast to similarly aged men, the labor force participation rates for women aged 55–59—who would not be eligible for social security early retirement or regular aged widow's benefits—increased substantially, from about 47 percent in 1965 to 57 percent in 1993. But for women aged 62 through 64, there was very little change from 1965 to 1993, varying by a couple of percentage points around 30 percent.

DISAGGREGATIONS BY RACE AND MARITAL STATUS

Further disaggregation of the labor force participation patterns highlights a number of interesting relationships. Among older men, the trend lines for white and African-American older workers have been fairly similar, though participation among African Americans has been somewhat lower. Apparently both groups have been affected by the early retirement trend. The lower participation of older African-American men may be explained in large part by higher rates of work-limiting health conditions and greater likelihood of participating in occupations requiring physical exertion (Coleman, 1993; Gibson, 1993). There is also reason to believe that financial need provides, on the average, more motivation for older African Americans to continue to work (Coleman, 1993). However, this is offset by factors such as health status, lower educational levels, the effects of past and current discrimination, and the occupational requirements for more strenuous activity among current cohorts of older African Americans.

Unlike their male counterparts, the labor force participation trends for older

Table 3.4
Labor Force Participation Rates, 1950 to 1993[1]

Sex	1950	1955	1960	1965	1970	1975	1980	1985	1990	1993
MEN:										
55 to 64	86.9	87.9	86.8	84.6	83.0	75.8	72.3	67.9	67.7	66.5
55 to 59	([2])	92.5	91.6	90.2	89.5	84.4	81.9	79.6	79.8	78.2
60 to 64	([2])	82.5	81.1	78.0	75.0	65.7	61.0	55.6	55.5	54.1
60 to 61	([2])	([2])	([2])	84.8	82.6	75.2	71.8	68.9	68.8	66.1
62 to 64	([2])	([2])	([2])	73.2	69.4	58.8	52.8	46.1	46.4	46.1
65 and over	45.8	39.6	33.1	27.9	26.8	21.7	19.1	15.8	16.4	15.6
WOMEN:										
55 to 64	27.0	32.5	37.2	41.4	43.0	41.0	41.5	42.0	45.3	47.3
55 to 59	([2])	35.6	42.2	47.1	50.4	47.9	48.6	50.3	55.3	57.1
60 to 64	([2])	29.0	31.4	34.0	36.1	33.3	33.3	33.4	35.5	37.1
60 to 61	([2])	([2])	([2])	40.4	41.4	39.5	39.8	40.3	42.9	45.2
62 to 64	([2])	([2])	([2])	29.5	32.3	29.0	28.6	28.7	30.7	31.8
65 and over	9.7	10.6	10.8	10.0	9.7	8.3	8.1	7.3	8.7	8.2

[1] Civilian labor force as percent of civilian noninstitutional population aged 16 or older.
[2] Data not available.
Source: U.S. House of Representatives (1994), 856.

African-American and white female workers are not similar. Among women aged 65 and over, African Americans have a somewhat higher rate of participation, possibly a function of greater need. Most of the increase in labor force participation among women ages 45–64 has been by white women. Older African-American women have participated for many years at levels that older white women have only recently realized. In fact, in this age group, white single women have also participated traditionally at fairly high levels, which white married women are beginning to duplicate.

IMPLICATIONS OF LABOR FORCE TRENDS

When considering lessons to be drawn with respect to future cohorts of older workers, one of the most important points to appreciate is that older workers are a heterogeneous group, leaving work—or in many cases, continuing to work—for a variety of reasons and in a variety of ways. Research indicates that it may be misleading to characterize retirement as an all-or-nothing event. Older "workers take a variety of routes between full-time work and full-time retirement. The paths are so varied that the phrase 'retirement' . . . may well conceal more than it reveals" (Quinn, Burkhauser, and Myers, 1990, 188). Part-time or part-year work options are increasingly exercised by older men continuing to work past age 62—with, for example, 62 percent of men age 65–69 who are labor force participants working less than full-time, full-year in 1985. These retirement transitions from a career full-time position "to part-time work on the same job or part-time or full-time work on a new job—are very important, but poorly understood" (Quinn, Burkhauser, and Myers, 1990, 239). Of course, many older workers leave the labor force permanently prior to age 65. The retirements of many are fully voluntary, often reflecting strong private and public-employee pension benefits and the desire for increased leisure. The withdrawals of others, however, are brought about primarily by health and limited employment options. Interestingly, groups of persons retiring prior to age 62 tend "to be composed of both very high income people and very low income people—with very few in the middle"—often reflecting the ability of higher income earners with second pension coverage to choose to retire early and the inability of more marginal or partially disabled older workers to maintain their links to the labor force (Schulz, 1992, 28). This phenomenon—termed the "Two Nations in Early Retirement" by researchers who have studied it in the context of the United Kingdom (see Atkinson and Sutherland, 1993)—presents one of the major challenges to policy makers concerned with developing equitable responses to the aging of the workforce. In addition, it raises important questions about whether, and which, older workers of the future will be healthier and able to work longer—a topic to which we turn now.

HEALTH, LONGEVITY, AND WORK ABILITY

One of the unknowns about the future with potentially important public policy implications is whether the health status of future cohorts of older workers will allow them, as a group, to work longer than today's elderly cohorts. Stated somewhat differently, the question is whether anticipated increases in life expectancy for today's "younger" older workers and those who follow will be matched by parallel reductions in morbidity and disability. A substantial literature addresses these questions but is not entirely conclusive (Butler, 1982; Feldman, 1983, 1991; Fries, 1991; Guralnik, 1991; Manton, 1983, 1993; Manton, Cordor, and Stallard, 1993; Verbrugge, 1991). Findings from recent research (Manton, 1993; Manton, Cordor, and Stallard, 1993), however, seem to point increasingly to the likelihood that there has been, and will continue to be, some aggregate increases in work ability among older populations, especially among more highly educated and high-income older persons.

Comparisons of the U.S. medicare elderly populations in 1982, 1984, and 1989 and analyses of the National Long Term Care Surveys of 1982, 1984, and 1989 by Kenneth Manton, Larry Corder, and Eric Stallard (1993) show a decline in disability prevalence among the elderly populations over this time period. For example, their analysis shows a drop in disability prevalence from 23.7 percent in 1982 to 22.6 percent in 1989. When this estimate is adjusted to account for changes resulting from population aging, it implies that there were 540,000 fewer chronically disabled elderly persons in 1989 than there would have been if there was no change in the prevalence of disability since 1982 (Manton, Cordor, and Stallard, 1993). Moreover, the "annual likelihood of staying non-disabled" for a year "adjusted for mortality for those age 65 to 74 was 96.5 percent (1982–1984) and 97.6 percent (1984–1989)" (Manton, 1993, 18).

James Fries outlined three scenarios. Under the first, life expectancy increases but disability occurs at roughly the same ages, with the result that we have "only added infirm years to life." Under the second, life expectancy and the typical age of disability increase by the same amount, resulting in the same amount of infirm years but increasing the number of years in which people could work. Under the third, life expectancy increases, but the average age of disability increases by even more, thereby greatly encouraging work among future old people (Fries, 1991, 17, 18).

On the one hand, there are experts such as Fries who have argued that the effective worklives of older persons in the future will be considerably longer because medical knowledge is reducing the risk of the onset of chronic illness, because the shift from manufacturing to service industry employment will reduce occupational trauma, and because the prevention of risk factors to health will result in a healthier and more functionally independent elder population. On the other hand, there is still merit to the view that we simply do not know whether older workers will, on average, be able to work longer. Analyzing data during the early 1980s, Jacob Feldman observed that "disability rates for the population aged fifty-five to seventy show no evidence of a decline in work incapacity during" the recent period of declining mortality (Feldman, 1991, 19–20). Other analysts also concur that there is little empirical evidence directly linking mortality declines to reduced disability, but they add that "experienced clinicians have noted that the health status of elderly persons have improved greatly in the last two decades"—leading them to speculate that the proportions of impaired and very healthy elders may be increasing simultaneously (Kane, Radosevich, and Vaupel, 1990).

Feldman highlights the great heterogeneity of circumstances with respect to changes in mortality and work ability among older age groups. His analysis shows that among men age 65–74, the gap in death rates increased substantially from 1960 to 1980 between those with less than eight years of education and those with at least one year of college. The differences with respect to work ability are even greater, leading Feldman to suggest a fourth scenario: life expectancy increases, especially for higher socioeconomic status groups, but although the age of onset of disability increases for persons of higher socioeconomic status, no change occurs for persons of lower socioeconomic status. If this scenario materializes, policies that encourage later retirement through raising the age of eligibility for full social security benefits—and do not provide for offsetting changes in eligibility for unemployment, disability insurance, or supplemental social security income benefits—will have deleterious consequences for those among future cohorts of middle-aged and elderly persons who experience health problems during their later working years (especially those with fewer years of education and fewer employment options).

Still others suggest that today's elderly and those of the next 20 years are transition cohorts—experiencing greater longevity and greater morbidity. These analysts speculate that as newer cohorts of elders enjoy the benefits of increasing numbers of biomedical innovations and more healthful behavior, most older people may experience a longer life with substantially less disabling disease (Harootyan, 1991).

In sum, although there seems to be progress with respect to unraveling the issues surrounding the question of work ability, much remains to be learned about the ability of new cohorts of older workers to work longer and about the variability of work ability across social classes and occupations.

CONCLUDING COMMENTS

In addition to demographic trends and trends in labor force participation rates, there is more that must be appreciated in order to speculate about tomorrow's older workers. Such speculation should be tempered by the knowledge that workforce aging is occurring in complex and changing institutional, policy, and economic environments and thus is characterized by a great deal of uncertainty. Growing pension costs, the possibility of labor shortages, and increasing life expectancy at older ages provide rationales for extending worklives. Legislative changes signal later retirement ages. The 1978 Age Discrimination in Employment Act and subsequent amendments virtually eliminated the practice of mandatory retirement. The 1983 amendments to the Social Security Act schedule a gradual increase in the age of eligibility for full social security benefits from age 65 to 67 over a period of 27 years, beginning in 2000. When asked, older workers and the elderly themselves often say they would like more opportunity for part-time work. Moreover, some policy makers and academicians have called for greater opportunity for skill development and retraining throughout the life course (Morris and Bass, 1988), as well as for the consideration of further increases in the age of eligibility for social benefits (Torres-Gil, 1992).

Nevertheless, retirement seems firmly fixed as a period of institutionalized leisure, and proposals to raise the age of eligibility for public benefits challenge existing norms and are considered by some as potentially undermining the well-being of vulnerable retirees (Crown, 1990). Today, over two-thirds of social security's newly retired worker beneficiaries first accept benefits prior to age 65. The practice of offering both early and very early (before age 62) retirement opportunities to older employees remains popular, in part because older workers generally favor these provisions, and also because early retirement offers a vehicle for defining some unemployment as retirement, particularly in contracting industries. Moreover, there are many older workers for whom work is but a remote possibility, and while there is some evidence of increased work ability, the jury is still out on the question of whether the health of older workers of the future will allow for longer worklives.

Certainly, much depends on the economy and the demand for labor, in interaction with social and demographic trends; there is still much to learn in these areas. For instance, we do not know what the demand for labor will be as the aging of baby boom cohorts swell the ranks of potential older workers or what future levels of immigration will be. If, for example, labor market shortages emerge around the time that the baby boom retires, then one scenario suggests that employers will take actions to encourage later labor force withdrawal— including higher wages, lifelong training opportunities, and flexible employment options such as partial and phased retirement. However, employers might seek to substitute capital for labor. Simultaneously (or alternatively), national policy could encourage later retirement through changes in social security and private pension regulation or through the manipulation of other policy variables (i.e., immigration laws).

Sorting through the multiple trajectories of demographic and labor force trends also requires an appreciation of the social and historical context giving rise to retirement as an institution and the choices before society as we prepare for an aging workforce; moreover, it should be based on the recognition that the transitions of cohorts into and through older worker status take a long time. Very importantly, as has been stressed throughout this chapter, proper analysis requires an understanding of the diversity of circumstances among today's and tomorrow's older workers so that preparations for workforce aging will be flexible enough to adjust to changing social and economic circumstances without devaluing or financially penalizing those who are unable to work. Thus, there is reason to be cautious when drawing implications from past and projected demographic and labor force trends.

4

Historical Trends in the Employment and Labor Force Participation of Older Americans

Christopher J. Ruhm

In 1960, there were 173 Americans over 65 years old for every 1,000 between the ages of 20 and 64; this fraction will increase to 379 per 1,000 by 2035, according to the Social Security Administration's intermediate demographic forecast (Burtless, 1993). At the same time that the population is aging, retirements are occurring at younger ages than ever before. This combination raises concern that the United States will not be able to support its elderly and places pressure on federal and state programs that provide financial assistance to older households.[1]

Earlier departures from the labor force also influence expectations of the roles of private employers and the government with regard to retirement. For example, in 1994 the Clinton administration proposed increased public support for health insurance benefits to early retirees. This proposal had implications for retirement policy because Americans frequently stop work prior to the age at which they qualify for federal medicare benefits and often receive either no health insurance or only inadequate coverage from their former employers. Government financed health benefits for early retirees would have created potentially strong, but poorly understood, incentives for still earlier retirement, which may run counter to public policy objectives.

This chapter has three aims. First, it describes historical trends in employment and labor force participation among older Americans. Gender and ethnic group differences receive some attention, but the majority of the discussion focuses on males. Second, previous research examining determinants of the secular changes is briefly summarized, with particular emphasis paid to recent investigations and emerging areas of study. Third, information is provided on the transition process into retirement. Although retirement has generally been portrayed as an abrupt event, recent studies indicate that it often represents the culmination of a more gradual process, which involves some type of "bridge" employment following the end of career jobs.

TRENDS IN EMPLOYMENT AND LABOR FORCE PARTICIPATION

Individuals are classified as participating in the labor force if they are either working or unemployed but looking for work.[2] Labor force participation thus abstracts from issues related to the intensity of employment, difficulties in finding positions, and intermittent job holding. Nonetheless, the labor force participation rate (LFPR) is probably the best single indicator of workforce involvement, particularly in light of the relatively low unemployment rates of mature adults.[3]

Historical trends in the participation rates of mature men are summarized in Figure 4.1. LFPRs in the United States have declined dramatically since the end of World War II, especially for the oldest groups.[4] For example, whereas participation probabilities of 45–54-year-olds fell by approximately 5 percent (from 96% to 91%) between 1948 and 1982, the corresponding reductions were 25 percent (from 90% to 67%) for those aged 55–64 and 66 percent (from 47% to 16%) among men 65 and over. Peracchi and Welch (1994) have recently shown that the reductions are particularly pronounced among men with low earnings. After declining steadily for four decades, however, LFPRs appear to have stabilized since the middle 1980s—participation rates averaged 91 percent, 68 percent, and 16 percent for 45–54-, 55–64-, and over-65-year-olds during the 1985–1987 period and a virtually identical 91 percent, 67 percent, and 16 percent between 1990 and 1992.

There is some question as to when the decline in participation rates of older men began. Census Bureau estimates reported by Ransom and Sutch (1988) indicate an uninterrupted downward trend in LFPRs beginning as far back as 1900. Ransom and Sutch (1986) have recently argued, however, that the early figures are biased upward by several important sources of error.[5] After correcting the data, they claim that participation rates of men 60 and over were essentially flat (at around 65%) or even trended slightly upward prior to the 1930s, after which they began their steady decrease.

A far different pattern is observed for women. As displayed in Figure 4.2, the participation rates of females 65 and older declined marginally over time (from 9% in 1948 to 8% in 1992), whereas the LFPRs of 55–64-year-olds and, particularly, of those between 45 and 54 grew rapidly; labor force participation of the latter group more than doubled, increasing from 35 percent to 73 percent over the 45 years. These trends reflect the combination of two patterns, which

Figure 4.1
Labor Force Participation Rates of Older Men, 1948–1992

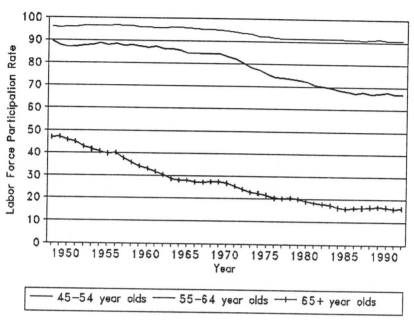

Sources: U.S. Department of Labor (1989a); U.S. Department of Labor, *Employment and Earnings* 37–40, no. 1 (January issues 1990–93).

have offsetting effects on the data for older women. First, workforce involvement of prime-age women has exploded since the end of World War II. This is shown directly for the 45–54-year-old group, and with even larger increases for females aged 20–44. Second, the participation rates of women 55 and over have fallen relative to those of their younger counterparts, just as they have for men.

Ethnic group differences in participation rates are detailed in Figures 4.3 and 4.4, with data for Hispanics separately broken out beginning in 1980. LFPRs are similar for persons 65 and over, although there is some indication that black males had lower participation rates than white men during the 1980s, while nonwhite women participated slightly more frequently than their white peers throughout the 1970s and 1980s. Larger disparities are observed among 55–64-year-olds, with black males typically around 10 percentage points less likely to participate in the labor force than white or Hispanic men. In contrast, the LFPR of black females is 2 to 4 percentage points higher than that for whites and up to 11 points higher than that for Hispanic females. The patterns for 55–64-year-olds largely mirror ethnic group differences in LFPRs observed at younger ages. Racial differences in participation are nearly eliminated by age 65 because so few persons of any group remain in the workforce beyond that age.

Figure 4.2
Labor Force Participation Rates of Older Women, 1948–1992

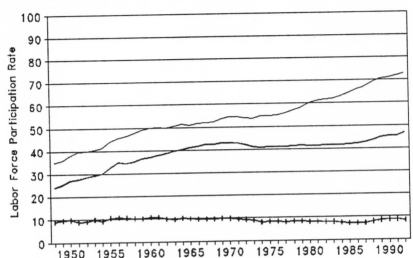

Sources: U.S. Department of Labor (1989a); U.S. Department of Labor, *Employment and Earnings* 37–40, no. 1 (January issues 1990–93).

Not only have older Americans become less likely to hold jobs over time, those that are employed work fewer hours. To illustrate, Figures 4.5 and 4.6 indicate the percentage of employed 45–64- and over-65-year-olds holding part-time jobs (fewer than 35 hours per week). The figures show a clear increase in the probability of working part time. For instance, 4 percent and 6 percent of 45–64-year-old working men held part-time jobs in 1960 and 1970, respectively, compared with 7 percent in 1982 and 1989. Even more dramatically, the percentage of men 65 and over who were employed less than 35 hours per week increased from 30 percent and 38 percent in 1960 and 1970, respectively, to 48 percent in 1982 and 1989. Women are much more likely to work part time than men, and the probability of working part time rises sharply with age for both sexes. Nonetheless, part-time employment continues to be the exception, rather than the rule, for workers 65 and younger. For example, only 20 percent, 26 percent, and 33 percent of employed 55–59-, 60–62-, and 63–65-year-olds, respectively, worked less than 35 hours per week in 1987 (Sum and Fogg, 1990b).

Surprisingly, recent cohorts of older workers hold part-year jobs less often than their earlier counterparts (see Figures 4.7 and 4.8). For instance, the proportion of male workers aged 55 and over who were employed between 1 and

Figure 4.3
Labor Force Participation Rates of Older Men By Race, 1972–1988

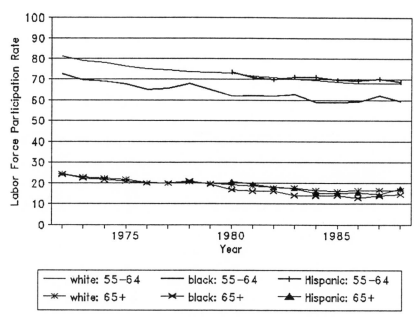

Source: U.S. Department of Labor, *Handbook of Labor Statistics* (Bulletin 2340), August 1989.

49 weeks of the year fell from 16 percent in 1967 to below 14 percent in 1986. The corresponding decline for women was from 12 percent in 1967 to 9 percent in 1986. Similarly, employed males in this age group averaged approximately 45 weeks of work per year throughout the 1967–1986 period, while weeks worked increased slightly over time for older females, from 40 per year in 1967 to 44 annually in 1986.

The failure of older workers to reduce their labor supply by moving to part-year work suggests the influence of labor market rigidities on their labor supply decisions. Hurd (1993) examined these labor market rigidities and documented movements into self-employment as one response to them by older workers. He calculated that the fraction of workers who were self-employed in 1990 differed substantially by age—from 14 percent of 55–59-year-old men to 24 percent of males over age 65 and from 8 percent to 13 percent for corresponding age groups of women. Sum and Fogg (1990b), however, showed that rates of self-employment have also fallen over time for older workers, indicating that these individuals have become less able to escape the effects of fixed costs by continuing in, or moving into, self-employment.

The vast majority of workers retire during their late 50s through their middle 60s. These are also the ages when private pension and social security incentives

Figure 4.4
Labor Force Participation Rates of Older Women By Race, 1972–1988

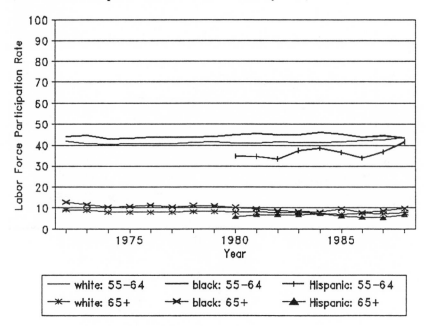

Source: U.S. Department of Labor (1989a).

are the most pronounced. With this in mind, Figure 4.9 provides information on age-specific participation rates of 58–67-year-old men. As expected, labor force participation falls with age and has trended downward over time for all groups. The secular reductions are particularly pronounced for 62–64-year-old men. For instance, 62-year-olds were less likely to participate in the labor force in 1992 (52%) than were 65-year-old men 30 years earlier (54%).

Probabilities that persons participating in the labor force at age $t-1$ no longer do so at age t (one year later) are shown in Figure 4.10. These conditional probabilities, which are known as *hazard rates*, indicate changes in LFPRs at exact ages. The ages listed on the table refer to the ending ages. (For example, the hazard rate for 65-year-olds refers to the conditional probability of leaving the labor force by age 65, conditional on participating in it at 64.) The most striking finding is the more than tripling, over the 30-year-period, in the probability that 61-year-old participants leave the workforce by age 62 (which rose from .063 in 1963 to .221 in 1992). The spike in hazard rates at 62, which was quite small in the late 1960s, is currently of approximately the same size as that occurring at age 65. Exit probabilities have also increased for 60–61- and 63–64-year-olds, although to a smaller extent than at 62, whereas 66- and 67-year-olds have become less likely to depart the labor force.

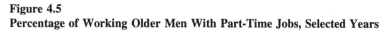

Figure 4.5
Percentage of Working Older Men With Part-Time Jobs, Selected Years

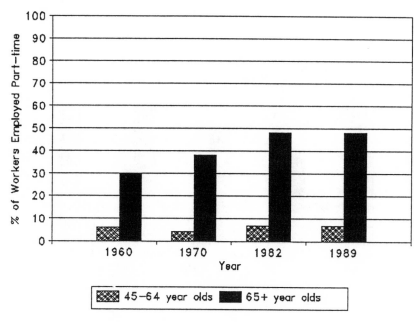

Source: U.S. Department of Health and Human Services.

The trends in participation hazards suggest an important role for the social security system, since 62 and 65 correspond to the ages at which early and normal retirement benefits can be received. Rising real benefit levels, combined with the existence of liquidity-constrained workers, may account for the increase in departures from the labor force occurring at 62. If the increased generosity of social security encourages persons to exit the labor force when early or normal benefits become available, the group continuing in the labor force after 65 may increasingly be accounted for by "workaholics" who plan to never retire.[6] This would explain the decline in hazard rates observed among 66- and 67-year-olds.

WHY ARE MEN LEAVING THE LABOR FORCE AT YOUNGER AGES?

This section summarizes research investigating the trend toward earlier retirement. Since much of the literature has been reviewed previously (e.g., by Mirkin, 1987; Ruhm, 1989; Hurd, 1990b; Quinn, Burkhauser, and Myers, 1990) and other chapters in this volume focus on some of the specific factors that have influenced the trend toward earlier retirement, this discussion highlights recent studies and emerging areas that have previously received limited attention.

Figure 4.6
Percentage of Older Working Women With Part-Time Jobs, Selected Years

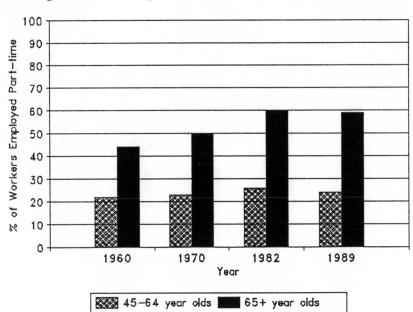

Source: U.S. Department of Health and Human Services (1991).

Before beginning, it is important to point out that factors that encourage early retirement at one point in time do not necessarily explain trends in declines of labor force participation rates. For example, the ability of firms to impose mandatory retirement was reduced in 1978, long before participation rates stopped declining, and it was subsequently eliminated for virtually all employees. Thus, although mandatory retirement provisions caused some older men to stop working in the past, they can not possibly explain recent reductions in LFPRs.[7]

Health, Disability Insurance, and Retiree Health Benefits

Persons with health problems retire at relatively young ages. For instance, Burtless (1986) estimated that men reporting poor health depart the workforce more than a year earlier than those describing their health as average or above average. There are at least two reasons, however, why self-classifications may be systematically biased in ways that overstate the deleterious impact of health problems on labor force participation. First, poor health may be considered a more acceptable reason to stop working than is the preference for leisure. Second, some income support programs (e.g., disability insurance) are only available to persons with health problems.

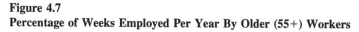

Figure 4.7
Percentage of Weeks Employed Per Year By Older (55+) Workers

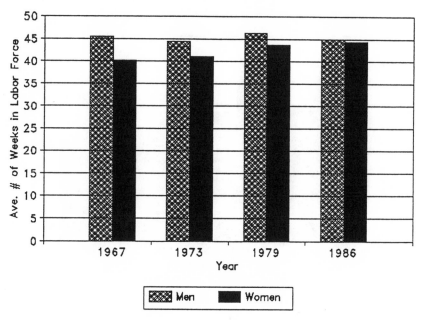

Source: Ruhm and Sum (1989), table 1.

Researchers have attempted to provide better estimates of the effects of health by using purportedly objective measures such as subsequent mortality rates (Anderson and Burkhauser, 1985; Burtless, 1987), self-classified health status in a period prior to retirement (Bazzoli, 1985), clinical diagnoses (Butler et al., 1987), or self-reports of specific health conditions (Bartel and Taubman, 1979; Ruhm, 1992b). When objective and self-classified measures of health are compared, the latter are more strongly associated with nonparticipation. Worsening health continues to appear to cause small reductions in labor supply, however, even when using objective indicators.

Bound (1991) argued that the objective measures are likely to understate the impact of health and overstate the influence of economic factors on retirement due to errors-in-variables bias. Although the objective indicators do not suffer from the same reporting biases as self-classified general health variables, they are likely to capture only a portion of the components of health that influence work capacity. For example, future mortality rates do not account for limitations (such as arthritis) that bear little relationship with life expectancy but may impact employment opportunities. Bound argued that the true health effect lies somewhere between the estimates obtained from self-classified and objective measures.[8]

Figure 4.8
Percentage of Older (55+) Participants Working Part-Year

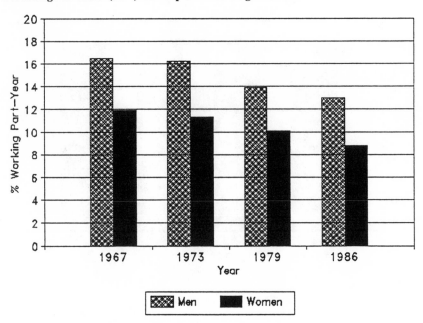

Source: Ruhm & Sum (1989), table 1.

Despite its contemporaneous effects, poor health cannot explain much of the trend toward earlier retirement. The most obvious indication is that life expectancies have increased substantially during the same period over which LFPRs have dramatically fallen. To the extent that rising lifespans correlate with improved health for men in their 50s and 60s, participation should therefore have been rising rather than decreasing over time. Even making the heroic assumption that all the additional longevity has occurred among unhealthy nonparticipants, Baily (1987) calculated that worsening health can explain, at most, a small fraction of the decline in labor force activity, and Bound and Waidmann (1992) estimated that deteriorating health can account for virtually none of the reduction for men over age 55.

It is possible that males with real or perceived health problems may now have the ability to stop working, due to the broadening of disability benefits. This argument has been made most forcefully by Parsons (1980). He estimated that the elasticity of male participation rates to the federal disability insurance (DI) wage replacement rate is .63, which is of sufficient size to explain the entire reduction in LFPRs of 48–62-year-old-men during the 1948–1976 period. There are, however, at least two problems with this argument. First, even if broadening DI benefits were a major cause of declining participation rates during the 1960s

Figure 4.9
Male Labor Force Participation Rates at Selected Ages

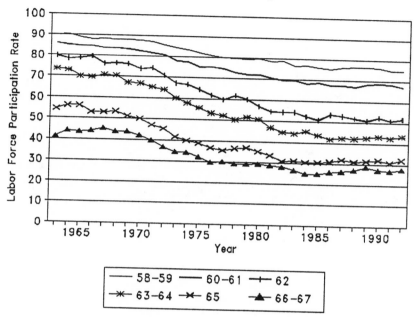

Source: Unpublished *Current Population Survey* data supplied by the Bureau of Labor Statistics.

and 1970s, the pattern of DI receipt and participation rates does not support a similar conclusion for the 1980s. In particular, eligibility restrictions for DI were tightened considerably beginning in the 1980s, with the result that the proportion of 16–64-year-olds receiving DI fell from 1.99 percent in 1980 to 1.76 percent by 1985 (Bound and Waidmann, 1992).[9] Participation rates of mature men continued to decline through the early 1980s, however, instead of increasing, as would be anticipated if DI incentives strongly influenced the labor supply of older males. Second, as demonstrated by Haveman and Wolf (1984) and Bound (1989), the estimation procedure used by Parsons is likely to overstate the elasticity of labor force participation to DI replacement rates because the latter are negatively correlated with past earnings and because persons receiving low pay typically exit the labor force at relatively young ages.

Upper-bound estimates of the impact of DI were provided by Bound (1989), who used rejected disability applicants as a natural control group, and by Bound and Waidmann (1992), who compared the percentage of men reporting specific health problems during periods when DI benefits were broadened and then subsequently restricted. They concluded that DI may explain a sizable portion of the drop in the participation rates of males aged 45–54 but little of the more substantial reduction observed among 55–64-year-old men. They also pointed

Figure 4.10
Participation Hazard Rates for Men of Selected Ages

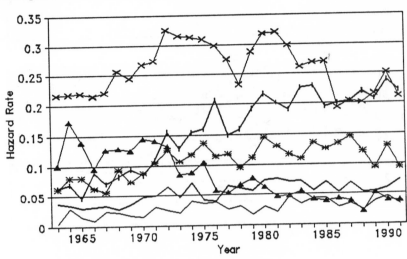

Source: Unpublished *Current Population Survey* data supplied by the Bureau of Labor Statistics.

out that most recipients do suffer from potentially disabling conditions and that many would have received other kinds of transfers or support in the absence of DI.

Recently researchers have become interested in the effects of employer-provided retiree health benefits (RHBs) on labor supply. RHBs are potentially important because federal medicare benefits do not become available until age 65 and privately purchased insurance is typically much more expensive than group plans obtained through a current or previous employer. Thus, the availability of RHBs may eliminate a significant financial barrier to leaving the labor force. With rapidly rising health insurance costs, this obstacle may have become more important over time.

It is unlikely, however, that changes in retiree health benefits can account for a substantial portion of the historical reductions in labor supply because relatively few retirees receive RHBs. Gustman and Steinmeier (1993) estimated that between 40 and 57 percent of privately employed men over the age of 40 holding full-time jobs in 1988 expected to receive health benefits from their employer in retirement. For corresponding women, the figures were 26–38 percent. Among part-time workers, just 11–14 percent of men and 6–9 percent of women anticipated obtaining RHBs. Gustman and Steinmeier further predicted that the expansion of RHBs would have a relatively small impact on LFPRs. For instance, the provision of benefits to all workers with health insurance on their current job is expected to reduce average retirement ages by less than three weeks.

On the other hand, Gruber and Madrian (1993) used data on the "continuation of coverage" mandates existing in many states during the late 1970s through the middle 1980s to argue that there are much stronger effects. One year of mandated continuation benefits was predicted to raise the number of retirements by 20 percent. Somewhat surprisingly, this increase appeared to occur fairly uniformly among 55–64-year-olds, rather than being concentrated near the age of medicare eligibility. Although retiree health insurance probably cannot explain much of the historical trend in LFPR, it may have a more important impact in the future—particularly if universal health insurance coverage is provided.

Wealth, Social Security, and Private Pensions

There is little question that wealth has risen over time among members of the older population and that this explains some portion of the secular reduction in labor supply.[10] Unfortunately, because accurate asset data is difficult to obtain, only limited research has been undertaken on the effects of nonpension wealth on retirement behavior. By contrast, the effects of incentives in both the social security system and private (employer-based) pensions have been extensively investigated. Given their complexity, this discussion highlights only a few key aspects of the impacts of the retirement plans.

In 1988, 92 percent of households with a member over the age of 65 received some income from social security, and this accounted for 38 percent of median household incomes (Chen, 1992). Private pensions were received by 29 percent of older households and accounted for 8 percent of median incomes.[11] The size of both social security and private pensions has been growing over time. The major increases in real social security benefits occurred during the 1960s and 1970s—average per capita benefit levels (in 1988 dollars) increased from $310 in 1964 to $501 in 1981 and have remained roughly constant subsequently (Levine, 1993). The percentage of private wage and salary workers covered by private pension plans rose from 19 percent in 1945 to 45 percent in 1970 and has been approximately constant since that time (Beller and Lawrence, 1992). Nonetheless, because coverage rates were lower for older cohorts, the proportion of retirees receiving private pension incomes continued to increase, rising from 12 percent to 29 percent between 1967 and 1988 (Chen, 1992).

Social security and private pensions create complicated economic incentives that influence the employment behavior of mature adults. For social security, the most significant incentives are the option to receive permanently reduced benefits beginning at age 62, a delayed retirement credit (DRC) for persons initiating benefits after 65, and an earnings test for individuals under the age of 70. Although the reduction in benefits for persons receiving early social security is approximately actuarially fair (i.e., the decrease in annual incomes is canceled out by the additional years over which benefits are received), the DRC is not, with the result that few individuals postpone social security past age 65.[12] Under the earnings test, 62–65-year-old recipients have their benefits reduced by $1 for every $2 of earnings above a threshold level ($7,680 in 1993).[13] Similarly, the benefits of 66–69-year-olds are reduced by $1 for every $3 of earnings exceeding $10,560 (in 1993). The earnings test does not apply to persons aged 70 and older. (See Barry L. Friedman, Chapter 8 of this volume, for a discussion of the effects of these social security provisions on social security wealth and retirement incentives.)

Although the incentives in private pensions are plan specific, a number of important generalizations can be made. Defined contribution (DC) plans, where the employer contributes a specified amount but does not guarantee benefit levels, essentially act as tax-advantaged savings vehicles and have relatively weak effects on retirement decisions. In defined benefit (DB) plans, the firm specifies a pension payment, which typically depends on some combination of earnings, years of seniority, and age at retirement. An additional year of employment, therefore, generally raises annual pension incomes but reduces the number of years over which benefits will be received. At some point, the latter effect dominates the former and the discounted value of pension wealth begins to fall. Thus, the individual is encouraged to remain with the firm prior to the point at which pension wealth is maximized and to leave it thereafter.

Both social security and private pensions have a "forced savings" component, to the extent that they cause individuals to accumulate more assets during their working lives than they otherwise would. Since social security and private pensions have been growing over time, increases in forced savings could be a cause of the trend toward earlier retirement. This effect is generally believed to be modest, however, when compared with social security and pension incentives existing at specific ages. (These are discussed next.)

The bunching of male retirements at 62 and 65 almost certainly results from the early and normal retirement provisions in social security.[14] The age 62 effect suggests that liquidity constraints prevent many individuals, who would otherwise do so, from retiring at earlier ages. The retirement spikes do not automatically imply that social security is responsible for a significant portion of historical reduction in older-male LFPRs. For example, the low retirement rates of 63- and 64-year-olds could occur because social security induces some persons to remain in the labor force until turning 65.

There are a number of reasons, however, to believe that social security is important. First, Ransom and Sutch (1986) suggested that the decline in the participation rates of mature men began at approximately the time when social security was put in place. Second, Levine (1993) showed that average benefit levels and relative participation rates of persons eligible for social security have tracked fairly closely during the last 30 years. In particular, the difference between the LFPRs of 62–64-year-old men and their 60–61-year-old counterparts almost doubled between 1968 and 1980, at the same time that average real social security benefits rose 40 percent. Conversely, there was little change in either relative participation rates or average real benefit levels between 1980 and 1990.[15] Third, the dramatic increase in retirements occurring at exactly age 62 is consistent with the hypothesis that the early retirement provisions of social security, combined with rising real benefit levels, have promoted departures from the labor force among liquidity-constrained workers.

Despite this evidence, some researchers continue to question the role of social security. When the most sophisticated econometric techniques are used (e.g., Burtless and Moffitt, 1984, 1985; Fields and Mitchell, 1984; Burtless, 1986; Gustman and Steinmeier, 1986), moderate changes in social security incentives yield only small predicted effects on LFPRs. As Hurd (1993) pointed out, however, these estimates will understate the true effect of social security if the variables that influence the retirement decision are not observed accurately. Furthermore, none of the models are able to predict the sharp reductions in labor force participation occurring at 62 and 65, which supports the notion that the observation errors are substantial.

Krueger and Pischke (1992) have argued that despite suffering a substantial unexpected reduction in social security wealth, the social security "notch" cohort (born between 1917 and 1921) did not have higher participation rates at ages 62–64 than individuals reaching these ages slightly earlier. Although this natural experiment suggests a fruitful line of future research, the results are less compelling than they at first appear. In particular, the measurement of social security wealth is quite crude, and other factors that influence LFPRs may not be adequately accounted for in the analysis.

The financial incentives in defined benefit pension plans are also frequently very large. For example, in Kotlikoff and Wise's (1989) case study of one large firm, the additional pension wealth obtained by remaining employed one extra year was $72,527 for a 54-year-old manager with 25 years of service, versus −$14,936 for a corresponding 65-year-old with 30 years on the job. Given their size, it is not surprising that previous research has uncovered strong worker responses to these pension incentives (see, e.g., Kotlikoff and Wise, 1989; Stock and Wise, 1990; Lumsdaine, Stock, and Wise, 1990). Furthermore, since pension wealth is maximized at relatively young ages for many workers (Kotlikoff and Smith, 1983; Fields and Mitchell, 1984; Lazear, 1986) and incentives to leave covered jobs early have been increasing over time (Mitchell and Luzadis, 1988; Mitchell, 1992; Ippolito, 1991), many researchers have concluded that private pensions are a key determinant of the trend toward earlier retirement.

There are, however, several reasons to doubt that a primary role can be attributed to private pensions. First, pensions continue to represent a relatively minor source of financial support for most of the elderly. According to Hurd (1990b), just 7 percent of households headed by a person older than 60 received more than half their income from pensions in 1986, compared to 57 percent who did so from social security. Second, pension and nonpension wealth are highly correlated. Without good asset data, the observed impact of pensions is, therefore, likely to be confounded with the effects of nonpension wealth. Third, departures from covered jobs will be reduced prior to the date at which pension wealth is maximized, which may actually delay retirements. For instance, Ruhm (1992a) found that pension coverage is associated with higher labor supply through age 61 and with negligible or small effects for 62–64-year-olds.

Pensions may have a bigger impact on retirement decisions when interacting with other types of wealth. Two recent studies have examined the joint effect of pensions and social security. Samwick (1993) incorporated detailed pension information into simulations predicting labor supply when both pension and social security accruals are accounted for, as compared to when only the latter is considered. The main result is that accounting for pension wealth raises predicted hazard rates out of employment prior to age 62, which Samwick attributed to their role in relaxing the liquidity constraints of early retirees. His model, however, does not include explicit interactions between social security and private pension wealth and is unable to explain the retirement spikes at ages 62 and 65. By contrast, Ruhm (1993b), examined how the likelihood of receiving pension income in retirement influences employment rates at specific ages. He found that increased pension probabilities are associated with substantial reductions in employment rates at 62 and 63 but have no effects at younger ages. This provides evidence that pension disincentives are important primarily for individuals with other financial resources (i.e., social security) in retirement.

Household Labor Supply

The rise of two-earner households may explain some of the fall in participation rates of older men, since the higher household incomes resulting from two earners could finance earlier retirement. Although there is a growing literature examining retirement decisions within a household context, it generally does not directly address the question of whether changes in household characteristics can explain historical trends in labor supply.

A common research finding is that household members coordinate retirement decisions. The form of coordination is less clear, with some studies finding a symmetric relationship between men and women (Hurd, 1990b) while others indicate that husbands' decisions precede those of their wives (Henretta and O'Rand, 1983; Clark and McDermed, 1989) or imply mixed or ambiguous behavior (Gustman and Steinmeier, 1993b; Ruhm 1993a). There is also evidence that household considerations play a greater role in the labor supply decisions of women, whereas economic factors predominate for men (Clark and McDermed, 1989; Pozzebon and Mitchell, 1989). Ruhm (1993a) showed that unmarried 55–59-year-old men and women with work experience after age 50 have identical rates of employment, whereas married females are only five-sixths as likely to hold jobs and work full time just 60 percent as frequently as their male counterparts. He also found that women were more likely to provide care to relatives, even after controlling for marital status and employment.

At present, we can only speculate whether the increase in two-earner house-holds has promoted earlier retirement. Evidence that the leisure time of husbands and wives are complements lends credence to this possibility, since a decision to stop working by either party may induce the other to leave the labor force. Furthermore, prime-age employment by both household members may represent a choice to jointly defer leisure to a lengthy period of retirement. Future research needs to focus directly on the relationship between household employment de-cisions and LFPR trends. Previous studies do suggest that the participation rates of mature women are likely to remain below those of their male counterparts, as long as most wives continue to be several years younger than their husbands.

Demand-Side Factors

Adults approaching the end of their working lives have greater difficulty than their younger peers in obtaining new positions following the loss of jobs (Sha-piro and Sandell, 1985; Hutchens, 1986, 1988, 1993). For instance, in January 1988, 36 percent of 55–59-year-olds were jobless one to four years after a permanent layoff, as compared to 22 percent of 40–44-year-olds (Hutchens, 1993). This could result from age discrimination or from several alternative possibilities (e.g., older workers may have unrealistic wage expectations).

Since it is illegal to explicitly discriminate on the basis of age, it is difficult to ascertain the extent to which this form of unequal treatment still exists. Survey responses suggest, however, that most older workers do not perceive themselves as subject to substantial discrimination. For instance, Hurd (1993) reported that over four-fifths of 51–65-year-old wage and salary workers in the new Health and Retirement Survey disagreed with statements that their employers gave pref-erence to younger people in promotion decisions and that coworkers made older workers feel as if they ought to retire before age 65.[16] Although some age discrimination undoubtedly persists, the passage and increased enforcement of antidiscrimination legislation makes it unlikely that the extent of bias has in-creased over time. Thus, age discrimination is probably not an important cause of the trends toward earlier retirement.

Older workers have greater adjustment problems following job loss, raising the possibility that increased economic turbulence has placed mature adults at a greater risk of exiting the labor force when their jobs disappear.[17] The limited available research (Parnes, Gagen, and King, 1981; Anderson, Burkhauser, and Quinn, 1986), however, provides little evidence that labor displacements reduce average retirement ages. This is a fruitful area for future research. Until further information becomes available, it is difficult to assess the role of demand-side factors.

TRANSITIONS INTO RETIREMENT

The previous discussion treats retirement as a discrete event rather than as the culmination of a gradual process. Increasingly, however, economists have realized that many workers do something other than permanently retire following the end of career jobs and that for these persons, the dichotomous distinction between employment (or labor force participation) and retirement is erroneous. Instead, it is useful to think of a transition process that may include, prior to permanent and complete retirement, one or more spells of partial retirement, bridge employment, part-time work, or reentry into the labor force following a temporary departure.

Much of the early research in this area examined the prevalence of partial retirement. Using the first four waves of the Social Security Administration's Retirement History Survey (RHS), Gustman and Steinmeier (1984) estimated that one-third of working men define themselves as partially retired at some point in their working lives. Honig (1985) and Honig and Hanoch (1985) showed that partial retirement is quantitatively important and that, especially for women, it should be viewed as a qualitatively different phenomenon from either full employment or complete retirement. More recently, Ruhm (1990) utilized all six waves of the RHS to demonstrate that approximately half of men partially retire, with the average spell duration exceeding five years. These estimates are somewhat sensitive to the definition of partial retirement. Supplementing self-classified status with a criterion based on earnings, Ruhm found that partial retirements occur even more frequently but last for shorter average durations. Recognizing the importance of partial retirement, a number of researchers have begun to include it as a separate labor market state in their structural models of employment and retirement (e.g., Gustmann and Steinmeier, 1986; Rust, 1989; Berkovec and Stern, 1991; Blau, 1992), although they often distinguish only between part- and full-time work.

A significant portion of workers also return to work after initially retiring. Ruhm (1990) found that one-quarter of RHS household heads retiring in 1971 reentered the labor force at some point during the next eight years. A large majority of these "reverse retirements" involved transitions into partial retirement and occurred within four years of the initial departure from the labor force. Blau (1992) presents evidence indicating that these estimates, which are based on biannual data, actually understate the frequency of labor force reentry, since short-lasting employment spells that begin soon after an initial survey date may not be observed.

Movements from career positions to bridge employment provide a second dimension over which the retirement transition process can be analyzed. Bridge jobs may involve some combination of fewer hours, less stress or responsibility, greater flexibility, and fewer physical demands. Bridge positions may also be taken when an individual is involuntarily displaced from a career job and is unable to obtain comparable reemployment.[18] Notice that these possibilities are far broader than can be captured by a simple distinction between full- and part-time work.

Researchers have used a variety of criteria for dating the end of career employment. Hurd (1993) pointed out that the vast majority of workers move directly out of the labor force from full-time jobs, with no intervening period of part-time work. In his view, this indicates that bridge employment is quite rare. These findings, however, simply reflect the infrequency of part-time employment, even for older individuals, and do not address the possibility that individuals may move into transitional employment at which they work more than 35 hours per week.[19]

At the other extreme, Ruhm (1990, 1991) focused on movements out of the longest job held during the individual's lifetime. Using this criterion, bridge employment is very common, with only around 40 percent of workers retiring directly from their longest employer. The subsequent positions are typically in a different sector of employment (industry, occupation, or both) and pay considerably less than the career job; moreover, partial retirement almost never occurs on the longest position. Some workers may begin second careers following longest jobs that terminate at relatively young ages. Ruhm's main findings continue to hold, however, when the analysis is restricted to persons leaving their longest employment relatively late in life. For example, 88 percent of persons ending their longest positions between the ages of 55 and 59, and 40 percent of those doing so between 60 and 64 remain in the labor force for at least some period of time (Ruhm, 1991). Changes in the sector of employment also become more common for individuals terminating career jobs at higher ages.

Quinn, Burkhauser, and Myers (1990) used an intermediate definition of career jobs. They classify as career employment full-time positions that have lasted at least 10 years. Thus, unlike Ruhm, they include some positions that are not the longest job held by the individual and, in contrast to Hurd, they recognize that short-lasting full-time jobs may represent transitional employment. They estimate that at least 27 percent of 58–63-year-old wage and salary workers who held full-time jobs in 1969 and changed their status during the next six years moved to some type of bridge employment. Among the self-employed, the comparable figure is 51 percent. These proportions are smaller than those obtained by Ruhm for two reasons. First, the definition of career employment is somewhat more restrictive. Second, by focusing on a narrower age range, they miss some types of transitional employment.

Although the exact number of bridge job holders is debatable, there is little doubt that retirement transitions are important for a substantial fraction of mature adults. This process is influenced both by the preferences of older workers to gradually reduce their labor force attachments and by institutional constraints such as the social security earnings test and Employee Retirement Income Security Act (ERISA) regulations that require firms to provide pension benefits to persons working more than a specified number of hours per year. Factors associated with early retirements are also typically correlated with movements from full employment to partial retirement. There are, however, important exceptions. For example, partial retirement is prevalent among higher-paid white-collar workers, who retire at relatively late ages (Honig and Reimers, 1987).

Most studies of gradual retirement have used RHS data, which is now quite dated and covers only a single cohort of (primarily male) household heads. Thus, it is difficult to infer much about trends in bridge employment or partial retirement from this research. A recent exception is Ruhm (1993b), who used information on men at ages 58 and 63 in 1969 and 1989, respectively. The 1969 data comes from the RHS and so is comparable to the previous research, while information for the 1989 cohort is from a recent Harris survey (Louis Harris and Associates, 1992). Ruhm considered transitions both out of the longest job and from career positions, where the latter are defined to include either the longest employment or jobs that have lasted more than 10 years. Notice that this definition is fairly close to that used by Quinn, Burkhauser, and Myers (1990).

Two of Ruhm's findings are particularly noteworthy. First, men appear to be retiring more abruptly in 1989 than 20 years earlier, as well as exiting the labor force at younger ages, based on the fact that the likelihood of holding bridge jobs at ages 58–63 has fallen for workers who are no longer employed in career positions and that the probability of employment at these ages has declined over time, even after controlling for the worker's age or number of years prior to the survey date at which the longest job had ended. Second, although attachments to longest jobs are virtually identical for the two cohorts through age 54, members of the 1989 group were much more likely to have departed their longest employment at 55 and beyond. Since 55 is the age for early retirement in many private pension plans, this suggests that pensions may be playing an increasing role in initiating the retirement transition.

WHAT WILL THE FUTURE BRING?

The analysis of historical trends is interesting in its own right but becomes even more relevant to the extent that it helps us forecast the future. Although we have learned a great deal, considerable uncertainty remains. Four factors help to explain why the LFPRs of mature adults have leveled out since 1985 and are likely to rise in the future. First, changes in the social security system will encourage longer worklives as benefits become less generous for future retirees, the age of "normal" retirement is raised, and the penalty for early retirement is increased. Second, primary pension coverage is shifting from defined benefit plans, which often contain incentives for early retirement, to defined contribution schemes, which generally do not. Levels of pension wealth are also generally lower in DC plans, which may further delay withdrawal from the labor force. Third, health insurance expenses are rising dramatically. This may be increasingly important for persons contemplating early retirement because many firms do not supply retiree health benefits or are in the process of eliminating them or limiting their scope. Fourth, persons approaching retirement age may have accumulated fewer assets than previous cohorts due to the stagnation of wages, lower savings rates, and a greater degree of economic turbulence.

On the other hand, several other influences could reinforce the trend toward early retirement. Perhaps most important is the rise of two-earner families, which implies increasing levels of wealth and may signify household decisions to reallocate nonmarket time to a lengthier period of joint retirement. Second, if future health care reforms result in universal coverage, the cost and uncertainty associated with obtaining health insurance by nonworkers may decrease. This could encourage more people to leave the labor force prior to becoming eligible for medicare. Third, public norms could shift toward a greater acceptance of, or even admiration for, those who retire early. To the extent that these attitudes are influenced by economic factors, however, they are subject to further modification, possibly in the opposite direction.

NOTES

1. See Crown (Chapter 20 of this volume).

2. Persons on temporary layoff with recall expected in the near future and those who have found jobs that they will start shortly are also classified as participants.

3. The unemployment rates of persons 65 and over averaged 3.1 percent between 1980 and 1988, as compared to 7.4 percent for 25–34-year-olds (U.S. Department of Labor, 1989a). Some researchers have argued that official unemployment statistics understate the labor market problems of older persons, because they are more likely than their younger peers to drop out of the workforce should they be unable to obtain jobs (see Sum and Fogg, 1990a, for further discussion of these concerns).

4. Similar patterns are evident in other industrialized countries. See the discussion in Stuart Dorsey and John A. Turner (Chapter 6 of this volume).

5. The main bias arises from the Census Bureau's use of sources of income to define employment. For example, persons were classified as "employed" landlords if they received property income and "employed" investors if they obtained stock dividends or bond interest. Moen (1987) criticized the adjustments made by Ransom and Sutch.

6. It is well known that some workers either plan to never retire or plan to do so long after economic incentives stop playing a major role. For example, Anderson, Burkhauser, and Quinn's (1986) analysis of the Social Security Administration's Retirement History Survey (RHS) revealed that in 1969, 11 percent of men employed at age 63 planned to retire beyond age 67 and 6 percent planned to do so at 70 or later.

7. Even during the 1960s and 1970s, when 30 to 50 percent of men worked in positions with mandatory retirement provisions, the majority chose to leave their jobs at or before the mandated departure age and so were not constrained (Parnes and Nestle, 1975; Halpern, 1978; Burkhauser and Quinn, 1983; Fields and Mitchell, 1986).

8. Stern (1989) also used detailed information on medical symptoms and conditions to test for biases in more general, self-classified health measures.

9. Similarly, expenditures on social security disability insurance, as a percentage of gross domestic product (GPD), fell from 1.65 to 1.50 percent of GDP between 1980 and 1985.

10. For example, the proportion of 58–63-year-old men owning homes increased from

67 to 87 percent between 1969 and 1989 (Ruhm 1993b). Real housing values also rose substantially during this period.

11. Assets, earnings, government pensions, and public assistance were responsible for 25, 17, 9, and 1 percent of the income of the median older households, respectively.

12. Individuals may also start social security at 65 in order to qualify for medicare health benefits. The DRC is gradually being raised from its current level of 4 percent per year to 8 percent annually by 2008, at which time the adjustment will be approximately actuarially fair. Other important changes in social security include raising the normal retirement age to 67 by 2027 and an increase in the penalty for early retirement. Leonesio (1993) provides an excellent review of the social security system.

13. However, benefit levels are recomputed at 65 to take account of the reduction in payments occurring between the ages of 62 and 64.

14. Even stronger evidence is provided by considering shorter time periods. Geweke, et al. (1992) showed that 20 percent of respondents begin receiving social security benefits in the first *month* of entitlement (the month of their 62nd birthday) and 80 percent of those not yet having done so initiate benefits during the month when they turn 65. Similarly, Blau (1992) found that 24 percent of men working on their 65th birthday were retired three months later.

15. Ippolito (1991) also showed a strong inverse relationship between social security benefit levels and participation rates between 1955 and 1980.

16. Similarly, the research summarized in Sandell (1987) generally singles out factors other than age discrimination as being the root cause of the problems of older workers.

17. Hamermesh (1989) estimated that displacement probabilities were 20 to 40 percent higher in the 1980s than during the 1970s. Farber (1993) showed that the relative displacement rates of older workers increased during the decade of the 1980s.

18. There is likely to be considerable overlap between bridge employment and partial retirement. A key distinction is that partial retirement refers to a subjective opinion of the individual's retirement status while bridge (versus career) employment is an objective criteria related to the type of position held at a given point in time.

19. As shown in Figures 4.5 and 4.6, a large percentage of older *workers* hold part-time jobs. Nonetheless, since relatively few individuals over the age of 65 remain in the labor force, only a small fraction of this age group are employed at all, and an even smaller proportion work part time.

5

Older Women Workers

Regina O'Grady-LeShane

Women have always worked. However, the contrast between today and earlier time periods is the numbers of women working outside the home and the timing of women's labor force participation, particularly for married women with children. Like their daughters, older women workers of today have faced the choice between work and family obligations, but few of them worked while their children were very young. The choice to work while their children were young was constrained by social norms and expectations. Consequently, they are a transitional group of individuals and represent a cultural shift between the norm of a stay-at-home mother and the working mother of today.

While many women resolved the dilemma of balancing work and child rearing by remaining at home, they again face a choice between working and family concerns in later adulthood (Moen, Robison, and Fields, 1994). Juggling parent care and work is both similar to, and different from, child care issues. However, the decision made in the past may influence how a woman resolves the choice between work and family concerns in late life (Pienta, Burr, and Mutchler, 1994; O'Rand, Henretta, and Krecker, 1992). A life course perspective offers a holistic view on the decision to work and incorporates the work/family choices faced by today's older women *throughout* their adult years.

Research that examines the decision to work may include different populations of women depending on the focus of the study. Studies of labor market participation focus on the decision to work and include *all women* in the sample population. Retirement studies, on the other hand, examine the transition from work to retirement and, consequently, focus on *women workers* (Weaver, 1994). The distinction becomes important when, and if, women workers are different than all women. Given the heterogeneity of today's older women workers and their diverse responses to the decision to work while raising children, the distinction between labor market and retirement studies can be important.

This review begins with a discussion of trends in labor force participation and discusses the job characteristics and labor market problems of current older women workers. Analyses that have been based on a life course perspective are also discussed. Finally, the growing literature on the pathways to retirement as viewed in the context of family life is examined.

TRENDS IN LABOR MARKET WORK

In the last 30 years there has been a steady increase in women's labor force participation rates, from 39 percent in 1965 to 58 percent in 1992 (U.S. Department of Labor, 1993d). The increase is due, in large part, to the change in behavior of married women with children. Today, three out of four married women with children work and more than one-third work full time (Hayghe and Bianchi, 1994).

Prior to the 1950s, the majority of women workers were young and single and exited the labor force at the time of marriage, although not always by choice (Goldin, 1990). Discrimination against married women resulted in the firing of women at the time of marriage and prevented the hiring of married women. The "marriage bars" were especially predominant in the occupations of teaching and clerical work. "In 1920 just 11% of all married women in the labor force were teachers and clerical workers, yet by 1970 the percentage nearly quadrupled, to 42%. The prohibitions covered what were to become the most frequent occupations for married women in the post-1950 era" (Goldin, 1990, 160).

The 1950s marked the decline of the marriage bars and a rise in the labor force participation rate of married women. For today's older women, the social constraints against working resulted in a pattern of work interrupted by child rearing. It is a pattern that has changed, both dramatically and incrementally, during the last 30 years. As Herz noted, "Women born at different times have had strikingly different worklife patterns" (1988, 4). Not only has the labor force participation rate for each birth cohort been increasing, fewer and fewer women of younger cohorts exit the labor force during the child-rearing years (Herz, 1988; Shank, 1988). Today it is no longer unusual for married women to work outside the home while raising young children (Avioli and Kaplan, 1992). Moreover, women today are more likely to work out of preference than economic necessity than women in the past (Herring and Wilson-Sadberry, 1994).

Whereas in recent years, more women of younger ages have entered the labor force, the participation rate of older women workers aged 55 years of age and older has not changed much. In 1972, 24.5 percent of women aged 55 years and older were working at a job, compared to 23.0 percent in 1992, but within that age group are distinct patterns (U.S. Department of Labor, 1993f). The labor force participation rate for women aged 55–59 has, in fact, increased during the last 20 years, from 48.2 percent to 56.8 percent. Little change has occurred among women aged 60–64 years of age (35.3% in 1972 and 36.5% in 1992), and there has been a slight decline among women 65 years of age and older (9.3% to 8.3%).

Part-time employment expanded following the end of World War II (Goldin, 1990). Although most women work full time (80% of women between 25 and 54 years of age), part-time employment has been increasing among older women workers, and especially among the oldest of women workers. Today, 35 percent of women between the ages of 60 and 64 and 60 percent of women over the age of 65 work part time (U.S. Department of Labor, 1993f). Many older women work part time because of family demands (Rones, 1988), reflecting the fact that even in later years, the work/family dilemma faces older women workers. Part-time employment is also characteristic among poor older women (Sum and Fogg, 1990a). Poor women, and especially unmarried women, continue to work after receiving Old Age and Survivors Insurance (OASI) benefits (Iams, 1986), indicating the fact that often they are not working out of choice but economic necessity.

CHARACTERISTICS OF OLDER WOMEN WORKERS

Many issues faced by today's older women workers are unique to this generation (Herz, 1988). They were prevented from working if they married, and they stayed at home while their children were young. The social constraints experienced by this generation were not always welcomed. Typical of many older women is the view expressed by Marjorie, a 56-year-old widow. "When I was young and wanted a career, every one told me I was nuts. Now, I really don't want a career, but I need one and can't get one" (Christensen, 1990, 189).

Today the majority of older women workers are employed in only three occupations—sales, administrative support (including clerical), and services (Herz, 1988, 5). Their concentration in sales and services is less related to a choice for part-time employment and flexible hours than the fact that these jobs tend to be a continuation of past employment (Herz, 1988; Iams, 1987). While occupational concentration is a strong similarity among older women workers, they are a diverse group, distinguished by marital status, education, and race.

Married women have lower labor force participation rates than unmarried women (U.S. Department of Labor, 1993f) and are less likely to work after receiving OASI benefits (Iams, 1986). For many women there is an economic advantage in being married. Divorced and separated older women are more likely to be poor than single or married women (Crown et al., 1993), and in 1992, among women between the ages of 55 and 59, labor force participation rates were 72 percent and 52 percent, respectively, compared to 63 percent for single women and 54 percent and 59 percent for married and widowed women, respectively (U.S. Department of Labor, 1993f).

Education is a very good predictor of whether a woman is working as well as if she is working full or part time (Herz, 1988). In an analysis of data from the Public Use Microdata files of the Decennial Census from 1940 to 1980 and the Current Population Surveys from March 1980 and March 1988, Coleman and Pencavel (1993) examined the number of hours worked by different cohorts of women. Although the increase in hours worked has not been as dramatic as the increase in labor force participation, important differences exist among women, particularly based on race and education. For example, the number of hours worked by white women with more than 16 years of education has increased since 1940; however, it has declined among white women with 13 to 15 years of education and among black women with 12 years or less. Coleman and Pencavel also noted that the overall labor force participation rate of unmarried black women with less than a high school education has fallen dramatically since 1940, when it was 38 percent, to 20 percent in 1988 (1993, 674).

The majority of older African-American women have less than a high school education and are employed in service occupations (Herz, 1988). Their wages are low, and they are generally less than wages earned by white women. In 1986, African-American women who worked full time, year-round, and were between the ages of 55 and 64 earned 84 cents for each dollar earned by white women (Herz, 1988). African-American older workers have more in common with one another than they do with their respective gender groups, having had a working life of accumulated disadvantages (Gibson, 1993). Despite not working, many African Americans age 55 years and older do not consider themselves retired, leading Gibson to refer to them as the "unretired-retired" (1993, 277–78). Similar to Weaver (1994), Gibson (1993) also underscored the point that retirement studies that focus on workers leaving the labor force may miss a large number of individuals in the "unretired-retired" category.

LABOR MARKET PROBLEMS

Many of the labor market problems of older women are similar to those experienced by older male workers. As more women work, they become vulnerable to job loss. Until recently, however, men, more so than women, have been vulnerable to job loss due to a recession (Goodman, Antczak, and Freeman, 1993). Part of the explanation can be attributed to the types of jobs in which men and women are employed. In each recession since 1964, the goods-producing sector of the economy has lost more jobs than the service sector. Women actually gained jobs in the recessions prior to 1981–1992. What was unusual about the recession of 1981–1982 was the loss of jobs in government, accompanied by a slight increase in private-sector service employment. During the recession of 1990–1991, government employment increased slightly and private-sector service jobs declined (Goodman, Antczak, and Freeman, 1993).

The protection that women workers have experienced against job loss during a recession would seem to be over. With the downsizing of government, women are again vulnerable to job loss.

Rones and Herz cited a study by McConnell in which he found gender differences in age discrimination against older workers, with women more likely to experience discrimination in hiring and men being forced out of their jobs through involuntary retirement or termination (1989, 40). Once unemployed, older women are more likely to be out of work longer than others, which could be interpreted as evidence of discrimination against older women (Sandell and Baldwin, 1990, 134).

The rate of reentry into the labor force has increased among women in mid-life but declined among women age 60 and older (Rones and Herz, 1989). Moen, Downey, and Bolger (1990) found that women who were in their 40s in the late 1970s (1975–1979) were more likely to reenter the labor force than women of the same age during the early 1970s (1970–1974). Among women who were out of the labor force, reentry was related to education (Moen, Downey, and Bolger, 1990). Women whose marriage ended, either through divorce or widowhood, were also more likely to reenter the labor force than women whose child-rearing responsibilities had ended (Smith and Moen, 1988).

Older women workers have the lowest median earnings of all workers, with the exception of young workers between the ages of 16 and 24. In 1987 the median earnings of year-round, full-time women workers aged 55–64 and 65+ were $16,721 and $15,200, respectively (Rones and Herz, 1989). While part of the discrepancy may be attributed to occupational segregation and the lower wages associated with the service occupations characteristic of older women (Rones and Herz, 1989), another explanation is the impact of new entrants into the labor force who have less experience and consequently receive lower wages, thereby decreasing the average wage for the group (Goldin, 1990). Examining women's labor force participation throughout the life course clarifies the experience of women workers.

WOMEN'S EMPLOYMENT: A LIFE COURSE PERSPECTIVE

The decision to work is often viewed as a choice made in the present moment and often conceptualized as a trade-off between the financial rewards of work and the value of leisure for an individual. But women's employment decision is more complex than the choice between work or leisure. As Mincer observed more than thirty years ago, "It is ... not sufficient to analyze labor force behavior of married women in terms of the demand for leisure. A predicted change in hours of leisure may imply different changes in hours of work in the market depending on the effects of the causal factors on hours of work at home" (Mincer, 1962, 65). However, the array of choices facing women cannot be explained separate, and apart from, the period of time in which those choices were made. Additionally, the influence of past decisions on present choices must also be considered.

A life course perspective on the decision to work incorporates the work/family choices faced by today's older women *throughout* their adult years. Consequently, a life course perspective assumes that the decision to work while raising children influences other work/family choices later in the life course (Pienta, Burr, and Mutchler, 1994). Moreover, the life course of a cohort is embedded in time, and therefore, the experiences of older cohorts may be very different from more recent cohorts (Moen, Robison, and Fields, 1994). Since the life course of today's older women is as yet unfinished, it is important to understand how women resolve the work/family dilemma in mid to late life as women are increasingly faced with the care of parents and other frail relatives.

Moen, Robison, and Fields (1994) examined how cohorts of women have combined caregiving (defined as excluding child rearing) and employment. Comparing four cohorts of women born between the years 1905–1917, 1918–1922, 1923–1926, and 1927–1934, Moen, Robison, and Fields found that caregiving typically occurred between the ages of 45 and 65 years of age. Each successive cohort had experienced increasing caregiving responsibilities. In contrast to interruptions for child rearing, women are more likely to combine employment and the provision of care to a relative.

Pienta, Burr, and Mutchler (1994) postulated a model of women's late-life labor supply based on the premise that early family events influence later decisions regarding labor force participation (see Kingson and O'Grady-LeShane, 1993, for the impact of family events, specifically withdrawal from the labor force for family reasons, on the level of social security accrued to the working wife). Utilizing data from the U.S. Census Bureau's 1984 Survey of Income and Program Participation, Pienta, Burr, and Mutchler examined the worklives of women born between 1920 and 1929 and developed a typology of work-family pathways, which they defined as continuous workers (24.0%), delayed entry (6.9%), work-oriented (32.2%), family-oriented (27.5%), and other interruption (9.4%). "Those women whose earlier life paths reflect a more stable attachment to the work force are more likely to be working later in life than women who have experienced disruptions for family reasons" (1994, S238).

WORK-TO-RETIREMENT TRANSITION

As people approach the end of their worklives, the factors that influence their decisions to work or retire are becoming increasingly important to researchers and policy makers. (Szincovacz, Ekerdt, and Vinick, 1992). While some studies focus on financial incentives to retire, primarily social security benefit amounts and pension wealth (see Weaver, 1994), other studies stress the influence of the family on, not only employment, but also retirement (e.g., Henretta, O'Rand, and Chan, 1993; O'Rand, Henretta, and Krecker, 1992). "The retirement process is appropriately viewed as temporally embedded in *current* incentive-discentive structures that mediate retirement decisionmaking and in *long-term* family relations that constitute the joint role pathways of couples through work and family domains'' (O'Rand, Henretta, and Krecker, 1992, 82; emphasis in original).

O'Rand, Henretta, and Krecker (1992) analyzed a sample of married women who were married at age 55. In 69 percent of the couples, both spouses were working. They found the following distributions of retirement patterns for working couples—joint retirement accounted for 22 percent; both continued working, for 15 percent; husband working and wife retired, 32 percent; wife working and husband retired, 31 percent. Having no children or working during those years increased the likelihood of joint retirement. ''The joint retirement pattern seems to be an economically and maritally advantageous state, benefiting from the enduring effects of early and sustained investments by both spouses to work and to family'' (O'Rand, Henretta, and Krecker, 1992, 94). Wives who continued to work were in families of lower financial resources, but if there was a family member in the household (i.e., sister or mother), the wife stopped working, suggesting that family care giving demands pulled her out of the labor force (96). Henretta, O'Rand, and Chan (1993) found that ''women who were not employed during child rearing are less affected by spouse's retirement than are men'' (163).

Other family effects may include husband's health and the presence of dependent children or parents. Of the 13 studies reviewed by Weaver (1994), only one (Pozzebon and Mitchell, 1989) found that husband's health resulted in a delay of wife's retirement. McBride (cited in Weaver, 1994) found that the presence of dependent children increased the probability of early retirement among married women but not among unmarried women. However, unmarried women had a 50.1 percent probability of retiring early if a parent lived with them and a 65.4 percent probability of early retirement if two parents shared the household.

CONCLUSION

The interrupted worklife experienced by older women workers has resulted in a unique set of circumstances, which may not be repeated by following generations of women (Herz, 1988). The oldest of today's women workers left their jobs when they married, and many companies would not hire married women. Part-time work did not become widespread until they were in mid-life. If they had worked before marriage, they returned to the labor force. Today they face similar work/family dilemmas. Those who wanted a career but felt pressured to remain at home with children have regrets (Christensen, 1990). Their daughters, however, may be envious of the financial freedom that allowed their mothers to remain in the home.

6

Social Security, Pensions, Disability, and Retirement: An International Perspective

Stuart Dorsey and John A. Turner

Governments around the world share a common goal of assuring adequate retirement income for their elderly citizens. The resulting policies are imbedded in institutions providing retirement income. In most countries, three labor market institutions have evolved that affect retirement income and, as a result, create incentives that affect workers in their decision to retire—social security, employer-provided pensions, and disability programs.[1]

Often, social security programs and private pensions are not age neutral but rather provide an incentive to retire early or to delay retirement. Social security pensions and private pensions may not be actuarially fair. The value of retirement wealth can be affected by retiring earlier or later than the "normal" retirement age or by special provisions such as early retirement bonuses.

This chapter examines current retirement policies and trends in selected industrialized countries. As background to the remainder of the chapter, the next section surveys the demographic and labor force participation trends that cause retirement to be an important social issue.

DEMOGRAPHIC TRENDS AND LABOR FORCE PARTICIPATION RATES

The relative size of the elderly population in industrialized countries is growing. Among the industrialized nations that are members of the Organization for

The material in this chapter is the responsibility of the authors and does not represent the position of the U.S. Department of Labor.

Economic Cooperation and Development (OECD), there is one person age 65 or older for each five persons age 15 to 64. This ratio is projected to increase to between one to three and one to four by 2010 (Incomes Data Services, 1993).

Japan is the most rapidly aging country in the world. The proportion of the population 65 and older in Japan more than doubled between 1950 and 1990 and is expected to double again by 2025, increasing from 12 percent in 1990 to 24 percent in 2025 (Clark, 1993). While the pace of aging is slower in France, the Netherlands, the United Kingdom, and the United States, people 65 and older are expected to represent between 20 and 25 percent of the population in those countries by 2025.[2]

Along with population aging, perhaps the most important change in the industrialized nations' labor markets over the last two decades was a massive movement among older workers to early retirement. Table 6.1 shows that labor force participation rates of males age 55 and older in OECD countries have declined for the last 20 years. The levels and downward trends differ between countries, but in all cases, the majority of males are now out of the full-time labor force several years before the age of legal entitlement to full social security retirement pensions.[3]

In every OECD country between 1975 and 1989, the labor force participation rate of males age 55–59 declined. That was also the case for males age 60–64, with the declines tending to be larger in percentage point terms for this older group. In many countries, a significant number of men are out of the full-time labor force several years before they are eligible to receive social security benefits. Consistent with this trend, in most countries few men remain in the labor force past age 65.[4] Less than 5 percent of men over age 65 are working in the European Community as a whole, with the highest rates in countries with a large agricultural sector (Incomes Data Services, 1993).

Austria provides a dramatic example of declining labor force participation and currently has one of the lowest labor force participation rates for older males. This is especially true of the 60–64 age group, where the rate has fallen below 15 percent, compared to considerably over 30 percent in most other countries. During the 1955–1985 period, the labor force participation rate for the 60–64 age group in Austria fell 58 percentage points (Zweimuller, 1991).

In contrast, Japan has high labor force participation rates for older males. For example, 36 percent of the men age 65 and older were in the labor force in 1989. Many male workers retire from their career jobs with a lump sum pension, often moving to some other, usually lower-paying, job for several years (Schulz, Borowski, and Crown, 1991).

Labor force participation rates among older women are much lower than for older males, but the downward trend is less apparent. The propensity for successive cohorts of women to have higher labor force participation rates has counteracted a tendency for earlier retirement among working women. In a number of countries, the labor force participation rate of women age 55–59 has increased over the past 20 years.

The rise in unemployment among industrialized nations is well known. The

Table 6.1
Labor Force Participation Rates by Sex and Age: Selected Years

Country	Year	Male			Female		
		55-59	60-64	65+	55-59	60-64	65+
Australia	1971	88.4	75.6	22.2	28.3	16.0	4.2
	1986	76.4	44.8	9.0	30.9	13.6	3.0
Austria	1971	83.7	44.9	8.0	35.8	13.2	3.2
	1988	65.3	14.2	1.8	24.6	5.7	0.9
Canada	1971	84.9	74.1	23.6	38.7	29.1	8.3
	1986	81.3	59.9	14.6	44.7	27.5	4.7
France	1975	81.8	54.6	10.7	42.1	27.9	5.0
	1990	68.6	18.1	2.8	46.8	16.7	1.5
Germany	1970	86.8	68.8	16.0	34.5	17.7	5.7
(West)	1988	79.8	34.5	4.9	41.1	11.1	1.8
Japan	1970	94.2	85.8	54.5	53.8	43.3	19.7
	1989	91.6	71.4	35.8	52.2	39.3	15.7
Poland	1970	90.9	83.0	56.4	68.1	51.1	33.0
	1978	81.5	62.4	34.9	57.9	37.4	19.4
Sweden	1970	88.4	75.7	15.2	41.1	25.7	3.2
	1985	85.3	63.2	11.3	72.5	45.6	3.1
United	1971	95.1	86.4	19.4	50.7	27.8	6.4
Kingdom	1986	80.3	53.4	7.5	51.5	18.8	2.7
United	1970	86.8	73.0	24.8	47.4	36.1	10.0
States	1991	79.0	54.8	15.8	55.7	35.1	8.6

Source: U.S. Bureau of the Census (1992).

increase in long-term unemployment for workers age 55 and over has been substantial. A general deterioration of labor markets, especially in Europe, may be a factor in increased early retirement. Thus, some portion of early retirement may not reflect optimal life-cycle labor supply decisions, but may instead be involuntary labor force withdrawal which, for older workers, is labeled retirement.

The trend toward earlier retirement has been supported by explicit social security and disability policies designed to induce early retirement among unemployed workers. In effect, social security and disability programs have become forms of long-term unemployment compensation for some older unemployed workers. For example, a growing number of older workers in several countries are claiming invalidity or disability benefits, apparently in response to unemployment. This has occurred especially in countries, such as the Netherlands, where entitlement to a disability benefit is based on the applicant's ability to find suitable work in the prevailing labor market, as well as his or her physical capability.

Social security and private pensions can reduce the age at which workers retire through four mechanisms. First, a rising level of benefits creates an income effect that induces greater leisure. Second, the age and conditions of eligibility for benefits can be liberalized. Third, benefits may not be actuarially reduced if a worker retires early, nor raised for late retirees. Finally, benefits may be offset by the earnings of retirement-eligible persons who continue working.

SOCIAL SECURITY

Rather than describe all features of institutions that affect the age at which workers retire in different countries, selected features from various countries are highlighted to indicate the range of practices.

Benefit Levels

Population aging is raising the cost of providing social security benefits. The old-age dependency ratio is a shadow price for social security benefits (Doescher and Turner, 1988). When the ratio of retirees to workers is one to four, it costs the average worker $.25 to raise average benefits by $1. If the ratio falls to one to three, it then costs the average worker $.33 to raise benefits. This increase in the price of social security benefits has caused countries to reduce the generosity of benefits.

Future social security benefits have been lowered by legislation in the United States (in 1983), in Japan (in 1985 and 1994), and in the United Kingdom (in 1986). In each case, legislation modified the benefit formulas to reduce the level of future benefits. The United States (in 1983), Germany (in 1989), and Japan (in 1994) scheduled increases in the age for full benefits and higher reductions in benefits at early retirement.[5] France, the Netherlands, the United States, and many other countries have increased contribution rates. In France, retirees at age 60 with 37.5 years of coverage receive 50 percent of the wage base.

The level of benefits is affected by indexing for postretirement inflation. In Japan, the United Kingdom, and most other developed countries, social security benefits are price indexed. In Germany, benefits of current pensioners are increased annually based on the increase in average earnings of workers, so that current pensioners share in the gains in real earnings. Earnings generally grow faster than prices; consequently, benefits that are earnings indexed will grow more rapidly than benefits that are price indexed.

In many countries, such as the United Kingdom, the benefit is higher for a married couple than for a single worker with the same earnings history. However, in some countries, such as Austria, Germany, and Italy, there are no additional benefits for a spouse.

Age of Eligibility for Benefits

The age of eligibility for social security benefits is substantially lower in poor countries than in high-income ones. The largest number of countries, including China and the republics of the former Union of Soviet Socialist Republics (USSR), allow the receipt of a pension at age 60 for men and 55 for women. Nearly as frequent is the use of age 60 for both sexes (Keesing, 1992). Five European Community countries—Germany, Greece, Italy, Portugal, and the United Kingdom—have lower retirement ages for women than men. Japan has a lower age of eligibility for social security for women than men, but that difference is being phased out, with the age for women gradually rising from 55 to 60 by the year 2005. The earliest age at which an individual can receive social security retirement benefits ranges within the European Community from age 60 (men and women in France, Belgium, and Germany and women in Italy, Greece, and the United Kingdom) to 67 (Denmark).

A European Court of Justice decision requires the United Kingdom and other European countries to have the same retirement ages in private pension plans for both men and women. This change is putting pressure on social security systems to also have the same ages for retirement for men and women.

In nearly all industrialized countries, the minimum age for retirement is now lower than when the social security systems were started (see Pilcher, Ramirez, and Swihart, 1968). The minimum retirement age has generally been lowered by allowing early retirement with reduced benefits. This permits a more flexible approach to retirement. It generally raises the cost of a pension system, however, because it allows individuals to pick the retirement age financially most favorable to them, given their expectations about their own mortality.

While most high-income countries have defined benefit social security systems, 20 nations have mandatory defined contribution systems, often called provident funds.[6] These funds may be managed by the government or by private sector financial organizations.

Most of the countries with provident funds are low-income countries, the largest being India. Chile and Singapore, which are middle-income countries, are two exceptions. These systems generally make benefits available at relatively young ages. In all the countries except Chile, benefits are available at either age 50 or age 55. (In Chile, benefits are available at age 60 for women and age 65 for men.) With defined contribution plans, however, when workers take benefits at young ages, the benefits are lower because the workers have had fewer years over which to accumulate assets.

Early Retirement

Many countries' public pension systems allow for early retirement, which may occur in exchange for reduced benefits or be based on one of the following:

- arduous, unhealthy, or dangerous work;
- being female and raising children;
- working in selected occupations;
- unemployment;
- years of covered employment completed.

Early retirement in selected arduous or unhealthy occupations is particularly prevalent in Eastern Europe. When early retirement is available based on occupation, miners are commonly included. In Hungary, for example, the age limit for retirement is set at the low ages of 60 for men and 55 for women. Moreover, individuals who have worked at least 10 years continuously under hard conditions are entitled to a reduction from these retirement ages by two years. Each five years of additional work increases the reduction by one year. The list of jobs covered by these rules has been extended to cover about 100 occupations, including not only coal mining but also oil drilling, the steel industry, the most difficult jobs in dockyards, some types of textile work and bakery work, and some types of health care work (e.g., ambulance drivers) (Szalai, 1991).

In the former Czechoslovakia, the retirement age for a woman varied from 53 to 57, according to the number of children she had reared. In France, women who have raised children can also retire at age 60 and receive the full benefit even if they have not worked a minimum of 37.5 years. Early retirement for women who have reared children is also available in Greece. Early retirement for career workers who become unemployed in old age is available in Austria, Finland, Italy, Sweden, and Mexico. Early retirement based on having completed 35 years of work is available in Italy. In Taiwan, 25 years of work suffices for retirement at any age. Early retirement for people in specific occupations is available in Japan (seamen and miners). For many years, benefits from the Canada and Quebec Pension Plans, the Canadian earnings-related social security plans, were only payable from age 65, but these plans now pay reduced benefits as early as age 60.[7] (This compares to age 62 in the United States.) Reduced early retirement benefits may be received at age 65 in Japan.

Under the German formula for social security benefits, a career worker retiring at age 63 has only a slight reduction in benefits in comparison to retirement at age 65. Suppose the worker has 35 years of service and retires at age 63. The worker's benefit will be 1.5 percent of his or her adjusted base wage multiplied by years of service, or 52.5 percent. A worker who remains in the labor force to age 65 will receive 3 percentage points more (55.5 percent). In other words, the age 63 benefit is 5 percent less than the age 65 benefit. This penalty for early retirement is substantially less than for a worker opting for early retirement at age 63 in the United States, where the actuarial reduction would be 13.4 percent of the age 65 benefit (Gordon, 1988).

In Germany there are several ways through which a worker can receive a pension before age 65. They include receiving a disability pension (receivable at any age) and pensions after long-term unemployment at age 60. In Germany, 35 years of coverage allows a person to retire at age 63. With 5 years of coverage, a man can retire at age 65 with a "normal" old-age pension. A woman can retire with a social security pension at age 60 if she has contributed at least 15 years and has worked 10 of the last 20 years. Women are allowed to retire earlier than men because that allows couples to retire together, given the normal age difference between husbands and wives. Because a woman is credited with one contribution year for each child, many women with a short employment history or none at all, who otherwise would not have been entitled to a pension of their own, are able to qualify. Workers can also qualify for a pension at age 60 if they have been unemployed at least 52 weeks within the last year and a half and have contributed at least 15 years.

In Germany, between 2001 and 2006, the retirement age for unreduced pensions is scheduled to rise to age 65 for both men and women. Early retirement at age 62 will be permitted with benefits reduced by 3.6 percent per year that retirement occurs before 65.

In the Netherlands, social security pays a flat benefit to men and women at age 65. There are no gains from delaying the acceptance of social security, except those due to having greater years of coverage. The benefit is paid whether or not the person stops working. To receive an unreduced retirement benefit, a person must have been covered by social security for 50 years between the ages of 15 and 65. Benefits are reduced by 2 percent for each year by which coverage falls short of 50 years, but years of coverage include periods of education and military service.

Early Retirement and Unemployment

During the 1960s and 1970s, early retirement incentives were incorporated into the national pension programs in several countries of Europe. By encouraging older workers to retire, it was expected that jobs would be made available for younger unemployed workers. (This, of course, assumes that older and younger workers are reasonably close substitutes for each other.) In these plans, the boundaries between retirement, disability compensation, and employment objectives are blurred. This has contributed to enormous strains on public systems, while the extent to which these plans have alleviated unemployment remains controversial (Mirkin, 1987).

The early retirement plan in Belgium in 1976–1983 stipulated that the employer must replace the retiring worker by a person under age 30, who must work for at least one year. These types of plans were intended as a short-term response to the rise in unemployment. The "preretirement" plan in Germany, introduced in 1984 to permit early retirement at age 58, was abolished at the end of 1988.

In France, a pension of approximately 70 percent of preretirement pay was made available to workers at age 60 if they agreed not to take other employment. Introduced in 1972, this plan was discontinued in 1984 when the normal retirement age for social security was lowered from 65 to 60. A government pension in France may be paid to persons age 55 or older who retire in order to be replaced on their job by an unemployed person.[8]

In the United Kingdom, the Job Release Allowance was introduced in 1977, making the retiree's receipt of a pension conditional on the employer hiring a person from the register of the unemployed. Unlike preretirement benefits in a number of other countries, the Job Release Allowance was not earnings-related but was instead paid at a flat rate. Not surprisingly, the overwhelming majority of recipients were low-paid, semiskilled and unskilled workers. This program was ended in 1988 (Laczko and Phillipson, 1991).

The Change in Benefits When Retirement Is Postponed

Besides provisions for early retirement, social security and private pension plans can encourage retirement by not making an actuarially fair adjustment to benefits for workers who postpone retirement. A majority of countries offer a higher monthly pension to someone who applies for a pension after working beyond the earliest age at which retirement is available. The higher the adjustment of benefits with postponed retirement, the greater is the incentive for workers to postpone retirement. The increase in benefits with postponed retirement is frequently compared with an increase that is considered to be actuarially fair. An actuarially fair increase provides the worker with the same lifetime expected present value of benefits for a given number of years of work, regardless of the age at which the worker retires.

An actuarially fair benefit increase takes into account three factors when a worker postpones retirement: (1) benefits are received for a shorter period of time, (2) benefits are received at a later date, and (3) the worker has a greater risk of dying before receiving the benefits. For countries—or groups of workers—with a high life expectancy at retirement age, the actuarial adjustment is lower than for countries or groups of workers with low life expectancy because the percentage reduction in the expected period of benefit receipt with a one-year postponement of retirement is relatively low. The actuarial adjustment increases with age because at progressively older ages, an additional year of postponed benefits is a progressively larger reduction in the expected period of benefit receipt.

The actuarially fair increase in benefits with postponed retirement is smaller when benefits are indexed for inflation after retirement than when they are not. When benefits are unindexed, workers compare the benefit they could receive at a certain age with the amount they would have if they had invested the benefit at the market interest rate. The higher the market interest rate, the greater must be the increase in benefits with postponed retirement.

Whether actuarially fair or not, the adjustment of benefits with postponed retirement will generally affect the age at which workers retire. Workers with higher-than-average mortality risk maximize the wealth from their retirement benefits by retiring early.

In Finland, benefits are reduced by 4 to 6 percent per year for retirement before age 65, depending on the worker's year of birth. The benefits of workers who defer retirement past age 65 increase by 12 percent per year of deferral.

In France, workers can retire at age 60 with unreduced benefits provided that they have at least 37.5 years (150 quarters) of coverage. Workers between ages 60 and 65 with less coverage can receive a reduced benefit. The pension is not increased for continued employment after age 60 unless the person has less than 150 quarters of coverage. For these workers, the pension is increased with continued work due to the increase in quarters of coverage.

In Germany, deferred retirement past age 65 (up to age 67) increases benefits by .6 percent per month. In addition, benefits are increased by 1.5 percent for each year of service. Thus, a worker who defers retirement until age 67 receives a pension about 18 percent higher than the amount he or she would have received at 65.

Hungary increases the monthly amount of the pension by 7 percent for each year by which the pension is deferred past the earliest retirement age.

Table 6.2 shows that in Japan, employment between ages 65 and 70 raises benefits by 88 percent instead of the actuarially neutral 40 percent (Myers, 1991). Thus, the Japanese system rewards retirement that is delayed past age 65. Benefits are not adjusted for the partial-year postponement of retirement. Thus, a worker who retires at age 60 years, 11 months, has the same reduction factor as one who retired at exactly age 60.

With the mortality and interest rate assumptions used to calculate actuarial reductions for the U.S. social security system, the age 60 factor would be 70 percent rather than the 58 percent figure used in Japan. The age 62 factor would be 80 percent rather than the 72 percent figure used in Japan. The greater penalties for early retirement reflect longer life expectancies in Japan than in the United States.[9]

Table 6.2

The Adjustment of Benefits with Postponed Retirement in Japan

Age at Initial Claim	Percentage of Age-65 Benefit
60	58%
61	65
62	72
63	80
64	89
65	100
66	112
67	126
68	143
69	164
70	188

Source: Myers (1991).

The Japanese adjustments were calculated using life tables for 1955 to make them actuarially fair on a unisex basis when calculated using a 5.5 percent interest rate. However, this interest rate is unduly high for price-indexed benefits. Using a 2 percent interest rate (appropriate for price-indexed benefits) and life tables for 1985, the actuarially fair age-60 reduction factor would be 73 percent (rather than 58%) and the age 70 adjustment factor would be 147 percent (rather than 188%).[10]

In Sweden, if a worker delays retirement past age 65, the pension benefit is increased by 0.6 percent a month. If a person retires earlier than age 65, the pension benefit is reduced by 0.5 percent a month for each month prior to age 65. In Denmark, Norway, and Switzerland, delayed retirement past the normal retirement age increases benefits by more than 7 percent per year (Gordon, 1988).

Earnings Test for Retirement Benefits

Some countries have an earnings test that stipulates that benefits cannot be received if earnings exceed a stated level. In countries with a restrictive earnings test, few workers will choose partial retirement. Retirement is a necessary condition for receiving a social security pension in most of the francophone countries of sub-Saharan Africa, most of the countries of the Middle East and North Africa, and a few countries in Latin America (Keesing, 1992). It is also a requirement in Spain and in the former Yugoslavia. Exceptions include Canada, the Netherlands, New Zealand, and Switzerland.

Several countries require retirement as a condition for receiving a pension at the earliest eligible age but then cease to require it if the pensioner is a few years older. In Sweden, there is no earnings test for the receipt of a pension benefit after age 65. Denmark specifies that the benefit be reduced for earnings up to the time of age 70 if they exceed a moderate amount. In France, an earnings test reduces benefits if beneficiaries work part time.[11] In Germany, retirees age 63–64 may earn no more than a certain amount per month, nor may they work more than 2 months a year. In Japan, at age 60–64 the pension is reduced for earnings above specified thresholds. At age 65 in both Germany and Japan, such restrictions cease. In Ireland, retirement is no longer required once the worker reaches age 66. In Luxembourg, "substantial retirement" is necessary until age 65. In the United States, the earnings test is not required once a worker reaches age 70.

In Finland and the Netherlands, a worker need not retire to qualify for a retirement benefit. In Finland, a part-time pension combined with part-time work is payable from age 60 to 65 to a worker who reduces his or her hours to less than 29 per week. Depending on age, the level of the part-time pension is between 44 and 64 percent of the difference between full- and part-time work (Jahunen, 1987).

In Sweden, workers age 60–64 may reduce their hours and combine part-time work with the receipt of a partial pension. This can be done through two different pension arrangements. In the first, it is possible to take a half pension and work half time, starting at age 60. In the second, working hours must be reduced by at least 5 hours per week but must be at least 17 hours. The partial pension covers 65 percent of the loss of earnings resulting from shifting to a part-time job.[12] The net income with partial pensions will, in most cases, be 80 to 90 percent of the income before taking a pension.

The labor supply effects of part-time pensions are unknown. One effect may be that workers who would otherwise have totally withdrawn from the labor force continue to work part time. On the other hand, workers who would have continued full time may have reduced their hours. Sweden is the only nation that actively seeks to prevent job loss among older wage earners rather than compensating them for it, and indeed, the labor force participation rate of persons over age 55 in Sweden has decreased little during the past 15 years.

PRIVATE PENSIONS

Employer-provided pensions have developed in different institutional settings in various countries. They have developed based on agreements between the government and unions (France, Germany, Italy), between industries and unions

(France, the United States), as well as based on company-specific plans (the United States, Canada, the United Kingdom). The terms of pensions are influenced by the terms under which social security is provided. For example, in countries where social security benefits are generous, such as in Italy, the private pension system is unimportant.

The percentage of the labor force covered by employer-provided pensions has increased in most countries. In addition, personal or individual pensions not tied to an employer have also increased in the United Kingdom, Canada, and other countries.

The percentage of the labor force covered by private pensions varies considerably across countries. In the late 1980s, less than a third of the labor force was covered in Australia (30%), Canada (29%), and the United Kingdom (29%). Less than half the labor force was covered by funded pension plans in Japan (39%) and the United States (46%).[13] The Netherlands was the only country with a voluntary private pension system under which more than half the labor force was covered (66%).[14] France and Switzerland both had mandatory private pension systems and thus both had universal or near universal coverage (Dailey and Turner, 1992).

In the United Kingdom, employees may opt out of the employer-provided pension plan and establish a personal pension with an insurance company, bank, or other financial institution.

Age of Eligibility

In the province of Ontario, Canada, employer-provided plans cannot set the normal retirement age later than the participant's 66th birthday. Participants may choose to retire at any time within 10 years of the normal retirement age specified in the plan documents. They may also choose to postpone retirement and continue accruing benefits if their employer permits. If a participant chooses to receive benefits while continuing to work for the same employer, no future benefits can be accrued (Pension Commission of Ontario, Canada, 1993).

In Canada, the usual, but not universal, practice is that a worker whose employment is terminated before qualifying for subsidized early retirement cannot subsequently qualify for those benefits. There is a trend in Canada toward pension plan provisions that favor early retirement (Pesando and Gunderson, 1987).

Often, employer personnel policies encourage early retirement. In Canada, one approach is to waive the reduction for early retirement provided additional age and service criteria are met, such as age 60 with 30 years of service. In that case, a retiring employee would receive a pension calculated with the formula used at normal retirement age. Some plans provide unreduced early retirement after 30 years of service or when an individual reaches age 62. Another possibility is for the reduction to be subsidized so that, rather than a reduction of 6 percent a year, it may be only 2 percent a year. This provides an additional incentive for participants to retire early. Another inducement to early retirement is the *open window policy*, whereby participants are given a limited time in which to take advantage of special early retirement rules. For example, for 3 months participants may be allowed to retire with no reduction in their pension if they are more than 55 years old and have 20 years of service, but after 3 months have elapsed, the window will be closed and the plan will revert to its normal rules (Jobin et al., 1991).[15]

In Germany, a worker receiving an early retirement pension from social security is legally entitled to an early retirement private pension. A range of collective agreements between unions and employers makes early retirement possible. For example, in most breweries, older workers are permitted to accumulate time, which can be used as a credit towards early retirement (Jacobs, Kohli, and Rein, 1991).

In periods of higher unemployment, many Japanese companies offer early retirement packages to their older employees. Many Japanese firms have moved back the age of compulsory retirement, but at the same time have increasingly offered early retirement options (Seike and Shimada, 1986).

In 1988, 47 percent of all Dutch firms with a pension offered a preretirement option to their employees. These options were generally the result of bargaining between a union and a firm or industry. A large segment of the working population—especially in small firms—did not have an early retirement option through a pension plan. In 80 percent of the plans, workers needed to have worked at least 10 years in the firm or industry and had to be at least 60 years old before they were entitled to benefits. Part-time workers were frequently excluded from eligibility (de Vroom and Blomsma, 1991). A number of temporary preretirement options have been negotiated by unions, involving options that generally last for a period of one to five years.

Most British pension plans offer early retirement provided the worker has worked a minimum number of years. This minimum may differ from that applying to eligibility for a pension at normal retirement age. Moreover, early retirement may require the employer's consent. Some plans have special provisions for early pensions if the worker is laid off (Haberman, 1991).

In the United Kingdom, for personal pensions that meet certain qualifying restrictions, the pension can be taken at any age between 50 and 75.[16] In certain occupations (for example, cricketers and trapeze artists), the pension may be taken as early as age 40.

Both employer-provided and personal pensions in the United Kingdom provide for flexibility in retirement. Nearly all (95%) employer-provided pensions allow early retirement (Laczko and Phillipson, 1991). However, in both employer-provided and personal pensions, the benefits may be reduced depending upon the recipient's age, length of service, and, in the case of personal pension plans, the amount contributed. In Germany, early retirement pensions are frequently reduced by 0.5 percent for each month by which retirement is early (Ahrend and Walkiewicz, 1991). Many pension plans provide enhanced benefits in the case of retirement due to ill health.

In the United Kingdom, many employers use early retirement to achieve reductions in their workforce. However, there is a trend away from open-access early retirement programs and toward targeted, closed-access programs. Closed-access programs are aimed at a particular target population, usually defined by the type of job or specific individuals. Such arrangements are used by employers to manage careers and aid organizational and technological change (Laczko and Phillipson, 1991).

In the United Kingdom, virtually all private sector plans base early retirement benefits on accrued service to retirement and then apply a reduction factor. Some plans provide, upon early retirement, an immediate pension without reduction based on accrued service, but such pensions tend to be available only under restricted conditions. For example, the eligibility may be limited to members over age 60 and with a long minimum period of service. Many plans provide a pension at normal retirement based on a formula incorporating a deduction to allow for the pension that will be provided by social security. Many of these plans do not apply this deduction when calculating the pension available on early retirement but instead reduce it only when social security commences. In a few plans, the person retiring early is given an option to exchange a pension at a certain level for a pension at a higher rate until social security begins and then will receive a lower one thereafter.

In the United Kingdom, the method of determining early retirement pensions depends frequently on whether the early retirement is initiated by the worker or the employer. Where members take voluntary early retirement, the accrued pension is likely to be reduced by normal actuarial factors. For 62 percent of participants, it is reduced by normal actuarial factors, while for an additional 21 percent of participants, there is either no reduction or a reduction smaller than an actuarial reduction. In contrast, when retirement is initiated by the employer, 32 percent of participants are in plans where either no reduction or a smaller-than-actuarial one is applied (Haberman, 1991).

In the United Kingdom, worker contributions to contributory defined benefit plans generally cease at the normal retirement age and subsequent service does not enter into the calculation of the pension benefit. However, the pension eventually awarded is increased to allow both for the amount of pension forgone during the further service and for the interest earned on the reserves backing the pension during the deferment period (Haberman, 1991).

Adjustment of Benefits for Postponed Retirement

There are four main ways in which postponed retirement benefits can be adjusted: (1) the continued accrual of pension benefits, with no actuarial increase of previously accrued benefits; (2) no further accrual, with an actuarial increase of previously accrued benefits; (3) continued accrual, with an actuarial increase of previously accrued benefits; and (4) no further accrual and no actuarial increase.

For example, in Canada, provision (1) is the most prevalent, and provision (3), the least common. Provisions (2) and (4) are about equally common (Pesando and Gunderson, 1987). If there is neither actuarial adjustment nor the continued accrual of benefits, the pension plan delivers a strong incentive for retirement. Revenue Canada, the taxing authority, requires that pension payments begin by the worker's 71st birthday, even if work continues beyond this age. After age 71, all workers cease to accrue additional benefits.

MANDATORY RETIREMENT

In some countries, firms that offer pension plans frequently also have mandatory retirement ages. While mandatory retirement because of age is no longer allowed in the United States, it is allowed in Japan, the United Kingdom, and elsewhere.[17] In the United Kingdom, a firm can have different mandatory retirement ages for different classes of workers. For example, one private school has mandatory retirement at age 60 for teachers and mandatory retirement at age 65 for maintenance staff. Virtually all large Japanese firms have mandatory retirement. Previously, the mandatory retirement age was set at age 55 in many Japanese firms. The Japanese government, however, has encouraged firms to increase their mandatory retirement age to 60 or later. As a result, by 1987, 54 percent of firms had adopted the age of 60 (Clark, 1991a, 16). Increases in the mandatory retirement age were especially prevalent in larger firms. In 1989, mandatory retirement at age 55 was used by 22 percent of firms with 30–39 employees but by only 5 percent of firms with 5,000 or more employees (Murakami, 1991).

In countries where mandatory retirement is allowed, pensions tend to be structured differently with respect to retirement age than in countries where mandatory retirement is illegal. In countries where mandatory retirement is illegal, firms that would otherwise have mandatory retirement often adjust the benefit formula so that it more strongly favors early retirement.

GENDER ISSUES

It has been common in the United Kingdom for pension plans to allow women to retire at earlier ages than men. That practice is consistent with the British social security system, which has allowed women to retire at age 60 but required men to work to age 65. The National Association of Pension Funds has estimated that 89 percent of employers have equalized retirement ages, 59 percent by raising the age at which women can retire to 65 (Cohen, 1993).

In the United Kingdom, the courts are still adjudicating whether it is permissible to pay men and women different lump sums for an equal monthly benefit. One argument is that since women on average live longer than men, they need a bigger lump sum to pay an annuity to provide them with an equal annual income for the rest of their lives. In the United Kingdom, the average life expectancy of a woman age 65 is an additional 20.5 years, while it is only 16.5 years for men. Thus, women need roughly 25 percent bigger lump sums. This issue primarily affects single people because a married couple's benefits are calculated jointly using both male and female life expectancies.

DISABILITY PENSIONS

Disability pensions have been a standard feature of social security systems in industrialized nations for several decades. Awarded to workers who have a physical or psychological disability that either prevents employment or only allows work at a reduced level, the payments have taken on growing prominence as a means for early retirement as definitions of disability have become increasingly broad. Broadening the definition of disability has enabled many more older persons to become eligible for a disability pension before they could receive a retirement benefit. Often in countries where early retirement benefits are unavailable through social security, many workers are able to qualify for early retirement through disability retirement programs. In times of an economic downturn, disability programs have tended to be adapted and made subject to less rigorous entry criteria in order to accommodate unemployed older workers who are unlikely to find other jobs. Labor market prospects have been considered along with medical criteria in Germany and the Netherlands.

In the former Federal Republic of Germany, Finland, and the Netherlands, a series of changes in the definition of disability in the 1960s and 1970s caused a substantial increase in the disability benefits awarded. In Germany—where there are practically no part-time jobs available—an older person will receive a full disability pension even if only partially disabled and able to work part time.

In Germany, employer-provided and general disability pensions are not dependent on reaching a given age limit; the only requirement is a contribution period of three years within the last five. This requirement mainly excludes housewives without recent work experience. Before the requirement, disability was the only way for many women to enter the pension system because of the short contribution period that it required. Frequently, a disability pension is more generous than a regular retirement pension. In Sweden, an actuarially reduced retirement pension taken at age 60 is 30 percent lower than a disability pension based on the same work history. In Sweden, it is possible to combine a disability pension with work. Three forms of disability pension are available—full, two-thirds, and one-half. There is no minimum age for eligibility.

Sometimes, private sector employers also provide disability plans or allow workers to retire early based on ill health. In the United Kingdom in 1987, 32 percent of private sector pension participants could retire early due to ill health with a pension equal to the normal retirement pension (i.e., without reduction for early payment). That percentage was up from 20 percent in 1983 (Haberman, 1991). About 30 percent of members of private sector pension plans receive only the pension accrued to the date of their retirement. About 14 percent of private sector participants belonged to permanent health insurance plans, which normally provide a pension up to normal retirement age only, when it is replaced by a pension from the pension fund itself, possibly at a different rate.

In Canada, in cases where the employer has a long-term disability plan, the employee will continue to be credited with years of service while disabled. Usually, these years of service will be based on earnings at the point of disability. Thus, when an employee reaches 65, the insured long-term disability payments stop and the pension begins, based on years of membership plus years of disability. Alternatively, if the employer does not have an insured long-term disability plan, the pension plan itself may pay a disability benefit to a member who becomes disabled. The level of benefit will likely be based on the plan formula and could either recognize service up to the date of disability or projected service up to normal retirement age (Jobin et al., 1991).

CONCLUSIONS

Countries have developed a wide variety of restrictions and incentives affecting retirement and the employment of older workers. If governments decide that they wish to either encourage or discourage early retirement, they have examples of such policies on which to draw. Around the developed world, the labor force participation of older men has declined over time, while the labor force participation of older women has been more stable. The policies of a country toward retirement age naturally evolve with its changing economic and demographic circumstances. With the aging of populations and the trend toward earlier retirement, several countries have changed their social security programs to encourage the employment of older workers in the future. Whether employers will do likewise with their private pension plans—and whether the employment of older workers will increase—remains to be seen.

NOTES

1. Unemployment compensation programs are another institution that may affect the transition between work and retirement, but they are not considered here.

2. See Kingson (Chapter 3 of this volume) for a discussion of demographic trends in the United States.

3. See Ruhm (Chapter 4 of this volume) and Leonesio (Chapter 12 of this volume) for discussions of retirement trends in the United States and their causes.

4. Japan is a notable exception.

5. In Germany, starting in 2001, the age limits for retirement with an unreduced pension will be raised from age 63 with 35 years of service to age 65 with 35 years of service. There will still be the possibility of early retirement up to 3 years before age 65, but each year prior to age 65 will be penalized by a 3.6 percent reduction of the pension amount. Each year of postponing retirement beyond age 65 will lead to a 6 percent increase in benefits.

6. Defined benefit plans typically specify a benefit based on the worker's earnings

and years of service. Defined contribution plans specify the amount to be contributed to the plan, with the benefit depending on the investment performance of the plan's assets.

7. There is also a flat rate benefit called old age security that pays all elderly residents the same amount.

8. This pension is not paid through the social security retirement program.

9. In Japan, life expectancy at age 65, according to 1988 life tables, was 19.5 years for females and 16.0 years for males, compared to 18.6 and 14.7 years, respectively, for the United States in 1986 (Myers, 1991).

10. These compare to the figures for the United States, with its slightly lower life expectancies, of 70 percent and 140 percent, respectively.

11. Much of the following discussion concerning the retirement incentives in the social security systems of different countries is from Clark (1991a).

12. The percentage was originally set at 50 percent but was raised to 65 percent in 1987.

13. The statistics for Japan are understated because they exclude workers who are in unfunded plans that provide lump sum benefits.

14. The statistics for the Netherlands are understated because they exclude workers that are in plans funded through insurance companies.

15. See Mutschler (Chapter 10 of this volume) for a discussion of window plans.

16. This applies only to personal pensions bought with contributions additional to the contracted-out rebate.

17. Mandatory retirement has also been banned in Canada in some jurisdictions.

7

Retirement before Social Security

W. Andrew Achenbaum

On June 8, 1934, Franklin Delano Roosevelt (FDR) sent a message to Congress reviewing the broad objectives and accomplishments of his administration during his first 15 months in office. The president offered the American people a New Deal. Recognizing that the nation's economic structure needed to be rebuilt, he signed into law sweeping reforms in farming, banking and commerce, and industry. He asked Congress to appropriate unprecedented sums of federal dollars for housing and relief for the hundreds of thousands of families whose lives had been disrupted by the Great Depression. Above all, he sought to restore citizens' faith in themselves and in the country's democratic, capitalist principles. FDR was ready to break new ground by proposing that Washington oversee a plan that would further "the security of the citizen and his family through social insurance" (Pifer and Chisman, 1985, 138). American workers, he declared, needed a measure of protection against the vicissitudes that accompanied the achievements of industrial progress:

I am looking for a sound means which I can recommend to provide at once security against several of the great disturbing factors in life—especially those which relate to unemployment and old age. . . . These three great objectives—the security of the home, the security of livelihood, and the security of social insurance—are, it seems to me, a minimum of the promise that we can offer to the American people. They constitute a right which belongs to every individual and every family willing to work. They are the essential fulfillment of measures already taken toward relief, recovery, and reconstruction.

... We must dedicate ourselves anew to a recovery of the old and sacred possessive rights for which mankind has constantly struggled—homes, livelihood, and individual security. The road to these values is the way to progress. (Pifer and Chisman, 1985, 138)

FDR was looking not for a panacea but something that dovetailed with other New Deal programs. An effective measure would promote insurance conscious-ness as it shored up the nation's safety net. These two objectives were intimately related in the president's mind, because they affected the workers' sense of security in the marketplace. A well-designed social insurance program would reaffirm the value that Americans traditionally placed on individual self-reliance and familial responsibilities. True to form, the president merely sketched out a vision; he left the details to others to negotiate.

Seven months later, FDR's Committee on Economic Security (CES) unveiled a package that included "economic assurance," unemployment compensation, old-age security, protection for children, insurance dealing with "risks arising from ill health," and residual relief. "The program for economic security we suggest follows no single pattern. It is broader than social insurance and does not attempt merely to copy European methods," the blue-ribbon panel declared. "In placing primary emphasis on employment, rather than unemployment com-pensation, we differ fundamentally from those who see social insurance as an all-sufficient program" (Pifer and Chisman, 1985, 70). The Committee on Economic Security went even further than Roosevelt in suggesting that U.S. workers deserved a plan that radically diverged from what was done in other countries. However, the CES strategy rested on "liberal traditions, through proc-esses which retain all of the deep essentials of that republican form of govern-ment first given to a troubled world by the United States" (Pifer and Chisman, 1985, 70). The fundamental flaw in European models of social insurance, ob-served U.S. experts, was that they did not sufficiently reinforce people's right, and obligation, to be gainfully employed. The CES plan thus forged partnerships around the primacy of work between the country's public and private sectors, between federal and state agencies, and between workers and employers.

Congress by and large accepted the committee's report, but the legislative history reveals much about the status of the elderly and the nature of retirement before the passage of the 1935 Social Security Act. FDR's experts had intended to make unemployment compensation the cornerstone of its measure. Indeed, as late as November 1934, the president admitted in a press conference that he was not certain that the bill being drafted would please Townsendites (who wanted more generous pensions to be given to senior citizens as a way of stimulating the economy), labor groups, and key social insurance advocates who wanted to include provisions for old-age security in the act.

The 74th Congress, however, gave old-age assistance top billing in its om-nibus legislation. In order to reduce the government's obligation to underwrite relief to needy senior citizens in the future, Title II authorized a program of old-age insurance that required employers and employees to make provisions for workers too old to remain in the labor force. Other titles focused on risks and hazards that affected opportunities for meaningful employment at earlier stages of life. They included aid to the blind and to crippled children, assistance for dependent children as well as for maternal and child health services, and funds for public health training. Even Section 702 of the 1935 Social Security Act which authorized the creation of a Social Security Board to study "the most effective methods of providing economic security through social insurance, and as to legislation and matters of administrative policy concerning old-age pensions, unemployment compensation, accident compensation, and related subjects" (Pifer and Chisman, 1985, 92) was consistent with a belief that welfare initiatives should care for people who could not be expected to find jobs.

Congress targeted particular needs of people at different ages in their life course. Due to changes in the work cycle (Achenbaum, 1986b), old-age dependency was, by 1935, unquestionably a "problem," so those who drafted social-security policies attempted to alter the social construction of retirement. Hence, the selection of age 65 to be the age of eligibility for old-age assistance and old-age insurance may be interpreted as a compromise choice. Picking age 70 was deemed too restrictive. Congress decided not to establish a younger age of entitlement, for which there were precedents abroad and in state-funded old-age pensions, because they feared such generosity would prove too costly (Cohen, 1957). Similarly, Congress did not create a nationwide floor for old-age relief or insist on universal coverage under the new retirement scheme. As a result, there would be considerable variations from place to place in the manner in which retirement under the new social-insurance legislation was defined and implemented.

The 1935 Social Security Act represents a watershed in the history of U.S. retirement. From the founding of the republic through the Great Depression, there were many ambiguities and variations in the ways people understood, and actually entered, retirement. Appreciating that retirement was shaped by various individuals and institutions in a historical process that was quite convoluted makes it easier to fathom the complexity of contemporary retirement trends and policies.

RETIREMENT AT THE INDIVIDUAL LEVEL

First a Stage, Then a Fixed Age

Like everybody else, older men in the early years of the republic were expected to remain economically and socially useful as long as they were physically able to work. An orator elaborated on this idea during July 4 ceremonies in 1825 in Ohio, where a new canal was being built. America's ability to tap the resources of citizens at different stages of life, he remarked, provided it "at once, all the vigor and firmness of youth, the strength and firmness of manhood, and the wisdom of age. Great as is the undertaking, your powers are equal to its completion; be but united, firm, and persevering, and if heaven smile on your labors, success is sure'' (Achenbaum, 1978, 9). Whatever the elderly lacked in "firmness," they made up in wisdom. The prevailing notion was that aged workers were seasoned veterans of productivity. Past experiences enhanced prospects that the old still offered good advice and could engage productively in the daunting task of nation building.

The converse to this proposition also held true: able-bodied older men who did not contribute to the well-being of society and to their own financial security were not esteemed by their contemporaries. Medical and popular writers asserted that deterioration in later years resulted more from disuse than from medical decay (Caldwell, 1846). In a comparatively youthful republic, where labor shortages were acute, wasting human resources at any age was foolish. In any case, although the notion of retirement itself was centuries old—Chinese bureaucrats had been granted stipends at advanced ages as early as the thirteenth century, and older British and French soldiers were assigned to garrison activities or officially discharged on account of age by the 1700s—there were few mechanisms in place in the United States prior to 1900 to entice or induce men to quit their jobs merely on account of old age.

Americans extolled the ageds' usefulness in farming, and articles in almanacs and farm journals routinely attested to their usefulness in rural settings. For example, the well-known *Farmer's Almanac*, originally compiled by Robert B. Thomas, annually featured suggestions by old "Father Simkins" on shoeing horses, caring for farm implements, and keeping account books in order (Thomas, ser.). Among "The Contents of an Old Man's Memorandum Book" in an edition of the *U.S. Almanack* was practical advice on naming sons and daughters, teaching children to be ambidextrous, traveling efficiently, exchanging ideas with friends, and selecting the best time to set a watch. Other writers noted older people's supervisory capacities. Even when the elderly slowed down, there were barnyard chores and other less physically demanding jobs to be done. The aged remained key figures in farm communities throughout much of U.S. history. After all, prior to the Civil War, 60 percent of all gainfully employed persons and a vast majority of all workers over 60 were farmers (Whelpton, 1926).

During the antebellum period, the election and appointment to high public office of men in their later years, moreover, attested to older men's presumed worth in handling public affairs as well as managing farms. In the heyday of Jeffersonian Democracy, septuagenarians were serving as chief wardens of the busy ports of Philadelphia and Boston and as key administrators in Connecticut, Pennsylvania, and South Carolina. Moreover, a number of octogenarians remained politically active at the city, state, and federal levels. Eleven of the 21 highest ranking naval officers were over 60 in 1839; 7 others were 59. Congressmen literally were often senior statesmen. "When persons of mature age and eminent for their experience, wisdom and virtue" were elected to Congress, Hezekiah Niles editorialized in the country's best-read weekly, "it is a subject for gratitude and congratulation'' (Achenbaum, 1978, 20). Years of service, it was said, ripened political sagacity.

In fact, the Founding Fathers of the Republic established many laws that forbade young men from voting and from holding public office, but there were only a few posts from which elderly citizens were disqualified. Most jurisdictions required voters to be at least 21 to cast a ballot. No one, however, was disenfranchised on account of advanced age. The U.S. Constitution set minimum ages for elections to Congress and to the presidency, yet there were no maximum age restrictions for any elected or appointed federal offices. States barred young men, not old ones, from running for governor or the legislature. Unlike the federal constitution, however, a few jurisdictions did impose definite limits on the number of years a person could serve as a justice. (Hence, James Kent did not write his famous *Commentaries* until he was forced off the New York bench at age 60; upon his death, 24 years later, the state abolished its mandatory retirement provision.) In addition, seven states followed a 1780 Massachusetts precedent requiring that licenses be renewed every seven years (Thorpe, 1909). Such restrictions were designed to guard against incompetency, and not to discriminate against old justices. That these are the *only* instances of discrimination against older men's right to hold elected or appointed office is revealing.

Nor was there extensive mandatory retirement in the private sector before the twentieth century. No U.S. profession, industry, business, craft, or trade organization prior to 1875 required people to leave the labor force because they had reached a predetermined chronological age. Thus, we must be careful not to impose modern definitions of retirement onto earlier concepts. Retirement once connoted a condition in life to be entered at various stages of the life course, not the attainment of a particular chronological age in late maturity. Boys and girls, men and women of all ages, and not just the elderly, were thought to retire under specific sets of circumstances. Farmers, according to almanacs, annually "retired" from winter storms to their family circles. In the first edition of *An American Dictionary of the English Language*, Noah Webster defined retirement as "1. The act of withdrawing from company or from public notice or station. 2. The state of being withdrawn. 3. Private abode; habitation secluded from much society, or from public life. 4. Private way of life" (Webster, 1828).

The Spread of Retirement as a Social Phenomenon in the United States

As late as 1900, many Americans still valued older men's contributions in the marketplace. Farming was the occupation of choice of more than half of all men over 65 who were still working. Since the most powerful committees went to those with the longest tenure, seniority counted more than ever in Congress. Many of the nation's most prominent professionals and best-known corporate executives had gray beards. Nonetheless, an increasing number of commentators sensed that the new urban-industrial order and Darwinian-inspired cultural norms were conspiring to change perceptions of the elderly's worth in the labor force.

In the search for increased efficiency, begotten in modern times by the practically universal worship of the dollar, . . . gray hair has come to be recognized as an unforgivable witness of industrial imbecility, and experience the invariable companion of advancing years, instead of being valued as common sense would require it to be, has become a handicap so great as to make the employment of its possessor, in the performance of tasks and duties for which his life work has fitted him, practically impossible. (*Independent*, 1913, 504)

A new trend in discharging employees who had attained a certain age provides a clear indication that ideas about older people's potential for productive careers were in flux. Frustrated by the inability of his naval officers to vanquish the Rebel forces, Abraham Lincoln demanded, in December 1861, the resignation of all men below the rank of vice admiral who were at least 62. Fifty-five years later, Congress raised the retirement age for military officers to 64 (U.S. Rev. Stats.). The practice of requiring federal officials to retire was not uniform. Each category of government workers was governed by a different set of age requirements. Retirement policies were also in the embryonic stages of development in the private sector and in various municipal and state bureaucracies.

The meanings of *retirement* and *superannuation* changed to embrace the new realities. According to lexicographers of the 1880 edition of Webster's *American Dictionary*, "retire" meant "to cause to retire; specifically to designate as no longer qualified for active service; as to retire a military or naval officer." Note the shift in agency: earlier definitions suggested that a person chose when and how to retire, but now, some third party could force a person to retire. Similarly, the verb *superannuate* now meant, among other things, "to give pension to, on account of age, or other infirmity." Reaching a certain age was associated with disability, with being incapable of meeting minimal standards (Graebner, 1980; Haber, 1983). Writers commented on "the tendency—visibly increasing in this country—of relegating the older and middle-aged men to the oblivion of 'innocuous desuetude' " (Dorland, 1908).

During the first third of the twentieth century, economic theorists and social commentators did not just rehearse earlier arguments about factories prematurely wearing out employees and making older workers seem obsolete. Agricultural productivity increased, thanks to mechanization and better applications of science. Modernization reduced farmers' reliance on aging hired hands. In a nation in which economies of scale and efficiency increasingly mattered, establishments that once served as "cushions for the scrap heap" declined in importance or ceased operations. Older workers were far more likely than younger ones to be engaged in traditional crafts and trades: they tended to be ticket collectors and hucksters, not locomotive engineers or telephone operators. As businesses became more bureaucratic, relations between employers and employees became more impersonal. Industries with advanced technologies and sophisticated production lines made little effort to recruit and retain older men. "In no other country does the basis of age alone furnish so definite a line of demarcation between a portion of the population recognized as economically efficient and socially attractive and that part of it which is neither useful nor particularly attractive" (Dallach, 1933, 50; see also Epstein, 1929).

Age grading pervaded every dimension of the country's social, economic, and cultural life. Rules that reinforced the prevailing bias against age compounded the predicament of elderly workers. Surveys of occupational groups, including professionals, revealed that workers' earnings declined past the age of 55 (Thorndike and Woodyard, 1926). Mandatory retirement programs increased in scope and specificity. In addition, the country's largest and most "progressive" corporations began to adopt the latest practices in scientific management. Personnel departments were established, with staffs of white-collar workers who were trained to use psychological tests and job profiles. Their battery of results indicated that older workers were less efficient than younger employees; the aged often caused morale problems (Hall, 1922). Such evidence warranted the rejection of aging job applicants on grounds of cost and efficiency. A federal study, *Recent Social Trends* (1933), reported that "there is much evidence to support the growing belief that industry is honeycombed with strict hiring limits (811)." On the eve of the Great Depression, finding meaningful employment was a major problem for older men.

DEMOGRAPHIC VARIATIONS

Gender

Obstacles imposed on account of gender exacerbated the employment discrimination based on age prejudice. Women have always worked in America, but until very recently, their employment and earnings patterns differed markedly from men's. Only certain types of jobs were available. Young women could become teachers, maids, nurses, or clerks. Generally, women were given low-paying positions and were paid less than their male counterparts for equivalent work. "Marriage bars" arose in teaching and clerical work during the last two decades of the nineteenth century: married women were not hired, and they generally were not retained after marriage (Goldin, 1990). Once they began to raise children, mothers were expected to stay at home. If necessary, wives might take in boarders, do laundry, or do piecework at home. More out of necessity than choice, widows very often became saloon keepers or hotel managers or took on any menial jobs outside the home that were not desired by younger female competitors.

Relatively few older women tried to reenter the labor force in the early decades of the twentieth century. Only 9 percent of all women over 65 were gainfully employed in 1900. Most engaged in agricultural pursuits or domestic service. Few were in trades or manufacturing. Those who attempted to resume earlier occupations often found that their skills had depreciated with the advance of technology. Hence, unlike those older women who returned to work during or after World War II, earlier cohorts of aging women with sketchy earnings records and dubious credentials found themselves marginalized.

The fact that so-called career women were often as disadvantaged around the turn of the century as other females who entered, left, and then reentered the labor force proves the virulence of sex discrimination. Generally enjoying even less job security and earning less than men, women were considered "older" workers at a relatively youthful 35 (Lobsenz, 1929). They rarely worked in jobs that enabled them to become eligible for pensions. Few career women could depend on an inheritance substantial enough to sustain them with advancing age. Thus, single older women were truly vulnerable.

Race

Any comparison of black and white employment patterns over the life cycle must begin by acknowledging the pervasiveness of racism in American culture. African Americans under slavery were considered property; they tried to do less than their masters wanted but still did more than if they had had freedom of choice. If the law did not expressly forbid it, some slave owners "emancipated" superannuated workers, thus "freeing" themselves of caring for elderly slaves. A few heartlessly banished their worn-out slaves like old horses to eke out an existence on their own. In the confines of the slave quarters, however, a different employment pattern emerged. There, the oldest members were accorded respect. They took care of children whose parents were in the fields. Black elders served as mentors to the young (Gutman, 1976; Genovese, 1971).

After the Civil War, most older African-American men remained in farming. Unlike their white counterparts, however, few became owners or managers of agricultural concerns. The percentage of aged black farm owners did not exceed the percentage of tenants until 1940. Those who migrated North or went to ghettos in southern cities invariably encountered job discrimination at the hands of whites. Opportunities were limited within the African-American community. There were exceptions, to be sure. There has always been a small middle-class, professional stratum. Blacks who owned newspapers or their own shops were able to prosper by retaining a controlling interest in late life (Lewis, 1993). Older African-American women, because of the economics of racial poverty and discrimination, very often had to find gainful employment in order to support their families. Prospects were slim—the chances that elderly black women could find decently paying jobs were thwarted by sexism and racism, which interacted with ageism.

Ethnicity

In addition to the segmentation of the labor force caused by gender and race, there were some ethnic variations that are worthy of note. Generally speaking, the most recently arrived immigrants took the most menial, hazardous, and lowest-paying jobs available. Certain groups acquired specialties—hence, the Chinese owned most of the laundries and Greeks owned many of the restaurants in Michigan's Upper Peninsula around the turn of the century. Newly arrived workers tried to stake a claim, so that their children and their children's children could realize the American dream. (Not all immigrants followed this path to retirement: roughly 30 to 40% of those who came to America to make their fortune left when they had saved enough money to buy a farm or shop in their homeland.) Successive generations were to build on the accomplishments of the "greenhorns," who relied on reciprocal arrangements within families and across kin networks (Gratton, 1985).

Consider the case of French-Canadian workers who took jobs in the mill in Amoskeag, New Hampshire, which at the turn of the century was the largest in the world. Irish supervisors counted on family elders to recruit immigrant workers, teach them the ropes (including how to cut corners), and keep them in line. Note the valuable, if informal, role that older workers played in promoting industrial efficiency. In the absence of formal retirement policies, aging workers were often rewarded for their loyalty by being given less demanding tasks. Young kin protected their elders by helping them with aspects of their jobs so that they appeared productive (Hareven, 1983). Disruptions in an aging person's work cycle, occasioned by layoffs, sickness, or physical decline, sometimes could be assuaged by support from family members who, in accordance with ethnic traditions, felt obliged to help their own in times of need.

The fate of immigrant women is difficult to summarize briefly. Ethnic customs mattered greatly. Hence, Italian working men frowned on their sisters, mothers, wives, and aunts working outside the home. The Irish were less ambivalent on this matter than Slovak immigrants, though both preferred that their women confine employment activities to the domestic sphere (Bell, 1941). Many Russian-Jewish women did piecemeal work in sweatshops in tenements or worked in cigar factories. Like the relatively more affluent, native-born widow, however, the older immigrant woman very often shivered at the thought of living to a ripe old age. Without their spouse's income for support and without assurances that their children would, or could, help in time of need, few of these women could eke out much of an existence relying on their own skills and pathways into the labor force.

Class

Though the citizens in the United States have usually considered theirs to be a "classless" society, divisions by race and ethnicity in the marketplace often served as surrogates for class. The impact of gender on late-life work opportunities was felt orthogonally, separating into distinct spheres by race and ethnicity. As late as 1930, 58.4 percent of all men over the age of 65 were gainfully employed, compared to 8.1 percent of all women. There was, moreover, a striking age-specific variation in the proportion (from 3 to 21%) of women working in clerical positions between 1890 and 1930. However, in 1930, less than 2 percent of all gainfully employed women over 65 held such jobs (Achenbaum, 1978; Schaie and Achenbaum, 1993). The luck and pluck of Horatio Alger novels inspired many youth, as did Andrew Carnegie's successes as a capitalist, risk taker, and philanthropist. Being born well was probably the best predictor of financial success and a comfortable old age, as America's elite tended to transmit wealth and positions of power along family lines. Upward social mobility over the life course was possible for the rest of the populace, but it was more modest in scope than American myths imply; often, it meant owning, not just renting, a home. With luck, workers could accrue some savings for the inevitable hard times ahead.

The structure of the nation's new urban-industrial order directly and indirectly widened the gap between the opportunities accorded aging workers whose career paths diverged even from birth (Haber and Gratton, 1994). Farmers had to be self-reliant; their fortunes over their lives depended on nature and their own capacity to produce. Managers of successful business ventures, in contrast, could find jobs for their aging relatives or grant them bonuses or pensions that would enable them to leave their posts with dignity and security. Large and established industries and firms were far more likely to provide pensions and benefits for older workers. The promise of a small pension was both a reward and an instrument of social control. Small, struggling concerns lacked the necessary resources to sustain welfare capitalism, even if they so desired (Shover, 1976; Brinkley, 1993).

The current two-tiered stream of older workers thus has deep historical roots. There have always been a privileged minority of employees who have had, or could expect, fairly generous compensation packages while they worked and then have sufficient income in retirement to replace lost income. Most workers, however, were not so lucky. Their working careers were interrupted by recessions, layoffs, strikes, firms going out of business, and other causes of unemployment. The specter of indigency in late life was a real possibility, but for most individuals, "retirement" was not an immediate concern. Men who had worked for two decades in the mills already were considered old by age 30 (Kleinberg, 1989). Should they survive to old age, most unskilled workers figured that their vulnerability would increase, but by late middle age they already would have acknowledged their fragility.

Disability

Indeed, sickness and disability constitute the last major demographic variation to be discussed in terms of how older workers prepared for their later years. Even in the early years of the republic, people recognized that debilities and infirmities restricted employment options. Declining health reduced Natty Bumppo and Daniel Boone from hunters to trappers and guides. Noah Webster's definition of "superannuate" connotes the critical importance of health: "To impair or disqualify by old age and infirmity" (1928, S.V.). The line between age and disease was always thin. When their disabilities accrued, the old were expected to phase down their activities. An old horse that trotted was respectable, Henry Hugh Brackenridge reminded readers in *Modern Chivalry* (1804), but one that tried to speed was contemptible: "The great secret of preserving respect is the cultivating and showing to the best advantage the powers that we possess, and the not going beyond them (36)."

The actual extent of physical and mental incapacity among the elderly before the twentieth century is unknown, but it undoubtedly was widespread. Even in the 1960s, 14 to 24 percent of all people over 65 in three industrial countries suffered from a major disability; the likelihood of incapacity was found to increase with advancing age, especially in the ninth decade (Shanas et al., 1968). Though it cannot be said that advances in medical technology and therapeutic interventions have dramatically reduced the incidence of disability in later years—we may have succeeded mostly in extending the lives of people sufficiently to put them at risk for impairment—it is reasonable to hypothesize that a significant minority of older men and women who wished to find jobs were physically unable to work prior to the enactment of social security.

It is important to bear in mind, however, that not all late-life impairments present themselves in old age. The disabilities that prevented the old from working might have occurred in the prime of their lives, as the nineteenth-century statistics on industrial accidents are grim. A young man who worked on the railroad was likely to become permanently disabled in five years. For the rest of his life, he would have to rely on the kindness of others; sometimes, foremen would permit these victims of industrial progress to beg outside the gates on payday. Engineers served as watchmen (Licht, 1933). Older workers frequently competed with their disabled sons for part-time jobs and small change. Putting the problems of older workers into a life course perspective helps to explain why Americans of a century ago were less concerned about their retirement options than they were about securing invalidity insurance, unemployment compensation, or mother's pensions. Few discounted the possibility that they might someday reach the biblical "three-score and ten" only to find themselves poor, out of work, and unable to find a job. However, workers had more immediate, omnipresent concerns; they already were too "old" for some jobs, their pay was minimal, they could not depend on steady employment, and they felt constantly at risk of losing everything they had secured. Not until a large segment of the work force found itself victimized by age discrimination and unable to make adequate preparations for the later years were remedies sought to the dependency of old age. In that context, a variety of approaches were taken, all of which shaped the institutionalization of retirement.

INSTITUTIONALLY BASED RETIREMENT STRUCTURES

Family Support

When aging individuals were no longer able to care for their own needs through gainful employment or reliance on savings, kith and kin were expected to provide support. If Scripture and the pressure of neighbors did not make that prescription clear enough, then officials in Colonial times backed up the custom by invoking common-law traditions. Nearly every colony modeled its statutes after the Elizabethan poor laws of 1601 and 1603, which made families morally responsible for the well-being of their poor and sick relatives, including members of the oldest generation. Few states, however, enacted family laws that distinguished between old-age dependency in particular and the general care of the impoverished (Schouler, 1870). Only three states (Colorado, Kentucky, and Ohio) imposed criminal charges on adult children who failed to furnish necessity to their aged parents. Families developed their own patterns of exchange.

Residency patterns reconstructed from state and federal censuses indicate that older people valued their privacy. They maintained independent households as long as possible. According to the 1895 Massachusetts census, fewer than 10 percent of all native-born men over eighty and 13 percent of their foreign-born peers lived with strangers or in institutions. However, widowed men were no more likely to head households than women who had lost their husbands. Causality is hard to determine, but the connection among age, employment, and marital status seems clear. Men who were ill, infirmed, and widowed generally had difficulty finding a new spouse. Inheritance laws tended to subordinate widows' interests. This heightened chances that older women would have no option but to seek aid from children or neighbors (Grigg, 1989; Smith, 1979).

Writers in the first decades of the twentieth century noted that multigenerational living arrangements provoked complaints and resentment among young and old alike. Even during the relative prosperity of the 1920s, surveys revealed that the middle-aged felt hard-pressed to raise their children as they wished; most recognized their responsibility to care for their parents, if the need arose, but the burden was significant. Adding to the squeeze was a change in domestic architecture. Newly constructed homes eliminated the spare bedroom. In a society in which privacy is greatly valued, it was hard for three or four generations to live under the same roof (Lynd and Lynd, 1929; *Recent Social Trends*, 1933).

Aging workers did have a third option besides trying to get and keep a job and relying on support from their children. Just as they bought disability insurance and life insurance, so, too, there were policies available that were expressly designed to protect people from the financial vicissitudes of late life. Even in the Colonial era, people of means could purchase annuities early in life, which would mature when they reached old age. Working-class people often deposited funds for "rainy days" into their savings account. Some states permitted savings banks to issue life insurance policies. Quite often, these funds had to be used in emergencies that arose before the onset of old age. Prior to the 1840s, most insurance policies covered short-term contingencies, while whole-life policies became fashionable thereafter. However, the insurance companies were prudent. They limited their liabilities—policies on a single life rose slowly from $10,000 to $100,000, with an average of $30,000. (Philadelphia department-store owner John Wanamaker, in 1888, became the first American to hold a million-dollar policy.) Moreover, they imposed age limits. Following cues from Elizur Wright, an authority at International of London, U.S. firms rarely issued policies or covered men over the age of 70 (Stalson, 1969).

The Tontine Plan, inaugurated in England in the 1860s, was popularized in the United States by the Equitable of New York (Bailey, 1967). Essentially, investors pooled their money. Those who died before their committed payments had been fulfilled forfeited dividends which, if things went according to plans, assured those who lived long enough a return on their contributions. The plan appealed to the wealthy and to speculators. However, when the federal government outlawed *tontine insurance* in 1906, many middle- and working-class Americans lost a popular way to protect themselves from the vagaries of the marketplace. Economists Ransom, Sutch, and Williamson (1993) contend, moreover, that the collapse of tontine insurance is a prime reason why Americans had to rethink their approach to the retirement years. There is no question that alternatives became increasingly prevalent.

Voluntary Associations

Philanthropists, churches and synagogues, and local charity agencies did little directly to effect the timing and implementation of retirement in the marketplace, but some acted on their concern for the well-being of older people who were not working. Andrew Carnegie, for instance, set aside $10 million in 1905 to enable college professors to retire in modest comfort. Benjamin Rose left $3 million six years later for "respectable and deserving" older people who needed help in the Cleveland area (Achenbaum, 1983). On a more modest scale, workers drinking in saloons often passed the hat to raise funds for aged and incapacitated comrades. Some of these arrangements provided the financial basis for immigrant banks in working-class districts of major cities or in rural communities.

Especially after the Civil War, various Protestant, Catholic, and Jewish organizations built institutions for the old. A few fraternal organizations also sponsored old-age homes for their fellow workers, but the religious ones are the most important. Of the 1,200 benevolent homes in operation in 1929, roughly 800 were constructed by religious bodies between 1875 and 1919 (U.S. Department of Labor, 1929). Once again, the country's diverse heritage becomes evident. Roman Catholics established residencies in ethnically homogeneous neighborhoods, which meant that funds were collected by Italian, Irish, German, and Polish parishes for their own. Protestants generally entered the homes established by their denomination. As a result, the homes differed in quality and standards. Few could accommodate more than 100 residents.

Notice the pattern emerging: At the grass-roots level, individuals and their families responded when necessary to the sicknesses and hard luck that may have occasioned retirement and the financial difficulties that this stage of life often entailed. At the local level, fraternal organizations, friends, and neighbors did the same thing. None of these efforts should be minimized, yet few of these gestures affected very many people. The same can be said of initiatives undertaken by larger organizations and public agencies.

Corporate and Union Responses to Retirement

Transportation companies inaugurated the earliest pension programs in the United States. In 1875, the American Express Company permitted workers past age 60 to receive some compensation upon retirement. Significantly, this gesture predated by a decade the company's establishment of a mutual benefit society (Hatch, 1950). The 1884 Baltimore and Ohio Railroad policy, which stipulated a minimum age (65) and service requirement (10 years), has been called "the pioneer in this country in the movement to pension its employees" (Squier, 1912, 78). Pension specifics varied considerably from company to company. Some companies required workers to make contributions toward their own financial well-being, while others were noncontributory. In addition, different age and service requirements were established.

Pension coverage grew slowly. Only 8 companies instituted programs during the last quarter of the nineteenth century. Another 23 implemented schemes between 1901 and 1905, and 29 more joined the ranks in the second half of the decade. However, 100 companies initiated policies in the short period of 1911–1915 (Latimer, 1932). By 1929, there were 140 plans in effect in the industrial sector alone. These companies disbursed $6.67 million to 10,644 beneficiaries. As was true in the past, small firms were less likely than larger ones to offer pension plans. Some companies, such as Westinghouse, General Electric, and Eastman Kodak, provided their pensioners with their products so that the retirees' leisure years would be happier.

However, without minimizing the altruism, it is important to recognize that corporate managers were more concerned with their own interests than with caring for the superannuated. Pensions were gratuities; they could be withheld in an economic downturn. Workers who were deemed disloyal or undeserving lost benefits. If retirement proved an efficient way to get rid of obsolescent employees, then pensions were used as a tool for enforcing efficiency and reducing labor turnover. Corporate plans also were a way of deterring skilled workers from joining unions. As a 1915 federal study concluded, pension plans served "to prevent [union] activity on the part of the employee" (quoted in Jacoby, 1985, 49). Nonetheless, by 1929, labor organizations had distributed $3.35 million to 11,306 recipients. Even though the American Federation of Labor declined to support the pension movement until the 1930s, local unions realized that retirement was becoming as much a bread-and-butter issue to their constituencies as hours and wages.

Public Initiatives

Well into the nineteenth century, public care for the aged, poor, and infirm devolved onto the local community. Sometimes the needy were given food and fuel so that they could remain in their homes; at other times, they were boarded out. Older men and women constituted from 16 to 25 percent of the poorhouse population before the Civil War. The ageds' relative numbers in almshouses soared as specialized facilities were created for juveniles, the deaf, and the mentally ill (Rothman, 1971). Faced with increasing numbers of elderly paupers, New York City converted a public facility into a Home for Aged and Infirm in 1903 (Johnson, 1911). Fighting considerable resistance, and after a few false starts, progressive legislatures in several states began to see the merits of financing old-age pensions for those in need. Relief was available in six states by 1928; another dozen started pension systems between 1929 and 1931, as the Depression worsened. Eligibility ages, means tests, and actuarial provisions varied from state to state (Lubove, 1968).

Taking cues from private initiatives, many public agencies started retirement plans for their employees. Nearly every city covered teachers, fire fighters, and police officers. Six states had plans in place by 1929. Perhaps the most comprehensive retirement system was created by the federal government, which in 1920 established a compulsory old-age and disability plan for its half-million civil service employees (Fogelson, 1984). Ironically, however, the most important source of support for elderly Americans came in the form of neither retirement insurance nor old-age relief. It resulted from Washington's desire to protect its veterans and their dependents. Less than 4 percent of all Americans over 60 were receiving military pensions in 1840. Seventy years later, however, veterans' benefits counted for a sixth of the federal budget. On the eve of the Great Depression, 80 percent of all senior citizens qualifying for any form of monetary assistance were receiving veterans' benefits. No president before FDR felt that the federal government should care for the needy aged, but even before the New Deal, Washington indirectly had created an old-age welfare state through its veterans' programs (Skocpol, 1993).

Not surprisingly, as the Depression deepened, senior citizens began to mobilize themselves to demand greater federal assistance. Huey Long and Upton Sinclair offered panaceas. Perhaps the most notable movement was headed by Dr. Francis Townsend, who wanted all Americans over 60 to receive a monthly sum of $200 on the condition that they be retired and that they spend the money within 30 days (Putnam, 1970). Whereas orators once had extolled the elderly's wisdom and contributions to nation building, Townsendites were banking on the advantages to be derived from viewing senior citizens as consumers whose departure from the marketplace would open jobs for younger workers.

CONCLUSION

Retirement in the United States in the years before social security was stitched into the American fabric in highly diverse ways resulted in a patchwork quilt of institutional arrangements and individual adaptations to leaving the workforce. For older men, unless they had private means, maintaining self-reliance generally meant remaining gainfully employed. Older women were far less likely to be in the marketplace unless forced to do so by lack of a husband or economic need. Age discrimination was increasingly rampant, exacerbated by racism, sexism, nativism, and class biases. Disabilities in late life impeded employment opportunities, though most Americans had greater sympathy for men in their prime who lost their jobs or limbs.

FDR's decision to create an omnibus social security measure was shrewd. He tried to build on existing partnerships, linking insurance and welfare concepts across public and private spheres. Pragmatically giving all interested parties a financial stake in the fledgling program assured social security a central role in the economy as it matured. In the process it made age 65 the benchmark for retirement. Unions, corporations, and public agencies all adjusted their rules to conform to social security guidelines. Workers became more eager to buy insurance to protect other spheres of their life.

8

Social Security Wealth and Labor Supply Incentives

Barry L. Friedman

Labor supply has long been a concern of social security policy, although it has been intertwined with other issues, such as adequacy and cost, in complex and varying ways. Social security has always had the goal of providing income support to older people but, as it originated at a time of high unemployment, it also served labor supply goals. Thus, the original program made the pension benefits virtually conditional on retirement through a full withdrawal from the labor force. Gradually, however, the policy focus has shifted from encouraging retirement to encouraging work.

There was a pronounced trend toward retirement at earlier ages during the years when the social security system was maturing. The shift toward encouraging work was partly a result of a growing belief that disincentives in the social security system may have contributed to the decline in work among older people. Partly, the shift also reflects increased interest in controlling the rising costs of the system.

Labor supply and cost could be complementary concerns if there were social security reforms that would induce people to work longer: there would be the double benefit of lower spending on social security pensions and increased contributions into the system from individuals still working. Moreover, even if a reform did cut benefits, the adverse effects for recipients might be partially offset by higher earnings for those who were induced to work more. Of course, the complementarity between cost and work breaks down to the extent that older people do not want, or are unable, to work longer. In this case, costs are cut by reducing benefits to some older people without offsets.

To explore the relationship between social security and work, this chapter first considers the incentives in the social security system and, second, the impact of these incentives on labor supply decisions. To explore the incentives, it focuses on *social security wealth*, which provides a measure of the overall net impact of the system on an individual. All the features of the social security system in one way or another affect this wealth measure. It presents illustrations of the impact on individual social security wealth of a number of features of the program. While social security wealth measures incentives in terms of the net impact of the features (or a reform therein) on the individual, in isolation it cannot tell us how the individual will react.

The second part of the chapter considers briefly the impact of the incentives on labor supply—on retirement and work decisions after retirement. This issue has been extensively studied, and there are several comprehensive reviews of the literature. The reviews have examined the effects of both social security and private pensions, including a comprehensive survey by Quinn, Burkhauser, and Myers (1990) and one focusing on research and data issues by Gustman and Mitchell (1992). Leonesio (1993) has reviewed literature on the effects of social security exclusively and provides a more general review of the retirement literature in Chapter 12 of this volume.[1] This chapter will not duplicate the reviews but will highlight some of the principal findings. It concludes by considering the uncertainty that remains about the future effects of social security on work.

WORK INCENTIVES AND DISINCENTIVES IN THE SOCIAL SECURITY SYSTEM

Social security program features may affect the timing of the retirement decision as well as work choices both before and after retirement. Retirement has been defined in a variety of ways, but given the focus of this chapter on social security, I will use it to mean the commencement of social security benefits. There is generally a significant change in the extent of work at this time, although work may continue afterward. This definition is thus related to, but not identical with, other possible definitions.

Several features of the social security program may affect decisions concerning benefit commencement (retirement) and work.

1. The early retirement penalty and the delayed retirement credit (as well as the normal retirement age, which defines ''early'' and ''delayed'') may affect the decision concerning the start of benefits.
2. The recomputation of benefits that occurs when a person works after the date of initial eligibility, 62, may provide an additional incentive to delay retirement.
3. The earnings test for those already drawing benefits may affect their work decisions.

4. The taxation of social security benefits may affect the work decisions of recipients.
5. The payroll tax on earnings may affect decisions concerning work both before and after the commencement of benefits.

From the point of view of an individual, the most visible impact of the system comes from the net benefit received, which includes the effects of features 1–4. However, the annual benefits, once commenced, continue for life, although program rules do permit some adjustments. The overall value of the benefits thus depends on their present expected value, which is the person's social security wealth. More specifically, to calculate social security wealth for a person at age s, (1) the payment in each future year $s+i$ is multiplied by the probability $p(s,s+i)$ that the person now age s will live through year $s+i$; this gives the expected benefit in year $s+i$; (2) each future expected benefit is discounted to its present value; (3) the discounted present values are added together.

Social security wealth compares present and future benefits in present-value terms and takes account of life expectancy. This allows it to reflect the fact that benefits continue over time. However, program features also confront people with choices in which the delay of benefits may result in larger benefits in the future for life. The net impact depends on comparing the benefit lost now with the gains in future expected benefits, which social security wealth does. Moreover, even if delaying commencement will increase annual benefits, there will be a shorter expected remaining life in which to collect them; social security wealth can account for this.

Social security wealth is also a good indicator of the incentive effects of the program. Any change in program features that changes social security wealth may have a *wealth effect*. Reduced wealth gives an incentive in the direction of increased labor supply, although the magnitude of the response may differ across people, with some not responding at all.

Even under a given set of rules, an individual's work decision may affect social security wealth. Some program features may penalize additional earnings, such as the earnings test, while others reward work, such as the delayed retirement credit (although the credit comes in the future only if benefits are given up in the present). Social security wealth helps to clarify the net effect of program features in relation to a decision concerning work. In examining the incentive effects of program features, we will focus on work decisions—postponing retirement or increasing postretirement work. Social security wealth can be calculated at a decision point separately for work and no-work options. The difference gives the net gain (or loss) in social security wealth of a decision in favor of work and is thus a measure of the incentive (or disincentive) to work resulting from relevant program features.

While this analysis identifies work incentive effects under a given set of rules, it can also be used to study the effects of changes in rules. A change in social security provisions can change the gain or loss and thus the strength of the incentive to choose work. Of course, in making work decisions, social security wealth is only one factor. The person will weigh the social security gain against changes in earnings, pension wealth, other income, and nonpecuniary benefits. It is quite possible that a person will choose work even if it reduces social security wealth because of these other factors.

We turn now to the various program features affecting work. We will give illustrations of work decisions in which these features affect social security wealth. Assumptions common to all the illustrations are presented in the Appendix.

Early and Delayed Retirement

The annual benefit is reduced for those who commence social security before normal retirement age, and is increased for those who delay benefits until after normal retirement age. Either way, the base for the calculation is the person's primary insurance amount (PIA). The PIA is calculated when a person turns 62 (although it may be recomputed later if the person subsequently has earnings higher than before) and is based on the person's lifetime earnings record. If the person starts benefits at the normal retirement age, the benefit equals 100 percent of the PIA (except for possible adjustments based on family status). The 1983 Amendments to the Social Security Act changed the normal retirement age and the early penalty and delayed credit rates, although the changes are being phased in gradually and will not be complete until 2027. The normal retirement age will rise from 65 to 67, but beginning only in the year 2000. The early retirement penalty also has not yet changed. Currently, as before, a person drawing social security beginning at age 62 receives a pension amounting to 80 percent of the PIA. Once the reform is completed, a 62-year-old would retire 5 years before the normal age and would receive only 70 percent of the PIA.[2] In contrast, the delayed retirement credit has already begun increasing from the original 1 percent per year (before 1981) to 5 percent in 1993–1994 and eventually to 8 percent for those who turn 62 by 2005.[3] However, although the credit is rising, the period over which it can be earned is shrinking because of the increase in the normal retirement age. A person retiring at age 70 before the reform would have received 105 percent of the PIA; he or she would currently get 125 percent but, once the reforms are complete, would in the future get only 124 percent.

Although each year of delay raises the amount of the benefit, it does not necessarily produce an increase in social security wealth since the higher benefit will be received for a shorter number of years. Thus, the expected value of the future benefits may go up or down depending on which of these effects predominates. Figure 8.1 gives an overview of the social security wealth of a female at the time of retirement under the old rules (before 1981), the current rules (1993–1994), and the new rules (after 2002) for each possible retirement age from 62 to 70.[4] The most important lesson of Figure 8.1 is that after the reform is completed, social security wealth will be smaller than it is now at all corresponding retirement ages, creating the possibility of a wealth effect. It also

Figure 8.1
Social Security Wealth under Alternative Program Rules

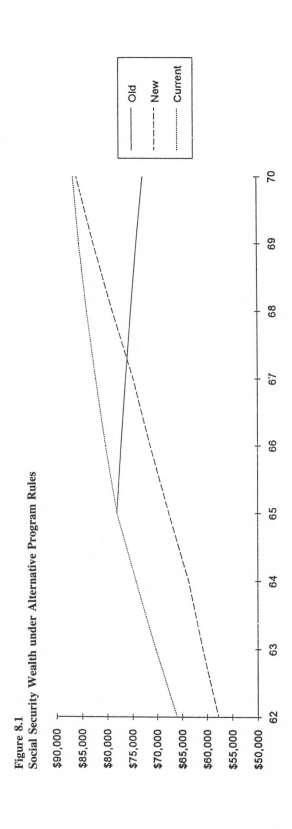

shows that before the reforms began, social security wealth would increase for each year of delay in benefits up to age 65 but decline thereafter: the delayed retirement credit was too small to offset the decline from a shorter period of receipt, thus creating an incentive to retire by age 65. However, the reforms have already eliminated the "hump" pattern of increase and then decrease.

Turning now to the effects of the credit on work incentives, we compare two values for social security wealth at each age, one assuming that the person retires now and the other that retirement is delayed one more year, both for a female who had always earned the average wage. In the case of delay, this year's benefit is lost and all future benefits will be higher, but for one year less of expected life. The results are shown in Table 8.1, which shows that under current rules, in spite of the increased future benefits there is a loss from a one-year delay in retirement at all ages at a 10 percent discount rate. Moreover, the amount of the potential loss relative to the annual benefit becomes larger, the later the age of decision, reflecting the effect of a shortened lifespan.[5] To test the effect of the discount rate, all wealth figures were recalculated at a 2 percent rate. At this low discount rate, there is a gain from delayed retirement, but only at ages 62 or 63. Thereafter, the losses resume—and grow with the age of decision—but they are always smaller than their counterparts at the higher discount rate. Even at a low discount rate, the credits cannot overcome the effect of diminishing life expectancy.

Table 8.1 shows similar comparisons for the reforms yet to be completed. The results are affected by the fact that under the new rules, the credit for a one-year delay in retirement rises at age 64 and again at age 67. There is generally a loss in social security wealth from delay, although at a 2 percent discount rate there is a gain at age 62, and again at ages 64 and 65. On the other hand, the magnitude of the loss is considerably smaller than in the case of the current rules (except at ages 62 and 63, when the credit under the new rules is small). At age 67, when the 8 percent credit becomes available, the loss is small, but it increases again at higher ages. It has sometimes been argued that the 8 percent credit is actuarially fair—that it is sufficient to make up for the initial loss in benefit. These calculations suggest that the 8 percent credit comes too late in life to offset fully the loss from delayed retirement. Actuarial fairness is conditional, depending on both the discount rate and age. It also depends on life expectancy.

To conclude, there is a disincentive to postpone retirement; neither the current credits for delay nor the additional proposed credits are sufficient to offset the current benefit lost except for people in their early 60s and at times when the discount rate is low. However, the new rules reduce the magnitude of the disincentive after age 64; people near the margin concerning work decisions could be affected. Moreover, by reducing social security wealth, the new rules may produce a wealth effect. As a result, the reform, once completed, could have an effect on the timing of retirement.

Table 8.1
Effect of One-Year Delay in Retirement on Social Security Wealth

	Age at Time of Decision							
	62	63	64	65	66	67	68	69
Current rules								
Benefit if retire now	$7,768	$8,416	$9,063	$9,710	$10,196	$10,681	$11,167	$11,652
10% discount rate								
If delay one year	$63,154	$66,688	$69,971	$71,855	$73,520	$74,950	$76,123	$77,008
If retire now	$65,979	$70,239	$74,250	$78,002	$80,211	$82,187	$83,908	$85,343
Net gain if delay	($2,825)	($3,551)	($4,278)	($6,147)	($6,691)	($7,237)	($7,785)	($8,335)
Gain as % of benefit	-36%	-42%	-47%	-63%	-66%	-68%	-70%	-72%
2% discount rate								
If delay one year	$122,759	$127,386	$131,327	$132,493	$133,164	$133,337	$133,002	$132,137
If retire now	$120,999	$126,602	$131,515	$135,752	$137,143	$138,035	$138,417	$138,267
Net gain if delay	$1,760	$784	($188)	($3,260)	($3,980)	($4,698)	($5,415)	($6,130)
Gain as % of benefit	23%	9%	-2%	-34%	-39%	-44%	-48%	-53%

	Age at Time of Decision							
	62	63	64	65	66	67	68	69
Rules for 2022								
Benefit if retire now	$6,797	$7,283	$7,768	$8,416	$9,063	$9,710	$10,487	$11,264
10% discount rate								
If delay one year	$54,653	$57,161	$60,642	$63,871	$66,836	$70,388	$73,586	$76,392
If retire now	$57,732	$60,784	$63,643	$67,602	$71,299	$74,715	$78,800	$82,498
Net gain if delay	($3,079)	($3,623)	($3,001)	($3,731)	($4,462)	($4,327)	($5,215)	($6,106)
Gain as % of benefit	-45%	-50%	-39%	-44%	-49%	-45%	-50%	-54%
2% discount rate								
If delay one year	$106,234	$109,188	$113,817	$117,771	$121,058	$125,221	$128,568	$131,080
If retire now	$105,874	$109,559	$112,727	$117,652	$121,905	$125,487	$129,991	$133,658
Net gain if delay	$359	($371)	$1,090	$119	($848)	($266)	($1,423)	($2,578)
Gain as % of benefit	5%	-5%	14%	1%	-9%	-3%	-14%	-23%

Note: All calculations assume person with PIA of $809.20 which was level in 1992 for a person who had earned the average wage over their lifetime; from U.S. Social Security Administration (1993), Table 2.A26, which gives an annual pension of $9,710 if the person retires at the normal retirement age.

Recomputation of Benefits

While the early retirement penalty and delayed retirement credit are based on a given PIA, the recalculation of benefits may raise the PIA itself for a person who works beyond age 62, and in this way may strengthen further the incentive to delay benefits. The PIA is based on a person's average indexed monthly earnings (AIME), which in turn depends on earnings over the 35 best years. The PIA is normally computed when a person turns 62, but it is recomputed if subsequent earnings are higher than those used initially; in this case, the new higher earnings replace lower earnings in the best 35 years. Before 1977, there was no indexing of previous wages, and hence, the most recent wages were often much higher than those for previous years just because of general wage growth.[6] With the introduction of indexing, the low wages from earlier periods were adjusted upward, reducing the potential gain from recomputation. Nevertheless, there could still be gains to those who had low or zero earnings in earlier periods of their career and comparatively high earnings after age 62. Indeed, periods of part-time work and even zero earnings may be common, especially for women, giving them the possibility of a substantial adjustment in their PIA.

To highlight the effect, consider an illustration for a person who had several years of zero earnings but then received the average wage upon returning to the labor force. We follow the same procedure as before, considering the gains from successive one-year delays in retirement. In each decision, the current year's benefit would be given up in exchange for an increase in all future benefits. The difference is that the increased benefit results from both the credit for delay and the recomputation of benefits.

Table 8.2 shows the delay decisions for a person who had 8 years of zero earnings included in the 35 years used to calculate the AIME but had earnings at the average level in all other years.[7] If he or she chooses to continue to work after age 62, he or she will also receive the average wage and thus qualify for recomputation. Table 8.2 shows that at a 10 percent discount rate, there is again a loss in social security wealth if a person delays retirement by one year—the present expected value of the extra benefits beginning the next year are not sufficient to offset the loss of the current year's benefits. However, the losses are consistently smaller when expressed as a percent of the current year's benefit than when there is no recomputation. Table 8.2 reproduces the percentage loss in the case of no recomputation from Table 8.1. Of course, the illustrative individuals in the two tables are different and have different benefit levels. However, in the no-recomputation case, the percentage gain from the decision to delay is the same for all initial benefit levels.[8] Thus, the two percentages can be compared for respective years of decision. The difference in the two percentages for any year provides an estimate of the gain from recomputation alone. This gain diminishes somewhat with each passing year, reflecting the lower life

Table 8.2
Effect of One-Year Delay with Recomputation of Benefits

	Age at Time of Decision							
	62	63	64	65	66	67	68	69
AIME, PIA, & Benefit if retire now								
AIME	$1,353	$1,403	$1,453	$1,503	$1,554	$1,604	$1,654	$1,704
PIA	$666	$682	$698	$714	$730	$746	$762	$778
Annual benefit	$6,389	$7,089	$7,814	$8,564	$9,194	$9,844	$10,513	$11,201
10% discount rate								
If delay one year	$53,196	$57,494	$61,712	$64,797	$67,755	$70,559	$73,171	$75,549
If retire now	$54,268	$59,164	$64,013	$68,794	$72,332	$75,743	$78,991	$82,034
Net gain if delay	($1,072)	($1,670)	($2,302)	($3,997)	($4,577)	(>5,184)	($5,820)	($6,486)
Gain as % of benefit	-17%	-24%	-29%	-47%	-50%	-53%	-55%	-58%
Gain as % of benefit, no recomputation	-36%	-42%	-47%	-63%	-66%	-68%	-70%	-72%
Difference in gains	20%	19%	18%	17%	16%	15%	14%	14%
2% discount rate								
If delay one year	$103,402	$109,824	$115,824	$119,478	$122,722	$125,525	$127,845	$129,632
If retire now	$99,522	$106,639	$113,384	$119,727	$123,672	$127,212	$130,307	$132,906
Net gain if delay	$3,880	$3,185	$2,441	($249)	($950)	($1,687)	($2,462)	($3,273)
Gain as % of benefit	61%	45%	31%	-3%	-10%	-17%	-23%	-29%
Gain as % of benefit, no recomputation	23%	9%	-2%	-34%	-39%	-44%	-48%	-53%
Difference in gains	38%	36%	33%	31%	29%	27%	25%	23%

Note: AIME at age 62 is $27/35$ of AIME in 1992 for person with average earnings; from U.S. Social Security Administration (1993), Table 2.A26. At age 63, AIME is $28/35$ of same 1992 figure (etc.). PIA is calculated using the 1993 bend points and delayed retirement credit. Gain as percentage of benefit; no recomputation: taken from Table 8.1 for respective discount rates. The person received an average wage in each year of paid work, but had eight included years of no earnings before 62.

expectancy. The loss from delay for this illustrative person who qualifies for recomputation, however, is consistently smaller than for a person who does not.

When a 2 percent discount rate is used, there is a clear gain from a one-year delay up to age 64. This compares to the no-recomputation case, where there is a gain only up to age 63. The difference in gains—the pure gain from recomputation—is considerably larger than in the case of the 10 percent discount rate. The size of the gain again diminishes with each passing year.

In short, recomputation can reduce substantially the disincentive to delay retirement, producing an outright gain at a low discount rate and ages in the early 60s. However, only a limited set of individuals has an earnings pattern such that they will gain from the recomputation—mainly those who had extensive periods of no work before age 62 or at least periods of no earnings. We considered an illustrative individual who would gain substantially from recomputation.

The Earnings Test

While the credit for delay and the recomputation of benefits affect incentives concerning the start of benefits, the earnings test affects work incentives for those who have already commenced their social security pensions. The earnings test differs somewhat for those below and those above the normal retirement age. For a person below age 65 in 1992, annual earnings less than $7,440 were permitted without penalty; for every $2 of earnings above this level, benefits were reduced by $1. For a person who had reached 65, the earnings threshold was $10,200; benefits were reduced by $1 for every $3 of earnings.

Those who work after the commencement of benefits can avoid the benefit reduction by keeping earnings low—working part-time or at a low wage. However, if a person were able to continue at the earlier earnings level, he or she would generally be subject to some earnings reduction. Even a person who worked full time at the minimum wage in 1991 would have earned $8,606, which was above the threshold for those under 65.[9] Indeed, if earnings are high enough, there is a second threshold at which benefits are reduced to zero. Whereas the first threshold is the same for everyone within each age bracket, the second depends on the level of annual benefits that the person receives. Table 8.3 shows the two thresholds for people with several patterns of lifetime earnings and their corresponding annual benefits. Both thresholds are considerably higher for those aged 65 or over.

Because the earnings test on its own reduces benefits while a person works, it clearly reduces social security wealth. However, since 1977, the delayed retirement credit has been available to a retiree 65 or over who works for each month in which the benefit is zero. (This happens when earnings are above the second threshold, at which benefits become zero.) This creates the familiar trade-off in which social security wealth is reduced by the loss of benefits but the loss may be offset by the increase in future benefits.

Table 8.4 illustrates the combined effect of the earnings test and delayed credit

Table 8.3
Earnings Levels Subject to Earnings Test (Illustration for Person Who Commenced Benefits in 1992)

Age in 1992	Lifetime earnings pattern	Earnings in 1991	Annual benefit if no work	Threshold earnings for: Benefit reduction	Threshold earnings for: Zero benefit	Diff. between thresholds: max. earnings subj. to benefit reduction
62	75% avg. wage	$16,359	$6,372	$7,440	$20,184	$12,744
62	avg. wage	$21,812	$7,764	$7,440	$22,968	$15,528
62	SS* max.	$53,400	$10,548	$7,440	$28,536	$21,096
65	75% avg. wage	$16,359	$7,974	$10,200	$34,122	$23,922
65	avg. wage	$21,812	$9,710	$10,200	$39,331	$29,131
65	SS* max.	$53,400	$13,196	$10,200	$49,789	$39,589

Annual benefit for each pattern based on monthly benefits reported in *Social Security Administration* (1993), Table 2.A26. Earnings in 1991 from U.S. Social Security Administration (1993), Table 2.A8. Threshold for zero benefit is first threshold plus two times annual benefit if less than 65; first threshold plus three times annual benefit if 65 or over.

*SS = social security

Table 8.4
Postretirement Work and Social Security Adjustment

			Age at Time of Decision		
	65	66	67	68	69
Retirement in 1992 at age 65, current rules					
10% discount rate					
1. No postret. work	$78,002	$76,391	$74,715	$72,963	$71,119
2. One year postret. work	$71,855	$70,178	$68,433	$66,608	$64,687
3. Loss (1 minus 2)	$6,147	$6,213	$6,282	$6,356	$6,432
4. Earnings subj. to ben. red.	$29,131	$29,131	$29,131	$29,131	$29,131
5. Loss as % of 4	21%	21%	22%	22%	22%
2% discount rate					
6. No postret. work	$135,752	$130,613	$125,487	$120,362	$115,222
7. One year postret. work	$132,493	$127,111	$121,743	$116,377	$110,995
8. Loss (6 minus 7)	$3,260	$3,502	$3,744	$3,986	$4,227
	11%	12%	13%	14%	15%

Rules for 2022; retirement at age 67; using 1992 PIA and earnings data

10 % discount rate			
10. No postret. work	$74,715	$72,963	$71,119
11. One year postret. work	$70,388	$68,511	$66,535
12. Loss (10 minus 11)	$4,327	$4,452	$4,584
13. Loss as % of 4	15%	15%	16%
2% discount rate			
14. No postret. work	$125,487	$120,362	$115,222
15. One year postret. work	$125,221	$119,702	$114,166
16. Loss (14 minus 15)	$266	$661	$1,056
17. Loss as % of 4	1%	2%	4%

Note: PIA = $809.20 in all calculations, which was level in 1992 for person with lifetime average wage. Initial benefit for person retiring at age 65 (or age 67 under new rules) is 100 percent of PIA. If no work, constant lifetime benefit equals initial benefit. Assumes person works for entire year and no benefit received in year of work (because of earnings test). Earnings subject to benefit reduction (Table 8.3). Assumes earnings at second threshold, the one for zero benefits. If person works after age 65, initial benefit increased by 5 percent for each year of work under current rules; under new rules, increased by 8 percent for each year.

on social security wealth for a female retiring in 1992 who had always earned the average wage. It is assumed that the person works for one year with earnings at the upper threshold, so no benefit is received. As in previous illustrations, social security wealth is calculated at the point of decision for two options: (1) working for one year and losing this year's benefit in exchange for a higher benefit in all subsequent years, and (2) not working.

Table 8.4 shows the loss in social security wealth from working, calculated at both a 2 percent and 10 percent discount rate relative to a person facing current rules and who retired in 1992 at age 65. In this illustration, the loss may be used to calculate the effective net rate of benefit reduction. The official benefit reduction rate for a person over 65 is 33 percent. However, the table shows that the net loss in social security wealth as a percent of earnings subject to benefit reduction is considerably less than this—21 percent at a 10 percent discount rate and only 11 percent at a 2 percent rate at age 65. The person does lose the full current benefit, and the higher future benefit does compensate in part for this loss—but not completely. The person who chooses to work loses social security wealth under the current rules even if he or she can take advantage of the delayed retirement credit.[10]

Under the new rules that will eventually prevail, the credit in the case of zero benefits will be 8 percent, available after age 67. Table 8.4 applies the new rules to a person retiring in 1992 at age 67 to see how the future rules would compare if applied now. The official benefit reduction rate is still scheduled to be 33 percent. However, the effective net benefit reduction rate based on the loss in social security wealth would be 15 percent at a 10 percent discount rate and only 1 percent at a 2 percent discount rate, both at age 67. Under the new rules, the credit for delayed benefits is almost enough to offset the current loss in benefits, at least at age 67 and at a low discount rate. It becomes a little less effective at later ages.

It is again clear that the credit in combination with full benefit reduction is actuarially fair only when evaluated at a low discount rate and relatively low age. Moreover, only those whose benefits are reduced to zero are eligible for the credit; retired workers whose benefits are only partially reduced experience only the disincentive from benefit reduction. Of course, only a minority of social security beneficiaries are affected by the earnings test—9.5 percent in 1989 (Bondar, 1993). Of these individuals, however, 36 percent had all benefits offset. The number affected by the credit is thus small, but not negligible.

Taxation of Benefits

The taxation of benefits is another program feature that could affect work decisions after the commencement of benefits. A portion of benefits is taxed only if the person's adjusted gross income, plus half of social security benefits, plus some additional adjustments exceeds a threshold level. The threshold for single individuals is $25,000 and for married couples, $32,000. It is total income that counts; thus, the higher the unearned income, the greater the chance that earnings will push the person over the taxation threshold. Consider a person with unearned income below the threshold who is considering work. Once earnings push the total income to the threshold, each extra dollar of earnings will subject one more dollar of social security benefits to taxation, up to a maximum of 50 percent of the benefit. In other words, within this range, each extra dollar of earnings increases the person's tax base, not only by itself, but by adding $1 of social security benefits as well until 50 percent are included. The tax is then determined by applying the person's regular rate calculations to this base. Beginning in 1994, there is a second threshold of $34,000 for single people and $44,000 for a married couple. If the relevant income figure exceeds this amount, up to 85 percent of the benefit may be subject to tax.

It is difficult to give simple illustrations since the outcome depends on a person's unearned income, earnings, and social security benefit, but there are three ways in which an extra dollar of earnings could raise a person's taxes. First, the extra earnings themselves will be taxed. Second, the person's social security benefit could be reduced if he or she is subject to the earnings test. Third, the extra dollar of earnings could push an additional dollar of benefits into the tax base if the person is just over the threshold for taxation. It is possible that all three circumstances will occur together. Consider, for example, a single person, age 64, who is drawing social security and has earnings of $12,000 (and so is subject to the earnings test). Suppose, further, that gross income is $27,000 (and so is subject to the taxation of benefits). Assume that the marginal tax rate is 28 percent, which is possible at this income level. Thus, if the person earns one more dollar, the regular tax is $.28, the social security benefit is reduced by $.50, and one more dollar of the social security benefit is taxed in the amount of $.28. The total effective tax from one more dollar of earnings is thus $1.06— thus, the net return is negative from the extra dollar of earnings. Of course, the triple taxation lasts over only a limited interval, coming down once 50 percent of the social security is included in the tax base, and again once the entire benefit has been taxed away under the earnings test.

Payroll Tax

The payroll tax must be paid on every dollar of earnings up to a maximum level ($57,600 in 1993 for the Old Age, Survivors, and Disability portion of social security), which is indexed upward each year for inflation. This tax could affect work decisions at any point in a career, including long before the time of retirement. As a tax, it would seem to provide a disincentive to work, but in fact, the effect may be complicated. Consider a person deciding on whether to increase work in order to earn one additional dollar. A portion of it will have to be paid as the payroll tax (in addition to other taxes), leaving less than one dollar as the net return from the work. On the other hand, the social security pension will also be higher for life if he or she earns the extra dollar. The net social security cost of working one more hour is thus the extra payroll tax minus the expected present value of the extra social security benefit to which the extra earnings will entitle the person.

Suppose social security is actuarially fair in the sense that the expected present value of earnings exactly equals contributions into the system through the payroll tax. Then, the net social security cost of one more dollar of earnings will be zero; it will provide no incentive or disincentive to a rational decision maker. In fact, social security rules are complicated in such a way that for some individuals, the present value of benefits will exceed costs, while for others, the opposite will hold. It is thus not possible to make a general statement about the incentive effects of the social security payroll tax on younger workers.

EFFECTS OF SOCIAL SECURITY ON LABOR SUPPLY

We have shown that the decision to work, either by postponing retirement or working after retirement, will generally reduce social security wealth, except at low discount rates or ages in the early 60s. The incentive features in the system—the credits for delay and the recomputation of benefits—are generally not strong enough to offset the lost benefits from delay or the adverse incentives such as the earnings test. In spite of this, some people do choose to work, indicating that other factors besides social security wealth are involved. Moreover, changes in program features can reduce the disincentives inherent in the social security system. For those near the borderline in terms of work decisions, a reduction in the loss of social security wealth could push them over the margin in favor of increased work. Added to this, a wealth effect is possible from the reduced social security benefits likely to be part of reform.

I thus turn briefly from the incentives in the social security system to its impact on labor supply. Within the vast literature, I focus on studies that examine the effects of specific features of the social security system. I examine the effects in relation to decisions on when to retire and whether to work after retiring. The general conclusion from this literature is that estimated effects of social security on labor supply tend to be small but significant, and they are larger for some particular groups. Although the illustrations used the probabilities of survival for females in calculating social security wealth, most of the estimates of the effects of social security on labor supply available from the literature are for males.

The Retirement Decision

Prior to the 1960s, men tended to retire at age 65—the age at which they could begin drawing social security benefits. Then, in the 1960s, a second cluster point emerged around age 62, following the introduction of early retirement for men in 1961, which allowed them to draw reduced benefits from ages 62 through

64. These patterns, widely observed in the literature, are suggestive of the idea that social security has an impact on retirement decisions.

More sophisticated tests have tried to estimate the magnitude of that impact. For example, Burtless and Moffitt (1984) found that a 20 percent cut in benefits would increase the mean retirement age in the entire population by .2 years, or about 2 months. Similarly, Fields and Mitchell (1984) found that a 10 percent cut in monthly benefits would delay retirement on average about a month. Some studies detected differences in response across groups. Quinn (1977), for example, found that the effect of social security appeared large. Disaggregating by health status, however, he found a reduction of 28 percentage points in labor force participation for those with health limitations, but only 4 points for those who were healthy. Burtless and Moffitt (1984) found that the effect of social security increased with age, from almost no effect at age 59 to a substantial effect at age 65.

Some studies focused on the effects of changes in social security benefits. For example, Hausman and Wise (1985) concluded that the increases in benefits between 1969 and 1974 may account for one-third of the reduction in labor force participation during that period. However, Burtless (1986) estimated that these unanticipated changes reduced the average retirement age of men by about one month; had the changes been expected, the effect would have been two months.

As the analytical models have become more sophisticated, it has become possible to test the effects of specific features of social security on labor supply. Among the features most related to the retirement decision are the normal retirement age and the adjustments for postponing benefits in the form of the early retirement penalty and the delayed retirement credit. The estimated models of retirement behavior have been used to simulate the effects of changes in these features. Burtless and Moffitt (1985) projected that an increase in the normal retirement age to 68 would reduce the probability of retiring at age 65 and increase it at subsequent years, perhaps eliminating the clustering at age 65. The change would delay retirement by .35 of a year, or 4.2 months. Fields and Mitchell (1984) estimated that the same policy change would delay retirement, on average, 1.6 months.

Burtless and Moffitt estimated that raising the delayed retirement credit to the "actuarially fair" level would delay retirement by about 4.7 months. Fields and Mitchell (1984) considered an increase in the credit to 6.6 percent and concluded that it would delay retirement by only a week, largely because most people have already retired. Gustman and Steinmeier (1985) considered the combined effect of increasing the normal retirement age to 67 and increasing the delayed retirement credit after 65 to 8 percent. They concluded that the percentage of men working full time at ages 65 and 66 would increase by about 6 percentage points and the percent working part time would decrease by about 2 points.

Work after Retirement

Earnings patterns of retirees show a clustering at earnings levels just below the threshold for the earnings test where benefit reduction begins. While this result has been often observed, Vroman (1985) found that the earnings cluster point increased as the threshold level was adjusted upward each year between 1970 and 1980, consistent with the idea that the earnings test has an influence.

Statistical evaluations of the earnings test have come to use models that estimate jointly retirement and postretirement work decisions. Burtless and Moffitt (1985) estimated that eliminating the earnings test would increase the average postretirement work effort from 3.2 to 4.4 hours per week, but these estimates reflect the fact that only 20 percent of retirees in their sample were working and only 12 percent were affected by the requirement altogether. For those who were affected, Burtless and Moffitt estimated that weekly hours would increase from 23 to 34. Gustman and Steinmeier (1991) estimated that eliminating the earnings test in conjunction with raising the delayed retirement credit would have an effect only marginally larger than increasing the delayed retirement credit alone.

CONCLUSION

As efforts to cut social security costs continue, social security wealth is likely to decline. However, increased work is likely to offset only a limited part of this loss. Social security creates inherent disincentives to work in that delayed retirement or postretirement work usually results in decreased social security wealth. However, the magnitude of the disincentive can be reduced by strengthening the credit for delayed retirement, and at low discount rates there could even be an increase from work in social security wealth. The literature on labor supply does suggest that social security has only a small, although significant, impact on it. Some studies do project that increasing the work incentive provisions would postpone retirement or encourage work by small amounts. Given current behavioral patterns, if social security reforms cut benefits, only a limited part of such losses are likely to be offset by augmented earnings from increased work.

On the other hand, the results of labor supply research depend on behavior from the past. It is conceivable that conditions in the future may change. Social security provisions are not the only factors affecting labor supply. If there is a significant change in other factors, the influence of social security itself could change. For example, one set of factors relates to private pensions. Should there be a reduction in private pension coverage and in private pension wealth, it is possible that people would be more eager to work and that a stimulus from social security provisions could have a larger effect. Another set of factors relates to the demand for older workers. If aging workers lose their jobs before their intended time of retirement, the income effect might induce them to seek new work and perhaps work longer to make up for the loss. On the other hand, if there were stronger demand for mature workers at wages they found attractive, they might be willing to retire later and be more responsive to a stimulus from social security provisions. Indeed, these two labor market possibilities could coexist if there were a loss of permanent jobs at the same time as an increase in the temporary and part-time work available to older workers. Of course, these are just possibilities that might affect the labor supply response to social security in the future. For now, it appears that features of social security that might provide an incentive to work are weak; workers do, nevertheless, respond, but the effects on retirement and work decisions are relatively small.

APPENDIX: ASSUMPTIONS COMMON TO ILLUSTRATIONS

The following common procedures were used in calculating social security wealth.

- To estimate real wealth, real benefits were used. Since social security benefits were adjusted for inflation, we assumed that real benefits remained constant over time.
- For a discount rate, the real interest rate was used, along with real benefits. The real interest rate has remained low for prolonged periods, although not always. On the other hand, Kahn (1988) has argued that liquidity constraints induce people to use higher-than-market interest rates. To accommodate the various possibilities, we present results for both a low rate, of 2 percent, and a high rate, of 10 percent, when the results are sensitive to the difference.
- The probabilities of survival are for females and are derived from the Commissioners' 1980 Standard Ordinary Mortality Table—Female Lives (Lavine, 1993). Social security wealth for males would be lower than the corresponding value for females because of the lower male probabilities of survival.
- Although actual benefits are adjusted for spouses, in order to concentrate on the pure effects of provisions related to labor supply we ignore such adjustments, instead presenting calculations for single people.

NOTES

1. In addition, Christopher Ruhm provides a summary of the retirement literature in Chapter 4 of this volume.
2. Currently, the amount is reduced by 6 ⅔ percent for each year of benefits prior to the normal retirement age of 65. Following the completion of the reform, the reduction rate of 6 ⅔ percent per year will remain the same for the three years preceding the then-normal retirement age of 67, but there will be an additional 5 percent reduction for each of the two years before this.
3. The delayed retirement credit had been 1 percent per year beginning in 1972. It was increased to 3 percent per year in 1977, effective in 1981. The 1983 amendments introduced a schedule for a further series of gradual adjustments up to 8 percent by 2005.
4. It is assumed that the earnings of this person always equaled the average wage, so in 1992 the PIA (which helps determine the monthly benefit) would be $810. It is

further assumed that the person will not work after retirement and thus that the benefit will not be adjusted as a result of the earnings test. Figure 8.1 uses a 10 percent discount rate, although a similar pattern emerges even at a 2 percent rate. For further assumptions, see the Appendix.

5. Although the calculations are based on the earnings record of one illustrative individual and the corresponding social security PIA and benefit schedule, the *percentage* gains are the same, no matter what the initial benefit. Social security wealth if one retires now assumes a constant real benefit in all future years. Social security wealth in the case of a one-year delay also assumes a constant benefit, although at a higher level. However, at any age, the postponed benefit is higher by a constant factor $(1 + c)$, where c is the credit for delay, and it does not depend on the size of the benefit. Thus, this year's benefit can be factored out as a proportionality factor in the formula for the difference in social security wealth examined here. When the difference is taken as a percent of this year's benefit, the benefit level cancels out, leaving a percentage that is invariant to the size of the benefit. At other benefit levels, dollar magnitudes would differ but the pattern of gains or losses would be the same.

6. Indexing is applied to all earnings from the years before the worker turned 60 and adjusts those earnings upward in proportion to the growth in general wages. Wages after age 60, including any used in the recomputation of benefits, are not indexed. However, in the case of recomputation, no matter what the person's age, the index factors used are the ones established in the year the person turned 62.

7. Since the AIME calculation uses the best 35 out of 40 years, the person must also have had an additional 5 years of no earnings, which are not included in the AIME.

8. See note 3.

9. In 1991, the minimum wage was $3.80 per hour in January–March; it then rose to 4.25 on April 1. The calculation assumes 2,080 hours of full-time work, spread evenly over the year.

10. This illustration does not consider the possibility of benefit recomputation.

9

Pensions and Retirement

John A. Turner and Tabitha Doescher

Superannuated employees pose a difficult problem for many firms. Reducing nominal wages to encourage retirement has never been a viable option for dealing with these workers, and mandatory retirement is no longer allowed. As a result, numerous firms rely on their pension plan (or plans) to influence their employees' retirement decisions.

This chapter examines the variety of ways in which pensions—in particular, defined benefit plans—can influence retirement. It begins with an overview of pensions, followed by a discussion of the major pension plan features that potentially affect workers' retirement decisions. The chapter then turns to an examination of the economics of pensions and retirement.[1] This section discusses a general economic theory of pensions and retirement, pension accruals and their role in this theory, and actuarial adjustments to pension benefits.

OVERVIEW OF PENSIONS

Many Americans are covered by a pension plan. Employer-provided pensions are almost universally provided to federal, state, and local government employees, who make up 17 percent of the labor force. For private sector workers (the remaining 83% of the labor force), employer pension coverage is less common—about half are covered.

The opinions in this chapter are the responsibility of the authors and do not represent the position of the U.S. Department of Labor.

Of those workers who are covered by a pension sometime during their career, many will end up receiving retirement income from their plan (or plans). In 1990, 45 percent of aged households (households in which at least one person is age 65 or older) received income from an employer-provided pension.[2] Thirty percent of aged households received a pension from a private sector employer, while 15 percent received a pension from a government employer (Grad, 1992). These percentages have increased over time. In 1980, 22 percent of all aged households received a pension from private employers and 12 percent received a pension based on employment in the government sector (Chen, 1992).

For most retirees receiving a private pension, social security was a somewhat more important source of income. In 1989, the median wage replacement rate for private pension recipients was 23 percent from a private pension and 33 percent from social security (Beller and McCarthy, 1992).

Types of Pensions

There are two basic types of pensions—defined contribution plans and defined benefit plans. Defined contribution plans are like individual retirement accounts. Each individual has an account, and the balance in the account represents the amount of money payable for the worker's retirement consumption. Thus, defined contribution plans are tax-free savings vehicles that may offer the benefits of economies of scale in comparison to individual plans such as individual retirement accounts.

Defined benefit plans are the second type of pension plan. In these plans, the worker's future benefits do not depend on an account balance but are generally determined based on the worker's earnings and years of service.

In 1990, there were 599,000 private sector defined contribution plans covering 35.5 million workers, and 113,000 defined benefit plans covering 26.3 million workers (U.S. Department of Labor, 1993b). Although defined benefit plans have long been regarded as the mainstay of the U.S. pension system, the number of these plans has declined in recent years, from a peak of 175,000 in 1983.

The 113,000 private sector defined benefit plans are the focus of this chapter. These plans can be structured as personnel tools, reducing the turnover of workers when young and inducing retirement when old. In contrast, defined contribution plans have only a limited effect as personnel tools.[3] Because the level of benefits they provide is based on the account balance, they cannot be designed to encourage retirement at a particular age or service level.

Perspectives on the Relationship between Defined Benefit Plans and the Retirement Decision

There are two different perspectives on the relationship between defined benefit pension plans and the worker's decision to retire. The first focuses on the use of defined benefit plans by firms as personnel tools, while the second focuses on the endogeneity of the pension contract.

Defined Benefit Plans as Personnel Tools. Defined benefit pension plans may aid the personnel policies of firms with respect to retirement in two situations. First, they may be used as part of a long-term strategy of deferring compensation to encourage long tenure, and then encouraging retirement at the desired age or years of service. Second, they may be used as part of a short-term strategy to reduce the workforce in periods of slack demand for the firm's product. Defined benefit plans provide a built-in mechanism to encourage workforce reduction through retirements and may be easily altered to add further incentives.

There are several different explanations for why firms might want to design pensions to promote retirement. One theory posits that it becomes increasingly difficult to monitor workers as they age because variability in worker productivity may increase with age (Parsons, 1983). Another explanation is that firms encouraging early retirement use their pension to "buy out" more expensive, older employees (Luzadis and Mitchell, 1992). Yet a different approach postulates that some firms use defined benefit pension plans as personnel tools to reduce older workers' compensation legally without violating age discrimination rules (Lazear, 1983; Hutchens, 1986a).

Firms differ in whether they want to use a pension to affect the timing of retirement. Some firms may have production processes in which it is desirable that most workers retire within a narrow age or tenure band. Those firms will be likely to offer a defined benefit plan with incentives for retirement over a narrow age band. Other firms may be indifferent over a broad range of ages as to the workers' age of retirement. These firms will be more likely to offer a defined contribution plan or a defined benefit plan that does not penalize early retirement.

The Endogeneity of the Pension Contract. A second perspective on the relationship between pensions and the retirement decision emphasizes the endogeneity of the pension contract. From this perspective, the financial terms of pension plans are not externally imposed on workers but are rather the result of bargaining between workers and employers. This theory argues that causation may go from desired retirement age to pension features rather than in the opposite direction. Workers with physically demanding, stressful, repetitive, or otherwise unpleasant jobs retire early. They also have relatively high pension benefits at early retirement ages. The theory argues that these workers negotiate compensation packages that make this feasible. Workers seek out firms offering, among other things, a pension plan that allows for retirement on favorable terms at the age at which they wish to retire.

Differences in retirement behavior by industry, occupation, and job characteristics are consistent with this interpretation. For example, the average age of retirement is less than 60 years for production testers, aircraft mechanics, explosives workers, stevedores, and air traffic controllers, while it is 65 years or more for child-care workers, lawyers, physicians, purchasing agents, and authors (Filer and Petri, 1988).

Pension plans are only one aspect of a job, and in searching over a limited number of job possibilities, it is unlikely that workers will generally be able to work in a firm with a pension plan that exactly fits their preferences concerning retirement age. The remainder of the chapter thus follows the generally accepted approach in the economics literature and assumes that workers are not perfectly sorted into firms with pension plans meeting their needs.

DEFINED BENEFIT PLAN FEATURES

Firms that wish to design defined benefit pension plans to influence the age at which their workers retire usually do so by manipulating the level and timing of benefits. In general, defined benefit pension plans provide benefits based on the worker's earnings and years of service. These plans typically include numerous provisions governing when, and under what conditions, plan participants can claim these benefits. In particular, plans frequently differ in the way they treat the receipt of benefits for normal, early, and late retirement.

Normal Retirement

In most defined benefit plans, the specified "normal retirement age," which is an element in the definition of the retirement benefit, is a key feature in the retirement incentives. Since plans generally lower benefits for early retirement and increase benefits for retirement postponed past the normal age, normal retirement age should be considered as a benchmark chosen by the plan to describe how benefits vary with age. In many plans, the normal retirement age varies with years of service. Thus, in these plans, there is not a single normal retirement age but a range of normal ages, varying by length of worker service.

In 1991, a majority of defined benefit plan participants in medium and large firms could receive normal retirement benefits before age 65, while 45 percent of participants were required to be age 65. This latter group of participants usually did not have to satisfy a length-of-service requirement, although some plans required that workers hired after age 60 complete at least five years of service (U.S. Department of Labor, 1993b).[4]

The plans that permitted normal retirement before age 65 generally imposed a minimum service requirement. For example, normal retirement at age 62 was available to 24 percent of participants in medium and large firms, but nearly 60 percent of these had to work 10 years or more. Few participants could retire with unreduced benefits before age 60, and those who could, usually had to work 30 years.

Plans that required combining a worker's age and service to reach a specified sum for retirement with full benefits covered 6 percent of participants in medium and large firms. This type of arrangement usually specified a minimum age of 55.

Early Retirement

Most defined benefit plans permit participants to retire before the age of normal retirement, usually with reduced (less-than-full) benefits. Many of these plans have features that discourage retirement before the early retirement age but encourage retirement at the point of eligibility for early retirement. These plan features include eligibility requirements for early retirement, early retirement reduction factors, supplementary early retirement benefits, backloading of benefits, nonaccrued early retirement benefits, requirement for employer's consent, suspension of payment, greater reduction factors for early leavers, and window plans (early retirement incentive programs that are offered during a limited time window).

Eligibility Requirements for Early Retirement. Typically, a defined benefit plan that allows early retirement specifies the criteria that a worker must meet to retire before the normal age. This criteria is usually in the form of a minimum age or service requirement.

Neither the Internal Revenue Code nor the Employee Retirement Income Security Act (ERISA) set a minimum age for early retirement in pension plans.[5] However, in practice, age 55 is the most common minimum age that plans permit for early retirement. In 1991, nearly 70 percent of all participants in medium and large firms were in plans that permitted workers to retire at that age, generally with 10 years of service required. If employees satisfied service requirements, 15 percent of all participants could retire earlier than age 55 and nearly half these participants could retire with reduced benefits at any age, usually after 30 years of service (U.S. Department of Labor, 1993b).

Eligibility requirements for early retirement have eased in recent years. Mitchell (1992) estimated that in 1980, 60 percent of defined benefit participants (in medium and large firms) could retire at age 55 if their service was sufficiently long; by 1989, this figure had risen to 66 percent. At the same time, the service components of these requirements have been liberalized. Between 1980 and 1989, the proportion of participants in plans requiring only 5 years of service to retire at age 55 rose from 5 to 9 percent, and those needing 10 years of service rose from 36 to 43 percent. However, plans requiring lengthy service for early retirement eligibility became less common: in 1989, 5 percent of participants needed 30 years of service, in comparison to 9 percent in 1980.

Early Retirement Reduction Factors. Benefits are usually reduced, by an early retirement reduction factor, for those workers who take early retirement. As will be discussed later in this chapter, this reduction factor can be either actuarially fair or it can subsidize or penalize early retirement.

Regardless of whether the reduction factor is actuarially fair, it may be uniform, or it may vary by age. In 1991, nearly half the defined benefit plan participants had uniform reduction factors, most commonly 3, 4, 5, or 6 percent for each year of early retirement. Eighteen percent of participants had reduction factors of 4 percent or less. Reduction factors that differed for each year of early retirement were used in plans covering 23 percent of participants (medium and large firms). For 26 percent of participants, the reduction factor differed for age brackets of several years instead of changing each year (U.S. Department of Labor, 1993b).

Reduction factors can differentially affect workers with different age and service. For example, consider a plan in which the "normal" retirement benefit at age 65 depends on earnings, age, and years of service at the time of departure from the firm. In this plan, a participant can retire and elect to start receiving benefits before age 65; however, the normal benefit is reduced by 5 percent for each year that receipt of benefits precedes age 65. Thus, a worker who retires at age 55 receives 50 percent of the normal retirement benefit of a worker who leaves the firm at age 65. However, in this plan, if a worker has 30 years of service and is age 60 or older, he or she is eligible for 100 percent of the normal benefit; if the worker has 30 years of service and retires before age 60, benefits are reduced 5 percent for each year that retirement precedes age 60. A worker who retires at age 55 with 30 years of service therefore receives 75 percent of the normal benefit. A worker who has 30 years of service and is age 60 or older no longer gains 5 percent a year from increased work, as occurs before age 60.

Supplemental Early Retirement and Integrated Benefits. In 1991, 9 percent of participants in defined benefit plans in medium and large firms were in plans that provided supplemental early retirement benefits. These were generally designed to augment the benefits workers received before they turned age 62 and became eligible to receive social security benefits.

Plans may impose special age requirements, length-of-service requirements, or both on eligibility for supplemental benefits. Therefore, a worker retiring with full benefits (but still too young to receive social security benefits) may receive a supplement, while a worker the same age with fewer years of service, and therefore reduced early retirement benefits, may not. For example, one large manufacturing plan offers early retirement to workers at any age with 30 years of service or at age 55 with 10 years of service. The plan's early retirement supplement, however, is available to all employees with 30 years of service but to employees age 55 only if their age plus service years total 85.

Plan sponsors are allowed to take into account social security benefits in formally structuring their pension plans. For example, a plan might provide, within limits, higher benefits relative to earnings for workers earning above the maximum level taxable under social security than for workers with lower earnings. Such plans are called *integrated plans*. In plans that are integrated with social security, the social security offsets are usually applied immediately on retirement, whether or not the retiree is eligible for social security benefits. Only 7 percent of participants in medium and large plans in 1991 had delayed imposition of the social security offset until social security payments began. Benefit formulas were integrated with social security for 54 percent of pension plan participants (U.S. Department of Labor, 1993b).

Backloading. In many defined benefit plans, pension accruals are a considerably higher percentage of earnings for workers near retirement than for younger workers. This feature, referred to as the *backloading of pension accruals*, provides an incentive for workers near retirement to postpone retirement until they become eligible for early retirement.

Nonaccrued Early Retirement Benefits. Many defined benefit plans offer benefits that are outside the ERISA definition of "accrued benefits" and are thus not required to vest. These benefits include subsidized early retirement benefits, subsidized joint and survivor's benefits, disability and death benefits, and health benefits for retirees. If a worker leaves the firm before eligibility for early retirement, the benefits may be lost. Thus, a worker who began working with a firm in his or her late 20s or early 30s may need to wait 25 or 30 years before being vested in these benefits (Bruce, 1988, 194). As is the case with the backloading of pension accruals, this type of arrangement can encourage workers to postpone leaving the firm at least until they are eligible for early retirement.

Requirement for Employer's Consent. A worker's receipt of early retirement benefits may require the employer's consent rather than occurring solely at the former's discretion. If the plans have established nondiscriminatory and uniformly and consistently applied standards for the exercise of consent, plans are allowed to actuarially subsidize early retirement benefits and require the employer's consent to receive those benefits (Bruce, 1988, 197). Although this could affect a worker's retirement decision, only 1 percent of plan participants (in medium and large firms) were in plans with this requirement (U.S. Department of Labor, 1993b).

Suspension of Payment. In certain cases, ERISA permits retirement benefits to be suspended month-by-month if a participant works more than 40 hours per month after normal retirement age. If the plan is a single-employer plan, payments can be suspended if the participant works more than 40 hours per month for the plan sponsor. If the plan is a multiemployer plan, payments can be suspended if the participant works more than 40 hours per month within the industry, trade or craft, and geographic area covered by the multiemployer plan, regardless of whether the employment is with an employer contributing to that plan.

In addition, subsidized early retirement benefits may be forfeited for reemployment within the same industry, trade or craft, or geographic area covered by the multiemployer plan. This is permitted as long as discrimination against lower-paid employees does not occur and several other requirements are met (Bruce, 1988, 255).

Similarly, forfeitures of benefit payments may occur because of employment in competition with a former employer or other reasons (such as malfeasance). However, forfeitures are limited to benefits that vest under standards more liberal than the minimum standards permitted by ERISA, and only if the worker has not worked long enough to satisfy the ERISA standards (Bruce, 1988, 241).

Greater Reduction Factors for Early Leavers. ERISA allows the reduction factor used to determine benefits for terminated and vested employees (early leavers) to be larger than that used to determine benefits for early retirees. Many plans, however, use the same factor; 49 percent of the participants in defined benefit plans with early retirement provisions (medium and large firms) were in plans that used identical factors. When reduction factors differed, the most common pattern was to provide actuarially fair (rather than subsidized) reductions to deferred vested benefits, thus eliminating the subsidy employers give to employees who stay with the firm until early retirement (U.S. Department of Labor, 1993b).

Window Plans. In addition to permanent features that permit or encourage early retirement, defined benefit plans sometimes have transient features available for a few months. These are called *window plans, golden handshakes,* or early retirement incentive programs (ERIPs). Window plans provide special bonuses to a specific group of workers—often defined by age, occupational group, or division within a firm—if they retire within a specified period of time. Often the goal of these plans is to reduce the size of the labor force without resorting to layoffs.[6] For employees, retirement windows offer enhanced pension benefits and a chance to leave a job or the workforce sooner than would have otherwise been possible.

A window plan may increase benefits by diminishing or eliminating the actuarial factor used to reduce the benefits of workers who have not yet reached the pension plan's normal retirement age. It may offer a fixed cash addition to monthly pension benefits and may be discontinued after workers become eligible for social security benefits at age 62. It may offer additional credits to age and years of service, permitting younger workers to meet the pension provisions for eligibility and increasing the amount of benefits they would have otherwise received. Other techniques include:

- making additional benefit forms available only at an early age (e.g., making lump sum distributions available only at an early age or only for a limited time),
- reducing or eliminating the early retirement reduction,
- using a shorter final average pay period, and
- using projected pay rather than actual pay.

Window plans are typically targeted at workers in their early or mid-50s.[7]

Approximately 80 percent of Fortune 500 companies sponsored an exit incentive or window program at least once between 1979 and 1988 (U.S. General Accounting Office, 1990). A majority offered age-specific, enhanced benefits. In these programs, certain enhanced benefits were provided exclusively to younger eligible workers so that they could receive benefits comparable to those received by older workers who were already at or near the pension plan's normal retirement age.

General Motors (GM) provides a good example of a window program. In 1992, GM and the United Auto Workers agreed on the terms of an early retirement program for hourly employees age 50 or older with at least 10 years of service. Under this program, workers who are age 50–61 and take early retirement receive a waiver of the existing rules that reduce pension payments to employees who accept new jobs in the automobile industry after retiring from GM. For workers age 62 or older, the additional incentives include a $10,000 certificate and $3,000 in cash toward the purchase of a new GM car. GM has estimated that the program will result in $1 billion savings in annual employment costs and that the success of the early retirement program will help the company reach its desired workforce reduction sooner than anticipated (LaRock, 1993).

Companies sometimes bar older workers from participating in exit incentive programs or exclude these workers from the enhanced benefits available to younger workers. This does not necessarily violate the Age Discrimination in Employment Act (ADEA). Passed in 1967, the ADEA prohibits arbitrary age discrimination in employment and promotes the employment of older persons based on their ability rather than age. It prohibits employers from discriminating against employees aged 40 and older.

The ADEA (modified by the Older Workers Benefit Protection Act of 1990, OWBPA) permits an employer to have an employee benefit plan that differentiates on the basis of age, as long as the plan is not designed to evade the general purpose of the act.[8] Under the ADEA, employee benefit plans may have benefits that (1) decrease with age, (2) end at a certain age, or (3) are only available to employees in a certain age bracket (U.S. General Accounting Office, 1990). However, when older workers receive lower benefits than younger workers, there must be a close correlation between older age and the greater cost for such an arrangement to be acceptable under the ADEA.[9]

Late Retirement

Finally, defined benefit pension plans can limit the benefits they provide to long-tenure workers. This feature suggests that there may be a maximum number of years of work that firms view as optimal for a typical worker to work, regardless of age. For example, 39 percent of plan participants in medium and large firms were in plans that limited the number of years of service included in benefit computations. For 16 percent of the participants, the limit was 30 years or less, while for 30 percent of the participants, the limit was 35 years or less (U.S. Department of Labor, 1993b).

The Age Discrimination in Employment Act requires employers to credit all service after normal retirement age, subject to any maximum credited service provision of the plan. When an employee delays retirement beyond the normal retirement date, benefits are usually withheld until the actual date of retirement, providing it occurs before age 70 ½. Participants generally must begin receiving their pensions no later than April 1 following the year they attain age 70 ½, regardless of whether they have actually retired. Participants who continue working past that age and receive benefits continue to accrue them based on their additional work.

Three alternative methods have been commonly used to determine the amount of monthly benefits payable upon deferred retirement. Under one method, the amount of the monthly pension is frozen at the normal retirement age and the amount paid upon actual later retirement is precisely the same dollar benefit that the participant would have been entitled to had she or he retired on the normal date. Under this method, there is neither a continued accrual of benefits nor an actuarial adjustment of benefits already accrued.

Under the second approach, the amount just described is increased to the actuarial equivalent of the amount that would have been payable at the normal retirement date.

Under the third approach, benefits continue to accrue beyond normal retirement, with any changes in the compensation base recognized in the benefit formula. The result is that if two employees, one age 45 and the other age 50, are hired at the same time and both work for 20 years at equal salaries, retiring at ages 65 and 70 (respectively), they will receive equal monthly payments under this method. The benefits determined under this third approach are sometimes greater and sometimes smaller than the normal retirement benefits adjusted to their actuarial equivalence. Since 1988, benefits credited upon deferred retirement generally may not be less than those determined under the third approach.

A fourth alternative could be used whereby benefits continue to accrue and there is an actuarial increase of previously accrued benefits. This method provides the most generous benefits of the four methods, but it is rarely used.

THE ECONOMICS OF PENSIONS AND RETIREMENT

When economists look at the effect of pensions on retirement, they focus on the financial incentives embedded in pension benefits. This section examines several dimensions of these financial incentives. First, it begins with a discussion of a general theory of pensions and retirement. It then turns to pension accruals and a discussion of how they fit into a theory of pensions and retirement. Finally, the section discusses actuarial adjustments to benefits.

A General Theory of Pensions and Retirement

Defined benefit pensions can influence the decision to retire through a wealth effect and a price effect.

Wealth Effects. The present value of the pension, rather than simply the size of annual benefits, is what matters in determining when workers retire (Burkhauser, 1979). Annual benefits are not the correct measure because they vary with both the age at which the worker retires and the form of the annuity. In addition, annual benefits may be affected by special supplements, such as those that cease when the worker reaches the age of eligibility for social security (age 62).

Pension wealth (i.e., the present value of the pension) is accrued over much of the worker's career. The theory of equalizing differences implies that workers give up wages in exchange for pension wealth.[10] If a worker gives up wages equal in value to pension wealth, then the pension wealth is not a net addition to his or her lifetime wealth. With no net addition to lifetime wealth, there is no wealth effect.

A wealth effect will occur only if workers are rewarded by more generous pensions that they have not fully paid for through forgone wages.[11] In this case, an increase in wealth would tend to lower the age at retirement because wealthier people take more leisure. However, the effect on age at retirement should be small even for a large amount of net pension wealth: the increase in leisure will presumably be spread over the individual's lifetime, assuming that the worker has anticipated the level of pension wealth provided by the plan.

Price Effects. According to the U.S. Internal Revenue Code, benefit payments from a defined benefit plan may not begin before a participant's separation from service, disability, death, or retirement. Thus, firms are not allowed to provide defined benefit pension benefits to a worker who has not left the firm.

If the acceptance of a pension were unrelated to leaving one's job, a worker would accept a pension at the age that yielded the stream of benefit payments with the greatest expected present value. However, accepting a defined benefit pension requires leaving one's job, and thus, loss of compensation must be taken into account. This suggests that the trade-off between present and future wages and present and future benefits is the crucial financial factor in the decision to retire.

The price effect reflects changes in this trade-off and the impact of these changes on the age at retirement. Typically, changes in the trade-off are measured by annual pension compensation, the amount by which an additional year's work increases the expected present value of the pension. An additional year's work will increase the annual pension compensation, both through the effect of tenure in the benefit formula, and through an increase in the nominal wage (in plans with earnings-related formulas).[12] Offsetting the factors that increase pension accrual is the loss in the current year's benefits for an individual who is eligible to receive pension benefits. Thus, through the price effect, year-to-year changes in annual pension compensation will affect the age at retirement.

Pension Accruals

In a typical defined benefit plan, the worker's pension benefit, B_t, at retirement is the product of the benefit formula generosity factor, k, the worker's years of service, S_t, and the worker's final average earnings, E_t:

$$B_t = ks_t\, E_t.$$

Suppose that for each year of service, a plan provides a benefit generosity factor, k, equal to 1 percent of average earnings over the final 3 years of employment. Then, a worker with 20 years of service and with 3-year average earnings of $25,000 will be eligible for a pension benefit of $5,000 per year due at normal retirement age.

The pension wealth, W_t, of the worker is the discounted present value of the worker's expected stream of retirement benefits

$$W_t = PV(B_t),$$

where PV is the expected present value function. Ignoring (for simplicity) the effect of mortality risk over the year of accrual, the pension compensation or pension benefit accrual, b_t, in a year is:

$$b_t = W_t - (1 + r)\, W_t - 1.$$

The pension benefit accrual equals the worker's pension wealth at the end of the year, minus his or her wealth at the beginning of the year, adjusted by an interest factor. The interest the worker would have earned on prior wealth regardless of whether he or she had continued working should not be included in the earned pension compensation.

Because both growth in earnings and increased tenure affect the benefit computation, nominal benefits generally increase when the worker continues working with the firm. However, the expected present value of benefits, or pension wealth, does not necessarily increase. With each year of continued employment past the worker's early retirement eligibility date, the worker forgoes a year of benefits. Typically, beyond some age (sometimes the early retirement age), the increase in benefits paid over the worker's remaining lifetime is insufficient to offset a year of forgone benefits.

Consider the example of a worker in a plan sponsored by a particular Fortune 500 firm (Kotlikoff and Wise, 1989). Until this worker reaches his or her 50s, pension accruals are small. However, at age 55 the worker becomes eligible for special early retirement benefits (available to all workers if they work to age 55), and the pension accrual jumps to 1.6 times earnings. Pension accrual becomes negative for this worker at age 61 because the plan provides no additional benefits for more than 30 years of service.

Defined benefit plan features affect pension accruals. For example, numerous plans offer a large increase in benefits (i.e., a large bonus) for remaining until early retirement. Workers covered by these types of plans make their retirement decisions based on a spike in pension accrual at the early retirement age.

In addition, many of these plans offer early retirement on actuarially favorable terms to workers who stay with the firm until that age. (Actuarial adjustments are discussed in detail later in this chapter.) This practice of using early retirement factors more favorable than the actuarially equivalent ones (resulting in benefits that are higher than actuarially reduced benefits) is referred to as *subsidized early retirement*, and this, too, affects the retirement decision.

Finally, early leavers (i.e., workers who leave the firm before the age of retirement) may be required to wait until after they reach the early retirement age to start receiving benefits. Alternatively, these early leavers may be able to receive benefits at the early retirement age but only on an actuarially neutral basis, causing them to receive lower benefits. A spike in benefit accruals occurs when a worker whose employment ends before qualifying for subsidized early retirement cannot subsequently qualify for these benefits.

Pension Accruals and a Theory of the Retirement Decision

The pension accrual rate for a given year does not fully capture the incentives facing a worker who is considering retiring in that year. A high accrual rate in a given year will provide workers with an incentive to continue working. However, if the accrual rate is low in one year but high the following year, the decision to retire based on the low accrual rate in the current year would be myopic. The high accrual rate the following year would provide an incentive to continue working. The value to the worker of working in year n includes the option of continuing to work in year $n + 1$ (Lazear and Moore, 1988).

One theory of retirement postulates that workers calculate the pension wealth they would expect to receive at each retirement age. They then compare the pension wealth they would receive if they retired at their current age with what they could receive at the age with maximum expected pension wealth. The maximum of the expected present value of retiring at each future age minus the expected present value of immediate retirement is called the *option value* of postponing retirement. If the former amount is sufficiently larger, then the worker will postpone retirement, while if it is not, the worker will retire.

Actuarial Adjustments

Defined benefit plans often adjust benefits for workers who retire either before or after the normal retirement age. Benefits are decreased for early retirement in large part because they are spread out over more years, and they are increased for late retirement to at least partially compensate workers for benefits lost. Thus, an actuarial adjustment increases (decreases) benefits for late (early) retirement to take the following into account: (1) benefits will be received for a shorter (longer) period of time, (2) benefits will be received at a later (earlier) date, and (3) the worker has a larger (smaller) risk of dying before benefit receipt when benefits are postponed (received early).

Actuarial Adjustments and Inflation. Social security benefits currently are increased for each month of postponed retirement by an amount equaling 6.7

percent per year of postponement of benefit receipt from age 62 to 65.[13] This increase is roughly actuarially fair, that is, it leaves the worker's present value of benefits constant in real terms.[14] However, an increase of 6.7 percent per year is not an actuarially fair increase for private pension benefits. This is because social security is fully indexed for postretirement inflation, while private pension benefits are generally not.

The extent of indexing of private pension benefits varies across plans. Some plans provide no indexing. Of those plans that do provide indexing, most offer only ad hoc partial indexing (Allen, Clark, and McDermed, 1992).

The actuarially fair adjustment for nonindexed plans is greater than that for indexed plans. This can be seen by considering the simplest possible case, in which there is no mortality risk and only one pension payment. Assume that the payment is $100 at age 62. Then, the actuarially fair adjustment for the benefit receipt at age 63 would be $100(1 + r)$, where r is the nominal interest rate.[15]

Because the nominal interest rate, r, varies with the rate of inflation, the actuarially fair adjustment will be higher for plans that are not indexed for postretirement inflation. For example, assume that the interest rate, r, is 10 percent. Then, in the absence of indexing, the actuarially fair adjustment of the postponed benefit is 10 percent. If, however, the benefit is inflation-indexed and the inflation rate is 7 percent, the actuarially fair adjustment is only 3 percent. Both cases yield a benefit of $110.[16]

Actuarial Adjustments and Mortality. If the adjustment of benefits with postponed retirement is actuarially fair, pension wealth for a worker with a life expectancy equal to that in the actuarial tables would be the same whether he or she retired this period and took benefits or retired this period and started receiving benefits next period. If the worker postpones retirement and continues working, his or her actual pension wealth will be higher because he or she will receive the actuarially fair increase plus the increase based on working an additional year.

Actuarial adjustments vary with the risk of mortality. For workers who have a long life expectancy, the postponement of retirement by one year has relatively little effect on the period over which benefits are expected to be received. Thus, the actuarially fair adjustment for postponed retirement would be lower for a worker with a long life expectancy than for a worker with a short one. However, the differences in actuarial adjustment are small when comparing across demographic groups with different expected mortality. Thus, in terms of economically significant effects, pension plans do not differentially affect the retirement decision across demographic groups that differ in their life expectancies.

Workers with below-average life expectancy would tend to retire earlier and, if possible, to take their benefits as a lump sum. Firms can, but rarely do, require proof of good health for a worker to receive a lump sum benefit at retirement.

Actuarial Adjustments and Interest Rates. To see how differences in interest rates affect retirement incentives, assume that there is zero postretirement in-

Table 9.1
Actuarially Fair Reduction Factors, Ages 55 to 65

Age	Interest Rate			
	0%	3%	6%	9%
55	59.0%	48.4%	38.9%	28.6%
57	64.5	55.0	46.2	36.2
59	71.0	63.0	55.3	46.0
61	78.9	72.8	66.7	59.0
62	83.4	78.5	73.5	67.1
63	88.4	84.9	81.2	76.4
64	93.9	92.0	90.0	87.3
65	100.0	100.0	100.0	100.0

Source: This table was calculated by Joseph Applebaum, Chief Actuary for the Pension and Welfare
    Benefits Administration, U.S. Department of Labor, using the Group Annuity Mortality 1983
    table for men.

dexing of benefits but that the interest rate fully adjusts for expected inflation.
Thus, higher interest rates compensate for the inflation erosion of assets. Table
9.1 shows that the higher the interest rate is, the higher the actuarially fair
reduction in benefits. For example, when there is a 6 percent interest rate, workers retiring at age 55 would receive 38.9 percent of the benefit they would have
received had they retired at age 65 with the same earnings and service. If the
interest rate dropped to 3 percent, the actuarially fair adjustment would rise to
48.4 percent.

In practice, pension plans do not adjust their early retirement factors when
the interest rate changes; the anticutback rules under the Employee Retirement
Income Security Act of 1974 (ERISA) prohibit them from doing so. Thus, when
interest rates are high, pension plans tend to provide a greater subsidy for early
retirement than when interest rates are low.

As indicated in Table 9.1, retirement at age 55 with an actuarially fair reduction in benefits results in a benefit less than half the normal accrued benefit
receivable at age 65 (assuming nonzero rates of interest). Because of the large
percentage reduction for retirement 10 years early, most plans do not permit
retirement more than 10 years before the normal retirement age (McGill and
Grubbs, 1989, 134).

Actuarial Adjustments and Economic Equivalence. While actuarial equivalence is a benchmark that is widely used for comparisons of benefit levels, an
actuarially equivalent reduction is usually not economically equivalent (Ippolito,
1990). To illustrate, suppose an actuary is setting an actuarially fair reduction

for workers retiring at age 55 rather than retiring with full benefits at age 65. In making the calculation, the actuary uses the benefit based on the workers' age 55 earnings. Thus, in the actuarially fair calculation, the full pension payable at age 65 is proportional to the workers' wage at age 55. The reduction factor is then applied to this amount. This approach would provide the economic equivalent if there were no inflation or merit wage increases. The problem with this approach for economic equivalence is that it uses nominal wages at age 55.

Economic neutrality occurs if the pension for retirement at age 55 equals the pension accrued to age 55 based on retirement at age 65. In that case, the worker's accrual to date is unaffected by the age at which he or she retires.[17]

CONCLUSIONS

By adjusting the incentives provided for workers to retire, defined benefit plans can provide employers with a flexible mechanism for managing the size and age structure of their workforces. First, they may be used as part of a long-term strategy of deferring compensation to encourage long tenure and then encouraging retirement at the desired age or years of service. Second, they may be used as part of a short-term strategy to reduce the workforce in periods of slack demand for the firm's product. Defined contribution plans, however, have little effect on the timing of retirement because they are based on a retirement investment account and there is no penalty or reward for choosing a particular retirement date.

The decline in the percentage of the workforce covered by defined benefit pension plans and the increase in the percentage covered by defined contribution plans (Turner and Beller, 1992) may significantly alter retirement behavior in the future. Workers may be more likely to retire over a broader range of ages and to retire earlier.

NOTES

1. See Mitchell and Fields (1982) for an early survey of the effects of pensions on retirement, and Quinn, Burkhauser, and Myers (1990) for a more recent discussion.

2. In comparison, 92 percent of aged households received income from social security.

3. Some defined contribution plans weight the employer contribution more heavily for long-service workers, which may encourage tenure (Turner, 1993). Defined contribution plans that require employee contributions may act as a sorting device, helping firms attract a particular type of worker.

4. The Employee Retirement Income Security Act (ERISA) requires that, for a worker who becomes a plan participant within five years of the plan's normal retirement age, no more than five years of participation in the plan can be required for eligibility for benefits.

5. A 10 percent tax is levied if distributions from a plan are made to a 5 percent or more employee-owner before age 59½, except for disability.

6. These plans are discussed in greater detail in Mutschler (Chapter 10 of this volume).

7. For very highly paid workers, the plan sponsor's flexibility in designing early retirement benefits may be constrained by the Internal Revenue Code. Section 415, which regulates the maximum benefits that can be provided by a tax-exempt pension plan, resulting in a steep reduction in the maximum amount of benefit that can be paid in an annuity form at early ages.

8. This exception was inserted to address concerns that employers would be discouraged from hiring older workers because of a higher cost of providing benefits to them.

9. The OWBPA permits subsidized early retirement benefits and social security supplements in defined benefit plans.

10. While it has proven to be difficult to verify econometrically the theory of equalizing differences, that theory is generally accepted as a requirement for equilibrium in competitive labor markets.

11. There may also be a wealth effect for short-tenure workers who forgo wages in anticipation of a pension based on long tenure but who then unexpectedly change jobs. These workers will experience a decline rather than an increase in lifetime wealth, which could affect their retirement behavior.

12. If the additional year's work occurs after the age of early retirement but before the normal retirement date, benefits will increase because the percentage reduction for early retirement will be less than if retirement had occurred a year earlier.

13. The 1983 amendments to the Social Security Act gradually change this adjustment starting in the year 2000.

14. Because differences in mortality risk between men and women are not large enough to significantly affect the actuarial adjustments, this increase is roughly actuarially fair for both men and women.

15. The benefit is adjusted by r because the worker could have taken the money at age 62 and invested it, yielding a sum of $100(1 + r)$ at age 63.

16. When the benefits are indexed for inflation after retirement, the initial year of benefits is a smaller percentage of the present value of benefits than when benefits are unindexed. Thus, the actuarial adjustment for forgoing a year of indexed benefits is smaller than is the adjustment for forgoing a year of unindexed benefits.

17. The worker's total wealth, however, is affected by income from earnings, which in turn is influenced by the age of retirement.

10

Early Retirement Incentive Programs (ERIPs): Mechanisms for Encouraging Early Retirement

Phyllis H. Mutschler

In 1978, the Age Discrimination in Employment Act (ADEA) was amended to increase the upper end of the age range for which workers were protected against arbitrary age discrimination from 65 to 70; it also eliminated all age limits for the majority of those employed by the federal government. Although the legislation passed easily, many policy analysts questioned whether such protection would lead to longer worklives for most employees. Rather, they argued, the legislation was largely irrelevant to the lives of most older workers, many of whom were being encouraged to retire before they reached their 65th birthdays. The Omnibus Budget Reconciliation Act of 1986 virtually eliminated mandatory retirement by extending ADEA coverage to all workers age 70 and older.[1]

Although the trend toward early retirement was already well established by the time the ADEA was amended, the new legislation made it imperative that firms facing the "stagflation" of the late 1970s and early 1980s find ways to pare their personnel costs without exposing themselves to charges of age discrimination. In such a climate, "golden handshakes," "open window plans," and other voluntary separation plans bloomed. Over the past two decades, hundreds of companies employing hundreds of thousands of workers have offered such programs to induce workers to leave. Some now consider these plans a durable feature of the employee benefits landscape:

Since 1982, at the bottom of the 1981–83 recession, it has become apparent that early retirement incentives are now a permanent device available to human resource planners whenever appropriate. Employers, private and public, have a good deal of latitude in targeting specific employee groups and still remain within the parameters of the Age Discrimination in Employment Act. (Charles D. Spencer and Associates, 1992, 1)

However, others are not all sanguine about these plans' longevity. A spokesperson for the American Management Association asserted that:

early retirement incentives continue to lose favor as an alternative to firings . . . [Since 1986, 16% of firms surveyed planned to cut workers] . . . but the percentage considering early retirement windows as part of downsizing declined from 47% in July, 1987 to 30% last July. (*Wall Street Journal*, October 30, 1990, p. 1)

Most observers, however, believe that if organizations continue to receive positive reactions to such plans from employees, the unions that represent them, and the press—and if they continue to achieve real reductions in costs—they are likely to continue to be offered.

Since the introduction of special early retirement programs in the mid-1970s, the programs have grown and enjoyed considerable popularity, with firms of all sizes employing them to reduce the number of older employees in the work force. In recent years questions have been raised about the fundamental fairness in the manner they are employed but, despite recent legislative restrictions, their continued use appears likely. (Grant, 1991, 10)

Information about these plans is not collected in any systematic way by the organizations that chart the progress of employer-sponsored pension plans. Hence, this chapter must reach beyond the scholarly journals and government reports to draw on press accounts, consulting firm reports, and law review articles to discern the parameters of early retirement incentive plans and other mechanisms for encouraging workers' exit; these are usually referred to as *voluntary separation programs*. This chapter will discuss the various forms of early retirement incentive programs, the motivation for offering them, their prevalence and cost, and the reaction of employers and employees to them. It also will review the legal and regulatory issues that surround plan designs. Finally, it will raise some questions about the way these plans impinge on public policy goals.

WHAT ARE EARLY RETIREMENT INCENTIVE PLANS?

Special early retirement incentive plans (ERIPs) extend the incentives already offered to workers through their pension plans and other employee benefits. ERIPs offer workers "an opportunity of limited duration to leave the company with higher benefits than would normally be available" (Hewitt Associates, 1986, 1). Three characteristics define such plans. First, participation in these programs is voluntary. In order to avoid charges of age discrimination, companies are careful to define eligibility to embrace an entire class of employees or a particular location. For example, a study of 100 firms with at least one such plan between 1983 and 1985 found that nearly 6 out of 10 offered the program to all those who met minimum age and service requirements.[2]

Second, these programs are short term. They are often called "open window plans" because the offers are made and must be accepted during a limited time period. Although firms and their advisors agree that it is most effective to offer such programs only once, when confronted with the need to continually trim costs and personnel, many organizations have offered such plans periodically— some as often as yearly. A Hewitt Associates 1992 survey of nearly 700 companies, for example, found that one-fifth had offered two programs since 1988; 7 percent had offered three, and 3 percent had offered four or more (Hewitt Associates, 1992). This practice—while perhaps unavoidable—threatens the program's objectives: unless workers believe that these offers will not be repeated (at least within their own personalized windows for retirement), they may wait for the next program—which they hope will be more generous. Others, who may have planned to retire at a specific date, wait for an incentive plan in order to retire. Firms that have offered several ERIPs can attest to just this result: almost no retirements take place outside a window plan.

Third, these plans provide *one-time* cash and/or pension plan adjustments. Some also provide a continuation of other benefits (e.g., health and life insurance) for a specified period. It should be noted, however, that the designs and eligibility requirements of employer pension plans have grown more selective over time and, in many cases, less generous.

HOW COMMON ARE THEY?

Recent surveys conducted by several benefits consulting firms have provided widely ranging estimates of the prevalence of ERIPs over the last two decades. One study of Fortune 100 companies found that 8 out of 10 had offered such programs.[3] Charles D. Spencer and Associates (1992) surveyed 362 firms and found that 13 percent of private sector and 28 percent of public sector employers had offered an ERIP in 1991. Moreover, nearly 9 out of 10 who had *not* offered such a plan had had a program at some point in the past. A Hewitt Associates survey of 700 firms found that 25 percent had offered a plan in the past five years (Hewitt, 1992). Other surveys (e.g., Buck, 1989) found rates closer to 40 percent. Various surveys conducted in the mid-1980s found that more than one-third of the largest U.S. firms had offered at least one special incentive program for their retirement-eligible employees.

Size of Organizations Offering Plans

Larger companies are much more likely to offer plans than smaller ones. For example, Buck Consultants (1989) found that while 46 percent of nearly 400 firms had offered a window plan, close to 60 percent of companies with 5,000 or more workers did so. Hewitt Associates' 1986 survey of 529 companies also showed that the likelihood of offering an ERIP rose with the size of the firm: only 13 percent of those with up to 500 employees offered such plans, compared with one-third of firms with 1,000 to 25,000 workers and 59 percent of firms with 50,000 or more employees.

Types of Organizations Offering Plans

While press accounts about such plans give the impression that ERIPs are offered solely by large, well-known firms, in fact, a diverse group of employers have used these plans to slim down. Organizations as large as the Department of Defense and the U.S. Postal Service and as small as the Minneapolis School Board have offered such programs.[4] A 1993 Hewitt Associates survey of 343 companies showed that nearly 11 percent of the organizations providing a severance pay plan were hospitals or health care organizations, 8 percent were retail businesses, another 8 percent were banks or financial firms, 7 percent were insurance companies, and 4 percent were utilities. Buck Consultants (1989) reported that 45 percent of those offering a window plan were in the service industry and 8 percent were government entities.

WHY ARE THEY OFFERED?

There are three concerns that lead organizations to consider adopting ERIPs: their likely economic impact, their reception by employees and their representatives, and the way they will be perceived by the public. In addition, some firms that want to achieve greater diversity in their workforce need to make reductions in order to create opportunities to hire new workers.

The American Management Association (1993) reported that in the five years from 1988 to 1993, 36 to 56 percent of companies had to take steps to downsize their workforce. "An actual or anticipated business downturn was the sole reason behind 32% of the reported reductions," the report said, but automation, information technology, and mergers also led to cuts in personnel. "For the first time in ... [seven years] ... a majority of the jobs eliminated belonged not to hourly workers but to ... supervisors, middle managers, professionals and technicians" (American Management Association, 1993, 4). As a consequence of workforce reductions, the report disclosed that operating profits increased for 45 percent of firms, but 80 percent experienced declining morale among those workers who survived the cuts.

It is the latter result that organizations offering ERIPs hope to avoid. Many benefits consultants agree with Robert Kryvicky of Towers, Perrin, Forster, and Crosby (TPFC) who said that windows are a "very humane and cost-effective way of downsizing."[5] Not only do ERIPs preserve the morale of current workers, they prevent the company from conveying a sense of crisis or panic, which often attends reports of layoffs. Instead, the company is able to announce a generous act, carefully planned and accounted for; in this way the firm is seen as being in control of its destiny. Finally, unions have responded quite favorably to ERIPs, seeing them as an extension of benefits for their members.

Surveys of companies offering such plans show the importance of these factors in the decision to initiate them. In the early 1980s, the reasons most often given for corporate decisions to offer an early retirement window plan were to reduce personnel and associated payroll costs and to avoid the need for generalized layoffs. More than half the companies in the 1986 Hewitt survey, 80 percent of the Conference Board's respondents (Rhine, 1984), and two-thirds of firms surveyed by Towers, Perrin, Forster, and Crosby (TPFC) cited one or both of these reasons.[6] A more recent study (Hewitt, 1992) showed that in addition to avoiding layoffs—cited by 52 percent of firms—61 percent of firms said they were responding to the need to restructure in response to mergers or a changed economic climate, and 25 percent wanted to improve productivity. Smaller proportions cited the cancellation of contracts (11%) or transfer of plant location (16%); 13 percent of those responding to the 1992 Hewitt survey said they wanted to create career opportunities for younger workers.

WHO IS ELIGIBLE FOR THESE PROGRAMS?

Eligibility requirements are dictated by the goals of the early retirement program. Companies responding to the effects of market forces have the greatest need to cut their work forces, and therefore they define eligibility quite broadly (i.e., all people in the retirement-eligible cohort or, simply, all workers). Companies responding to changes in technology are more focused in defining the eligible group—which is generally restricted to certain geographic locations or specific work classes where employees are no longer needed. Companies that are attempting to restructure due to mergers also define eligibility along lines of divisions or work classes.

Several surveys have found that plans most frequently target a firm's salaried employees. Sixty percent of the companies in the TPFC study targeted nonunion workers only, while 29 percent of the 1986 Hewitt survey respondents targeted executives.[7] In its 1992 survey, Hewitt Associates found that 38 percent of ERIPs were offered to nonunion hourly workers; 32 percent to union workers and "others" (e.g., faculty); 48 percent to executives; more than 70 percent to those in middle management, supervisory, administrative, and technical positions; and 68 percent to other salaried workers. These figures confirm those already presented here, showing that in the 1990s, downsizing has hit middle management with new vigor (American Management Association, 1993).

Another recent development in defining the conditions for eligibility is the greater sophistication that firms are exercizing in targeting their ERIPs. Grant asserted that "companies are careful not to define the target group too broadly for fear of losing needed workers" (1991, 5). As a result, "increasingly they're becoming more deliberate in crafting . . . packages. Instead of just trying to reduce total employment, companies are targeting positions—or even particular individuals—they want to remove" (Hemp, 1991, 41). Indeed, International Business Machines (IBM) was roundly criticized for the generosity and lack of selectivity in targeting its most recent buyout offers. The price tag for the 115,000 exits achieved by the company since 1989 has been estimated at $11 billion, causing analysts to conclude that the firm "has not managed its cuts well" (Fatsis, 1993, 57).

Most organizations offering ERIPs rely on age and years of service to determine who is eligible. Because these are sweeteners for potential retirees, the companies obviously want to encourage those who would not otherwise retire to do so. Minimums for age and service, therefore, reflect the firms' rules regarding early pension receipt, having been liberalized somewhat for the special incentive program. Sixteen percent of the plans in the 1992 Hewitt survey allowed workers to participate at ages 50 and younger, and 27 percent granted eligibility to workers who had been with the firm for less than ten years. Some companies, particularly those with "30 and out" rules for regular pension receipt, relied only on service requirements, while a few, like Chevron, allowed workers of any age to have as little as 5 years of service and still qualify for program participation.

Federal workers, and employees of other governmental entities frequently are entitled to retire with full benefits when they reach age 62 with 5 years of service, age 60 with 20 years' service, or age 55 with 30 years' service. After many years of discussion, Congress approved "early outs" that were offered to those who had reached age 50 with 20 years of service and to those of any age with 25 years' service.

WHAT IS OFFERED?

"Unlike many benefits, which often appear cut from the same cloth, there is considerable variety in open window programs offered, and it appears that employers often attempt to tailor their programs to perceived employee needs" (Grant, 1991, 4). Most companies offer one or a combination of three things: cash payments, pension plan adjustments, and other benefits. Cash payments— either salary continuance or severance pay—are most often based on length of service and typically are paid out over six months to two years. Sometimes there is an option to receive a lump sum, but more often they are distributed periodically. "Bridge" payments are a form of salary continuance, typically replacing some portion of earnings until a worker becomes eligible for social security benefits at age 62.

Pension plan adjustments usually take one of two forms. Either they reduce or eliminate the actuarial adjustment, or "penalty" for early retirement, or they add a certain number of years to an employee's age, length of service, or both in calculating pension benefits. This latter provision is frequently called "the 5 plus 5" or "the 5 plus 5 plus 4" (in which five years are added to a person's age, five are added to length of service, and, in addition, four weeks of severance pay are provided). Although five is a common number of years to add in this manner, some plans, notably those targeting workers who are close to normal retirement age, offer only three or even two years.

Another method of using age and service limits is for a firm to specify that an employee's age and service must sum to a certain number, say 70 or 80. In that way, persons who have long service with the firm, having started at a young age, can retire earlier than those who joined the company later in their lives.

When ERIPs were originally introduced, a few companies reduced the benefits that currently existed in plans, but today such a scheme would be rare. Not only would those actions jeopardize relationships with unions and with nonunion workers whom companies hope to retain, companies offering such plans would leave themselves exposed to lawsuits. Moreover, the positive image that companies hope to project would be imperiled.

A 1983 survey of 108 companies indicated the variety and incidence of methods used in ERIPs.[8] Fifty-four percent offered a monthly supplement, sometimes along with some other incentive, such as a pension unreduced for early retirement. Thirty-eight percent offered salary continuation; one in five offered this in combination with other incentives. Fifteen percent offered one-time-only cash payments. Fifty percent of these companies said that they had put other cost-cutting measures in place prior to, or at the same time as, the offering of incentives. These measures included freezes on salary, workhour reductions, delays on merit increases, or suspension of executive bonuses.

Salary continuation arrangements varied widely. Examples of monthly supplements included 25 percent of salary for two years; $400 a month until age 62; $650 a month until normal retirement age; and 15 percent of pay (up to $450) for employees age 58–61 and 20 percent of pay (up to $550) for employees age 62–65. However, there are far less generous plans, as well. California Portland Cement, for example, offered a monthly payment of $150 for life, plus a cash bonus of $2,000. Severance pay may be as short as one or two months, or may extend for one or two years. One advantage that a firm realizes in offering severance pay rather than adjusting their pension plans is that they will not be subject to the regulations and legislation that apply to qualified pension plans under ERISA.

It is plain that the more generous the incentive, the more likely eligible employees are to retire from the firm. Acceptance rates are as variable as the benefits proffered. Some plans garner only 10 percent or less, while others may see up to 70 or 80 percent of the eligible group leave. There have been well-publicized "surprises," such as Du Pont's 1985 plan, which aimed to achieve about 6,000 acceptances but instead caused 12,000 to leave the firm. However, in recent years, one in three workers who were offered such schemes have accepted. For that reason, advisors to companies planning ERIPs tell them to target three times as many employees as needed and to be moderate in what is offered (Hawthorne, 1983).

PROGRAM TIMING

The Older Workers Benefit Protection Act (OWPBA) of 1990 (see the section titled, ''The Alphabet Soup of Legal Issues'') requires that workers have sufficient time—at least 21 days—to consider an ERIP offer, if their decisions are to be considered voluntary. A plan is subjected to increased scrutiny in this regard when employees leaving the firm are asked to sign waivers holding the employer harmless. Since waivers are only enforceable if workers are given at least 45 days to consider their participation (Dunn, 1989), companies that decide to use them set their window period accordingly.[9]

For most companies, the window period during which incentives are offered runs from 60 to 90 days, although for some it may be as short as 1 month or as long as 1 year. The window period during which workers must decide whether to participate is often shorter than that—usually 1 to 2 months. Companies prefer a shorter period because it both reduces the coverage by the media of its need for attrition and avoids giving benefits to those workers who would have retired without any incentive.

Further, companies that aim at workforce reductions want to achieve cost savings over as short a time as possible. Moreover, they want to minimize the effects of these programs on employee morale and productivity. Experience with these plans has also shown that workers make their decisions to participate in these programs at the very beginning or at the end of the window period. Hence, companies see no benefit to dragging out the middle.

Workers, however, say they feel rushed into an important decision; and some personnel administrators worry about the consequences of such rushed retirement planning for retirees' future well-being. Most companies offer some counseling to workers in individual sessions or in groups. Some prefer to use their own personnel department staff; others contract counseling to a professional counseling firm.

COSTS

ERIPs are costly for companies, but most firms offering ERIPs recover the costs within two years. The expenses associated with such schemes obviously depend on the size of the target group, the rate of acceptance, and the generosity of the benefits offered. Media General reported costs of only $10.6 million for their 1991 plan, Motorola's 1989 program cost $43 million, Du Pont took $350 million in fourth-quarter charges for its 1991 plan, and Digital is reported to have posted up to $1 billion in charges for its 1992 exit incentives.[10] Costs for General Motors' plans, however, dwarf even these substantial expenses. It has been estimated that in the late 1980s and early 1990s, GM took $11 billion in accounting charges for 115,000 worker exits (Fatsis, 1993).

The Financial Standards Accounting Board (FASB) Statement 88 now requires that costs for special benefits must be accounted for in the quarter they are incurred (Wiber and Adams, 1991); this applies even to pension plan adjustments, if they are offered on a "one-time basis." Consequently, profits for the quarter in which incentives are provided will dwindle or disappear, affecting the attractiveness of the company to current and future investors, at least for a short time.

EMPLOYER AND EMPLOYEE REACTIONS

Employers

Most employers profess pleasure at plan results. However, if the number of workers accepting the incentive plan exceeds employer expectations, the employer may face the necessity of hiring replacements. There have been several examples of such an occurrence—New York State's incentive plan left the state without sufficient workers and depleted so many individuals with critical skills that vital work could not be carried out. The issue of the skill level or productivity of plan participants is also of real concern to employers who design and offer such schemes. If those leaving are highly productive workers or employees with needed skills, the losses may be very great indeed. One writer, describing the penchant of newly retired ex-executives to start their own businesses with the generous severance benefits they receive, said: "Downsizing exacts a terrible toll on a company's resources. Though it is difficult to quantify the loss, the exit of highly skilled, talented employees reduces the overall quality of personnel" (Zoghlin, 1989, 82). If critical functions are left uncovered, there can be less savings realized than expected, since new hires will need to be trained and paid. Some studies report that at least half the firms offering ERIPs are forced to hire replacements, usually within one year.

Employees

Many studies have found that workers are generally positive about the plans. In fact, in recent years there have been a number of news reports of employees suing their prior employers over being denied the opportunity to participate in such schemes.[11] However, not all employees have been pleased with ERIP offers. Some workers report that they feel pressure to leave from either other, frequently younger, employees or from supervisors. Workers who have rejected an earlier plan that was more generous feel cheated if the plan they are offered does not measure up, and workers who are certain they will find another job or consulting opportunities are bitterly disappointed if these opportunities do not materialize. In this instance, the payments they had thought of as a windfall have to be spread out over a much longer period and retirement income is much smaller than anticipated. This situation has faced many who have left a firm in recent years: finding no jobs are available, they have received a blow to both ego and pocketbook.

THE ALPHABET SOUP OF LEGAL ISSUES: ADEA, ERISA, AND OWBPA

There are several laws that must be taken into consideration by employers wishing to offer an ERIP. Two of these laws—the Age Discrimination in Employment Act (ADEA) and its 1990 amendment, the Older Workers Benefit Protection Act (OWBPA)—concern challenges that may be raised regarding age discrimination. These are discussed further here and in Chapter 11 by Steven Sandell and Marc Rosenblum.

The Consolidated Omnibus Budget Reconciliation Act of 1987 (COBRA) also affects ERIPs by specifying that: "In the event of certain types of separation from service, the exiting employee must be provided with the opportunity to participate in the employer's health care plan for up to 36 months" (Grant, 1991, 4).

ERISA regulations must also be considered. If the plan provides severance pay, it must meet the requirements of a welfare benefit plan; if it uses pension plan assets to fund the buyouts, plan fiduciaries must demonstrate that they have not violated their responsibilities to all pensioners. Plans offered to union members must comply with federal labor laws, and there may be state contract law to consider as well. Finally, financial considerations are addressed by Section 415 of the Internal Revenue Code, which speaks to the maximum early retirement pension allowed and the Financial Accounting Standards Board (FASB) Statement 88.

When ERIP plans were first offered more than a decade ago, employers believed that they had only to observe the proper procedures to assure the voluntary nature of plan acceptance to avoid litigation. Firms admonished those administering the programs to be sure that no worker felt threatened or pressured to leave, and eligibility rules were drafted to affect entire groups of workers rather than singling out only the oldest ones.

In the last 15 years, however, contradictory court decisions and the passage of the OWBPA have complicated the matter. Grant (1991) reported that more than 30,000 age discrimination claims are filed with the Equal Employment Opportunity Commission each year, many due to ERIPs. There are two basic issues involved: (1) the permissibility of ERIPs under the ADEA, and (2) whether eligibility for, or benefits under, such plans can terminate or decrease with advancing age. Prior to passage of the OWBPA, ERIPs were permitted under the ADEA so long as they were a "bona fide employment benefit plan" and were not designed as "a subterfuge to evade the purposes of the Act" (Stith and Kohlburn, 1992, 264).

Then, in 1985, a 66-year-old speech pathologist who was in poor health left her job and tried to claim disability benefits. Instead, her employer—the state of Ohio—insisted on providing the normal retirement pension, which yielded $197 less per month than disability benefits. The ensuing litigation concluded when the Supreme Court reversed the decision of the appellate court that had found for the plaintiff; it stated that Ohio's plan was not discriminatory on the basis of age. As a result of this decision, Congress amended the ADEA to include explicit language that would reflect congressional intent when the ADEA was enacted.

The OWBPA permitted ERIPs provided that they could be shown to be a bona fide benefit plan, that they were voluntary, and that the employer's payments or cost for each benefit or benefit package would be no greater for younger workers than for older employees. It is this last consideration that has caused the greatest worry for employers.

Generally, the OWBPA prohibits discrimination in employee benefits against workers except when age-based reductions . . . are justified by significant cost considerations. . . . [It] permits employers to provide older workers fewer benefits when the actual amount of payment made or cost incurred on behalf of an older worker is no less than that for younger ones. (Williams, 1991, 92)

Due to the ambiguities in interpreting the law, employers confer with their lawyers and benefits consultants in designing eligibility requirements, program timing, and the structure of benefits so as to avoid costly litigation. Stith and Kohlburn (1992) reported that temporary plans, while less effective, are more likely to provide a safe harbor than are the longer-term or permanent plans, such as retirement bonuses, terminating benefits plans, or "bridge" or "actuarial" plans.[12] It is hoped that final regulations, currently due for release, will clarify some of these issues.

POLICY QUESTIONS

There are two types of concerns voiced when ERIPs are discussed: (1) the long-term effect of taking early retirement on workers who accept such offers, and (2) the impact of the widespread use of these plans on achieving public policy objectives.

In discussing employees' reactions to ERIPs, some fraction of those participating do so with the expectation that they will be able to return to work elsewhere when they determine that they require additional funds. In periods in which there is high inflation, the adequacy of pension and special benefits is eroded quickly, but even with modest increases in the cost of living, elders' standard of living is compromised over time.

Some observers of ERIPs offered to federal workers and those in the military claim that these incentives have an impact on the federal deficit, but such contributions are too meager to cause serious concern. More troublesome is the fact that these plans run counter to the goals of public policy that seek to encourage later labor force withdrawal and increased reliance on retirement savings. Extending the age at which one can receive full social security benefits, for example, and the taxation of benefits both provide incentives to remain in the labor force and to begin a sound program of saving prior to middle age. Inducing workers to leave their jobs prior to their planned date of retirement frequently curtails individual savings or may cause retirees to withdraw funds sooner than they had planned. Clearly, in these instances, what is good for GM is *not* good for the nation.

NOTES

1. See the discussion in Sandell and Rosenblum (Chapter 11 of this volume).

2. *BNA Pension Reporter*, February 10, 1986, 277.

3. *BNA Pension Reporter*, May 15, 1989, 852.

4. On the Department of Defense and the U.S. Postal Service, see the *Washington Post*'s series of articles in "The Federal Diary" column, in May, June, August, and October 1992. On the Minneapolis School Board, see *BNA Pension Reporter*, May 8, 1989, 825.

5. *Wall Street Journal*, October 30, 1990, 1.

6. *BNA Pension Reporter*, February 10, 1986, 277.

7. On the TPFC study, see *BNA* Pension Reporter, February 10, 1956.

8. Charles D. Spencer Associates (1983).

9. See *Business Week*, February 27, 1989, 134. According to a 1989 Bureau of National Affairs report (1989, 852), the use of waivers increased between 1985 and 1988 but peaked in 1987, when 35 percent of firms offering exit incentives required participants to sign waivers. A General Accounting Office (U.S. General Accounting Office, 1990) survey found that only 14 percent of those offered ERIPs or severance pay had to sign waivers.

10. On the Media General claim, see *New York Times*, September 5, 1991, D6.

11. See "200 Retirees Charge Deception by Kodak," *Boston Globe*, October 15, 1991, 41, for example.

12. Actuarial plans provide early payment of benefits which would be earned if the employee continued to work (Stith and Kohlburn, 1992, 274).

Age Discrimination in Employment: Economic and Legal Perspectives

Steven H. Sandell and Marc Rosenblum

Age discrimination in employment encompasses a gamut of practices that are detrimental to older workers—failure to hire, dismissals, lower pay, and denial of promotions—because of age. It is both a malfunction of the labor market and an injustice against individuals. The economy loses the potential contributions of a valuable segment of the population, and older persons suffer both financial harm and great personal distress. The Age Discrimination in Employment Act (ADEA) of 1967, as amended, provides the primary legal redress for older workers and now prohibits workplace discrimination against most persons 40 years old and over.

Virtually no one doubts the existence of age discrimination. Private litigation and the 19,880 age cases filed with the Equal Employment Opportunity Commission (EEOC) in fiscal year (FY) 1993—a 29 percent increase from four years earlier—attest to this.[1] Although its overall magnitude is almost impossible to measure, the prohibition of age discrimination is an important legal protection for individual workers.

This chapter provides both economic and legal perspectives on age discrimination in employment. Age discrimination combines with economic and demographic factors to affect the employment conditions of older workers. It is important to consider the earnings and labor supply of such workers to under-

When this chapter was drafted in late 1993, some of the issues discussed here were influx. Obviously, very recent developments are not included.

stand the context of age discrimination and legal protections for them. The second section describes the labor market circumstances of older workers, in general, and the situation of displaced workers, women workers, and workers with disabilities, in particular. The latter groups suffer from special labor market problems that appear to interact with age discrimination. The third section examines federal legal protections against age discrimination. The legislative and judicial histories of ADEA are emphasized, and we address differences between the treatment of age and other legally protected worker categories (e.g., race, sex, national origin, and religion). Conclusions are presented in the final section.

LABOR MARKET CIRCUMSTANCES OF OLDER WORKERS

Three labor market measures—earnings, unemployment and labor force participation (retirement)—describe the labor market circumstances of older workers, and potentially reflect the impact of discrimination. Age discrimination in compensation implies lower pay for older workers than they would have earned in the absence of discrimination. Discrimination in hiring and termination—especially reductions in force (RIFs)—affects labor force participation and unemployment rates.

Age discrimination is not necessarily the sole cause of older workers' labor market problems. Four distinct, but not mutually exclusive, factors explain the problems: factors totally unrelated to age, such as living in a high-unemployment area; factors correlated with age and also associated with low earnings, such as low levels of education or having health problems; skill mismatches between older workers and available jobs; and age discrimination. The interplay of these sources of labor market difficulties, rather than age discrimination alone, should be the focus of labor market policies toward older workers.

Older workers in general do well in the labor market. (See Levy and Murnane, 1992, for a recent examination of earnings.) The relatively high earnings of older persons who continue to work is accounted for by two factors. First, general and firm-specific skills and experience accumulate with age. These lead to greater productivity and pay. Second, older workers benefit from institutional factors, particularly increased pay for greater seniority. Older workers' formal education, however, is lower than that of younger workers, and some of their formal training may be obsolete. Older persons' relatively low unemployment rates, however, reflect retirement induced by labor market opportunities that are inferior to retirement-income options (Shapiro and Sandell, 1987).

Earnings

The earnings of older workers employed year-round and full time (more than 35 hours per week) compares favorably to that of other workers. Table 11.1 presents the median earnings of year-round, full-time workers by age and sex

Table 11.1

Median Earnings of Year-Round, Full-Time Workers, by Age and Sex in 1992

Sex	Age					
	25+	25-34	35-44	45-54	55-64	65+
Men	$31,408	$26,197	$33,949	$36,802	$31,904	$27,356
Women	$22,178	$21,510	$22,972	$23,367	$21,250	$17,848

Source: U.S. Bureau of the Census (1993), 116–143, Table 29.

in 1992. The earnings of men 65 and older who work full time, full year, are close to the overall median ($27,356 compared to $31,408). A large drop in the earnings of men 65 and over occurs because they no longer work full time, full year. The median earnings of men 65 and over is $9,093, compared to $26,472 for all men 25 and over. The implications of full time, full-year work are similar for women. The median earnings for all women 65 and over is $6,292, compared to $16,227 for all women 25 and over. The comparable statistics for women who work full time, year-round are $17,848 and $22,178.

It is difficult to conclude from these statistics whether age discrimination in earnings is present. To do so, a standard by which wages of workers can be compared is needed to measure wage discrimination. In a world without discrimination, we could define an ideal standard. Without that, the best we can do is estimate the relationship between chronological age and earnings, after accounting for the influence of other factors (e.g., education) that affect earnings.

Because of the limitations of econometric models and the availability of appropriate data, few studies purport to quantify age/earnings discrimination. One study (Shapiro and Sandell, 1985) used a sample of older workers who were forced to look for new jobs to examine the relationship between age and wages and look for possible age discrimination. By analyzing the factors determining earnings at the previous job and the age/earnings relationships on the postdisplacement jobs, the effects of age and age discrimination on earnings are inferred. Other studies on displaced workers that do not attempt to measure age discrimination (see, for example, Carrington, 1993) have confirmed the relevance of the factors for more recent samples.

Older displaced workers' reduction of earnings is largely attributed to the loss of *firm-specific human capital*, meaning skills and experience useful only in particular jobs. The loss of firm-specific skills, measured by seniority with the previous employers, and of associated pay premiums accounted for 90 percent of the average earnings loss for the sample of job losers examined by Shapiro and Sandell.

Older workers' greater seniority and firm-specific experience compared to younger workers imply greater reductions in pay associated with involuntary job changes. For example, workers who were over age 60 when they lost their jobs averaged more than 11 years of seniority, while those age 45–49 averaged 6 years on their previous jobs. This implies an average 6 percent wage loss for those over 60, compared with only a 3 percent loss for those age 45–49.

Overall economic conditions, measured by the unemployment rate, explained the extent of wage changes among older job losers. While the average loss in average hourly earnings was 4 percent for the entire study period, years of high national unemployment were associated with greater average losses. Job searches conducted during periods of high labor market demand provide a means of recouping pay premiums associated with the lost seniority.

Except for workers over age 65, age/wage discrimination was not evident for displaced older workers. The significant age-related drop in earnings for the sample seemed to be explained by the loss of pay premiums associated with seniority rather than age discrimination by the new employers. The drop in pay for men over 65 was partially explained by occupational changes and the shift to part-time work.

Unemployment and Retirement

The incidence of unemployment declines with age for most groups. However, the duration of unemployment spells is higher for persons over 45. Many older workers who would prefer to work may drop out of the labor force when they become discouraged about finding new jobs and believe further search would be futile (Rosenblum, 1975). Adding the category of discouraged workers to the number of persons officially counted as unemployed increases the unemployment rates. Age discrimination, as it affects the likelihood of older persons finding new employment, will increase unemployment rates, the average duration of unemployment, and the proportion of older persons not in the labor force.

Age discrimination also influences retirement rates. Although mandatory retirement is illegal for most employers, age-related incentives embodied in pension provisions and the benefit rules in social security penalize working at older ages, thereby affecting retirement ages.[2] In social security, actuarial penalties are paid by workers who continue to work past the normal retirement age, which is currently 65. Essentially, the higher benefits received each year after retirement do not fully compensate for the benefits lost by delaying retirement.

Special Concerns

Four groups warrant special attention, if only because their age-related earnings problems may be compounded by age discrimination. Older persons who are also members of minority groups, displaced workers, women, or those who have disabilities may be particularly sensitive to age discrimination. However, while persons in these categories may suffer from age discrimination, the source of their labor market problems is more fundamental.

The incidence of employment problems, defined as a combination of low income and unemployment or underemployment, is higher for members of minority groups, women, and persons with health problems (National Commission for Employment Policy, 1985). Older blacks are four times as likely, and Hispanics more than three times as likely, as whites to have labor market problems. Although the likelihood of having problems drops for whites as they grow older, age does not affect the incidence of labor market problems for blacks or Hispanics.

Table 11.1 showed that women's earnings, even for full-time, full-year workers, are below men's and that the earnings difference increases with age. In general, this earnings pattern has less to do with age discrimination than with the current cohort of older women workers' lifetimes of low-paying jobs, interrupted work experience, and sex discrimination in the labor market. Recent increases in women's wages, annual hours of work, and lifetime labor force participation patterns imply higher earnings for future cohorts of older women workers, but not current ones (Sandell, 1994).

The incidence of health problems and disabilities increases with age (U.S. Department of Health and Human Services, 1982). About 20 percent of working men age 55–64 have disabilities that limit their work, compared to 15 percent of men age 45–54 and less than 10 percent of men age 18–34. Disabilities, in turn, are associated with lower pay (Martini, 1990). Thus, the interaction between age and disability may complicate analyses of age discrimination.

Older displaced workers are another group that warrants special attention in analyses of age discrimination (see Baldwin and Sandell, 1988). Not only will these workers have difficulty finding new jobs and suffer wage reductions when they do, but some may be induced to retire earlier than they might have otherwise (Shapiro and Sandell, 1987). Job losers are more likely to retire than comparable older persons who have not lost their jobs. Thus, the combination of wage reductions, potential retirement income, weak labor markets, and age discrimination induces retirement.

LEGAL PROTECTIONS FOR OLDER WORKERS

Legal Background

Congress passed the Age Discrimination in Employment Act (ADEA) in 1967[3] as the final segment of that decade's effort to address workplace discrimination, following statutes covering gender-based compensation differences in 1963[4] and race, color, national origin, religion, and gender generally in 1964.[5] The ADEA followed specific legislative proposals by the secretary of labor that Congress had expressly requested,[6] and it enjoyed substantial backing from President Lyndon Johnson[7] and key legislative leaders.[8]

The original emphasis behind the ADEA was to promote older worker employment on the premise that age stereotypes (rather than the type of overt animus underlying the racial or religious discrimination addressed by the companion statutes) was primarily responsible for the arbitrary reduction of workplace opportunities for older persons.[9] Earlier congressional intent to provide older workers with the same types of protection that Title VII extended to race and gender proved politically infeasible, leading instead to the further study and legislative debate that occurred between 1964 and 1967.

As originally enacted, ADEA was enforced by the Department of Labor, and covered employees between ages 40 and 65. The law combined Title VII's substantive provisions with the Fair Labor Standards Act's procedural features.[10] In a 1978 reorganization, ADEA enforcement authority was transferred to the Equal Employment Opportunity Commission (EEOC) from the Department of Labor.[11] EEOC now administers almost all federal workplace laws against discrimination.[12]

ADEA coverage, as expanded by successive amendments, now extends to all workers age 40 and above, with several exceptions.[13] The act protects against age-discriminatory hiring, termination (including forced retirement), promotion, compensation, and all other terms and conditions of employment. Similar to Title VII, it also expressly forbids retaliation by employers against persons filing ADEA complaints.[14] The statute extends to all firms employing 20 or more persons as well as labor organizations, and employment agencies' roles in the employment process and in advertising practices.[15]

Persons with ADEA complaints may pursue a private course of action, but only after filing a charge of discrimination with EEOC within 180 or 300 days of the discriminatory event, depending on the presence of a state regulatory agency.

If filed, the lawsuit may be brought any time from 60 days after the charge is filed up to 90 days after receipt of the closure notice from EEOC.[16] EEOC may represent complaining parties, but it also has independent statutory authority to investigate ADEA claims and bring suits directly.[17]

Unlike the parallel provisions of Title VII, an EEOC lawsuit terminates an individual complainant's right to bring or maintain a separate cause of action. Like Title VII, workers or applicants affected by the same employment practice may bring a class action to gain relief as a group. Because of the procedural differences between the two statutes, prospective ADEA class members must affirmatively agree to participate, or "opt in."[18] In contrast, potential Title VII class members are automatically included and bound by the outcome unless they expressly opt out of the litigation.

Age Discrimination in Employment Act

The Age Discrimination in Employment Act is unique in the sense that all workers (as they reach age 40) are eventually covered. In contrast, statuses protected by Title VII and the Equal Pay Act are based on permanent characteristics. For some workers without other protected characteristics such as race, ethnicity, or gender, ADEA provides the sole statutory source of workplace protection.

Thirty years ago, older workers faced widespread stereotyping that was negatively associated with job performance and age. Those attitudes, however pervasive, were somehow seen by some people as different from the type of overt prejudice affecting minorities and women in the workplace. The decision to delay older worker protection until discrimination against blacks and women had been addressed separately in the Civil Rights Act of 1964 resulted in the creation of separate regulatory systems that later had to be merged. Over time, the political coalition of civil rights and older workers' advocates has not remained strong, due perhaps to declining economic growth and structural change in the post-Vietnam era and the resultant scarcity of adequate job opportunities for many older workers, as well as others (see, for example, Levy and Murnane, 1992).

Legislative History of the ADEA

The Act and Its Initial Amendments. In drafting the ADEA, Congress adopted Title VII's substantive framework with only minimal changes, indicating that the judicial construction of the two laws was intended to be similar. This was merged with the procedural mechanism established under the Fair Labor Standards Act (FLSA)[19] and the time limits for bringing suit contained in the Portal-to-Portal Act of 1947.[20]

Congress rejected several alternatives, including (a) one modeled after the National Labor Relations Act (NLRA), which would have authorized the secretary of labor to issue cease and desist orders that could be enforced in the courts of appeals, and (b) one that would have adopted Title VII's statutory pattern in its entirety and placed enforcement of the act with EEOC.[21] The outcome and structure are best understood as reflecting the preferences of key legislators that the act be enforced by the Department of Labor, using that agency's enforcement model.

Only after ADEA enforcement authority shifted to EEOC in 1978 was the act's structure seen as imposing time limits on complaints that were inconsistent with Title VII. In the 1991 Civil Rights Act amendments, ADEA was modified to make the time periods for filing complaints and lawsuits parallel to Title VII's time requirements.[22]

Congress has amended ADEA several times, both expanding and limiting coverage. State and local government employment was added in 1974, along with most federal employment.[23]

The 1978 amendments, which were the most substantial changes in a decade,[24] raised the upper limit for coverage from age 65 to 70 and prohibited mandatory retirement at lower ages even under an otherwise permitted employee benefit plan.[25] The same amendments also set mandatory limits on air traffic controllers (age 56), federal law enforcement officers and firefighters (55), and Panama Canal and Alaska Railway employees (age 62).

The 1978 amendments also contained several occupation-specific exceptions, reflecting particular interest group legislative influence. The first exception permits the retirement of corporate executives and policy makers who qualify for substantial pensions.[26] A temporary exemption for tenured professors in higher education was included, permitting their involuntary retirement at age 70. After one extension, that exception finally expired at the end of 1993, when Congress refused to reenact it.

The police and firefighter exception was first enacted in 1978; it was extended by the 1986 amendments through 1993.[27] This provision has generated more controversy and litigation than almost any specific ADEA issue, in that the bona fide occupational qualification (BFOQ) defense, which is generally raised to justify specific retirement ages for many jobs, remains under relentless attack. Sustained only in cases where an employer can demonstrate that the fitness of "all or substantially all" its employees cannot be individually determined, the BFOQ defense is at increasing odds with the increased accuracy of medical technology that objectively measures fitness irrespective of age.

Although Congress appeared ready to permanently codify this provision into the ADEA, legislative wrangling over the past 2 years has thus far blocked its enactment.[28] Proponents justify the provision as enhancing public safety, despite the growing body of empirical evidence that fitness can be accurately measured rather than rely on age-based proxies.[29]

Congress further amended ADEA in 1984 to protect health care coverage for employees' spouses age 65–69[30] and to cover Americans employed abroad by U.S. corporations.[31] This extraterritoriality provision is not contained in Title VII, marking one area where ADEA coverage is more extensive.[32]

More Recent Amendments. Throughout the early to mid-1980s, advocates for older workers sought improved coverage in health care and the complete elimination of mandatory retirement. Legislation in 1986 achieved both those goals.

Under the Omnibus Budget Reconciliation Act of 1986 (OBRA), employers' nondiscriminatory ADEA health care obligations were extended to workers age 65–69, subject to several exceptions.[33] Congress "uncapped" the act, effectively eliminating mandatory retirement for most workers by extending ADEA coverage to workers age 70 and older in all private sector and most government employment, other than the exceptions referred to here.[34] The amendments also banned mandatory retirement because of a collective bargaining agreement between an employer and a labor organization representing age-protected employees. Where an existing labor agreement contained such provisions, however, it was permitted to remain in effect for the life of that agreement or until January 1, 1990, whichever occurred first. Obviously, that exception has been completely phased out.

The 1986 amendments also extended until 1993 the exception for tenured university faculty. That exception has now expired. Also extended through 1993 was the permissibility of maximum hiring and mandatory retirement ages for state and local police and firefighters. The secretary of labor and EEOC were directed to study the validity of physical and mental tests as determinants of fitness for older police and firefighters.

Sponsors of legislation to make the police and firefighters exception permanent were unable to secure full passage by the end of 1993, or during the subsequent 2 years. Thus, while the exception no longer applies, Congressional Republicans may again seek its passage in 1996.

Another amendment in 1987 covered age-based differences in employee pension plans.[35] Requiring employers to continue making benefit accrual payments without reference to age, it was passed after many employers were found to have terminated benefit accruals for employees remaining active beyond the "usual" retirement age of 65.[36]

The Older Workers Benefit Protection Act (OWPBA) further amended the ADEA in 1990 and is another illustration of quick congressional action to overturn a Supreme Court decision found contrary to the legislative consensus.[37] The Court had held in *Public Employees Retirement System* v. *Betts* that employee benefit plans that discriminate on the basis of age do not violate ADEA unless also shown to be a subterfuge for other age-based discrimination.[38]

Title I of OWBPA overruled *Betts* to limit employers' benefit plan defenses, where those defenses raised doubts concerning several key appellate decisions restricting severance pay denials to retirement-eligible employees. Title II articulated standards to evaluate the lawfulness of claim releases that employees are asked to sign in return for conditional exit incentive compensation.[39]

In particular, the changes codified EEOC's "equal benefit or equal cost" test to ensure that employer benefit plans are not biased against older employees on the basis of age.[40] OWBPA also recognized two areas of legitimate concern to employers, allowing them to offset severance pay against retiree health benefits or incentives received by employees, and also allowing an offset of pension benefits an employee has elected or was eligible to receive against disability benefits to which an employee was entitled, eliminating duplicative benefit payments.[41]

OWBPA resolved a range of benefit issues that had generated substantial litigation over the preceding decade.[42] Most employers revised various practices to comply with the amendments, substantially lessening the number and nature of benefit cases left for the courts to decide.

As discussed in other chapters of this volume,[43] private pension plans often penalize older persons who continue to work. Although OWBPA prohibits specific age-related pension benefit provisions, de facto age-related incentive provisions serve employer downsizing aims. As long as the expected remaining lifespan diminishes with each passing year, pension plans that do not contain full actuarial adjustments have larger work disincentives for older workers. This is reinforced if plans that base their benefits in part on number of years with the firm do not credit years beyond a specific limit (i.e., 30 years). Because firm tenure is correlated with age, these provisions adversely impact older workers. When pension provisions provide large disincentives to continued work, de facto mandatory retirement takes place. Such workers have the option of seeking other employment, but many exit the workforce instead.

A provision of the 1991 Civil Rights Act revises the maximum time period for ADEA complainants to file suit.[44] Under the Portal-to-Portal Act, suits could be brought within 2 years of the complaint (three years if a willful violation was claimed). Now, this right to sue ends 90 days after EEOC issues a closure notice on the complaint.

This provision was added for two reasons: first, to make ADEA's filing limits congruent with Title VII, and second, to avoid unfairly penalizing complainants whose time for filing court actions expired before EEOC acted on their charges.

Court Decisions Under ADEA

The litigation of older worker issues under ADEA spans the past quarter-century and cannot easily be summarized, in part due to the changing nature over time of key topics. Some matters, especially procedural questions during the act's first decade, arose, were resolved, and have become part of the body of settled law. Other problems, particularly those paralleling Title VII legal standards, continue to be litigated.

Looked at another way, some matters are resolved by Congress and avoid litigation; some are resolved by the Supreme Court; and some go back to Congress when the Court's decision is regarded by key lawmakers as contrary to the legislative consensus of what the law should be.

Nonetheless, certain ADEA cases were significant when issued by the Supreme Court and are summarized here first. The section that follows reviews the Court's most recent decisions affecting older workers. Next, several major unresolved areas that are likely to require resolution by the Supreme Court, Congress, or possibly both are identified.

Supreme Court Cases of Historical Significance. In addition to statutory challenges to mandatory retirement under ADEA, a number of cases have been argued under the Constitution's equal protection provisions. None have succeeded. In *Massachusetts Board of Retirement* v. *Murgia*, the Court held that the state could, consistent with the Equal Protection Clause of the 14th Amendment, require uniformed state police officers to retire at age 50 because fitness "presumably" declines with age.[45] The Court also held that State Department foreign service officers could be required to retire at age 60 without violation of the equal protection component of the Fifth Amendment's Due Process Clause.[46]

Similarly, the Court also ruled that state constitutional provisions requiring judges to retire at age 70 did not violate the U.S. Constitution.[47] In contrast to the highest level of judicial scrutiny reserved for cases involving race or national origin, the Court held federal and state governments (as employers) in these cases to a lower (and easily satisfied) "rational basis" standard. A similar broad deference to governmental retirement policies by lower federal courts is illustrated by the rejection of constitutional challenges covering tenured professors in higher education,[48] police officials,[49] and postal inspectors,[50] among others.

Lorillard v. *Pons* resolved the question of whether a private ADEA plaintiff seeking lost wages could obtain a jury trial.[51] The case stemmed from the hybrid nature of ADEA alluded to here because Title VII plaintiffs pursuing equitable claims were not (prior to the 1991 Civil Rights Act amendments) entitled to a jury trial. Because of the FLSA procedural underpinning of ADEA, plaintiffs seeking legal relief (such as wage claims) were entitled to a jury trial.

The Court subsequently held that federal employees are not entitled to jury trials for ADEA claims because Congress did not unambiguously authorize them.[52] Interpreting the 1978 amendments, the Justices ruled that if Congress wanted to authorize jury trials for federal employee age claims, it could have included clear language to that effect.

Oscar Mayer & Co. v. *Evans* resolved the question of whether employees living in states with age discrimination laws enforced by state agencies must comply with a waiting period after complaining to the state agency and before bringing an ADEA lawsuit in federal court.[53] Following parallel Title VII procedures designed to encourage the resolution of discrimination complaints short of litigation, the Court ruled that deferral was required. This gave the state agency at least some opportunity to resolve the problem in administrative, rather than legal, proceedings.

Western Air Lines v. *Criswell* represents a conclusion to the most substantial ADEA issue resolved in litigation, the use of age as a bona fide occupational qualification (BFOQ).[54] The Supreme Court emphasized that the BFOQ defense was a very narrow exception to the otherwise clear prohibition on age-linked employment criteria and rejected an airline's reliance on the Federal Aviation Administration (FAA) rule that required commercial pilots to retire at age 60.[55]

A BFOQ can only be established when age is not simply a convenient proxy for the job performance but rather the employer demonstrates that it is both impossible or highly impractical to measure individual employee performance and that it has a clear basis in fact to believe that all, or substantially all, employees above a certain age cannot safely perform their job duties.

The application of the *Criswell* standard remains at issue primarily where it involves public safety employees, because of the expired and presently pending legislation referred to here. Elsewhere, most employers have abandoned the BFOQ argument as too difficult and costly to establish, in favor of stringent qualification standards that limit older worker employment in many occupations and industries.

Significant Recent Supreme Court Cases. In *Hazen Paper Co.* v. *Biggins* the Court resolved two ADEA issues, one of them for the second and, presumably, last time.[56] The Court first held that an employer's interference with the vesting of pension benefits is not a per se ADEA violation, although it could be unlawful under ERISA. Justice Sandra Day O'Connor distinguished between an employer action based on employee age—which would be illegal—and an action based on some other factor—pension status—that empirically correlates with age. Biggins, age 62, was fired just several weeks before becoming vested in Hazen's pension plan.

The Court next held that the standard it articulated for liquidated damages based on a formal, facially discriminatory employment policy also applied to informal polices that were motivated by an employee's age. In revisiting the term "willful violation" which, when present, triggers liquidated (doubled) monetary damages, the Court confirmed that its 1985 *Thurston* interpretation applied to both.[57] Under *Thurston*, a willful violation is one where the employer "knew or showed reckless disregard for the matter of whether its conduct was prohibited by ADEA."[58] Since the *Thurston* ruling, several courts of appeals have declined to award liquidated damages in the absence of formal employment policies, a distinction that *Hazen Paper Co.* dispels.

Another 1993 Supreme Court case with substantial application to ADEA, even though it was decided under Title VII, addresses the burden-of-proof framework for disparate treatment plaintiffs. After three decisions, in 1973, 1981, and 1983, most observers feel that the burden paradigm is clear.[59] To prevail, a plaintiff must first establish a prima facie case, or quantum of evidence, to support further litigation of the claim.

Under the prevailing Title VII approach, this is done by proving protected class status (here, being at least age 40), being qualified for the job (often a matter of contention), undergoing an adverse employment action, and (other than in a RIF situation) being replaced by a younger worker. Age act plaintiffs can either use this paradigm or establish the prima facie case through statistical evidence that older workers as a group were disadvantaged, direct evidence of discrimination, or other types of circumstantial evidence.[60]

Once established, the prima facie case can then be rebutted by the defendant, who must then provide a legitimate, nondiscriminatory explanation of the challenged action. At this point, the plaintiff must be given the opportunity to show, by a preponderance of the evidence, that the employer's stated explanation is untrue. If the plaintiff proves that all the defendant employer's proffered reasons are pretextual, it is generally assumed that the plaintiff is entitled to judgment as a matter of law.

Addressing that final presumption in *St. Mary's Honor Center* v. *Hicks*, a divided Supreme Court held that the plaintiff must not only prove that the defendant's explanations are pretextual but must also prove that the real reason was the intent to discriminate and not simply some other excuse.[61] In dissent, Justice David Souter argued that employers must be bound by their choice of explanation; otherwise, plaintiffs would face an impossible evidentiary burden.[62] ADEA courts routinely apply the Title VII burden standard, and they have already incorporated *Hicks* (referred to as the *pretext plus standard*) into the judicial calculus.

Major Unresolved Areas of Litigation

Disparate Impact Theory. One key issue that could possibly attract Supreme Court review is the applicability of Title VII disparate impact theory to ADEA. Under the theory, a race-neutral (here, age-neutral) employment practice that disparately harms a protected class of workers may be judged illegal unless the employer articulates a legitimate, nondiscriminatory reason for the disparity.

Like Title VII, a majority of ADEA cases involve the disparate treatment of individuals and are distinguished not by the formality or informality of the employment practice but rather by whether the protected characteristic is directly implicated. Disparate impact theory applies when the protected characteristic is not directly implicated but the end result disproportionately affects members of the protected group—in this instance, older workers. Disparate impact evidence often involves statistical analysis of employer decision patterns, usually covering applicants who charge hiring discrimination or former workers who claim to have been discharged due to age.

Many appellate courts have applied disparate impact to ADEA cases, starting with *Geller* in 1980.[63] Nevertheless, Justice Kennedy's concurring opinion in *Hazen Paper Co.* noted that "nothing in the Court's opinion should be read as incorporating in the ADEA context the so-called 'disparate impact' theory of Title VII."[64] Adhering to that view, several Courts of Appeal rejected ADEA impact claims more recently.[65] If the Supreme Court ultimately adopts Justice Anthony Kennedy's view, Congress will be under strong pressure to legislatively nullify that reasoning. In the meantime, disparate impact theory continues to apply, albeit uncertainly, to ADEA.[66]

Waivers. Another important unresolved ADEA issue concerns the validity of waivers under OWBPA, where employees agree to forgo all legal claims against their employer in return for financial incentives to retire. Some courts of appeals have held that employees may sue for age discrimination even though they signed release forms in return for severance pay. Typifying this view, the seventh circuit court held that because the employer had not complied with the OWBPA requirement that employees be given 45 days to consider the waiver agreement, it could not claim that, by signing, the employees had ratified the agreement as a contract.[67]

OWBPA requires all waivers to be "knowing and voluntary," setting certain validating criteria. Key among these are adequate time for employees to evaluate the offer, advice to consult an attorney, and a seven-day cooling-off period during which the waiver may be revoked.[68]

Other courts have divided on the issue of returning the severance pay, setting up possible Supreme Court resolution. The eleventh circuit court is in agreement with the seventh that the employees need not return their severance pay in order to sue.[69] The fifth circuit court, however, holds that no suit is permissible whenever employees keep the exit incentive compensation, thereby ratifying releases that might otherwise be invalid.[70]

After-Acquired Evidence. Another issue unresolved when this chapter was intially drafted has subsequently been resolved by the Supreme Court. This legal issue crossed over from Title VII to affect ADEA litigation, involving the "after-acquired evidence" doctrine. Under this theory, candidates who obtain jobs through falsified resumes are subject to dismissal without liability to the employer whenever the fraud is discovered, even if in the interim that employee is subjected to employment discrimination.[71] Opponents of this doctrine argue that resume fraud does not "offset" discrimination and that plaintiffs are entitled to legal relief for unlawful harms even if they might not otherwise have been hired.

Reflecting disagreement on this issue by several appeals courts, the Supreme Court first agreed in 1992 to review the legality of after-acquired evidence in a Title VII context.[72] The parties then settled, causing the case to be withdrawn from the Supreme Court docket and leaving the underlying legal issue unresolved.[73] Given the courts' growing tendency to merge ADEA and Title VII law into an interchangeable employment discrimination law, this issue again came before the Supreme Court in 1995, this time involving an age claim. The Court held that after-acquired evidence of misconduct is not a complete bar to recovery in an ADEA action. Rather, it affects only the amount of changes an employee may recover, and generally precludes reinstatement or front-pay.[74]

Age-Based Remarks as Evidence of Discrimination. Following Title VII's prohibition of racial slurs, ADEA courts initially treated most employer statements and remarks deprecating older workers as evidence of age bias. Recently, however, in contrast to heightened judicial sensitivity to sexist comments in gender cases, some courts have drawn more benign inferences regarding age-based remarks in the workplace.[75] Thus, observations that older workers "moved in slow motion," or "couldn't 'at your age' pass a physical examination" were not held to infer prejudice toward age.[76]

Similarly, characterizing the rejection of older applicants as "overqualified" may be a pretext for discrimination. Several courts have refused to treat this defense as an adequate basis for summary judgment, and instead left the question to trial by a jury.[77] The employers in these cases argued that more senior workers, forced by economic cutbacks to apply for less desirable positions, would become disgruntled and nonproductive. The courts rejected that view, holding instead that employers cannot presume, without inquiry, that the downgraded higher-level employee would not diligently perform a lesser job rather than be terminated or unemployed.

Other Legislation Affecting Older Worker Employment

Older employees and, in some instances, applicants for employment are protected in the workplace by federal statutes other than ADEA, although the latter applies exclusively if age is the sole basis for the action. If age and other criteria are violated, employees may seek redress for all the employer's discriminatory acts in a single suit. The other statutes include: (1) Title VII of the Civil Rights Act, covering race, color, gender, national origin, and religion, (2) the Equal Pay Act, requiring that women receive the same compensation as men for equal work, (3) the Family and Medical Leave Act (FMLA), and (4) the Americans with Disabilities Act (ADA) of 1990.[78]

The Medical Leave Act establishes standards for employees who need up to 12 weeks of unpaid leave to care for a seriously ill spouse, child, or parent or in connection with the birth, adoption, or placement through foster care of a child, and it requires employers to grant such leave. The ADA prohibits discrimination on the basis of disability and requires the reasonable accommodation of a defined disability. Under this act, persons are defined as disabled who have physical or mental impairments that substantially limit a major life activity and either have record of, or are regarded as having, such an impairment.

CONCLUSION

Age discrimination in the labor market will receive increased attention in the future as the aging labor force confronts the dynamics of the global economy. Dramatic changes in the economic prospects of individual firms will affect older persons along with other workers. Relatively well-paid older workers present a target of opportunity for firms facing the necessary downsizing of their workforces.

As the population projections presented in Chapter 3 suggest, the portion of the labor force covered by the ADEA is already starting to grow. The number of persons reaching usual retirement ages will begin to increase dramatically around 2015. With these demographic trends on the horizon, age discrimination issues will become more salient.

Legal protections against discriminatory treatment are vital to the economic security of older workers. Almost 30 years ago, Congress intended that ADEA would remove barriers and facilitate the hiring of older workers. In practice, however, the statute's main success has been to eliminate most mandatory retirement and provide some RIF protection for incumbent jobholders. It has been less effective as a vehicle to change hiring practices.

Moreover, the law is an expensive and uncertain remedy for most workers, given the ambiguity surrounding many personnel decisions and the costs—monetary and emotional—of pursuing legal action. ADEA as amended provides a framework for the fair treatment of older workers and a set of rules to be followed by employers. A prosperous economy and strong labor markets, however, are clearly the best prerequisites for the well-being of older Americans.

NOTES

1. EEOC carried into FY 1994 a backlog of 19,420 uninvestigated ADEA charges (about one year's worth). The commission estimates a further 25 percent increase by FY 1995 of age discrimination complaints that cannot be addressed immediately.

2. Pension provisions and other incentives for early retirement are discussed elsewhere in the volume and will not be elaborated here. See Lazear (1979) for a discussion, perhaps dated, of the relationship between the structure of pay and mandatory retirement.

3. Pub. L. No. 90–202, 29 USC §§ 621–634 (Supp. IV 1992).

4. Equal Pay Act of 1963, Pub. L. No. 88–38, 29 USC § 206(d) (Supp. IV 1992).

5. Civil Rights Act of 1964, Title VII, Pub. L. No. 88–352, 42 USC § 2000e et seq (Supp. 1993).

6. U.S. Department of Labor (1965).

7. Older Americans Message, 113 Cong. Rec. 34743–44 (1967).

8. See U.S. Senate (1967).

9. 29 USC § 621(b) (Supp. IV 1992). See also Bendick et al. (1993), where 25.6 percent of older job-seekers were treated less favorably than similarly qualified younger applicants in a controlled, matched-pairs study.

10. 29 USC §§ 216(c), 217 (Supp. IV 1992).

11. Reorganization Plan No. 1, 43 Fed. Reg. 19807 (1978), as amended by Pub. L. No. 98–532 (1984). Section 9 of ADEA, 29 USC § 628 (Supp. IV 1992) authorizes EEOC to exempt from ADEA those otherwise covered if it is in the public interest. The secretary of labor initially invoked this provision to exempt union apprenticeship programs, permitting them to set enrollment limits that exclude older workers. EEOC retained this exemption after assuming authority to administer ADEA, codifying it at 29 CFR § 1625.13 (1993).

12. There are only two exceptions. First, the Office of Federal Contract Compliance Programs (OFCCP), a unit of the Department of Labor, monitors federal contractors under Executive Order 11246 and may debar violators from contracts. Second, while EEOC may sue state and local governments under ADEA, Title VII litigation authority against governmental entities was retained in the 1972 amendments by the Justice Department.

13. The ADEA itself permits mandatory retirement of bona fide business executives and policy makers at age 65, and of law enforcement officials, air traffic controllers, and commercial airline pilots as limited by other federal statutes. A parallel exception permitting state and local governments to set retirement age limits for police officers and firefighters expired at the end of 1993, but may, after some delay, be reinstated by Congress.

14. *Passer* v. *American Chemical Society*, 935 F.2d 322 (CADC 1991), held that an employer unlawfully retaliated against a 70-year-old executive's filing of an ADEA charge by canceling a symposium planned to honor him.

15. In *EEOC* v. *Plumbers and Pipefitters Local 350*, 982 F.2d 1305 (CA9 1992), it was ruled that a union policy of barring retired members who receive pension benefits from seeking work through its hiring hall violated ADEA. The court ruled that the union's practice frustrated the act's policy of promoting older worker employment on the basis of ability rather than age.

16. Prior to the changes affecting ADEA in the 1991 Civil Rights Act, suits were required to be brought within two years of the event, or three years if a willful violation was claimed. See *McLaughlin* v. *Richland Shoe Co.*, 486 U.S. 128 (1988).

17. See *EEOC* v. *American & Efird Mills, Inc.*, 964 F.2d 300 (CA4 1992) (EEOC was authorized to investigate the claim even though the employee's own charge was filed too late), and *EEOC* v. *Harris Chernin, Inc.*, 10 F.3d 1286 (CA7 1993) (dismissal

of an employee's action was ruled no bar to a subsequent EEOC suit against the same employer for injunctive relief against further violations).

18. The Supreme Court interpreted this provision, 29 USC 216(b), to permit representatives of a potential class to discover the identity of, and contact similarly situated, persons. See *Hoffman-LaRoche* v. *Sperling*, 493 U.S. 165 (1989).

19. 29 USC §§ 200–219 (Supp. IV 1992).

20. 29 USC § 255a (Supp. IV 1992).

21. National Labor Relations Act, 29 USC §§ 151–169 (Supp. IV 1992).

22. Pub. L. No. 102–166 (1991).

23. On state and local government employment, see Pub. L. No. 93–259 (1974). The Supreme Court ratified extension of ADEA to the states, *EEOC* v. *Wyoming*, 460 U.S. 226 (1983), ruling that the Tenth Amendment does not limit congressional Commerce Clause power to extend coverage to state and local government employment.

24. Pub. L. No. 95–256 (1978).

25. This provision rejected the Supreme Court's decision in *United Air Lines, Inc.* v. *McMann*, 434 U.S. 192 (1977), which permitted the forced retirement of pension-eligible older employees.

26. Originally at least $29,000 per year, that amount was later raised by Congress to at least $44,000 per year.

27. Pub. L. No. 99–592 (1986).

28. H.R. 2722 was approved by the House of Representatives, in November 1993, to continue the exemption covering bona fide hiring and retirement plans for state and local firefighters and law enforcement officers. The proposed legislation also set aside $5 million for EEOC to develop standards to evaluate older employee fitness and guidelines for performance testing. Senate passage and presidential approval in 1994 were initially expected, but failed to materialize. See H. Rep. 103–314 (1993).

29. See Landy (1992). The study found only a small risk that otherwise qualified officers would compromise public safety by experiencing a catastrophic medical event while on duty.

30. Pub. L. No. 98–369, Sec. § 2301(b) (1984).

31. Pub. L. No. 98–459 (1984).

32. In *EEOC* v. *Arabian American Oil Co.*, 499 U.S. 244 (1991), the Supreme Court rejected Title VII claims on behalf of a U.S. citizen employed by an American company in Saudi Arabia, expressly noting that Congress had amended ADEA to provide extraterritorial coverage but had not done so for Title VII.

33. Omnibus Budget Reconciliation Act of 1986, Pub. L. No. 99–272 (1986).

34. Pub. L. No. 99–592 (1986).

35. Pub. L. No. 99–509 (1987).

36. For accrual purposes, the Employee Retirement Income and Security Act (ERISA) defines the "normal" retirement age as 65. See 29 USC § 1002 (Supp. IV 1992).

37. Older Workers Benefit Protection Act, Pub. L. No. 101–433 (1990).

38. 492 U.S. 158 (1989).

39. *Runyan* v. *National Cash Register Corp.*, 787 F.2d 1039 (CA6 1986); *EEOC* v. *Westinghouse Electric Corp.*, 869 F.2d 696 (CA3 1989), *vacated & remanded*, 493 U.S. 801 (1989). More recently, one commentator recommended a ban on all conditional exit incentives, arguing that OWBPA has failed to prevent subtle employer coercion of retirement-eligible older workers. See Harper (1993).

40. 29 CFR § 1625.10 (1993).

41. 29 USC §§ 623(e)(2), (3) (Supp. IV 1992).

42. See, for example, *EEOC* v. *Borden's, Inc.*, 724 F.2d 1390 (CA9 1984), which held that denying severance pay to pension-eligible employees violates the act. See also, *AARP* v. *Farmers Group*, 943 F.2d 996 (CA9 1991), *cert. denied*, 112 S.Ct. 937 (1992), holding that an employer was not required by ERISA to cut off contributions and accruals to profit-sharing and pension plans for persons remaining employed after age 65, nor permitted to design a benefits package so unattractive for employees over age 65 that it would force them to retire at that age, and in both instances had willfully violated ADEA.

43. See Ruhm (Chapter 4); Dorsey and Turner (Chapter 6); Friedman (Chapter 8); Turner and Doescher (Chapter 9); Leonesio (Chapter 12).

44. Pub. L. No. 102–166, § 115 (1991).

45. *Massachusetts Board of Education* v. *Morgia*, 427 U.S. 307 (1976).

46. *Vance* v. *Bradley*, 440 U.S. 93 (1979).

47. *Gregory* v. *Ashcroft*, 501 U.S. 452 (1991).

48. *Crozier* v. *Howard*, 11 F.3d 967 (CA10 1993).

49. *McCann* v. *City of Chicago*, 968 F.2d 635 (CA7 1992).

50. *Thomas* v. *U.S. Postal Inspection Service*, 647 F.2d 1035 (CA10 1981).

51. 434 U.S. 575 (1978).

52. *Lehman* v. *Nakshian*, 453 U.S. 156 (1981).

53. 441 U.S. 750 (1979).

54. 472 U.S. 400 (1985).

55. In a case decided the same day as *Criswell*, the Supreme Court, in *Johnson* v. *Mayor and City Council of Baltimore*, 472 U.S. 353 (1985), also rejected reliance by state and local governments on federal law requiring mandatory retirement of federal government firefighters at age 55 as the basis to establish a BFOQ defense that would have permitted the retirement of analogous local firefighters at age 55.

56. 113 S.Ct. 1701 (1993).

57. *TWA* v. *Thurston*, 469 U.S. 111 (1985).

58. 469 U.S. at 128.

59. *McDonnell-Douglas Corp.* v. *Green*, 411 U.S. 792 (1973); *Texas Dep't. of Community Affairs* v. *Burdine*, 450 U.S. 248 (1981); *USPS Board of Governors* v. *Aiken*, 460 U.S. 711 (1983).

60. Concerning the argument that older workers as a group are disadvantaged, see, for example, *Barnes* v. *GenCorp, Inc.*, 896 F.2d 1457 (CA6 1990), *cert. denied*, 498 U.S. 878 (1990).

61. 113 S.Ct. 2742 (1993).

62. 113 S.Ct. at 2759 (Souter, Justice, dissent).

63. *Geller* v. *Markham*, 635 F.2d 1027 (CA2 1980), *cert. denied*, 451 U.S. 945 (1981). See also *Allison* v. *Western Union Telegraph Co.*, 680 F.2d 1318 (CA11 1982); *Leftwich* v. *Harris-Stowe State College*, 702 F.2d 686 (CA8 1983); *Rose* v. *Wells Fargo & Co., Inc.*, 902 F.2d 1417 (CA9 1990).

64. 113 S.Ct. at 1710 (Kennedy, Justice, concurring). Justice Clarence Thomas and Chief Justice William Rehnquist joined the concurring opinion. Rehnquist had dissented when the Supreme Court refused to review *Geller* in 1981, arguing then that disparate impact theory was inapplicable to ADEA cases.

65. *Ellis* v. *United Airlines*, No. 94–1351 (CAIO 1/4/96); *EEOC* v. *Francis W. Parker School*, 41 F.3d 1073 (CA7 1994), *cert. denied*, 515 U.S. (1995).

66. Both ADEA and Title VII's legislative history are silent on disparate impact the-

ory, which emerged several years later from a Supreme Court decision, *Griggs* v. *Duke Power Co.*, 401 U.S. 424, 429–32 (1971). As a result, arguments rejecting disparate impact theory in ADEA cases due to an absence of supporting legislative history are undermined by the Title VII parallel. See Kaminshine (1990).

67. *Oberg* v. *Allied Van Lines, Inc.*, 11 F.3d 679 (CA7 1993). See also Imbrogno (1993).

68. 29 USC § 626(f)(1) (Supp. IV 1992).

69. *Forbus* v. *Sears, Roebuck & Co.*, 958 F.2d 1036 (CA11 1992), *cert. denied*, 113 S.Ct. 412 (1992).

70. *Grillet* v. *Sears, Roebuck & Co.*, 927 F.2d 217 (CA5 1991); *Wamsley* v. *Champlin Refining & Chemicals, Inc.*, 11 F.3d 534 (CA5 1993).

71. Under this theory, if the employee would not have initially been hired or would have been terminated if the resume fraud became known sooner, the employer is insulated from liability even though evidence of the employee's true qualifications was not revealed prior to the discrimination charge.

72. *Milligan-Jensen* v. *Michigan Technological University*, 975 F.2d 302 (CA6 1992), *cert. granted*, 113 S.Ct. 2991 (1992), *cert. dismissed*, 114 S.Ct. 22 (1993).

73. See *McKennon* v. *Nashville Banner*, 9 F.3d 539 (CA6 1993), holding that after-acquired evidence is a complete bar to any recovery for either resume fraud or employee misconduct during employment, and *O'Driscoll* v. *Hercules, Inc.*, 12 F.3d 176, 180–81 (CA10 1994), ruling that plaintiff misconduct precludes any relief for termination. Other courts bar the claim only where the employee would clearly have been fired for the misconduct once the employer learned of it—see *Washington* v. *Lake County*, 969 F.2d 250 (CA7 1992)—or limit relief only to back pay from the date of the discriminatory event until the employee misconduct is uncovered—see *Wallace* v. *Dunn Construction Co.*, 968 F.2d 1174 (CA11 1992).

74. *McKennon* v. *Nashville Banner Pub. Co.*, 115 S.Ct. 879 (1995).

75. *Cone* v. *Longmont United Hospital Ass'n.*, 14 F.3d 526, 1045 (CA10 1994), a chief executive officer's (CEO's) statement that "long-term employees have a diminishing return" was characterized by the court as a "stray remark" and "not linked to plaintiff's termination."

76. *Young* v. *General Foods Corp.*, 840 F.2d 825 (CA11 1988); *Barnes* v. *Southwest Forest Industries, Inc.*, 814 F.2d 607, 610–11 (CA11 1987).

77. *Taggart* v. *Time, Inc.*, 924 F.2d 43 (CA2 1991); *Binder* v. *Long Island Lighting Co.*, 933 F.2d 187 (CA2 1991).

78. The Family and Medical Leave Act, 29 USC § 2601 et seq (Supp. IV 1992), covers certain employers with 50 or more employees. Americans with Disabilities Act of 1990, 42 USC § 12101 et seq (Supp. 1993): initially covering employers with 25 or more employees, ADA was extended to employers with 15 or more employees as of July 26, 1994.

12

Economic Model of Work–Leisure Choice

Michael V. Leonesio

Since the 1970s there has been a considerable resurgence of interest among economists in the study of older workers' labor supply and retirement issues. Much of the impetus for this research has been generated by public concern about a set of issues surrounding the aging of American society that will occur over the next several decades. These issues include the probable impact of an aging workforce on American productivity and living standards, the continued financial soundness of social security and private pension plans in the face of large increases in the number of retirees, and the changes in the economy and society that will be necessitated by the demands of a larger elderly population (e.g., increased demand for health services, changes in living accommodations).

Empirical research on retirement issues has also been stimulated by the development of databases that provide much of the information needed to explore aging issues. Most prominent among these was the Social Security Administration's Retirement History Study, a 10-year study of approximately 11,000 Americans who were aged 58–63 in 1969. During the 1969–1979 survey period, in which the respondents were interviewed every 2 years, most of the sample members retired, permitting researchers to collect and analyze a large amount of data on the circumstances surrounding the timing of retirement. Much of what is currently understood about the labor supply and retirement behavior of older workers derives from studies based on this very rich database.[1]

The purpose of this chapter is to provide a nontechnical explanation of the basic ideas that underpin economists' thinking about work and retirement decisions, and also to discuss and elaborate on the basic economic model of retirement. The plan of the chapter is to begin with a simple economic model of an individual's work decision, to explain the construction and logic of this model, and to show how the model can be used to make predictions about factors that might plausibly affect the timing of retirement. From this starting point—which essentially describes the economic retirement models before the late 1970s—the chapter then explains how the model has been extended during the past two decades. The increasing sophistication and complexity of the models reflect scientific progress in which new retirement research incorporates the findings of previous efforts, the desire to incorporate more realism into the models, and the availability of improved data. The progress in economic modeling is emphasized as the contributions of various influential studies are reviewed.

THE ECONOMICS OF TIME USE

Conventional, or neoclassical, economics assumes that individuals make choices that maximize self-perceived well-being in light of available opportunities. That is, the supposition is that, given their circumstances, individuals attempt to do as well for themselves as possible. Of course, other social sciences such as psychology or sociology are also concerned with how individuals make such decisions. The distinguishing feature of the economic perspective is an emphasis on how options are nearly always limited by the availability of key resources—such as money or time. Economics focuses on how, in the face of limited resources, choices can be made efficiently to ensure that individuals achieve their highest attainable level of well-being. This very general formulation of the nature of economic decisions opens a wide range of behavior to economic analysis—for example, consumption, work, play, saving, household formation, educational attainment, altruism, thievery, and retirement. Economic theory also can readily account for the typical variation in the specific choices made by different individuals in that allowance is made for differing tastes and preferences among individuals. Contrary to some popular misconceptions, economics does not claim that people are primarily money oriented or that their behavior is narrowly self-interested. In fact, it is perfectly consistent with economic thinking for individuals to give money to causes they deem worthy, to work at low-paying but satisfying jobs in lieu of higher paid, albeit disagreeable, employment, or to forgo a lucrative earnings opportunity to enjoy a leisure pursuit.

One important set of economic decisions involves how people allocate their time among alternative uses. Decisions about work, retirement, leisure, and so forth are all part of the general problem of deciding how to use time. For any particular person, the answer to this question depends on many factors, which include tastes and preferences for particular uses of time (e.g., what activities are enjoyable?), employment opportunities, financial needs, health, and so on. In the face of many alternative uses of time, the individual chooses which activities to pursue and how much time to devote to each. The solution to this problem emphasizes the true economic cost of pursuing any specific action, not merely out-of-pocket expenses. Assessing the economic cost entails identifying what opportunities are forgone when a particular course of action is followed, and then assigning values to these alternatives. The economic cost of an activity is the value that can be assessed to the *best* alternative that must be forgone. For example, if a person chooses to play tennis for an hour rather than read a book during the same interval, the "cost" of an hour of tennis is the value he or she places on the pleasure that would be derived from an hour of reading.

The Basic Model of Work–Leisure Choice

The most fundamental time-allocation decision in economics is the decision whether to work, which is the central question addressed by the *theory of work–leisure choice*. In its simplest form, the decision concerns how an individual can best allocate total available time (T) between two competing uses, the amount of time given to market work (H) and the amount of time devoted to leisure (L). That is, $T = H + L$.[2] Further assume, for simplicity's sake, that the person's level of satisfaction or well-being (called *utility* by economists) depends solely on the consumption of goods (X), a unit of which can always be purchased at price P in the marketplace, plus the amount of leisure that is enjoyed.[3] If income can always be earned at a wage rate of w dollars per hour worked, then the total income available to the individual during time interval T consists of total earnings (wH) plus any nonwage income (V). The individual's attainable well-being is, therefore, limited by the restriction that $XP \leq w(T - L) + V$, which is referred to as the *budget constraint*, an expression that summarizes the relationship between time and income. Given the wage rate, the amount of money that can be spent on X could vary from a minimum of V (i.e., no hours are worked) to a maximum of $wT + V$, the situation in which no leisure is consumed. The cost of an hour of leisure is always w, the amount of forgone earnings.

In this simple model, the individual's decision amounts to choosing how much time to work. In addition to the budget constraint, the answer depends on the person's tastes and preferences for leisure and consumption goods.[4] The solution to the problem is given by the worker's *labor supply function*, $H = H(P, w, V)$, which states mathematically that the number of hours worked depends on the price of consumption goods, the wage rate, and the amount of nonwage income available.[5] Because many people choose not to work, the case where $H = 0$ is so prevalent that the labor supply decision is often thought of as comprising two closely related stages. In the first stage—called the *labor force participation decision*—the question concerns whether to work at all. The decision is made by comparing the real wage rate (w/P) offered by a prospective employer with the subjective value (w^*) that the individual places on an hour of leisure.[6] If the real wage rate exceeds the value of an hour of leisure, then well-being is improved through labor force participation and $H > 0$. For many individuals, however, the real wage offered by an employer provides an insufficient incentive to work and the person opts out of the labor force. Conditional on a decision to work, the second-stage decision—called the *hours of work decision*—concerns how many hours to work. The optimum is found by selecting the number of hours for which the subjective value of an additional hour of leisure, w^*, exactly equals the real wage rate.[7]

A typical analysis of labor supply concerns how the individual's hours of work would be likely to change in response to changes in financial circumstances and, in particular, to changes in the wage rate or income. Economic theory suggests that the effect of an increase in the wage rate on the probability of labor force participation is positive (a higher wage increases the likelihood of working), but that the effect on hours of work for someone who already works is unclear. The latter ambiguity arises because there are two opposing incentives to consider. First, a higher wage rate effectively raises the cost of consuming an hour of leisure, namely, more income is sacrificed when an hour is not worked. This effect—called the *substitution effect*—provides an incentive to work more and consume less leisure.[8] Second, at the new, higher wage, the original number of hours of work yields a higher income that would enable the individual to afford more consumption and leisure. Thus, the higher income could finance a reduction in hours of work through the *income effect*. In the end, whether the labor supply of workers undergoes a net increase or decrease depends on which of these two opposing incentives dominates—a question that can only be answered empirically. Finally, if the wage rate is unchanged, increases in nonwage income should both reduce the probability of participating in the labor market (i.e., w^* increases) and reduce hours of work through an income effect.

These ideas constitute the essential features of the economic theory of work–leisure choice, which serves as the basis for most labor supply research, and considerable supportive evidence has been found.[9] In the actual empirical analysis of work behavior, economists try to determine through statistical procedures specific labor supply functions that best explain the work patterns found in the economy. A statistical labor supply function can be formulated by introducing a stochastic (i.e., random) element ε into the hours-of-work equation. A rudimentary statistical labor supply function can thus be written as:

$$H = H(P, w, V, Z, \varepsilon) \tag{1}$$

where Z represents a set of individual characteristics that plausibly affect the decision to work (e.g., age, health, marital status).[10] The inclusion of the random term ε explicitly recognizes that statistical labor supply models are inherently imprecise and can at best only approximate the actual decisions made by workers, especially given the limitations imposed by available data.

The statistical model described by Equation (1) can be extended in numerous ways. Successful extensions include the inclusion of more alternative uses of time into decisions about time allocation; the consideration of individual choice within models of household or family behavior; the integration of saving, borrowing, taxes, and transfer payments in budget constraints; and the development of life-cycle models that incorporate multiperiod planning. These refinements augment the basic theory by incorporating more realistic features of economic life while leaving intact the essential characteristics of the simplest model.

Older Workers and Life-Cycle Models

The most basic retirement models are straightforward applications of the single-period, work–leisure choice model described by Equation (1). An older person might be categorized as "retired" if he or she chooses not to work during some specified time interval—typically the reference period used in the survey that generated the research data.[11] Retirement models share many of the properties and characteristics of labor supply models for younger workers, but they generally have two distinguishing features. First, social security and private pension plans are institutional features that play unique and important roles in the labor market decisions of older workers, and retirement models usually incorporate the relevant details. Second, the models for older workers are more likely to be cast in a life-cycle framework than are many of the labor supply models for younger, prime-aged workers. This orientation reflects the fact that workers tend to plan their eventual withdrawal from the labor force over many years. The act of retirement is, therefore, sensibly evaluated in the context of a plan that allocates time between work and leisure over the remaining lifetime.

In a life-cycle model of labor supply, the individual formulates a long-term plan for work and consumption that maximizes well-being over the expected lifetime. The remaining lifespan can be thought of as a sequence of N subperiods of equal finite length (e.g., a year, month, week, or generally, T). A *life-cycle utility function* can be written as:

$$U = U(X_1, L_1, X_2, L_2, \ldots, X_N, L_N, \rho, Z) \tag{2}$$

where utility (U) depends on the amounts of consumption (X_1) and leisure (L_1) enjoyed in each period, on the individual's *rate of time preference* (ρ), and on Z, a vector of relevant personal characteristics such as tastes and preferences, gender, marital status, and health. The rate of time preference denotes the extent to which an individual prefers consumption and leisure now rather than in the future. A person with a high rate of time preference values the immediate enjoyment of a unit of consumption or leisure much more highly than his or her prospective enjoyment at some future date, while at the extreme of someone with no time preference ($\rho = 0$), the individual is indifferent about the timing of consumption or leisure (i.e., it makes no difference whether it occurs today or sometime in the future).[12]

Current and future consumption can be financed through various income sources including earnings, savings, pensions, social security benefits, and other public and private transfers. The individual's objective is to plan a sequence of consumption and work activity from now (i.e., $t = 0$) through period N that maximizes Equation (2) subject to a *life-cycle budget constraint* of the form:

$$\sum_{t=0}^{N} (1 + r)^{-t}P_tX_t \leq A_0 + \sum_{t=0}^{N} (1 + r)^{-t}[w_t(T - L_t) + TR_t - TX_t + PENS_t + SS_t] \quad (3)$$

where the new variables defined are assets held at the beginning of the first period (A_0), transfer payments (TR_t), taxes (TX_t), private pension income ($PENS_t$), and social security benefits (SS_t). The lifetime budget constraint simply says that the present value of remaining lifetime consumption cannot exceed the current value of assets plus the present value of all anticipated net income (earnings plus transfer payments less taxes plus pension income plus social security benefits). The rate of interest (r) is used to convert all future income flows to present values.[13] If the equality holds for Equation (3), the individual consumes all assets and lifetime income; otherwise, unspent resources represent a bequest to heirs. The utility-maximizing desired amount of work (H_t) in each period is given by the solution to this problem and can be generally stated as:

$$\begin{aligned}
H_t = T &- L_t, (P_1, P_2, \ldots, P_N, w_1, w_2, \ldots, w_N, A_0, \\
&TR_1, TR_2, \ldots, TR_N, TX_1, TX_2, \ldots, TX_N, \\
&PENS_1, PENS_2, \ldots, PENS_N, SS_1, SS_2, \ldots, \\
&SS_N, \rho, r, Z) \ t = 1, 2, \ldots, N
\end{aligned} \quad (4)$$

The empirical work on the work and retirement decisions of older workers essentially consists of determining from data the variants of Equation (4) that best explain the behavior that has been documented in specific data sets.[14]

Several features of this model should be noted. First, the estimation and empirical testing of a life-cycle model of this type require a large number of additional assumptions. A specific functional form must be selected to represent Equation (4), a choice that implicitly dictates the properties of the underlying utility function (2), which describes tastes and preferences.[15] In fact, to make the problem tractable both mathematically and statistically, numerous explicit assumptions about the nature of tastes and preferences are usually made.[16] Second, the apparent simplicity of the lifetime budget constraint (3) presented here brushes aside the real-world complexity of income flows and interactions among flows. The rules that determine current and future income from various sources must be precisely specified in order to calculate the net incentives to work during each period. To cite several examples, the amount of earnings in one period can affect the value of social security benefits and private pension income received in another period, integrated private pension plans dictate that pension payments depend on the amount of social security benefits received, and both taxes paid and government transfers received depend on the level of earnings. When all tax and transfer programs are taken into account, individual budget constraints are exceedingly complicated. Third, the model as presented thus far implicitly assumes that the future is always known with certainty. In reality, all planning occurs in an uncertain environment that requires considerable personal forecasting skill. In formulating long-range plans, individuals confront uncertainties such as their own life expectancy, future health status, and the security of various sources of future income. Fourth, in order to simplify the analysis, this life-cycle model takes as given (i.e., includes as conditioning elements in the Z vector) the results of other personal decisions that are co-determined with lifelong work and consumption paths. Some of these items are marital status, family size and composition, education and training levels, and occupational choice.

Fifth, there are various methods by which a constrained optimization problem of this type can be solved mathematically, and the choice of solution technique depends on the details of how the problem is formally structured, which itself depends on how the model presupposes that the decision is made. For example, if the model assumes that future income streams under various desired work scenarios are known and that there is no uncertainty with regard to health and mortality, there is no need for any replanning to occur during the life cycle. In such a case, the utility-maximizing work and consumption plans can be generated as the solutions to an optimal control problem in which the individual knows the complete solution at the start of the first period and then simply executes the plan as time passes. Alternatively, if uncertainty is permitted, the model might allow for replanning in which the individual revises or updates work and consumption plans for the expected remaining lifetime as more information becomes available.

Finally, economic research attempts to verify the theoretically predicted nature of the determinants of retirement and, where possible, to measure the effects of the various retirement influences. This process requires detailed information on the various factors that influence retirement decisions. No actual database contains all the relevant information, and these shortcomings necessitate that empirical implementations omit some features of the theoretical models. Furthermore, some causal factors are notoriously difficult to measure accurately (e.g., health status), while others are both unobservable and difficult to gauge (e.g., motivation). Although all empirical studies involve compromises between theory and data, conclusions that are repeatedly verified with different models and different data sources attain higher levels of credibility among retirement experts.

ECONOMIC RETIREMENT MODELS IN PRACTICE

This section reviews the development of economic retirement models over the past two decades. It is by no means intended to be an exhaustive survey. Rather, the idea is to sketch the development of economists' views about retirement by examining some of the most influential research.[17] The central theme is how increasingly sophisticated implementations of the work–leisure choice framework have been used to explain observed retirement patterns and trends. As the models and statistical procedures have evolved, three explanatory factors have received particular scrutiny: the social security program, private pension plans, and health.

Early Models

Nearly all the early modern retirement studies (circa the late 1970s) consisted of efforts to determine whether retirement trends for American male workers could be explained by single-period work–leisure models. Up to that point, retirement was often regarded as involuntary; it was commonly thought that workers retired either because of health problems or when their employers terminated their employment.[18] The modern research introduced a decidedly different view in which retirement decisions were characterized as largely *voluntary*. The idea was that as a worker aged, eventually the subjective value of leisure might exceed the rate of compensation offered by his or her employer and the individual would decide to withdraw from the labor force. Note that this circumstance could arise either due to an increase in the subjective value placed on leisure or a decrease in the rate of compensation—or some combination of the two.

In one of the earliest of the modern studies, Boskin (1977) sought to explain the long-term decline in the labor force participation of virtually all male age groups. In 1948, for example, the labor force participation rates for white and nonwhite males aged 65 and older were 46.5 and 50.3 percent, respectively; by 1974 these had fallen to 22.5 and 21.7 percent, respectively. The study's central hypothesis was that rising income levels were associated with voluntary reductions in work (through the income effect). In particular, the expansion of the social security retirement program during the post–World War II period might have prompted the decline in labor force participation among men over the age of 65. This idea led to the development of a statistical retirement model in which the value of annual social security benefits for which a retiree was eligible is a key explanatory factor.[19] Boskin's model also included measures of before- and after-tax wages, nonwage income, and indicators of bad health, compulsory retirement, and presence of both a wife and children.

Boskin found that the value of current annual social security retirement benefits had a pronounced effect on the decision to retire (defined as working less than quarter time). A $1,000 increase in annual benefits was associated with an increase in the probability of retiring from .075 to .16, implying that the expected number of years of work between ages 61 and 70 falls by slightly more than a year. The effect of a $1 increase in social security benefit amounts is seven times as large as the effect of a like increase in income from assets. Other statistically significant factors included the level of net earnings, which had a strong negative effect on the probability of retirement, and especially the simple

attainment of age 65. The results indicate that this "age 65" effect had a powerful influence on the propensity to retire—an effect that was very much more
powerful than the effects of the social security program's apparent monetary
incentives. This finding is consistent with the views that social security might
have established age 65 as a social norm for retirement and that the tastes of
older workers shift toward leisure and away from work.

Boskin's research was one of the first attempts to consider the retirement
decision as a matter of individual choice. His results demonstrated that retirement behavior is amenable to analysis using a relatively simple form of the
work–leisure choice model. Particularly noteworthy is the strong role found for
social security in this model—a result that has not been well supported in subsequent research.[20] Note, however, that his model dictates that any work and
retirement incentives associated with social security are allowed to influence
work decisions only through the current-period income effect associated with
annual benefits received. The actual structure of the social security program and
its rules for benefit computation are not taken into account, nor is the structure
of private pension plans for covered workers. The potential influence of private
pensions in the retirement decision is limited to counting pension income as one
component of total nonwage income for individuals already receiving benefits.
Although Boskin's empirical model was influential, it is decidedly inferior to
the richer structure of more recent applied work.

Pellechio (1978) also examined how social security affects the retirement
behavior of married men aged 60–70 using a labor force participation model.[21]
In Pellechio's model, an individual will work if the wage offer exceeds the
subjective value placed on an hour of leisure when no market work is performed.
Social security wealth (SSW) is hypothesized to affect the subjective value of
time; that is, larger amounts of wealth are thought to increase the value placed
on a unit of leisure time.[22] Separate models are estimated for the 60–61, 62–64,
and 65–70 age groups. The SSW variable is statistically insignificant for the
60–61 group but has significant negative effects on participation for individuals
aged 62–70. When SSW increases from $35,000 to $55,000, the probability that
a married man aged 62–64 will withdraw from the labor market increases by
.15 (from .41 to .56). For persons aged 65–70, the predicted probability of
retirement increases by .22 (from .78 to virtual certainty). Although this research
also presents evidence of social security's influence on older men's work decisions, the reliability of these results are suspect due to the lack of information
on health status and private pensions.

Parsons (1980) also attempted to explain the declining male labor force participation rates during the post–World War II era through the increased availability of income for nonworking men. Like Boskin, Parsons thought that the
primary cause of the downward trend was the increased availability of nonlabor
income. The Parsons model is predicated on the view that declining labor force
participation rates for U.S. males aged 55–64 are likely to be caused by a substitution of women's market work for men's labor force participation within

families and by a large expansion of welfare programs that provide substantial nonlabor income. In contrast to Boskin and Pellechio, Parsons focused his efforts on the social security disability program.[23]

Parsons's (1980) research found that nonworking men in this age group tended to have low earnings potential, as indicated by their low levels of education. Their families did not appear to have large amounts of pension, rent, dividend, or interest income, the usual sources of retirement income (i.e., 13 percent of total family income for whites, 6 percent for blacks). Thus, the decline in labor force participation was not primarily an increase in early retirement prompted by accumulated savings and assets. In contrast, welfare programs account for 33 and 59 percent, respectively, of total income for white and black families. Because most general welfare programs disallow aid to households headed by men who are capable of working, disability programs account for the bulk of the transfer income to these families (29 and 48 percent of family income for whites and blacks, respectively).

The determinants of labor force participation in 1969 were estimated using financial variables, age, and a mortality index as explanatory variables (Parsons, 1980). The key hypothesized explanatory factors were (1) the ratio of potential monthly social security disability benefits to monthly wages, (2) an index of local welfare generosity normalized by the monthly wage, (3) the fraction of the year unemployed in 1966, (4) the interaction of factor (1) with a mortality index, and (5) the interaction of factor (2) with a mortality index. All these factors, and especially the two interaction terms, were found to be significant predictors, suggesting that persons with health problems are especially sensitive to the availability of sources of income support that permit withdrawal from the labor market. Parsons concluded that the falling labor force participation rate for older men was explained largely by the increased generosity of welfare transfers, especially social security disability payments. Low-wage workers were particularly affected. These conclusions have been subsequently disputed by Haveman and Wolfe (1984).

Of course, health status and financial incentives are probably only part of any comprehensive explanation of declining labor force participation among older men. Older workers' labor supply decisions are also likely to be influenced by the nature and requirements of available jobs, factors examined in research by Joseph Quinn. Quinn (1977) investigated the relative impact of three sets of factors in explaining older men's labor force participation decisions: (1) personal and financial characteristics, (2) local labor market conditions, and (3) job attributes.[24] Quinn's labor force participation model also included measures of health status, indicators of current eligibility for social security and private pension benefits, both the husband's and wife's hourly wage rates, the amount of asset income (from rents, interest, and dividends), the presence of dependents, the local unemployment rate, the most recent annual rate of local employment growth, and indicators of three job characteristics (low job autonomy, physical or mental strain, and bad physical working conditions). Quinn found that the health variable was the single most influential determinant, lowering the probability of participating by .2 (from a mean of .9). Eligibility for social security and pension benefits made work less likely, as did higher income from assets. A significant contribution of Quinn's study was the finding that the influence of financial incentives varies by health status. The effect of social security is eight times as large for those with poor health; private pension and asset income effects are three times as large. Both health and the availability of financial support are important influences in the early retirement decision, but persons in poor health are more likely to respond to financial incentives to retire—a finding consistent with Parson's conclusion regarding disability benefits.

Quinn (1978) further explored the importance of the nonmonetary nature of the job in men's decisions to retire early (i.e., before age 65).[25] Again, the central idea was that, other things equal, people tend to retire earlier from jobs with undesirable attributes. The seven job characteristics used in this analysis were: whether the worker was engaged in the whole production activity, repetitiveness of tasks, specificity of instructions for completing tasks, stress, strength, the physical nature of work, and the existence of bad working conditions. The first of these is a favorable characteristic; the last six are undesirable. There was clear support for the view that people with bad jobs are more likely to retire. Similar analysis for groups of men categorized by health status revealed that those with bad health were more sensitive to characteristics of bad jobs. Persons with poor health, and especially those who were eligible for social security retirement benefits, were consistently more sensitive to job characteristics.

Nearly all the early retirement research addressed the behavior of men. Hanoch and Honig (1983), however, conducted a study of the determinants of labor supply behavior of unmarried women as well as older married men, aged 58–69 in 1969–1975.[26] The determinants of labor force participation for married men and unmarried women were found to be remarkably similar. Age and health limitations had substantial negative effects on the probability of working. The social security primary insurance amount (PIA) value had a negative effect, particularly for women, and the effects of this income source were larger than for other nonwage income.[27] Other variables such as education, private pension coverage, and time trend had statistically significant predicted influences. Hanoch and Honig found that once the decision whether to participate in the labor force was made, wage opportunities had surprisingly modest effects on the number of hours worked.[28] Social security PIA values had no statistically significant effect on the hours worked for either gender. Hanoch and Honig concluded that economic variables explain surprisingly little of the labor supply decision of older men and older unmarried women. Instead, age, perhaps through sociological and biological factors, appeared to be the single most important determinant of work activity.

In the Retirement History Study (1969–1979) data, over half of all men eligible for social security retirement benefits retired before the social security normal retirement age of 65. In contrast to previous researchers, who had treated the retirement decision as a single-period choice problem, Burkhauser (1980) implemented a more explicit life-cycle approach in estimating a model of early retirement (the acceptance of social security benefits at age 62). Burkhauser speculated that workers determined the present value of social security benefits and forgone market earnings associated with retirement at age 62, and then considered how the present value of private pensions and social security benefits would change if retirement was postponed.

In the statistical model, Burkhauser hypothesized that early retirement is positively related to the asset value of social security entitlements and the probability of an early private pension; it is negatively related to market earnings, later private pension eligibility, education, and marriage.[29] Evaluated at the mean values of the model's explanatory variables, a 10 percent increase in the asset value of social security increases the probability of retirement at age 62 by .03 (from .21). Unfortunately, there was no information on health status available in Burkhauser's data set, so the statistical model lacks any health indicator. Other research, such as that by Quinn (1977) and Boskin and Hurd (1978), suggests that this is a serious omission in a model of the early retirement decision. Nonetheless, these results are consistent with a life-cycle theory of work–leisure choice, and they imply that social security induces early retirement.

Gordon and Blinder (1980) were also among the first researchers to examine retirement decisions within the work–leisure framework. The main contribution of their research was to estimate a *structural* retirement model. Previous empirical studies of retirement had estimated *reduced-form* equations for labor force participation or for the act of retiring (variously defined). In the reduced-form approach, economic theory suggests which explanatory factors are likely to influence labor supply or retirement and might also provide some indication about the type and form of statistical model to select. The resulting statistical model essentially confirms and measures the influence of the explanatory factors thought to be associated with the outcome. The reduced-form model is usually neither directly nor uniquely linked to the researcher's theoretical model.[30] In fact, it is often consistent with various similar, yet distinct, underlying theoretical specifications. An estimated reduced-form model can be subsequently used to explain or predict changes in outcomes that are likely to be associated with hypothetical changes in the specific explanatory factors included in the model. A limitation of this approach is that the impact of factors not explicitly included in the reduced-form model can be estimated only if the omitted factors can be believed to affect behavior in a manner equivalent to some included factor, in which case the equivalent influence is calculated. Thus, it is usually difficult, if not impossible, to use estimated reduced-form models to predict the consequences of altering many specific features of private pension programs or social security that, nonetheless, would plausibly influence behavior.[31]

The defining nature of a structural model is that the underlying preferences believed to have generated the observed behavior are specified and estimated. The advantage of the structural modeling approach is that once a mathematical representation of preferences has been determined, it is then possible to predict the response to a considerably larger variety of changes in the individual's opportunities than in the case of reduced-form models. That is, once individual preferences (i.e., the utility function) are known, it is possible to predict how behavior will respond to changed opportunities.[32] It is only through developing increasingly detailed and realistic structural models that one can determine the influence of plausible factors such as the specific features of the social security system, the structure of private pension plans, and so forth. The Gordon-Blinder (1980) model demonstrated how a structural modeling approach could be used to understand retirement behavior.

Gordon and Blinder's (1980) model integrates the effects of health, declining wage offers as workers age, social security benefits to retired workers, private pensions, and changing preferences on the retirement decision using a labor force participation framework with two structural equations: a marginal rate of substitution function and a market wage equation.[33] Preferences, as represented by a utility function, were hypothesized to shift in favor of leisure as the person ages, generating an explicit marginal rate of substitution function that depends on age, health, social security wealth (as a ratio to full income,)[34] pension availability, blue-collar work status, education, an indicator of birth cohort, and the present value of lifetime potential earnings.[35] The market wage equation contained measures of experience, job tenure, occupational group (broadly defined), age, health, education, a pension coverage indicator, and an indicator of birth cohort. Market wage offers were expressed (in logarithmic form) as hourly wage rates in terms of 1969 dollars. The work–retirement decision hinges on whether the market wage exceeds the value placed on an hour of leisure (given by the marginal rate of substitution function) when there is no labor force participation. Note that many of the plausible explanatory variables affect the decision to retire through both structural relationships.

The results indicated that pensions play a substantial role in workers' hourly compensation offers; each dollar that an employer contributes to an employee's pension plan was estimated to be equivalent to approximately \$.52 in direct monetary compensation. Real wages were observed to decline with age, with poor health having a large negative impact on wage offers. Social security wealth had no discernible impact on retirement prior to age 62, and afterward it had a statistically significant, but small, effect. Age apparently played an important role in the retirement decision by simultaneously lowering market wage offers and increasing the value placed on leisure. Private pensions appeared to provide strong incentives to retire at the onset of eligibility; the social security effects were very much weaker and were judged not to have contributed significantly to the trend toward earlier retirement.

In its early estimation of a structural life-cycle model of the retirement decision, the Gordon and Blinder (1980) article was an influential contribution in the evolution of the retirement literature, even though subsequent research has raised concerns about the reliability of the specific findings. The decision to retire at a given age should probably be cast in terms of the relative rewards to another year of work. The Gordon-Blinder model uses net present values of income streams as explanatory variables in a current-period, labor force participation model, a formulation that weakens the life-cycle nature of the retirement decision. It would be preferable to include the *change* in the present value of income streams associated with working another year.

Retirement research in the 1970s and early 1980s was not limited to the United States. Zabalza, Pissarides, and Barton (1980) investigated the determinants of retirement decisions in Great Britain in the late 1970s, confirming that the work–leisure model could explain retirement patterns outside the United States.[36] Similar in approach to U.S.-based research, Zabalza and colleagues modeled labor force participation as a function of income and personal characteristics. The individual's net income position—inclusive of taxes, pensions, and social security payments—was calculated for each of three possible levels of work: full-time work, part-time work, and complete retirement. Personal characteristics included in the model were health status, age, an indicator of whether a person was old enough to receive social security payments, indicators of a "waiting wife," marital status, a working spouse, and the involuntary loss of the main job.[37] Women were found to be more responsive to financial incentives than men. Old age and poor health were strong indicators of retirement. There was also evidence of a discrete shift in preferences for leisure at the normal retirement age for both sexes.

More Recent Research

As the study of older workers' labor supply has proceeded, models have become increasingly dynamic and structural. The early models were usually *static*—in contrast to *dynamic*—in the sense that labor force status was determined by a set of causal factors but there was no allowance within the model for how either the causal factors or the outcome might change over time. In contrast, *dynamic models* explain the timing of a change in labor force status. These types of models usually allow at least some of the model's explanatory factors to change as time passes, and the sequencing and timing of events is held to be critical to the behavior being investigated. Retirement is naturally considered within a dynamic model, where the focus is on the timing of a change in labor market status rather than simply on work status during some reference period.

As shown in the Gordon and Blinder (1980) study and subsequent research, structural models offer the advantage that they can potentially incorporate much of the detail of individuals' life-cycle budget constraints. These types of models allow economists to measure the specific effects of numerous features of social security and pension plans rather than restricting their financial incentives to operate through one or two summary measures, such as a monthly benefit amount or a coverage indicator. In the end, the main obstacle to the structural approach is the extent to which relevant information is included in the database used to support the investigation.

To illustrate with a specific problem, the early research on the effects of social security on retirement decisions tended to use simple program measures such as benefits amounts or social security wealth to ascertain the effect of the program. In fact, a complex program such as social security generates a complicated pattern of substitution and income effects through various program features that affect the individual at different ages (e.g., payroll taxes, the retirement test, the delayed retirement credit), and the net effect on work incentives over the life cycle is often theoretically ambiguous and only possible to determine through careful empirical investigation.

To elaborate further, consider the complicated way in which social security can influence work and retirement decisions over the life cycle. For those workers who will be fully insured by the time of retirement age, the potential monthly benefit amount can influence the timing of retirement in several ways. Other things being equal, the income effect of increased benefit levels would be expected to promote earlier retirement dates, decrease the likelihood of working among retirees, and reduce hours of work by labor force participants.[38] Note, though, that the age at which benefits are first received itself affects the monthly benefit amount via three separate channels. First, at any time between the ages of 62 and 70, the monthly benefit rises when benefit receipt is postponed. Between the ages of 62 and 64, early retirement is penalized by reducing the monthly benefit amount by ⅝ of 1 percent for each month the person is under the age of 65. The delayed retirement credit (DRC) increases monthly benefits when benefit receipt is postponed between ages 65 and 70. Second, as long as annual earnings are greater than the smallest value included in the computation years for determining average indexed monthly earnings (AIME), postponing retirement will increase the primary insurance amount (PIA).[39] Third, for some individuals, a delay in retirement can result in him or her accumulating the minimum number of quarters of covered employment to qualify for retirement benefits.

In all three instances, the delay in retirement increases the monthly benefit amounts which, other things held equal, will lower the probability of labor force participation. Therefore, there is a two-way relationship between work and benefit amount; each affects the other. In addition to benefit amounts, two other features of the social security system might influence work decisions. The payroll tax decreases the marginal after-tax wage rate for covered workers with annual earnings less than the taxable maximum.[40] Because the resulting work incentives associated with the income and substitution effects work in opposite directions, the net effect of the payroll tax is theoretically ambiguous. For those workers with annual earnings above the taxable maximum, the marginal net wage is not altered and the tax produces an income effect that encourages work; that is, the payroll taxes paid on the earnings below the taxable maximum reduce disposable income and lower the capacity to afford leisure. Finally, the earnings test for beneficiaries aged 62–69 operates similarly to a tax on earnings when workers earn more than the annual earnings limit.[41] As long as some benefits are received, the earnings test reduces the marginal net wage and produces both income and price effects with opposing effects on work incentives. When all benefits are lost because of the test, the loss of income should stimulate work effort through a pure income effect. In sum, this type of complexity can be addressed only with a structural retirement model. The Retirement History Study, with its inclusion of administrative data on survey respondents provided by the Social Security Administration, provides much of the detail required for a thorough examination of social security program incentives. This feature of the database probably accounts for its continued use by retirement researchers despite the fact that most of the data were collected two decades ago.

In order to examine the financial incentives of social security and private pensions, Fields and Mitchell (1984) developed a structural life-cycle retirement model that examined how monetary incentives affect the age of retirement (defined as leaving the principal employer and accepting a pension). They used two complementary databases, the Retirement History Study—a source with good information about social security benefits but little information about pensions—and the U.S. Department of Labor's 1978 Benefit Amounts Survey—a source with excellent pension data but little information about social security benefits. Their model assumes that individuals maximize lifetime utility by selecting a consumption path and retirement age subject to a lifetime income constraint. This constraint has as its main components (1) the expected level of earnings at each age and (2) streams of anticipated private pension and social security benefits contingent on retirement at each age. In choosing a retirement age, individuals weigh the monetary advantage to be gained by postponing retirement another year against the value of forgone retirement leisure.

Fields and Mitchell (1984) constructed lifetime budget constraints for the individuals in their database.[42] The critical explanatory factors were the present value of total expected income if retirement occurs at age 60 (YBASE), and the change in present value of expected income if retirement were postponed until age 65 or age 68 (YSLOPE65 and YSLOPE68, respectively). Components of YBASE, YSLOPE65, and YSLOPE68 were included as separate explanatory factors in several variants of the model. The results show that people with greater base period wealth retire earlier, and that the greater the monetary gain to delaying retirement, the later the retirement age, other things being equal. The size of the effects of monetary incentives on the timing of retirement, while in accord with theoretical predictions, are modest. For example, in one variant of the model, a $1,000 increase in the present value of income from delaying retirement is associated with a .03 to .05 year increase in age of retirement; a 10 percent increase in retirement benefits lowers the retirement age by about 1 month, on average. Results were robust across specifications. Note that an important feature of the Fields-Mitchell model is that it assumes that all changes in income streams, including social security, are fully anticipated by workers.

Gustman and Steinmeier (1985, 1986) also estimated a structural life-cycle model of retirement in which preferences for either income or leisure gradually shift in favor of leisure as individuals age. An important novelty offered in their work is an explicit treatment of the empirically important phenomenon of partial retirement, whereby some workers work part time at reduced wage rates between full-time career work and complete retirement.[43] The empirical model assumes that individuals develop optimal work plans over the period from age 25 to 85.[44] The model allows preferences to vary both across individuals and over time with age and health and by cohort. The pension component of compensation is the estimated change in present value associated with working an additional year; the value of social security is the change in accrued value from working an additional year. The individual chooses a lifetime path of leisure consumption in which the person works full time, is partially retired, or is completely retired during each period.

The results indicate that the effect of age on preferences appears to be the dominant influence on the retirement decision, although preferences for leisure exhibit a high degree of variation across individuals. In a number of simulations, social security and private pension provisions accounted for the peaks in the distribution of retirement ages at 62 and 65. Because of the detailed structure of their model, Gustman and Steinmeier (1985, 1986) were also able to simulate the effects of changes in specific features of the social security program. For example, increasing the retirement age to 67 and increasing the delayed retirement credit to 8 percent reduced the propensity to retire at 65 and increased the number of people working full time at ages 65 and 66. Lowering the retirement test penalty rate from 0.5 to 0.33—a reform that actually took place in 1990 for beneficiaries aged 65–69—was predicted to lead to fewer retirements at 65 and to an increase in the number of full-time workers thereafter.

The Gustman and Steinmeier (1985, 1986) retirement research is an impressive blend of theory and application. Their approach imposes substantial structure on the model at the outset and, as in the case of the Fields and Mitchell (1984) research, assumes that all changes in potential income streams from various sources are foreseen with certainty. In the context of their own data, it is unlikely that the large real increases in social security benefits that occurred during the early 1970s could have been anticipated by many beneficiaries. In light of subsequent research on the role of private pensions, the lack of pension plan details for covered workers in the RHS database also raises questions about the extent to which inaccuracies are introduced into this analysis through the use of imputed pension plan information for covered workers.

A third dynamic life-cycle model by Burtless and Moffitt (1984, 1985) estimated the effects of social security on the work–retirement choices of the elderly. Their model assumes that decisions about retirement date and post-retirement hours of work are made jointly.[45] As in the case of the Gustman-Steinmeier (1985, 1986) model, a critical feature is that individuals are assumed to have preferences that shift in favor of leisure as they grow older. Prior to retirement, utility is hypothesized to be (linearly) dependent on hours worked, the preretirement hourly wage, and socioeconomic characteristics (e.g., health, age, race, education, private pension vesting). Utility declines with age until the negative contribution of the age term becomes sufficiently large that the person is better off retiring. Postretirement utility is a nonlinear (i.e., logarithmic) function of consumption, hours of work, education, and marital status. The model's structure also dictates that only one type of labor supply adjustment is permitted per person: work to partial retirement or work to complete retirement. Although the RHS database lacks the requisite detail to ascertain the specific role played by private pensions, the authors reported that social security influenced both retirement age and choice of postretirement hours of work, but the magnitude of the effect on the age of retirement was small. Estimated magnitudes were generally consistent with those reported by Fields and Mitchell (1984) and Gustman and Steinmeier (1985, 1986).

If individuals are the long-term planners described in life-cycle labor supply models, saving behavior would likely be an important related phenomenon. Accordingly, Diamond and Hausman (1984a) examined the effects of social security and private pensions on both retirement (stopping full-time work) and saving decisions.[46] Life-cycle theory suggests that a rise in future resources, perhaps due to an increase in social security benefits, will lead to increased consumption in all periods, including the present. In fact, this may fail to occur for two reasons. First, individuals may not be able to convert the additional wealth into current consumption. Second, people may be backward- rather than forward-looking when making their consumption decisions. For instance, current consumption could be strongly influenced by persistent habit.

In the Diamond-Hausman (1984a) model, both pensions and social security were shown to have strong positive effects on the probability of retirement, as did permanent income and bad health. The onset of a health problem had the same measured impact as an increase in yearly pension income of about $1,600. Social security had a positive effect on early retirement, but its effects were dominated by the other explanatory factors. The conclusion was that even without social security, the trend to earlier retirement observed in the data would have likely occurred. In the analysis of savings and wealth accumulation, higher pensions and social security led to decreased personal savings; a $1 increase in social security benefits received per year was associated with a $.25 to $.40 decline in other personal savings. Therefore, social security appears to have had a significant effect on retirement decisions, both directly, through the provision of income, and indirectly, through its effect on savings.

Numerous studies have underscored the key role of health in the decision to work. Hausman and Wise (1985) measured the importance of both health and social security wealth on the retirement decision (persons are retired if they claim to be either completely or partially retired).[47] The graph of the hazard by age computed for the RHS sample shows that the hazard rises to a peak at age 63–64, declines slightly at age 65, and is relatively constant thereafter.[48] The

Hausman-Wise model examined the influence of monthly social security payments (and their change if retirement is delayed another year), social security wealth (and its change if retirement is delayed another year), earnings, the value of liquid assets, education, the number of completely supported children, age, and indicators of bad health and private pension eligibility. After age 62, larger social security payments were associated with a higher probability of retirement, and greater monthly rewards for working made retirement less likely (i.e., there was a dominant substitution effect associated with the increased wage rate). Between the ages of 62 and 64, poor health had the equivalent effect of a $10,000 increase in social security wealth. Most variables had their predicted effects, except for the pension indicator which was statistically insignificant. The results suggest a substantial effect of social security benefits on the probability of retiring. Benefit increases in the 1969–1975 period probably accounted for a 3–5 percentage point increase in the probability of retirement for men aged 62–66.

Sickles and Taubman (1986) considered a more complex relationship between health and retirement and explored how financial factors such as social security benefit amounts might influence both (retirement was defined as not working full time). Retirement and health status equations were jointly estimated using panel data.[49] Explanatory variables in the retirement equation included age, race, marital status, number of dependents, job type, various income sources, the estimated financial gain from postponing retirement, and health. Health status was assumed to influence retirement, but the model did not permit retirement status to affect health. The key income variable in the retirement equation was the monetary gain from postponing retirement. A transition from good to poor health increases the probability of retirement by .21. Social security and pension payments, however, have positive effects on health that partially offset their direct influence on retirement. There was a large amount of individual variation in both the retirement and health equations. The authors concluded that an effective way to increase work among the elderly is to raise the age at which early retirement benefits are paid.

Although life-cycle models have usually assumed perfect foresight and information, some analysts have explicitly addressed the importance of uncertainty in the timing of retirement. Diamond and Hausman (1984b) investigated the impact of two common sources of uncertainty: the onset of poor health and involuntary unemployment.[50] Their research modeled the probability of retirement (an individual describes him- or herself as retired or unable to work) as dependent on both personal characteristics and financial variables. The estimated model indicated that both private pensions and social security had strong positive effects on the probability of retirement. Larger permanent incomes were associated with a somewhat lower probability of retirement—an anomalous finding that is contrary to what theory would lead one to predict. Health also played a key role, especially in the decision to retire early. The onset of poor health was equivalent in its effect on retirement to a $540 monthly increase in pension entitlement.

The analysis also considered the response of older workers to involuntary unemployment. In the National Longitudinal Survey data, 36 percent of men aged 60–64 whose employment was terminated subsequently retired instead of moving to another job. Higher levels of pension income, social security benefits, poor health, age, wealth, and a wife's (permanent) income level were positive influences on the decision to retire after losing a job. Both private pensions and social security retirement benefits had strong positive effects on the probability of retirement, with the effect of social security especially strong at age 62.

Although the preponderance of evidence has identified the social security program as a significant factor in American retirement patterns, empirical results have been somewhat mixed about the extent to which social security has contributed to the marked trend to earlier retirement in recent decades. In another effort to incorporate the role of uncertainty into the analysis, Burtless (1986) developed a life-cycle model in which predictable benefit increases are distinguished from unanticipated changes.[51] Between 1969 and 1972 there was a 20 percent increase in the real value of social security retirement benefits—an increase that followed a 15-year period in which the level of real social security benefits for a worker with a specific earnings history was approximately unchanged. It is unlikely that this sudden, sizable increase was anticipated by beneficiaries.

Burtless's (1986) research confirmed that retirement is a function of health, marital status, household size, and financial variables from the budget constraint.[52] Poor health, household size, an indicator of wealth in excess of $25,000, and total family wealth in 1969 all lowered the age of retirement; lower levels of wealth, being married, and the rate at which family wealth accrues when retirement is delayed for one year (i.e., the slope of the lifetime budget constraint) are positive influences on retirement age. Men who reported bad health retired about 1.1 years earlier, on average. Evaluated at sample mean values, the implicit rate of time preference of retirees appeared to be slightly greater than 5 percent. The estimated model was used to calculate the effects of the presumably unanticipated benefit increases in 1970 and 1972. Burtless estimated that the average retirement age was about .09 years (4.7 weeks) earlier due to these unanticipated increases; had the change been anticipated, the long-run effect would have been to reduce the average retirement age by .17 years (8.8 weeks). The estimated magnitudes reported by Burtless are consistent with those studies that have found that changes in social security benefit levels have a modest effect on the timing of retirement.

Sueyoshi (1989) attempted to identify and measure factors that determined the timing of retirement during the 1970s, as well as whether initial labor force transitions were made to partial or complete retirement. Transitions to partial retirement are empirically important; approximately one-third of the RHS sample claimed to be partially retired at some point during the 10-year survey period.

The mean duration of the partial retirement state was estimated to be 5.5 years, with a median of about 20 hours of work per week reported among partial retirees. Graphs of the simple hazards for the two types of retirements showed that the "risk" of (probability of first entering) partial retirement remained roughly constant with age, but the risk of complete retirement increased sharply at age 65.

Sueyoshi's (1989) model permitted the competing risks of partial and complete retirement to be analyzed together and allowed for their potential correlation. The variables used in the analysis controlled for individual differences as well as economic factors.[53] Social Security was found to decrease the labor market activity of older workers. The probability of complete retirement increased as the benefit amounts available at age 62 increased; however, there was little impact of benefit levels on the likelihood of partial retirement. Increases in the benefit amount payable when retirement is delayed between ages 62 and 65 had little effect on the decision to retire completely, but it lowered the probability of partial retirement. Sueyoshi's results imply that policies that increase benefit levels and increase the amount by which benefits increase when retirement is postponed between ages 62 and 65 will prompt people who might otherwise partially retire to retire fully.

The most technically ambitious approach to retirement modeling has been described in a series of articles by Rust (1989, 1990) and Phelan and Rust (1991). Nearly all retirement models have assumed that individuals accurately foresee income consumption possibilities under alternative work scenarios and make lifetime work plans that are subsequently carried out without change. In view of the pervasive uncertainty that attaches to future events, a more realistic approach would allow individuals the opportunity to update and revise their plans as new information becomes available. In Rust's model, individuals formulate and routinely revise a utility-maximizing plan for work and consumption over their remaining lives. Planning must be based on expectations about longevity, health, marital status, income, and wealth—all of which are retirement determinants whose future values cannot be known with certainty when long-term plans are formulated. A key innovation of Rust's model is its elaborate modeling of the formation and revision of these expectations. The full model simultaneously explains employment status, consumption expenditures, and the timing of the first application for social security benefits. As individuals age and acquire additional information, they can update their consumption and work plans to reflect changed circumstances (e.g., on the onset of a disabling health condition). Rust's treatment of these decisions as a dynamic stochastic-programming model is fully structural; individual utility functions are estimated and then used to examine the impact of life-cycle budget constraints.[54]

In reporting preliminary estimates of the utility function parameters from their model, Phelan and Rust (1991) note that the model predicts the timing of retirement from full-time employment by higher-paid workers quite well but is somewhat less successful for lower-wage and part-time workers. The model's predictions capture the popularity of first receipt of social security benefits for retired workers at age 62, but they underestimate the frequency with which benefits are first collected at age 65. Anomalies are also noted regarding the predicted behavior of workers with health impairments; the model overestimates their propensity to work. The authors observe that expanding the model's capability to address disability issues and the demand for insurance under medicare is a promising extension that might improve its predictive power in several of these areas.

The dynamic-programming approach has also been used by Berkovec and Stern (1991) in a model that explains how older men choose among the alternatives of full-time employment, part-time employment, and complete retirement.[55] Individuals are assumed to maximize utility when they make decisions about employment at the beginning of each period. The decision is based on observed values of monetary payments and leisure associated with each employment state in the current period, as well as expected values of these variables in future periods, contingent on current and past choices. Poor health, age, and lack of education are shown to increase the probability of retirement. The major weaknesses of the empirical work are that (1) it assumes that a number of magnitudes (e.g., future health status) are known with certainty, and (2) the potential influence of the social security system is not treated. The primary contribution of this article is methodological; it demonstrates how the method of simulated moments can be used to estimate a dynamic work–retirement model with a complex error structure.

Dynamic-programming retirement models can potentially incorporate enormous amounts of detail about lifetime budget constraints and, given the power of modern computers, are limited only by data availability and the ingenuity and diligence of the researchers. This approach clearly assumes substantial rationality on the part of individuals and a predilection for carrying out long-term plans. As pointed out by Phelan and Rust (1991), two of the leading contributors to this literature, it is uncertain in what direction this approach will eventually evolve. One option would be the development of increasingly detailed optimizing models where observed behavior is explained by a level of mathematical complexity that in reality is understood by only a tiny fraction of the population. Although many successful behavioral models involve computational processes that relatively few individuals can actually perform, one can be rightfully skeptical if it is hard to see how individuals can approximate the results of sophisticated analysis by trial-and-error methods or by employing rules of thumb. Alternatively, dynamic-programming models might eventually give way to other types of models that attempt to mimic real human decision processes. One might reasonably expect that researchers will opt for whatever approach best explains the observed variation in labor supply and retirement behavior. For now, it is interesting that in one attempt to compare the predictive power of simpler empirical retirement models with that of a dynamic-programming model, Lumsdaine, Stock, and Wise (1990b) found that a simpler option value approach performed about as well as the more complex model—although it must be emphasized that the dynamic-programming model they tested has far less complexity than Rust's model.[56]

Most of the economic retirement research conducted since the late 1970s has used data from the Retirement History Study (RHS), whose inclusion of the Social Security Administration's information on respondents' lifetime earnings and benefits in good part accounts for the intensive efforts by researchers to determine the effects of social security on American retirement behavior. The consensus of this research has been that social security's program features have statistically significant, but relatively modest, effects on the overall retirement picture. Behavioral estimates from the best-quality studies suggest that social security probably has caused the average age of retirement for men to decline by several months. Social security probably accounts for the current popularity of retirement at age 62, primarily by helping to supply the wherewithal for workers with few assets, undesirable jobs, or poor health to leave the labor force when early retirement benefits are first available. Unfortunately, an increasingly evident shortcoming of the database is its minimal information about private pension plans for the RHS respondents. This aspect of the database severely limits any RHS-based investigation of the effects of pensions on the timing of retirement for covered workers. Recent studies using other data sources have identified the important role played by pensions and sought to determine how the structure of private pensions influences retirement.

Private pensions are a key source of retirement income for a significant portion of the population and, in their function of providing a means of financing consumption during the retirement years, they would, at first blush, appear to encourage retirement and deter work via their income effect. This is particularly the case with respect to *defined contribution* plans, in which retirement savings accumulate as the employer makes periodic payments to a worker's retirement account, as specified by a formula. In these plans, pension wealth eventually depends on the returns on the retirement account's assets as well as on the employer's contributions.

More complex are the incentives for work and retirement posed by *defined benefit* plans, which constitute the predominant primary pension plan type for workers covered by private pensions. As pointed out by Kotlikoff and Wise (1987), defined benefit plans are usually structured in ways that will motivate employees to behave consistently with the firm's personnel goals. Specifically, firms usually aim to discourage quitting among experienced, skilled workers, and particularly those who have received costly training; they seek to promote worker effort on the job while discouraging shirking; and they often want older, higher-paid workers to retire so that high-priced labor can be replaced by younger, lower-paid workers. All these objectives can be advanced by establishing a career compensation profile that rises with job tenure until workers reach the firm's chosen retirement age, after which the rate of compensation levels off or declines. One way to achieve this compensation payment schedule is through defined benefit pensions. The pension component of total compensation is actually deferred compensation—payments that will be received only at the end of the worker's career. Early departure from the firm, both voluntary and involuntary, is discouraged because both vesting rules and the nonportability of benefits mean that early departure can impose large capital losses on workers. Because the pension amounts eventually paid by defined benefit plans depend on a worker's highest earnings (typically received late in the career) and the number of years of employment with the firm, the annual accumulation of pension wealth represents a significant component of total compensation for older workers. Gustman and Steinmeier (1989) estimate that the annual increment to pension wealth amounts to 15 to 16 percent of total compensation for workers during the several years prior to the typical employer's early and normal retirement ages. To encourage older workers to retire at the firm's preferred age, the employer can offer extra monetary incentives in the form of retirement bonuses to workers who leave the firm at that age. When pension receipt is conditional on full retirement from the firm, workers who remain with the employer past the firm's normal retirement age often experience negative pension wealth accruals because the present value of increments to anticipated future benefits is less than the value of pension payments currently being foregone. This type of pension structure means that the older worker effectively faces a large decrease in annual total compensation for working past the normal retirement age, providing a strong incentive for workers to leave the firm.[57]

Although earlier empirical work (e.g., Burkhauser, 1979; Fields and Mitchell, 1984) explicitly modeled the effects of pension wealth accrual on the timing of retirement, more recent research has provided stronger evidence on the importance of pensions for covered workers by incorporating a conceptual innovation offered by Lazear and Moore (1988). The earlier studies that attempted to include measures of pension wealth accrual as a component of a worker's total annual compensation simply included the difference in the net present value of the anticipated stream of future pension payments associated with another year of work. Measures of annual pension wealth accrual can then be incorporated in an individual's budget constraint. However, this procedure does not generally provide an effective indicator of the incentive created by a private pension plan for an individual to continue working. For example, in the year prior to the year in which cliff vesting occurs, actual pension wealth accrual might be calculated to be zero; that is, retirement that year would lead to no higher expected future pension payments than retirement in the previous year—prior to vesting, the worker has not earned a pension right.[58] In fact, private pensions provide a fairly strong incentive to remain with an employer in the year prior to vesting since leaving at that point terminates the prospect of a future income from the firm's pension plan.

The *option value* approach to the analysis of pension incentives focuses on the notion that at any point in time, the decision to continue working retains an option to retire at a future date, and that option has value that typically changes appreciably over time. At any point in time, the present value of all expected future pension payments can be calculated, assuming that the worker retired immediately. A similar calculation can be made assuming retirement at other dates in the future and discounting future income streams to the same point in time. The option value of continued work is the difference between the highest present value associated with retiring at any future date and the present value of retiring in the current period. The pension plan provides an incentive for continued work as long as the option value is positive. The optimal retirement date occurs at that point where the option value first falls to zero, or a negative value.

Stock and Wise (1990a, 1990b) used an option value approach to model the retirement decisions of 1,500 salesmen employed by a large, Fortune 500 firm in 1980. In the Stock-Wise option value model, at each age the worker calculates the present value of the stream of utilities associated with expected income and leisure over the anticipated remaining lifetime if the worker were to leave the firm immediately. A similar calculation is made assuming that retirement occurs at each year in the future. If the utility level is higher for a future retirement date, the individual continues to work. When the option value or gain from postponing retirement—now measured in utility units—is zero, the individual retires from the firm. Using a very parsimonious model in which the effects of social security must be estimated on the basis of imputed earnings histories, Stock and Wise were able to predict the retirement behavior of the sample very well. Simulations using the model suggest that the effect of changes in either social security's normal retirement age or the early retirement reduced-benefit rate are easily offset by relatively minor changes in the private pension rules. Because the underlying data are drawn from only one employer, the results should be considered preliminary and should not be extrapolated to larger segments of the population. Nonetheless, the findings are sufficiently promising to encourage further research and represent key evidence supporting the current view that, for covered workers, defined benefit pension plans are a very important element, if not the dominant factor, in the timing of retirement.

During the 1980s many American firms reduced the size of their workforce in reengineering efforts designed to increase competitiveness. Rather than resort to morale-depleting layoffs, employers often targeted older, higher-paid workers with special incentives to leave the firm voluntarily. One personnel tool for accomplishing this objective is to offer a *retirement window* in the firm's pension plan. A private pension plan offers a retirement window when a group of workers is promised a specific bonus beyond the usual pension plan rules for leaving the firm within a specified time period. The window provision might take the form of a cash bonus or a temporary change in the rules for calculating pension benefits that leads to higher benefits if the worker retires by a specified date. It is common for the window to be offered only to a specific category of workers, a category that might be defined by age, seniority, occupation, division within the firm, and so forth.

Lumsdaine, Stock, and Wise (1990b) examined the effect of a window provision on the retirement behavior of a sample of 1,000 randomly selected male office workers, aged 50 or older, working for a Fortune 500 firm in 1980.[59] The window provision offered retirement bonuses of 3 to 12 months' salary, the amount varying with age and years of service. The study uses the option value model developed by Stock and Wise (1990a), whereby workers retire at the point where their perceived value of immediate retirement exceeds the expected present value of retiring at any future date. The estimated model shows a sizable effect of the window plan on retirement behavior. The proportion of employees working at age 52 who subsequently retire by age 60 increases by approximately 50 percent (i.e., 79 percent retired, compared to the 52 percent predicted in the absence of the window). The results suggest that firms can significantly influence employee retirement decisions through the use of well-designed retirement windows.

Hogarth (1988) provided confirmatory evidence of the effectiveness of a somewhat different retirement window offered by the New York State government in 1983 in a large downsizing effort. During that spring, vested workers aged 55 and older were given an additional 3 years' service credit if they retired by May 31, 1983. In response, 30 percent of eligible employees accepted the offer. Hogarth estimated a pension-acceptance equation that included economic, sociological, and psychological factors including the present value of future earnings, health status, employment status of spouse, perceived adequacy of retirement income, and a DIFFERENCE measure of the change in value of the pension (measured in thousands of dollars) associated with retiring immediately compared with waiting until the planned retirement date.[60] The DIFFERENCE variable was statistically significant and raised the probability of acceptance by .03 above its mean of .30. Most variables performed in a predictable manner, with bad health and greater age increasing the probability of early retirement, and the present value of earnings decreasing the probability. A notable finding is the importance of expectation variables in the decision. An expectation of a layoff increased the probability of accepting the pension offer by .15, while an expectation that retirement income would not be adequate lowered the probability of acceptance by .06. This article provides additional evidence that retirement decisions are responsive to monetary incentives associated with additional years of work, although these effects appear to be relatively modest, consistent with the earlier findings of Burkhauser (1979) and Fields and Mitchell (1984).

DISCUSSION AND CONCLUSIONS

A substantial body of research has assessed the relative importance of financial incentives, particularly social security and private pensions, in the retirement decision. Financial incentives have been shown to affect retirement and work choices in a manner consistent with the theory of work–leisure choice, but they are sometimes overshadowed by noneconomic factors, particularly age and health. The secular rise in the real incomes of the elderly has helped finance earlier withdrawal from the labor force through an income effect. Convincing evidence exists establishing a link between increasingly generous social security benefits and reduced labor market activity of older workers over time. Social security is probably responsible for the particular popularity of retirement at ages 62 and 65. As documented by Kahn (1988), workers with relatively low amounts of non–social security wealth who would like to retire early are probably liquidity-constrained prior to age 62, the point at which social security provides the means to leave the labor force. This is likely to be particularly true for workers with health problems or for those who work at unpleasant or physically demanding jobs. Social security probably has accounted for the longtime, but declining, popularity of retirement at age 65 through the retirement test and an actuarially unfair delayed retirement credit. The continued liberalization of the retirement test and scheduled increases in the delayed retirement credit lessen the impact of these provisions with time (Leonesio, 1990a). Finally, it cannot be ruled out that, in its declaration of age 65 as the program's normal retirement age (i.e., the first age at which full benefits for retired workers can be collected), social security might have given impetus to retire at that age through the establishment of a social norm.

Recent evidence indicates that older workers covered by defined benefit, private pensions are likely to be strongly influenced by the structural features of those plans. Firms can create sharp incentives to continue working or to retire at specific ages through the pension wealth accrual profile. Changes in the slope of this profile are tantamount to large proportional changes in the annual rate of total compensation paid to workers. In fact, these incentives can be sufficiently powerful so that employers could easily offset the effects of most prospective changes in the social security program aimed at changing the nation's retirement behavior. For example, the scheduled increase in the social security normal retirement age provides an incentive to work longer, but firms will have the option to adjust pension wealth accrual profiles to ensure that the timing of retirement of their older employees remains unchanged.

Further progress in retirement modeling now awaits the development of new databases whose information content reflects the current state of knowledge. The more that is learned about retirement, the greater becomes our awareness of the deficiencies in the data sources that have been used in the past. The estimation of dynamic structural models requires comprehensive and detailed information about the life-cycle budget constraints that critically influence observed behavior. As this chapter has shown, modern retirement models consider the labor market decisions of older workers to be largely voluntary. In order to understand these choices, it is necessary to have detailed information about the various options at different points in time that were *not* chosen, as well as the circumstances attending those that were. Certainly, good, new data sources for retirement modeling will have to contain sufficient details about individual work histories to permit researchers to mimic the computations done by the Social

Security Administration to calculate benefits for retirees. In addition, the database should include the specific rules that are used to determine any pension benefits for which the worker might be eligible since these are required to calculate the incentives to remain on the job or retire. The database should ideally have good information about all other potential sources of retirement income including earnings opportunities, savings, and both private and public transfers. The University of Michigan's new Health and Retirement Survey is an ambitious data collection effort that attempts to address all of these needs.

Improvements in models that exploit new data sources will enable researchers to address a number of questions that have not been satisfactorily addressed to date.

The Interaction between Health and Retirement

Until the new Health and Retirement Survey, no single database has contained both comprehensive information about individuals' budget constraints as well as good measures of health status and ability to work. Studies that have used self-reported measures of health status have often found health status to be more influential than financial considerations in explaining retirement. Quinn (1977) reported that health and eligibility for social security and private pension benefits are equally influential in the early retirement decision for white married men.[61] Gordon and Blinder (1980), Boskin and Hurd (1978), and Hanoch and Honig (1983) found that poor health increases the probability of retirement in a given year. More recent work suggests that studies that purport to show health to be more influential than financial variables in the retirement decision may have incorrectly measured both magnitudes (Anderson and Burkhauser, 1985). Bazzoli (1985) investigated how the estimated effect of health on early retirement responds to alternative measures of health status and concluded that studies that measure health by asking individuals whether their health limits work activity overstate that factor's true effect. Inaccurate measures of health status have probably caused the impact of health on work and retirement to be overestimated, but the amount of bias is uncertain.[62] Health status, the functional capacity to work, and closely related issues such as a family's long-term care needs, access to quality medical care, the availability of private and public insurance, and the incidence of out-of-pocket medical expenses are clearly important considerations when older individuals make decisions about work and retirement. Real advances in this area will require new data.

Demand for Older Workers

Most studies of older workers have concentrated on the supply side of the market, leaving the demand for older workers relatively underexamined, as pointed out by Straka (1992). Older workers often complain that suitable work opportunities are limited. Many older full-time workers would prefer to continue working part time for their employer rather than retire completely, but few employers appear to offer this option. Using data from a survey of 267 work establishments conducted by the American Society of Personnel Administration and the Bureau of National Affairs, Gustman and Steinmeier (1983, 1984) reported that only ten percent of employers appear to permit full-time employees to reduce hours prior to complete retirement. Private pension plans usually require that a worker leave the firm before pension receipt can begin. Continued employment for the older worker usually entails a change in employer and a sharply reduced wage rate, with few fringe benefits. The constraints that govern the individual choices examined in the retirement literature are, in large part, determined by employer attitudes and policies regarding older workers. Further empirical analysis of the demand for older workers would significantly enhance our understanding of observed work and retirement patterns and perhaps inform the development of appropriate public policies. Again, data limitations currently proscribe the research possibilities—a situation that generally applies to the empirical study of labor demand. The ideal database would include considerable detail on firm decisions about production technologies, personnel policies, and the use of factors of production, along with considerable detail about individual employees. A large, nationally representative database of this type does not currently exist.

Research on Women's Retirement and Family Retirement Models

Most retirement research has concerned the behavior of men, with relatively few studies examining women's retirement decisions. Notable exceptions have been provided by Clark, Johnson, and McDermed (1980), Pozzebon and Mitchell (1989), Hurd (1990a), Vistnes (1994) and Gustman and Steinmeier (1994). This small and uneven literature was reviewed and criticized by Weaver (1994). To date, the results are inconsistent and should probably be viewed with some skepticism. The main impediment has been a lack of suitable data, especially with respect to married women. The Retirement History Study, the information source for much of the men's retirement literature, primarily collected data for men and for single women; data for married women were included mainly to illuminate the behavior of their husbands. This is another shortcoming to be remedied by the new Health and Retirement Survey—a database whose design recognizes the central place women now occupy in the labor market.

Married women's labor market decisions are best understood within the context of their families, where husbands and wives jointly make choices about work, consumption, and eventual retirement in light of family wants and needs. Although it has long been recognized that men's labor supply is influenced by factors such as marital status, family size, and income amounts earned by other family members, most economic models of male labor supply decisions have simply taken the labor market decisions of spouses to be independently determined events. That is, apart from counting a wife's earnings as a component of family income that is not earned by the husband, the husband's labor supply decisions have often been modeled taking the wife's current labor force status to be an unchanging, external event.[63] This simplifying assumption—which becomes increasingly less tenable as the labor force activity of women increasingly resembles that of men—has long been recognized as even less satisfactory when attempting to understand the labor supply of married women.

Ideally, retirement models for married men or women would take into account the complex life-cycle budget constraints that jointly influence the timing of retirement for both spouses, including the Social Security Administration's treatment of couples, private pension rights that have been earned by each spouse, and the influence of factors such as the deteriorating health of a spouse or the burden of providing home-based care to an elderly parent. Our confidence in measurements of the impact of financial incentives on work and retirement behavior will likely increase as researchers increase the scope of potentially confounding nonmonetary factors that are simultaneously evaluated.

NOTES

1. Other U.S.-based data sources frequently used in retirement research include the Department of Labor's National Longitudinal Survey of Mature Men, the University of Michigan's Panel Study of Income Dynamics, various samples selected from the Census Bureau's Current Population Surveys (CPS), the Social Security Administration's (SSA) New Beneficiary Survey, and the 1973 CPS-IRS-SSA Exact Match file. The latter data source was created by matching CPS data with administrative data on the survey respondents maintained by the SSA and the Internal Revenue Service (IRS). Details concerning these and other surveys may be found in publications reporting research findings based on them. These publications are cited throughout the remainder of this chapter. Alternatively, readers may wish to contact sponsoring agencies or institutions of each survey to learn more about them. Readers may also contact the Interuniversity Consortium of Political and Social Research at the University of Michigan, which maintains an archive of these and other data bases.

2. Note that this theory uses an unconventional definition of the term *leisure*; leisure refers to all time not devoted to paid work. Of course, however, not all nonwork time is accurately characterized as voluntarily chosen leisure. Considerable amounts of time need to be devoted to sleeping, eating, and other routine personal hygiene. Some time must be allocated to activities more accurately described as chores than as leisure. In a very influential article, Becker (1965) extended the basic work–leisure choice model by explicitly accounting for the large number of potential uses of time. In Becker's model, labor supply decisions are made jointly with decisions about the amounts of time to devote to the many distinct activities that the simple model aggregates as "leisure."

3. One can think of X as a hypothetical generic commodity that satisfies all consumption needs or, more realistically, as a vector (or collection) of many goods and services, units of which sell at prices given by the respective elements of conforming price vector, P.

4. In economic models, tastes and preferences are expressed mathematically by *utility*

functions, which relate the level of well-being, or utility (U), to the level of consumption and leisure enjoyed. In this example, a strictly concave utility function can be written in general functional notation as $U = U(X, L)$, where it is assumed that $\partial U/\partial X > 0$, $\partial U/\partial L > 0$, $\partial^2 U/\partial X^2 < 0$, and $\partial^2 U/\partial L^2 < 0$. These four assumptions about the properties of $U(.)$ imply that utility always increases as the amounts of consumption goods or leisure increase, but at a decreasing rate. The optimal amounts of consumption and leisure are given by the solution to the constrained optimization problem:

$$\text{Max}_{X,L}\ U = U(X, L) \text{ s.t. } XP \le w(T - L) + V.$$

5. Economists often express theories in terms of mathematics because of the precision that these formulations permit. Once a problem has been defined, the solution can be found using appropriate mathematical techniques. Note that this methodology does not imply that people literally use formal mathematics to make their economic decisions. Rather, the argument is that through normal decision-making processes, intuition, rules of thumb, solicited advice, and the like, individuals arrive at decisions that are quite similar to those generated by economic models. Thus, people are thought to act "as if" they had arrived at their decisions through the more formal analytical methods used by economists to solve the problem. The ultimate test of the theory rests with its power to explain behavior. These ideas have been forcefully espoused by Milton Friedman (1953).

6. The *real* wage offer, w/P, indicates the rate at which leisure can be transformed into goods. For example, if a unit of good, X, sells for \$3 and the worker's wage rate is \$12 per hour, the real wage is 4. That is, for every hour of leisure that the individual gives up by working, 4 more units of good X can be consumed. The theory is founded on the view that individuals never suffer from "money illusion." Regardless of nominal price, wage, and income levels, people are always assumed to understand precisely what real resources any particular sum of money can command.

The subjective value that the individual places on time is given by the *marginal rate of substitution function*, $w^* = w^*(X, L)$, which is given by the expression $(\partial U/\partial L)/(\partial U/\partial X)$. The decision whether to work at all depends critically on the value of w^* when $L = T$. Other things held equal, w^* increases as L declines.

7. The rationale for this result lies with the nature of the utility function (see note 6). Because utility increases—but at a decreasing rate—as more leisure is consumed, additional hours of work will always increase the subjective value of the $(T - H)^{th}$, or *marginal*, hour of leisure enjoyed. That is, the less we have of something desirable, the greater value we tend to place on each unit. If the individual works, w/P must exceed w^*, the subjective value placed on the Tth unit of leisure. As the number of work hours increases, the subjective value of an hour of leisure will increase. Utility will be at its highest when the number of hours worked is such that the subjective value of the Lth hour of leisure just equals the wage. If an even greater number of hours were worked, the subjective value of leisure would exceed the wage, and utility could be increased by reducing the number of hours worked.

8. The term *substitution effect* connotes that if the price of a commodity increases, people will tend to consume less of it by substituting the consumption of now relatively cheaper commodities. Conversely, if the price falls, individuals will tend to consume more of a commodity.

9. Good surveys are provided by Killingsworth (1983), Killingsworth and Heckman (1986), and Pencavel (1986).

10. These factors can account for tastes and preferences that vary across individuals.

11. It is possible to choose different definitions of *retirement*, various of which might

be better suited to particular purposes. A labor supply–oriented definition that focuses on hours of paid work has the advantage of being based on behavior that is observed and documented in many databases and, hence, is readily amenable to statistical analysis. Other common definitions of retirement include departure from a career job; a sustained, sizable reduction in annual earnings; receipt of social security benefits or private pension income; or merely the self-assertion that a person is retired. See Ekerdt and Deviney (1990).

12. A person with a high rate of time preference gives large weight to current events and highly discounts the importance or value of future events. Thus, a young worker with a very high discount rate would place little or no value on a pension plan that generates benefits that will not be received for many decades, while someone with a very small ρ values a distant dollar of pension income nearly as highly as a dollar of current income. One way to think about ρ is that it is akin to an individual's own personal interest rate used to calculate how he or she currently values a future event. Thus, if my ρ equals .10, the present value that I place on \$100 to be received in 1 year equals \$100/ $(1 + .10) = \$90.91$. Note that ρ need not equal the market rate of interest.

13. As indicated in the simple, one-period model, it is usually assumed that individuals are not fooled by any inflation of nominal values of wages, prices, and income. That is, if wage rates, prices, and nonwage income all double, people will realize that they are no better or worse off; their real compensation rate is unchanged and their command over real resources is no different. Typically, life-cycle models convert all nominal values to real magnitudes by deflating the values of variables by an appropriate price index. Similarly, the interest rate used in the budget set is the *real rate of interest*, the nominal interest rate *minus* the premium that lenders require to compensate for any anticipated inflation.

14. A life-cycle formulation of the theory of work–leisure choice can underpin empirical models that are either static or dynamic in spirit. That is, a life-cycle model can be used to generate hypotheses about behavior (or an outcome) that is observed during a specific sample period in which only a small fraction of the entire life cycle is observed. Explanatory variables might include measures of causal factors that represent information about circumstances that occur in nonsample periods. For instance, the work activity of a 63-year-old man observed in 1995 likely depends to some extent on his social security wealth (i.e., the present value of future net social security payments) and the rate at which additional social security wealth will accrue with additional earnings. The far-sighted planner anticipates future income needs when current-period work decisions are made. Alternatively, the life-cycle framework can be used to develop a dynamic model that explains the timing of retirement as one aspect of a planned sequence of work effort over the lifetime.

15. The most common statistical procedures used to estimate retirement models are regression techniques, hazard models, and the method of nonlinear maximum likelihood.

16. One common assumption about tastes and preferences in life-cycle models is that the utility function exhibits intertemporal separability. This property means that the marginal utility derived from consumption or leisure in any given period is independent of consumption or leisure in all other periods. This assumption substantially simplifies the nature of any influences that the values of financial variables in one period can have on behavior in another period. See Deaton and Muellbauer (1980, ch. 5).

17. For more comprehensive reviews, consult Hurd (1990b), Leonesio (1990b), or Quinn, Burkhauser, and Myers (1990).

18. Surveys of retirees conducted by the Social Security Administration and academic researchers between 1941 and 1963 usually indicated that a majority of respondents retired because of health problems or employer-initiated terminations. See Boskin (1977), 3.

19. Boskin's data set comprised 131 households headed by white males from the 1968–1972 waves of the University of Michigan's Panel Study of Income Dynamics. Selection was governed by the requirement that these heads be aged 66–70 in their last interview. Unfortunately, this data source has little information about private pension entitlements.

20. Although, Hurd and Boskin (1984) also report a fairly large effect for social security.

21. The data source was the 1973 CPS-IRS-SSA Exact Match File.

22. The SSW variable is based on the husband's and wife's primary insurance amounts (PIA). It is calculated by taking the present value of the husband's benefits as a retired worker and adding the present value of the wife's benefits (i.e., the higher of her expected benefits as a retired worker and the benefits she would receive as a spouse).

23. The statistical work used data for 3,219 men, aged 45–59 in 1966, selected from the 1969 wave of the National Longitudinal Survey of Mature Men.

24. This study examines data for 4,354 white, married men, aged 58–63, selected from the 1969 wave of the Retirement History Study.

25. The statistical analysis uses data for 4,845 white, married males, aged 58 to 63, selected from the 1969 wave of the Retirement History Study.

26. The study uses observations on 12,520 white, married men (spouse present in 1969) and 5,436 white, unmarried women from the 1969–1975 waves of the Retirement History Study.

27. The PIA values were calculated under the assumption of retirement in the survey year.

28. They estimated a wage elasticity of .17, and compensated wage elasticity of .19 for men, with corresponding measures of .15 and .21 for women.

29. The data are from the 1973 CPS-IRS-SSA Exact Match File, supplemented with information from the 1971 wave of the Retirement History Study. Models were estimated on a sample of approximately 700 men eligible for social security retirement benefits at age 62 and who had not received social security disability payments.

30. To elaborate on this point, economists assume that individuals make decisions about consumption and leisure that maximize utility. Utility theory suggests that financial incentives (i.e., price and income variables), as well as other nonfinancial control variables, influence the choices that are made. One approach to the empirical work would be to estimate the relationship between the outcome variable (e.g., hours worked per period) and all available explanatory variables using statistical regression techniques, largely ignoring the properties of any particular utility function. Although this *reduced-form* method, in principle, enables us to predict how changes in the various explanatory factors would affect the explained behavior, the estimated relationship is usually consistent with many specific utility functions. That is, from the reduced-form model it is impossible to determine the underlying mathematical representation of preferences that generated the observed behavior. As a consequence, the reduced-form approach makes it difficult to attribute differences in observed choices between individuals to differences in budget constraints as opposed to differences in their tastes and preferences.

31. For example, a reduced-form labor supply model for older workers might explain

annual hours of work using currently available benefits and the anticipated increment to the present value of anticipated social security benefits as explanatory factors. Even if the model includes many other precisely measured variables, the model lacks sufficient detail about how social security can affect work incentives to allow one to compare and contrast the effects of changes in many specific program features such as the benefit formula, the taxation of benefits, or the retirement test.

32. The *structural* approach begins by assuming a specific utility function (or functional transformation, such as the marginal rate of substitution function, indirect utility function, or expenditure function) whose parameters are to be estimated. The database typically contains information that allows the investigator to reconstruct the opportunities embodied in the individual's budget constraint. The statistical estimation procedure involves determining the values for the utility function parameters that maximize the likelihood of occurrence of the observed outcomes documented in the data. Once the specific utility function is determined, it is possible to predict the response to changed opportunities since behavior would adjust to maximize utility in light of the new circumstances.

33. The study used data for 5,327 white males who were not self-employed, selected from the 1969–1973 waves of the Retirement History Study. Since three waves of information are used for each individual, the total number of observations is 15,981. Ages 58 through 67 are represented in the sample.

34. "Full income" is the total amount of income that would be available to spend if all time were devoted to work.

35. The measure of lifetime potential earnings is calculated by taking the present value of earnings assuming full-time work until age 67, and no work thereafter.

36. The empirical work is based on cross-section data for 1,483 men and 1,207 women collected for 1977 by the British Office of Population Censuses and Surveys.

37. "Waiting wives" are women older than 60 whose husbands were not yet 65 and who thus could not receive a state pension.

38. Whether the social security system as a whole promotes earlier retirement in this way depends on the extent to which individuals are forced by the program to save more for their retirement than they would have otherwise. In the case of forced savings, older workers end up with greater assets to finance retirement.

39. For retired workers the AIME is calculated by first adjusting annual social security taxable earnings prior to age 60 for average wage growth in the economy. Earnings at later ages are not adjusted. The number of computation years (call this number y) is then determined; namely, the number of years worked after 1950 (or the year of attainment of age 21, if later) up to the year in which the individual attains 62, minus dropout years (usually 5). The actual computation years are then selected based on the y years over the individual's lifetime with the highest taxable earnings, after making the wage-growth corrections for pre–age 60 earnings. The AIME is then calculated by summing the adjusted earnings in the computation years and then dividing by the total number of months in the computation years.

The primary insurance amount (PIA) is the monthly amount payable to a retired worker who begins receiving benefits at age 65, and is calculated as follows for persons attaining age 62 in 1992 or later. The PIA is computed using a formula consisting of three brackets in which different percentages are applied to the worker's AIME. The two *bend points* that define the three brackets are different for each calendar year of attainment of age 62, a program feature intended to account for average wage growth in the economy. For example, the 1995 bend points are $426 and $2,567. To compute the PIA for a retired worker who attains age 62 in 1995, take 90 percent of the first $426 of the AIME, add 32 percent of the next $2,141 of the AIME, and add 15 percent of the amount of the AIME that exceeds $2,567. The result of this computation is the "age 62 PIA." The PIA of a new beneficiary who is older than age 62 is further adjusted for cost-of-living increases granted to beneficiaries since the year in which the individual attained age 62. These are simplified explanations that can vary with an individual's circumstances. For more accurate details consult the *Social Security Handbook, 1993* (U.S. Department of Health and Human Services, 1993).

40. In 1995 the taxable maximum was $61,200.

41. In 1995, beneficiaries aged 62–64 faced an annual earnings limit of $8,160. Earnings in excess of this amount led to a benefit reduction of $1 for every additional $2 earned. For beneficiaries aged 65–69, that annual earnings limit was $11,280, and excess earnings resulted in a $1 reduction in benefits for every $3 earned over the limit. For some exceptions to these rules, see Myers (1985), ch. 3.

42. Fields and Mitchell estimated variants of their model using data for a sample of 1,024 men aged 59–61 in 1969 selected from the Retirement History Study, and information for 8,733 men who retired between the ages of 60 and 68, as documented in the Benefit Amounts Survey.

43. The model permits transitions among three states: not retired, partially retired, and completely retired. Respondents were asked in each survey year whether they considered themselves to be completely retired, partially retired, or not retired at all.

44. The model was estimated using data for 494 white males drawn from the 1969–1975 waves of the Retirement History Study.

45. The study uses data for 4,603 men selected from the 1969–1977 waves of the Retirement History Study.

46. The model was estimated using data for 1,335 respondents from the National Longitudinal Survey of Mature Men for the years 1965–1975. Those with wealth below $4,000 in 1966 were excluded from the sample.

47. Information comes from all six waves (1969–1979) of the Retirement History Study. The sample consists of 2,000 men who were not self-employed.

48. The *hazard* is defined as the probability that the particular event of interest (in this case, retirement) occurs during a specified interval, given that the occurrence of the event is possible (i.e., in this case, given that the person has not yet retired).

49. The study used data for approximately 8,500 male heads of households selected from the 1969–1977 waves of the Retirement History Study.

50. Data were used for 1,356 respondents for the years 1966–1978, selected from the National Longitudinal Survey of Mature Men. Of these men, aged 45–71, 428 were fired during the period of observation, and provided sufficient information to estimate a competing risks model.

51. The study was based on the behavior of 4,193 men selected from the Retirement History Study. Data from all six waves were used. Excluded were farmers and men who reported substantial income from welfare programs, civil service pensions, or railroad retirement benefits.

52. Burtless (1986) defined retirement as occurring at the first discontinuous drop in annual hours of work not connected to a spell of unemployment that ends in return to full-time work.

53. Data were taken from 1,633 males selected from the 1971–1979 waves of the Retirement History Study.

54. The model was estimated using data on 8,131 men selected from the Retirement History Study. Note that the final estimated retirement model uses the information on considerably fewer than the initial 8,131 respondents. The initial larger sample serves to supply data for that estimation of preliminary information on worker beliefs about future values of the retirement determinants included in the model. The final retirement model is estimated on a subsample of respondents who receive social security retirement benefits but no private pensions, and who have fairly complete data in the RHS.

55. A total of 2,497 job histories were constructed from the 1966 to 1983 waves of the National Longitudinal Survey of Mature Men. The estimation procedure uses a subsample of 500 persons aged 55 and older at the start of the survey.

56. The option value approach is discussed later in this chapter.

57. See Gustman, Mitchell, and Steinmeier (1994) for a recent review of current thinking on the economic role played by pensions in the labor market.

58. In *cliff vesting*, an individual's pension status changes from nonvested to 100 percent vested (i.e., eligible to receive accrued pension benefits at the normal or early retirement age regardless of whether he or she remains with that employer) at a particular point in service tenure.

59. The sample comprises nonmanagerial office personnel and is different from the sample of salesmen used in other research by Stock and Wise (1990a, 1990b), although the employer is the same.

60. The study used data from a sample of 4,000 (1,720 women and 2,280 men) New York state government employees.

61. There is also an important interaction between the two, with individuals who claim health limitations approximately eight times as responsive to social security benefits.

62. This conclusion was reached in Sammartino (1987).

63. More technically, husband's labor supply functions frequently treat the labor supply of wives as strictly exogenous.

13

Social Gerontological Models of Retirement and Employment of Older Persons

Robert M. Whaples and Charles F. Longino, Jr.

As the previous chapter explains, economists model the retirement and employment of older persons as a special case of the more general work–leisure choice. Economic models tend to examine the relation between an individual's economic environment (budget constraint) and his or her preferences (indifference curves). The act of retirement occurs when one or both of the curves shift so that the indifference curves and budget constraint are no longer tangent at a positive (or full-time) amount of hours worked. Economists focus primarily on shifts in the budget constraint, because they are much easier to observe and operationalize. Less attention is paid to the shape and shifts of the indifference curves, because preferences are hard to measure and, perhaps, because of the traditional belief among economists that preferences are generally stable (Stigler and Becker, 1977).[1] The goal is usually prediction about labor force participation, so the strategy is to measure the regression coefficients of independent economic variables, with a focus on the levers of public policy. Understanding the timing of retirement and its proximate causes are issues that have attracted the most attention.

This approach has been very fruitful. Ruhm summarized the empirical findings of these models by noting that "economics researchers have suggested that most persons respond to economic incentives in choosing when to retire" (1989, 294). However, Ekerdt's comments on Ruhm's article underline the difference between economic models of retirement and social gerontological models. The standard economic view is "a rather blinkered view of work and retirement behavior in later life," asserted Ekerdt, because it focuses almost exclusively on changes in labor market behavior (1989, 707).

An adequate analysis of why people stop or don't stop working should consider people's feelings about work, their jobs, their workplaces, and their attitudes and expectations about retirement. It is also useful to acknowledge the organizational matrices, normative structures, corporate cultures, and occupational contexts in which older people are employed. (Ekerdt, 1989, 707)

These broader concerns are the focus of social gerontological models of retirement, which are informed by a tradition of advocacy for the elderly. Thus, social gerontologists focus less on shifts in the budget constraint, and more on the *genesis* of the budget constraint. Rather than focusing on the rate at which individuals wish to trade off leisure and income, they examine the reasons *why* individuals are willing to make these trade-offs. Moreover, social gerontological models go beyond economics models by examining the social and psychological consequences of retirement. Social gerontology adopts this broader view because it conceptualizes retirement as a process and a role, not merely as an act or a state.

The economic and social gerontological models of retirement are not mutually exclusive. Their emphases are only different. An interdisciplinary approach incorporating both is needed to fully understand retirement behavior.

This chapter will begin by examining social gerontological models that focus on the economic constraints faced by the elderly, then it will turn to broader models about preferences and the process of retirement. Finally, an original model of retirement adjustment will be presented.

SOCIAL GERONTOLOGICAL MODELS OF CONSTRAINTS FACING THE ELDERLY

The chief constraints influencing the choice between employment and retirement are the wage and salary rates available in the labor market, and the income available through public and private pensions, and other sources. While economists modeling retirement behavior generally take these constraints as a given, social gerontological models have attempted to endogenize them.

The social security system is at the heart of public policy concerning retirement. Social security benefits are received by approximately 90 percent of retired people, and account for about half their incomes. Social security taxes are levied on income from employment, and the size of the social security payment is largely determined by the amount of wages a worker earned while employed. However, low earners receive a higher expected rate of return on their "contribution." In addition, payments are reduced for individuals under age seventy who earn enough labor income and cannot pass the "retirement test," and benefits are taxed if the beneficiary's income is too high. These payments are indexed to current average wages and inflation.

Surprisingly, there is little evidence that social security has influenced the average retirement age. Michael Leonesio summarized recent research by economists who find that it "appears to be a minor force in the long post–World War II trend to retire at earlier ages" (1993, 193).[2] Economic historians confirm this when they examine retirement rates between the Civil War and the present (Whaples, 1994). However, "in virtually all studies, social security system incentives are found to cause a moderate increase in retirement probabilities at age 62 (when workers first become eligible for benefits) and a much larger spike at 65 (after which the actuarial value of benefits declines)" (Ruhm, 1989, 296). Hence, social security is important to the study of retirement because it can have a substantial influence on the precise timing of retirement, and more so because its rules can have a profound impact on retirees' life styles and standards of living.

Where did the system and these rules come from? A leading sociological theory cites "modernization" as the root cause of social security (Cowgill and Holmes, 1972; Atchley, 1976).[3] It posits that the demands of the capitalist industrial economy have marginalized the elderly, while the same capitalist system has yielded a bounty of output. As "the corporate bureaucracy became the dominant organizational form" in the American economy, "the growing power of the private sector *produced* the government bureaucracy as a means of protecting the public interest" (Atchley, 1976, 13). International case studies are invoked to show that these developments were ubiquitous. As the failures of the market system became apparent, establishing a social security system became inevitable.

Political economy models argue that the development of social security systems have been much more complex, citing unique and historically evolving economic, demographic, political, and cultural factors within each country. For example, Quadagno (1988) attributed the relatively late development of social security in the United States to the late unionization of mass-production workers, a powerful private sector pension initiative, and divergent economic systems in the northern and southern states. The Great Depression galvanized support for a social insurance system, but the influence of business leaders, as well as the opposition of southern planters to direct government aid, shaped the Social Security Act, and is still reflected in today's program, which "rewards" those retired from the work force, but "penalizes" those who have not participated in the labor force.

Socialist-feminist models of retirement stress power relationships and contend that social security is based on "androcentric notions of work and production, as well as traditional notions about the private sphere." As Calasanti (1993) put it, "Most private and public pensions assume that white men's work history is the norm" (1993, 140). Critics of these models point out that social security is designed to yield a higher rate of return for those who earn less than average and that it redistributes wealth toward women.

Achenbaum's (1986b) model of the "politics of incrementalism" explains the social security system's subsequent development. Prosperity and favorable demographic ratios up to the early 1970s allowed activist bureaucrats to expand the system, making it ever more generous to retirees, and papering over the inherent conflict in the system between "individual equity" (a fair rate of return on one's "contributions") and "adequacy" (providing an adequate standard of living for those who contributed little). Political models find that a strong "welfare orientation" among voters has strengthened support for the program (Klemmack and Roff, 1983).

Graebner's widely cited theory argues that social security was designed to induce retirement in an effort to solve the problem of unemployment for younger workers (1980). The "retirement test" is still with us, even as there is a growing concern that too few of the elderly work. Most historians argue that the Social Security Act was part of a response to late-nineteenth- and early-twentieth-century beliefs that the status of the elderly was in decline. During this period, activists argued that economic developments and ageism had made older workers less employable, throwing them onto the industrial scrap heap. Haber and Gratton (1994) have recently questioned these claims about the declining status of the elderly, and argue that reformers' beliefs were based on a misinterpretation of the evidence. Whether or not these beliefs were correct, however, these models suggest that the public pension constraints facing the elderly today are shaped by the perceptions of the economy over a half-century ago and by subsequent political developments.

The individual's budget constraint is also shaped by the various employment packages and pension options he faces. Economists generally assume that these offers represent profit-maximizing behavior by employers and are closely tied to the productivity of the worker and attempts to influence worker turnover. Social gerontologists often question these assumptions. Do employers try to maximize profits? Do they know individual workers' productivity?

The ageism model points to institutions such as mandatory retirement (now illegal in most cases) and negative cultural stereotypes of aging to posit that discrimination against the elderly is widespread. Ageism among employers would tend to make employment less remunerative than it would otherwise be (rotating the budget constraint) or eliminate employment opportunities all together. However, these ageist models rarely confront economic models which show that mandatory retirement need not be a product of ageism (Lazear, 1979). Moreover, we should be wary of blanket statements about pervasive ageism. David Schonfield builds a convincing case that "evidence does not support [the] judgement" that "a negative attitude toward older people is common in America" (1982, 267). Schonfield warns that advocates of the elderly often misinterpret the evidence because of their vested interests.

A more productive approach is to use case studies to develop typologies of "corporate cultures" in relation to aging workers. For example, Barbara Hirshorn (1988) interviewed managers at 25 "Fortune 500" companies and analyzed their organizational behavior regarding older workers. According to Hirshorn, each company has its own "personality," which, together with constraints facing the company, help determine its treatment of older workers. She identified five distinct responses to older white-collar workers: the "proactive" response (acceptance of change rather than resistance to it); the "at cross-purposes" response (different policies are inconsistent with one another); the "performance-focused" response; the "positive means–negative ends" response (those with performance-focused policies whose policies are "biased" against or "unresourceful" toward older workers); and the "older worker antagonism" response (1988, 204–10).

While the idea of identifying different responses and company personality types is potentially fruitful, many economists would object that some of Hirshorn's categories are quite normative. More needs to be done to develop more objective criteria for categorizing companies and to carefully explain why company personalities differ. An increasing numbers of firms systematically assess age performance through "age audits," these models must explain why employers would systematically underestimate the performance of older workers. In addition more must be done to explain how employers assess the productivity of older workers and how they formulate employment and pension policies.

SOCIAL GERONTOLOGICAL MODELS OF THE RETIREMENT PROCESS

The mainstream of social gerontological models of retirement and work in old age deal with the preferences, decision-making and adjustment processes, and the physical and psychological well-being of individuals as they go through the retirement process. These models must explain two patterns of the retirement behavior in the contemporary United States: why have retirement rates risen so much, and why are most retirees satisfied with their retirement experiences? The second question answers the first. Most people accept retirement when an adequate income is secure, because they prefer it to continuation of work—because they enjoy retirement. Why do they have these preferences? How do they successfully adjust to retirement? In answering these questions, sociological gerontologists go beyond the economist's proximate questions about the shapes of indifference curves, to wrestle with questions about why indifference curves have these shapes.

While economists see retirement as a relationship between income and leisure, social gerontologists see it as a relationship between people and jobs. In this model, retirement is the final stage of the occupational life cycle. The retirement process begins when an individual recognizes that eventually he will permanently withdraw from the work force in old age.

Following Robert Atchley's model of the phases of retirement, the early recognition of impending retirement is the remote phase of preretirement (1976). The near phase of preretirement begins when the individual becomes aware that he or she will take up the retirement role very soon and begins to gear up for separation from the job and the social situation within which it was carried out. This theory of a process of preretirement role exit was operationalized well by David Ekerdt and Stanley DeViney (1993), who found that men evaluate their jobs as more burdensome when drawing closer to retirement, regardless of age and other factors (the "short-timer's syndrome"). Thus, "time left at work organizes the experience of the older worker" (1993, S35). However, David Karp's (1989) research warned that the social construction of retirement varies greatly. Among professionals in their 50s, retirement is anticipated in diverse ways. For example, those with "unfinished agendas" are not likely to exhibit the short-timer's syndrome.

After the event of retirement, individuals may proceed through a number of phases (honeymoon, disenchantment, reorientation), but a long stability phase usually precedes the end of the retirement role. This model suggests that people expect more out of retirement than just extra leisure, and that a job may or may not be considered something more than time that is traded to earn income. What do people expect in retirement, and how do they feel about leaving their jobs?

The dominant paradigm for approaching these questions is continuity theory, which has arisen out of the ashes of the conflicting disengagement and activity theories. Disengagement theory argues that retirement is part of two withdrawal processes. Elderly people voluntarily withdraw from roles and activities (such as paid work), reducing their sense of involvement and cutting themselves off from society. This happens more or less in concert with the second process, whereby society withdraws from elderly persons in order to dampen the impact on society of their eventual death. The theory maintains that the turning inward (interiorization of ego) is typical of aging people, who have an increasing pre-occupation with the self and decreasing involvement with others. However, re-search has made it clear that this type of disengagement is neither natural nor inevitable; consequently, it cannot explain retirement as a social phenomenon.

Activity theory opposed disengagement theory. In this model, the decreased economic and social interaction that characterizes old age results from the with-drawal by society from the aging person. The older person who ages optimally is the person who stays active and manages to resist the shrinkage of his or her social world, rather maintaining the activities of middle age as long as possible and then finding substitutes for those activities when forced to relinquish them. Activity theory predicts that substitutes for the work role will be sought when one is forced to retire. This theory has also been found to be overly simple. Empirical research has shown that many older people do not want to find a substitute for a job and that most retirement is "voluntary," and not forced. Chambré (1984), for example, finds that levels of volunteering are similar among retirees and workers of the same age. Thus, volunteer work is not a substitute for role loss in old age. This finding also questions disengagement theory because volunteering does not generally decline upon retirement, either.

Continuity theory has supplanted these theories. As Robert Atchley explained it:

Continuity is first and foremost a subjective perception that changes are linked to and fit with individual personal history. Continuity can be either internal or external. Internal continuity is defined by the individual in relation to a remembered inner structure, such as the persistence of a psychic structure of ideas, temperament, affect, experiences, preferences, disposition, and skills. (1989, 184)

Moreover, "individuals have strong motives for wanting to preserve internal continuity. They perceive that internal continuity acts as a foundation for effective day-to-day decision making because internal continuity is an important part of individual mastery and competence" (Atchley, 1989, 185). Internal continuity is essential to a sense of ego integrity and helps meet the need for self-esteem. In addition, the predictability of an individual's identity, self, and temperament is an important part of that individual's personal attractiveness because it makes him or her comfortable and predictable to be around and promotes an easy maintenance of social interaction and social support.

"External continuity is defined in terms of a remembered structure of physical and social environments, role relationships, and activities" (Atchley, 1989, 184). Various pressures and attractions move people toward external continuity as well. First, people are expected by others to present themselves in a way that is obviously tied to, and connected with, their past role performances. Second, external continuity of relationships is motivated by a desire for predictable social support. External continuity is seen as an important means of coping with physical and mental changes that may accompany aging. Finally, external continuity reduces the ambiguity of personal goals that can come with the changes of old age. Continuity is an efficient way to narrow the field from which new goals are sought. Thus, continuity theory predicts that a common pattern of adjustment to retirement is to maintain the same general set of personal goals that were held prior to this phase of life.

Research has shown that both internal and external continuity are very common aspects of aging.[4] (See, for example, Palmore, Fillenbaum, and George, 1984.) The central premise of continuity theory is that in making adaptive choices, middle-aged and older adults attempt to preserve and maintain existing internal and external structures, and that they prefer to accomplish this objective by applying familiar strategies in familiar areas of life; this is exactly what is found empirically. "We find older people using familiar skills to do familiar things in familiar places in the company of familiar people. . . . [T]his continuity is not a boring sameness for most but rather a comforting routine and familiar sense of direction" (Atchley, 1989, 188). Thus, while models of stages of life and role theory often imply that retirement is an epochal, disruptive event, continuity theory argues that it need not be, and usually is not.

Activity theory attempted to account for these empirical findings, but it was a homeostatic or equilibrium model. It assumed that when change occurred, the typical response was to restore the previous equilibrium. However, aging produces changes (in health, productivity, or tastes, for example) that cannot be completely offset, so there is really no way to return completely to the prior state. On the other hand, continuity theory assumes evolution, not homeostasis, and this assumption allows change to be integrated into one's prior history without necessarily causing upheaval or disequilibrium. Continuity theory contends that the positive outcomes of normal aging occur because large numbers of aging people use continuity strategies to adapt to changes associated with normal aging and maintain the same general set of personal goals.

As retirement releases people from external role demands, they are freer to concentrate their activities in areas they define as their strengths and to avoid areas they define as weaknesses. This makes adaptation easier. Furthermore, when people retire, they may no longer play the job role, but they often retain the occupational identity, easing the transition.

Atchley (1976) argued that a necessary condition for the emergence of retirement as a social institution is that "people in the society must be able to accept the idea that one can legitimately live in dignity as an adult without having a job" (Atchley, 1976, 16). Ekerdt (1986) argues that the "busy ethic" and the "ideology of pensions" are the continuity mechanisms used by retirees and society in the United States. His theory suggests that "retirement is legitimated on a day-to-day basis in part by an ethic that esteems leisure that is earnest, active, and occupied. [This busy ethic] endorses conduct that is consistent with the abstract ideal of the work ethic. The busy ethic justifies the leisure of retirement, defends retirement against judgments of senescence, and gives definition to the retirement role. In all, it helps individuals adapt to retirement and in turn adapts retirement to prevailing societal values" (Ekerdt, 1986, 239).

Our "cultural map of the life course has now been altered to include a separate stage of life called retirement. [The busy ethic] represents people's attempts to justify retirement in terms of their long-standing beliefs and values" (Ekerdt, 1986, 239). This has altered the shape of the indifference curve, making individuals more willing to trade off income for leisure, because society deems it acceptable.

The work ethic, like any ethic, is a set of beliefs and values that identifies what is good and affirms ideals of conduct. It provides criteria for the evaluation of behavior and action. The work ethic historically has identified work with virtue and has held up for esteem a combination of such traits and habits as diligence, initiative, temperance, industriousness, competitiveness, self-reliance, and the capacity for deferred gratification. (Ekerdt, 1986, 239)

Among persons approaching retirement, surveys show no falloff in subscription to values about work. Thus, assuming that a positive value orientation toward work is carried up to the threshold of retirement, the question becomes: what do people accomplish with a work ethic when they no longer work?

Transitions are easier when beliefs are continuous between two positions, that is, when action in the new position is built upon or integrated with the existing values of the person. Moral continuity is a benefit for the individual who is in transition, and for the wider social community as well. "But the work ethic is not unlearned in some retirement resocialization process. Rather, it is transformed" (Ekerdt, 1986, 240). The busy ethic defends the daily conduct of retired life. The ideology of pensions legitimates retirees' claims to income without the obligation to work, due to status as a veteran.

Economists assume that people retire because they value the leisure they gain more than the income they give up, implicitly assuming that work is viewed as an instrumental means to an end and a "bad" rather than a "good." This ignores the importance of the work role and the work ethic. In contrast, continuity theory and the model of the busy ethic help explain why leisure in old age is valued and how older workers are able to slip out of the work role.

Continuity theory can potentially overcome the biases that Maximiliane Szinovacz, David Ekerdt, and Barbara Vinick (1992) identified in earlier models of retirement and family. Many models, including those most widely used by economists, are afflicted by a "triple bias." These models contain an "individualistic" bias, frequently ignoring linkages between family and retirement experiences; lack a life-course perspective; and suffer from an "isolationist" bias, failing to explore whether life events surrounding the retirement transition impinge on individuals' retirement experience.

Szinovacz, Ekerdt, and Vinick (1992) argue for a more eclectic, holistic approach to retirement that is informed by several sociological and social psychological theories. In particular, the assumptions contained in systems theory, role theory, exchange theory, and life event and life course theories underline the importance of linking the retirement experience to individuals' other life spheres. Systems theory is functionalist in that it is grounded on the assumption that changes in one system part will bring about changes in other system parts. This means that the retirement transition will effect changes in family relationships; and also implies that changes in parts of the family system can have an impact on family members' work and retirement status and experience. It assumes that individuals' self-concepts are closely linked to the roles they play as well as to others' evaluation of these roles. Hence, the importance in transforming the retirement role through the "busy ethic" to mimic the work role.

Exchange theory assumes that a person's power in relationships is equal to others' dependence on his or her resources. The income loss caused by retirement may significantly alter an individual's power position within a marriage as well as in other family relationships. The central assumption of life-event theory concerns the timing and accumulation of life events. Specifically, both the accumulation of life events (such as illness or death of a spouse) and the inappropriate timing of these events is presumed to cause difficulties in coping with life transition. Continuity theory is most compatible with life-course (or life-cycle) theory, which stresses the impact of earlier life experiences and events on individuals' attitudes, behaviors, and coping abilities.

Antonovsky and Sagy (1990) used a developmental model first produced by Erikson (1963) to argue that retirement is a major discontinuity in the stage-like life cycle. The dominant cultural values of Western societies place a premium on overt and evident active involvement in life: on doing, belonging, and making. Upon retirement, one confronts the task, in the literal sense of the word, of deciding what is to be done. Retirement forces a reevaluation. One is compelled to take stock and to justify the decision. They propose that the continuum of reintegration–disintegration best expresses that dimension of personality that is central to the retirement transition outcome. The more people succeed in actively reevaluating the important areas of life, and in maintaining a sense of health integrity, the more they will succeed in reintegrating their lives upon retirement. The less this is the case, the more they will be characterized by disintegration. This model helps generalize continuity theory, which applies well to "normal" aging. Nonetheless, it must be amended to include retirement decisions that are triggered by "critical events," such as health problems or job loss.[5]

The major criticism of continuity theory is that its level of abstraction and lack of operational definitions make it inadequate for research and theory testing. For example, as Henretta, Chan, and O'Rand showed, a standard practice in social gerontological research is to examine the "reasons for retirement." This practice implicitly ignores the conceptualization of retirement as a process. Furthermore, the most commonly used reason-for-retirement typology (reasons that are health based, voluntary, or compulsory) is neither analytically nor empirically exhaustive, but the "fundamental conceptual difficulty with the reason typology as an indicator of the retirement pathway is that it uses outcome as a measure of process, thereby ignoring those subject to the process who do not retire" (1992, S1) and failing to reflect the complexity of retirement. Thus, most sociological gerontologists find that standard economic budget constraint variables, such as wages, pensions, and health, explain most of the variance in decisions about when to retire, and rarely operationalize variables related to continuity theory in models of satisfaction with retirement and life satisfaction among the elderly.

In light of these limitations, a major research task in the future is to get beyond these broad models of aging and retirement, and develop operational models that integrate social forces into economic models of retirement in empirical work. By way of illustration, in the brief section below, the conceptual form of one such social-psychological model is outlined.

RETIREMENT ADJUSTMENT: SHIFTING RESOURCES IN QUEST OF MEANING

A new model of retirement adjustment, congenial to continuity theory, emphasizes goals, meaning, and resources of two types. This shifting resources model (Longino, 1993), takes as its starting point the concept of productive activity, and posits that all productive activity, including work, involves the use of resources in the quest of meaningful goals. Meaning can be rooted in the cosmos, in our social identities and commitments, and in ourselves as individuals. In this context, Americans more often turn to individual sources of meaning such as our achievements, accomplishments, and self-investments, or our contributions to entities with which we identify, such as family, community, ethnicity, and nation, and, of course, our intimate relationships. The devotion to religious and philosophical principles and systems also provide meaning. These principles provide the value or moral dimension that serves to prioritize our tendency to emphasize one source of meaning above others. Therefore, what we set out to do productively is not random but guided. Wanting to do something valued and meaningful, however, does not make it automatically happen; productivity requires resources.

Resources can be conceptually sorted into two categories, as facilitating or contextual. This is, in fact, an artificial distinction because contexts can also facilitate. Facilitating resources include such factors as health, wealth (or credit), income, education and experience. Facilitating resources may also be inhibiting if they are not present; for example, a low level of education.

Contextual resources, like parenthood, marriage, work, school, and organizations, provide the contexts in which we seek meaning for our lives, guided by our values. Without the context of marriage or parenthood, or enduring friendships, for example, intimate relationships could not provide much meaning.

Resources are not fixed. They come and go; they strengthen and weaken. Seeking meaning for our lives in the face of changing resources requires adjustment. Seen in this way, the adjustment to retirement is just one example of a more general process. Employment, both as a context and facilitator, by providing income, contributes meaning to the lives of most workers. Retirement ends one complex resource. Retirement adjustment, therefore, can be seen as the shifting of resources in the quest of meaning.

Almost all human beings have a lifetime of adjustment experience behind them when they reach retirement. Resources have come and gone; goals have shifted in importance several times. It is just one more in a long series of adjustments.

The adjustment to retirement actually begins before the event, in anticipation of it, as Atchley (1976) pointed out. Anticipatory adjustment requires us to invest our selves or personhood into other meaning contexts. These include intimate relationships, organizations, leisure activities and hobbies, education, or second career lines, among others. This means emphasizing less the personal satisfaction and meaning that has come from our job and emphasizing more the meaning that comes from other contexts.

Speculating about such conceptual models is intellectually enjoyable. However, operationalizing them in quantitative terms is a challenge. Perhaps such models are most appealing to qualitative studies of small numbers of persons in research strategies more congenial to sociology or anthropology than to economics. Such studies, however, often have heuristic value for later quantitative efforts.

CONCLUSION

Economists, in focusing primarily on the work/leisure choice, make a vital contribution but miss many aspects of the process. In examining the relationship between the individual's budget constraints and indifference curves, economists fail to observe the dynamics of preference. We share Ekerdt's (1986) view that although such research is very useful so far as it goes, it is a rather blinkered view of retirement because it focuses almost exclusively on the labor market. It misses less measurable but no less important factors such as people's feelings about work, their jobs, their workplaces, and their attitudes and expectations about retirement.

As indicated in continuity theory and the shifting resources model (Longino, 1993), it is also useful to acknowledge the organizational matrices, normative structures, corporate cultures, and occupational contexts as well as the contextual resources other than work in the quest of the productive and meaningful life in middle and old age. These broader concerns are characteristic of social gerontological models of retirement. Moreover, social gerontological models go beyond economics models by examining the social and psychological consequences of retirement and by seeing retirement dynamically as a process— not merely as an act or a state.

We would emphasize in conclusion that the economic and social gerontological models of retirement are not mutually exclusive. They only have different emphases. An interdisciplinary approach would do well to incorporate both in order to fully explicate retirement behavior.

NOTES

1. "On our preferred interpretation . . . the economist continues to search for differences in prices or incomes to explain any differences or changes in behavior" (Stigler and Becker, 1977, 76).

2. See also Michael Leonesio's discussion of the retirement literature (Chapter 12 of this volume).

3. Andrew Achenbaum also discusses the events leading up to the passage of the Social Security Act of 1935 (Chapter 7 of this volume).

4. Continuity theory is implicitly linked to theories of personality. Reis and Gold discuss some of the links between personality theories, including five-factor personality theory, attachment theory, and the adaptation-level phenomena, to studies of retirement and life satisfaction. "Even accident victims who are paraplegics generally adapt and revert to their usual levels of happiness after an initial period of adjustment" (1993, 271), so it would be odd if there were no ability to adjust in the face of an event as relatively benign as retirement.

5. Ekerdt, Vinick, and Bosse (1989), for example, found that retirement is an "orderly," predictable event for about two-thirds of men, but not for the remainder.

14

Theoretical Perspectives on Productive Aging

Scott A. Bass and Francis G. Caro

Over the last decade in the United States, there has been a growing interest in involving older people in significant economic and social roles. Encouraged by elder advocates and policy makers, the subject of elder engagement and the barriers older people face in maintaining significant involvement later in life has captured the imagination of numerous researchers and several foundations.

Initially, the literature was primarily based on ideas and qualitative studies, but more recently, a number of large-scale surveys have provided a detailed quantitative examination of involvement of older people in a variety of productive activities including work, volunteering, caregiving, and education. These activities of older Americans are included in an area of study termed *productive aging*, which in recent years has received increased attention among gerontologists. One result has been a clarification of concepts and definitions of the term.

Productive aging has evolved to a point where broader theoretical work is needed. This chapter is an attempt to introduce a theoretical perspective that will provide a useful framework for continuing development of this field.

THE MEANING OF PRODUCTIVE AGING

The term *productive aging* is used here to refer to any activity by an older individual that produces goods or services, whether paid or not, or develops the capacity to produce them. Productive aging is restricted to activities that contribute to the community or society. They are activities that are *socially valued* in the sense that, if they were not performed by one person or group, there would be demand for them to be performed by another individual or group. The term *excludes* activities that are simply enriching to the older person who performs them. Physical exercise and intellectual and spiritual activity, for example, are excluded. More specifically, the term includes paid employment, unpaid volunteer work for service organizations, certain unpaid tasks performed for family members such as care of grandchildren, and unpaid care at home to relatives, friends, or neighbors who are sick or disabled. Education or training that strengthens an older person's ability to be effective in paid work, in volunteering for organizations, or in informal productive family or community activities is also included as productive aging. Education for personal growth is not included. Productive aging analysts disagree on some of the specifics. Herzog et al. (1989), for example, included housework; Caro, Bass, and Chen (1993) did not. In this case, there is ambiguity about the extent to which housework left undone by an older person would have to be done by someone else.

The fact that the productive aging discussion focuses on *aging* rather than *the aged* implies that the chronological ages included vary from one discussion to another and are often loosely defined. In some cases, the lower age limit is set at 40 years of age, since federal legislation on age discrimination in employment specifies it as a lower boundary. Other analysis begins at 50 or 55 years of age because this is when age-related departure from the workforce begins to be substantially evident. A pervasive theme in the productive aging literature is that chronological age is a weak predictor of *capacity* for productive performance (Sterns & Sterns, 1995). A great deal of evidence has been accumulated to show that older people have the physical and mental capacities to perform all but the most physically demanding tasks; further, there is evidence that they have the ability to learn new skills that may be required for work or other productive activities.

The use of the term *productive aging* for analytic purposes should not be confused with aging advocacy issues. Advocates for productive aging emphasize the need for expanded opportunities for older people to engage in productive activities (e.g., Morris and Bass, 1988). Critics have expressed concern that expectations for more extensive productive activity may arise, with adverse effects on more vulnerable older people, notably women and members of minority groups (Holstein, 1993).

Attention to productive aging as defined here does not, by implication, devalue *successful aging* or *healthy aging*, terms that describe activities older people undertake to promote their own physical and mental health, their appreciation for life, or their satisfaction with their lives.

The knowledge base for various aspects of productive aging is highly uneven (O'Reilly and Caro, 1992). Extensive research has been conducted on employment among older people with particular emphasis on circumstances surrounding retirement. A number of studies have also been conducted on volunteering for

Table 14.1
Age and Productive Activity (percentages)

Age	One or More Productive Activities	20 or More Hours Per Week of Productive Activity
55-64	87.4	64.5
65-74	73.1	35.7
75 and older	48.0	17.4

service organizations among older people; that literature emphasizes the extent of volunteering and personal characteristics associated with volunteering. The community-based long-term care literature, in spite of its focus on the recipients of care, provides extensive evidence of the role played by older people, particularly spouses, as caregivers. Informal help to the younger generation, including care of grandchildren, has received modest research attention. Some studies have been conducted on grandparenting (Cherlin and Furstenberg, 1986) and some general research has been conducted on reciprocal patterns of assistance between older parents and their children (Rossi and Rossi, 1990; Shanas et al., 1968). Several studies have been conducted that examine the circumstances under which older people enroll in college courses (Lowy and O'Connor, 1986); however, retraining to strengthen work or volunteering skills has received much less research attention (Peterson and Wendt, 1995).

The 1991 Commonwealth Fund Productive Aging Survey was unique in examining the productive activity of older people across institutional sectors.[1] The study surveyed a representative sample of noninstitutionalized people in the United States 55 years of age and older. Evidence was collected on the extent of employment, volunteering for service organizations, provision of help to the younger generations, and informal caregiving to sick and disabled relatives, friends, and neighbors. In addition, participation in work-related education and training was covered. Aggregate analysis focused on four sectors: employment, volunteering for organizations, help to children and grandchildren, and help to the sick and disabled.

The survey showed evidence of extensive involvement in productive activity (Table 14.1). Among those 65–74 years of age, 73.1 percent were engaged in at least one of the four forms of productive activity; even among those 75 years of age and older, 48 percent reported at least one form of productive activity. The extent of productive activity varied enormously, with some people engaged only a few hours a week and others engaged almost around-the-clock, seven days a week. A substantial percentage were active at least the equivalent of a half-time job (20 hours a week or more). Of those 65 to 74 years of age, 35.7

percent were active at least half time. Even among those 75 years of age and older, 17.4 percent were active half time or more.

The relationship between chronological age and participation varied among the four sectors. These relationships are shown in Figure 14.1 through quadratic regression lines. The relationship between age and employment was relatively strong; employment rates of those in the older age groups were much lower than those close to 55 years of age. Other curves were much flatter. The percentage volunteering was clearly lower only among those 75 years of age and older. The percentage helping the sick and disabled was also relatively stable across ages. The differences among the four figures are important for two reasons. First, among older people, employment is highly deceptive as a general indicator of productive activity. The sharply lower rates of employment in older age groups should not be taken as an indicator of general decline in productive activity associated with age. In contrast, volunteering and informal caregiving to the sick and disabled are remarkably stable across older age groups. Second, the data suggest that characteristics of the institutional sectors themselves must be examined to explain how they provide opportunities for productive activity for older people.

Both participation and the extent of participation in any one of the four sectors is, at best, weakly related to participation or the extent of participation in the three other sectors. Older people often answer "other obligations," for example, as a reason for not volunteering at all or limiting their volunteer effort. However, among healthy older people who have recently stopped working, the percentage volunteering to help organizations is not higher than it is among healthy older people who are employed.

THE CONCEPTUAL SHIFT IN PRODUCTIVE AGING

Scholarly work on the subject of productive aging comprises more than the analysis of individual characteristics that affect productive activity. It involves an examination of the larger social structures, policies, programs, and norms that influence individual behavior. The study of productive aging includes attention to the older person within the situational context of societal structures. This is not to say that research on individual behavior is excluded, as this is not the case; it is merely to indicate that the individual is envisaged in a societal context.

As Campbell (1992) points out in his book, *How Policies Change*, much of the policy and conceptual work in gerontology within the United States has focused on aging per se, that is, centered on older people themselves with emphasis on the aged and frail. Traditional theoretical work about aging has been driven by the established disciplines of psychology and sociology, and the allied health professions. Only recently has economic theory been applied extensively to issues in gerontology. Much of the research in gerontology has been criticized as fragmented, and has contributed too little to the development of a theoretical

Figure 14.1
Age and Four Productive Activities

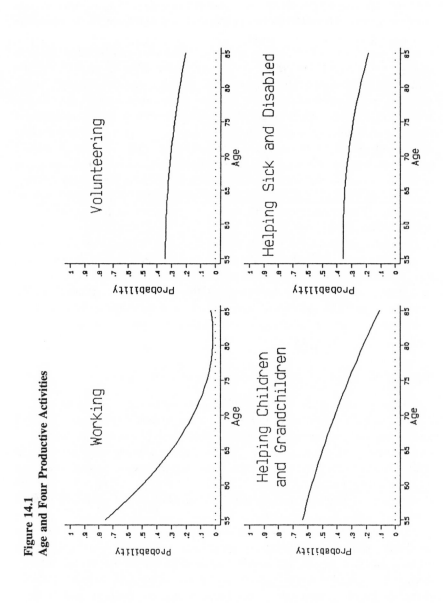

understanding of individual aging and the implications for society (Thornstam, 1992). The notion of shifting from the study of individual aging to the study of aging in a societal context is particularly appealing to researchers interested in the interaction between individual and social structures. From a societal perspective, issues such as long-term care, pensions, social supports, housing, career training, employment, and health care delivery are primary areas of inquiry. The issue of productive roles for older people is particularly significant in an aging society.

As in the earlier theoretical work in sociology (Rosow, 1985), status and role are important in examining productive aging. Within the typology of status–role permutations developed by sociologists, there are two relevant groupings: (1) institutional, where roles and status are defined and institutionalized with clear positions and attributes (these roles are most commonly found among defined occupations or obligations such as workers, managers, doctors, etc.); and (2) tenuous, where roles are unclear (e.g., the chronically unemployed) and status is undefined (e.g., the chronically unemployed and frequently the role of the elderly).

Writing from a static sociological perspective, Rosow (1985) argued that the tenuous roles older people face in America are the result of a normative process in which older people are removed from more highly valued institutional roles (are devalued) and are ascribed less-defined, and more ambiguous, roles. The devaluing process is fairly universal for an entire cohort of people who individually seek to adjust to old age, a different phase of their lives.

Alternatively, some psychologists have looked toward intrapsychic causes to explain the decline of participation among older people in the engagement in productive activities. In this view, the decline in participation is viewed individually based on personality and opportunities for engagement. Indeed, there are different adjustment patterns in later life—to loss of loved ones, to withdrawal from work, to economic stress, to chronic ailments, and to changing social conditions. Nevertheless, an individually based description of the participation in productive activities later in life cannot be fully explained without an understanding of the economic and social context that confront the aged.

Economists have also contributed to the examination of certain aspects of productive aging. They have been particularly interested in the changing patterns of employment of older adults and have found that pension policies act as incentives or disincentives regarding individual retirement decisions (Schulz, 1992). The finding that workers respond to economic incentives in the timing of retirement is consistent with the microeconomic theory that people seek to maximize their economic advantage. Although, for the most part, these economists have not been identified with productive aging, their contributions to the understanding of the linkage of economic incentives and disincentives to individual behavior provide important theoretical groundwork for the multidisciplinary study of productive aging.

Thus far, research about productive aging contributed by scientists from the disciplinary perspectives has documented the current activity of older people and explored their interest in expanded roles; it has just begun to analyze the established policies and practices that can be altered through litigation, education, programmatic change, and policy reformulation to expand the opportunities for enhanced roles and status in later life. A conceptual framework for productive aging needs to draw on the earlier work in psychology, sociology, and economics and acknowledge that societal norms evolve and change over time.

A CONCEPTUAL FRAMEWORK FROM WHICH TO VIEW PRODUCTIVE AGING

In Figure 14.2, we have developed a conceptual scheme from which to view productive aging that involves three sectors: situational, individual, and structural. The description is dynamic and interactive with the expectation that change is possible in each of the three sectors, which in turn will influence the others. As items in the three sectors change, the participation of older people in productive activities can change.

Sector A includes the situational variables over which the individual has little control. They include formal institutional roles and also more tenuous roles that are assigned through both opportunity and circumstance. Included are family obligations to spouse, children, relatives, grandchildren, and so forth; financial standing and available economic resources; race; gender; health status; educational level; and current economic conditions. An older person often has little flexibility in altering these situational variables, and they can have a significant influence on the subsequent levels of participation in productive activities in later life.

Mediating these situational variables are individual variables such as motivation, initiative, creativity, attitude, flexibility, and skill level, which are identified in Sector B. Although older individuals may face discrimination and unfair treatment, how they mediate these circumstances will vary from individual to individual. There are those remarkable individuals who may be able to navigate a course that leads to high levels of participation in later life. These individuals—"super-elders" as they are sometimes called—are often individuals who have overcome major obstacles to achieve significant productive roles in later life. Although we all can point to individuals who obtain their college degree in their late 70s, people who find new jobs after retirement, and older adults who are providing extraordinary community service, these super-elders are the exception rather than the rule. The evidence indicates widespread productivity among older people, but survey findings also indicate significant untapped potential (Caro and Bass, 1995). Early research on older people has provided a substantial body of knowledge on the cognitive ability, physical ability, motivation, and personality attributes of older people.

It is Sector C, encompassing structural factors, that has received the least scholarly attention, though elder advocates and elected officials have sought to

Figure 14.2
Theoretical Perspectives on Productive Aging

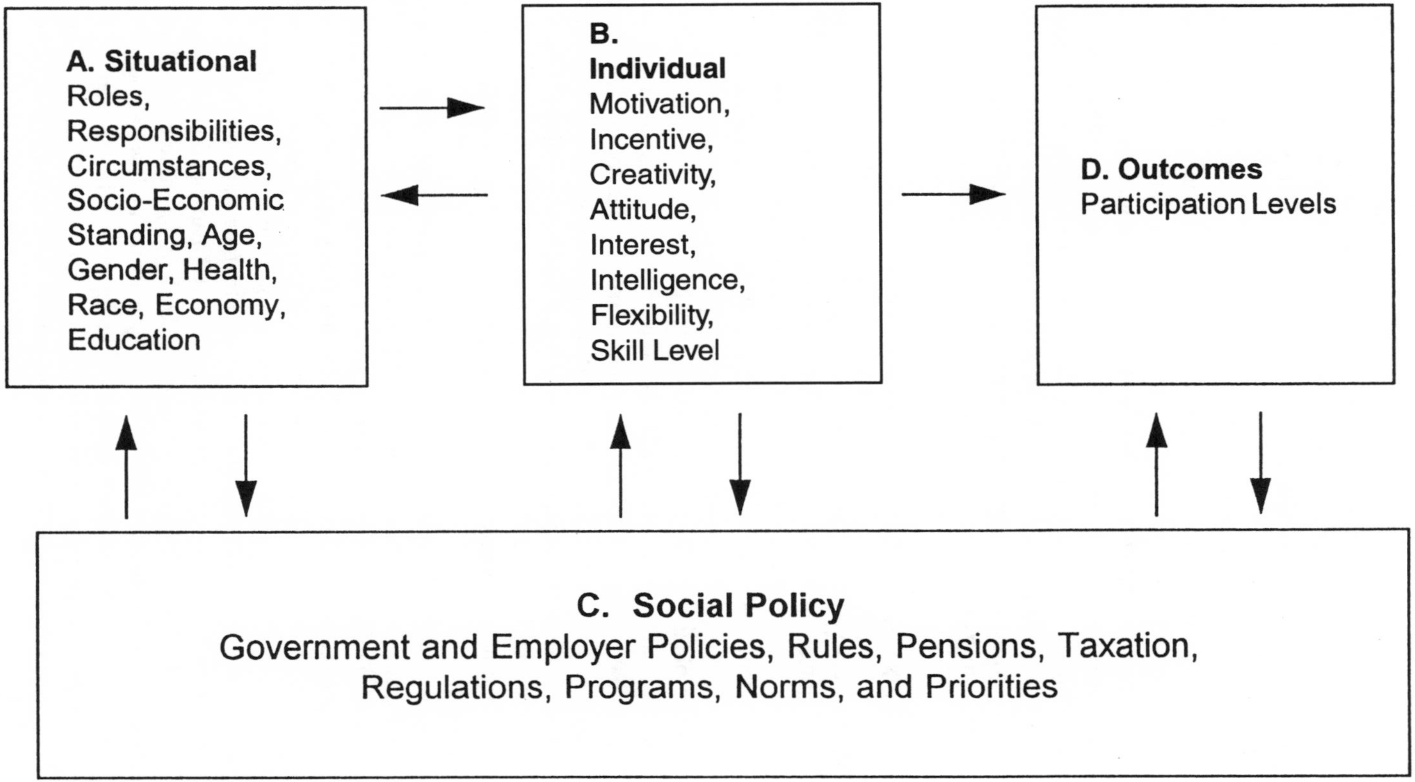

A. Situational
Roles,
Responsibilities,
Circumstances,
Socio-Economic
Standing, Age,
Gender, Health,
Race, Economy,
Education

B.
Individual
Motivation,
Incentive,
Creativity,
Attitude,
Interest,
Intelligence,
Flexibility,
Skill Level

D. Outcomes
Participation Levels

C. Social Policy
Government and Employer Policies, Rules, Pensions, Taxation,
Regulations, Programs, Norms, and Priorities

develop legislation, programs, and policies to protect older people from employment discrimination, provide resources for retraining, and change employers' attitudes toward older workers. If the prevailing rules and regulations change, older people may experience changes in both the situational variables and the individual variables that ultimately affect their productive participation in society.

For example, under the 1992 Americans with Disabilities Act (ADA), all workers with disabilities are given new protections in the workplace. Among these protections is included the requirement that employers adapt and modify working environments for disabled adults. Although this does little to influence the situational variable of the disability itself, it opens doors for those with disabilities. The act will have implications for older people who may develop disabling conditions later in life and seek to continue to work. Prior to passage of the ADA, these older people might have been forced to retire or leave work; now there is the possibility of paid employment being sustained.

THEORIES OF PRODUCTIVE ACTIVITY

Productive aging researchers have sought to explain the obstacles to productive aging. Their particular focus has been to consider the importance attached by our society to economic institutions. Not only is paid work the major source of personal income, but occupation is central to adult identity. The decline in labor force participation that has taken place in recent decades (particularly among older men), in spite of major gains in health and longevity among older people, has received extensive research attention. Those studying productive aging have also tried to identify ways in which volunteering for organizations might be increased. Their interest is less in the characteristics of individual older people that would explain their patterns of productive activity than it is in the institutional forces that both account for opportunities for productive participation and help to shape public opinion on productive participation among older people.

Caro, Bass, and Chen (1993) hypothesized that the obstacles in this society to the successful employment of older people are so widespread that the term *institutionalized ageism* should be used to describe them. They argued that these obstacles are often so subtle they are not recognized. They may include not only discrimination against older people in the hiring process, but also a lack of full recognition of the achievements of older workers, lack of consideration of promotions, less-than-equal access to retraining that may be key to job retention or promotion, and exclusion from full participation in informal work groups dominated by younger workers. Underlying these discriminatory practices may be unjustified beliefs that older workers are less productive than their younger counterparts, less capable of being retrained, less open to change in organizational practices, more vulnerable to injury and illness, and more costly than younger workers from a fringe benefit perspective. The institutionalized norms that minimize the capabilities of older people in the workplace may be so pervasive that they are internalized even by older people themselves. Through negative images of aging, older people may underestimate their own capabilities and accept the notion that they should leave productive roles at relatively young ages.

A fundamental question about the institutionalized ageism hypothesis concerns the evidence supporting it. The extent to which there are *patterns* of discriminatory practices and prejudicial attitudes against older people in work organizations is an empirical issue. From a scientific perspective, it is not sufficient to invoke institutionalized ageism as a residual explanation of various employment problems of older people. While there is scattered evidence of discriminatory practices and prejudicial beliefs directed toward older workers, no pervasive patterns have been documented. However, because of the difficulty of obtaining such data, the absence of evidence does not provide a basis for ruling out the possibility of institutionalized ageism in the workplace. To the extent that such ageism can be established, an explanation of the phenomenon is needed.

A basic hypothesis to explain the relatively low levels of participation of older people in the workforce might be termed the *affluence/leisure preference* hypothesis, reflecting both the relative affluence of many current older Americans and the preference of many of them for leisure activities. Implicitly, according to this hypothesis, prevailing social norms define old age as a time in which older people are encouraged to pursue leisure activities. Older people are relieved of their obligations to be economically productive. Again, according to the hypothesis, people work largely for economic reasons, that is, because they "need the money." When they can afford to, older people retire. In this framework, the decline in the typical retirement age is attributed to societal as well as individual affluence. The economic prosperity of the United States and Western European countries after World War II has made it possible for many older people, through government pension programs and employer-financed pension programs, to live comfortably without working. Essentially, the hypothesis asserts that prosperity makes it economically possible for many older people to retire; a great many of them not only take advantage of the opportunity for leisure activities but also concentrate on them rather than on other productive activities such as volunteering for organizations.

Intergenerational conflict is a second potential explanation of both the current low levels of workforce participation of older people and institutional ageism more generally. According to conflict theory, social groups make competing claims on scarce resources. Each group pursues its own interest, attempting to maximize its share of societal rewards without regard for the welfare of other groups. The pursuit of competing claims need not always be overt. On the surface, groups with conflicting interests may maintain civil relationships, but they may be engaged in energetic covert struggles to maximize their advantages. Older and younger people sometimes have conflicting economic interests. When jobs are scarce, older people can be seen by younger people as competitors. If older people hold attractive positions within a firm, this is sometimes seen as blocking opportunities for younger people. Thus, the removal of an older person from such a position is interpreted as an opportunity to make the position available to a younger person. Institutional arrangements that encourage older people to leave jobs, such as early retirement incentives, can be instruments of conflict between older and younger people over jobs.

Conflict theory predicts that pressure to exclude the elderly is affected by labor market conditions. During recessions when jobs are scarce, pressure to remove the elderly from the workforce is expected to increase. In periods of economic prosperity when workers are in short supply, conflict theory predicts that older workers will be seen in a much more favorable light, and therefore, the employment of older people is then more likely to be actively encouraged.

Cultural lag is a third potential explanation for the limited participation of older people in attractive, paid work roles and is also a potential explanation of institutional ageism. Cultural lag theory, which was introduced by Ogburn (1964) to explain slow societal responses to the improved conditions made possible by technological advances, differs from conflict theory in its assumptions about the underpinnings of institutional patterns. The cultural lag hypothesis asserts that as a society, we simply are slow to adjust our institutions in response to changing conditions. The premise is that institutional arrangements are inherently difficult to change because of their complexity and rigidity and our short-sighted satisfaction with them. According to cultural lag theory, a learning process is required to understand the implications of technical and social change and to make sound adjustments in institutional policies and practices. Our society may not recognize, for example, that contemporary retirement policies which encourage early retirement are premised on an oversupply of labor. As a result, though the labor supply may diminish to a point where greater numbers of older workers are needed, those who control pension policies may be slow to recognize the need to adjust them to reflect the economic value of continuing the employment of older workers. Certain existing pension policies may be formalized in contracts that cannot be modified quickly. Similarly, our society may simply be slow in reorganizing its educational institutions to provide the lifelong training for work necessary in a changed economy characterized by sharper competition and rapid technological advances. Moreover, according to cultural lag theory, we may be slow to recognize that people now have the potential for remaining productive later in life as a result of improved health and reduced physical demands in the workplace.

Although the three theories have been developed to explain the underutilization of older people in a historical context, they can be used also to explain certain present-day variations in productive activity among older people. The affluence/leisure preference theory, for example, predicts that among older workers, the greater the accumulated savings and the stronger the pension benefits, the earlier the likely age of retirement. Further, the more intrinsically satisfying the occupation, the later the likely age of retirement. Conflict theory predicts that policy toward the older worker is a function of an industry's prosperity. More specifically, in expanding industries, employer policies will tend to encourage the retention of older workers. In contracting industries, employers' policies will tend to discourage it. On the other hand, cultural lag theory predicts that receptivity to older workers is a reflection of industry "enlightenment." To the extent that industry leaders are well informed about the potential contribution of older workers and make efforts to modify industry policies accordingly, opportunities for older workers will be relatively better.

The three theories differ in their implications for change. The affluence/leisure preference theory suggests that older people will seek to remain in the workforce longer if their economic circumstances are less favorable or if their lifestyle preferences shift from less to more productive activities. On the economic dimension, there is some evidence that future cohorts of older people may prefer to stay in the workforce longer because their pension coverage will fall short of that of recent retirees (Holden, 1993). Further, if legislative proposals to weaken social security benefits in the name of deficit reduction are successful, early retirement will seem less attractive from an economic perspective.

Conflict theory suggests that change is most likely to occur when there are shifts in the relative strength of opposing forces. The baby boom generation has the potential to assert itself effectively in the political process because of its extraordinary numerical strength. As time goes on, the baby boom generation will find itself affected by older worker issues. In the coming decade, the number of young people entering the workforce will be declining. To the extent that votes reflect political strengths, older workers will have the potential to improve their relative position through legislative measures that strengthen their position in the workforce. At the same time, the underlying tension between older and younger workers will remain. In periods of economic recession when jobs are scarce, competition for jobs will be an issue, and age will be one of the factors considered when workers contest for access to jobs.

Cultural lag theory offers a basis for optimism about the potential for improved opportunities for the productive participation of older people. It suggests that the basis for change lies in part in education. Further, it suggests that social engineering can be successful in adapting societal institutions to changing conditions. Through the education of employers and older workers, myths about the liabilities of older people as workers can be replaced by a more accurate understanding of their potential. As a result, employers will make it more attractive for older workers to remain in the workforce and older workers will be more eager to remain.

POLICIES TOWARD WORK THAT NEED RECONSIDERATION

The current participation levels among older people as they age in paid work reflects a very different pattern than that of their participation in other productive activities. Findings from the 1989 Commonwealth Fund Laborforce 2000 Survey (Commonwealth Fund, 1993b), a nationally representative sample of older people, indicated that a small but sizable percentage of those who had already retired were interested in returning to work. In addition, of those then working, 26 percent of men and 24 percent of women would work longer than they had then planned to if their employer pension contributions were to continue past the age of 64; 31 percent of men and 30 percent of women indicated that they would do so if they were offered fewer hours and responsibilities with the attending reduction in pay. Recent secondary analysis of this data set by Quinn and Burkhauser (1994b) indicated that of those who responded that they would like to work longer, 59 percent wanted to return to work for economic reasons and 41 percent wanted to return more for social and psychological reasons. In either case, these are powerful reasons to work and Quinn and Burkhauser believe this data indicates a trend toward increased interest in later-life paid work. They point to increased longevity, better health, a reduction in corporate pensions, declining interest rates, and the social rewards for work as reasons to expect more older people remaining on the job or returning to work after retirement. Still, powerful disincentives exist in public policy that discourage people from working past the age of 65.

Bass, Quinn, and Burkhauser (1995) identified a series of policy changes that would make it much easier for those older people who want to work to continue working beyond the traditional retirement years. Their suggestions are rather specific; undoubtedly, the significance of each will change over time. They are based on the belief that social outcomes are alterable through macro level policy changes. New and different work incentive policies will need to be adopted in the future if we choose to be proactive about encouraging able-bodied individuals to remain in the workforce. Policy changes that could be implemented in the future include the following: (1) provide part-time employees with prorated fringe benefits, depending on the number of hours they work. This would be a significant incentive for older people to return to work. (2) As part of health care reform, reduce private health care costs for the employer employing older workers. (3) Allow the over-65 worker to opt out of social security contributions—saving the older worker and the employer money. (4) Allow low-income older workers without children to qualify for the Earned Income Tax Credit. (5) Provide tax credits to employers who provide or pay for older worker retraining. (6) Expand federal employment training programs to older people. (7) Provide a personal tax credit to older workers who pay for work-related educational expenses. (8) Mandate through federal legislation that employer pensions be age neutral. (9) Develop state plans for older workers to encourage their retraining and hiring. (10) Expand the enforcement of age discrimination laws.

Some of these changes will cost money, but older people who work are taxpayers and generate new revenues for the state and federal governments. Further, if older people work, they are less likely to draw on social security resources. There are economic reasons as well as social benefits to consider in expanding the roles of older workers in an aging society that is nonetheless productive.

CONCLUSION

In this chapter, we have attempted to develop a theoretical perspective from which to consider the productive engagement of older people in our society. Within this framework is the explicit examination of the interplay between situational variables, individual variables, and social policy regarding their involvement and engagement. It is hypothesized that changes in prevailing social policies will alter the interactions between situational and individual variables resulting in different participatory outcomes. Either increasing or decreasing participation among older people can be achieved through various social policies, rules, and regulations.

In addition, we have examined the theories of affluence/leisure preference, intergenerational conflict, and cultural lag as potential explanations for the relatively low levels of participation by older people in the United States in certain productive activities. Finally, we have identified specific policy directions for increasing participation levels in such activities among older people.

NOTE

1. For a description of this survey, see Bass (1995).

15

The Productivity and Functional Limitations of Older Adult Workers

Anthony A. Sterns, Harvey L. Sterns, and Lisa A. Hollis

For many decades we have been aware of the increasing numbers of older individuals in the United States. Increasing budgetary demands have put pressure on social policy planners to define the protections, entitlements, services, and benefits that this large and growing group receives. Related to these issues are questions concerning how older Americans will participate in our economy and our society. This chapter will examine the potential of aging to affect the productivity of workers. It will also focus on the many changes members of this group will experience, both within themselves and in the environment around them, and examine how these may impact on productivity. We will also suggest mechanisms for coping with and adapting to these changes.

To examine recent trends in older workers it is important that a definition of this group is stated clearly. Sterns and Doverspike (1989) looked at five ways of defining who is an older worker: chronological, functional, psychosocial, organizational, and life-span developmental.

Chronological age is the most common approach to examining older workers. According to the 1967 Age Discrimination in Employment Act (ADEA) and amendments (1978, 1986), an older worker is any individual 40 and over who is still an active worker (Snyder and Barrett, 1988). Chronological age has been preferred by courts (over functional age) in the assessment of individual performance capacity, and it has been found to be a bona fide occupational qualification (BFOQ) when reasonably related to job performance. Commercial airline pilots, for example, are still subject to mandatory retirement based on their chronological age (Avolio, Barrett, and Sterns, 1984).

Functional age is a performance-based definition of age and is conceptualized as a single index that considers biological and psychological changes, including both declines in abilities as well as increases in skill, wisdom, and experience (Birren and Stafford, 1986). We will examine examples of functional age approaches including physical abilities analysis and functional capacity assessment.

Psychosocial definitions of older workers focus on social perceptions of this group. When a worker is perceived as older, the attitudes toward older workers and the implications for personnel decisions of labeling a worker as older are addressed in this view. Research on how older workers are perceived has found both negative and positive perceptions. Negative perceptions include older workers being regarded as more difficult to train, less receptive to technological changes, more accident prone, less promotable, and less motivated (Avolio and Barrett, 1987; Bird and Fisher, 1986; Schwab and Heneman, 1978; Stagner, 1985). On the positive side, older adults are perceived as more dependable, cooperative, conscientious, consistent, and knowledgeable (Schwab and Heneman, 1978).

The organizational approach considers the roles of individuals in an organization and the organization as a whole. This perspective emphasizes seniority and tenure rather than age. At the aggregate level, an organization is considered old if the average age of its members is old. As the average age of personnel increases, attitudinal and financial demands on the organization may change. This approach focuses on the nature of the organization. The mix of cognitive and physical requirements required by the nature of the work will be important considerations when examining the impact of aging on workers in an organization.

The life-span orientation combines these approaches with a recognition that behavioral change can occur over the entire life cycle. This approach emphasizes substantial individual differences in aging (Baltes, Reese, and Lipsitt, 1980). Individuals are influenced by normative, age-graded biological and environmental influences (physical and cognitive changes as one ages); normative, history-graded factors (generational events); and nonnormative influences unique to every individual. The influences interact to determine an individual's career path and the strengths and limitations that person brings to a job. Individuals begin with different potentials and will improve and decline at differing rates.

How older workers are defined tempers how the impact of future technological changes, employment opportunities, and incentives to remain in the workforce are viewed. Each definition will emphasize different viewpoints and lead to different recommendations. For example, the chronological viewpoint emphasizes legal issues, while functional age perspectives focus on the physical capacity of the worker. Psychosocial perspectives consider the attitudes an individual holds. Organizational perspectives focus on the use of human resources to maximize productivity and efficiency. The life-span perspective reminds us of the individual differences and to be cautious of overgeneralizing. All these must be kept in mind as the issues of productivity and functionality are considered with regard to the older workers.

In order to understand how aging interacts with the productivity of a workforce or places limitations on individuals, it is important to understand the tasks involved in a job and the requirements of the person doing it. These are determined by a process known as job analysis.

JOB ANALYSIS AND JOB DESCRIPTIONS FOR A DIVERSIFIED WORKFORCE

Job analysis is the fundamental methodology for determining the knowledge, skills, and abilities required for a person to successfully perform a job. Determining the knowledge, skills, and abilities of a job is important for several reasons. First, the employer will want to consider only those applicants who possess the appropriate qualifications for the position. This allows the employer to determine the availability of qualified persons in the population, which is important if the company has an affirmative action program. Second, job analysis provides criteria for evaluating the qualified candidates to determine who is the most qualified. This is especially important for a company that seeks a diversified workforce from the general population.

From a functional age perspective, health can impact a person's physical and psychological capabilities. Avolio, Barrett, and Sterns (1984) proposed an approach based on job analysis techniques that would assess intrinsic attributes directly related to performance on the job, independent of physical health problems. Information obtained from specific job analysis is used to establish criterion performance levels. Above the criterion level, an individual's performance on the job is expected to be satisfactory.

Once criteria for a job are established, tests are then developed that significantly correlate with the job's critical abilities. Cutoff scores are developed and validated for the established performance levels. The repeated assessment of individuals can track their performance levels over time and determine when substantial drops have occurred. A word processor who develops arthritis would be allowed to continue the job until (or unless) his or her performance drops below criterion levels. Arthritis would affect a switchboard operator less dramatically and might never impact substantially on job performance or play a role in retirement. This approach provides the means for a legally defensible method of performance appraisal that is job related, sensitive to disabilities and limitations, and not directly related to age.

The job analysis process allows an employer to attain information about observed behavior on a job. This information is used for compensation to describe job tasks and the abilities, skills, and behaviors required by the position. Different methods are used to get the required information. The most common method requires a combination of observation, interviews with job incumbents and supervisors, and occasionally some surveying. Other methods may include checklists, the use of diaries, activity sampling, or using a critical incidents technique. The job analysis process results in a job description detailing the knowledge, skills, and abilities required of the position as well as essential and marginal functions performed on the job.

A number of steps are required when conducting a job analysis. First, preliminary job information is gathered, such as a job description from the *Dictionary of Occupational Titles (DOT)* (U.S. Dept. of Labor, 1965) or an existing job description. Next, an initial tour of the work site is conducted to evaluate the working environment. Interviews are then conducted with job incumbents and supervisors. A second tour of the work site is done to confirm the information obtained from the interviews, and the job information is consolidated into a new job description, which should then be verified by the supervisor.

NEEDS ANALYSIS

A needs analysis (Goldstein, 1986) is also essential to thoroughly understand the requirements of a job. A needs analysis consists of three separate analyses, which examine the organization, the personnel, and the job tasks.

Organizational analysis is concerned with issues of manpower, organizational strategy, and organizational climate (Wexley and Latham, 1981). The person conducting the organizational analysis should be on the lookout to determine potential obstacles, whether the desired skills will be reinforced by supervisor and peers, job objectives, and how to measure and evaluate those objectives.

Personnel analysis examines such issues as the need for performance appraisal, a consideration of trainability of the person, and the existing abilities, motivation, perceptions of the work environment by job incumbents (Noe, 1986), training readiness, and motivation for trainability (Wexley and Latham, 1981).

Task analysis is closely tied to job analysis (Wexley and Latham, 1981), which reveals testing concerns and allows for a consideration of potential obstacles. Other authors have also suggested that testing applications such as tailored testing be considered at this stage in the needs analysis (Barrett and Mauer, 1992).

Needs analysis supports and enhances the human resource functions present in most organizations, such as planning and career management, and the writing of job descriptions (Schneier, Guthrie, and Olian, 1988). Products of needs analysis include the identification of the knowledge, skills, and abilities (KSAs) required to perform jobs, ability to assess which training program would be best for a job, designing future training across jobs, and the creation of a database of pertinent KSAs throughout the organization. These activities will also be used for many other essential human resource functions, such as determining benefits and compensation.

Job and needs analysis techniques emphasize the tasks required to perform the job. However, other analysis techniques focus on defining the capabilities and capacities of the person. These approaches originate from the functional age perspective. Two of these approaches are the physical abilities analysis and functional capacity assessment. Neither approach concerns itself directly with aging or disabilities. Rather, the physical demands of the job are defined and the applicants are evaluated to determine if they can achieve and maintain those demands.

PHYSICAL ABILITIES ANALYSIS

This approach concentrates on defining the physical abilities required of the worker, rather than emphasizing the physical demands of the job tasks. In other words, this approach focuses on the person more than the job. The demands can then be used as a guideline against which the employee can be measured. The physical abilities analysis attempts to measure job effort using job incumbent's perceptions of effort or exertion experienced while performing work.

A number of scales have been developed to perform a physical ability analysis. These include the rating of perceived exertion (RPE) scale (Borg, 1962), acceptability scaling (Snook, 1978; Ayoub et al., 1979), and the *Physical Abilities Analysis Manual* (PAAM) (Nylander and Carmean, 1984).

The PAAM is based on the assumption that the performer's subjective report of perception associated with physical work can be used to obtain information about physiological responses to work and workload to make a determination of capacity and work demand (Fleishman, Gebhardt, and Hogan, 1984). It is comprised of three parts which ask job incumbents to give biographical data and to rate 34 different sets of working conditions and 22 physical abilities, each with a unique set of anchors.

The steps required for a selection procedure using the PAAM are as follows:

1. Employer collects information on physical abilities required for all jobs being assessed and prepares a physical ability analysis.

2. The applicant is offered a position pending a medical review.

3. A health professional conducts an assessment of the job candidate.

4. If any impairments are revealed, the health professional consults the standards derived from the PAAM and compares the conditions of the job to the capacity of the candidate.

5. If conditions of the job do not exceed the capacity of the applicant, the applicant is acceptable.

6. If the conditions required of the job do exceed the capacity of the applicant, the PAAM will assist in defining any accommodations that might be required or provide evidence for the unsuitability of the candidate (Fraser, 1992).

FUNCTIONAL CAPACITY ASSESSMENT

Successfully evaluating an employee applicant in terms of the capacity to perform essential functions of a job is the goal of a functional capacity assessment (FCA). The FCA is comprised of a number of procedures used to evaluate fitness for work and is done in conjunction with a physical demands analysis (PDA). The PDA provides the context against which to measure applicants. It addresses only the assessment of fitness for those duties that are necessary for the safe and efficient performance of the job. The FCA and PDA provide the necessary detail to recommend accommodations should the assessment indicate less-than-adequate capacity.

The FCA is composed of a medical fitness evaluation and a work capacity evaluation. Medical fitness is determined by examining occupational health history, general medical history, lifestyle history, and a physical examination. The focus of the medical fitness evaluation is to determine within broad limits the state of medical health.

The work capacity assessment examines the compatibility of the demands of the job to the capacity of the worker. In general the work capacity of a person is the integrative sum of the function of that individual's physiological systems. Fraser (1992) defined those systems in terms of the following:

1. ability to breath
2. ability to transfer oxygen effectively in the lungs
3. ability to increase cardiac output to meet a given workload
4. ability to transport oxygen to the working muscles
5. ability to exert adequate muscular force

These physiological functions can be assessed by examining posture, exertion of appropriate strength, reaching, grasping, holding, manipulating, pushing, pulling, lifting, and carrying. The functions are also assessed during physical fitness testing or other specialized testing such as hearing, vision, or lung function testing.

The requirements of a physical examination for evaluation of fitness to work are job oriented and determined by the demands of the work and the working environment, as modified by the nature of the occupational and general medical histories. The objective is to ensure that the subject can undertake the essential demands of the job (Fraser, 1992).

AGE-RELATED WEAKENING OF FUNCTIONAL CAPACITY

Aging research has indicated that age and job performance are generally unrelated (McEvoy and Cascio, 1989; Waldman and Avolio, 1986; Rhodes, 1983).

The problem, therefore, is not the general skill performance of older workers as much as it is their ability to maintain skill competency in response to changes in technology. Certainly, learning capabilities do not significantly decline with age (Sterns and Doverspike, 1989). Therefore, it is important to review age-related decline factors for older workers (e.g., sensory decline) and propose appropriate ergonomic interventions which an organization may utilize to support the work-life extension of older adults.

IMPACT OF THE ADEA AND ADA ON THE WORKPLACE

The basis of the chronological perspective is the Age Discrimination in Employment Act (ADEA) of 1967. The ADEA protected workers with a chronological age greater than 40 years to an age of 65. In 1978, the ADEA was amended to extend its coverage to age 70. In addition, the amendment abolished mandatory retirement for federal employees. The most recent amendment, 1986, removed the maximum age restriction with certain exceptions. In terms of the ADEA, an older worker is any individual 40 and over who is still an active worker (Snyder and Barrett, 1988). Being classified as an older worker affords certain protections against discrimination. Stereotypes about declining abilities and declining productivity may contribute to discrimination against older workers which these laws were designed to defend against.

The Americans with Disabilities Act (ADA) of 1990 offers additional protection to older adults, as well as the disabled. Many of the ailments associated with older adults are now classified as disabilities. To fail to hire or promote an older worker because of some belief about older workers abilities in general is illegal and leaves an organization open to potential litigation.

The ADA defines disability as any physiological disorder, or condition, cosmetic disfigurement, or anatomical loss affecting one or more of the following body systems: neurological, musculoskeletal, special sense organs, respiratory, cardiovascular, and it also includes infectious and contagious diseases. A communicable disease, such as tuberculosis, is also considered a disability.

The ADA requires that an employer make reasonable accommodations in administering employment tests to eligible applicants or employees with disabling impairments in sensory, manual, or speaking skills. The test must be in formats that do not require the use of the impaired skill. Reasonable accommodation may be acceptable in one instance but not in another. Very specific position analysis must now be used to determine the essential skills, required experience and education level for a position and to test only those skills. The job analysis techniques described here, if done correctly and thoroughly, will provide the level of detail required.

It is important to understand that employers do not have to alter the qualification requirements for the position. In addition, a medical exam cannot be required prior to hiring the individual. These changes should aid older adults as

well as the disabled. The ADA requires that individuals be allowed to demonstrate their qualifications. If an employer does not select the most qualified
applicant, this is discrimination and the applicant has grounds to pursue litigation. Again it must be emphasized that an employer does not have to alter
standards and does not have to initiate an affirmative action program. Any function that is critical to the job such as attendance can be an essential function.
Critical tasks, such as a firefighter carrying a person out of a building, though
seldom done, must be able to be performed in order to hold that job (Landy,
1992).

The ADA should provide additional protections for older adults, especially
those returning from illnesses, such as heart attacks and strokes. The employee
has demonstrated qualification by already holding the position prior to illness.
The employee must be allowed to return to work, even with impairments, if he
or she can perform the essential functions of the position with reasonable accommodation (Sterns and Barrett, 1992).

Though disabilities and limitations become more likely as people age, these
changes do not affect most older adults. Further, disabilities are not a result of
normal aging. They are a result of genetics, accidents, or disease. Laws now in
place protect older workers with disabilities as well as young workers. When
older adults are impaired by a disability they should seek the support necessary
to accommodate their disability and continue receiving the intrinsic and extrinsic
rewards of working.

AGE-RELATED PHYSICAL CHANGES AND LIMITATIONS

Changes in Strength

There is some indication that physical strength declines beyond the age of
40, but the extent of decline is not clear, nor is the effect of decline on work
performance. Shephard (1984) reports that, by the age of 65, the aerobic power
of the average man and woman declines to the point that physically demanding
work becomes too strenuous for continued involvement, such as activities involving walking, carrying, and climbing steps (e.g., mail carriers).

Welford (1988) cited research suggesting that moderately heavy muscular
work is well tolerated by older adults, especially if it is intermittent. Other
research has found, however, that older workers are more likely to leave jobs
that are highly physical in nature (Hayward and Grady, 1986). It has been argued
that repetitive loading, twisting of the torso, and rapid lifting may result in
special risk to older workers who have decreased strength (Chaffrin and Ashton-
Miller, 1991). Thus, it has been suggested that design/redesign efforts should
be used to reduce some of the physical demands on older workers (Welford,
1988).

Changes in Physical Mobility

With regard to mobility, it is a well-known fact that peripheral nervous system slowing gradually occurs with increasing age and can impact task performance, as in slowed responses during calculations of simple multiplication problems (Allen, Ashcraft, and Weber, 1992). Research by Welford (1988) indicated that the number of workers on conveyor lines is dramatically reduced after age 40.

Human factors designs are utilized to enhance work performance for older workers by minimizing the effects of declines in physical or mental abilities while supporting the use of well-established skills (Rabbitt, 1991). It is clear that characteristics of the work environment can affect the work experience of older workers. The next step is to develop and test interventions designed to aid the older worker. Many suggestions have been made about methods to design work environments that will enhance the performance of older adults. These interventions may be a critical ingredient for maintaining the competence of an older workforce in a changing technological environment.

Anthropometry

Another set of physical changes that may occur with age are changes in body dimensions. Annis and colleagues (Annis et al., 1991) reviewed the findings of research on anthropometric changes with age. The general conclusions from this set of research are that weight gains are seen into the fifth or sixth decade of life, followed by declines. The individual's body dimensions change also, characterized by increases in the size of the stomach and hips. Height, on the other hand, steadily decreases from the fourth decade on. Annis and colleagues (1991) compared the changing body dimensions of adults with the anthropometric standards that are currently used in designing an individual's work space (e.g., seat height and width) and concluded that the standards are adequate for older workers as well as younger workers. Research has not given enough evidence to support different workspace designs for older workers (Annis et al., 1991).

The incidence of arthritis increases with age, causing a reduction in joint mobility. Because of this, an employer may want to pay particular attention to postures required of older workers. Static postures may be especially problematic for older workers. In fact, poor work postures have been shown to significantly contribute to physical strain, disability, and impairment of older workers (Annis et al., 1991).

Tayyari and Sohrabi (1990) raised another important work-related issue of factors associated with carpal tunnel syndrome (a condition in which wrist tendons become irritated and swollen) developing among employees in the workplace. The following have been identified as occupational risk factors related to the onset of this condition: (1) performing tasks involving highly repetitive manual actions and the use of small hand tools, (2) performing manual tasks which involve using force, (3) awkward hand motions, (4) carrying small objects (e.g., a book) which requires it being held between thumb and fingers of the hand, (5) using tools with low-frequency vibrations, (6) using short-handled tools, (7) wearing gloves which do not fit properly, and (8) working in conditions of low temperature (Tayyari and Sohrabi, 1990).

These eight factors should be eliminated or reduced to a minimum during work activity to insure that this does not impact the functioning capabilities of both younger and older workers. Specifically, tool redesign efforts (e.g., longer-handled tools), proper temperature control in workspaces, and systematic variations in movement during task performance would help in preventing carpal tunnel syndrome from developing among employees in an organization.

Changes in Health and Rehabilitation

A recurrent theme in work-life extension is the health of the older worker. There are implications that health is one of several variables affecting the functional capacity of older persons. Thus, the working capacity of older workers needs to be assessed.

Historically, health status has been measured by mortality rates alone. No ongoing, valid, uniform measure of the nation's health level beyond mortality statistics have been available. Today, health measures are used as direct and indirect indicators of health status. The commonly used health indicators measure poor health, presence of disease, disability or death, rather than good health. Therefore, with regard to extending the work life of individuals across the life span, the standard health indicators can only measure disability, not functional capacity, and thus do not reflect the extent to which people are able to work.

It is important to identify what aspects of health are central to measuring disability and its impact on work life. Health may be defined in several ways, such as total well-being and absence of disease. Further distinctions between chronic and acute disease and subjective feelings of sickness must be made clear.

These distinctions highlight that disability or functional capacity are not directly tied to the presence of disease or impairment. The population of the United States is growing older and problems posed by chronic and disabling conditions demand increasing attention. Heart disease, cancer, stroke, and lung and liver disease are major conditions that increase with age. Other disabling conditions that affect people in all ages include arthritis, deformities or orthopedic impairments, hearing and speech impairments, and mental retardation. These disabilities may limit the kind of work an individual can do, but they do not prevent work altogether.

Disability is defined by its impact on one or more major life activities an individual is to perform. Disabilities affected more than 9 percent of Americans in 1988. This means that 37 million people have functional limitations that prevent them from working, attending school, or maintaining a household (U.S. Dept. of Health and Human Services, 1990).

One of the best reviews of health and implications for work-life extension carried out in the early 1980's (Newquist and Robinson, 1983) indicated that older persons over 65 have more health problems compared to middle-aged persons (45–64). However, there are not major differences between the age groups. Large numbers of middle-aged and older persons are able to work. Age 65 was not found to be a point where dramatic changes in health patterns take place. A sizable minority of the older population experiences functon impairment. A sizable percentage of older persons experience partial work disability. Health patterns differ by sex with women frequently reporting more problems than men. The health states of older Hispanics and blacks is poorer than that of older whites. Older blacks are especially disadvantaged in terms of health status.

Health problems increase gradually across groups as age increases. Only small differences are found between groups close in age. Young elders (ages 65–74) are more like the middle-aged (ages 45–64) in their health level than older elders (ages 75 and over). The majority of the population 45 years and over report no functional limitations due to chronic conditions. Over two-thirds of persons age 45 and above rate their health as good or excellent; thus, a large segment of the older population can be characterized as able-bodied. Thirty-two percent of individuals ages 45 and older report some level of impairment due to health limitations. Ten percent of this population report that they are unable to work or do house work because of chronic conditions.

While health problems are more frequently experienced by older compared to younger persons in their groups, differences between the groups were small. In terms of continuing work, there is a sizable percentage of older people who report partial work disability (defined as limited in amount or kind of major activity they can perform). Eighty-four percent of those individuals ages 45 and over, as well as 86 percent of the 55–61 year olds, 84 percent of the 62–64 year olds, 80 percent of the 65–68 year olds, and 78 percent of the 69–74 year olds report that they are not limited in the amount or kind of major activity they can perform (Newquist and Robinson, 1983).

It is of utmost importance that older adults not be treated as one homogeneous age group. The life-span perspective emphasized the unique development of each individual and this is especially true of health. There is greater variability in the older population compared to the younger population. Reporting older workers as a single group can distort the reality of health and aging. The result is that the young elders (ages 64–75) are portrayed as less healthy than they actually are (Newquist, 1986).

There are a number of generalizations about age differences in the health of the working population, however, same-age people differ greatly on measures of health and functional capacity. Some data is available from the military and the Metropolitan Life Insurance Company personnel suggesting that age differences in physical work capacity may exist and that there is an increase in the number of days of work lost due to injury or illness as age increases to 65 (Robinson, 1986). However, generalizations are limited, as other factors affect job performance as well. In general, variability in performance measures within age groups far outweighs differences between age groups. Age differences can be observed more readily in some occupations than in others.

Health and functioning do not inevitably decline in the middle and later working years. Furthermore, there are some interventions in the workplace that can prevent or reduce health decrements. Reducing work hazards and promoting health-related behaviors in the work environment may reduce health decrements associated with aging. The workplace is a reasonable site for interventions because of the high proportion of time spent at work. In addition, workplace interventions to reduce the impact of age-related health declines in job performance may be accomplished via assessment (which may reveal reduced capabilities), workplace accommodations, and retraining. The major obstacles associated with the area of age-related declines in health and subsequent effects on job performance are the lack of awareness of the business sector, and the lack of published data on health and job performance. Workplace interventions offer many benefits for business in terms of reducing health hazards, promoting good health, assessing change, providing alternate working arrangements, redesigning jobs, and retraining.

AGE-RELATED COGNITIVE CHANGES AND LIMITATIONS

To appreciate the real complexities of the relationship between cognitive change and work ability, we have chosen to look at a few examples: changes in intelligence, changes in cognitive task performance, and changes in creativity across the life span. The purpose is to move beyond a simple discussion of changes in intelligence, memory, and learning. We would like to show how current thinking regarding effortful and automatic processing, expertise, and related discussions of well practiced skills can be affected by changes in cognitive ability. Complex approaches may not be well understood or palatable to managers and researchers, but the efforts of the cognitive sciences over the past decades have produced mental models, which reflect the diverse and individual changes of adult and older adult workers. These models are beginning to help us understand the combined effects of increasing knowledge, skills, and practice with declines in perceptual and motor speed. This understanding can be further put to use to suggest interventions to aid those with changing abilities or existing disabilities.

Changes in Intelligence

Over 25 years of gerontological research has provided important information regarding intellectual ability and learning and memory. Major longitudinal studies (Schaie, 1985) have shown that most individuals maintain stable intellectual functioning well into the 70s and beyond. Unless there is a major health problem most people remain at the same level of intellectual ability up to very late life.

There are age-related changes in the central nervous system. While there may be neuronal loss with age in the brain, such changes vary within and between individuals. Recent evidence suggests plasticity and modifiability in brain function continue well into late adulthood. In cases where adults must divide attention and process complex information, performance goes down with age. As people grow older, information processing may be affected. The speed and efficiency of processing may be affected by aging. However, most job situations do not involve maximal levels of performance and most adult and older adult workers can perform satisfactorily (Hayslip and Panek, 1993). For many work-related cognitive abilities, there is no age variation across the working years (Warr, 1993).

This raises the methodological issue of proper measurement of changes across the life span and potential limitations of such research. Specifically, there are different results when examining age-related change if the research design of a study is cross-sectional, time lag, or longitudinal (Schaie, 1965). Studies involving cross-sectional design tend to show changes in cognitive ability (Schaie, 1974) when longitudinal designs do not show such significant changes, each with respective confounds of selective sampling, selective dropout, selective survival, practice effects (longitudinal), and generation effects (cross-sectional) (Schaie, 1965).

Another issue of life-span development psychology is why there are apparent changes in some capabilities (e.g., fluid intelligence in problem-solving capabilities), while there is stability in other areas of performance (e.g., areas of expertise, crystallized knowledge). This has direct implications for industrial gerontology in terms of understanding ways to improve older workers' training (e.g., transfer) and job-related performance through the use of their existing knowledge bases (i.e., proceduralized knowledge bases).

Baltes (1993) talked of the importance of "selective optimization with compensation" in the maintenance of older adult performance. This idea of compensatory behaviors has direct relevancy for industrial gerontology, as in the transcription typing study by Salthouse (1984) in which it was found that older expert typists were able to compensate for age-related slowing in reaction time (e.g., finger tapping) through the utilization of an expanded eye-hand span and parallel processing (overlapping) of underlying performance segments of input, parsing, translation, and execution (Salthouse, 1984). Job experience has certainly been a better predictor of job performance than the age of an employee in the workplace ($r = .18$) (Giniger, Dispenzieri, and Eisenberg, 1983; McDaniel, Schmidt, and Hunter, 1988; Avolio, Waldman, and McDaniel, 1990).

There is a need to identify the legitimate age-related changes in performance potentiality and the limitations they impose in order to develop appropriate remedial and preventative interventions for older adults (Kliegl and Baltes, 1987).

Only then can appropriate organization-based policies be developed and interventions implemented.

Skill obsolescence is an area which has received attention from life-span developmental and industrial gerontological research (Willis and Dubin, 1990). Organization-based policies have been studied to better understand how motivational (Rosen and Jerdee, 1990; Stagner, 1985) and organizational-based factors impact on the phenomena of skill obsolescence among older workers.

For example, Fossum et al. (1986) emphasized the idea of applying human capital theory to the phenomena of skill loss. This idea is reflected in earlier research, such as a study by Shearer and Steger (1975), in which a sample of civilian civil engineers exhibited greater skill obsolescence than a sample of military civil engineers. It may be argued that organizational culture, such as the continual training and practicing stressed in the military, impacts the rate and degree of skill loss among older workers. An organizational culture that emphasizes a frequent updating of skills will prevent or lessen skill loss among older workers.

Changes in Cognitive Task Performance

Research presents an apparent paradox between laboratory and real-world job performance. Older adults demonstrate age-related declines in performance on lab-related cognitive tasks but they are still capable of maintaining a good level of work-related performance in the workplace. It is important to discuss the relevant research which supports the existence of this paradox.

Examining the findings of job performance data, Rhodes (1983) conducted a qualitative review of several studies examining the relationship between age and job performance and concluded that there is a mix in the conclusions of studies, but overall there appears to be no significant relationship between the age of a worker and job performance capabilities. Similar results were found by two meta-analytic studies investigating the same topic (McEvoy and Cascio, 1989; Waldman and Avolio, 1986).

Giniger, Dispenzieri, and Eisenberg (1983) conducted a series of studies to determine the extent of age differences in performance of speed (sewing) and skill (quality inspectors) tasks in the garment industry. The studies revealed that older workers' performance was superior to younger workers' performance; this was attributed to older workers' increased experience on the job, which ameliorated any age-related decline factors.

Perlmutter, Kaplan, and Nyquist (1990) found that older food-service workers showed age-related declines on measures of reaction time but were comparable in job knowledge and performance to younger workers on the job.

In terms of learning and memory, the general conclusion for learning is that older adults can learn as well as younger individuals, but it will take them more time. This means that people maintain intellectual and learning ability and should be able to continue to perform in familiar job roles and be trained for new ones.

The main issue for the individual worker is how to remain current and competitive (Rosen and Jerdee, 1990). The best way is to take advantage of relevant training, both within as well as outside the current employment situation (Sterns and Doverspike, 1989).

It is important to realize that older adults are capable of learning and growing through educational experiences (Peterson, 1986) and this has direct implications for the availability of older adult education opportunities for older learners.

Barriers to such opportunities (i.e., institutional barriers such as a "rejection" attitude toward older adults in education) are serious in terms of limiting the true growth potential of individuals across the life span (Cross, 1981). Moreover, they present the issue of blatant ageism (Kimmel, 1988) and age discrimination in the context of availability of updating skill opportunities for older workers, who may be in the position of losing their jobs and work skill competency in the workforce (Sterns and Alexander, 1987, 1988).

Willis and Dubin (1990) proposed that a preventive approach to skill obsolescence, the maintenance of professional competency, is an important issue for older workers. An organization that encourages maintaining and improving the skills required to excel at one's job, provides challenging work and the opportunity to inject new ideas will not only be more likely to stay ahead of competitors, but also will have reduced turnover and retain more productive employees.

An organization can measure the success of their efforts by examining organizational-based self-esteem (OBSE), which has been assessed by measuring the degree to which organizational members believed they could satisfy their needs through their participation in roles within the organizational context. The focus was on individuals' assessments of their organizational worth (Peirce et al., 1989).

Matheson (1991) explored age-related differences between OBSE and other work satisfaction and commitment measures. Matheson (1991) found age was significantly and positively related to organizational satisfaction, perceived alternatives commitment, and global self-esteem. However, after controlling for job and organizational tenure, two variables that have been found to co-vary with age, only global self-esteem was significantly associated with age. Employees over age 50 had significantly higher global self-esteem than did younger age groups. Employees who perceived that they were valuable as organizational members were more satisfied with their jobs and organizations, were committed to the organization, both effectively and in terms of perceived sacrifice, and less likely to leave. This finding shows the importance of understanding an employee's perceptions and interpretations of organizational policies, procedures, and culture.

Older adults bring experience and extensive skills to any job. They have had a lifetime of communicating, overcoming hardships, solving problems, and acquiring lessons learned. Older employees have had years to integrate their knowledge with practical experience to develop efficient methods of accomplishing their work. When new techniques arise, open-minded older workers are often the best source to determine how successful new ideas will be and how best to implement them.

Evidence is mounting that intrinsic rewards of work, job satisfaction, relationships with coworkers, and a sense of participating in meaningful work become more important as an individual ages. Most jobs allow older adults to continue to participate in these benefits until they feel that they have the financial resources and personal network outside of the workplace to retire (Brady et al., 1989).

Expertise, Problem Solving, and Decision Making

Older adults are responsible for many of the most complex decisions made in the world everyday. A majority of executives, senior politicians, and world leaders are older adults and successfully carry out their responsibilities. However, how cognitive changes over the life span affect performance is not well understood.

Research into the effects of aging on managerial functioning have produced mixed results (Stagner, 1985). Meyer (1970) reported performance decrements with age on an in-basket task. Taylor (1975) found that older managers made slower decisions but took greater advantage of available information by considering more problem facets. Other reviews indicate a mix of age-related decrements and sustained performance (Davies and Sparrow, 1985; Rhodes, 1983).

Even if performance does decline with age, this still leaves open the source of the decline. Knowledge, skills, and abilities (KSAs) which affect job-specific performance may become obsolete (Fossum, et al., 1986). KSA obsolescence resulting in inadequate performance may be due to changes over time in job characteristics, motivation, individual orientations, organizational factors, and organizational structure (Howard and Bray, 1988). If obsolescence is the cause of decline, this would be encouraging, because with training, this is correctable. However, other evidence supports other causes of decline which may be more fundamental.

In a study of age and management team performance by Streufert et al. (1991), four-person, age-homogeneous groups were assessed using a day-long, decision-making simulation. Older subject groups (75 and older) demonstrated significantly different performances and strategies from middle age (45–55) and young (28–35) subject groups. Strategy differences included asking for less additional information, having less breadth to their overview of the simulation (having a more restricted conceptualization of the task), using fewer avenues to effect changes, and planning which was less effective and less optimal. Older subject groups performed more poorly in the simulation, and their planning was less complex than other groups. Older subject groups were similarly motivated and expressed satisfaction with their performance, unaware of their much longer decision making and less extensive information searches as compared to younger groups. Interestingly, no differences emerged in responding to emergencies between the different age groups, perhaps due to shorter information searches. Importantly, cognitive processes, rather than motivational differences, appear to play a strong role in the differences between older and younger managers, though these differences may be cohort specific rather than age related.

Clearly, older workers are in positions of responsibility in every occupation and make important decisions affecting employees throughout their organizations. Is their decision making affected by the aging process, and if so, to what extent?

Light (1991) examined the research in older adult cognitions and compared various approaches to explaining the cause of changes that have been found in research over the last several decades. Their evaluation included meta-memory, semantic deficits, impairment of deliberate recollection (effort exerted in retrieval), and reduced processing resources (attention, working memory, and cognitive slowing). Light clearly shows that to understand where these changes are occurring researchers must focus on understanding the cognitive processes themselves.

Turning to expertise research, studies by Charness and colleagues have indicated that expertise in a given field of performance (chess, bridge) can ameliorate the effects of cognitive aging. For example, Charness (1981) found that grandmaster chess players were able to utilize the knowledge of different patterns of piece positions on a chess board to encode and chunk information for later recall purposes. Charness (1983) investigated the effect of cognitive aging on ability to do bridge bidding during play. It was found that expertise in knowledge of bidding strategies could ameliorate the negative effects of cognitive aging until approximately the age of 60 among experienced players. As previously stated, experience assisted older typists in transcription typing through the utilization of increasingly overlapping steps of input, parsing, translation, and execution (Salthouse, 1984).

Changes in Creativity and Idea Productivity

Creativity is an important area of study in life-span changes in cognitive abilities. Creativity may be indicative of originality and productivity. Researchers have found that creativity may decline in the later years (see Kausler, 1992; Simonton, 1990; for reviews). Research focusing on creative productivity has led to conclusions of decline in later career production compared to that in the earlier stage of a career. Other researchers have considered the relationship between age and creative processes using more standardized measures and more controlled conditions.

Simonton (1990) looked at the quantity and quality of products produced by professionals over the course of their careers. Quantity measures that considered the number of publications, patents, paintings, etc. tended to decline in the later years. Simonton's findings suggest that quantity peaks in the late 30s or early 40s and declines gradually over later decades. Productivity in the later decades was half that of peak performance.

To assess quality, Simonton (1990) examined important contributions such as publications in well respected journals. Quality was studied by comparing the ratio of minor works (e.g., publications in mediocre journals) to major works (e.g., publications in well respected journals). The ratio fluctuated randomly over the course of careers. Simonton's (1990) findings indicate that age differences in quantity rather than quality explain apparent declines over the life span.

Researchers have also examined the cognitive processes involved in creative endeavors to identify the specific abilities and cognitive processes involved in creativity. Age differences favoring younger adults have been found on many measures of creativity (McCrae, Arenberg, and Costa, 1987; Ruth and Birren, 1985).

Alpaugh and Birren (1977) studied variables affecting creativity across the life span. They found age differences favoring younger adults for specific creativity abilities including originality (providing unusual answers), adaptive flexibility (ability to modify and use strategies for more efficient functioning), fluency of ideas (the ability to generate appropriate ideas in a limited amount of time), and preference for more complex situations.

McCrae, Arenberg, and Costa (1987) conducted the first longitudinal study of creativity to separate differences due to age and cohort. Longitudinal analysis, assessing initial performance and then six years later, showed decline over time for group means.

Alpaugh et al. (1982) studied young and older adults on a creative writing task. They concluded that standardized measures of creativity have predictive validity in measuring age differences favoring young adults. Standardized measures of creativity, however, lacked construct validity. The tests did not converge on the hypothesized factors of creativity, originality fluency, and flexibility. Alpaugh and colleagues (1982) concluded that older adults may rely on different cognitive abilities in creative problem solving than younger adults. One of these abilities is crystallized intelligence. This implies an interesting link between creativity and expertise.

If previous knowledge is linked to creativity in older adults, than it is important to understand how previously stored information can be optimally transferred from one problem to another. If this process is understood, interventions can be designed and applied to the training of older employees.

Research on transferring information from one problem to another has focused on the distinction between surface and deep-structure problem features. Surface features are defined as the characteristics of a problem. Deep-structure features are the underlying relationships between the problem characteristics. Deep structures can be thought of as the rules necessary for solving a problem.

Stein (1989) argues that both surface and deep-structure features must be present to guarantee transfer of knowledge from one situation to the next. In contrast, Kotovsky and Fallside (1989) argue that transfer of knowledge from one problem to another is optimized when the task is designed to evoke established, naturally organized memories.

Novick (1988) considered expert and novice differences in transferring information from one problem to another. When two problems share deep-structure features, experts are more likely than novices to appropriately transfer information from the first problem to the second. When the two problems shared surface-structure features but not deep-structure features, novices were more likely than experts to inappropriately transfer information from the first problem to the second.

Thus, the findings from expertise research, such as the studies mentioned here, offer valuable information in the design of training programs and job design that utilize existing knowledge bases of older workers to optimize transfer and maintain professional competencies across the life span.

Age-Related Sensory and Perceptual Changes and Limitations

Two recent reviews by Fozard (1990) and Kline and Schieber (1985) present information pertaining to sensory and perceptual capabilities in hearing and vision that exhibit different degrees of age-related decline across the life span. Keeping in mind that there are always individual differences in the degree of decline with age (Kline and Schieber, 1985), the following aspects of the aging process still must be noted.

Before proceeding, the point needs to be mentioned that different aspects of age-related sensory decline may potentially be ameliorated to some degree with proper ergonomic interventions (Charness and Bosman, 1990); however, more empirical research in the workplace is needed before definitive conclusions regarding this issue can be made.

It is important to reiterate that most significant decline probably does not begin until approximately age 70 or older, and there are always individual differences in decline such that some individuals in the workplace may not be affected by any of the following decline factors.

Changes in Vision

Reactions to Illumination. Older adults are more likely to be adversely affected by changing levels of illumination. Reactions to light and dark adaptation may not be as quick or complete, although recent research suggests that dark adaptation may not be as problematic as had been previously thought (Fozard, 1990). In addition to adaptation, older adults have been shown to be more affected by glare from light sources (Fozard, 1990).

In response to these age-related changes, it has been suggested that conditions causing glare at work should be modified or eliminated if possible (Charness and Bosman, 1990; Welford, 1988). For example, installation of lighting that has soft white reader bulbs, allowing a diffusion of light in the workspace and a reduction of glare, would be an effective intervention. Glare on computer screens is another relevant source to focus on for intervention purposes; the installation of a glare-free computer screen on a computer terminal would help in reducing glare in the workplace. The design of workstations should include adjustable light sources in order to alter lighting in the workspace according to the perceptual needs of the employee over the course of the day. The consideration of placement of a computer or other equipment in relation to windows in an office is another related workspace design issue. Additionally, covers should be placed on light bulbs and furniture should be arranged to face away from the source of glare. Lastly, sudden shifts in illumination should be avoided in the workplace; walking from one area of the workplace to the next area, an employee should not perceive a drastic shift in lighting of rooms (Charness and Bosman, 1990).

Poorer Contrast. A second change in vision with age is that older adults have more difficulty detecting differences between visual stimuli. Older workers need greater contrast between the stimuli to be able to distinguish them (Fozard, 1990). This could create problems for an older worker with respect to navigating stairs at work or accurately utilizing visual information.

In response to this, it has been suggested that the work environment should be designed to avoid difficult contrasts for older workers (Charness and Bosman, 1990; Garg, 1991). Difficult contrast, such as blue-green, should not be used for visual displays (computerized or written) that older workers will use. In fact, it has been suggested that black print on a white computer screen is the most effective for older adults (Charness and Bosman, 1990).

Useful Field of View. A third age-related change in vision concerns the useful field of vision (UFOV). Older adults have a smaller UFOV in which to process information from the environment. Stimuli outside the UFOV may not be processed as well by older adults (Fozard, 1990). Driving research by Owsley and colleagues has indicated that older adult performance can be impaired due to a shrinking UFOV in their perceptual range (Owsley et al., 1991). The findings from driving research are applicable to the workplace context; older workers may be impaired in their information processing capabilities if their attention to environmental stimuli is outside the periphery of their reduced field of view.

A possible ergonomic response to this would be to create workspaces organized such that important information for task performance on the job is easily perceived within an older worker's UFOV perceptual span. Additionally, it has been suggested that lighting should be focused on select areas in a workspace (Garg, 1991; Fozard, 1990) in order to assist in enhancing the perceptual and selective attention capabilities of workers across the life span.

Reduced Visual Acuity. Older adults, in general, are less able to make fine visual discriminations, although the extent of this difficulty is not clear from the existing research (Fozard, 1990; Kline and Scheiber, 1985).

Researchers have suggested that employers should revise printed material to ensure an adequate size for legibility (Garg, 1991; Charness and Bosman, 1990). Such measures as the use of larger print on signs or having a larger font on a computerized display will aid older adults especially.

Changes in Hearing

Some auditory changes that occur with age include difficulty hearing sounds at high frequencies, greater distractibility, and increasing difficulty with the speed of presentation (Fozard, 1990; Stine, Wingfield, and Poon, 1989). In addition to these auditory changes, older adults are sometimes able to hear a pure tone at a given loudness yet unable to understand a spoken word at the same noise level. This is known as a phonemic regression effect. Older adults also may respond more dramatically to slight increase in volume (Stine, Wingfield, and Poon, 1989). New research indicates, however, that consonants and consonant-vowel combinations may have different intensity without causing the overall noise level to be too high for older adults. This could lead to potentially interesting interventions, both in and out of the workplace (Fozard, 1990).

Suggestions have been given for improving the auditory characteristics of the work environment for older adults (Charness and Bosman, 1990). Noise levels in general should be decreased to reduce distracting noise. Noise from machinery, heating equipment, etc., should be muffled if possible (e.g., use of sound-absorbing materials such as curtains). Eliminate possible echoes in a room (e.g., position the speaker and audience to best utilize the room acoustics). Avoid high frequency sounds (i.e., 4,000 hertz and above) in the work or living space. To assist the older adult in selectively attending to important noises (e.g., a smoke alarm), increase the volume of such noises so there is a good auditory contrast effect. In a group discussion format, it is important to enhance visual cues of communication to compensate for older adult decline in auditory functioning capabilities (e.g., a speaker should facilitate use of visual cues when speaking and listening; place seating arrangement of the group such that it is in a circle to improve visual cue attendance of older adults; limit the size of the group to help integration of auditory and visual communications).

Changes in Perceptual Speed

The generalized slowing hypothesis proposes that age-related deficits are spread throughout the cognitive-processing system, and that performance declines are tied to the amount of processing rather than any specific component (Salthouse, 1985). Cerella (1990) attributed these declines to random breaks in the neural connections in the brain that build linearly over time but exponentially affect the pathways along which thoughts and motor responses travel. Cerella described two slowing functions for older adults, finding they take 1.22 times longer to complete perceptual-motor function and 1.82 times longer to complete cognitive functions. Using these functions, Cerella ignored higher-level cognitive processes, instead taking the position that generalized slowing can adequately account for age-related declines.

Another generalized approach has theorized that age-related changes can be attributed to changes in the quantity of mental resources. Resources which have been proposed are working memory and processing rate. Researchers, however, have found support for multiple aging mechanisms (i.e., several factors) that contribute to age-related declines (Salthouse, Kausler, and Saults, 1988). Future research is still required to understand these cognitive declines.

Changes in Motor Speed and Reaction Time

Excitation and inhibition have been found to be the major mechanisms which influence what people attend to in their surroundings (Tipper, 1992). Excitation enhances attention and speeds up reaction-time responses (Gernsbacher, 1990). In terms of the schema model discussed above, priming creates an association between two nodes and speeds recall of that information. Inhibition involves the suppression of distractors. Inhibition suppresses unrelated or weak associations. Negative priming tasks are used to demonstrate active inhibition (Tipper, 1992).

Most negative priming tasks have demonstrated inhibitive effects of very short duration, typically under one second. Recently, several studies have shown inhibitive effects over longer durations. Tipper et al. (1991) have shown negative priming to cause inhibition to endure for at least seven seconds and survive intervening tasks. Diefendorff et al. (1993) showed significant suppression effects involving higher-level cognitive tasks (associating words to goals, e.g., *productivity* and *hard-working*), though it was unclear that suppression was due to the same inhibitory mechanism found in traditional negative priming tasks.

Lord and Levy (1994) propose that the capacity to inhibit competing cognitions is the primary mechanism by which one maintains focus on a particular task or problem, and thus makes a cognitive connection between goals and motivation. This inhibition mechanism would have implications to the process of attending to information which is not the focused goal.

Recent research has demonstrated that older adults have significantly smaller negative priming effects than younger adults on various tasks. Stolzfus et al. (1993) conducted two experiments to clarify the differential pattern of suppression effects found in older and younger adults. In a previous study, Hasher et al. (1991) reported that older adults exhibited no suppression effects in a letter-naming reaction time task. Combining the data of four experiments across the above two studies, Stolzfus et al. found that older adults demonstrated no evidence of suppression effects while younger adults exhibited a consistent suppression effect across the time courses that have been examined (300, 500, 1,200, and 1,700 milliseconds). In addition, two experiments involving measures of inhibition and interference suggested that inhibition is not related to interference in either younger or older adults.

Farrell et al. (1994) offered additional support for differences in suppression between younger and older adults. They proposed the lack of variability in effects (many nonsignificant results) found in many studies was due to sampling error and low power of small sample sizes (Hedges and Olkin, 1985). Their meta-analysis found that the younger adults showed a significant negative priming effect and older adults had a priming effect which approached significance. Age was found to be a clear moderator.

The absence of a reliable relationship in the above study, supported by evidence that older adults have greater difficulty maintaining a line of coherent thought (Gold et al., 1988; Kemper et al., 1990), and that older adults have greater difficulty abandoning no-longer-relevant information as effectively as younger adults do (Hamm and Hasher, 1992; Hartman and Hasher, 1991) call into question the role of suppression in selection among concurrent targets.

PROLONGING PRODUCTIVITY OF WORKERS ACROSS THE LIFE SPAN

Designing a workplace that supports older workers in their efforts to remain updated and competent is one important application of motivation research. The design of training equipment that has age-sensitive considerations which take into account age-related factors (e.g., decline in visual acuity) has many advantages for an older adult learner and the employer.

First, the equipment will assist older workers in adopting compensatory behaviors to adapt to the work demands of the task, such as giving more attention to monitoring oneself for safety reasons. Second, a deeper degree of learning the training material may be achieved if the training design allows the avoidance of distractions that may detrimentally affect the allocation of working memory in learning the task. It is hypothesized that there will be an increase in trainees' feelings of trainability and job performance competency, especially among older trainees, if age-related factors are accounted for in training-program design.

From an organizational perspective, the potential loss of productivity that can occur if proper design/redesign of training and job equipment is not taken into account may be substantial. Organizations may have to use limited time, capital, and human resources to correct for this oversight through implementation of corrective training programs, changes in selection process, or supervision techniques (Howell, 1992). It is pragmatic for organizations to evaluate and understand the underlying cognitive subsystem of the man–machine system to insure that there is a proper match between employee and equipment characteristics in equipment design, especially for older adults.

The following section will address specific examples of workplace interventions that could be designed to best enhance the work experience of older adults.

SUGGESTIONS FOR ORGANIZATION-BASED INTERVENTIONS

The following will be a discussion of some specific workplace design considerations that have been addressed in the ergonomic literature and their implications toward older workers. For example, workspace and computer design are two areas that can be examined with specific consideration for the needs of older workers. In addition, the transfer of trained skills to the workplace is a special issue that should be considered when discussing how to design training programs suited for the learning needs of older workers.

General Workplace Design

According to Charness and Bosman (1990), it is recommended that there should be an increase in the level of illumination (e.g., at the top and bottom landings of stairs, hallways, and elevators) for older adults. To compensate for decreasing dark adaptation capabilities of older adults, sudden and pronounced transitions in the level of illumination should be avoided. For example, lighting in a workplace should be designed with considerations of consistent lighting levels between different areas of an industrial manufacturing plant, especially avoiding a transition from high- to low-level lighting in a room which may contain disability-related dangers for older employees (e.g., steps descending to a lower level).

Since older adults have more difficulty with some color discriminations, it is recommended that materials, for example, should not be used which are within the blue-green range of colors and avoid using colors that are of the same hue (e.g., do not have carpet colors of the same hues when there is a step or transition from one level of the house to another level).

The installation of lighting with soft white bulbs and a glare-free computer screen on computer terminals would help in reducing glare in the workplace, and the design of workstations should include adjustable light sources; these are important workspace design issues.

The age-related decline in ability to read certain sizes of print necessitates the increase of print size in text material (i.e., recommended type size for older adults of, at least, 8) and the lettering on signs (i.e., recommended print size of letters on a sign to be at least 15 millimeters in size).

Last, a recommendation to compensate for age-related visual decline with age is to increase contrast (target luminance) in a room to enhance the visual discrimination capabilities of older adults.

Workspace Design

The importance of a well-designed workstation can not be stressed too much. In the design of office equipment, for example, it is usually the standard to design them so they can be adjusted to the needs of most individuals, covering the range of 5th to 95th percentile of the relevant population characteristics (e.g., anthropometric consideration of arm reach and sitting height of workers in the workspace). The standards of equipment design tend to focus on the average worker's physical characteristics, but as will be discussed, there are physical dimension changes that occur with age (e.g., decrease in height of the worker).

Although age-related physical changes of older workers may not require significant equipment design measures, it is a consideration for organizations as the percentage of individuals over age 65 is projected to be 17 percent of the total population by the year 2000 (Sanders and McCormick, 1987). Considerations that future research may focus upon are age-related changes in physical stature (e.g., height, weight). Horizontal work-surface design, seated work-surface heights, and standing work-surface heights in reference to older worker anthropometric needs would be areas in which to conduct further ergonomic research.

Significant increases in the use of video display terminals (VDTs) in the workplace necessitates an examination of proper seating design to assist in computer operator comfort and bodily support through an examination of the relationship between the body structure of the employee and the physical demands of the workspace (e.g., the reaching distance according to the design of the desk or table, the keyboard, and the placement of the chair) (Sanders and McCormick, 1987).

To compensate for losses in strength, an older worker could use a mechanical lift to carry heavy objects overhead. If lifting is required of the older worker, it has been suggested to keep the load close to the body, and eliminate lifting that requires bending, stooping or twisting. This can be done by rearranging storage facilities and providing lifting aids for heavier objects. Moreover, workers should be given rest between lifts and given good foot traction to reduce tripping hazards.

With regard to changes in mobility, one suggestion has been to use "buffer" stocks between assembly line positions (Welford, 1988). Buffer stocks are small surpluses of assembly items either feeding into or along assembly lines or process lanes used to minimize the impact of those items requiring more labor time. The stock moves out of the buffer at the line pace, but the stock is replenished at a slower pace. The buffer may be replenished by working additional hours off-shift, or increasing the number of workers filling the buffer.

Computer Design

In addition to designing the workspace of computer users, the design of the computer itself is relevant (Charness and Bosman, 1990). While older adults can effectively use computers (Jay and Willis, 1992; Gist, Rosen, and Schwoere, 1988; Elias et al., 1987; Hartley, Hartley, and Johnson, 1984), they are less likely to do so.

Huutanen (1988) found, for example, that Finnish workers age 50 years and older reported the lowest use of computers. Jay and Willis (1992) discovered that in their sample, only 1 percent of individuals over the age of 65 used computers. These findings could be related to a general reluctance to use computers on the part of older adult workers.

Training older adults on the computer has been shown to improve attitudes toward that technology (Jay and Willis, 1992; McNeely, 1991). From an ergonomic standpoint, the design of the computer can influence its user-friendliness. Researchers have only recently begun to determine which design is most effective for older adults. We have already mentioned that installation of a glare-free computer screen on a computer terminal is a viable workplace intervention to ameliorate age-related increases in glare sensitivity. Another work-related issue for older adults is that they may wear eyeglasses with bifocal or trifocal lenses, which cause difficulties in reading information off a stationary computer screen; older employees who wear these types of eyeglasses would benefit from a computer screen that is adjustable, and thus permits easier readability of information on the screen. Charness and Bosman (1990) also reviewed research suggesting that a computer system offering the use of a computer mouse (controlling device) may help in reducing speed differences between older and younger adults in operating computers. Another workspace design issue suggested by the research of Jaschinski-Kruza (1990) is that older VDT users may be more comfortable with somewhat longer viewing distances from a computer screen; thus, an adjustable workstation that permits such adjustments should be a consideration.

CONCLUSION

It is clear that older adults experience declines in physical, sensory, and, to some extent, facets of cognitive abilities on an individualistic basis. Some individuals may not experience significant cognitive decline across a life span. What is not clear, however, is how these declines affect performance at work, for example, and how such effects can be ameliorated through effective ergonomic design.

It is important to reiterate the point that although recommendations can be made about probable ergonomic interventions to assist in ameliorating age-related decline factors (e.g., sensory decline), there may be no significant age-related decline for some individuals across most of their adult life span. Moreover, there has been a relative paucity of research to test whether these ergonomic interventions actually do have significant ameliorating effects for older employees. Thus, more research efforts to understand the real impact of ergonomic interventions for older adults in the workplace is recommended.

An additional work-related issue to be considered is stress in the workplace. Sources of stress at work may include task-related factors such as information overload, equipment underload and deficiencies of equipment design; interpersonal factors such as overcrowding; environmental factors (e.g., noise, heat, lighting, dirt, and squalor); and personal threats to physical safety, economic security, or self-esteem.

In dealing with stress, individuals have mediating factors such as personality, attitudes, and coping skills. These help ameliorate the subjective or perceived effects of stressors. In addition, mediating factors concerning health impacts on how the perceived stress will manifest itself physically are important to understand. For older workers, some stressors such as information overload or poor air quality may be exaggerated. For example, older adults are more affected by carbon monoxide, a common indoor air pollutant, than younger workers. This combined with less physical reserve to mediate effects of perceived stress puts older workers at greater risk of stress-related difficulties. Not only does stress have physical outcomes, but performance and job satisfaction may also be sacrificed. Controlling sources of stress such as task design and environment will bolster older workers' capability to withstand stress.

Workplace design characteristics have been linked to the incidence of disability, but the specific effects of design on the performance of older workers have not been investigated. Results of various studies provide indirect, albeit conflicting, evidence concerning this issue. (Fuller, 1981, 1984; Zedeck, Jackson, and Summers, 1983; Snook, 1971).

Some research suggests that older adults may be less able to work in physically demanding occupations. Older males are more likely to leave physically demanding occupations (Hayward and Grady, 1986), while women are more likely to leave mentally demanding jobs. Past research addressed by Welford (1958) discovered that older workers were less often found in positions characterized by high time pressures. Thus, the possibility exists that older workers can compensate for the negative physical effects of work in some occupations, but not in others. Research should be conducted to identify the characteristics of the work environment, whether physical, functional, or psychological (e.g., stress associated with task), that could influence an older worker's performance.

This topic of research is especially relevant when older workers are faced with the likelihood of entering into a second career (e.g., an entrepreneurial role in a smaller business) or a "bridge" job that is similar to the former primary career.

In addition to the effects of physical characteristics of the work environment, the research has also shown that psychological characteristics of work, such as possibilities for development, can help alleviate the negative effects of poor physical design (Hayward and Grady, 1986). Therefore, the psychological characteristics of the job as well as the physical aspects of the job must be considered. The workplace should be designed to best promote health for older adults (e.g., implementation of a "wellness" program). Additionally, the job should be designed to promote mental stimulation, autonomy, and room for development.

In conclusion, a combination of changing demographics with an increasingly sophisticated workplace puts greater emphasis on ergonomic interventions in workspace design to extend the worklife of older adults who desire to participate in the workforce. More empirical research in this area is greatly needed in order to understand and meet the needs of an aging workforce.

16

Investing in the Future: What Role for Older Worker Training?

Sara E. Rix

THE NEED FOR TRAINING IN THE UNITED STATES

Concern about America's competitiveness in the global economy begs the question of how well workers are being prepared to meet the demands of that economy. Technological advances, structural change throughout entire industries, increasing job complexity, and an aging workforce heighten the salience of employee training and retraining.[1]

The U.S. Department of Labor's Commission on Workforce Quality and Labor Market Efficiency minced few words when it spoke of America's workforce crisis and warned of the grave consequences facing a nation unwilling to invest substantial resources in human capital: "America's workforce will be under-educated, undertrained, and ill-equipped to compete in the twenty-first century" (U.S. Department of Labor, 1989b, vii). While new entrants to the labor force will increasingly comprise groups that are less job-ready and hence more in need of skills development than entrants of recent decades, current labor force participants are themselves not immune to the risks of skills obsolescence.[2] Obsolescence may begin to manifest itself well before workers reach old or even

In this chapter, *training* is defined as learning what is necessary to qualify for a job, perform in an entirely new job, or improve or upgrade job skills. This word is used throughout the chapter, even when the term *retraining* might be the more precise choice of words. The views expressed in this chapter are those of the author and do not necessarily represent the views of any organization with which she may be associated.

middle age (Andrisani and Daymont, 1987; Shearer and Steger, 1975). According to one estimate, three-fourths of workers already employed at the end of the 1980s will need retraining by the year 2000 (Galagan, 1988).

Albeit seldom the focus of training or retraining programs or policies, older workers should not assume that their training days are necessarily over. Much of the job security associated with long tenure has evaporated in recent years as older workers find themselves disproportionately affected by corporate restructuring and downsizing (Hall and Mirvis, 1993; Useem, 1993).[3] Once unemployed, older workers remain out of work longer than their younger counterparts, are less likely to be reemployed, and suffer greater earnings losses when they do find work (U.S. Congressional Budget Office, 1993). For a large percentage, labor force withdrawal is the ultimate response to job loss. At a time when technological competence is regarded as critical to business functioning (American Association of Retired Persons, 1989), employers' suspicions about older workers' comfort with new technology—whether legitimate or not—serve as a formidable employment barrier.

Although there seems to be a general perception that America lags behind its major trading partners when it comes to worker training, deficiencies may not, in fact, extend to spending. Acknowledging the difficulties inherent in crossnational comparisons among countries using different accounting procedures, Lynch (1993a, 1993b) nonetheless observed that U.S. training expenditures as a percentage of total wage bill compare quite favorably to expenditures in six other industrialized nations.

What appears to distinguish the United States from the countries studied by Lynch is not so much *what* is spent on training but rather how the monies are spent. On average, European and Japanese trainees are better grounded in basic or fundamental skills than are American trainees, which enables their instructors to teach new and advanced skills sooner than can be done in the United States.

In the United States, where changing job demands increasingly require workers with the ability to read, write, and communicate (Eck, 1993), an estimated 20 percent or more of workers in some firms are deficient in basic skills (Fletcher and Robison, 1991)—skills that large numbers of U.S. employers say will be their primary training need in coming years (Opinion Research Corporation, 1992).[4] Time that can be spent teaching advanced skills in European and Japanese training programs must be devoted to basic skills in the United States. Consequently, as Lynch (1993a, 1993b) concludes, program content and outcome vary markedly across countries, even though relative expenditures may not.

Aggregate data such as those used by Lynch often mask significant age-related differences. One is tempted to ask how training expenditures, course content, and outcomes vary by age, but a complete answer would not be forthcoming. Training resources disproportionately go to workers between the ages of 25 and 44 (Carnevale, 1993), but otherwise, age-specific data on the participants in and payoffs to formal or informal employer-provided training are limited (Mangum,

1989; Organization for Economic Cooperation and Development, 1991; U.S. Department of Labor, 1990a).

Similarly lacking is information on the intriguing possibility of age differences in training readiness. On the one hand, years of job-related experience and the productivity associated with that experience should count for something. On the other hand, stereotypes or doubts about older workers' ability to master new skills, fear of failure, and approaching retirement may undermine any training advantages older workers might have.[5]

Assessment of the nature and extent of worker training in the United States is hampered by the fact that most training occurs in the private sector, much of it is informal in nature and thus hard to identify, and training expenditures, particularly for informal training, are not always clearly or thoroughly itemized.[6]

The problem of identifying who is getting what training is compounded by the lack of a standard, widely accepted definition of training. While providing no evidence in support of its contention, the Bureau of Labor Statistics (BLS) asserted that survey respondents tend toward a narrow definition of training; economists, in contrast, were said to regard training as almost any learning or skill enhancement that "will be applied in the work place" (U.S. Department of Labor, 1990a, 9). The distinction is more than a matter of semantics, for what "training" means to respondents will obviously affect both their answers and subsequent estimates of training experiences based on those answers.

WHO GETS TRAINED? THE WORKER'S PERSPECTIVE

Regardless of how training is defined, older workers seem to get less of it (e.g., Carnevale, 1993; Fletcher and Robison, 1991; U.S. Department of Labor, 1990a).[7] One of the more recent sources of data on the training experiences of the entire labor force is the 1991 Bureau of Labor Statistics update of a 1983 survey of how workers get their training (U.S. Department of Labor, 1985, 1992c). Surveys conducted in both years asked workers about the training they needed to qualify for their jobs, as well as about skills improvement training received since obtaining those jobs. Of course, workers may receive both types of training in middle or old age. In view of the long tenure of so many older workers, however, it seems reasonable to assume that much of the job-qualifying training for this age group occurred when they were younger workers.

Unfortunately, because respondents were asked simply whether they had taken any training to improve their skills since taking their current jobs, recency of skills improvement training can at best only be approximated. For many older workers, skills updating may also have taken place when they were considerably younger. That possibility, coupled with the problem of recalling training that might have occurred some time ago, points to the need for caution in drawing conclusions about when and how much training has taken place.

Data for both 1983 and 1991 show that the proportion reporting skills improvement training rises up to the age of 44 (Table 16.1), after which it begins

Table 16.1
Percent of Workers Taking Skills Improvement Training on Current Job: 1983 and 1991

Age Group	1983	1991	Percent Change
16-19	18	18	--
20-24	28	31	11
25-34	39	41	5
35-44	41	48	17
45-54	37	46	24
55-64	31	37	19
65+	19	25	32
Total	35	41	17

Source: U.S. Department of Labor (1992), Table 38.

to drop, a finding consistent with observations that training expenditures are concentrated on prime-age workers. Significantly, while skills updating increased for all age groups except the very youngest (ages 16–19) between the two surveys, the increase was greatest among the oldest (i.e., workers ages 65 and older). Even so, this oldest age group remained substantially less likely than all but the very youngest workers to report skills improvement training in 1991.

A Gallup poll conducted for the American Association of Retired Persons (1986) is at marked variance with the BLS figures for either 1983 or 1991. In that survey, two-thirds of the 1,300 respondents, all of whom were 40 or older, said that they had received some job training over the previous three years, a much higher figure than reported by any age group in the BLS survey.

If anything, the restricted time frame in the Gallup survey—the past three years as opposed to any time since obtaining one's current job—would be expected to yield a lower figure (offset to some extent, perhaps, by better recall of recent training), but insights into how respondents in the Gallup poll interpreted the training question—broadly, one can only surmise—are unavailable. In any case, the Gallup survey also reveals a decline in training with age, although the proportion of the oldest workers (63+) who had received training within the past three years remained high—over 50 percent.

Also noteworthy is the finding that more than four-fifths of the Gallup respondents expressed interest in further, generally job-related, training and, again, age differences stand out. Nearly one-third of the oldest respondents wanted no additional training.

Since relatively few people remain in the labor force much beyond age 62, proximity to retirement may explain at least some of the lack of interest in training on the part of the oldest workers. For workers on the threshold of retirement, additional work-related training probably doesn't make much sense, as there may be too little time left for the investment to generate sufficient return. Even so, findings such as these are troublesome if they serve to reinforce a belief on the part of employers and supervisors that older workers in general would not be receptive to training opportunities. Hence, one should bear in mind that even among the oldest respondents, interest in training outweighed disinterest.

Asking a different question ("Since your fiftieth birthday, have you taken any kind of courses or training specifically to improve your job skills or employment opportunities, or not?"), the Commonwealth Fund recently obtained yet a different estimate of older worker training.[8] Just over one-fourth of the respondents in that survey said they had engaged in job-related courses or training since turning 50, a figure below that for the most comparable age groups in either the BLS or Gallup surveys.

The discrepancy between the Commonwealth Fund survey (conducted by Louis Harris and Associates, 1992) and the 1991 BLS survey is most likely due to the more open-ended timeframe in the BLS question (i.e., *"Since you obtained your present job* did you take any training to improve your skills?"). Undoubtedly, at least some older BLS respondents were recalling training taken before their 50s, thus increasing the total affirmative answers.

The Commonwealth Fund survey is one of the few available studies that attempts to discern how workers happen to participate in training efforts. Over half of the workers who had received training since reaching age 50 said that they had taken it upon themselves to get some training; it had, in other words, been their own idea. However, for about one-fourth, the training had been required, and for another one-fifth, an employer had encouraged it.

Workers whose employers required or encouraged them to obtain training were in the minority. Nevertheless, few though they were, their very numbers indicate that some employers, at least, place a value on training their older workers. It is doubtful, however, that even these employers would wax enthusiastic about training all of them.

On the whole, access to training is not spread equally across all workers at every educational level or in all occupations. The better educated, as well as professionals, managers, and technical workers, are among those most likely to receive post-qualifying job-related training (American Association of Retired Persons, 1986; Levitan, Mangum, and Mangum, 1992; U.S. Bureau of the Census, 1992d; U.S. Department of Labor, 1985, 1992c).[9] The fact that such workers get more training than their less educated or blue-collar peers most likely helps explain why corporate executives tend to believe that older professionals and managers are no less likely than younger ones to keep abreast of developments in their fields (Rhine, 1984).

WHO IS TRAINED? THE CORPORATE PERSPECTIVE

Employer and establishment surveys provide little evidence that older worker training and retraining are corporate priorities. Senior workers are widely viewed by their employers as costing too much and as having "plateaued" or become obsolete, even though these problems are often blamed on "insufficient organizational investment in training and development" (Commerce Clearing House, 1988, 4). Analyzing a number of cross-sectional and panel surveys, Lillard and Tan (1992) showed that compared to young men, mature workers (ages 45–59 at the start of the National Longitudinal Surveys in 1966) got the short shrift when it came to training. Perhaps most troubling was the finding that they were about half as likely as their younger counterparts to receive company training.

Fossum et al. (1986) suggested that by withholding developmental resources from workers such as these, the relationship between obsolescence and age is enhanced. Certainly, the classic age discrimination study by Rosen and Jerdee (1977) left no doubt about the extent to which managers pass over older workers when it comes to training referrals. A decade later, Bové complained that there was still "no statistical evidence to indicate that [older worker training] programs are anything more than the efforts of a few enlightened corporations to grapple with a problem that should interest all" (1987, 77).

In the more than 400 Conference Board member firms surveyed by Louis Harris and Associates in 1991, retraining employees to keep them current was a "somewhat or very serious human resource issue" for over 70 percent (Barth, McNaught, and Rizzi, 1993). However, these companies were far less likely to invest in training older workers than younger ones. Greater exposure to older workers seems to matter little: companies with relatively high proportions of older workers were no more disposed toward training older workers than other firms, even though one would assume that overall skills deficiencies and the corresponding need for training would be greater.[10] In fact, companies with "older" workforces were more apt than all companies to view older workers as less flexible about accepting new assignments and less suitable for training than the average worker (Hall and Mirvis, 1993).

Companies also shy away from adjusting training programs to meet what Barth, McNaught, and Rizzi (1993) say are the needs and learning styles of older workers. They are even less inclined to target older workers in their training programs: for example, just three percent of the firms represented in a survey of Society for Human Resource Management (SHRM) members have formal retraining programs for older workers (American Association of Retired Persons, 1993). On a more positive note, one-fourth of the respondents maintained that they try to retain older workers through routine retraining. If it is true that these firms routinely include older workers in their corporate training programs, then that is indeed good news. However, since retention of older workers is hardly the corporate norm today, it is unclear how to interpret those responses.

In the main, employers are disinclined to invest substantial resources in training older workers. Despite their awareness of population aging, they are not convinced that labor shortages will force them to turn to this group of nontraditional workers anytime soon (Johnson and Linden, 1992).[11] Employers are not faced with the tight labor markets of the 1950s and 1960s, which might have encouraged them to concentrate on retaining older workers and keeping them productive through such efforts as retraining and program design (Standing, 1986). Still, employers are worried about skills shortages, particularly on the part of entry-level workers.

Such concern may be what prompted three-fourths of the several hundred human resource executives in one study to say that their "younger employees represent the future of the industry and we should focus our training and development efforts on them" (American Association of Retired Persons, 1989, 14), a sentiment that does not augur well for older worker training.

In firms where early retirement is the downsizing tool of choice, employers will have few incentives for training their older workers. Older workers who have captured the eye of corporate cost cutters are hardly likely to be marked for training, unless it is to prepare them for work outside the corporation. The same seems likely to be the case for workers approaching "normal" retirement age. But even in firms that are not downsizing, older workers may be considered unsuitable for training because employers question their trainability, their interest in training, and the payback to their training.

At a recent conference on U.S. competitiveness and an aging workforce, the suggestion was made that employers may deem older workers "unfit for faster paced jobs, unsuitable for retraining, and too expensive to keep on the payroll" (Hall and Mirvis, 1993, 1). Assuredly, these "undesirable traits" reinforce one another. Being unfit for faster paced jobs would seem to underscore a need for remedial action—training perhaps—to increase job fitness and help ensure that workers are not being paid more than they are worth. Chances are that workers who are denied the opportunity to prove their flexibility, adaptability, and ability to develop new skills will live up to negative stereotypes about them. Lack of training hinders older workers' ability to counteract the pervasive view that they are inflexible and unwilling to adapt (American Association of Retired Persons, n.d., 1989; Commerce Clearing House, 1988; Rhine, 1984).

However, even high-performing older workers—those who are fit, flexible, and unquestionably suitable for training—can find their access to training restricted by supervisors reluctant to excuse highly productive and better-paid workers from their duties (Sterns and Doverspike, 1988). In other words, the opportunity costs involved in training older employees (National Commission on Employment Policy, 1985) work to the disadvantage of these workers as far as training is concerned.

The Age Discrimination in Employment Act of 1967 protects older workers against discrimination in "all terms of employment," including training, so denial of training might well be grounds for a grievance (National Commission for Employment Policy, 1985). Workers themselves, however, are apparently not bothered much by limited training opportunities, if charges filed with the Equal Employment Opportunity Commission (EEOC) are any guide. Training discrimination was alleged in fewer than 1 percent of the age charges filed with the EEOC during the 1980s.[12] Whether older workers are unaware of differential treatment, do not know it may be illegal, or simply do not care is not known.

When it comes to older worker training, the United States marches in step with other industrialized nations, where training also tends to peak in the age 35–45 group (Organization for Economic Development and Cooperation, 1991). The exceptions to this pattern involve countries with extensive apprenticeship programs (e.g., Germany), where the incidence of training among any but the very youngest workers tends to be low, and Japan, the one country that has begun to take an aggressive approach to older worker training.

A cross-national study by the International Labor Office (ILO) actually paints a rather bright, but perhaps misleading, picture of older worker training in the United States, especially as compared to Canada and a number of European countries (Plett, 1990). The ILO's final report described more than 40 different approaches to older worker training and provided illustrative models of those approaches; all but a handful of the models came from the United States.

In fact, however, the United States stands out not because it is doing so much on behalf of older workers but because most other countries, with the prominent exception of Japan, are doing so little. The U.S. country report prepared as a part of the ILO study presents a somewhat more balanced view of older worker training in the United States (Sheppard and Rix, 1989), lending support for Nusberg's conclusion that in the United States, as well as in other industrialized nations, "good recommendations continue to outpace good practice as far as employment-related training for older persons ... is concerned" (Nusberg, 1990, 23).

FEDERAL TRAINING FOR OLDER WORKERS

Because most postqualifying employment training occurs in the private sector, where the large majority of workers are employed, this chapter focuses on private sector training. However, the federal government also invests in worker training, although to a far lesser extent than many other countries (Organization for Economic Cooperation and Development, 1991). At least 125 different federal programs offer some form of training assistance, according to the U.S. General Accounting Office, in a "fragmented 'system' [that] creates a variety of problems that hamper attempts to help workers obtain training and find jobs" (Crawford, 1993, summary). Many of the programs prove inadequate for moving trainees into decent-paying jobs (Heckman, Roselius, and Smith, 1993; Levitan, Mangum, and Mangum, 1992).

Like private sector training programs, few federal programs (10) specifically single out older workers, although again, as is the case with private sector programs, older workers as well as younger ones can be served in "age-neutral" federal programs. Government-supported, older worker training programs differ from those in the private sector in that they emphasize services to job losers or the economically disadvantaged. Updating the skills of the currently employed to lessen the risk of job loss or obsolescence is not the thrust of federal training policy or programs in the United States.

The Senior Community Service Employment Program (SCSEP) is one of the better known and politically popular federally funded older worker "training" efforts, despite the fact that program participants actually receive very little in the way of skills training. Funded under Title V of the Older Americans Act, the SCSEP has traditionally been more of a subsidized community service employment program than a job training program, but it serves an important function in finding jobs for hard-to-place workers. These are disproportionately female, minority, poorly educated, and unlikely to be regarded as suitable to train almost anyplace else. SCSEP has served about 96,000 to 97,000 persons 55 and older annually in recent years, a very small proportion of the potentially eligible population.[13]

Efforts to increase training that would lead to more private-sector employment in high-technology and other growing fields have been encouraged in experimental 502(e) programs under Title V; however, the lack of supplemental funding for those programs has limited what SCSEP program operators could do. On the other hand, money alone would not have been enough to encourage substantial increases in the number of older workers placed by 502(e) programs. An evaluation of the 502(e) programs indicates that program operators themselves may have doubts about the willingness of older participants to invest in the training required for more desirable jobs, e.g., in high-technology, high-growth fields (Centaur Associates Inc., 1986).

A second effort worth mentioning is the Job Training Partnership Act (JTPA). As enacted in 1982, the JTPA was to serve older workers, defined as persons 55 and older, under Title II-A, which offers training to disadvantaged youths and adults, and under Title III, designed to assist displaced workers, many of whom are older. In addition, a 3 percent set-aside under Title II-A was reserved for training programs for persons ages 55 and older.[14]

Older workers have typically been underrepresented in Title II-A and Title III training programs; for instance, during the late 1980s, roughly 35 percent of the Title II-A enrollees and about 8 percent of the Title III enrollees were 55 or older (see U.S. Department of Labor, 1992c; U.S. Senate, 1993). While older participants have been assigned to all of the types of programs offered under JTPA, they have been somewhat overrepresented in programs stressing job-seeking assistance.[15] Regardless of where and how they have been served, there is very little evidence that JTPA training has prepared older workers to compete successfully for good jobs in the turbulent market of the present.[16]

As this publication goes to press, efforts to consolidate 80 to 100 federal job training programs into 1 to 3 block grants are underway in Congress. The most recent versions of both the House and Senate bills set funding for the consolidated programs at below the current level. What consolidation, which has considerable bipartisan support, might mean for older worker training remains to be seen.

PAYOFFS TO TRAINING

If employers are to provide or support worker training and if workers are to participate in training, rewards must accrue to both of them. Higher wages have traditionally rewarded the human capital investment of education and training (Becker, 1975; U.S. Bureau of the Census, 1992d; U.S. Department of Labor, 1990a). As Eck (1993) has shown in his analysis of the 1991 BLS training data, there can be little doubt that education and training, especially qualifying and skills improvement training, are associated with higher earnings. However, Lynch (1993a) reminds us that estimates of the returns to investments in education and training may be biased upward because of the selectivity of persons who are chosen or who opt for education and training.

For employers, too, the return on training investments must outweigh the costs, and either the costs of training older workers must not exceed the costs of training younger workers or the return must be just as great. As the National Commission on Employment Policy pointed out, "Unless employers determine that these training costs will have a similar return on investment for older workers and younger workers, they have less incentive to provide training to older workers and hence are less likely to offer [it]" (1985, 18).

In particular, there is the question of just what training has what returns, and under what circumstances. Lynch (1993a) discussed research on younger and entry-level workers that found relatively little sustained productivity or wage improvement associated with certain types of training. Informal training, the second most common form of skills upgrading (U.S. Department of Labor, 1992), produced rapid productivity growth for the first month after training, but its value dwindled quickly. In contrast, formal employer-provided training from a current employer tended to have a more lasting positive effect on wages, productivity, and worker innovation. Previous employer training was found to lower subsequent training requirements substantially, but its impact diminished if no further on-the-job training were provided, which would seem to highlight the need for and value of on-going training opportunities. Unfortunately, most research has focused on youth; comparable studies on returns to training for older workers are in short supply.

Barth, McNaught, and Rizzi speculated that managers' "calculations of the immediate costs and return-on-investment of retraining and redeploying them" (1993, 165) may influence their judgments about older workers' suitability for training. Cost-benefit calculations undoubtedly run through the minds of employers and supervisors as they make policy and decisions about whom to train, but their calculations may be no more than rough estimates. Only 1 in 10 firms surveyed by the Commerce Clearing House in 1988 reported that they had actually tried to assess the costs and benefits associated with training senior workers (Commerce Clearing House, 1988).

Training costs for the employer involve not only the direct costs of any training activity itself but worker wages, possible expenditures for replacement work-ers, and productivity decline. Costs to workers may involve forgone wages, at least in the case of entry-level workers, lost leisure if training is not provided during work hours, and some or all of the training costs if not supplied or reimbursed by the employers. Even if employers lack ''hard'' numbers on all the costs, their assessments will be colored by the fact that the direct and easy-to-measure expenditures for wages and benefits typically rise with age. A major impediment to older worker training is their expected shorter remaining work-lives when compared to younger workers. Straka stated baldly that ''an older worker (though unlikely to quit) can seldom credibly signal to an employer a plan of long tenure in comparison to a settled prime-age worker'' (1992, 18). The common counterargument that older workers are less mobile than younger workers is only valid, he contended, when older workers are compared to very young workers, who are in the process of job shopping. These young workers are typically not in competition with older workers for jobs or training slots. Instead, older workers compete with ''settled prime-age workers,'' whose job stability, at least until recently, has been comparable to that of ''older'' workers (Carey, 1988; U.S. Department of Labor, 1987).

Older workers who may be trained in entirely new lines of work are hardly eager to accept wages lower than they had been earning before training; the prospect of entry level wages for these retrained workers is likely to be accept-able only to the most desperate of job seekers. Straka suggests that an added training constraint is the higher training costs resulting from the fact that older workers seek to enter or remain in firms at higher levels than younger workers. However, most important, he feels, is the ''short tenure [that] lowers the return to a firm's investment in a worker's productivity'' (1992, 18).

It is conclusions such as these that underscore the need for some specificity in defining old. ''Old age'' as a protected category under the Age Discrimination in Employment Act encompasses almost half the average life expectancy. In fact, the ''settled workers'' to whom Straka refers are actually likely to be older workers. The shorter tenure constraint may be valid when talking about older workers who are close to 60, but it may be far less significant in the case of workers in their mid-40s.

Whether they are 45, 50, or 60, workers who see no payoff to training may be as reluctant to participate in training programs as employers seem to be to train them. If older workers are less likely to invest the time and whatever else skills updating requires, it may be because they too are influenced by the belief that the payoff time is shorter. That reluctance might make sense for workers close to retirement age. How far away from retirement must they be to regard training as a worthwhile investment? Surely the answer will depend in part on how long it takes before a newly acquired skill needs to be updated. If change is rapid and frequent updating is required, the influence of expected worklife on training decisions should be lessened (Sterns and McDaniel, 1994).

At present, it is not clear to what extent investments in skills updating at the upper ages pay off in terms of higher wages, better job options, increased job security, or whatever else may be important to workers as they age. Nor is it clear just how congruent older worker and employer expectations are with regard to appropriate training payoffs. Presumably, both parties would agree that the training should improve performance, but should it be rewarded with better wages or promotion opportunities?

Two recent surveys provide some indication of how workers thought they benefitted from work-related training. In one, conducted for the Commonwealth Fund, older workers felt that training had enabled them to do their work more effectively; however, they were less convinced that it helped them get a better job or promotion.[17] Of considerable interest is the fact that nearly two out of five thought that training had helped them keep their jobs, no small accomplishment for workers today.

Complementary responses were obtained in the second survey of over 500 workers in firms that do train their employees. Regardless of age (under 40, 40–54, and 55+), the overwhelming majority of workers maintained that recent job training had improved their job performance (Opinion Research Corporation, 1992). They were less certain that it had improved their performance evaluations or helped them get raises or promotions, and the proportion mentioning these positive outcomes tended to decline with age.

There is no way to prove that the skills training received by respondents in either survey actually had the reported rewards; what is significant is that respondents saw some positive payoff, particularly when they evaluated their own performance. However, for many older workers, the return to training may not be especially tangible, which could affect enthusiasm for getting it. Moreover, it seems likely that older workers who opted to forgo, or who were denied, training would have held very different opinions from the respondents in these studies.

AGE AND ABILITY TO LEARN

Decisions about training are based, at least in part, on employer attitudes about worker flexibility, ability to learn, and receptivity to training; employers understandably prefer to invest in the "trainable." While the relative lack of investment in older worker training would appear to reflect a sense that older workers are less trainable, the data are not consistent on this point. Some surveys find that employers do not believe that older workers have greater difficulty mastering new skills (Rhine, 1984; Barth, McNaught, and Rizzi, 1993), while others suggest just the opposite (American Association of Retired Persons, 1989; Commerce Clearing House, 1988).

On average, learning time does appear to increase with age: older workers generally take more time than younger ones to master new subjects (see, for example, Czaja and Sharit, 1993; Poon, 1987; Sterns and Doverspike, 1989; Sterns and McDaniel, 1994), although the extent to which age is the culprit is problematic. Educational attainment, in particular, may contribute more than chronological age to learning success, and instructors' and supervisors' negative stereotypes about older worker trainability may undermine older trainees' confidence in learning new skills. Moreover, differences among individuals may be marked (Stagner, 1985); some older workers may be more successful learners than their younger peers.

In their massive review of the literature on older workers, Doering, Rhodes, and Schuster observed that older workers can "continue to learn and learn well" (1983, 113), especially with a programmed instruction methodology. However, this conclusion was based on only five "relatively recent" (i.e., since the late 1960s) studies of learning performance that the authors had been able to identify. Not only were the training studies few in number, but sample size tended to be very small: subjects numbered 60 or fewer in all but one of the studies.

Nonetheless, most research, starting with the pioneering work of Belbin and Belbin, leaves little doubt that ability to learn continues well into the upper years, even though older individuals may not learn as well under the pressure of fast-paced learning situations as they do in other learning environments. Broad generalizations about older people—in this case, learners—are always risky, in view of the fact that variability among individuals actually increases with age (Meier and Kerr, 1976). Some older workers are very rapid learners or can be under the right circumstances.

The research on age and learning or training suffers from a number of limitations, the main one being that there isn't enough of it. Other limitations include:

- Little replicability of studies.
- Typically small samples restricted to very narrow and specialized groups, which limit the generalizability of any findings.
- Little consistency among studies in the definitions of "young" and "old," and generally very few cases of trainees in their 60s or older.
- Insufficient evaluation of background factors or moderators that intervene in, or help explain, learning (Sterns and McDaniel, 1994), and understandable but still unfortunate limitation of small sample studies in which age may be the only possible control.
- Relatively little follow-up of the long-range effects of training, particularly formal and informal company training.
- A preponderance of "classroom" or experimental studies whose relevance to real work-related training may be marginal.
- Dated studies that do not necessarily apply to the workplace of today.

Doering, Rhodes, and Schuster went on to evaluate three studies of posttraining performance, concluding rather tentatively that "the outcomes of training the older worker are better than when training the younger worker" (1983, 115).

In fact, however, this conclusion depends in part on how a "positive" outcome is defined.

In general, the research available through the early 1980s as reviewed by Doering, Rhodes, and Schuster (1983) tended to confirm that although older workers take somewhat longer to complete training programs, they also tended to be effective learners (e.g., Jamieson, 1969; Siemens, 1976). Moreover, when training time was measured against the probability that trainees would remain with the firm that trained them, older workers "outperformed" younger ones.

Treat, Poon, and Fozard (1981) found that while younger individuals were better learners than older ones, experience and practice appeared to have a substantial and positive effect on performance over time. This finding is consistent with that of an earlier study by Newsham (1969), who reported that the longer the training (i.e., the more practice), at least up to a limit, the better older workers did. Treat, Poon, and Fozard have suggested that "a truer measure of performance capabilities may be obtained only after a considerably longer time given to task familiarization than generally has been afforded in the past" (1981, 341), a finding that trainers might keep in mind as they develop programs for training workers of various ages.

More recent research suggests that older learners take more time, often considerably more time, to master some of the new technology and make more errors in the process, although samples tend to be small, and the results not consistent. Elias et al. (1987), for example, tested a total of 45 older (55–67), middle-aged (37–48), and younger (18–28) women who were being trained to use a common word-processing system under conditions supposedly optimal for older persons (Sterns, 1986). With the exception of one of the lessons, the oldest group took significantly longer to complete all tasks, did significantly worse on the review exam, and tended to require much more assistance from the trainer. The other two groups generally did not differ from one another.

Much of the help was trainer-initiated when it became apparent that a trainee was floundering. Time spent being assisted naturally increased the length of time it took to complete a training session, but the authors suggest that without this help, the oldest subjects might have taken even longer to learn to use the word processor. Elias et al. also noted that age-related differences seemed greatest "when the procedure produced very fast, extensive screen changes or when characters were included that indicated commands or document parameters but were not printable text characters" (1987, 346). These procedures were, in other words, ones that were relatively far removed from the procedures that trainees were used to as typists.

Sterns and Doverspike (1989) raised the somewhat disturbing possibility that when it comes to learning new technologies, expertise gained over the years might not have the mediating effect on training that it has had in the past, a fact that may explain some of the findings in the Elias et al. (1987) study. However, it might also be the case that, as individuals become more familiar and comfortable with new technologies, they will once again bring new relevant expertise to other "high tech" training situations. Moreover, it should be emphasized that Elias et al. found that regardless of age, subjects made few overall errors and all of the trainees were capable of learning the basics.

The Elias et al. (1987) findings about length of learning are contradicted to some extent by Hartley, Hartley, and Johnson (1984), who also taught word processing to an unspecified number of older (age 65–75) and younger (18–30) subjects. In this study, older trainees apparently acquired information at the same rate as younger trainees, although it took them longer to select and carry out correct procedures. Again, what seems critical was access to assistance. In a second study in which access to assistance was severely restricted, older adults did worse than they did in the first.

Two admittedly dated training studies indicate that even relatively unskilled workers with low educational attainment can be trained for rather complex tasks involving new technology (Stewart, 1969; Mullan and Gorman, 1972). While a worker's motivation undoubtedly contributes to the success or failure of a training exercise, an employer's motivation to retrain may be equally important. In these cases, absolute job guarantees (a promise of lifelong employment in one of the enterprises) almost certainly served as an incentive to train workers. In one study, airline operatives were slated to shift from a "shelf-and-forklifts technology" to a new semiautomated system with an associated computer documentation system. In the other, baggage and mail handlers and stevedores, all of whom ranged in age from 41 to 60, were retrained for much more highly specialized, complex jobs requiring a high degree of accuracy.

Whatever the motivation, retraining in both cases proved successful, regardless of the age of the trainee. What is perhaps most notable about these two efforts is the fact that operatives were not merely part of an academic training exercise, but rather participants in a real training program with real employment consequences.

In an effort to evaluate recent studies of age and training performance, Sterns and McDaniel (1994) were confronted with a continuing dearth of research on topic. However, new research techniques, specifically meta-analysis, enable reviewers to use statistical methods to draw conclusions from many separate studies and so expand upon the work of Doering, Rhodes, and Schuster (1983).

Sterns and McDaniel (1994) assessed a paper by Haslett et al. (1994) that reviewed several decades of research on aging and training. Examining data on more than 1,700 individuals in 20 independent samples, Haslett et al. reported a negative relationship between age and knowledge learned ($r = -.39$), indicating that increases in age were associated with a decline in effective learning. The negative relationship was somewhat stronger for computer than noncomputer training. This review also confirmed that older adults took longer than younger ones to learn ($r = .42$) and had a higher error rate as well ($r = .29$).

What is perhaps most striking about the Haslett et al. (1994) review is that 20 years of research yielded data on less than 2,000 individuals. Thus, some caution about attaching too much significance to the correlations is probably in order. In addition, Sterns and McDaniel (1994) have stressed that these age-related differences do not necessarily have any meaningful effect on productivity.

The key point in virtually all available research is that older adults do master training material, even when it involves complex new tasks and technologies. From a practical (i.e., job-related) perspective, age differences in learning may be trivial, especially if any additional costs associated with longer training are recouped through such cost-effective attributes of older workers as lower absenteeism or accident rates.

Larger studies and more multivariate analyses of age-related learning experiences are clearly called for, as are more studies of skills training for real jobs in the real work world. Controls for health, education, and motivation, for example, to say nothing of experience and that elusive factor "survival of the fittest," are clearly impossible in sample sizes of most of the studies reviewed. Also needed are productivity studies in a range of environments, using a range of training techniques attempting to teach subjects a range of new or advanced skills or activities. However, the most important question is whether even statistically significant differences in trainability have any true practical significance, especially for private and public sector employment policies.

TRAINING FOR WHAT?

Caro and Morris have argued that "explicit efforts are needed both to recruit older people for retraining and to persuade employers to invest in the retraining of older workers" (1992–1993, 22). The fact of the matter is, however, that employers will invest in older workers when they perceive that (1) it is in their own best interest to do so and/or (2) they have no choice. At the moment, employers do not seem to feel that such an investment is in their best interest, in part because they now have a choice.

Whatever advantages older workers bring to the workforce—and they are many according to employers' own reports—they do not outweigh real or perceived disadvantages, including greater costs and less technological competence when they are compared to younger workers. The skills shortages that so many employers bemoan have caused them to focus on the training needs of younger and entry-level workers, not on their older ones.

Whether employers can be convinced that it *is* in their best interest to train older workers is a key question. Any concerns that employers may harbor about the ability of older workers to succeed in training programs can be refuted by available research, which demonstrates that learning ability is not the gift of youth exclusively. Where the research is weakest is in demonstrating how efficiently the oldest workers, particularly those in their 60s and 70s, master new technology. However, those are not the older workers who are going to flock to employment training programs, whatever the inducement. It is workers in their early 40s and 50s, with 10 to 20 or more work years ahead of them before eligibility for social security benefits, who are likely to grasp the implications of technological advances, structural change in industry, and increasing job complexity and to see the value of skills updating.

These are workers who qualify as "old" under the Age Discrimination in Employment Act, although they might not view themselves as such and they might not even be seen as old by employers and supervisors. Are all of these workers such poor investments?

More and better research on older worker training in the United States is badly needed. Research is needed not only on who is and is not getting trained, disaggregated by age, but on just what type of training workers are getting, where they are getting it (e.g., in formal programs or informally on the job), how intensive the training is, and what its costs and rewards are to both employers and employees.[18] How both workers and their employers define training also needs to be explored. For example, is informal training regarded as "training" by workers and their employers? What really qualifies as formal skills updating? Would a single hour's introduction to a new office telephone system or copy machine qualify, or must it be something more intensive? What factors actually come into play in employers' decisions to encourage or discourage older worker training? Is there an age at which workers are generally perceived, by themselves as well as by their employers, as too old to train? What incentives, if any, serve to persuade employers and workers to invest in training?

If older workers are going to want or need training, then over the short run at least, Hall and Mirvis are probably correct in their "hard conclusion" that "aging workers will simply have to invest more of their own monies to further their formal education in the future" (1993, 38). In particular, firms that are being streamlined will not be training their older workers, unless it is to train them to find work outside the company. Small firms lack the resources to make substantial investments in worker training, while firms of all sizes will deemphasize older worker training if they perceive a greater need for and return on developing the skills of young or entry-level workers.

It will not be the case that all older workers will have to shoulder the burden of their own training, but it will be the case for many, particularly those who seek more general as opposed to firm-specific skills, since employers are understandably reluctant to pay for workers to acquire easily transferable skills.

Employers who question the interest of older workers in training opportunities might be convinced to the contrary if those workers made it clear that they would like to avail themselves of whatever training opportunities may exist. Older workers ought to be aware that denial of training, when based solely on age, is illegal and that they do have some recourse in the Age Discrimination in Employment Act. However, the search for legal remedy is hardly likely to foster good relations between workers and their employers, so it is not a step to be taken lightly.

Assuming that workers—and perhaps even employers—acknowledge the need for older worker training, the question is "training for what?" A former

U.S. Commissioner of Labor Statistics recently lamented that "we simply have not done a very good job in focusing on relevant training" (Janet Norwood, quoted in Labich, 1993). What type of training will ensure that America's older workforce, however defined, is *not* undereducated, undertrained, and ill-equipped to compete with younger U.S. workers in the twenty-first century?

To be sure, relevant training will include training to equip workers with technical skills. However, Levitan and Gallo (1991) have cautioned that job demands are simply not changing all that rapidly, so it is by no means certain that jobs of the near future, anyway, will require significantly different skills from those of today.

While some of the so-called "high tech" jobs are among the fastest growing, some of the biggest job producers—namely, the occupations whose numbers are projected to increase the most—are relatively low tech, for example, sales, cashiers, general office clerks, and janitors among them (Silvestri, 1993). Many of these and others will require less in the way of technical skills than competence in some of the basic skills of reading, writing, and communication.

"Workers," said Friedman, "will fare better to the extent that their skills allow them to move from one kind of work to another" (1992, 70), an observation that holds true for older as well as younger workers in a changing labor market. Relevant training will be training that keeps workers flexible and adaptable and thus able to meet the changing needs of their employers and the society.

In the final analysis, research to date shows us that the answer to the question "training for what?" depends in great part on who is answering the question. Employers, policy and advocacy institutions, and workers themselves have divergent views depending on their economic interests and goals. To formulate a national policy or even a coordinated approach to training will be difficult. To find a coordinated solution to the problem of "America's workforce crisis," which includes far more than worker training, will be even more difficult. Researchers can play an important role by producing accurate and relevant data on all aspects of this crisis. The final answer to worker training for successful competitiveness in the global economy of the twenty-first century, however, will have to come through constructive compromise among employers, workers of all ages, and their advocacy and policy institutions. Such compromises, one hopes, will lead to action to achieve an equitable and effective national employment and training policy.

NOTES

1. An emerging factor that may increase the need for training is the widely touted flattening of the organizational pyramid. In the vertical career path, one's current job frequently provides the training needed to reach the next step on the occupational ladder. In a workplace characterized by horizontal mobility, the current job may be far less relevant to future employment options than is the case today. Horizontal mobility may involve substantially different responsibilities and a greater need for training.

2. Even professionals and managers in healthy firms in growing industries may find themselves subject to skills obsolescence, with a corresponding impact on earnings, according to Andrisani and Daymont (1987). In the specific case of scientists and engineers, this type of obsolescence alone might have accounted for an earnings difference of some 18 percent between workers aged 50 and 65.

3. While older workers are generally less likely than younger ones to lose their jobs (U.S. Congressional Budget Office, 1993), firms with the greatest reductions in the late 1980s tended to be those with higher proportions of older workers, wrote Hall and Mirvis, who go on to note that "the favored downsizing measures of [such] firms were to close plants and make across-the-board layoffs, eliminate layers of management, and offer employees early retirement incentives (which, respectively, discount seniority, affect more older workers, and encourage them to get out while the getting is still good)" (1993, 1).

4. This observation comes from a 1992 survey of older worker training in nearly 450 large manufacturing, banking, diversified financial services, and related firms that was conducted by Opinion Research Corporation for the American Association of Retired Persons.

5. Not surprisingly, Hill and Elias (1990) found that midcareer managers who doubted their ability to be retained were unreceptive to training *even before* they attended a training session.

6. Training expenditures are difficult to calculate with any precision. One of the most widely quoted figures on corporate expenditures for formal employee training is the $30 billion estimate that comes from the American Society for Training and Development. Up to $180 billion is believed to be spent on informal training (Carnevale, 1986). These figures are now several years old, so some adjustment is undoubtedly in order.

7. Most studies indicate that men are more likely to participate in employer-provided training than women; however, it is still possible that any age-associated decline in training rates is greater among men. Such could be the case if, for example, employers were reluctant to invest substantially in training younger women whom they fear might leave the labor force for family reasons (see Green, 1993).

8. The figures in this section are unpublished, unweighted partial counts of the responses made available to the author by the Commonwealth Fund (1992 data).

9. Education appears to be positively related to acquisition of skills training among older workers as well (Bass and Barth, 1992).

10. If 30 percent or more of the employees were aged 50 or older, a workforce was classified as "older."

11. The respondents to the Conference Board survey are not alone in questioning dire warnings of labor shortages (see Mishel and Teixeira, 1991).

12. Author's calculations for this chapter.

13. Because more than one person can fill a slot in any year, the number of funded SCSEP slots is actually lower than these figures would suggest.

14. Subsequent amendments restructured Title II-A and eliminated the 3 percent setaside. Currently, roughly 5 percent of all adult funds are to be spent on older worker programs.

15. To some, job search assistance may appear to stretch the definition of job "training." However, it does seem to be somewhat effective (Heckman, Roselius, and Smith, 1993; U.S. Congressional Budget Office, 1993).

16. Short-term training and job-search assistance are key components of the Economic

Dislocation and Worker Adjustment Assistance Act (EDWAA) Program, funded under Title III of the JTPA. In addition, older workers stand to be assisted by Trade Adjustment Assistance (TAA) programs that provide income replacement benefits and training to workers who have become unemployed as a result of increased imports.

Little can be said about the effectiveness of EDWAA or TAA when it comes to training workers, in view of a scarcity of research on programs funded under either act (Heckman, Roselius, and Smith, 1993; U.S. Congressional Budget Office, 1993). However, preliminary results from a TAA study are not encouraging. According to the Congressional Budget Office (1993), those results indicate that TAA has done little to improve earnings or reemployment probability.

17. See Green (1993).

18. This would include research on training goals. In order to evaluate the effectiveness of any training program, its objectives must be clear. Employers and workers may differ in those objectives. Employers undoubtedly seek enhanced productivity, while workers may look to training to promote job security, give them a leg up on finding another job, or lead to a raise or promotion.

17

The Costs and Benefits of Older Workers

Michael C. Barth, William McNaught, and Philip Rizzi

If media attention is any indicator, there currently is a great deal of interest in the topic of increasing work opportunities for older people (Labich, 1993).[1] Some of this interest grows directly from the large number of older people who are having difficulty finding work.[2] Additional interest stems from the growing unease felt by many older workers about the security of their jobs. This situation exists despite a substantial body of literature suggesting that older people are, on a broad range of criteria, excellent employees.

The popularity of early retirement incentive programs (ERIPs) within the American business community suggests that corporate decisionmakers believe the cost of older employees exceeds their benefits.[3] That this chapter is devoted to a careful examination of the validity of this common belief may surprise many readers who might reasonably expect that it had long since been reliably verified. In fact, we believe that comparisons of the relative costs and benefits of older and younger workers have not been sufficiently examined within the literature and that the available evidence does not convincingly support prevailing management views.

It is not surprising that American corporations hold beliefs that are not supported by the research evidence, although the reason for this disparity is not

The authors of this chapter worked on the Americans over 55 at Work Program sponsored by The Commonwealth Fund from 1988 to 1993. Many of the studies referenced in this chapter were commissioned by the program, and the chapter itself was prepared with the financial support of The Commonwealth Fund, for which we are grateful.

entirely clear. One possibility is that managers are biased against older workers. Substantial evidence supports this theory; for example, suits under the Age Discrimination in Employment Act have increased steadily since it was first passed in 1967 (McEvoy and Cascio, 1989).[4] In addition, as we will describe later, controlled studies typically find that negative stereotypes about older people are quite common.

A second possibility is that employers are using age as an inexpensive screening device in order to simplify a complex, expensive, and often politically charged decision about whom to hire, fire, train, reward, and promote. Age serves as an easy proxy for the much more difficult task of fairly and objectively assessing a worker's productive potential. As an example, corporations rarely receive bad publicity for offering retirement programs to their workforce but are routinely excoriated when laying off middle-aged and younger workers.

A third possibility is that, like lemmings, some employers are more comfortable as members of a pack moving in the same direction rather than risking an original approach to layoff decisions. Once some firms showed how easy it was to downsize using ERIPs, others have naturally followed suit.[5]

A fourth possibility, consistent with business decision making in other areas, is that American managers often resort to shortsighted strategies in response to immediate problems without considering the long-term consequences.[6] If managers believe that older workers are more expensive in the short term, then they are prime candidates for terminations, whether through ERIPs or layoffs, regardless of their value over the longer term. Thus, in an era of corporate retrenchment and downsizing, cutting costs quickly and deeply substitutes for any strategic planning that aligns human resource policies with corporate objectives. All of the above explanations appear to be relevant when examining the complex labor market for older people, with the relative importance of each explanation varying under different circumstances.

Before we explore the facts on the benefits and costs of older workers, we note that the skills, attributes, and abilities of people vary. Thus, it is incorrect and misleading to speak of older workers as if they all were identical or suggest that average values reasonably represent the diversity of the older worker population. Indeed, there is a distribution among all older workers, and younger ones as well, along any dimension of interest, whether, for example, productivity, attendance, or health care costs. To the extent that we discuss older workers as a group or mention average values, we do so merely to ease the flow of our exposition of the issues surrounding their employment.

In the remainder of the chapter, we first present a brief overview of the age distribution within the American labor force so that readers will understand the scope and importance of the issue we address. We then examine prevailing management attitudes toward older workers assembling both survey evidence and conclusions from the literature on this topic. Next, we discuss the costs and benefits of older workers. A brief conclusion ends the chapter.

THE DEMOGRAPHICS OF THE AMERICAN LABOR FORCE

While older Americans comprise a growing proportion of the population, they make up a declining fraction of the U.S. workforce. Table 17.1 shows the distribution of the working-age population (i.e., those aged 16 and older) and also the age distribution of those in the labor force and those with paying jobs. The data indicate that older people are underrepresented in the labor force (i.e., those working or actively looking for work) and employed populations (i.e., those with jobs). Twenty-seven percent of the working-age population are age 55 or older, while 12 percent are employed.

The importance of older people in the labor force will increase in the future. The over–age 45 population and labor force is expected to grow rapidly over the coming years relative to other segments of the population and labor force, as shown in Table 17.2. Growth of the overall labor force is expected to slow between now and the early years of the twenty-first century. However, the growth rate of the over–age 55 portion of the labor force is expected to rise from the one-half of a percent annual average experienced between 1975 and 1990 to 2.4 percent per year between 1990 and 2005 (Fullerton, 1991). After 2005, adverse swings in the retirement environment for older people may make continued work an increasingly attractive, or necessary, option and further accelerate growth rates in the older labor force (Barth and McNaught, 1991).

PREVAILING MANAGEMENT ATTITUDES TOWARD OLDER WORKERS

In examining management attitudes toward older workers, we are trying to understand the motives of those we might call "gatekeepers" of American business—those who develop and implement employment policies. The views of human resource gatekeepers have been documented in two recent surveys.[7] In 1989, the Daniel Yankelovich Group surveyed senior human resource executives in 400 randomly selected companies (AARP, 1989).[8] In 1992, on behalf of the Commonwealth Fund and The Conference Board, Louis Harris and Associates interviewed 406 senior human resource gatekeepers in a random sample of Conference Board member firms (Mirvis, 1993).

The results of the two surveys were consistent. The AARP/Yankelovich study (AARP, 1989) found gatekeepers responded positively regarding the work ethic of older workers, praising their commitment to quality and loyalty to the company. Older workers also received high marks regarding coolness in a crisis and practical knowledge. On the negative side, employers reported "lingering questions" about older workers' adaptability to new technology and serious concerns regarding the costs of their health insurance.

The Commonwealth Fund/Louis Harris survey (Mirvis, 1993) also indicated ambivalence toward older workers among gatekeepers. They rated older workers

Table 17.1
Age Distribution of the Population, Labor Force, and Employed Population in 1992

Ages	Population (millions)	Labor Force (millions)	Employment (millions)
16 to 24	30.9 (16%)	20.5 (16%)	17.6 (15%)
25 to 34	41.9 (22%)	35.1 (28%)	32.4 (28%)
35 to 44	39.5 (21%)	33.6 (26%)	31.7 (27%)
45 to 54	27.5 (14%)	22.4 (18%)	21.2 (18%)
55 to 64	21.1 (11%)	11.9 (9%)	11.3 (10%)
65 to 74	18.5 (10%)	3.0 (2%)	2.9 (2%)
75+	12.3 (6%)	0.5[a]	0.5[a]
All ages 16+	191.6 (100%)	127.0 (100%)	117.6 (100%)

Note: [a]Less than 0.5 percent. Column percentages may not add due to rounding.
Source: U.S. Department of Labor (1993c).

positively on reliability, skills, and attitude, and negatively on health care costs, flexibility in taking new assignments, and suitability for training. Table 17.3 summarizes the overall conclusions of the survey.

Despite the mixed ratings, it appears that the negative factors—suitability for training, flexibility, and health care costs—are more important to corporate gate-keepers than the positive ones. This interpretation is certainly consistent with management's behavior of offering incentives to induce many older workers to retire early. This practice is now so widespread that a substantial minority, about one-eighth, of America's middle-aged and older workers (age 50 to 64) do not expect to be allowed to work up to the age at which they would like to retire (Quinn and Burkhauser, 1991).

Survey evidence of employer attitudes on the qualities of older workers is fairly consistent, but surveys may disguise latent biases of managers about the capabilities of older workers. One compelling piece of evidence of bias comes from a meta-analysis of studies investigating the productivity of older workers by David Waldman and Bruce Avolio (1986).[9] Waldman and Avolio found evidence that studies based upon the opinions of managers usually conclude that age negatively influences a worker's productivity. However, when similar studies of the influence of age on productivity used objective or co-worker evaluations, age was generally found to have a positive influence on productivity.

A striking analysis of the opinions of managers about older workers is that of Benson Rosen and Thomas Jerdee (1977). They conclude that managers hold conscious opinions that are generally favorable toward older workers, but unconsciously discriminate against them when making practical personnel deci-

Table 17.2
Percentage Change in Population and Labor Force, 1990 to 2005

Ages	Percentage Change in Population	Percentage Change in Labor Force
16 to 24	8.3%	13.2%
25 to 34	-15.4%	-11.5%
35 to 44	13.0%	16.4%
45 to 54	66.1%	74.8%
55 to 64	40.4%	52.3%
65 to 74	2.6%	10.5%
75+	37.3%	40.4%
All Ages 16+	16.4%	20.8%

Source: Authors' calculations based on data from U.S. Bureau of the Census (1992c) and Fullerton (1991).

sions. Rosen and Jerdee divided a representative sample of managers into two groups and asked them to imagine themselves to be administrators who had to make recommendations to solve a set of troublesome personnel situations. Unknown to the managers, the incidents presented to each group were identical except for the age of the employee involved. Managers in the group presented with problems involving older workers handled the incidents differently than the group dealing with younger workers. The managers perceived older workers as more resistant to change and were less inclined to attempt corrective action to help the older worker.[10] Managers also were more inclined to train and promote younger workers than equally qualified older workers. Rosen and Jerdee conclude that "age stereotypes clearly influence managerial decisions" (1977, 105).

Sonnenfeld (1978) suggested that part of the explanation is the tendency of managers to consider an employee's potential—including the employee's remaining years until retirement and perceived age-based declines in a worker's capabilities—in making current evaluations. To the extent that age stereotypes influence managerial decisions beyond performance evaluations such as decisions about promotions, job assignment, and access to training, these stereotypes become self-reinforcing by undermining the skills and motivation of older workers that are critical to their continued productivity.

THE COSTS OF OLDER WORKERS

We initiate our discussion of the costs of older workers with a simple comparison of wages and salaries of older workers with those of younger workers and then move to the costs of fringe benefits. In this second area, we concentrate

Table 17.3
Percentage of Companies Reporting Older Workers as Better or Worse Than Average Workers

Work attribute	All companies	Companies with an older workforce[a]
Better than average		
Work attitudes	57	64
Turnover	76	74
Absenteeism	66	60
Job skills	48	45
Worse than average		
Health care costs	64	79
Flexibility	57	62
Suitability for training	37	50

Note: [a]Companies with at least 30 percent of the workforce age 50 or older.
Source: Barth, McNaught, and Rizzi, 1993, Exhibit 6.6.

heavily on the question of health care costs, the item employers frequently cite as a concern about older workers. Next, we consider the indirect costs of employment, such as the costs of recruitment and training. Throughout this section, we treat costs as those activities resulting in actual expenses to the employer as a consequence of employing a worker.[11]

In the next section, we consider the other side of the coin—the benefits of older workers—by examining how their job performance compares to that of younger workers.

Wage and Salary Costs

If expenses are measured only by the wages and salaries received, an older worker costs more than a younger worker. There is a simple reason for this. Traditionally, workers and corporations have concluded an ''implicit contract'' in which workers have promised corporate loyalty and exemplary work behavior (punctuality, attendance, diligence, and consistency) in return for the firm's provision of employment security and relatively steady annual wage increases over the course of a working career (Fay, 1993).[12] Since most U.S. workers matured in such a system, it is not surprising to find that wage and salary levels rise steadily with age, and only begin to level off in the age range when workers traditionally retire (Burkhauser and Quinn, 1993).

Table 17.4 compares the usual earnings of workers of various ages who are employed full time. These data clearly show the upward progression in salaries

Table 17.4
Usual Weekly Earnings of Full-Time Wage and Salary Workers in 1990

Ages	Men	Women	Both Sexes
16-24	$285	$267	$277
25-34	$470	$383	$424
35-44	$584	$419	$504
45-54	$636	$417	$523
55-64	$578	$376	$483
65+	$421	$328	$378

Source: U.S. Department of Labor (1993).

through the prime of the working career, at about age 50 for men and slightly younger for women, and then a steady fall in these salaries through the 50s, with more drastic reductions during the 60s.

These earnings patterns are the product of historical practices of setting wages, reflecting a society in which a worker remained with the same firm for a large portion of his or her career. The idea of an implicit lifetime employment contract appears to be fast disappearing from large segments of the economy as companies move increasingly to "employment-at-will" arrangements and tighter linkages between current pay and current performance (Fay, 1993).[13] If the lifetime bargain between employers and employees is becoming less and less tenable throughout the economy, it will be increasingly difficult for older workers to retain their relatively high income levels and at the same time remain competitive in a job market characterized by low job security—unless they are demonstrably more productive than other workers.

Health Care Costs

Health care is the single most widely cited area where the costs of older workers are perceived to exceed those of younger workers and an issue of urgent competitive concern to corporate gatekeepers (Mirvis, 1993; American Association of Retired Persons, 1989). Respondents in the 1989 AARP/Yankelovich (AARP, 1989) survey estimated that, on average, the health insurance costs of older workers were 15 percent higher than those of the average age worker.

As shown in Table 17.5, the average cost to employers for workers' health care coverage generally increases with age, confirming managers' perceptions that health care costs are indeed higher for older workers than for younger workers (Commonwealth Fund, 1993a). The increase is very strong for men, but less so for women, whose costs peak in the age range of 45 to 54 and then decline modestly. The increase in average cost with age for men is significantly greater than for women for three reasons:

Table 17.5
Annual Employer Health Care Costs for Insured Workers by Age and Sex

	Men		Women	
Ages	Cost	Percent of Earnings	Cost	Percent of Earnings
18 to 24	$710	4.1%	$900	6.7%
25 to 34	1,500	6.1	1,780	8.5
34 to 44	2,380	6.6	2,410	9.0
45 to 54	3,200	8.4	2,580	8.5
55 to 64	3,960	14.5	2,300	7.7

Note: Estimates are based on an analysis of 1987 data from the National Medical Expenditure Survey (1987), inflated to 1994 dollars.

Source: Commonwealth Fund (1993).

- Average health expenditures for young women are higher than those for young men because of maternity costs;
- Average health expenditures for older men are higher than those for older women because of higher rates of cardiovascular disease, which is expensive to treat;
- The percentage of women with dependent coverage declines more rapidly with age than that of men. (Commonwealth Fund, 1993a)

The higher health care costs of older men stand out even more when considered as a percentage of total earnings, which provides a more accurate picture of the burden of health care coverage to employers (Commonwealth Fund, 1993a; U.S. Senate, 1984). As described earlier, average earnings of men increase with age until around age 50 and then decline, but employer health care costs for older men increase steadily with age. Consequently, for insured men between ages 55 to 64, employer health care costs are nearly 15 percent of earnings, twice the average for all male workers.[14] For women, employer health care costs as a share of earnings do not change significantly with age, ranging from about 7 percent for working women age 18 to 24 to a peak of approximately 9 percent for women age 35 to 44.

Whether the higher health care costs of older workers influences managerial perceptions of the costs of older workers depends in part on the company's method of financing health care coverage. Companies that self-insure pay their actual claims and, therefore, will bear directly the higher health care costs of their older workers. Companies with experience-rated health insurance coverage provided by a third-party insurer will bear the higher health care costs of older workers in the form of increased annual premiums.[15] Companies with community-rated coverage—meaning that the cost for coverage is based on the claims history of an entire community rather than only the company's workforce—

Table 17.6
Average Annual Health Expenditures for Older Workers and Nonworkers

	Men		Women	
Ages	Employed	Not Employed	Employed	Not Employed
55 to 59	$1,957	$4,508	$1,768	$2,622
60 to 64	1,885	4,198	1,378	2,911
65 to 69	2,441	4,518	2,929	3,759

Source: Commonwealth Fund (1993a).

would not incur additional costs by having an older workforce. Instead, the higher health care costs of their older workers would be spread out over many companies and individuals in the community risk pool.

As shown in Table 17.6, health care expenditures for older people who are working are substantially less than those of older people out of the labor force because the state of their health affects when people stop working. Older people who continue to work past normal retirement age tend to be healthier than their nonworking contemporaries (Barth, McNaught, and Rizzi, 1994).[16]

Likely changes to the existing health insurance system will undoubtedly alter workers relative health care costs and perhaps significantly reduce them. If health reform reduces the overall burden of health costs on business, it will likely reduce both the total and relative costs of older workers because health costs are a larger share of their total employment costs than they are for other workers.

However, incremental changes to the current system may not eliminate the gap in health care costs between older and younger workers. Melissa Barringer and Olivia Mitchell (1993) found that older workers are more likely to select a traditional fee-for-service plan over other options, such as managed care, if both options are available. In general though, Barringer and Mitchell found that older workers respond much as younger workers do to increases in health plan premium costs and deductibles by moving to prepaid plans when it becomes cost-effective to do so.

Pension Costs

Pensions usually are structured in two basic forms: defined benefit plans, in which a worker receives a guaranteed monthly amount for life, normally some fixed percentage of his or her final pay, with the percentage based on years of service; or defined contribution plans, in which the company annually contributes a set percentage of the worker's pay into a fund that is not taxed until disbursement and is legally set aside only for the payment of retirement benefits.

The distinction is important for any discussion of the pension costs of older workers. To support defined benefit plans, actuaries calculate how much money a firm must set aside annually to cover the costs that will eventually result from the company's promises to pay future benefits. These estimates are based on actuarial projections about future wage increases, turnover rates among employees, the rate of return to be earned on pension investments, age of retirement, and life expectancy. Thus, calculating the costs of a defined benefit plan in any given year is inherently uncertain. In addition, the risk that these pension accruals will not be sufficient to meet actual pension obligations to retirees is born principally by the employing firm.[17]

Under most standard actuarial models, the "accrual cost" of a defined benefit plan increases rapidly as employees age. This means that as a worker approaches the age of normal retirement, the percentage of pay that must be set aside increases rapidly. Although defined benefit pension plans differ substantially in structure, Laurence Kotlikoff and David Wise (1989) provided estimates of the age-related differences in pension costs based on data from the Bureau of Labor Statistics' 1979 Level of Benefits Survey, which covered nearly 18 million plan participants in 3,248 pension plans. For percent-of-earning plans with provisions for early retirement at age 55 and normal retirement at age 65, the accrual rates for an average employee who joined the company at age 30 increased steadily from 1.3 percent (pension accrual as a ratio of the wage) at age 41 to 9.7 percent at age 55. The differences by age were even greater under other scenarios.

Malcolm Morrison and Anna Rappaport (U.S. Senate, 1984) also analyzed pension costs by age.[18] They compared the cost of a life annuity for men beginning at age 65 assuming a 7.5 percent rate of interest. As shown in Table 17.7, using costs for a 47-year-old male employee as a standard of reference, accrual costs grew rapidly as workers aged, and costs for workers at age 65 were more than four times greater than the 47-year-old reference.

The calculations underlying defined contribution plans are much simpler. Each year, a constant share of the worker's pay is placed in an individual pension fund to be invested. The worker gains legal title to the funds per a vesting schedule and is entitled to the accrued (vested) money in this fund upon separation from the firm. There is no promise of a specific retirement entitlement, and the risk of investment performance is born entirely by the employee.

Defined contribution plans are roughly "age neutral" because generally, the same percentage of earnings is set aside annually for all employees regardless of their ages. Consequently, the employer's expense is a function of each worker's individual earnings and will reflect whatever age-related differences exist in the earnings of the company's workforce. As discussed in the section on salary and wages, older workers typically earn more than younger workers and, therefore, will have higher pension costs under a defined contribution plan. Because, under most plans, the amount set aside annually is on the order of 3 to 5 percent of wages or salary, the differences will be modest but accentuating.[19]

Recently, the establishment of defined contribution plans has exceeded that

Table 17.7
Cost of an Annuity for Male Workers at Various Ages Relative to Cost for a 47-Year-Old

Age	Relative Cost
25	19.9%
30	28.6
35	41.3
40	59.5
45	86.1
47	100.0
50	125.4
55	184.4
60	274.5
65	417.1

Source: U.S. Senate (1984).

of defined benefit plans. As noted, the risk of investment performance (and the possibility of having insufficient retirement income) rests with the employee under a defined contribution plan. This eliminates future financial uncertainty for the company as a result of poor actuarial assumptions as well as the need for management to monitor current financial performance of its pension assets.[20]

By 1988, defined contribution plans accounted for 80 percent of all pension plans, up from 70 percent in 1980 (Employee Benefits Research Institute, 1992). Participation in defined contribution plans during this period grew even faster from 34 percent of all eligible employees to 48 percent. This trend continues; between 1990 and 1992, more than 30,000 defined benefit pension plans were terminated, with most of these plans replaced by defined contribution plans (Fay, 1993). Despite these trends, defined benefit pension plans remain a formidable presence on the pension landscape, accounting for approximately 60 percent of all pension assets (Employee Benefits Research Institute, 1992).

For purposes of considering cost differentials, then, the lesson is straightforward. In terms of pension costs for all employers in the economy, older employees are more expensive than younger employees, especially for companies with generous defined benefit plans. However, as more employers convert their existing pension plans into defined contribution plans (or supplement defined benefit with defined contribution plans), this cost differential will decrease, possibly to the point of insignificance.

Other Fringe Benefits

Paid time off (holidays, sick leave, and vacation) can be an expensive fringe benefit provided by employers, often accounting for approximately 10 percent of total compensation (U.S. Senate, 1984; Jondrow, Brechling, and Marcus, 1987). Paid time off may increase the cost of older workers relative to younger workers in two ways. First, if the worker is not replaced while absent, there is an opportunity cost attributable to the forgone production.[21] If this cost is estimated based on the salary of the worker, it will be higher if there is a positive correlation between the salaries and age of employees.[22] Second, many companies increase the number of vacation days based on seniority, typically at five-year intervals.

Although pension, paid time off, and health care insurance are the most common and expensive benefits typically offered by employers, the list can be much longer and include: life insurance, disability insurance, supplemental retirement income, employee stock ownership, dues and membership fees for unions or professional societies, and company-provided transportation (company car or subsidized mass transportation). Some of these benefits may be offered as a percentage of salary or wages and, therefore, will increase whatever age-related differences in salary and wages exist in the company's workforce. Here again, however, this is not true if employers are able to backshift the higher costs of fringe benefits to older workers in the form of less pay (i.e., smaller pay increases). It also is not true for some so-called *cafeteria plans*, in which all workers have the same amount of money or credits to spend on their choice of benefits. Under these cafeteria plans, any age-related differences in costs are spread out among all employees in the form of higher ''prices'' for each benefit on the menu.[23]

For other benefits, the age of an employee directly accounts for the cost difference. The cost to an employer of providing life insurance is based on actuarial tables of mortality and the composition of its workforce (e.g., age, gender). Consequently, life insurance is more expensive for an older worker, but the difference is typically small compared to health care insurance costs or pension costs under a defined benefit plan (U.S. Senate, 1984).

Some fringe benefits are more complex to analyze. The age-related cost of disability insurance is complicated by two considerations: the incidence rate of disability, and the duration of benefit payments, which typically terminate at a specified age, thereby reducing the payout period in the event of disability. For example, an older worker may be more likely than a younger worker to become disabled, but benefits will be paid for fewer years. How these factors offset each other depends on the specifics of each company's plan but overall, Morrison and Rappaport (U.S. Senate, 1984) conclude that disability insurance premiums are unlikely to differ significantly for employees of various ages.

Absenteeism

Absenteeism imposes either a direct or an opportunity cost on employers depending on whether management and other workers compensate for the absence by hiring a temporary employee, reassigning workloads, or foregoing the worker's output.

As shown in Table 17.8, rates of absenteeism for full-time older workers are modestly higher than those for younger workers with the exception of workers ages 16 to 19. However, when absences are divided into avoidable (i.e., casual, voluntary, or unsanctioned) and unavoidable (i.e., sickness, involuntary, or sanctioned), a different picture emerges. Older workers generally have the same or fewer absences for personal reasons than younger workers. These findings are consistent with managers' perception of older workers as having high levels of loyalty and reliability and better work habits than younger workers.

In reviewing numerous studies, Rhodes (1983) found that avoidable absences for men generally declined with age. For women, the results are conflicting and inconclusive. Studies on unavoidable absences and age have generally revealed positive or nonsignificant relationships for men and predominantly nonsignificant relationships for women. In two corporations we studied, Days Inns of America (McNaught and Barth, 1992) and B&Q plc (Hogarth and Barth, 1991), older workers were found to have a considerably lower incidence of absenteeism than younger workers.

Workplace Injury

Work-related injuries impose costs associated with the worker's absence while recovering. Workplace injury also adds to health care costs, directly in the case of companies that self-insure and indirectly in the form of higher future premiums for companies using traditional third-party insurers and experience rating, and results in higher worker compensation premiums.

Most studies examining the relationship of age to workplace accidents conclude that younger workers are more likely to be injured on the job than middle-aged or older workers chiefly as a result of their lack of experience (Mitchell, 1990). The picture is somewhat less clear when the severity of injury is taken into account. Mitchell (1990) reported that for temporary disability, the recovery period of older workers tends to be longer than that of younger workers. Findings on rates of permanent disabilities and fatalities vary from study to study and generally do not test for statistically significant differences, which makes it difficult to draw firm conclusions. However, injury rates appear to rise for workers age 65 and older, and these employees also are more likely to suffer permanent disabilities and fatalities (Mitchell, 1988).

Table 17.8
Absence Rate of Full-Time Workers in 1992

Age	Men			Women			Total		
	Total	Illness	Other reasons	Total	Illness	Other reasons	Total	Illness	Other reasons
16 to 19	6.4%	1.8%	4.6%	8.5%	3.6%	4.9%	7.3%	2.5%	4.7%
20 to 24	4.0	1.8	2.1	6.6	3.3	3.2	5.1	2.5	2.6
25 to 54	3.4	2.0	1.4	6.3	3.3	3.0	4.6	2.5	2.1
55+	4.8	3.0	1.7	6.6	3.7	2.8	5.5	3.3	2.2
All Ages	3.7	2.1	1.6	6.4	3.3	3.0	4.8	2.6	2.2

Note: Absences refer to work missed due to illnesses or other personal reasons. Excluded is work missed due to vacation, holiday, labor-management dispute, or bad weather resulting in an employer temporarily curtailing business activity. The absence rate is the ratio of workers with absences to total full-time employment. To be counted as having an absence, a person who usually works 35 hours or more per week must have been at work fewer than 35 hours or have not been at work at all during the survey reference week.

Source: U.S. Department of Labor (1993c).

As for absenteeism, the data on workplace injury are inconclusive as to whether older workers are more or less expensive than other workers.

Training

Surveys indicate that corporate gatekeepers have reservations about both the ability of older workers to adapt to new technologies and their suitability for training. Corporate actions are consistent with these attitudes. In a recent survey, large companies reported that they had invested more money in training workers under age 35 than workers age 51 or older (Barth, McNaught, and Rizzi, 1993).

Older workers' lack of access to training appears to result from a combination of beliefs by managers that "old dogs cannot learn new tricks" and that sufficient returns on the training investment will not be realized before an older worker retires.[24]

Evidence supporting the first belief is weak. Our case studies of two corporate settings revealed that older workers learn as easily and as well as younger workers (McNaught and Barth, 1992; Hogarth and Barth, 1991). Days Inns of America began hiring workers age 50 and older as reservations agents at its national reservations center in Atlanta, Georgia, in 1986 after experiencing high rates of employee turnover and difficulty recruiting young workers. The job is not simple: a reservation agent must simultaneously engage in conversation with a prospective client, query information from the computer system, and obtain information on the local area from binders. Further, the reservation center is staffed at a level that ensures that agents receive a steady volume of calls and have little idle time between calls. Initial concerns by Days Inns management about the trainability of older hires proved to be unfounded. The managers had planned to give older workers more training than younger ones but found that extra training was unnecessary. After a half-day of computer familiarization training, older workers learned the complicated system in two weeks, just as quickly as younger workers (McNaught and Barth, 1992).

B&Q plc, England's largest chain of home and houseware stores, was experiencing significant labor problems in 1988. Meeting recruiting targets was difficult, and the turnover rate among sales personnel was above 100 percent. B&Q's senior management decided to adopt a new strategy that included hiring older workers. In 1989, B&Q opened a store in Macclesfield entirely staffed by workers over age 50.[25] Out of concern that older workers would require more training, eight weeks of training were offered instead of the usual four. This turned out to be excessive, and when the company opened a second all-older-worker store in 1990, the training period was cut back to the standard level. B&Q's management noted, however, that older workers typically asked many more, and more demanding, questions during training than younger workers, which required corporate trainers to be more extensively prepared.

Doubts about the learning abilities of older workers arise in part because the design and delivery of training seldom incorporate techniques proven effective for older learners. More than 80 percent of large companies report no adjustment in their training for workers of different ages, even though older workers have generally been away from the classroom for a long time and have considerable work experience that can be leveraged for new learning (Bass and Barth, 1992).

Evidence for the second proposition that returns on training investments in older workers are diminished by retirement appear to be largely impressionistic since technological obsolescence is so rapid in many fields today. As the useful life of equipment and production methods shortens, the payback period for re-lated training similarly shrinks, as should employers' concern that the value of the training will be lost upon a worker's retirement.[26] For example, Motorola, the semiconductor and electronics manufacturer, spends approximately 2.6 per-cent of payroll just to maintain the competency level of its employees in the face of technological change (Brody, 1987).[27]

Our case studies suggest that managers have largely overestimated the training costs of older workers. From the limited evidence available, if access to training is equal for all workers, the costs will probably not vary by age because older workers are capable of learning as quickly and thoroughly as younger workers, and the value of training "lost" on retirement is likely to be less than is com-monly believed. However, because older workers have received less training than younger workers in the past, it may now be more difficult to train the typical older worker to the same level of competency as a younger worker.

In summary, older workers are, on average, more expensive with regard to wages and salary, health care costs, and pension costs (especially in the years just before retirement). On paid time off, other fringe benefits such as life and disability insurance, absenteeism, and workplace injury, it is either not clear that any cost differences exist between younger and older workers or the differences are so modest that it is unlikely to be a significant influence on managers' decisions about employing older people. In addition, we believe that managers have largely overestimated the training costs of older workers, resulting in older workers being shortchanged on training. This lack of training may be short-sighted, having the effect of holding down current employment costs of older workers but eroding their productivity in the future.

Further, while it may be true that in most circumstances older workers cost more than younger workers, this is not always the case. One innovative program using older workers actually is saving money for a corporation. In the late 1970s, the Travelers Corporation, an insurance and financial services company based in Hartford, Connecticut, decided to start a customer service hotline and needed employees familiar with the range of the company's operations to staff it. Re-moving full-time employees from their regular work assignments would have disrupted the company's continuing operations. Instead, Travelers decided to rehire recent retirees to staff the hotline on a part-time basis.[28] The success of this small program soon convinced Travelers to expand the use of retirees as temporary workers throughout the firm.

Using data from 1989, the last year Travelers operated an internal job bank exclusively using their own retirees, Travelers saved nearly $900,000 in labor costs (McNaught and Barth, 1991).[29] By hiring its own retirees, Travelers does not have to incur additional benefit costs such as health insurance and pensions. Further, by concentrating its temporary hires on workers already familiar with firm operations, Travelers avoids continually having to train newly placed workers.

BENEFITS OF OLDER WORKERS

Perhaps the most important question underlying the future employment of older workers concerns their productivity relative to other employees. Ultimately, the wages or salary of any worker and his or her employability are determined by that individual's productivity (within the limits of being able to accurately and efficiently assess an individual's productivity).

Earlier, we summarized the opinions of management about the relative strengths and weaknesses of older workers as employees. These opinions include the widespread belief that a worker's contribution to the firm generally increases throughout the worker's career or increases and then reaches a plateau until retirement (Barth, McNaught, and Rizzi, 1993). If, as the previous section suggests, older workers are more expensive to employ than younger workers, then their ability to compete in the labor force will largely depend on their productivity compared to younger workers. If older workers are more productive than younger workers, they could be worth their higher costs.

Empirical Evidence on the Benefits of Older Workers

This section provides a brief review of the empirical evidence about the productivity of older workers.[30] Measuring the productivity of older workers is much more difficult than measuring costs, which can be readily identified and counted. Productivity is highly variable from industry to industry and measuring it with accuracy at the level of an individual worker is often virtually impossible. Thus, of the many studies attempting to determine whether age is related to productivity, few provide a satisfactory basis for reaching general conclusions.

Bivariate comparisons of job performance and workers' ages, the method most commonly used, do not control for other possible determinants of productivity, such as job tenure or amount of training, despite evidence that these are important factors (Avolio, Waldman, and McDaniel, 1990; Andrisani and Daymont, 1987). Second, objective measures of individual worker productivity are rare except in piece-rate settings such as craft positions and certain clerical positions. Such settings are the exception rather than the norm, diminishing confidence that what may be true for one industry also is true for another. Finally, most studies are cross-sectional, which may miss generational effects (e.g., quality of education) and "survivor" effects (i.e., biases resulting from the nonrandom departure of workers over time).

With these limitations in mind, it is not surprising that studies of the relationship between age and productivity across a wide variety of occupations reveal no clear answer to this important question. In a comprehensive review of the literature, Rhodes (1983) found studies describing positive, negative, and nonsignificant relationships between age and performance for production and blue-collar workers. Studies of clerical and office workers also were mixed, suggesting that one can find as many situations in which productivity increases with age as where it decreases. In all studies, there was considerably more variation in productivity within each age group than across age groups, indicating that chronological age alone is a poor indicator of productivity, and that managers' focus on age may be miscast.

Our case studies of two companies with special programs targeting older workers support the conclusion that age is a poor indicator of job performance. Both case studies analyzed profitability and, by inference, productivity, since in both cases, the costs of older workers exceeded those of younger workers. In a simulation model of total employment costs and revenue generated at the Days Inns reservation center, the net value of older and younger workers was virtually the same (McNaught and Barth, 1992). In the other case, B&Q's Macclesfield store, entirely staffed by older workers, was 18 percent more profitable than a comparison group of five other B&Q stores and 9 percent more profitable than the storewide average (Hogarth and Barth, 1991). The success of the Macclesfield store led B&Q to open another store entirely staffed by older workers and to set a companywide goal to increase employment levels of older workers to 12 percent of the total workforce.

Although studies of the relationship of age to worker productivity yield no definitive conclusions, there is evidence that older workers possess distinct competencies, which may make them particularly suitable for certain jobs. The foremost example of jobs that we believe capitalize on the particular strengths and minimize the relative weaknesses of older workers are those involving customer service. At the Days Inns reservation center, older workers took about 45 more seconds to handle each customer's inquiry than younger workers but achieved higher reservation rates than younger workers—booking an additional room for about each 200 calls received (McNaught and Barth, 1992). Bass and Barth (1992) and Krieger (1991) have offered other evidence of the customer service attributes of older workers in the financial services industry and quick-service restaurant industry, respectively.

Examples of improved customer service attributable to older workers are not confined to the United States. When B&Q plc decided to open a store entirely staffed by older workers, management hoped to improve the level of product knowledge within its sales staff. Among the advantages of older workers was a lifetime of experience carrying out repairs around their own houses. The store has proven to be very successful, in part because employees leveraged their product knowledge and actual experience to provide superior customer service. B&Q's marketing surveys consistently show that customers rate Macclesfield

Table 17.9

Characteristics of Those Working and Not Working

Characteristic	Age 55 to 64		Age 65 to 74	
	Working	Not Working	Working	Not Working
Percentage in Good or Excellent Health	82%	60%	84%	58%
Percentage Very Satisfied with Life	66	57	71	62
Percentage with Some College or More	40	24	36	21
Percentage with Professional or Technical Skills	52	38	51	31

Source: Louis Harris and Associates (1992).

(the test store) service levels as far superior to similarly sized stores. A supporting piece of evidence is that pilferage rates have been reduced considerably from those observed in similar stores. Management attributes this pilferage decline to lower rates of shoplifting, in part because of the high levels of attention that older workers gave to all shoppers.

The apparent divergence between studies of older worker productivity and managerial perceptions may be explained in part by inappropriate stereotyping by managers. Managers' perceptions about the abilities of older *workers* may derive largely from their impressions about the abilities of older *people* in general, but the two groups are quite different. As noted in discussing health care costs, older people who work are significantly healthier than their nonworking peers. Such differences extend across other attributes important to productivity, as shown in Table 17.9.

Rosen and Jerdee (1977) found that managers believe that older workers are less aggressive than younger workers, and conventional corporate wisdom holds that older workers are less conversant with current technology. On this point, the conventional wisdom may be correct, but the fault for the lack of their technological sophistication may not rest with older workers. Throughout most of their career, older workers looked to their companies to keep them abreast of technological developments, and they did. When they reach mid-career, however, many find their employers less willing to retrain them than younger workers. The Commonwealth Fund/Louis Harris survey found that only 17 percent of companies report spending ''a lot of money'' to retrain workers age 51 or over, whereas 29 percent spend a lot to retrain employees under age 35, and 26 percent spend a lot to retrain employees age 35 to 50 (Barth, McNaught, and Rizzi, 1993). Based on what evidence is available, we would fault the older worker him- or herself less than the company that has failed to provide training opportunities to older workers. Thus, although companies may believe that older workers lack the flexibility and adaptability needed to succeed in the rapidly changing competitive environment today, the solution to this *perceived* problem lies within the companies' grasp—provide equal access to training to older workers so that they can maintain their technical knowledge and skills, which are critical to remaining versatile and productive.

Lower Turnover

Perhaps the principal characteristic of an older workforce that benefits an employer is its increased stability (Rhodes, 1983), which reduces an employer's recruitment and training costs for new employees. As shown in Table 17.10, job tenure increases with age. Our research at both B&Q plc and Days Inns of America found turnover rates of older workers to be only a fraction of those of younger workers. At B&Q's Macclesfield store, the turnover rate among its staff of older workers was about one-sixth of the average turnover rate of comparable stores and less than one-third of the rate for the entire firm (Hogarth and Barth, 1991).

At Days Inns, a newly hired older worker had an expected job tenure of more than three years while the average tenure of other workers was less than one year (McNaught and Barth, 1992). As a result, the annualized costs for recruiting and training an older worker at Days Inns was $618, compared to $1,752 for a younger worker. Other estimates of the cost of turnover range from 1 to 2.5 times a worker's annual salary (Spencer, 1986; Knowles, 1988) suggesting that employers enjoy a considerable cost advantage as a result of an older, more stable workforce.[31]

In addition, numerous economic studies show the primary reason most workers leave their "career" employment is the economic incentives within their pension plan (Quinn, Burkhauser, and Myers, 1990; Barth and McNaught, 1989). In other words, the primary reason why most older employees usually leave a firm is within the firm's control.

In conclusion, older workers offer employers clear benefits in the form of lower turnover, the costs of which are frequently underestimated. In addition, older workers appear to be particularly suited for certain roles, such as customer service jobs where making a sale depends heavily on the quality of product information provided and the attention paid to the customer. On the critical issue of whether the higher average costs of older workers are justified by superior job performance, the issue is unresolved, although there is ample reason to believe that age itself is a poor indicator of productivity.

Table 17.10
Years with Current Employer, 1991 (Percent Distribution)

Ages	Men			Women			Total		
	1 year or less	2 to 5 years	6 or more years	1 year or less	2 to 5 years	6 or more years	1 year or less	2 to 5 years	6 or more years
25 to 34	27.9	42.4	29.7	33.0	43.0	24.0	30.2	42.6	27.2
35 to 44	16.7	27.5	55.8	22.9	34.2	42.9	19.5	30.6	49.9
45 to 54	12.9	18.8	68.3	16.3	28.0	55.7	14.5	23.0	62.5
55 to 64	10.5	17.9	71.7	12.2	23.5	64.3	11.2	20.3	68.4
65+	10.2	21.9	67.9	12.9	25.0	62.0	11.4	23.2	65.4
All Ages	24.5	30.6	44.9	29.9	34.2	35.9	27.0	32.2	40.9

Source: U.S. Department of Labor (1992d).

CONCLUSION

The studies done to date do not completely elucidate the costs of benefits of older workers, but our review of the available studies and our own research suggest that older workers frequently compare favorably with younger workers and are far more productive than they are usually thought to be. Older workers also appear to have distinct competencies in areas frequently cited as key attributes for competitive success in today's fast-paced and service-oriented markets. Further, in cases where older workers are less productive, the gap may be largely explained by their reduced access to the training necessary to remain productive.

At the same time, older workers generally are more expensive than younger workers. In some instances, particularly where pension and health care coverage differentials are great, the costs of older workers may outweigh their productivity and mitigate against their employment, especially in companies focused on cutting costs immediately. On a more encouraging note, trends such as national reform of the health insurance system and shifts by corporations toward defined contribution pension plans will tend to reduce these cost differentials over time. Our overall optimistic conclusion about the employability of older workers seems to stand in contrast to that of many managers, who, we believe, tend to overestimate the costs of older workers and underestimate their benefits.

The future will differ from the past. Demographic projections suggest that the relative need for older workers may increase and, depending on the rate of economic growth, this demand could be significant. Taking advantage of the skills of older workers may become increasingly important in a future labor market where skilled young workers are rare, and experienced, dedicated older workers are plentiful. In anticipation of this possibility, companies would do well to reconsider their current perceptions about older workers and investigate further changes in the structure of work and compensation to make the workplace more age neutral.

NOTES

1. The definition of the term *older* varies within the literature. In this chapter, we generally mean persons age 55+ or some subset of this population. Using chronological age is simple and, in most instances, raises no problems. However, the concept of *functional ability*, meaning whether a person can function in a given situation, is often more meaningful than chronological age.

2. The Bureau of Labor Statistics (BLS) reports only about 1 million persons over age 55 as unemployed based on census data (U.S. Department of Labor, 1993). However, there is substantial reason to doubt this accounting. Previous studies of ours suggest that the number of discouraged workers (i.e., those who would like to work and are able to but have given up attempting to find work) is quite large—perhaps several times the BLS/census estimate (Barth, McNaught, and Rizzi, 1993).

3. See Marks (1993) and Mutschler (Chapter 10 of this volume).

4. See also Sandell and Rosenblum (Chapter 11 of this volume).

5. Lemming-like behavior in human resource policies is quite common. Salaries, fringe benefit packages, and retirement policies are examples of human resource policies heavily influenced by what "competitors" or other comparable firms are doing in these areas. See Woodbury (1991).

6. Kaufman (1986) and Porter (1992) both have provided compelling arguments of the role of American capital markets in creating pressure on managers to focus on short-term financial performance. Reich (1989, 1993) contended that the adverse effects of this short-term focus are ultimately borne by the American labor force.

7. Less recent but comparable surveys include over 300 medium- to large-sized companies by The Conference Board (Rhine, 1985) and 544 Texas businesses (Jackson, 1986).

8. The Yankelovich survey was commissioned by the American Association of Retired Persons (AARP) and followed up a similar AARP survey conducted in 1985 that found that American business viewed older workers favorably with respect to their work ethic, experience, and knowledge and unfavorably with respect to flexibility, adaptability to technology, and aggressive spirit. Respondents to the 1985 survey overall reported that older workers were not more costly than younger workers (American Association of Retired Persons, 1985). Both AARP surveys defined older workers as employees age 50 and over.

9. Other studies by Avolio and Waldman (1984, 1989) further support the finding that managers rarely assess job performance without taking into account the age of the job holder. For example, a supervisor may rate a younger worker's technical knowledge as superior to an older worker's even if the two are equal by objective measures because the supervisor expects that the technical knowledge of the older worker to be less current than that of the younger worker. Such subtle biases, favorable or unfavorable, are likely to persist in decisions about training, promotion, and job assignment. The Avolio-Waldman conclusions regarding biases in assessing the abilities of older workers are supported by other meta analyses (McEvoy and Cascio, 1989).

10. See also Sonnenfeld (1978); Doering, Rhodes, and Schuster (1983); and previous work by Rosen and Jerdee (1976).

11. A complete discussion of the costs of older workers cannot be limited simply to "out-of-pocket" or even just actuarial costs. Opportunity costs—the costs incurred should the older workers prove less productive than other workers—should also be considered.

12. For a review of the literature on "implicit contracts," see Straka (1992) and Rosen (1985).

13. This system is even breaking down in Japan, often held up as a model of human resource practices for developing a stable and loyal workforce (Ogawa and Clark, 1993).

14. In many cases, the costs of fringe benefits appear to be passed on by employers to workers in the form of smaller pay increases (Gruber, 1994; Gruber and Krueger, 1991). Such backshifting of costs to employees might explain in part the decline in earnings for older workers.

15. Experience-based rating means that the costs of coverage are based on the claims history of the company's workforce.

16. In certain situations, health care costs for older workers may be comparable to, or even less than, those of other workers (McNaught and Barth, 1992).

17. Part of the risk is shared with the Pension Benefit Guaranty Corporation (PBGC)

through its insurance system. The risk also is shared indirectly by the worker because, in the event of bankruptcy, benefits from the PBGC may be lower than those promised under the defaulted corporate pension plan.

18. Their analysis did not address differences in defined benefit pension plans such as early retirement options and integration with social security even if these features typically further accentuate any age-related differences in accrual costs.

19. The analysis is complicated somewhat by the higher turnover rate of younger workers. Employees who leave before becoming fully vested lose part or all of their pension accrual upon departure under either a defined contribution or defined benefit plan. The money put aside for younger workers who leave before becoming fully vested is returned to the plan and can be used to defray administrative costs or allocated to other plan participants. The higher turnover of younger workers thus increases the average pension cost difference between younger and older workers.

20. Companies with overfunded pension plans were inviting targets in the merger and acquisition frenzy of the 1980s as these overfunded plans could be terminated, thereby freeing up large amounts of cash (see Pontiff, Shleifer, and Weisbach, 1990; Shleifer and Summers, 1988). Conversely, underfunded pension plans are likely to provoke intense scrutiny and criticism from employee groups, public officials, and regulators.

21. If the worker is replaced, the cost of hiring a substitute or reassigning another worker is incurred. In some cases, the worker's absence may be absorbed by the "slack" that typically exists in organizations, thereby resulting in nearly no additional measurable cost.

22. Using salary to measure the opportunity cost of a worker's time is to choose precision over accuracy. A better measure of opportunity cost is the value of the marginal product of the worker, which may differ from salary over the course of a career (Becker, 1964; Lazear, 1979). Employers assessing the opportunity cost of personnel time, therefore, should focus on productivity, not on compensation.

23. The Age Discrimination in Employment Act, as amended by the Older Workers Benefit Protection Act, allows companies to offer less benefits to older workers under the "equal benefit or equal cost standard." Under this standard, an older worker may receive less benefits than other workers provided that the actual payment for the benefits is equal. In fact, few companies avail themselves of this option, with the exception of pension and disability benefits for workers over age 65.

24. An alternative explanation is that managers provide less training to older workers because the cost of training older workers is higher than for younger workers as a result of the generally higher salaries of older workers (Sandell, 1987).

25. It is legal in Britain for help wanted advertisements to specify the desired age of job applicants.

26. This issue is more problematic for training in general skills (e.g., public speaking) which are assumed to be relevant throughout an employee's career. For such training, the longer expected work career of a younger employee may make that employee a preferential candidate for training but this consideration needs to be weighed against the shorter job tenure (i.e., higher turnover) of younger workers compared to older workers. In the next section, we offer evidence that older workers stay on the job longer than younger workers.

27. The company's most famous forum for technical and professional education is Motorola University, its collection of 11 in-house training centers, whose faculty is mostly made up of Motorola *retirees*.

28. The company's pension system regulations restricted retirees to part-time work.

29. In 1990, Travelers expanded the job bank to include other companies' retirees and younger workers as well.

30. See Sterns, Sterns, and Hollis (Chapter 15 of this volume) for a detailed review of the literature on productivity and the functional limitations of older workers.

31. These costs include the expense of recruiting and hiring the new employee, training and orientation, and "learning curve" inefficiencies (that is, lost productivity while the employee gains experience and efficiency). For certain professions, such as salespeople of complex machinery, learning curve costs alone are estimated as much as six times annual salary (Spencer, 1986).

18

The Economics of Occupational Labor Shortages

Burt S. Barnow

Major changes in the economy in recent years have generated more than the usual interest in how well the U.S. labor market is functioning. Three general issues have been widely discussed by economists and policy makers. First, because of recent declines in the U.S. birthrate, some analysts are concerned that there will simply be too few workers to maintain growth in the American economy (Levitan and Gallo, 1989). Second, there has been a growing concern that there is or will be a serious mismatch between the skills of the American labor force and the needs of employers, resulting in a serious "skill gap" characterized by unfilled vacancies in many high-skill occupations along with high unemployment for less-skilled workers.[1] Finally, there has long been concern that shortages sometimes develop and persist in specific occupations, leading to market inefficiencies in the U.S. economy. It is this third topic, occupation-specific shortages and the opportunities and challenges they present for the employment of older workers, that is the subject of this chapter.

I begin with a brief overview of the concept of labor shortages, focusing on the alternative definitions that have been used to identify occupational-specific labor shortages. This is followed by a discussion of the causes and consequences

This chapter is based on research supported by the Employment and Training Administration, U.S. Department of Labor. The larger study, prepared by John W. Trutko, Burt S. Barnow, Amy B. Chasanov, and Abhay Pande, includes four case studies of labor shortages. All views and opinions expressed in the chapter are those of the author and do not necessarily reflect the views of the U.S. Department of Labor.

of occupational labor shortages. The chapter concludes with a discussion of the implications of occupational shortages for older workers.

BACKGROUND ON LABOR SHORTAGES

The term *labor shortage* has no universally agreed upon definition. It sometimes refers to a shortfall in the total number of individuals in the labor force, and sometimes denotes the possible mismatch between workers and jobs in the economy. Even when the term is used to refer to a particular occupation, a number of definitions have been proposed and used. In this chapter, the definition of a labor shortage provided by the Department of Labor is used: "a market disequilibrium between supply and demand in which the quantity of workers demanded exceeds the supply available and willing to work at a particular wage and working conditions at a particular place and point in time."[2]

This definition considers a shortage as a *disequilibrium* condition where the amount of labor workers are willing to supply is less than employers are willing to buy at the prevailing wage. A market is said to be in equilibrium when the amount of labor that workers (i.e., sellers) are willing to provide at the market price is equal to the amount that firms (i.e., purchasers) wish to buy at the market price. When the quantities that workers wish to provide and firms wish to buy are not identical at the prevailing price, the market is said to be in a disequilibrium situation.

If the quantity of labor offered exceeds the quantity that firms wish to purchase, there is a surplus, and if the quantity of labor desired by firms exceeds the amount workers offer at the prevailing price, there is a shortage. In general, the quantity that workers are willing to provide is an increasing function of the wages (i.e., price) they can obtain, and the relationship between the amount that workers are willing to provide at various prices, with other factors held constant, is referred to as the supply curve.[3] Figure 18.1 shows a typical upward-sloping supply curve for labor. As the wage rate is increased, more workers are willing to enter a particular occupation and current workers are generally willing to provide more labor.

In Figure 18.1, the amount of labor that employers will wish to hire at alternative prices is indicated by the downward-sloping demand curve. Demand curves slope down because as the price of a factor increases, the employer will generally substitute other factors of production for the factor whose price has increased. In addition, higher factor prices will generally lead to higher product prices, which in turn will lead to a reduction in the quantity of the product demanded and the factors of production.

The point labeled E in Figure 18.1 is the market equilibrium point. If the wage is equal to W_E then the quantity of labor that workers are willing to supply at that wage (Q_E) is exactly equal to the quantity of labor that employers will wish to hire. The market is said to be in equilibrium because the quantity supplied is equal to the quantity demanded.

Figure 18.1
Illustration of a Labor Shortage

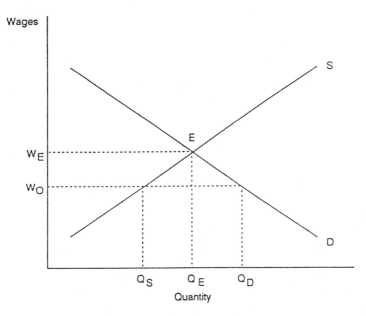

If for some reason the prevailing wage rate in the market is W_0 rather than W_E, then the quantity of labor workers are willing to supply is equal to Q_S—the point on the supply curve corresponding to W_0. Employers, however, would like to hire Q_D at that wage rate. The difference between the amount of labor that employers wish to hire and the amount that workers are willing to provide $(Q_D - Q_S)$ is the amount of the shortage. In the next section we discuss how such shortages might arise.

Economists and other analysts have proposed several alternative definitions of occupational shortages.[4] Although these definitions are not used in this chapter, it is important to note that others use the term differently. It is particularly important to keep the definition in mind when interpreting other studies of shortages.

The Social Demand Model

Some analysts consider a shortage to be present if the number of workers in an occupation is less than what is considered the socially desired number. Under this definition, a shortage of engineers exists if the analyst making the determination concludes that society would be better off if there were more engineers. This type of definition does not imply that the labor market is in disequilibrium; instead it describes a situation where the person who claims there is a shortage does not like the market's results. Arrow and Capron explain the problem with the following definition:

In particular, careful reading of such statements indicates that the speakers have in effect been saying: There are not as many engineers and scientists as this nation should have in order to do all the things that need doing such as maintaining our rapid rate of technological progress, raising our standard of living, keeping us militarily strong, etc. In other words, they are saying that (in the economic sense) demand for technically skilled manpower *ought* to be greater than it is—it is really a shortage of *demand* for scientists and engineers that concerns them. (1959, 307)

The Secretary of Health and Human Services' Commission on Nursing states in its final report that: "In the most general terms, a registered nurse [RN] shortage exists when the supply of RNs is insufficient to meet the 'requirements' for RNs. RN requirements can be defined based on either economic demand or clinical need," (U.S. Department of Health and Human Services, 1988, 3). The commission rejected the use of clinical need for defining a shortage because they concluded that there is no objective method of quantifying the degree of the shortage and relating it to specific factors.

The fact that we do not use this type of definition for a shortage does not mean we believe that it is unimportant for the nation to consider whether it is satisfied with market-produced results. Quite the contrary, it is important for society to consider whether or not the market solutions are desirable, and, if not, to take appropriate actions.[5] The concern in this chapter is with the operation of labor markets, the reasons why they sometimes fail to achieve equilibrium, and actions that can be taken to improve their efficiency.

The Blank-Stigler Model

One of the first major studies of occupational shortages was conducted by David S. Blank and George J. Stigler, who defined a shortage as follows: "A shortage exists when the number of workers available (the supply) increases less rapidly than the number demanded at the salaries paid in the recent past" (1957, 24). Blank and Stigler then argue that to alleviate the shortage, wages in the occupation must rise and some of the work formerly performed by the occupation with the shortage will now be performed by others.

The Blank-Stigler shortage concept is illustrated in Figure 18.2. Initially the market is in equilibrium at E with wage rate W_E and Q_E workers. If demand increases, the demand curve will shift to the right to the line D_1. A shortage will result if the wage remains at W_E because employers will wish to hire Q_1 workers—but only Q_E workers will be available at that wage. Market pressures will then lead to an increase in the wage, and equilibrium will eventually be restored with a new wage of W_2 and Q_2 workers.

There are several problems with the Blank-Stigler model. First, an increase

Figure 18.2
Illustration of Blank-Stigler and Arrow-Capron Shortages

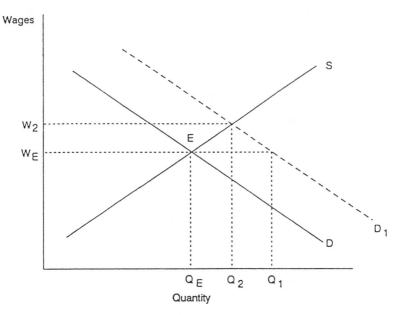

in demand is only one of the possible causes of a shortage. Thus, the Blank-Stigler model ignores other possible causes of occupational shortages. Second, Blank and Stigler indicate that a shortage can be identified by rising wages in the affected occupation. Wages may not rise, however, because of market imperfections such as controls on wages or imperfect information.

The Arrow-Capron Dynamic Shortage Model

Kenneth J. Arrow and William W. Capron (1959) developed an alternative model of occupational shortages. Their definition, which they refer to as a *dynamic shortage*, is based on the premise that "a steady upward shift in the demand curve over a period of time will produce a shortage, that is, a situation in which there are unfilled vacancies in positions where salaries are the same as those currently being paid in others of the same type and quality" (1959, 301).

The Arrow-Capron model is also illustrated in Figure 18.2. Like the Blank-Stigler model, the Arrow-Capron model is characterized by increased demand. However, Arrow and Capron note that markets are characterized by a "reaction speed," and that institutional arrangements (such as long-term contracts) and the time it takes for information to spread will affect the time required for employers to adjust wages. Thus, Arrow and Capron conclude that shortages will be characterized by vacancies. In Figure 18.2, the number of vacancies initially resulting from the increase in demand will be equal to $Q_1 - Q_E$. If demand continues to grow, then the market may not achieve equilibrium. The Arrow-Capron dynamic shortage model is consistent with the general model used here, but it may be considered a specific case.

Other Definitions of Shortages

In addition to the definitions presented above, several other definitions for shortages have been proposed. Paul E. Harrington and Andrew M. Sum (1984) reviewed several other possible definitions of occupational labor shortages, and two of them are briefly discussed below.

The "rate of return model" is based on the application of internal rate of return analysis to alternative occupations. The costs of investing in a particular occupation are defined as the sum of the direct costs for higher education, training, and supplies, plus the indirect costs of foregone wages that are incurred during periods of training. The benefits are the earnings typically derived from the occupation each year. The internal rate of return is then calculated by finding the interest rate that equates the present value of the costs and benefits.[6] Occupations with shortages are thus defined as those occupations with higher than average rates of return.

Harrington and Sum note that the rate of return approach is "beset with numerous methodological and measurement difficulties" (1984, 9). One important problem is that we cannot observe the future earnings streams from various occupations. Relying on cross-sectional or historical data may provide a misleading picture of what the earnings will eventually be. In addition, the returns to various occupations may differ for reasons having little to do with a shortage. For example, some occupations may pay higher wages because they have high health or safety risks—what economists refer to as compensating differentials.

Finally, we consider the monopsonistic labor market model. A market where there is only one buyer for a particular good or type of labor is referred to as a monopsony. The monopsonist differs from an employer in a competitive labor market because the monopsonist can set the wage rather than act as a price taker. The situation for a monopsonist is illustrated in Figure 18.3.[7] Because the monopsonist is the only buyer for the occupation of interest, the monopsonist observes the labor supply curve for the occupation; this is in contrast to an employer in a competitive market who can hire all the labor desired at the market wage. Because the monopsonistic employer must pay all workers the same wage, the monopsonist faces a steep upward sloping marginal labor cost curve—if an additional worker is hired, wages must be increased for all currently employed workers as well as the marginal worker. Figure 18.3 also illustrates the marginal revenue product curve for the firm. To maximize profits, the monopsonist employer will hire labor until the marginal labor cost is equal to the marginal labor product, corresponding to the point X in the figure. The wage paid by the mon-

Figure 18.3
Illustration of Labor Demand by a Monopsonist

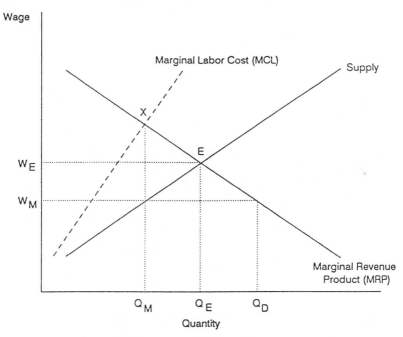

opsonist will then be W_M, and Q_M workers will be hired. Note that the number of workers hired is less than in a competitive market (Q_E) and the wage is lower than the competitive wage (W_E).

The monopsonist might consider the resulting situation to be a shortage because the monopsonist would like to hire more workers at the monopsony wage. However, because the monopsonist faces an upward sloping labor supply curve, the wage must be increased to attract additional labor into the occupation. Ronald G. Ehrenberg and Robert S. Smith (1993) conclude that the labor shortage faced by a monopsonist is more apparent than real. In addition, Ehrenberg and Smith point out that monopsony situations are likely to be very rare.

Summary of Shortage Concepts

Some of the labor shortage concepts that have been proposed, such as looking at the total amount of labor supplied and the potential economy-wide mismatch between employer needs and worker qualifications, are important, but they are not relevant to the study of occupational shortages. Like the Secretary of Health and Human Services' Commission on Nursing, the social demand concept is not used because there is no objective way of determining the optimal number of workers in various professions.

Definitions proposed in the 1950s by Blank and Stigler (1957) and by Arrow and Capron (1959) are closer to the concept of a labor shortage that is used here. The principal advantage of these definitions is that they provide relatively straightforward tests for the existence of a shortage—rising relative wages in the case of the Blank-Stigler definition and increasing vacancies in the case of the Arrow-Capron definition. However, these definitions are too narrow to capture all the types of shortages of interest. Both the Blank-Stigler and Arrow-Capron definitions do not include in their definitions labor market situations classified as shortages by the other definition, and both omit situations where excess demand results from market imperfections. The more general definition employed here covers such cases.

The use of a broad definition does have some disadvantages. As Walter Franke and Irving Sobel noted in using a similar definition, "The definition is neither altogether concrete and precise nor is it susceptible to precise measurements" (Franke and Sobel, 1970, 7). However, we also concur with Franke and Sobel's conclusion that: "Viewed in the context of a study whose purpose is to examine the degree to which labor market institutions respond to and facilitate adjustment to varying degrees of labor market tightness, the definition is, however, meaningful and operational" (1970, 7–8).

CAUSES AND CONSEQUENCES OF LABOR SHORTAGES

There are several reasons why it is important to address the causes and consequences of labor shortages. First, because we have adopted a fairly broad definition of a shortage, we will have no single indicator that a shortage exists. By reviewing the economic theory of the causes and consequences of shortages, we will be aware of the appropriate market signals to look for in assessing whether or not a shortage exists. This is especially important because under certain conditions various interest groups have incentives to argue that a shortage is present or absent. For example, employers and trade associations sometimes have an incentive to claim that there is a shortage to increase immigration quotas for particular occupations, giving them access to a broader pool of applicants. At other times, employers might find it in their interest to claim there are no shortages in order to gain better leverage in contract negotiations with their workforce.

Another important reason for analyzing the causes and consequences of shortages is to help identify and assess potential public and private policies for dealing with shortages. Being able to identify causes will help interested parties focus on the relevant developments in labor and product markets. Understanding the consequences will help us to assess what interventions, if any, are appropriate by government, employers, and workers.

Before turning to the causes and consequences of labor shortages, it is useful to note some of the dimensions of shortages:

- *Geographic scope of the shortage*: Depending on the occupation and the nature of the market, labor markets can be national or regional in scope. Similarly, a particular occupation may have a nationwide shortage, or the shortage may be confined to a few labor markets or a single region of the country.

- *Longevity of the shortage*: Various forces act to bring markets into and out of equilibrium. Thus, shortages can be relatively brief, lasting for a few weeks or months, or prolonged, lasting for one or more years.

- *Severity of the shortage*: Unlike the two dimensions discussed above, it is not easy to develop good measures of the severity of a shortage. Conceptually, we can measure the severity of a shortage in terms of the magnitude of the changes in wages required to restore equilibrium or in terms of the number of workers added to the occupation to alleviate the shortage. There are several difficulties with these concepts. First, we do not generally observe the supply and demand curves for specific occupations. Thus, we cannot directly estimate the size of the labor or wage gap of a shortage. Second, even if we could measure supply and demand, it would not be easy to classify a particular gap as large or small, especially when comparing across occupations—occupations vary significantly in their normal vacancy rates and wage dispersion. Thus, a high vacancy rate for one occupation with a shortage may be characteristic of another occupation in equilibrium.

- *Subspecialty shortages*: Up to this point we have considered occupations as if they are uniform. For some occupations this may be correct, but for others there may be differentiation by subspecialty (e.g., emergency room nurses), years of work experience, or specialized training. In such cases, a shortage may exist for the entire occupation or only for workers with selected characteristics. For example, training for engineers has changed considerably over the past 20 years, and older electrical engineers may not be good substitutes for new engineers who have more training in designing integrated circuits. Likewise, new tool and die makers may not be good substitutes for experienced tool and die makers who have gained additional skills through their work. The key determinant of whether there can be shortages for some parts of an occupation is whether all workers within the occupation are reasonable substitutes for each other. If not, a shortage can exist within an occupation while other subcategories are in equilibrium or even in surplus.

For an occupation to have a shortage, two conditions are necessary. First, the occupation must be in disequilibrium, where the number of workers employers wish to hire exceeds the number willing to work at the prevailing wage. Second, the market must adjust slowly, if at all, with the achievement of equilibrium requiring a substantial period of time. This chapter first discusses the reasons why markets are sometimes in disequilibrium. It then examines the adjustments that employers make to alleviate the disequilibrium, followed by a discussion of the reasons why disequilibria may persist. We then discuss the consequences of prolonged shortages. The chapter concludes with a discussion of the implications of the theory for the case studies.

Reasons Why Occupational Labor Markets Are in Disequilibrium

Labor shortages can result from a number of different causes. In this section we discuss the reasons why the labor market for a particular occupation might leave an equilibrium situation where the market wage equates supply and demand.

Increase in the Demand for Labor. Figure 18.4 illustrates how a labor shortage can result from an increase in the demand for labor; several variants of this scenario were discussed previously. Suppose that the labor market is initially in equilibrium at point E. If the demand for labor increases, the demand curve will shift to the right. If the supply curve remains the same and the prevailing price (wage) remains at W_E, employers would like to hire Q_D workers, but only Q_E will be available. Thus, there will be a shortage of $Q_D - Q_E$ workers.

The demand for labor by employers can increase for several reasons. Perhaps the most likely reason for an increase in the demand for labor is an increase in the demand for the goods or services produced by employers. An increase in the demand for the product can result from an increase in the number of consumers, an increase in the income or wealth of consumers, a change in the composition of the population of buyers, or changes in the tastes of consumers.

Another reason for an increase in the demand for labor is an increase in the prices of substitute factors of production. For example, in a hospital the demand for nurses might increase if the wage rates of doctors and/or nurses' aides increases. The demand for a given type of labor will also increase if the price of a nonlabor factor (e.g., raw materials or machinery) increases and the labor can be used as a substitute in the production process.

Both the Arrow-Capron (1959) and Blank-Stigler (1957) labor shortage models discussed in the previous section are demand-driven shortage models. The Arrow-Capron dynamic model is somewhat more complex because it deals with a situation where demand continually grows more rapidly than supply.

An increase in demand for labor in a particular occupation does not necessarily lead to a shortage. If the supply of labor to an occupation can respond to the increased demand, the result will be a new equilibrium with more workers employed and a higher wage rate than at the previous equilibrium, as is illustrated in Figure 18.4. An increase in demand will almost certainly require some time for the market to reach a new equilibrium, but if vacancies persist for a sustained period, the occupation can be characterized as experiencing a shortage. Reasons why occupational labor markets may adjust slowly are discussed below.

Decrease in the Supply of Labor. A decrease in the supply of labor to a particular market can also create a labor shortage. This situation is illustrated in Figure 18.5. Once again suppose that the market is originally in equilibrium at point E. If the labor supply curve is shifted to the left, indicating fewer workers available at each wage rate, there will be a labor shortage if the prevailing wage remains at W_E. Employers will still be trying to hire Q_E workers, but only Q_S

Figure 18.4
Illustration of Labor Shortage Arising from Increases in Labor Demand

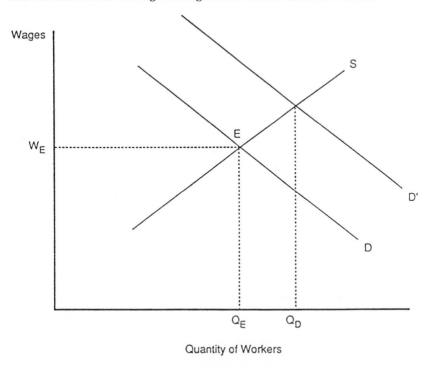

workers will be available after the supply decreases. Thus, there will be a shortage of $Q_E - Q_S$ workers.

The labor supply curve for the labor market in question might shift for several reasons. One potential cause is a decrease in the size of the population that works in the relevant jobs. For example, as the baby boom generation has aged, employers who generally hire youth as they complete high school have suddenly faced a much smaller supply of entry-level workers from the so-called baby bust generation (the population cohort following the baby boom generation), whose population is much smaller.

The supply curve might also shift to the left because wages in other occupations have risen, making employment in the market of interest less attractive, or because non-work opportunities, such as welfare, crime, and retirement, have become more attractive. Finally, the labor supply curve for an occupation might shift to the left because of restrictions on entry into the relevant labor market. Such restrictions may be implemented by the government (through licensing requirements and restricting the number of licenses granted), by professional organizations that set standards for practice, by labor unions, or by training institutions (e.g., universities, community colleges).

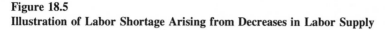

Figure 18.5
Illustration of Labor Shortage Arising from Decreases in Labor Supply

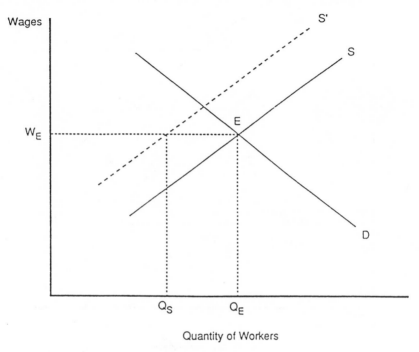

Quantity of Workers

Restrictions on Prices. Although most prices are determined competitively by
the market in the United States, in some industries the price of labor or the price
of the final product is regulated. For example, cities generally regulate the price
that taxi drivers can charge. In such instances, the supply curve is truncated at
the regulated price. This situation is illustrated in Figure 18.6. The wage rate is
restricted to be no higher than W_M, so the supply curve at higher wages is
indicated by a dashed line. The labor that will be supplied at that wage is Q_S.
At that wage, however, the demand is for Q_D workers, so there is a shortage of
$Q_D - Q_S$ workers. An example of this type of shortage is the federal government's market for entry-level Ph.D. economists. The federal government traditionally hires entry-level economists at the GS-12 level, and agencies are
generally not permitted to pay a higher wage rate. The current market wage for
entry-level economists is higher, so in many government agencies there is a
shortage of entry-level Ph.D. economists.

More commonly, the government regulates the prices of products and services
rather than labor. In industries where labor comprises a relatively small share
of the product's price, such as in the generation of electric power, the product
price regulation is not likely to cause a labor shortage. In very labor-intensive
industries, however, output price regulation can be tantamount to regulating the

Figure 18.6
Illustration of Labor Shortage Arising from Restrictions on Wages

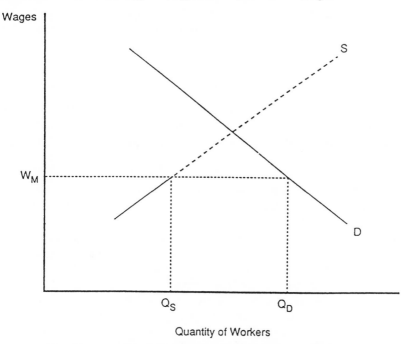

Quantity of Workers

price of labor. Examples include the health care industry in general and the home care industry in particular. A large share of the health industry is financed by the medicare and medicaid programs. In the case of medicare, the federal government limits the reimbursements that providers can obtain for treating covered elderly patients. State governments provide similar regulation under medicaid programs for the poor. By restricting the charges that providers can make, the providers face limits on what they can pay workers and still cover their costs.

Adjustments to Occupational Shortages by Employers

This section describes some of the actions that firms are likely to take to deal with labor imbalances. Because employers will note the problems first, as they are unable to fill vacancies at current wage rates, employers will take actions to deal with the unfilled positions. Some actions are more costly than others, so employers should undertake the least expensive and most easily reversed actions first. The potential actions that employers can take are listed roughly in order of desirability from the employer's point of view. In particular cases, of course, some of the potential actions may be inapplicable or employers may undertake the actions in a different order. Note that all the potential actions employers can take are the opposite of the actions that lead to vacancies: increasing supply, decreasing demand, and increasing wages. Finally, many of the actions described below may be undertaken by employers for reasons other than trying to fill vacant positions.

Increase Recruiting Efforts

A logical first step to fill vacancies is to increase recruiting efforts. Although employers will incur short-term costs in expanding recruiting, there are no long-term or permanent costs involved. Recruiting can be increased through several approaches:

- *Increased advertising in the usual outlets*: for example, employers who advertise in newspapers can increase the frequency of the advertisements or the size of the advertisements to attract more attention to vacancies.

- *Advertise in other media*: to reach a wider audience of potential employees, firms can expand their advertising campaigns. Firms that traditionally recruited through newspaper advertisements can add other newspapers in the community, radio, and television. The use of job fairs is another such technique.

- *Expand the recruiting area*: employers who believe that the problem is local rather than regional or national can increase the geographical scope of their recruiting efforts. For example, a firm having difficulty recruiting machinists in Chicago might expand its recruiting efforts to nearby Milwaukee. Some occupations, generally those with highly skilled jobs, already have national labor markets. For these firms, and for firms recruiting for occupations with a national shortage, the only way to increase the recruiting market is to recruit abroad.

- *Use public and private employment agencies*: firms that do not already do so can make use of public and private employment agencies. Public agencies, referred to as the employment service or job service, are free to both workers and employers. In some states the employment service may tend to specialize in serving particular types of workers, but all employers can list their openings with the employment service. Private employment agencies charge a fee to either the worker or the firm, with the fee based either on the time spent by the agency or as a percentage of the hired worker's salary.

- *Pay recruiting bonuses to employees who bring in new workers*: for many employers, current workers are often the best source of potential new hires. Employees are likely to be hesitant to recommend individuals who are unqualified, and the candidates they recommend are likely to know more about the work and working conditions than other job candidates. Thus, for many firms current employees are a major source of job applicants. To encourage workers to assist in the recruiting process, employers sometimes offer a bonus for referring qualified applicants or applicants who are hired.

Increase Use of Overtime. A relatively simple solution to the problem of filling vacancies is to have current employees work more hours. Employers who anticipate that the problem will not last for a substantial period of time are likely to use this approach. If the workers are exempt from the overtime provisions of the Fair Labor Standards Act (FLSA) and do not receive a premium for hours in excess of 40 hours per week, overtime may actually save money relative to hiring additional workers. This is because many fringe benefits, such as health insurance, unemployment insurance, and workers compensation, are fixed and the firm will not experience any increase in costs for these benefits when current employees work additional hours.

As a long-term measure, however, increased use of overtime may not be a viable option. For workers not exempt from the FLSA, the employer must pay a premium of at least 50 percent for overtime work, which gives employers a strong financial incentive to try other means to deal with vacancy problems. In addition, many workers prefer not to work overtime, so increased use of overtime may lead to employee dissatisfaction and increased turnover, thereby exacerbating the vacancy problem instead of reducing it.

Reduce Minimum Qualifications for the Job. Another method of filling vacancies is to reduce the minimum hiring standards for the occupation. At first this may appear damaging, but this is not necessarily the case. The firm may have set the minimum hiring qualifications higher than necessary when labor was abundant. For example, a firm may have required a college degree for sales workers when a high school diploma would have been adequate. For professional jobs, the firm may have selected graduates from the most prestigious schools, or have had a minimum grade point average or test score cutoff.

If the productivity of less-qualified workers is lower, the firm may be able to train the workers to reach the productivity levels of the more qualified workers after a reasonable period of time. When a firm reduces the minimum hiring qualifications, the labor supply is effectively increased, and the firm may be able to reduce the wages offered or at least avoid increasing wages.

Restructure Work to Use Current or New Employees in Other Occupations. If employers have difficulty filling vacancies with workers in one occupation, it is sometimes possible to restructure the work to make use of workers in other occupations. For example, in a hospital services are performed by workers in a number of occupations (e.g., physicians, nurses, nurse's aides, and orderlies). Although some duties cannot be readily reassigned (only physicians can make diagnoses), nurses can perform some of the testing, and care-taking functions can be assumed by virtually any of the staff. Likewise, some engineering tasks can be performed by drafters, and some tasks performed by teachers can be performed by aides.

For several reasons, firms will not always make use of this option. For example, hospitals are unlikely to use physicians to perform care-taking tasks because physicians are so costly that other measures will generally be less expensive. In addition, assigning what is perceived to be low-level work to employees may hurt morale and productivity. Finally, reassigning tasks may involve considerable expense and disruption because of training and rescheduling that must be conducted.

In some cases, complex jobs can be decomposed into simpler tasks that can be handled by less-skilled workers. For example, a tool- and diemaker's work could be split among metalworkers who possess some, but not all, of the skills of a tool- and diemaker. In general, shortages are more likely to occur for high-skill than low-skill occupations.[8]

Substitute Machinery and Equipment for Labor. Employers can sometimes alter the production process to replace workers with equipment. As technology has advanced in recent years, the types of tasks performed by machines have also changed. Formerly, machines typically replaced humans in unskilled tasks such as lifting and moving. More recently, computer-based technology permits machines to perform more sophisticated tasks including voice recognition, drawing, designing, and (to some extent) teaching. Artificial intelligence "expert system" models even permit computers to substitute for professional judgment under certain circumstances.

There are obviously limits to how much technology can substitute for labor, and in many situations technology will be used to substitute for labor for reasons other than difficulty in filling job openings. However, substituting technology for labor is sometimes a viable method of dealing with difficulty in filling vacancies.

Train Workers for the Jobs. For some occupations, training is traditionally performed by employers, either formally through apprenticeship or other training programs, or informally through on-the-job training. For many other occupations, however, training for entry-level jobs is performed by other means— typically, colleges and universities for professional occupations and vocational schools and trade schools for skilled craft and service occupations. Employers who traditionally do not train their own workers may resort to offering or sponsoring training if they are experiencing difficulty filling vacancies.

Offering training for an occupation is often a major commitment for employers, and it is typically not provided unless most other approaches fail. There are several related reasons why firms are reluctant to offer occupational training. First, the training is generally time-consuming. Training new employees for a skilled occupation can sometimes take years, and by the time the workers are trained, the problem of filling vacancies may have disappeared. Second, establishing and operating a training program to bring new employees into an occupation is costly. Employers must feel confident that they can recoup their investment before they are willing to underwrite these costs. Finally, training new hires for occupations with vacancies carries several risks for employers. The individuals selected may not be able to successfully complete the training, or if the skills are transferable to other employers, they may quit shortly after they are trained.[9]

For occupations that do not require a college degree, establishing an apprenticeship program is one potential method of training workers for occupations through a combination of classroom and on-the-job training. The Department of Labor recently moved to expand apprenticeship opportunities through its Apprenticeship 2000 program. Other possibilities include training current or new workers in-house or in cooperation with local colleges, vocational schools, and proprietary schools. In some cases the employer may not pay for the training—the courses can be partially or fully funded under federal programs—primarily the Job Training Partnership Act (JTPA)—state training programs, or educational institutions.

Training for entry into an occupation can be illustrated by an extreme but interesting case. The uniformed services need physicians, but they are prohibited from paying market wages to physicians (a shortage induced by market restrictions). To get around this problem, the uniformed services established their own medical school to train physicians at no cost to the students. To prevent the students from leaving soon after being trained, the students are required to sign contracts agreeing to stay in the military for a specified number of years.

Improve Working Conditions. Improving working conditions sometimes is an effective way to attract new workers or reduce turnover. Working conditions include factors such as hours worked, upgrades in equipment and facilities used by workers, level and type of supervision, involvement in operation of the firm, training to deal with stress related to the job, and recognition of the importance of workers in the occupation. Improvements in working conditions can be especially useful in situations where vacancies are created by high turnover. High turnover is often associated with occupations with high stress, low wages, or low prestige. A concomitant benefit of improving working conditions is that productivity may increase as well.

Improving the number or timing of work hours can also help in recruiting or reducing vacancies. Some occupations may require split shifts (e.g., driving buses), night and weekend work (e.g., health occupations), or downtime between productive periods (e.g., home care). Employers sometimes deal with these unpleasant working conditions by offering premiums for work at undesirable times, but they often believe they cannot afford a sufficiently high shift differential to eliminate the problem. Although shift differentials are still often necessary for undesirable shifts, employers can sometimes improve recruiting and reduce turnover by working with employees to structure shifts to be as desirable as feasible. For example, hospitals have experimented with a number of shift structures to fill the most undesirable shifts. In the home care industry, where workers sometimes have a great deal of travel time and downtime between cases, some employers have been successful in restructuring caseloads to minimize these problems.

Offer Bonuses to New Employees. Although this approach is not commonly used, firms sometimes offer new employees bonuses for joining the firm. Signing bonuses are similar to paying current employees bonuses (or "bounties") for recruiting new employees for occupations that are difficult to fill, except that bonuses go to the new employees rather than the current employees.

For workers, this option provides an extra incentive to join the firm offering the bonuses. This approach is more advantageous for employers than raising wages because it is a one-time cost and only affects the employees added in the occupation of interest. The disadvantage for employers is that the employees lured by such bonuses may not be as interested in long-term careers with the firm, and they may be "pirated" away by other firms offering similar bonuses. Signing bonuses are most frequently used when employers feel that they are under intense pressure to fill vacancies in the short run. They have been used by hospitals to recruit nurses and by data-processing firms to recruit programmers. When employers recognize this to be the case, they sometimes resort to using hiring bonuses to lure employees from other firms.

Improve Wages and Fringe Benefits. Increasing wages or fringe benefits would, at first glance, appear to be the logical way for a firm to attract more workers into an occupation. Based on the simple supply and demand curve analysis, increasing wages is an obvious way to increase the number of workers willing to work in a particular occupation. Employers are generally reluctant to increase wages for several reasons. First, an increase in wages will affect the entire workforce in the occupation with vacancies, not just the new workers the firm wishes to attract. Thus, the employer incurs costs for more than just the added workers.

Second, the employer might have to increase wages for workers in other occupations as well. Employers generally attempt to maintain equity among workers in various occupations. Thus, if an employer increases wages for one occupation because of difficulties in filling vacancies, wages may have to be increased for other occupations as well to maintain what are viewed as appropriate differentials. Another problem with raising wages is that wages tend to be "sticky" in terms of moving down. That is, once market conditions change, employers will generally have less flexibility to reduce wages later. Finally, raising wages might not be an effective means of recruiting in the short run if supply is not responsive to changes in wages (i.e., the supply is inelastic). In the extreme case, if the supply is totally fixed in the short run, higher wages cannot induce any change in the number of workers qualified to work in the occupation.

Improving fringe benefits is similar to increasing wages, but in some instances employers will reduce their vacancy rates more by improving benefits rather than increasing wages by a similar amount. For example, health insurance is often an important fringe benefit to provide. Because group health insurance rates are usually substantially less expensive than individual policies, the value of health insurance to the employee will often be greater than the cost to the employer. Health insurance is especially a concern for employers trying to fill vacancies for relatively low-paying jobs if Aid to Families with Dependent Children (AFDC) recipients are potential workers. This is because AFDC recipients receive excellent health insurance through the medicaid program, and they are often hesitant to take jobs if they will lose coverage for themselves and their children.[10] Unfortunately, many employers who do not provide health insurance are small and pay low wages. Thus, adding benefits such as health insurance may be most burdensome in those cases where it would be most important.

Contract Out the Work. If a firm is unable to hire all the employees it needs in particular occupations, the firm may be able to contract out the work to another employer who is not experiencing the problem. In some instances the labor problem may be regional in nature, and the firm can contract out the work to a firm in another part of the country. If the problem is nationwide, the firm can sometimes have the work performed overseas.

Turn Down Work. If a firm has exhausted all means that it considers reasonable and can find no reasonable way around its occupational vacancies, the firm always has the option of turning down work. Employers generally use this ''solution'' only as a last resort because they do not like to give up customers to competitors and, more basically, the only way to make a profit is to sell goods and services.

If the firm has limited capacity to conduct its business because of occupational shortages, there are more subtle measures than simply refusing work. For example, the firm might reduce its marketing activity, and thus reduce the demand for its products as well as its advertising costs.

Reasons Why Labor Markets May Adjust Slowly

Labor markets, and other markets as well, constantly experience changes in supply and demand that cause them to deviate from an equilibrium situation. In most cases, firms and workers will take actions to move the labor market toward equilibrium. In some instances, however, the market adjusts slowly and equilibrium is not restored, resulting in a shortage for the occupation. The literature suggests several factors that may result in the market failing to clear reasonably quickly. These factors will be discussed here.

Slow Reaction Time by Employers. In most industries, each individual firm employs a small share of the workers in a particular occupation. Thus, individual employers may be unaware of an increase in demand, and they are almost certainly unaware of the magnitude of the increase. As the firm recognizes that workers cannot be attracted at what they believe to be the market wage, they may then take actions described above to deal with the vacancies.

A number of factors can influence the reaction time of employers. If the firm does not recruit frequently for the occupation, either because of low turnover or because it employs few workers in the occupation, it may not know what the typical period is for filling vacancies for that occupation. The firm also may not have a good idea of what the market wage is, and thus may tend to set its offer wage too low.

Several institutional factors are likely to affect reaction time by employers. Occupations characterized by long periods of vacancies are more likely to have slow reaction times by employers because employers expect to take a significant amount of time before they fill vacancies. Lengthy recruiting periods are more characteristic of occupations with high salaries, typically professional and managerial occupations and highly skilled craft jobs. Occupations where employment is concentrated in small firms are likely to be characterized by slow reaction times because the employers are likely to recruit for fewer positions and less frequently than larger employers.

Other institutional factors that can influence employer reaction time include the extent to which employers and workers in the occupation are organized and exchange information. For example if employers have a trade association that monitors and publishes data on wages, vacancies, and other employment-related factors, employers will be aware of the occupational situation early in the search process. Of course, national-level data is not as useful as local data for an employer who recruits locally. For some occupations, hiring is done in conjunction with the trade union representing the workers. Even if most firms are small, the centralization of the hiring process will help employers gain a quicker grasp of the supply available.

Slow Response Time by Employers. After firms recognize that there is excess demand for an occupation, they may delay taking actions to fill their vacancies. Most strategies that a firm might try could be risky, expensive, or both. Relatively minor responses, such as intensifying the recruiting effort, will waste the firm's money if the positions would be filled without them. More significant responses, such as changing the occupational structure of the firm and training workers, require major commitments to plan and implement. Such actions are unlikely to be taken unless the employer believes that the firm is facing a prolonged period of difficulty in hiring.

Increasing wages can also be a major step for employers, as the wage increases must in addition be passed on to current workers as well as the newly hired workers, and sometimes workers in other occupations must receive increases as well. If the firm is in a competitive product market, it must carefully balance two competing interests. If it sets the wage too high, the firm's costs will be higher than the costs of its competitors, and the firm is likely to either lose market share (if it passes the costs on to consumers), profits (if it absorbs the increased costs), or both. Thus, firms are likely to be conservative in increasing wages as a method of filling vacancies.

Slow Reaction Time by Workers. Workers in other occupations and individuals who are unemployed or out of the labor force may not immediately recognize that wages or working conditions have improved in the occupation with the developing shortage. If workers who might be attracted to jobs in the occupation with the excess demand are unaware of the opportunities, they will not be able to consider entering that occupation. The time required for workers to become aware of the new opportunities depends on how effective firms' recruiting strategies are and how sensitive workers are to the recruiting effort. Moreover, workers may have a certain amount of loyalty to their current employer, occupation, or industry; the greater such loyalty, the slower will be the reaction time by workers.

Slow Response Time by Workers. Once workers are aware of the opportunities, their response time will depend on the time required to qualify for the positions and the costs and benefits of obtaining any needed qualifications, applying for the positions, and changing jobs. Typically, the greater the incentives provided by employers to induce workers into the occupation of interest, the quicker and greater will be the response by potential entrants.

For many occupations, training time is the most important factor slowing worker response time. Occupations requiring a specialized college degree, such as engineering, will be very slow in adjusting because the "pipeline" for producing new engineers is four years. The lag might be more extensive if some potential engineers must adjust their mathematics course load in high school. Some specialized occupations, such as architecture and medicine, require even longer preparation.

Many occupations requiring less than a college education still demand several years of training and will have a substantial lag before interested individuals qualify for the occupation. For example, many technician and skilled craft positions take two or more years of training. At the other extreme, some low-skill jobs, including paraprofessional home health care workers, may require as little as one week of formal training. Thus, the worker response lag generally will be shorter.

Response time can also be slowed if training institutions lack the capacity to train additional workers. For instance, the supply of nurses cannot be readily expanded if there are too few nursing instructors.

Restrictions on Occupational Entry. In some cases institutional barriers to occupational entry will slow down the adjustment process. These restrictions are generally instituted to achieve certain purposes, so removing or modifying the barriers is not always appropriate. However, in times of occupational shortages, consideration is often given to modifying these restrictions.

One example of a barrier to occupational entry is limits in the enrollment capacity of training institutions that supply workers for the occupation. Suppose, for instance, that hospitals needed to hire more physicians and there were enough individuals interested in attending medical school to meet the hospitals' demands. If the nation's medical schools could not admit the extra students because of limited capacity, the supply of physicians could not increase. Note that hospitals do not regulate the capacity of medical schools, so it would be difficult for this market to adjust.

Other institutional barriers include licensing and certification requirements. Employers might be willing to lower the standards for a particular occupation, but if entry to the occupation is regulated, the regulatory or licensing board would have to agree. These boards, which are often state bodies, might not wish to lower the standards, and current members of the occupation might object to relaxation because it would cheapen their credentials and possibly result in lower wages. Restrictions on immigration may operate as a similar institutional barrier to achieving equilibrium in occupational labor markets. Trade unions or associations, at the time of contract negotiations or through other activities, may restrict the supply of workers or hiring requirements for workers. An example of this type of barrier is restrictions on the ratio of apprentices to journey workers in an occupation. In some instances such restrictions could constrain employers and potential entrants from increasing the number of entrants in an occupation making use of apprenticeships.

All of the barriers mentioned above were established for particular reasons, usually to assure quality for workers in the occupation. Although consideration should be given to changing or eliminating the barriers, their original intent should not be forgotten.

Continuous Increases in Labor Demand. If the labor demand schedule continuously increases faster than the amount supplied can increase, then the market will not achieve equilibrium. This scenario is the basis of the Arrow-Capron (1959) dynamic model of labor shortages, and it can occur in periods of rapid sustained growth in one or more industries that employ workers in the shortage occupation. Such a period of sustained rapid growth for a particular sector of the economy can prevent the market from clearing for a substantial period of time. According to Arrow and Capron, this situation occurred for engineers following World War II. Note that in this situation the problem is not necessarily that workers or employers cannot adjust; rather, the problem is due to continued shocks to the equilibrium levels of employment and wages.

Consequences of Labor Shortages

Labor shortages can lead to a number of consequences for the firms experiencing them, and the rest of the economy as well. In economic terms, the major consequence of a sustained shortage is that the economy will operate less efficiently than it could. Until the market achieves equilibrium, resources are not put to their most productive use. Thus, aggregate production for the nation will be below capacity. Workers may have to work more hours than they desire, or they may be assigned to jobs they do not want. Employers may have to use their workers and equipment less efficiently than they desire, and this may result in lower output and reduced profits. Consumers will be denied the goods and services they wish to buy. In some cases, the impact on consumers will be relatively modest, but if, for example, they cannot obtain needed health care because of a labor shortage, the consequences can be severe. Finally, the impact of a shortage can extend beyond the firms directly experiencing the problem. A shortage of home health workers or nursing home workers, for example, may result in hospitals having to keep patients longer than is desirable. Thus, it is difficult to trace all of the effects of an occupational shortage.

IMPLICATIONS OF OCCUPATIONAL SHORTAGES FOR OLDER WORKERS

Occupational shortages will often present labor market opportunities for older workers in need of employment. As employers seek to alleviate a shortage, they will often turn to nontraditional sources of labor, and in many instances older workers will benefit. The opportunities provided by occupational shortages will vary, and in this section the circumstances that provide the best opportunities for older workers are considered.

Shortages can arise from increases in the demand for labor, decreases in the supply of labor, or restrictions on wages. When the shortage arises from a change in supply or demand, opportunities will generally exist for older workers to obtain some of the jobs available. Shortages due to restrictions on prices, however, are a different matter. By definition, such shortages stem from regulatory or institutional constraints that prevent the market from reaching the equilibrium wage. Although older workers would find employment opportunities in such situations, the positions would pay less than the market-clearing wage.

The characteristics of the occupation experiencing a shortage will affect the potential responses by older workers. Occupations with long training periods or expensive training expenses for the worker will be less appealing for older workers. Skilled occupations such as tool- and diemakers require many years to achieve journeyperson status; because older workers have fewer years of expected worklife, a long training period could significantly reduce the proportion of time over which they could recoup the investment. In addition, long training periods also increase the likelihood that by the time the worker obtains the skills, the shortage will be gone. Occupations that require less time to gain the required skills will be more attractive, but if there are extensive training costs, these occupations will also be of limited interest. If employers bear the cost of training, then older workers will not care about the expense, but employers will be reluctant to hire older workers if they must pay substantial training costs because they have less time on average to recoup the investment.

Employers have many potential ways to adjust to occupational shortages, and in some situations hiring older workers, or other workers as well, may not be an attractive option. If an employer believes that a shortage is likely to be temporary, management is more likely to have the existing labor force work overtime rather than hire new workers, particularly if the fixed costs of recruiting and training new workers are high. Other options available to employers that are unlikely to provide many opportunities for older workers include substituting machinery and equipment for labor and turning down work. On the other hand, raising wages is usually an unattractive option, so employers are more likely to try options such as expanding their recruiting efforts, reducing the minimum qualifications for the job, or training applicants rather than increase wages. In these situations, older workers will have opportunities to compete for the jobs, and in cases where employers increase their recruiting effort, older workers may even be a specific target for the recruitment.

It is important to close on a note of caution. Occupational shortages, as defined here, are not easy to identify. Moreover, in many situations employers or worker organizations may have incentives to claim a shortage exists even when the labor market is functioning well. Employers may argue that a shortage exists to help persuade the Department of Labor to admit more immigrants with the desired skills and curtail wage increases. Trade unions may find it advantageous to argue that a shortage exists in seeking higher wages. In a recently completed series of case studies, Trutko et al. (1993) found that two occupations that are often cited as having shortages, tool- and diemakers and electrical engineers, were not experiencing shortages at the national level, although there were shortages among special education teachers and home care workers.[11] Thus, although occupational shortages can sometimes offer excellent opportunities for older workers, it should be kept in mind that not all claims of shortages represent actual shortages; moreover, employers or older workers may not always find it advantageous to target occupations with shortages for expansion.

NOTES

1. See, for example, Commission on Workforce Quality and Labor Market Efficiency (1989), and Johnston and Packer (1987). For a critical review of this literature, see Barnow and Bawden (1991).

2. This definition, which was provided by the U.S. Department of Labor in a Request for Proposals (RFP) for a study of labor shortages, is essentially identical to the definition used by Franke and Sobel in their study of labor shortages: "A situation existing over an extended period of time in which employers were unable to hire at going wages or salaries sufficient numbers of qualified persons to fill positions for which there were budgeted funds and for which personnel were required to meet existing demands for services" (Franke and Sobel, 1970, 7).

3. Technically, the supply curve for labor may be *backward bending*, which means that at very high wages workers actually reduce the amount of labor they are willing to supply. We do not consider this concept further in our discussion because it is unlikely to be relevant in a study of labor shortages.

4. There are different definitions of labor surpluses as well. For example, the Bureau of Labor Statistics concludes that the nation has a surplus of college graduates while John Bishop concludes that there is a shortage. For a review of this issue, see Barnow and Bawden (1991).

5. See Barnow and Bawden (1991) for a review of recent studies that have concluded that the United States should increase education and training.

6. Formally, the internal rate of return is found by solving the equation

$$0 = (W_0 - C_0) + (W_1 - C_1)/(1 + i) + (W_2 - C_2)/(1 + i)^2 + \ldots + (W_n - C_n)/(1 + i)^n,$$

where W_t represents earnings in year t,
C_t represents costs incurred in year t,
and i is the internal rate of return that is solved for.

7. For a more detailed discussion of monopsonistic employers, see Ehrenberg and Smith (1993).

8. Other factors can also contribute to changes in the mix of skill levels desired by employers. There is currently debate over whether computers and other microchip applications have led to "upskilling" or "deskilling" of jobs.

9. The arguments presented above apply primarily to training new hires for entry into a new occupation. The arguments do not apply, or do not apply to the same extent, to training workers already on the payroll to improve their skills. Moreover, even if training does not pay for an individual employer, it might pay for society as a whole. See Barnow, Chasanov, and Pande (1990).

10. The Family Support Act of 1988 partially alleviates this problem by providing transitional medicaid benefits for up to one year for AFDC recipients who leave the program to take employment. Some AFDC recipients may still be reluctant to leave AFDC if their employer does not provide health insurance, or they may quit to regain medicaid coverage later if they or their children require health care.

11. For a summary of the case studies, see Trutko, Barnow, Chasanov, and Pande (1993).

19

Impacts of an Aging Workforce on Productivity and Economic Growth

William J. Serow

The fundamental question to be addressed in this chapter is the relationship between the probable aging of the labor force and the level and rate of economic growth. This question in turn is a consequence of the assumption of sustained low levels of fertility and the likelihood that rates of mortality will remain low and continue to decline. While particular demographic dynamics will vary among countries, the continuation of both of these tendencies seems at least to be highly probable in economically advanced nations. In the present context, this chapter is somewhat less concerned with the overall aging of the population and growth in the relative and absolute size of the older population than with changes in the structure of the population of working age and, by extension, of the labor force.

The chapter will begin with an overview of the prospective course of population change and especially with changes in the relative size and structure of the working-age population.[1] This is followed by a discussion of the relationship between the size and, particularly, the structure of the labor force and economic growth, as mediated through the mechanism of labor productivity. As an economy goes through the transition from primary to secondary and from secondary to tertiary modes of production, the measurement of labor productivity becomes increasingly difficult. While at the most general level, labor productivity is simply output per unit of input, the measurement of output is difficult when services rather than goods are produced. Productivity per worker—and in the aggregate—is properly viewed as being a function of both individual worker characteristics and the overall economic milieu in which the workers function, with the latter represented by both current economic conditions and current economic policies.

In this context, the arguments for changes in the aggregate level of productivity as a function of the age structure of the workforce are considered. However, it is also necessary to consider changes in the labor market behavior of individuals as they pass through the life course; of particular concern here is the extent to which older workers become increasingly self-selected. In other words, and abstracting from temporal fluctuations in economic conditions, the question of future productivity levels associated with an aging labor force will depend not merely on the age structure of the labor force, but also on its skill and experience levels.

Ultimately, the question of productivity leads to the question of output and income per worker. Growth here necessarily implies growth in the total level of income. Economic policies (especially those dealing with measures intended to influence individual labor force participation), as well as underlying demographic change in the size and composition of the nonlabor force population, will then determine the level of income per person, providing a convenient, if imperfect, measure of the overall level of economic well-being. Labor productivity ultimately rests on previous policy decisions made regarding capital formation and investment and current policies regarding labor force participation. The implications for economic growth in the context of an aging labor force are considered in the final section as a function of the issues of productivity, labor force participation, and investment/capital formation.

CHANGES IN DEMOGRAPHIC AND LABOR FORCE AGE STRUCTURES

Over the course of the 60-year period centered on 1990, there appear to be remarkably consistent changes in the age structures of presently industrialized nations. Table 19.1 illustrates that in 1960, between 25 and 30 percent of the total population in all such regions were below working age (here defined as those under 15 years of age), 60 to 65 percent were of working age (here defined as 15 to 64 years old), and 5 to 10 percent were above conventional working age. These figures have evolved, and are likely to continue to do so, in a remarkably consistent manner through the year 2020, according to current United Nations (1993) projections. By that year, only 15 to 20 percent will be below conventional working age, and 15 to 25 percent will be above age 65. While the dramatic aging of the population of Japan clearly emerges from this table, it is also the case that there has been and, within the limited future time horizon employed here, will be almost no change in the proportion of the population that is of working age. In other words, during this period the overall demographic change is likely to be in the nature of a shift of some 10 percentage points *from* the share of children *to* the share of older persons, with little changes

Table 19.1
Population by Broad Age Group for Selected Industrialized Regions 1960–2020
(Percent Distribution)

	1960			1980			2000			2010		
	0-14	15-64	65+	0-14	15-64	65+	0-14	15-64	65+	0-14	15-64	65+
EUROPE:	25.8%	64.5%	9.7%	22.4%	64.6%	13.1%	18.6%	66.5%	14.9%	17.5%	64.4%	18.0%
NORTH AMERICA:	31.3%	59.7%	9.1%	22.6%	66.3%	11.1%	21.6%	66.1%	12.3%	18.4%	65.2%	16.4%
AUSTRALIA-NEW ZEALAND:	30.6%	60.9%	8.5%	25.5%	64.8%	9.7%	21.8%	66.7%	11.5%	19.7%	65.1%	15.2%
JAPAN:	30.2%	64.1%	5.7%	23.6%	67.4%	9.0%	16.4%	67.4%	16.2%	15.6%	60.2%	24.2%
TOTAL:	27.9%	63.1%	9.0%	22.6%	65.5%	11.9%	19.3%	66.5%	14.2%	17.6%	64.2%	18.2%

Source: United Nations (1993), medium variant projections.

in the share of population of working age and little change in crude measures of economic dependency.

From an economic perspective, this demographic regularity suggests that concerns for the long-term funding of support for older persons may well be mitigated by the lesser demand for support by the young, although as Easterlin noted: ''The real issue to be faced is not economic, but political, namely, how to capture via taxation the savings of households from supporting fewer younger dependents, so that these funds can be used to meet the rise in public expenditures needed to support older dependents'' (1991, 306). From the perspective of the overall economic performance of an economy, however, this type of analysis needs to expand to consider the characteristics of members of the labor force.

The characteristic detail of the labor force is determined by the number of individuals of given characteristics (age, gender, race/ethnicity, etc.) and their specific probability of participating in the labor force (that is, working or actively seeking work). Before addressing the question of labor force participation, it may be well to consider prospective changes in age structure. Table 19.2 illustrates changes in the distribution of those aged 15–64 between 1990 and 2020. Once again, for the presently industrialized regions there is a remarkable degree of uniformity apparent. At present about one-third of individuals of working age are under age 30 and one-fifth to one-fourth are at least 50. Over time, the proportion of potentially younger workers declines by about five percentage points and that of middle-aged workers by only one or two points, with an increased proportion being observable among older workers. In other words, during this period the overall demographic change is likely to be in the nature of a shift of some five percentage points *from* the share of younger workers *to* the share of older workers, with little change in the share of the potential labor force of middle age. Other things being equal, then, the central issue here may well be the differences in actual and prospective productivity between younger and older workers.

In addition to age, other individual attributes may contribute to differences in labor productivity. Consider Figure 19.1, which illustrates trends in the age, gender and racial structure of Americans aged 15–64 between 1990 and 2020. With greater disaggregation by age, there appear to be more salient shifts in the age structure of the potential working age population, with declines of four to five percentage points among those aged 25–34 and 35–44 and corresponding increases among those over the age of 45. There is very little change in the share who would be considered probable new entrants to the labor force. Hence, the U.S. case will hinge on the relative productivity of those aged 45–64 versus those 25–44. The data also suggest increases in the share of all races other than white in the potential labor force and a pronounced increase in the share of Hispanics. The proportion of females in this age range remains almost perfectly constant throughout the period. To the extent that productivity changes are em-

Table 19.2
Population of Working Age by Broad Age Group for Selected Industrialized Regions 1990–2020 (Percent Distribution of Persons Aged 15 to 64)

	1990			2000			2010			2020		
	15-29	30-49	50-64	15-29	30-49	50-64	15-29	30-49	50-64	15-29	30-49	50-64
EUROPE:	34.3%	40.9%	24.8%	30.5%	44.1%	25.4%	28.1%	43.1%	28.8%	28.5%	39.8%	31.7%
NORTH AMERICA:	35.4%	44.8%	19.9%	30.5%	46.5%	22.9%	30.4%	40.7%	28.9%	30.8%	38.9%	30.3%
AUSTRALIA-NEW ZEALAND:	37.0%	43.1%	19.9%	32.6%	44.5%	22.9%	30.4%	42.5%	27.2%	31.4%	40.1%	28.5%
JAPAN:	31.5%	42.3%	26.2%	30.0%	38.9%	31.1%	25.6%	42.7%	31.7%	27.9%	41.6%	30.5%
TOTAL:	34.3%	42.3%	23.4%	30.5%	44.2%	25.3%	28.6%	42.2%	29.2%	29.3%	39.7%	31.0%

Source: United Nations (1993), medium variant projections.

Figure 19.1
Estimated and Projected Population by Age, Gender, and Race/Ethnicity: United States, 1990–2020 (Persons Aged 15–64)

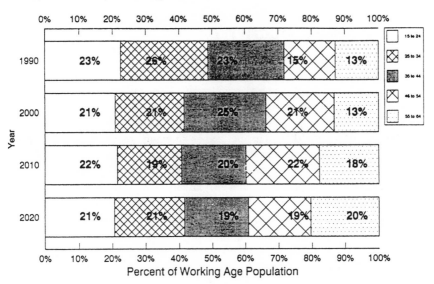

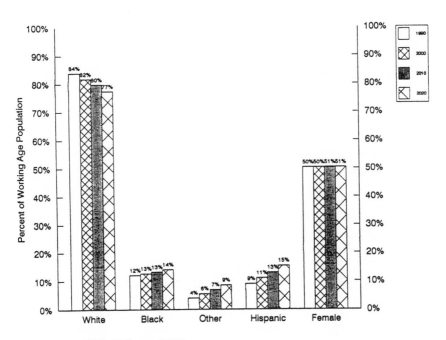

Sources: Day (1992); Hollmann (1993).

bedded in these demographic characteristics, there will be consequences for the overall level of labor productivity and for economic growth and well-being.

THE RELATIVE SIZE OF THE LABOR FORCE, ECONOMIC GROWTH, AND PRODUCTIVITY

The recent demographic history of most industrialized nations has been largely favorable for the relative size of the working age population and hence for quite favorable labor force to population ratios. *Other things being equal,* the higher this ratio, the higher will be the level of income per person, simply because relatively fewer nonworkers need be supported by the earnings of workers. Recent history could be characterized as showing gradual increases in these ratios as falling fertility reduced the relative number of children without any totally offsetting increase in the relative number of retired persons. However, there are not likely to be any further increases in the ratio.[2] Moreover, as Terleckyj (1990) argued: "Economic growth over the next thirty years in the United States will depend largely on growth of productivity" (p. 68). Underlying this contention is the simple identity that total output equals total workers multiplied by their level of productivity. As the number of workers rises only at the same rate as total population (reflected in the constant share of the population aged 15–64), then increases in per capita income (ultimately determined by the value of output and population size) rely solely on enhancements in the average level of productivity per worker. This could come about through either or both of the following mechanisms:

- a change in the composition of the labor force so that the proportion of workers characterized by relatively high productivity increases;
- sustained increase in savings and capital formation in human resources, plant and equipment, technology and infrastructure. (Terleckyj, 1990)

There have been several previous reviews of the relationship between worker age and productivity (Serow and Espenshade, 1978). More recent reviews by Jablonski, Kunze, and Rosenblum (1990) and by Richter (1992) suggest that the situation is quite dependent on the type of work performed and that in the aggregate, there is little effect until the attainment of quite advanced age. Increased experience and acquired skills may overcome whatever losses in strength and agility accompany aging. The current context, though, does preclude the immediate adaption of an entirely sanguine answer to this question. Richter, as well as Clark (1993), make statements quite similar to the observation by Boes and von Weizsaecker (1989): "In general, population aging is likely to have its most substantial effect on the overall level of productivity in an economy where technical knowledge is changing rapidly and strong competition necessitates a high degree of adaptability in the labor force" (p. 349) or that made a generation earlier by Brennan, Taft, and Schupack (1967): "It is a decline in the ability to make rapid adjustments that appears most important in putting the older worker at a productivity disadvantage" (p. 208). Although it may be tempting to equate adaptability with chronological age, other attributes such as educational attainment (Serow, 1976) and prospects for individual mobility and advancement (Keyfitz, 1973) are also extremely important. While an aging labor force certainly retards the speed at which newer entrants may expect occupational advancement, more flexible types of employment arrangements may alleviate some of these concerns (Copperman and Keast, 1983; Doyle, 1990). Questions of individual motivation are quite important in establishing productivity on the margin, above and beyond the question of individual endowments of capital, human or otherwise.

The question of the measurement of productivity has been a thorny one and despite many efforts to answer it (see Jablonski, Kunze, and Rosenblum, 1990), it remains the case that in order to make statements of comparability across industries and cohorts and over time, it usually becomes necessary to resort to wages or earnings as a proxy for productivity, following economic theory, which asserts that workers are paid the value of their marginal product. This is conventionally adopted recognizing the fact that seniority arrangements in union contracts or in civil service pay scales frequently provide more-or-less automatic salary increases. From a theoretical perspective, workers should become more productive as they age and gain experience. However, at some point (which will vary considerably across individuals and occupations), declines in functional status and obsolescence of skills will set in, leading to lower productivity and, theoretically at least, lower wages.

Bearing this in mind, one might consider the hypothetical age-earnings profiles shown in Figure 19.2.[3] These profiles are designed to suggest a constant shape in the age-earnings profile over time, but also a profile that rises over each successive time period due to sustained technical progress and/or capital formation. At any given *time period*, then, the level of earnings and, theoretically, the level of productivity per worker would reach a maximum at age 45–49 in this example. This does *not* apply to the actual experience of any individual worker over the course of his or her working life. As the profile rises for each time period, the peak for actual earnings and (presumably) productivity would shift to an older age. Thus, as shown by the heavy line in Figure 19.2, the lifetime earnings for an individual entering the labor force at what is termed "time 1" in the illustration would peak in this hypothetical case at ages 50 to 54.

The conclusion reached from this exercise is that the most important issue is not the age of the labor force itself but the ability of the economy to continue to generate constantly upward moving age-earnings profiles, or, in other words, the necessity to maintain technical progress and capital formation. In this manner, the potential decline in worker productivity is "postponed" as new tech-

Figure 19.2
Period and Cohort Perspectives on the Hypothetical Age-Earnings Profile

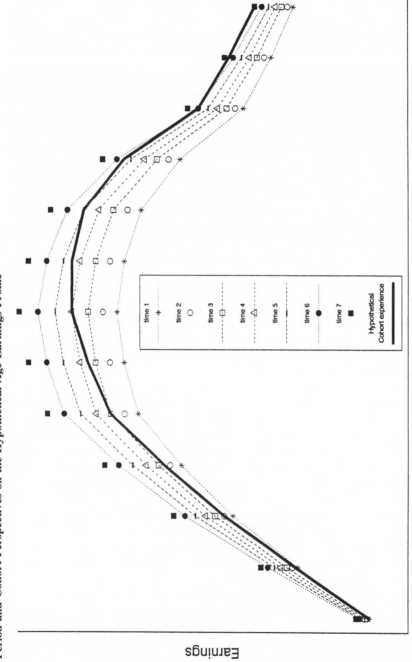

nology and/or increased capital endowments per worker offset the age-linked decline in productivity that would have otherwise occurred.

Before moving away from this topic, it would also be well to consider attributes that interact with age to determine the overall level of labor productivity. Education as a measure of human capital would seem to be an excellent proxy for potential labor productivity and as shown by data for the United States (1991), the age-earnings profile classified by educational attainment shows an almost perfect pattern of monotonic increase by educational attainment, holding current age constant (Figure 19.3). The importance of this for future productivity in light of the probable trends in the age structure is suggested by current data on educational attainment by age and gender, which are shown in Table 19.3. Substantial differences clearly exist between the two youngest age groups who will have substantially completed their education (those aged 25–44) and all older individuals, particularly those aged 55+. As those now at the oldest range of the labor force gradually withdraw through death or retirement, they will effectively be replaced by members of the next older cohorts, whose level of educational attainment is much higher. To illustrate this point, consider only the cohorts now aged 45–54 and 55–64. Precisely half of males and 42 percent of females in the younger group have at least some postsecondary education; among those 10 years older, these proportions are 40 and 31 percent, respectively. While the tendency for gains in educational attainment has slowed down appreciably (reflected by the great similarity between the 25–34 and 35–44 groups), it is unlikely that the educational attainment of future labor force entry cohorts will be substantially less than that of current 25–34-year-olds. However, as noted, the racial and ethnic mix of the American labor force will be shifting in future years. Future changes in this mix, especially those attributable to immigration, could conceivably exert downward pressure on future levels of educational attainment.

The relationship between population change and technical progress has become the subject of considerable debate among scholars interested in the topic. Among others, Steinmann (1989) argued that sustained population growth (which would deter aging of both the population and the labor force) is necessary for technical progress to ensue. While Richter (1992) reviewed many of the arguments pro and con this assertion, the overall notion that technical progress is determined simply by the demographic dynamics of a given country or countries ignores the globalization of the world economy. To argue that innovation will slow due to lack of growth of numbers in a domestic market seems to fly in the face of current international economic realities.

Technical progress certainly implies additional capital formation and a demand for investment funds. To accommodate technical progress, the argument must note the relationships between the propensities of different age groups to earn and invest and the relative sizes of these groups within the labor force (Lee, Arthur, and Rodgers, 1988, part 1: Fair and Dominguez, 1991). While conventional economic wisdom asserts that older persons dissave (and hence impede

Figure 19.3
Educational Attainment and the Age-Earnings Profile: U.S. Males Aged 25-64, 1991

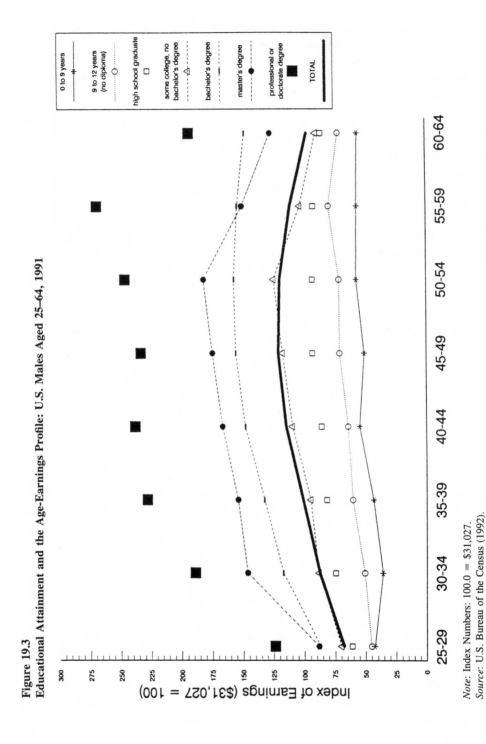

Note: Index Numbers: 100.0 = $31,027.
Source: U.S. Bureau of the Census (1992).

Table 19.3
Educational Attainment by Age: United States, 1991 (Percent Distribution)

	0-8 grade	9-12 grade no diploma	high school graduate	some college no degree	bachelor's degree	master's degree	professional/ doctorate
Male:							
25-34	4.3%	9.7%	38.4%	24.2%	17.4%	4.1%	1.8%
35-44	4.4%	7.6%	32.7%	26.7%	17.9%	6.9%	3.8%
45-54	7.5%	9.7%	32.8%	21.1%	15.9%	8.7%	4.4%
55-64	13.9%	14.0%	32.3%	17.3%	12.6%	5.8%	4.1%
65+	25.9%	14.6%	29.3%	14.2%	9.6%	3.3%	3.1%
Female:							
25-34	3.6%	9.4%	37.0%	26.9%	18.3%	3.5%	1.2%
35-44	3.9%	7.7%	35.6%	27.6%	16.9%	6.8%	1.5%
45-54	6.3%	11.1%	40.4%	22.6%	11.9%	6.3%	1.3%
55-64	11.4%	14.5%	43.1%	17.7%	8.5%	4.0%	0.8%
65+	24.0%	16.1%	37.2%	14.0%	6.2%	2.0%	0.5%

Source: U.S. Bureau of the Census (1992).

385

the formation of additional capital), recent empirical evidence not only questions this assertion (Wiseman, 1989), but actually finds that the sort of population and labor force aging that is probable in most industrialized nations will act to enhance the availability of funds needed for the "supply side" of capital formation.

Much of the demand for capital formation will come from the private sector acting in response to its own perceptions of the long-term economic outlook. Again, in light of the economic realities of the present day, such considerations would appear to have little to do with population changes or changes in the structures of the labor force of the domestic economy, and much more to do with the world marketplace. Other components of demand for capital stem from the public sector and, ultimately, the level and composition of such demand becomes a matter of public policy. This is partially a matter of infrastructure development and maintenance, but from the perspective of enhancing productivity, it is difficult to argue against improvements in the educational system as the principal means to this end.

As is well known, the labor force participation rates of American males have declined somewhat in recent years, while those for women continue to increase. There are also considerable differences in the relative degree of attachment to the labor force as a function of educational attainment and, presumably, productivity as well. The data shown in Table 19.4 show the course of participation rates for Americans between the ages of 25 and 64 during the 1980s.[4] While there were very few instances of increases in male participation rates, it was certainly the case that the smallest declines within most age groups were observed among those with the highest level of educational attainment and that withdrawal from the labor force was substantially highest among those who had not completed secondary school, regardless of age. Among females there were only scattered instances of reduced labor force participation, and these always occurred among the most poorly educated. In general, the highest rates of increase were to be found among those with at least some college education.

The upshot of these tendencies is that investment in education may tend to enhance the level of labor productivity, both directly, through the human capital endowments associated with education, and indirectly, through the favorable influence of education on labor force retention. Workers who are the most educated tend to be those who are most productive, assuming that the hypothesized relationship between earnings and productivity is valid. These same workers are also those who are most prone to remain in the labor force over time, thus enhancing the overall level of labor productivity. It is certainly possible that, as Mitchell (1990) speculated, those who remain in the labor force for longer periods of time are those with fewer health problems. Such an outcome is by no means inconsistent with our conclusions regarding the role of educational attainment, given the negative association between educational attainment and mortality or morbidity.

CONCLUSIONS

Productivity levels in the context of the aging workforce, which will characterize all industrialized economies in coming decades, should not deter the course of economic growth so long as appropriate policy measures are adopted. The enhancement of productivity depends on a sustained commitment to the process of capital formation, and the demographic changes that should occur will permit much more attention to be paid to the process of *capital deepening*, or increasing the ratio of capital to labor. While the future labor force will undoubtedly be older, it will also possess a higher standard of educational qualification on average than has been the case in the past. This is the result of cohort differences in educational attainment and the certainty that as older cohorts move out of the labor force, they will be replaced by new cohorts with higher levels of education. In general, the future older labor force will tend to include relatively more individuals who are at or near their peak earnings and (presumably) productive years.

In order to maximize the productivity of the older workforce, measures need to be adopted to overcome the lack of mobility and flexibility that may, indeed, characterize such a labor force. Schulz, Borowski, and Crown (1991) argued strongly for continuous education as a means of ameliorating such problems. Serow (1981) added to this the need to assure the full portability of pensions and the possibility of gradual, rather than abrupt, withdrawal from the labor force. Older workers need to be viewed as a productive resource and not as being excessively compensated and unproductive. Crown (1990) suggested programs that both encourage participation (such as measures suggested above) and discourage retirement. Any and all efforts that cause workers to remain in the labor force have the desirable consequences of adding to the level of national output, adding to savings through continued contributions to social security and reducing the immediate expenditure from the trust funds. Such efforts are particularly appropriate when targeted to the most potentially productive individuals.

From the perspective of assuring adequate supplies of investment funds, Burtless (1993) argued that increases in the size of the U.S. social security trust fund (through higher withholding taxes) would have a very positive impact on productivity if these funds were saved rather than continuing to be spent on non–social security, federal government operations. Such savings would enhance savings, investment, the size of the capital stock, labor productivity, wage levels, and overall levels of income. According to Burtless, "Sacrifices today could make a significant difference in raising the living standards of future workers and reducing the burden on them of paying for higher social security benefits" (1993, 251).

Our discussion here has concentrated nearly entirely on aggregate measures of economic well-being. There are also issues of the distribution of income and wealth which, while of paramount importance, lie outside the scope of this

Table 19.4

Educational Attainment and Receipt of Earnings by Age and Gender: United States, 1981 and 1991

	1981		1991		percent change	
	Male	Female	Male	Female	Male	Female
25-34:						
0-8 years	82.2%	45.5%	82.3%	44.2%	0.1%	-2.7%
9-11 years	90.3%	52.9%	85.9%	55.4%	-4.9%	4.7%
12 years	95.4%	70.9%	93.8%	76.4%	-1.7%	7.8%
13-15 years	95.5%	78.4%	95.5%	83.5%	0.0%	6.5%
16 years	97.1%	85.5%	96.3%	89.5%	-0.8%	4.7%
17 + years	96.2%	87.3%	95.2%	90.0%	-1.0%	3.1%
TOTAL	94.8%	72.8%	93.5%	78.2%	-1.4%	7.4%
35-44:						
0-8 years	85.9%	51.0%	76.5%	49.9%	-10.9%	-2.2%
9-11 years	92.0%	61.4%	86.1%	62.4%	-6.5%	1.5%
12 years	95.9%	72.2%	92.6%	79.4%	-3.4%	10.0%
13-15 years	96.2%	76.9%	95.1%	83.2%	-1.1%	8.2%
16 years	98.3%	73.9%	97.6%	83.6%	-0.8%	13.1%
17 + years	99.0%	88.0%	98.4%	91.0%	-0.7%	3.3%
TOTAL	95.4%	71.3%	93.6%	79.6%	-1.9%	11.7%

45-54:

0-8 years	82.4%	44.6%	72.0%	43.4%	-12.7%	-2.7%
9-11 years	87.9%	57.3%	78.8%	56.0%	-10.3%	-2.3%
12 years	92.7%	68.0%	92.0%	74.4%	-0.7%	9.3%
13-15 years	93.1%	69.5%	95.0%	82.5%	2.0%	18.7%
16 years	95.7%	72.1%	96.7%	85.4%	1.1%	18.6%
17+ years	98.3%	88.2%	97.4%	92.6%	-0.9%	5.1%
TOTAL	91.5%	64.8%	91.3%	74.9%	-0.2%	15.6%

55-64:

0-8 years	64.8%	33.3%	57.7%	27.2%	-10.9%	-18.3%
9-11 years	71.4%	42.2%	65.4%	39.8%	-8.4%	-5.6%
12 years	78.0%	48.1%	71.9%	54.0%	-7.8%	12.4%
13-15 years	82.6%	52.7%	78.8%	57.0%	-4.6%	8.1%
16 years	88.1%	54.8%	80.0%	63.5%	-9.2%	15.9%
17+ years	90.9%	69.9%	86.6%	77.3%	-4.7%	10.6%
TOTAL	76.6%	45.9%	72.7%	51.4%	-5.0%	12.0%

Source: U.S. Bureau of the Census (1983, 1992).

chapter. The sort of policy measures discussed here have the desirable effect of increasing total and per capita incomes, but in and of themselves, they do not address the distribution of that income. As Ermisch and Joshi (1987) suggested, much work in this context needs to be done in the context of gender and economic inequality, and generalized answers probably need yield to specific analyses within given national contexts. The recently released Final Report of the Carnegie Inquiry into the Third Age (1993) provides (for the specific case of the United Kingdom) an example of a carefully considered set of recommendations which deal simultaneously with both labor market policies for older workers and income security policies for older individuals.

NOTES

1. See Kingson (Chapter 3 of this volume) for a detailed discussion of population aging.

2. Although there have been remarkable increases in labor force participation among women, there has also been some tendency for earlier withdrawal from the labor force especially among men. Current projections by a variety of U.S. government agencies have suggested a broad continuation of these trends, although Levine (1993) has argued for more research on this issue. Given the recent role of women's labor market activities in enhancing the labor force-population ratio and current proposals for tax increases, one should note Apps's (1991) finding that such an increase could act to reduce the labor force participation of married women in middle income households.

3. These are based on the age-earnings profile for full-time U.S. male workers in 1991. It is important to recognize in this context that earnings are a function of both wage levels and hours worked. Our discussion here deals with the former, but one must bear in mind that these factors interact and will affect the labor market behavior of older workers. Thus, an increase in wage levels could engender a decline in hours worked (due either to workers opting for more leisure instead of more income or to employers seeking to control payrolls), leaving actual earnings largely unchanged.

4. The data shown are proportions of each age-gender-educational attainment group who *earned* income during the year in question. From a technical perspective, the educational attainment categories are not strictly comparable for the two years, as the most recent data are grouped by completion of a level of education rather than a given number of years of schooling.

20

The Political Context of Older
Worker Employment Policy

William H. Crown

The labor force participation decisions of older workers are enormously complex. They are influenced by retirement incentives and disincentives in social security and private pension plans, the health status of workers, retirement decisions of spouses, workers' earnings levels, and many other factors. Employers and public policy makers who attempt to alter the timing of retirement decisions invariably are able to influence only a portion of the total set of factors that enter into the retirement decision.

Earlier chapters have discussed these factors in considerable detail, but they have not examined their implications for older worker policy. This chapter begins with a summary of programs and policies that influence the retirement decisions of older workers. It then considers the objectives of these programs and policies within the current political context characterized by concerns related to population aging and federal budget deficits. Finally, it attempts to draw implications for the future direction of older worker employment policy.

POLICIES INFLUENCING THE EMPLOYMENT OF OLDER WORKERS

Social Security

When the Social Security Act was originally passed in 1935, the creation of jobs was a major objective. One way to create jobs was to move older workers out of the labor force to make room for younger workers. The social security program did this by linking the receipt of benefits to an earnings test, thereby ensuring that those who accepted social security benefits really left the labor force. In recent years, however, policy makers have become increasingly concerned about the need to encourage older persons to work *longer*, rather than less. Consequently, changes made to social security since the early 1980s have tended to emphasize work incentives.

As a result of shifts in policy emphasis with regard to the employment of older persons, the social security program contains a mix of provisions that influence the retirement decision. Some of these provisions encourage early retirement; others encourage delayed retirement. The main social security provisions influencing the retirement decision are the:

- early retirement penalty;
- delayed retirement credit;
- earnings test;
- taxation of benefits for "high-income" beneficiaries;
- payroll tax on earnings; and
- recomputation of benefits for persons who continue to work after beginning to receive benefits.

The effects of these provisions on social security wealth are examined in Chapter 8 by Barry Friedman, who concludes that, on balance, social security provisions create incentives for early retirement.

This conclusion is supported by most of the empirical evidence from the retirement literature. As reviewed by Christopher Ruhm in Chapter 4 and Michael Leonesio in Chapter 12, numerous studies have examined the effects of social security on the retirement decision. Most studies have found that social security *does* influence the timing of retirement. Although the most sophisticated econometric models indicate that the magnitude of these effects is fairly small, there is no denying the existence of retirement spikes at age 62, the earliest age at which social security benefits become available, and age 65, the current normal retirement age under social security.

Employer Pensions

A major difficulty with assessing the effects of social security provisions on the retirement decision is that the retirement decision is also influenced by other financial incentives such as those in public and private pensions. As with social security, studies of the history of employer pensions indicate that a major reason for their creation was to remove older workers from the labor force to make room for younger workers (Graebner, 1980). Most studies of the effects of private pensions on the retirement decision indicate that pensions exert powerful influences on retirement decisions through their effects on retirement wealth. Pension wealth is often maximized at relatively early ages. Moreover, in many plans, workers are eligible to begin drawing benefits at age 55 if years of service criteria have been met. When one considers that much of the decline in labor force participation rates took place over the same time period as the maturation of the private pension system and that nearly two-thirds of workers retire *before* initial eligibility for social security at age 62, it seems clear that pensions are a major reason for the trend toward early retirement.

On the other hand, Hurd (1990b) pointed out that a relatively small proportion of the population age 60 and older receive more than half their income from private pensions (7 percent), compared to 57 percent who receive more than half their income from social security. In addition, persons with high pension wealth also tend to have high nonpension wealth, making it difficult to separate the effects on retirement behavior. These results suggest that the *combination* of social security and private pension incentives may be especially important in inducing early retirement (Samwick, 1993; Ruhm, 1993b).

Early Retirement Incentive Programs

Early retirement incentive programs (ERIPs) further complicate the retirement decision. ERIPs are often designed to work in concert with private pensions to "bridge" retirees over to the point where they can begin receiving social security benefits. In Chapter 10, Phyllis Mutschler discusses the development of ERIPs, in the late 1970s and early 1980s, as a mechanism for employers to reduce their personnel costs without exposing themselves to charges of age discrimination. ERIPs can involve cash payments, pension plan adjustments, or other types of benefits. In deciding whether to accept an ERIP, individuals must consider the value of the ERIP itself, as well as the influence of the retirement decision on their private pension and social security wealth. Such calculations are enormously complex and will yield different decision rules for individuals with different characteristics (e.g., age, years of service, and wage level).

Pension and Age Discrimination Legislation

The Employee Retirement Income Security Act. The Employee Retirement Income Security Act of 1974 (ERISA) was designed to protect the pension rights of workers covered by private pension plans. ERISA, however, contains a variety of provisions that may inhibit the employment of older workers (see, e.g., Kahne, 1985; Munnell, 1984). Under ERISA, workers are not allowed to work more than 40 hours per month for a company from which they are receiving a pension. Consequently, older persons who are receiving a pension and wish to work more than 40 hours per month must change jobs—often at a reduction in pay and job status. Workers must also work a minimum of 1,000 hours per year (about half time) to earn credits toward becoming vested in a pension plan. This encourages employers hiring older workers to limit them to under 1,000 hours. In an effort to address this problem, ERISA allows firms to exclude from the plan workers who are hired within five years of a plan's normal retirement age. This addresses the pension cost concerns of employers hiring such workers, but it may also limit the supply of older workers willing to work because it reduces their effective compensation.

The Age Discrimination in Employment Act. The Age Discrimination in Employment Act (ADEA) of 1967 was designed to protect workers aged 40–65 against age discrimination in the workplace. Under the original law, age 65 was the "normal" age of retirement. In 1978, the ADEA was amended to raise the mandatory retirement age to 70 (with certain exceptions, such as tenured faculty in colleges and universities). In 1986, the retirement age was eliminated completely.

The 1978 ADEA amendments spawned a number of studies attempting to measure the impact of mandatory retirement and age discrimination on labor force participation rates of older persons. Most studies estimated that the labor force participation response was fairly small (e.g., Halpern, 1978; Barker and Clark, 1980; Burkhauser and Quinn, 1983; Sherman, 1985; Lawlor, 1987). For example, using data from the Social Security Administration's New Beneficiary Survey, Sherman (1985) found that only 6 percent of older men and 3 percent of older women responded that they felt compelled to leave the labor force because of mandatory retirement or age discrimination. Lawlor (1987) found *no* evidence that the ADEA amendments of 1978 had any impact on the labor force participation rates of aged men.

On the other hand, several studies have indicated that substantial numbers of workers aged 50+ face age discrimination in the labor market (Brudney and Scott, 1987). Victims of age discrimination often do nothing about it because (a) they do not know their rights under the ADEA, (b) they do not feel that the ADEA can be an effective mechanism for getting their jobs back, (c) the costs and delays involved in the litigation process are often large, and (d) they are influenced by, or fearful of, age discrimination from younger coworkers. These factors suggest the need for greater educational efforts to inform older workers of their rights under the ADEA, as well as reforms in the implementation of the ADEA to make it a more effective piece of legislation. In Chapter 11, Steven Sandell and Marc Rosenblum provide a recent review of the literature dealing with age discrimination in employment.

Federal Employment Programs

There are two primary employment programs for older workers: The Job Training Partnership Act (JTPA) and the Senior Community Service Employment Program (SCSEP). Both are federal programs that are implemented at the state and local level. The JTPA established a nationwide network of job training programs, some of which are targeted specifically to older workers. JTPA legislation established two principal training programs. The first of these, Title II, is targeted toward disadvantaged youths and adults (it has no upper age limit). The second, Title III, is targeted toward dislocated workers, including long-term, unemployed older workers. In addition, under Section 124(a-d) of the JTPA, states are required to set aside 3 percent of their Title III allocation for the training of economically disadvantaged workers aged 55+. JTPA programs are meant to be jointly administered by local governments and private agencies. Thus, they provide an appropriate focal point for state and local policy in developing employment programs for older workers.

The emphasis of JTPA programs on training, however, has been criticized as being less effective than direct job placement. In contrast to the JTPA, the SCSEP is designed to provide part-time jobs in community service agencies for low-income persons aged 55+. Very little has been written about the SCSEP. One study found that, of the 11 million persons estimated to be eligible for the program in 1980, less than 1 percent participated (Sheppard, 1988). Other analysts (Rupp et al., 1987; Leavitt and Crown, 1995) have reached similar conclusions. Part of the reason for the low participation rate is inadequate funding. Sheppard (1988) found that fewer than 75,000 jobs per year could be funded under the SCSEP, but he estimated that at least 500,000 persons would apply for the SCSEP if funding levels were adequate.

Leavitt and Crown (1995) compared the characteristics of SCSEP participants to other older workers and found that SCSEP participants were different along several dimensions:

- they are more likely to be female than other older workers. Seventy-two percent of the SCSEP enrollee population is female, versus 44 percent of the 55+ working population;
- they tend to be older than other workers in the 55+ age group. For example, 21 percent of SCSEP workers are age 70 or older, compared to 10 percent of workers in the age 55+ group;
- they are more likely to be members of a racial or ethnic minority group than other older workers. For example, 22 percent of SCSEP enrollees are black compared to 8 percent of the general older worker population; and
- they tend to be less highly educated than other older workers. For example, 6 percent of SCSEP participants are college graduates compared to 15 percent of other older workers.

The disadvantaged characteristics of SCSEP participants relative to other older workers, of course, makes SCSEP participants difficult to place in unsubsidized employment. Perhaps for this reason the program has remained limited in scope. (As of June 30, 1994, there were 63,318 enrollees in the program.) On the other hand, SCSEP has demonstrated remarkable longevity for a jobs program—having started as a demonstration program (Operation Mainstream) in 1965. It remains to be seen whether SCSEP will continue to survive in the current era of fiscal austerity.

Private Sector Employment Programs

Although anecdotal information on older worker programs is found in the media (e.g., Labich, 1993), there does not appear to be a groundswell of interest in older worker programs among private employers. In fact, the early retirement incentives that employers create through private pensions and ERIPS indicate that most employers wish to move older workers out of the labor force to make room for younger employees. In Chapter 17, Michael Barth, William McNaught, and Philip Rizzi point out that even though employers view some attributes of older workers in a positive light (e.g., commitment to quality and company loyalty), on balance, these positive perceptions are outweighed by concerns regarding health insurance costs of older workers and their ability to adapt to new technologies.

Nevertheless, some companies do offer older worker employment programs, which take a variety of forms. For example, part-time, employer-sponsored programs can take the form of job sharing, work sharing, phased retirement, or retiree labor pools. In most part-time programs, employees are limited to less than 1,000 hours per year so the employer will not have to provide fringe benefits. Typically, firms prefer to rehire their own employees. Older workers continue to receive their pension benefits but do not receive fringe benefits other than those they receive as retirees.

Phased retirement enables older workers to make a gradual transition from full-time employment to full retirement; it does, however, raise some thorny technical issues. For example, most pensions are based on the last several years of an employee's earnings. If a worker gradually retires from the workplace, earnings, and hence pension benefits, will be lower than if the employee withdrew from the labor force abruptly upon retirement. Perhaps for this reason, phased retirement programs have not been as popular among older workers as sudden retirement, even when they have been available (Jondrow, Brechling, and Marcus, 1987).

Part-time employment can also take the form of job sharing and work sharing. Although job sharing and work sharing are often confused because they both involve the reconfiguration of full-time positions into part-time jobs shared by two or more workers, they are quite different. Job-sharing arrangements are usually initiated at the request of one or more employees. The reasons for such arrangements are as varied as individual workers. Some workers may have caregiver responsibilities at home; others may wish to reduce their hours because they are not yet ready to fully retire. Individuals initiating a job-sharing request often take the responsibility for any associated increased administrative activities (e.g., delineating responsibilities). This helps reduce the higher administrative costs usually associated with part-time jobs. The full-time benefits associated with the original job are often prorated among the job sharers. Job-sharing programs can be attractive to employers because they provide a mechanism for enlarging their labor pool, maintaining valued employees, and enhancing employee morale.

In contrast, work-sharing arrangements are usually initiated by employers during periods of economic retrenchment. Work sharing may involve a reduction in hours worked per day, days worked per week, or the rotation of weeks worked and not worked. Work-sharing arrangements enable employers to maintain their workforce while instituting cost-containment measures (Kahne, 1985).

Finally, job redesign and transfer programs are generally used to restructure job characteristics for workers who are having difficulty dealing with the physical or mental aspects of their job. These types of programs are most often used to reemploy workers who have been receiving long-term disability or workers' compensation (Root and Zarrugh, 1983). However, few employers offer such programs to older workers (Paul, 1987). Job redesign and transfer schemes are seldom formal programs at all; instead, they tend to be arrangements made between individual employees and their supervisors (Paul, 1987).

Private Sector Training Programs

Some employers are concerned about maintaining the productivity of their workers in a rapidly changing workplace. These employers view retraining programs as a way of upgrading the skills of older workers who are currently "coasting" toward retirement because their skills no longer enable them to be as productive as they once were. Evidence regarding training programs for older workers offered by employers is provided by many sources (e.g., Jessup and Greenberg, 1989; Opinion Research Corporation, 1992; Hirshorn and Hoyer, 1994). Nevertheless, training programs for older workers are uncommon in the private sector. Sara Rix (Chapter 16) points out that this is probably due to the basic incompatibility of training objectives with the reasons employers hire or retrain older workers. Employers usually hire or keep older workers because of their job skills or experience or because the firm needs to fill a part-time position. Training is not necessary in the first instance, and may be perceived as too expensive in the second.

Moreover, we know comparatively little about the relative productivity of older and younger workers, and even less about how this relative productivity may be influenced by training (Sterns, Sterns, and Hollis, Chapter 15). In the absence of evidence that it is more cost-effective to train older workers than to hire and train younger ones, employers have little incentive to develop training programs for older workers.

THE INCREASED INTEREST IN OLDER WORKER POLICY

It is clear that many factors influence the retirement decisions of older workers. Some of these factors are influenced by employer programs and policies; others are influenced by public policy—but what are the underlying motivations for the increased interest in older workers on the part of employers and policy makers? An understanding of these motivations is a necessary precondition for the design of effective programs for older workers. After all, programs are effective only to the extent that they satisfy their intended objectives. Moreover, program objectives are, of course, closely linked to the concerns prompting interest in program development in the first place.

Several reasons for the growing interest in older workers are evident from the literature: (1) concerns about future labor shortages, (2) concerns about financing pension and health care benefits, (3) equity issues stemming from the age distribution of public expenditures and rising life expectancy levels, and (4) the desire to enhance opportunities for productive roles for the elderly in society. Public policy is concerned with all of these areas; employers are concerned primarily with labor shortages and retiree benefit costs.

Labor Shortages

Several demographic trends currently underway could cause older workers to become more attractive to employers over the next several decades. Of these, population aging is the one most frequently cited as leading to a future growth in demand for older workers. Several studies have predicted that population aging, in conjunction with rapid growth in the industries that are the major employers of older persons, will lead to an increased demand for older workers (Drucker, 1985; Olson, Caton, and Duffy, 1981; Kieffer, 1983; Work in America Institute, 1980). Employers and policy makers alike are concerned that, as the population ages, the number of young, new labor force entrants will decline, possibly causing widespread labor shortages. Eric Kingson (Chapter 3) points out, however, that the labor force will, in fact, continue to grow—though at a slower pace than in the past. In addition, evidence from other countries also indicates that population aging does not necessarily lead to labor shortages. Stuart Dorsey and John Turner (Chapter 6) point out that several European countries are already demographically as old as the U.S. population will be when the baby boom cohort reaches retirement age. However, retirement ages in these countries remain below those of the United States because of high unemployment rates (i.e., these countries are experiencing labor surpluses, *not* labor shortages).

In his review of the economic theory of occupational labor shortages, Burt Barnow (Chapter 18) points out that the opportunities offered to older workers by occupational shortages depend on the cause of the shortage. Shortages can arise because of increases in demand, decreases in supply, or restrictions on wages. Barnow argues that changes in demand or supply will often lead to job opportunities for older workers. Although this is also true of restrictions on wages, the available jobs will tend to pay less than the market-clearing wage. If employers believe the shortage to be temporary, there may be no opportunities for any additional workers of any age. Instead, employers may have members of their existing labor force work additional hours. Older workers will also generally find it difficult to take advantage of opportunities in occupations where they lack experience if employers are reluctant to provide training.

Although some employers are interested in older workers as a potential labor supply pool to help them fill anticipated labor shortages, most are concerned about the higher costs and possible lower productivity of older workers relative to younger workers. The evidence to date indicates that older workers are more expensive than younger workers, but there is no strong evidence that older workers are also more productive. Consequently, it is not surprising that most employers remain more concerned with structuring incentives to encourage older workers to retire, rather than remain in the labor force.

Although infrequently mentioned in policy discussions, a second demographic trend may have even more important implications than population aging for the future demand for older workers—the rapid growth in minority population groups. Minority groups such as Hispanics and African Americans have traditionally had lower education levels than the population as a whole. As a consequence, many of the new entrants to the labor supply pool may have poorer job skills than older white workers. If so, it is hard to predict how employers will react. Employers may place stronger emphasis on the retraining of existing workers to keep workers' skills up to date. If so, the productivity of older workers may be enhanced and employers may choose to encourage older workers to remain on the job. On the other hand, employers may opt for training new labor force entrants, banking on a longer period to recoup their investment. Or, employers may decide to reduce their need for workers altogether by substituting capital (e.g., computers or robotics) for labor. The important point is that employers will *only* encourage the continued labor force participation of older workers if it is in the employers' economic interest to do so.

To the extent that employers decide to encourage continued labor force participation on the part of older workers, the most effective tools at their disposal are the retirement incentives created by private pension provisions and ERIPs. In all likelihood, the demand for older workers will differ substantially across industries because of variations in the growth of demand for different industries' products and the types of workers that these industries require. Some industries will experience shortages; others will not. Individual employers (especially those offering defined benefit plans) have the capability of responding to their labor force needs by altering private pension incentives or by offering (or not offering) ERIPs.

Although most employers are taking a "wait and see" approach to encouraging increased labor force participation of the elderly, the interest among policy makers is much stronger. From its inception, an important public policy objective of social security has been to remove older workers from the labor force. More recently, however, policy makers have become increasingly interested in changing social security provisions to encourage continued labor force participation on the part of older workers. For example, the 1983 Social Security

amendments introduced several policy changes that could cause older persons
to delay the date that they plan to retire:

- including up to 50 percent of benefits in taxable income for high-income beneficiaries (defined as $32,000 for a couple filing jointly and $25,000 for an individual);
- increasing the delayed retirement credit;
- liberalizing the earnings test; and
- gradually increasing the "normal retirement age" from 65 to 67 over the period 2000–2027.

The 1993 Omnibus Budget Reconciliation Act further increased the taxation
of social security benefits.

Studies of the impact of the 1983 social security amendments indicated that
the amendments probably would have relatively small effects on the retirement
decisions of older workers. The small effects stem from the health and economic
status of early retirees. Early retirees can be grouped into two categories. One
group tends to have significant health limitations and relatively low incomes,
while members of the other group tend to be healthy and have relatively high
retirement incomes. Individuals with health limitations may have little flexibility
in the timing of retirement (Podoff, 1986). As a result, the increased actuarial
penalties for early retirement will have the effect of lowering their retirement
incomes. Many older workers with adequate incomes may not alter the timing
of their retirement even though the policy changes have the effect of lowering
their income somewhat; for these workers the economic disincentives are outweighed by the desire to consume more leisure time. On the other hand, raising
the normal retirement age may have comparatively large effect on "encouraging" the increased labor force participation of low-income workers, many of
whom may be compelled to continue working until they reach the new (higher)
normal retirement age in order to obtain a higher retirement income. These
considerations raise serious equity issues regarding social security policies that
attempt to encourage the continued labor force participation of older workers
through retirement disincentives such as raising the normal retirement age.

If potential labor shortages were the only problem, social security policies to
encourage extended labor force participation on the part of older workers would
probably not be the most effective approach. In the absence of another econo-
mywide depression, labor shortages are likely to be concentrated in specific
industries and can be dealt with more effectively through private pension policies and ERIPs. In fact, social security policies that encourage continued labor
force participation may work at cross-purposes with employer attempts to encourage older workers to retire.

Pension and Health Care Financing

Potential labor shortages, however, are not the only policy concern driving
the interest in encouraging older persons to remain longer in the the labor force.

Another important motivation is concern about the affordability of an aging population. These concerns are shared by employers and policy makers alike. Employers have seen pension and health care benefit costs rise as their retiree populations have grown. Policy makers are concerned about the future solvency of the social security trust funds as members of the baby boom cohort enter retirement, and perhaps even more worried about the costs of health care for the elderly.

Although employers are concerned about the rising pension and health care costs associated with retirees, this concern has not translated into an increased demand for older workers to forestall their retirement. Rather, many employers have attempted to shift the responsibility for pensions to workers by switching from defined benefit to defined contribution plans. Similarly, many employers have reduced the generosity of health care coverage offered to retirees. Everything else equal, rising retiree benefit costs will reduce employer demand for older workers.

Like employers, public policy makers are concerned about rising pension and health care benefit costs associated with an aging workforce. The emphasis of public policy, however, has been to encourage increased labor force participation of older persons. The concerns of public policy makers about the financial implications of population aging are understandable. In 1950, there were about 7.5 persons aged 16–64 (of labor force age) for each person aged 65 and over; by 2025, this ratio will decline to about 3 younger persons to one senior. It is easy to conclude, based on these figures, that the support burden for each worker will rise dramatically when the baby boom enters the retirement years over the period 2015–2040 (Samuelson, 1988; Wattenberg, 1987). However, this conclusion is based on an oversimplified view of the problem.

The elderly are not the only population group that is largely outside the labor force. Children and many adults of labor force age also fall into this category. Moreover, many elderly persons *are* employed. Studies that take account of the labor force participation rates of all age groups invariably conclude that the support burden on members of the labor force age will be *lower* in the future than it was in the 1950s or 1960s (Adamchak and Friedmann, 1983; Crown, 1985). The reason is that the same individuals who were the baby boom children of the 1950s and 1960s will be the baby boom retirees of 2015–2040. In the meantime, however, the labor force will more than double in size. In short, despite rhetoric to the contrary, there is little evidence of a demographic "time bomb."

Of course, it can be argued that if the support costs of older people are higher than those of children, the support burden on workers may rise nevertheless. Again, however, studies that account for the relative costs of supporting children and older persons conclude that the support burden will be lower when members of the baby boom retire than it was when they were children (Clark and Spengler, 1978; Dixon and Thame, 1984; Wander, 1978; Schulz, Borowski, and Crown, 1991; and Cutler et al., 1990).

Finally, *any* measure of the support burden arising from population aging—even those that take account of the relative costs of supporting younger and older persons—will *underestimate* the degree to which relative support costs could rise before an increased burden would be placed on workers. This is because, to the extent that real economic growth occurs over time, there is the potential to allocate some of this growth to nonworking members of society without imposing an increased burden on workers. Crown (1988) estimated that if the real rate of economic growth averaged 2.0 percent over the period from 1985 to 2050, the real costs of supporting each nonworking person could be 5.6 times higher than in 1960 without any increased burden to society. Moreover, there is an exponentially increasing relationship between real economic growth rates and the support costs that could be sustained without an increased burden on workers. Thus, although the implications of population aging need to be closely monitored, there is no convincing evidence that the burden on future members of the labor force will be too great to bear.

Equity Issues

In the current environment of limited fiscal resources, an equity issue has arisen with respect to trends in the incomes of older and younger persons over the last two decades. Stated bluntly, some have argued that the old are getting richer at the expense of the young (Chakravarty and Weisman, 1988). Over 1970–1989, the real median income of older households increased by 41 percent. The real median incomes of younger households, however, increased by less than 4 percent over the same period. Most disturbing of all, the poverty rate for children stood at 23 percent in 1991. However, despite the superficial appearance of a relationship between improvements in the economic status of the elderly and the rise in poverty among children, several studies have concluded that the income gains of the elderly are independent of the factors creating the rise in poverty among children (Scholl and Moon, 1989; Ryscavage, 1987; Smolensky, Danziger, and Gottschalk, 1988). The rise in poverty among children is a complex phenomenon related to the impacts of the baby boom on labor markets, the increased labor force participation of women, and the rise in single, female-headed households with children. In contrast, since the mid-1970s the economic gains of the aged have come about primarily from improvements in employer pension and asset income. Thus, as with concerns regarding future labor shortages and the affordability of an aging population, there is little evidence to support the claim that the income gains of the aged have come at the expense of the young.

A second equity issue has emerged from the rising life expectancy of older persons. Podoff (1986) pointed out that several advisory panels considered raising the social security normal retirement age during the late 1970s and early 1980s. In each case, the motivation was concern about social security financing and the need to take account of improvements in life expectancy that have occurred since the passage of the Social Security Act in 1935. Although it is undeniable that improvements in life expectancy have taken place over the last six decades, analysts are much less certain about improvements in the ability to work (see Kingson, Chapter 3 of this volume).

Enhancing Productive Roles for Older Persons

Advocates for the elderly have long argued that expanded employment opportunities for older workers would have a variety of socially desirable outcomes. From the perspective of older persons, greater employment opportunities would enhance their sense of self-esteem, provide them with a mechanism for remaining socially connected, and avail them of earnings opportunities. From society's perspective, enhanced employment opportunities for older workers may reduce public pension costs and enable the economy to take full advantage of older workers' experience and productive capacity.

On the other hand, we are prone to forget, in our haste to deal with concerns about future labor shortages and pension financing, that there is a potential opportunity cost to encouraging increased labor force participation on the part of older persons. In Chapter 14, Scott Bass and Francis Caro describe a variety of roles for older persons that constitute productive aging. For example, in addition to participation in the paid labor force, productive aging roles include volunteering and informal caregiving. To what extent would the increased labor force participation of older persons come at the expense of other roles for the elderly persons in society? Perhaps it is possible to increase the labor force participation of older persons without reducing the availability of older persons for other socially productive roles, but this is unclear. At a minimum, the opportunity cost of encouraging increased labor force participation of the elderly needs to be considered in public policy discussions.

WHAT ROLE FOR OLDER WORKER POLICY?

Crown (1990) has noted that older worker programs and policies can be broadly categorized into two types—those that use employment incentives and those that use retirement disincentives. Programs and policies that use employment incentives (e.g., employment or training programs, enforcement of the ADEA) usually involve visible costs. Employment incentives can also involve reductions in government revenues. This would be the case, for example, if the earnings test in social security were eliminated. The benefits of programs that use employment incentives can be measured in terms of jobs created, but it is often not always obvious whether these benefits are worth the costs or whether they would have taken place even in the absence of the incentives. Finally, the opportunity costs of *not* pursuing such programs are almost never considered.

In contrast, programs and policies using retirement disincentives (e.g., raising the normal retirement age under social security and the taxation of benefits) usually do not involve direct expenditures. On the contrary, retirement disincentives may have (or appear to have) positive revenue implications. For example, raising the normal retirement age for receipt of social security benefits is intended to reduce total social security payments. The costs of retirement disincentives, however, are generally borne by older workers. This distinction in approaches to employment policies and programs is important because the use of the "carrot" (employment incentives) versus the "stick" (retirement disincentives) tends to differ systematically with the issues that motivate the creation of these programs and policies in the first place.

Concerns about future labor shortages, intergenerational equity, and pension financing tend to result in policies that rely on retirement disincentives. In contrast, policies that strive to give older persons broader employment opportunities tend to rely on employment incentives. In recent years, public policy concerns have placed the emphasis on retirement disincentives. Policy makers must recognize that this emphasis has important equity implications for those with low incomes or poor health. It may also reduce the availability of older persons for other socially productive roles, such as volunteering and informal care. Finally, public policy to encourage delayed retirement currently runs counter to early retirement incentives in private pension plans.

This does not mean that policy makers need to give up altogether on encouraging the increased employment of older workers, but there is clearly a need to broaden the set of factors that they consider when developing older worker initiatives. These factors include the relative merits of retirement disincentives versus employment incentives, the distributional consequences and opportunity costs associated with alternative policies, and some serious soul-searching about why the policies are being pursued in the first place.

References

Abel, N., and Folbre, M. 1990. "A Methodology for Revising Estimates: Female Market Participation in the U.S. before 1940."*Historical Methods*, 23(4):167–76.

Achenbaum, W. A. 1978. *Old Age in a New Land*. Baltimore, Md.: Johns Hopkins University Press.

———. 1983. *Shades of Gray*. Boston: Little, Brown.

———. 1986a. "The Meaning of Risk, Rights, and Responsibilities in Aging America." In *What Does It Mean to Grow Old?* ed. T. R. Cole and S. Gadow. Durham, N.C.: Duke University Press.

———. 1986b. *Social Security: Visions and Revisions*. Cambridge, Cambridge University Press.

Adamchak, D., and Friedmann, E. 1983. "Societal Aging and Generational Dependency Relationships: Problems of Measurement and Conceptualization." *Research on Aging*, 5:319–38.

Age Discrimination in Employment Act of 1967. 29 U.S.C. Sec. 621 et seq. (1976 and Supp V. 1981 & 1986).

Ahrend, P., and Walkiewicz, N. 1991. *Private Pensions in the Federal Republic of Germany*. Country Report for the Organization of Economic Cooperation and Development. Paris, France.

Allen, F. 1989. "U.S. West Offers Retirement Plan to Cut Costs." *Wall Street Journal* (December 1): A6.

Allen, P. A., Ashcraft, M. H., and Weber, T. A. 1992. "On Mental Multiplication and Age." *Psychology and Aging*, 7(4):536–45.

Allen, S., Clark, R., and McDermed, A. 1992. "Post-Retirement Benefits Increases in the 1980s." In *Trends in Pensions 1992*, ed. John A. Turner and Daniel J. Beller. Washington, D.C.: U.S. Government Printing Office.

Alpaugh, P. K., and Birren, J. E. 1977. "Variables Affecting Creative Contributions across the Adult Life Span." *Human Development*, 20:240–48.

Alpaugh, P. K., Parham, I. A., Cole, K. D., and Birren, J. E. 1982. "Creativity in Adulthood and Old Age: An Exploratory Study." *Educational Gerontologist*, 8:101–16.

American Association for Retired Persons. 1985. *Workers over 50: Old Myths, New Realities*. Washington, D.C.: American Association for Retired Persons.

———. 1986. *Work and Retirement: Employees over 40 and Their Views*. Washington, D.C.: American Association of Retired Persons.

———. 1989. *Business and Older Workers: Current Perceptions and New Directions for the 1990's*. Washington, D.C.: American Association of Retired Persons.

———. 1993. *The Older Workforce: Recruitment and Retention*. Washington, D.C.: American Association of Retired Persons.

American Management Association. 1993. *AMA Survey on Downsizing and Assistance to Displaced Workers*. New York: American Management Association.

Anderson, K., and Burkhauser, R. 1985. "The Retirement-Health Nexus: A New Measure of An Old Puzzle." *Journal of Human Resources*, 20(3): 315–30.

Anderson, K., Burkhauser, R., and Quinn, J. 1986. "Do Retirement Dreams Come True? The Effect of Unanticipated Events on Retirement Plans." *Industrial and Labor Relations Review*, 39(4):518–26

Andrisani, P. 1977. Effects of Health Problems on the Work Experience of Middle-Aged Men. *Industrial Gerontology*, 4(2):97–112.

Andrisani, P., and Daymont, T. 1987. "Age Changes in Productivity and Earnings Among Managers and Professionals." In *The Problem Isn't Age: Work and Older Americans*, ed. S. H. Sandell. New York: Praeger.

Annis, J. F., Case, H. W., Clausen, C. E., and Bradtmiller, B. 1991. "Anthropometry of an Aging Work Force." *Experimental Aging Research*, 17(3):157–76.

Anrig, G., Jr. 1988. "How to Retire Early and Comfortably." *Money*, 17(12):58–66.

Antonovsky, A., and Sagy, S. 1990. "Confronting Developmental Tasks in the Retirement Transition." *The Gerontologist*, 30(3):362–68.

Apps, P. 1991. "Tax Reform, Population Ageing and the Changing Labour Force Supply Behaviour of Married Women." *Journal of Population Economics*, 4:201–16.

Arrow, K., and Capron, W. 1959. "Dynamic Shortages and Price Rises: The Engineer-Scientist Case." *Quarterly Journal of Economics* 73(2):292–308.

Atchley, R. 1976. *The Sociology of Retirement*. Cambridge, MA: Schenkman.

———. 1989. "A Continuity Theory of Normal Aging." *The Gerontologist*, 29(2):183–90.

Atkinson, A., and Sutherland, H. 1993. "Two Nations in Early Retirement? The Case of Britain." In *Age, Work and Social Security*, ed. A. B. Atkinson and Martin Rein. New York: St. Martin's Press.

Avioli, P. S., and Kaplan, E. 1992. "A Panel Study of Married Women's Work Patterns." *Sex Roles*, 26:227–42.

Avolio, B., and Waldman, D. 1984. "A Job Analytic Assessment of Age Bias: The Neglected Error in Personnel Research." *The Gerontologist*, 24 (special issue): 247.

———. 1989. "Ratings of Managerial Skill Requirements: Comparison of Age and Job-Related Factors." *Psychology and Aging*, 4(4):408–70.

Avolio, B., Waldman, D., and McDaniel, M. 1990. "Age and Work Performance in

Nonmanagerial Jobs: The Effects of Experience and Occupational Type." *Academy of Management Journal*, 33(2):407–22.

Avolio, B. J., and Barrett, G. V. 1987. "The Effects of Age Stereotyping in a Simulated Interview." *Psychology and Aging*, 2:56–63.

Avolio, B. J., Barrett, G. V., and Sterns, H. L. 1984. "Alternative to Age for Assessing Occupational Performance Capacity." *Experimental Aging Research*, 10:101–5.

Ayoub, M. M., Dryden, R., McDaniel, J., Kniper, R., and Dixon, D. 1979. "Predicting Lifting Capacity." *American Industrial Hygiene Association Journal*, 40:1075–84.

Bailey, R. C. 1967. *The Equitable Life Insurance Society of New York*. 2 vols. New York: Appleton-Century-Croft.

Baily, M. 1987. "Aging and the Ability to Work." In *Work, Health, and the Elderly*, ed. Gary Burtless, 59–97. Washington D.C.: Brookings Institution.

Baldwin, S., and Sandell, S. 1988. "Older Workers and Employment Shifts: Policy Responses to Displacement." In *The Aging Workforce*, ed. Irving Bluestone, Rhonda Montgomery, and John Owen. Detroit, Mich.: Wayne State University Press.

Baltes, P. B. 1993. "The Aging Mind: Potential and Limitations." *The Gerontologist*, 33(5):580–94.

Baltes, P. B., Reese, H. W., and Lipsitt, L. P. 1980. "Life-Span Developmental Psychology." *Annual Review of Psychology*, 31:65–110.

Barker, D., and Clark, R. 1980. "Mandatory Retirement and Labor Force Participation of Respondents in the Retirement History Study." *Social Security Bulletin*, 43(11):20–29.

Barnow, B., and Bawden, D. 1991. *Skill Gaps in the Year 2000: A Review of the Literature*. Washington, D.C.: The Urban Institute.

Barnow, B., Chasanov, A., and Pande, A. 1990. *Financial Incentives for Employer-Provided Training: A Review of Relevant Experience in the United States and Abroad*. Washington, D.C.: Urban Institute Policy Memorandum prepared for the U.S. Department of Labor.

Barrett, G. V., and Maurer, T. J. 1992. "The Task/Job Analysis Predictor Development Process: Critical Issues in Tailored Employment Ability Testing." Unpublished manuscript.

Barringer, M., and Mitchell, O. 1993. "Health Insurance Choice and the Older Worker." In *As the Workforce Ages*, ed. Olivia S. Mitchell, 125–46. Ithaca, N.Y.: ILR Press.

Bartel, Ann, and Taubman, Paul. 1979. "Health and Labor Market Success: The Role of Various Diseases." *Review of Economics and Statistics*, 61(1):1–8.

Barth, M., and McNaught, W. 1989. *Why Workers Retire Early*. Americans over 55 at Work Program. Background paper no. 1. New York: Commonwealth Fund.

———. 1991. "The Impact of Future Demographic Shifts on the Employment of Older Workers." *Human Resource Management*, 30 (Spring): 31–43.

Barth, M., McNaught, W., and Rizzi, P. 1993. "Corporations and the Aging Workforce." In *Building the Competitive Workforce: Investing Human Capital for Corporate Success*, ed. Philip H. Mirvis, 156–200. New York: John Wiley and Sons.

———. 1994. "Work and Work Effort among Older People." In *Active and aging*, ed. Scott Bass. New Haven, Conn: Yale University Press.

Bass, S. 1995. "Older and Active." In *Older and* Active, ed. Scott Bass. New Haven, Conn.: Yale University Press.

Bass, S., and Barth, M. 1992. *The Next Educational Opportunity: Career Training for Older Adults*. Americans over 55 at Work Program. Background paper no. 7. New York: Commonwealth Fund.

Bass, S., and Caro, F., 1992. "The New Politics of Productive Aging." *In Depth*, 2(3): 59–79.

Bass, S., Quinn, J., and Burkhauser, R., 1995. "Towards Pro-Work Policies and Programs for Older Americans." In *Older and Active*, ed. Scott Bass. New Haven, Conn.: Yale University Press.

Bazzoli, G. 1985. "The Early Retirement Decision: New Empirical Evidence on the Influence of Health." *Journal of Human Resources*, 20(2):214–34.

Beck, S. 1985. "Determinants of Labor Force Activity among Retired Men." *Research on Aging*, 7(2):251–80.

Becker, G. 1962. "Investment in Human Capital: A Theoretical Analysis." *Journal of Political Economy*, 70:9–49.

———. 1964. *Human Capital*. New York: National Bureau of Economic Research, Columbia University Press.

———. 1965. "A Theory of the Allocation of Time." *Economic Journal*, 75 (September): 493–517.

———. 1975. *Human Capital*. 2nd ed. New York: National Bureau of Economic Research.

Bell, T. 1941. *Out of This Furnace*. Pittsburgh, Pa.: University of Pittsburgh Press.

Beller, D., and Lawrence, H. 1992. "Trends in Private Pension Coverage." In *Trends in Pensions 1992*, ed. John A. Turner and Daniel J. Beller. Washington, D.C.: U.S. Government Printing Office.

Beller, D., and McCarthy, D. 1992. "Private Pension Benefits." In *Trends in Pensions 1992*, ed. John A. Turner and Daniel J. Beller. Washington, D.C.: U.S. Government Printing Office.

Bendick, M., Jr., Jackson, C., and Romero, J. H. 1993. *Employment Discrimination against Older Workers: An Experimental Study of Hiring Practices*. Washington, D.C.: Fair Employment Council of Greater Washington, Inc.

Berkovec, J., and Stern, S. 1991. "Job Exit Behavior of Older Men." *Econometrica*, 59(1):189–210.

Bird, C. P., and Fisher, T. D. 1986. "Thirty Years Later: Attitudes toward the Employment of Older Workers." *Journal of Applied Psychology*, 71:515–17.

Birren, J. E., and Stafford, J. I. 1986. "Changes in the Organization of Behavior with Age." In *Age, Health, and Employment*, ed. J. E. Birren, P. K. Robinson, and J. E. Livingston, 1–26. Englewood Cliffs, N. J.: Prentice-Hall.

Blank, D., and Stigler, G. 1957. *The Demand and Supply of Scientific Personnel*. New York: National Bureau of Economic Research.

Blau, D. 1992. "Labor Force Dynamics of Older Men." University of North Carolina at Chapel Hill. Mimeographed.

Boa, R. 1987. "Work and Response to Low and Decreasing Real Income during Retirement." *Research on Aging*, 9(3):428–40.

Boes, D., and von Weizsaecker, R. K. 1989. "Economic Consequences of an Aging Population." *European Economic Review*, 33:345–54.

Bondar, J. 1993. "Beneficiaries Affected by the Annual Earnings Test, 1989." *Social Security Bulletin*, 56 (Spring): 20–28.

Borg, G. 1962. *Physical Performance and Perceived Exertion*. Copenhagen, Denmark: Ejnar Munskgaard.

Boskin, M. 1977. "Social Security and Retirement Decisions." *Economic Inquiry*, 15 (January): 1–25.

Boskin, M., and Hurd, M. 1978. "The Effect of Social Security on Early Retirement." *Journal of Public Economics*, 10 (December): 361–77.

Bound, J. 1989. "The Health and Earnings of Rejected Disability Insurance Applicants." *American Economic Review*, 79(3):482–503.

———. 1991. "Self-reported versus Objective Measures of Health in Retirement Models." *Journal of Human Resources*, 26(1):106–38.

Bound, J., and Waidmann, T. 1992. "Disability Transfers, Self-Reported Health, and the Labor Force Attachment of Older Men: Evidence from the Historical Record." *Quarterly Journal of Economics*, 109 (November): 1393–419.

Bouvier, L., and DeVita, C. 1991, November. *The Baby Boom—Entering Midlife*. Washington, D.C.: Population Reference Bureau.

Bové, R. 1987. "Retraining the Older Worker." *Training and Development Journal*, 41(3):77–78.

Brackenridge, H. H. (1804) 1965. In *Modern Chivalry*, ed. L. Leary. New Haven, Conn.: College and University Press.

Brady, E. M., Fortinsky, R. H., Norland, S., and Eichar, D. 1989. *Predictors of Success among Older Workers in New Jobs*. Final Report. Gorham, Maine, University of Southern Maine, Human Services Development Institute.

Brennan, M., Taft, P., and Schupack, M. 1967. *The Economics of Age*. New York: W. W. Norton.

Brinkley, A. 1993. *The Unfinished Nation*. New York: McGraw-Hill.

Brody, M. 1987. "Helping Workers to Work Smarter." *Fortune* (June 8): 86–89.

Bruce, S. 1988. *Pension Claims: Rights and Obligations*. Washington, D.C.: Bureau of National Affairs.

Brudney, J., and Scott, H. 1987. *Forced Out*. New York: Simon and Schuster.

Buck Consultants. 1989, December. *Pre-Retirement Planning Survey*. New York: Buck Consultants.

Bureau of National Affairs, Inc. 1989. "Waivers used by 28% of Firms with Exit Incentive Programs, GAO says." *BNA Pension Reporter* (6):852.

Burkhauser, R. 1979. "The Pension Acceptance Decision of Older Workers." *Journal of Human Resources*, 14 (Winter): 63–75.

———. 1980. "The Early Acceptance of Social Security: An Asset Maximization Approach." *Industrial and Labor Relations Review*, 33 (July): 484–92.

Burkhauser, R., and Quinn, J. 1983. "Is Mandatory Retirement Overrated? Evidence from the 1970s." *Journal of Human Resources*, 18(3): 337–58.

———. 1993. "Changing Policy Signals." In *Age and Structural Lag: Essays on Changing Work, Retirement and Other Structures*, ed. Matilda White Riley, Robert L. Kahn, and Anne Foner. Washington, D.C.: American Association for the Advancement of Science.

Burtless, G. 1986. "Social Security, Unanticipated Benefit Increases, and the Timing of Retirement." *Review of Economic Studies*, 53 (October): 781–805.

———. 1987. "Occupational Effects on the Health and Work Capacity of Older Men."

In *Work, Health, and the Elderly,* ed. Gary Burtless, 104–42. Washington, D.C.: Brookings Institution.

———. 1993. "The Fiscal Challenge of an Aging Population." In *As the Workforce Ages: Costs, Benefits, and Policy Challenges*, ed. Olivia Mitchell, 225–52. Ithaca, N.Y.: ILR Press.

Burtless, G., and Moffitt, R. 1984. "The Effect of Social Security Benefits on the Labor Supply of the Aged." In *Retirement and Economic Behavior*, ed. Henry J. Aaron and Gary Burtless, 135–74. Washington, D.C.: Brookings Institution.

———. 1985. "The Joint Choice of Retirement Age and Postretirement Hours of Work." *Journal of Labor Economics*, 3(2):209–36.

Butler, J. S., Burkhauser, R., Mitchell, J., and Pincus, T. 1987. "Measurement Error in Self-Reported Health Variables." *Review of Economics and Statistics*, 69 (February): 644–50.

Butler, R. 1982. "Testimony before the National Commission on Social Security Reform." Washington, D.C.: National Commission on Social Security Reform.

Calasanti, T. 1993. "Bringing in Diversity: Toward an Inclusive Theory of Retirement." *Journal of Aging Studies*, 7(2):133–50.

Caldwell, C. 1846. *Thoughts on the Effects of Age on the Human Condition*. Louisville, Ky.: John C. Noble.

Campbell, J. C. 1992. *How Policies Change*. Princeton, N.J.: Princeton University Press.

Carey, M. 1988. "Occupational Tenure in 1987: Many Workers Have Remained in Their Fields." *Monthly Labor Review*, 111(10):3–12.

Carnegie Inquiry into the Third Age. 1993. *Final Report: Life, Work and Livelihood in the Third Age*. Dunfermline UK: Carnegie United Kingdom Trust.

Carnevale, A. 1986. "The Learning Enterprise." *Training and Development Journal*, 40(1):18–26.

———. 1993. "Developing the New Competitive Workforce." Paper prepared for a conference of the National Planning Association/National Council on the Aging, Joint Project on U.S. Competitiveness and the Aging American Workforce. Washington, D.C.

Caro, F., and Bass, S. 1995. "Dimensions of Productive Aging." In *Older and Active*, ed. S. Bass. New Haven, Conn.: Yale University Press.

Caro, F., Bass, S., and Chen, Y. 1993. "Introduction: Achieving a Productive Aging Society." In *Achieving a Productive Aging Society*, ed. S. Bass, F. Caro, and Y. Chen, Westport, Conn.: Auburn House.

Caro, F., and Morris, R. 1992–1993. "Retraining Older Workers: An Emerging Economic Need." *Community College Journal*, 63(3):22–26.

Carrington, W. 1993. "Wage Losses for Displaced Workers: Is It Really the Firm That Matters?" *Journal of Human Resources*, 28(3):435–62.

Centaur Associates, Inc. 1986. *Report on the 502(e) Experimental Projects Funded under Title V of the Older Americans Act*. Washington, D.C.: Centaur Associates.

Cerella, J. 1990. "Aging and Information Processing Rate." In *Handbook of the Psychology of Aging*, ed. J. E. Birren and K. W. Schaie, 201–21. 3rd. ed. New York: Academic Press.

Chaffin, D. B., and Ashton-Miller, J. A. 1991. "Biomechanical Aspects of Low Back Pain in the Older Worker." *Experimental Aging Research*, 17(3):177–87.

Chakravarty, S., and Weisman, K. 1988. "Consuming Our Children?" *Forbes* (November 14): 222–32.

Chambre, Susan. 1984. "Is Volunteering a Substitute for Role Loss in Old Age? An Empirical Test of Activity Theory." *The Gerontologist*, 24(3):292–98.

Chapman, S., LaPlante, M., and Wilensky, G. 1986. "Life Expectancy and Health Status of the Aged." *Social Security Bulletin*, 49(10):24–48.

Charles D. Spencer and Associates. 1983. "Early Retirement Incentives: A Survey of Corporate Employers."

———. 1992. "Survey of Early Retirement Incentives 1991; Components of Private, Public Employers' Offers." Newsletter. (April 24): 1–10, 10A.

Charness, N. 1981. "Aging and Skilled Problem Solving." *Journal of Experimental Psychology: General*, 110:21–38.

———. 1983. "Aging and Problem-Solving Performance." In *Aging and Human Performance*. New York: Wiley.

Charness, N., and Bosman, E. 1990. "Human Factors and Design for Older Adults." In *Handbook of the Psychology of Aging*, ed. J. E. Birren and K. W. Schaie, 446–63. 3rd ed. New York: Van Nostrand Reinhold.

Chen, Yung-Ping. 1992. "The Role of Private Pensions in the Income of Older Americans." In *Trends in Pensions 1992*, ed. John A. Turner and Daniel J. Beller, 393–417. Washington, D.C.: U.S. Government Printing Office.

Cherlin, A., and Furstenberg, F. 1982. *The Shape of the American Family in the Year 2000*. Trends Analysis Program. Washington, D.C.: American Council of Life Insurance (Fall).

———. 1986. *The New American Grandparent: A Place in the Family, a Life Apart.* New York: Basic Books.

Christensen, Kathleen, 1990. "Bridges over Troubled Water: How Older Workers View the Labor Market." In *Bridges to Retirement*, ed. Peter B. Doeringer. Ithaca, N.Y.: ILR Press.

Clague, E., Pahli, B., and Kramer, L. 1971. *The Aging Worker and the Union.* New York: Praeger Press.

Clark, R. 1990. "Pensions in an Aging Society." In *The Aging of the American Workforce*, ed. Irving Bluestone, Rhonda J. V. Montgomery, and John D. Owen, 75–100. Detroit, Mich.: Wayne State University Press.

———. 1991a. "Population Aging and Retirement Policy: An International Perspective." Pension Research Council Working Paper 91-7. University of Pennsylvania.

———. 1991b. *Retirement Systems in Japan*. Homewood, Ill.: Irwin.

———1993. "Population Aging and Work Rates of Older Persons: An International Comparison." In *As the Workforce Ages*, ed. Olivia S. Mitchell. Ithaca, N.Y.: ILR Press.

Clark, R., Johnson, T., and McDermed, A. 1980. "Allocation of Time and Resources by Married Couples Approaching Retirement." *Social Security Bulletin*, 43 (April): 3–16.

Clark, R., and Spengler, J. 1978. "Changing Demography and Dependency Costs: The Implications of Future Dependency Ratios and Their Composition." In *Aging and Income: Programs and Prospects for the Elderly*, ed. B. Herzog. New York: Human Service Press.

Cohen, N. 1993. "Sigh of Relief on Pensions." *Financial Times* (April 29).

Cohen, W. J. 1957. *Retirement Policies under Social Security.* Berkeley: University of California Press.

Coleman, L. 1993. "The Black Americans Who Keep Working." In *Aging in Black America*, ed. James S. Jackson, Linda M. Chatters, and Robert Joseph Taylor. Newbury Park, Calif.: Sage Publications.

Coleman, M., and Pencavel, J. 1993. "Trends in Market Work of Women since 1940." *Industrial and Labor Relations Review*, 46 (July): 653–76.

Commerce Clearing House. 1988. *1988 ASPA/CCH Survey: Managing the Aging Work Force*. Washington, D.C.: Commerce Clearing House (CCH).

Commission on Workforce Quality and Labor Market Efficiency. 1989. *Investing in People: A Strategy to Address America's Workforce Crisis*. Washington, D.C.: U.S. Department of Labor.

Commonwealth Fund. 1993a. *Health Care Costs and Older Workers*. New York: Commonwealth Fund.

———. 1993b. *The Untapped Resource: The Final Report of the Americans over 55 at Work Program*. New York: Commonwealth Fund.

Copperman, L. F., and Keast, F. D. 1983. *Adjusting to an Older Work Force*. New York: Van Nostrand Reinhold.

Cowgill, D., and Holmes, L. 1972. *Aging and Modernization*. New York: Appleton-Century-Crofts.

Crawford, C. 1993. *Multiple Employment Programs: National Employment Training Strategy Needed: Testimony before the Subcommittee on Education, Labor, and Health and Human Services, Committee on Appropriations, U.S. Senate*. Washington, D.C.: U.S. General Accounting Office.

Cross, K. P. 1981. *Adults as Learners*. San Francisco, Calif.: Jossey-Bass.

Crown, W. 1985. "Some Thoughts on Reformulating the Dependency Ratio." *The Gerontologist*, 24 (April): 166–71.

———. 1988. "The Prospective Burden of an Aging Population." In *Retirement Reconsidered*, ed. R. Morris and S. Bass, 89–106. New York: Springer Publishing Co.

———. 1990. "Economic Trends, Politics, and Employment Policy for Older Workers." *Journal of Aging and Social Policy*, 2(3/4):131–51.

———. 1993. "Projecting the Costs of Aging Populations." *Generations*, 18(4):32–36.

Crown, W., Mutschler, P., Schulz, J., and Loew, R. 1993. *The Economic Status of Divorced Older Women*. Waltham, Mass.: Brandeis University, Heller School, Policy Center on Aging.

Cutler, D., Poterba, J., Sheiner, L., and Summers, L. 1990. *An Aging Society: Opportunity or Challenge?* Vol. 1 of *Brookings Papers on Economic Activity*. Washington, D.C.: Brookings Institution.

Czaja, Sara J., and Sharit, Joseph. 1993. "Age Differences in the Performance of Computer-Based Work." *Psychology and Aging*, 8(1):59–67.

Dailey, L., and Turner, J. 1992. "U.S. Pensions in World Perspective." In *Trends in Pensions 1992*, ed. John A. Turner and Daniel J. Beller. Washington, D.C.: U.S. Government Printing Office, 11–34.

Dallach, M. 1993. "Old Age, American Style." *New Outlook*, (October): 162.

Davies, D. R., and Sparrow, P. R. 1985. "Age and Work Behavior." In *Aging and Human Performance*, ed. N. Charness. Chichester: John Wiley & Sons, 293–332.

Davis, K. 1991. *Life Satisfaction and Older Adults*. Americans over 55 at Work Program. Background paper no. 6. New York: Commonwealth Fund.

Day, J. C. 1992. "Population Projections of the United States, by Age, Sex, Race, and Hispanic Origin: 1992 to 2050." *Current Population Reports*, Series P-25, No. 1092. Washington: U.S. Government Printing Office.

Deaton, A., and Muellbauer, J. 1980. *Economics and Consumer Behavior*. Cambridge, UK: Cambridge University Press.

de Vroom, Bert, and Blomsma, Martin. 1991. "The Netherlands: An Extreme Case." In *Time for Retirement: Comparative Studies of Early Exit from the Labor Force*, ed. Martin Kohli, Martin Rein, Anne-Marie Guillemard, and Herman Van Gunsteren. Cambridge, England: Cambridge University Press, 97–126.

Diamond, P., and Hausman, J. 1984a. "Individual Retirement and Savings Behavior." *Journal of Public Economics*, 23 (February-March): 81–114.

———. 1984b. "The Retirement and Unemployment Behavior of Older Men." In *Retirement and Economic Behavior*, ed. Henry J. Aaron and Gary Burtless, 97–134. Washington, D.C.: Brookings Institution.

Diefendorff, J. M., Quickle, T., Lord, R. G., Sanders, R. E. and Hepburn, E. T. 1995. "Goal-related Inhibition: Application of a Negative Priming Paradigm." Unpublished paper presented at the annual convention of the Society for Industrial/Organizational Psychology. Orlando, Florida.

Dixon, R., and Thame, C. 1984. "The Relative Costs to Government of the Young and Old." *Australian Quarterly*, 56(1):41–52.

Doering, M., Rhodes, S., and Schuster, M. 1983. *The Aging Worker: Research and Recommendations*. Beverly Hills, Calif.: Sage Publications.

Doescher, T., and Turner, J. 1988. "Social Security Benefits and the Baby Boom Generation." *American Economic Review*, 78 (May): 76–80.

Dorland, W. 1908. *The Age of Mental Virility*. New York: Century Company.

Doyle, F. P. 1990. "The Effect of Older Work Forces on Individual Firms, Labor Unions and Industries." In *The Aging of the American Work Force*, ed. I. Bluestone, R. J. V. Montgomery, and J. D. Owen, 290–95. Detroit, Mich.: Wayne State University Press.

Drucker, P. 1985. *Innovation and Entrepreneurship: Practice and Principles*. New York: Harper and Row.

Dunlop, D. 1980. *Mandatory Retirement Policy: A Human Rights Dilemma*. Ottawa, Canada: Conference Board.

Dunn, D. 1989. "Early Retirement: It Pays to Plan Early." *Business Week* (February 27): 134–35.

Easterlin, R. A. 1991. "The Economic Impact of Prospective Population Changes in Advanced Industrial Countries: An Historical Perspective." *Journal of Gerontology: Social Sciences*, 46:S299–S309.

Eck, A. 1993. "Job-Related Education and Training: Their Impact on Earnings." *Monthly Labor Review*, 116(10):21–38.

Ehrenberg, R., and Smith, R. 1993. *Modern Labor Economics: Theory and Public Policy*. 5th ed. New York: HarperCollins.

Ekerdt, D. 1986. "The Busy Ethic: Moral Continuity between Work and Retirement." *The Gerontologist*, 26(3):239.

———. 1989. "Economic Blinkers in Retirement Research." *The Gerontologist*, 29(5): 707.

Ekerdt, D., and DeViney, S. 1990. "On Defining Persons as Retired." *Journal of Aging Studies*, 4:211–29.

———. 1993. "Evidence for a Preretirement Process among Older Male Workers." *Journal of Gerontology: Social Sciences*, 48(2):S35–S43.

Ekerdt, D., Vinick, B., and Bosse, R. 1989. "Orderly Endings: Do Men Know When They Will Retire?" *Journal of Gerontology: Social Sciences*, 44(1):S28–S35.

Elias, P., Elias, M., Robbins, M., and Gage, P. 1987. "Acquisition of Word Processing Skills by Younger, Middle-Age, and Older Adults." *Psychology and Aging*, 2(4): 340–48.

Epstein, A. 1929. "Facing Old Age." *Commonweal*, 11 (December 1): 3–6.

Erikson, E. 1963. *Childhood and Society*. 2nd ed. New York: Norton and Company.

Ermisch, J., and Joshi, H. 1987. *Demographic Change, Economic Growth and Social Welfare in Europe*. Discussion paper no. 179. London: Centre for Economic Policy Research.

Fair, R. C., and Dominguez, K. M. 1991. "Effects of the Changing U.S. Age Distribution on Macroeconomic Equations." *American Economic Review*, 81:1276–94.

Farber, H. 1993. "The Incidence and Costs of Job Loss: 1982–91." Working paper no. 309. Princeton University, Industrial Relations Section.

Farrell, J., Alexander, R., Lord, R., Deiffendorf, J., and Sanders, R. 1994. "Age-Related Declines in Negative Priming: A Meta-Analysis." Unpublished manuscript. University of Akron, Ohio.

Fatsis, S. 1993. "IBM to Cut Its Buy-Out Packages." *Boston Globe* (April 6): 41, 57.

Fay, C. 1993. *A New Look at Compensation and Related Human Resource Management Systems*. Americans over 55 at Work Program. Background paper no. 10. New York: Commonwealth Fund.

Federal Old-Age and Survivors Insurance and Disability Insurance Trust Funds. Board of Trustees. 1994. *Annual Report of the Federal Old-Age and Survivors Insurance and Disability Insurance Trust Funds*. Washington, D.C.: U.S. Government Printing Office.

Feldman, J. 1983. "Work Ability of the Aged under Conditions of Improving Mortality." *Milbank Memorial Fund Quarterly/Health and Society*, 61(3):430–44.

———. 1991. "Has Increased Longevity Increased Potential Worklife?" In *Proceedings of the Second Conference of the National Academy of Social Insurance*, ed. Alicia Munnell. Washington, D.C.: National Academy of Social Insurance.

Fields, G., and Mitchell, O. 1984. *Retirement, Pensions, and Social Security*. Cambridge, Mass.: Massachusetts Institute of Technology Press.

———. 1986. "Early Retirement in the United States." Cornell University, Cornell, N.Y. Mimeo.

———. 1987. "Restructuring Social Security: How will Retirement Ages Respond?" In *The Problem Isn't Age: Work and Older Americans*, ed. S. Sandell. New York: Praeger Publishers.

Filer, R., and Petri, P. 1988. "A Job Characteristics Theory of Retirement." *Review of Economics and Statistics*, 70:123–29.

Fleishman, E. A., Gebhardt, D. L., and Hogan, J. C. 1984. "The Measurement of Effort." *Ergonomics*, 27:947–54.

Fletcher, W. W., and Robison, A. J. 1991. "Worker Training: Competing in the New International Economy." *Looking Ahead*, 13(½):26–33.

Fogelson, R. M. 1984. *Pensions*. New York: Columbia University Press.

Fossum, J., Arvey, R., Paradise, C., and Robbins, N. 1986. "Modeling the Skills Obsolescence Process: A Psychological/Economic Integration." *Academy of Management Review*, 11(2):362–74.

Fox, A. 1984. "Income Changes at and after Social Security Benefit Receipt: Evidence from the Retirement History Survey." *Social Security Bulletin*, 47(9):3–23.

Fozard, J. L. 1990. "Vision and Hearing in Aging." In *Handbook of the Psychology of Aging*, ed. J. E. Birren and K. W. Schaie, 150–70. 3rd ed. New York: Academic Press.

Franke, W., and Sobel, I. 1970. *The Shortage of Skilled and Technical Workers*. Lexington, Mass.: Heath-Lexington Books.

Fraser, T. M. 1992. *Fitness for Work*. London: Taylor and Francis.

Friedman, B. 1992. "Job Prospects for Mature Workers." *Journal of Aging and Social Policy*, 4(¾):53–72.

Friedman, M. 1953. "The Methodology of Positive Economics." In *Essays in Positive Economics*, 3–43. Chicago, Ill.: University of Chicago Press.

Fries, J. 1991. "The Workspan and the Compression of Morbidity." In *Proceedings of the Second Conference of the National Academy of Social Insurance*, ed. Alicia Munnell, 17–18, Washington, D.C.: National Academy of Social Insurance.

Fuller, R. G. 1981. "Determinants of Time Headway Adopted by Truck Drivers." *Ergonomics*, 24(6):463–74.

———. 1984. "Prolonged Driving in Convoy: The Truck Driver's Experience." *Accident, Analysis, and Prevention*, 16(⅚):371–82.

Fullerton, H., Jr. 1991. "Labor Force Projections: The Baby Boom Moves On." *Monthly Labor Review*, 114 (November): 31–44.

Galagan, P. 1988. *Gaining the Competitive Edge*. Alexandria, Va.: American Society for Training and Development.

Garg, A. 1991. "Ergonomics and the Older Worker: An Overview." *Experimental Aging Research*, 17(3):143–55.

Genovese, E. 1971. *Roll, Jordan, Roll*. New York: Vintage.

Gernsbacher, M. A. 1990. *Language Comprehension as Structure Building*. Hillsdale, N.J.: Lawrence Erlbaum Associates.

Geweke, J., Zarkin, G., Slonim, R., Hiedemann, B., and Atkinson, P. 1992. "The Social Security Acceptance Decision." University of Minnesota. Mimeo.

Gibson, R. 1993. "The Black American Retirement Experience." In *Aging in Black America*, ed. J. S. Jackson, L. M. Chatters, and R. J. Taylor. Newbury Park, Calif.: Sage Publications.

Giniger, S., Dispenzieri, A., and Eisenberg, J. 1983. "Age, Experience, and Performance on Speed and Skill Jobs in an Applied Setting." *Journal of Applied Psychology*, 68(3):469–75.

Gist, M., Rosen, B., and Schwoerer, C. 1988. "The Influence of Training Method and Trainee Age on the Acquisition of Computer Skills." *Personnel Psychology*, 41: 255–65.

Gold, D., Andres, D., Arbuckle, T., and Swartzman, A. 1988. "Measurement and Correlates of Verbosity in Elderly People." *Journal of Gerontology: Psychological Sciences*, 43:27–33.

Goldin, C. 1990. *Understanding the Gender Gap*. New York: Oxford University Press.

Goldstein, I. 1986. *Training in Organizations: Needs Assessment, Development, and Evaluation*. Pacific Grove, Calif.: Brooks/Cole Publishing.

Goodman, W., Antczak, S., and Freeman, L. 1993. "Women and Jobs in Recessions: 1969–92." *Monthly Labor Review*, 116 (July): 26–35.

Gordon, M. 1988. *Social Security Policies in Industrial Countries*. Cambridge: Cambridge University Press.

Gordon, R., and Blinder, A. 1980. "Market Wages, Reservation Wages, and Retirement Decisions." *Journal of Public Economics*, 14 (October): 277–308.

Grad, S. 1983. "Minimum Hours Constraints and Retirement Behavior." *Contemporary Policy Issues, 3* (April): 77–91.

———. 1992. *Income of the Population 55 or Older, 1990*. Prepared for U.S. Department of Health and Human Services. Washington, D.C.: U.S. Government Printing Office.

Graebner, W. 1980. *A History of Retirement: The Meaning and Function of an American Institution, 1885–1978*. New Haven, Conn.: Yale University Press.

Grant, P. 1991. "The Open Window—Special Early Retirement Plans in Transition." *The Employee Benefits Journal* (March 4): 2–9.

Gratton, B. 1985. *Urban Elders*. Philadelphia: Temple University Press.

Gratton, B., and Haber, C. 1984. *Old Age and the Search for Security*. Bloomington: Indiana University Press.

Green, F. 1993. "The Determinants of Training of Male and Female Employees in Britain." *Oxford Bulletin of Economics and Statistics*, 55(1):103–22.

Grigg, S. 1989. "Women and Family Property: A Review of U.S. Inheritance Studies." *Historical Methods*, 22(3):116–22.

Gruber, J. 1994. "The Incidence of Mandated Maternity Benefits." *American Economic Review* 84(3) (June): 622–41.

Gruber, J., and Krueger, A. 1991. "The Incidence of Mandated Employer-Provided Insurance: Lessons from Workers' Compensation Insurance." In *Tax Policy and the Economy*, ed. David Bradford, 111–43. Cambridge, Mass.: Massachusetts Institute of Technology Press.

Gruber, J., and Madrian, B. 1993. "Health Insurance Availability and the Retirement Decision." National Bureau of Economic Research working paper no. 4469.

Guralnik, J. 1991. "Comment." In *Proceedings of the Second Conference of the National Academy of Social Insurance*, ed. Alicia Munnell. Washington, D.C.: National Academy of Social Insurance.

Gustman, A., and Mitchell, O. 1992. "Pensions and Labor Market Activity: Behavior and Data Requirements." In *Pensions and the Economy*, ed. Zvi Bodie and Alicia H. Munnell, 39–87. Philadelphia: University of Pennsylvania Press.

Gustman, A., Mitchell, O., and Steinmeier, T. 1994. "The Role of Pensions in the Labor Market: A Survey of the Literature." *Industrial and Labor Relations Review*, 47 (April): 417–38.

Gustman, A., and Steinmeier, T. 1983. "Minimum Hours Constraints and Retirement Behavior." *Contemporary Policy Issues, A Supplement to Economic Inquiry*, 21 (April): 77–91.

———. 1984. "Partial Retirement and the Analysis of Retirement Behavior." *Industrial and Labor Relations Review*, 37(3):403–15.

———. 1985. "The 1983 Social Security Reforms and Labor Supply Adjustments of Older Individuals in the Long Run." *Journal of Labor Economics*, 3 (April): 237–53.

———. 1986. "A Structural Model of Retirement." *Econometrica*, 54(3):555–84.

————. 1989. "An Analysis of Pension Benefit Formulas, Pension Wealth, and Incentives from Pensions." In *Research in Labor Economics*, vol. 10, ed. Ronald G. Ehrenberg, 33–106. Greenwich, Conn.: JAI Press.

————. 1991. "Changing the Social Security Rules for Work after 65." *Industrial and Labor Relations Review*, 44 (July): 733–45.

————. 1993. "Employer Provided Health Insurance and Retirement Behavior." National Bureau of Economic Research working paper no. 4307.

————. 1994, January. "Retirement in a Family Context: A Structural Model for Husbands and Wives." Dartmouth College.

Gutman, H. 1976. *The Black Family in Slavery and Freedom*. New York: Vintage.

Haber, C. 1983. *Beyond Sixty-Five*. New York: Cambridge University Press.

Haber, C., and Gratton, B. 1994. *Old Age and the Search for Security: An American Social History*. Bloomington: Indiana University Press.

Haberman, S. 1991. *Private Provision of Retirement Incomes in the United Kingdom*. Country Study for the Organization for Economic Cooperation and Development. Paris, France.

Hagestad, G. 1986. "The Family: Women and Grandparents as Kin-keepers." In *Our Aging Society: Paradox and Promise*, ed. Alan Pifer and Lydia Bronte. New York: Norton and Company.

Hall, D., and Mirvis, P. 1993. "The New Workplace and Older Workers." Paper prepared for a conference of the National Planning Association/National Council on the Aging, Joint Project on U.S. Competitiveness and the Aging American Workforce. Washington, D.C.

Hall, G. S. 1922. *Senescence*. New York: D. Appleton and Co.

Halpern, J. 1978. "Raising the Mandatory Retirement Age: Its Effect on the Employment of Older Workers." *New England Economic Review* (May/June): 23–35.

Hamermesh, D. 1989. "What Do We Know about Worker Displacement in the United States?" *Industrial Relations*, 28 (Winter): 51–59.

Hamm, V., and Hasher, L. 1992. "Age and the Availability of Interferences." *Psychology and Aging*, 7:56–64.

Hanoch, G., and Honig, M. 1983. "Retirement, Wages, and Labor Supply of the Elderly." *Journal of Labor Economics*, 1 (April): 131–51.

Hareven, T. K. 1983. *Family Time and Industrial Time*. New York: Cambridge University Press.

Harootyan, R. 1991. *Aging in the 21st Century: The Quiet Revolution*. Washington, D.C.: American Association of Retired Persons, New Roles in Society Program.

Harper, Michael C. 1993. "Age-Based Exit Incentives, Coercion, and the Prospective Waiver of ADEA Rights: The Failure of the Older Workers Benefit Protection Act," *Virginia Law Review* 79:1271.

Harrington, P., and Sum, A. 1984. *Skills Shortages and Employment and Training Policy in the U.S.: Past Relationships and Desirable Future Directions*. Boston: Northeastern University, Center for Labor Market Studies.

Hartley, A., Hartley, J., and Johnson, S. 1984. "The Older Adult As Computer User." In *Aging and Technological Advances*, ed. Pauline K. Robinson, Judy E. Livingston, and James E. Birren. New York: Plenum Press.

Hartman, M., and Hasher, L. 1991. "Aging and Suppression: Memory for Previously Relevant Information." *Psychology and Aging*, 6:587–94.

Hasher, L., Stolzfus, E. R., Zacks, R. T., and Rypma, B. 1991. "Age and Inhibition."

Journal of Experimental Psychology: Learning, Memory, and Cognition, 17:163–69.

Haslett, T., Kubeck, J., Delp, N., and McDaniel, M. A. 1994. *Age and Job-Relevant Training Performance: A Comprehensive Review and Meta-Analysis*. Cited in Harvey L. Sterns and Michael A. McDaniel. 1994, January. "Job Performance and the Older Worker" (draft). Paper prepared for the American Association of Retired Persons. University of Akron, Ohio.

Hatch, A. 1950. *American Express*. New York: Doubleday.

Hausman, J., and Wise, D. 1985. "Social Security, Health Status, and Retirement." In *Pensions, Labor, and Individual Choice*, ed. 159–91. David Wise, Chicago, Ill.: University of Chicago Press.

Haveman, R., and Wolfe, B. 1984. "The Decline of Male Labor Force Participation: Comment." *Journal of Political Economy*, 92(3):532–41.

Hawthorne, F. 1983. "Rigging the Early Retirement Game." *Institutional Investor*, 27(5): 79–80, 83–84, 86.

Hayghe, H, and Bianchi, S. 1994. "Married Mothers' Work Patterns: The Job-Family Compromise." *Monthly Labor Review*, 117 (June): 24–30.

Hayslip, B., and Panek, P. E. 1993. *Adult Development and Aging*. New York: HarperCollins College Publishers.

Hayward, M. D., and Grady, W. R. 1986. "The Occupational Retention and Recruitment of Older Men: The Influence of Structural Characteristics of Work." *Social Forces*, 64(3):644–66.

Heckman, J., Roselius, R., and Smith, J. 1993. *U.S. Education and Training Policy: A Reevaluation of the Underlying Assumptions behind the "New Consensus."* Chicago: University of Chicago, Center for Social Program Evaluation.

Hedges, L. V., and Olkin, I. 1985. *Statistical Methods for Meta-Analysis*. New York: Academic Press.

Hemp, P. 1991. "Easing Employees Out the Door." *Boston Globe* (October 15): 37, 41.

Henretta, J., Chan, C., and O'Rand, A. 1992. "Retirement Reason versus Retirement Process: Examining the Reasons for Retirement Typology." *Journal of Gerontology: Social Sciences*, 47(1):S1–S7.

Henretta, J., and O'Rand, A. 1983. "Joint Retirement in the Dual Worker Family." *Social Forces*, 62 (December): 504–20.

Henretta, J., O'Rand, A., and Chan, C. 1993. "Gender Differences in Employment After Spouse's Retirement." *Research on Aging*, 15 (June): 148–69.

Herring, C., and Wilson-Sadberry, K. R. 1994. "Preference or Necessity? Changing Work Roles of Black and White Women, 1973–1990." *Journal of Marriage and the Family*, 55 (May): 314–25.

Herz, D. 1988. "Employment Characteristics of Older Women, 1987." *Monthly Labor Review*, 111 (September): 3–12.

Herzog, A., Kahn, R., Morgan, J., Jackson, J., and Antonucci, T. 1989. "Age Differences in Productive Activities." *Journal of Gerontology: Social Sciences*, 44:129–38.

Hewitt Associates. 1986. "Plan Design and Experience in Early Retirement Windows and in Other Voluntary Separation Plans." Mimeographed.

———. 1992. "Early Retirement Windows, Some Options, and Postretirement Increases in Pension Plans." Mimeographed.

———. 1993. "Employee Experience in Work Force Reductions." Mimeographed.

Hill, L., and Elias, J. 1990. "Retraining Midcareer Managers: Career History and Self-Efficiency Beliefs." *Human Resource Management*, 29(2):197–217.

Hill, R., and Dwyer, P. 1990. "Grooming Workers for Early Retirement." *HR Magazine*, (September): 59–63.

Hirshorn, B. 1988. "Organizational Behavior Regarding Older Workers: Prototypical Responses." *Journal of Aging Studies*, 2(3):199–215.

Hirshorn, B., and Hoyer, D. 1994. "Private Sector Hiring and Use of Retirees: The Firm's Perspective." *The Gerontologist*, 34(1):50–58.

Hogarth, J. 1988. "Accepting An Early Retirement Bonus: An Empirical Study." *Journal of Human Resources*, 23 (Winter): 21–33.

Hogarth, T., and Barth, M. 1991. "The Costs and Benefits of Older Workers: A Case Study of B&Q's Use of Older Workers." *International Journal of Manpower*, 12(8):5–17.

Holden, K. 1993. "Continuing Limits on Productive Aging: The Lesser Rewards for Working Women." In *Achieving a Productive Aging Society*, ed. Scott Bass, Frank Caro, and Yung-Ping Chen. Westport, Conn.: Auburn House.

Hollmann, F. W. 1993. "U.S. Population Estimates, by Age, Sex, Race, and Hispanic Origin: 1980 to 1991." *Current Population Reports*, series P-25, no. 1095. Washington, D.C., U.S. Government Printing Office.

Holstein, M. 1993. "Women's Lives, Women's Work: Productivity, Gender, and Aging." In *Achieving a Productive Aging Society*, ed. Scott Bass, Frank Caro, and Yung-Ping Chen, 235–48. Westport, Conn.: Auburn House.

Honig, M. 1985. "Partial Retirement among Women." *Journal of Human Resources*, 20(4):613–21.

Honig, M., and Hanoch, G. 1985. "Partial Retirement as a Separate Mode of Retirement Behavior." *Journal of Human Resources*, 20(1):21–46.

Honig, M., and Reimers, C. 1987. "Retirement, Re-entry, and Part-Time Work." *Eastern Economic Journal*, 13(4):361–71.

Howard, A., and Bray, D. 1988. *Managerial Lives in Transition: Advancing Age and Changing Times*. New York: Guilford Press.

Howell, W. C. 1992. "Human Factors in the Workplace." In *Handbook of Industrial and Organizational Psychology*, Vol. 2, ed. M. D. Dunnette and L. M. Hough, 210–69. Palo Alto, Calif.: Consulting Psychologist Press.

Hurd, M. 1990a. "The Joint Retirement Decision of Husbands and Wives." In *Issues in the Economics of Aging*, ed. David A. Wise, 231–54. Chicago: University of Chicago Press.

———. 1990b. "Research on the Elderly: Economic Status, Retirement, and Consumption and Saving." *Journal of Economic Literature*, 28 (June): 565–637.

———. 1993. "The Effect of Labor Market Rigidities on the Labor Force Behavior of Older Workers." National Bureau of Economic Research working paper no. 4462.

Hurd, M., and Boskin, M. 1984. "The Effect of Social Security on Retirement in the Early 1970s." *Quarterly Journal of Economics*, 99 (November): 767–90.

Hutchens, R. 1986a. "Delayed Payments and a Firm's Propensity to Hire Older Workers." *Journal of Labor Economics*, 4 (October): 439–57.

———. 1986b. "Do Job Opportunities Decline with Age?" *Industrial and Labor Relations Review*, 42 (October):89–99.

———. 1993. "Restricted Job Opportunities and the Older Worker." In *As the*

Labor Force Ages: Costs, Benefits, and Policy Challenges, ed. Olivia Mitchell, 81–102. Ithaca, N.Y.: ILR Press.

Huutanen, P. 1988. "The Aging Worker in a Changing Work Environment." *Scandinavian Journal of Work, Environment, and Health*, 14:21–23.

Iams, H. 1986. "Employment of Retired-Worker Women." *Social Security Bulletin*, 49 (March): 5–13.

———. 1987. "Jobs of Persons Working after Receiving Retired-Worker Benefits." *Social Security Bulletin*, 50 (November): 4–18.

Imbrogno, Linda. 1993. "Can You Have Your Cake and Eat It Too? Ratification of Releases of ADEA Claims." *Fordham Urban Law Journal* 20:311.

Incomes Data Services European Report. 1993. "Europe Focuses on the Role of Older Workers." (May): 9–17.

"Independent Opinions." 1913. *Independent*, August 28, 75.

Ippolito, R. 1990. "Toward Explaining Early Retirement after 1970." *Industrial and Labor Relations Review*, 44:520–35.

———. 1991. "Towards Explaining Earlier Retirement after 1970." *Industrial Relations*, 43(5):556–69.

Jablonski, M., Kunze, K., and Rosenblum, L. 1990. "Productivity, Age and Labor Composition Changes in the U.S. Work Force." In *The Aging of the American Work Force*, ed. I. Bluestone, R. J. V. Montgomery, and J. D. Owen, 304–38. Detroit, Mich.: Wayne State University Press.

Jackson, R. 1986. "Employer's Attitudes towards Older Workers: Implications for an Aging U.S. Labor Force and National Employment Policy." Ph.D. dissertation, University of Michigan.

Jacobs, K., Kohli, M., and Rein, M. 1991. "Germany: The Diversity of Pathways." In *Time for Retirement: Comparative Studies of Early Exit from the Labor Force*, ed. Martin Kohli, Martin Rein, Anne-Marie Guillemard, and Herman van Gunsteren, 181–221. Cambridge: Cambridge University Press.

Jacoby, S. M. 1985. *Employing Bureaucracy.* New York: Columbia University Press.

Jamieson, G. H. 1969. "Age, Speed, and Accuracy: A Study in Industrial Retraining." *Industrial Gerontology* (Summer): 50–51.

Janhunen, J. 1987, February. "Tyoelake." Central Pension Security Institute (report).

Jaschinski-Kruza, W. 1990. "On the Preferred Viewing Distances to Screen and Document at VDU Workplaces." *Ergonomics*, 33(8):1055–63.

Jay, G. M., and Willis, S. L. 1992. "Influence of Direct Computer Experience on Older Adults' Attitudes toward Computers." *Journal of Gerontology*, 47(4):250–57.

Jessup, D., and Greenberg, B. 1989. "Innovative Older-Worker Programs." *Generations* 14(Summer): 23–27.

Jobin, G., Koskie, R., Longhurst, P., and Zigler, M. 1991. *Employee Benefits in Canada.* Brookfield, Wisc.: International Foundation of Employee Benefit Plans.

Johnson, A. 1911. *The Almshouse.* New York: Charities Publications Committee.

Johnson, A, and Linden, F. 1992. *Availability of a Quality Work Force.* New York: Conference Board.

Johnston, W. B., and Packer, A. 1987. *Workforce 2000: Work and Workers in the Twenty-First Century.* Indianapolis, Ind.: Hudson Institute.

Jondrow, J., Brechling, F., and Marcus, A. 1987. "Older Workers in the Market for Part-Time Employment." In *The Problem Isn't Age*, ed. Steven H. Sandell, 84–99. New York: Praeger.

Jones, L. 1980. *Great Expectations: America and the Baby Boom Generation.* New York: Coward, McCann and Geoghegan.

Kahn, J. 1988. "Social Security, Liquidity, and Early Retirement." *Journal of Public Economics*, 35 (February): 97–117.

Kahne, H. 1985. *Reconceiving Part-Time Work.* Totowa, N.J.: Rowman and Allanheld.

Kaminshine, Steven J. 1990. "The Cost of Older Workers, Disparate Impact, and the ADEA." *Florida Law Review* 42:229, 291.

Kane, R., Radosevich, D., and Vaupel, J. 1990. "Compression of Morbidity: Issues and Irrelevancies." In *Improving the Health of Older People: A World View*, ed. R. L. Kane, J. G. Evans, and D. Macfadyen. New York: Oxford University Press.

Karp, D. 1989. "The Social Construction of Retirement among Professionals 50–60 Years Old." *The Gerontologist*, 29(6):750–60.

Kaufman, H. 1986. *Interest Rates, the Markets, and the New Financial World.* New York: Time Books.

Kausler, D. H. 1992. *Experimental Psychology, Cognition, and Human Aging.* New York: Springer-Verlag.

Keesing, D. 1992. "Old-Age Security throughout the World: A Survey." World Bank, Washington, D.C.

Kemper, S., Rach, S., Kynette, D., and Norman, S. 1990. "Telling Stories: The Structure of Adults' Narratives." *European Journal of Cognitive Psychology*, 2:205–28.

Keyfitz, N. 1973. "Individual Mobility in a Stationary Population." *Population Studies*, 27:335–52.

Kieffer, J. 1983. *Gaining Dividends of Longer Life: New Roles for Older Workers.* Boulder, Colo.: Westview Press.

Killingsworth, M. 1983. *Labor Supply.* Cambridge: Cambridge University Press.

Killingsworth, M., and Heckman, J. 1986. "Female Labor Supply: A Survey." In *Handbook of Labor Economics*, vol. 1, ed. Orley C. Ashenfelter and Richard Layard, 103–24. Amsterdam: North-Holland.

Kimmel, D. C. 1988. "Ageism, Psychology, and Public Policy." *American Psychologist*, 43:175–78.

Kingson, E. 1992, April. *The Diversity of the Baby Boom Generation: Implications for their Retirement Years.* Washington D.C.: American Association of Retired Persons, Forecasting and Environmental Scanning Division.

Kingson, E., and Berkowitz, E. 1993. *Social Security and Medicare: A Policy Primer.* Westport, Conn.: Auburn House.

Kingson, E., and Cornman, J. (forthcoming). *The Social Security of the Baby Boom.* New York: Columbia University Press.

Kingson, E., Hirshorn, B., and Cornman, J. 1986. *Ties That Bind: The Interdependence of Generations.* Cabin John, Md.: Seven Locks Press.

Kingson, E., and O'Grady-LeShane, R. 1993. "The Effects of Caregiving on Women's Social Security Benefits." *The Gerontologist*, 33 (April): 230–39.

Kleinberg, S. J. 1989. *In the Shadow of the Mills.* Pittsburgh, Pa.: University of Pittsburgh Press.

Klemmack, D., and Roff, L. 1983. "The Role of Social Security in Retirement Income: Factors Affecting Public Attitudes." *Research on Aging*, 5(3):301–18.

Kliegl, R., and Baltes, P. B. 1987. "Theory-Guided Analysis of Mechanisms of Development and Aging through Testing-the-Limits and Research on Expertise." In

Cognitive Functioning and Social Structure over the Life Course, ed. C. Schooler and K. W. Schaie. Norwood, N.J.: Ablex.

Kline, D. W., and Schieber, F. 1985. "Vision and Aging." Cited in J. E. Birren and J. Cerella, 1990. "Aging and Information Processing Rate." *Handbook of the Psychology of Aging*, ed. K. W. Schaie, 296–331, 2nd ed. New York: Van Nostrand Reinhold.

Knowles, D. 1988. "Dispelling Myths about Older Workers." In *Employing Older Americans: Opportunities and Constraints*, ed. Helen Axel, 16–19. New York: Conference Board.

Kotlikoff, L., and Smith, D. 1983. *Pensions in the American Economy.* Chicago, Ill.: University of Chicago Press.

Kotlikoff, L., and Wise, D. 1987. "The Incentive Effects of Private Pension Plans." In *Issues in Pension Economics*, ed. Zvi Bodie, John B. Shoven, and David A. Wise, 283–336. Chicago: University of Chicago Press.

———. 1989. *The Wage Carrot and the Pension Stick.* Kalamazoo, Mich.: W. E. Upjohn Institute for Employment Research.

Kotovsky, K., and Fallside, D. 1989. "Representation and Transfer in Problem Solving." In *Complex Information Processing*, ed. D. Klahr and K. Kotovsky, 69–108. Hillsdale, N.J.: Lawrence Erlbaum.

Krieger, M. 1991. "Case Study Analysis of Older Workers Programs in the Quick Service Restaurant Industry." Master's Thesis, Eastern Michigan University.

Krueger, A., and Pischke, Jörn-Steffin. 1992. "The Effect of Social Security on Labor Supply: A Cohort Analysis of the Notch Generation." *Journal of Labor Economics*, 10:412–37.

Labich, K. 1993. "The New Unemployed." *Fortune* (March 8): 40–49.

Laczko, F., and Phillipson, C. 1991. "Great Britain: The Contradictions of Early Exit." In *Time for Retirement: Comparative Studies of Early Exit from the Labor Force*, ed. Martin Kohli, Martin Rein, Anne-Marie Guillemard, and Herman van Gunsteren, 222–51. Cambridge: Cambridge University Press.

Landy, F. J. 1992. "Alternatives to Chronological Age in Determining Standards of Suitability for Public Safety Jobs." Technical report. Pennsylvania State University.

LaRock, Seymour. 1993. "Retirement Plan Experience." *Employee Benefit Plan Review*, July:10–15.

Latimer, M. W. 1932. *Industrial Pensions in the United States and Canada.* 2 vols. New York: Industrial Relations Counselors.

Lavine, A. 1993. *Your Life Insurance Options.* New York, N.Y.: John Wiley and Sons.

Lawlor, E. 1987. "The Impact of Age Discrimination Legislation on the Labor Force Participation of Aged Men: A Time-Series Analysis." *Evaluation Review*, 10(6): 794–805.

Lazear, E. 1979. "Why Is There Mandatory Retirement?" *Journal of Political Economy*, 87(6):1261–84.

———. 1983. "Pensions as Severance Pay." In *Financial Aspects of the United States Pension System*, ed. Zvi Bodie and John Shoven. Chicago, Ill.: University of Chicago Press.

———. 1986. "Retirement from the Labor Force." In *Handbook of Labor Statistics*, ed. Orley Ashenfelter and Richard Layard. New York: Elsevier Science Publishers.

Lazear, E., and Moore, R. 1988. "Pensions and Turnover." In *Pensions in the U.S.*

Economy, ed. Zvi Bodie, John B. Shoven, and David A. Wise. Chicago, Ill.: University of Chicago Press.

Leavitt, T, and Crown, W. 1994, December. *Labor Force Characteristics of Older Americans.* (*December*) Needham, Mass.: Analytic Resources.

———. 1995, January. *The Senior Community Service Employment Program: An Analysis of Enrollee Characteristics.* Needham, Mass.: Analytic Resources.

Lee, R. D., Arthur, W., and Rodgers, G. 1988. *Economics of Changing Age Distributions in Developed Countries.* Oxford, U.K.: Clarendon Press.

Leonesio, M. 1990a. "Economic Retirement Studies: An Annotated Bibliography." ORS working paper no. 45. Social Security Administration, Office of Research and Statistics, Office of Policy.

———. 1990b. "The Effects of the Social Security Earnings Test on the Labor-Market Activity of Older Americans: A Review of the Evidence." *Social Security Bulletin*, 53 (May): 2–21.

———. 1993. "Social Security and Older Workers." In *As the Workforce Ages: Costs, Benefits, and Policy Challenges*, ed. Olivia Mitchell. Ithaca, N.Y.: ILR Press.

Levine, P. 1993. "Examining Labor Force Projections for the 21st Century." In *As the Labor Force Ages: Costs, Benefits, and Policy Challenges*, ed. Olivia Mitchell, 39–56. Ithaca, N.Y.: ILR Press.

Levitan, S., and Gallo, F. 1989. "The Shortsighted Focus on Labor Shortages." *Challenge* (September/October): 28–32.

———. 1991. "Preparing Americans for Work." *Looking Ahead*, 13(½):18–25.

Levitan, S., Mangum, G., and Mangum, S. 1992. *A Training Program for the 1990s: Reflecting on Campaign Proposals.* Washington, D.C.: Center for Social Policy Studies.

Levy, F., and Murnane, R. 1992. "U.S. Earnings Levels and Earnings Inequality: A Review of Recent Trends and Proposed Explanations." *Journal of Economic Literature*, 30 (September): 1333–81.

Lewis, E. 1993. *In Their Own Interests.* Berkeley: University of California Press.

Licht, W. 1993. *Working for the Railroads.* Princeton, N.J.: Princeton University Press.

Light, L. L. 1991. "Memory and Aging: Four Hypotheses in Search of Data." *Annual Review of Psychology*, 42:333–76.

Light, Paul C. 1988. *Baby Boomers.* New York: W. W. Norton and Company.

Lillard, L., and Tan, H. 1992. "Private Sector Training: Who Gets It and What Are Its Effects?" *Research in Labor Economics*, 13:1–62.

Lobsenz, J. 1929. *The Older Woman in Industry.* New York: Scribner's Sons.

Long, C. D. 1958. *The Labor Force under Changing Conditions of Income and Development.* Princeton, N.J.: Princeton University Press.

Longino, Charles F., Jr., 1993, September. "Aging and the Productive Life." Retirement in Georgia Conference, Georgia Council on Aging, Atlanta.

Lord, R. G., and Levy, P. E. 1994. "Moving from Cognition to Action: A Control Theory Perspective." *Applied Psychology: An International Review*, 43:335–67.

Louis Harris and Associates. 1981. "Agency, Earnings Profiles, Productivity, and Hours Restrictions." *American Economic Review*, 71:1261–84.

———. 1992. *Productive Aging: A Survey of Americans Age 55 and Over.* New York: Louis Harris and Associates.

Lowy, L., and O'Connor, D. 1986. *Why Education in the Later Years?* Lexington, Mass.: Lexington Books.

Lubove, R. 1968. *The Struggle for Social Security.* Cambridge, Mass.: Harvard University Press.

Lumsdaine, R., Stock, J., and Wise, D. 1990a. "Efficient Windows and Labor Force Reduction." *Journal of Public Economics*, 43 (November): 131–59.

———. 1990b. "Three Models of Retirement: Computational Complexity Versus Predictive Power." NBER working paper no. 3558. Cambridge, Mass.: National Bureau of Economic Research (NBER).

Luzadis, R., and Mitchell, O. 1992. "Buying-Out Older Workers: Sectoral Differences in Pension Incentives." Paper presented at Current Pension Policy Issues, a conference sponsored by the Center for Pension and Retirement Research, Miami University, March 27, 28.

Lynch, L. 1993a. *"Payoffs to Alternative Training Strategies at Work."* Paper prepared for a conference of the National Bureau of Economic Research, Working under Different Rules. Washington, D.C.: May 7.

———. 1993b. *Strategies for Workplace Training: Lessons from Abroad.* Washington, D.C.: Economic Policy Institute.

Lynd, R., and Lynd, H. 1929. *Middletown.* New York: Harcourt, Brace, Jovanovich.

Mangum, S. 1989. "Evidence on Private Sector Training." In *Investing in People: Background Papers*, vol 1. Washington, D.C.: U.S. Department of Labor.

Manton, K. 1983. "Changing Concepts of Morbidity and Mortality in the Elderly Population." *Milbank Memorial Fund Quarterly/Health and Society*, 60:183–244.

———. 1993. "Trends for the Elderly—Implications for Income Support, Health, and Provisions for Long Term Care." Paper presented at conference sponsored by the Public Trustees of the Social Security and Medicare Board of Trustees on the *Future of Health Care Needs and Resources for the Aged.* Washington, D.C., October 7.

Manton, K., Corder, L., and Stallard, E. 1993. "Estimates of Change in Chronic Disability and Institutional Incidence and Prevalence Rates in the U.S. Elderly Population From the 1982, 1984, and 1989 National Long Term Care Survey." *Journal of Gerontology: Social Sciences*, 48(4):S153–66.

Marks, M. 1993. "Restructuring and Downsizing." In *Building the Competitive Workplace: Investing in Human Capital for Corporate Success*, ed. Philip H. Mirvis, 60–94. New York: John Wiley and Sons, Inc.

Martin, L. 1989. "The Graying of Japan." *Population Bulletin*, 44 (July): 2–42.

Martini, A. 1990. *A Labor Force Profile of Persons with Disabilities.* Report prepared for the Office of the Assistant Secretary for Planning and Evaluation, U.S. Department of Health and Human Services. Washington, D.C.: Mathematica Policy Research.

Matheson, N. S. 1991. "The Influence of Organizational-Based Self-Esteem on Satisfaction and Commitment: An Analysis of Age Differences." A dissertation manuscript. University of Akron, Ohio.

McBride, T. 1988. "Women's Retirement Behaviors: Implications for Future Policy." Paper presented at the American Economic Association meetings (December).

McCrae, R. R., Arenberg, D., and Costa, P. T. 1987. "Declines in Divergent Thinking With Age: Cross-Sectional, Longitudinal, and Cross-Sequential Analysis." *Psychology and Aging*, 22:130–37.

McDaniel, M. A., Schmidt, F. L., and Hunter, J. E. 1988. "Job Experience Correlates of Job Performance." *Journal of Applied Psychology*, 73(2):327–30.

McEvoy, G., and Cascio, W. 1989. "Cumulative Evidence of the Relationship Between Employee Age and Job Performance." *Journal of Applied Psychology*, 74 (February): 11–17.

McGill, Dan M., and Grubbs, Donald S., Jr. 1989. *Fundamentals of Private Pensions*. 6th edition. Philadelphia, Pa.: Wharton School of the University of Pennsylvania, Pension Research Council.

McNaught, W., and Barth, M. 1991. *Using Retirees to Fill Temporary Labor Needs: The Travelers' Experience*. Americans over 55 at Work Program, background paper no. 5. New York: Commonwealth Fund.

———. 1992. "Are Older Workers 'Good Buys'?: A Case Study of Days Inns of America." *Sloan Management Review*, 33 (Spring): 53–63.

McNaught, W., Barth, M., and Henderson, P. 1989. "The Human Resource Potential of Americans over 50." *Human Resource Management*, 28 (Winter): 455–73.

McNeely, E. 1991. Computer-Assisted Instruction and the Older-Adult Learner. *Educational Gerontology*, 17:229–37.

Meier, E., and Kerr, E. 1976. "Capabilities of Middle-Aged and Older Workers: A Survey of the Literature." *Industrial Gerontology*, 3(3):147–56.

Meyer, H. H. 1970. "The Validity of the In-Basket Test as a Measure of Managerial Performance." *Personnel Psychology*, 23:297–307.

Mincer, Jacob, 1962. "Labor Force Participation of Married Women: A Study of Labor Supply." In *Aspects of Labor Economics*. Princeton, N.J.: Princeton University Press.

Mirkin, B. 1987. "Early Retirement as a Labor Force Policy: An International Overview." *Monthly Labor Review*, 110(3):19–33.

Mirvis, Philip H. 1993. *Building the Competitive Workforce*. New York: John Wiley and Sons.

Mishel, L., and Teixeira, R. 1991. *The Myth of the Coming Labor Shortage: Jobs, Skills, and Income of America's Workforce 2000*. Washington, D.C.: Economic Policy Institute.

Mitchell, O. 1988. "The Relation of Age to Workplace Injuries." *Monthly Labor Review*, 111(7):8–13.

———. 1990. "Aging, Job Satisfaction, and Job Performance." In *The Aging of the American Work Force*, ed. I. Bluestone, R. J. V. Montgomery, and J. D. Owen, 242–72. Detroit, Mich.: Wayne State University Press.

———. 1992. "Trends in Pension Benefit Formulas and Retirement Provisions." In *Trends in Pensions 1992*, ed. John A. Turner and Daniel J. Beller. Washington, D.C.: U.S. Government Printing Office.

Mitchell, O., and Fields, G. 1982. "The Effects of Pensions and Earnings on Retirement: A Review Essay." In *Research in Labor Economics*, vol. 5, ed. Ronald G. Ehrenberg. Greenwich, Conn.: JAI Press Inc.

Mitchell, O., and Luzadis, R. 1988. "Changes in Pension Incentives through Time." *Industrial and Labor Relations Review*, 42 (October): 100–108.

Moen, J. 1987. "The Labor of Older Men: A Comment." *Journal of Economic History*, 47 (September): 761–67.

Moen, P., Downey, G., and Bolger, N. 1990. "Labor-Force Reentry Among U.S. Homemakers in Midlife: A Life-Course Analysis." *Gender and Society*, 4 (June): 230–43.

Moen, P., Robison, J., and Fields, V. 1994. "Women's Work and Caregiving Roles: A Life Course Approach." *Journal of Gerontology,* 49 (July): S176-S186.

Moody, H. 1988. *Abundance of Life.* New York: Columbia University Press.

Morgan, J. 1980. "Retirement in Prospect and Retrospect." In *Five Thousand American Families: Patterns of Economic Progress,* vol. 8, ed. G. Duncan and J. Morgan, 73–105. Ann Arbor, Mich.: University of Michigan, Institute for Social Research.

Morris, R., and Bass, S. 1988. *Retirement Reconsidered: Economic and Social Roles for Older People.* New York: Springer Publishing Company.

Morrison, M. 1983. "The Aging of the U.S. Population: Human Resource Implications." *Monthly Labor Review,* 106(5):13–19.

Mullan, C., and Gorman, L. 1972. "Facilitating Adaptation to Change: A Case Study in Retraining Middle-Aged and Older Workers at Aer Lingus." *Industrial Gerontology,* 15 (Fall): 20–39.

Munnell, A. 1984. *The Economics of Private Pensions.* Washington, D.C.: Brookings Institution.

Murakami, K. 1991. "Severance and Retirement Benefits in Japan." In *Pension Policy: An International Perspective,* ed. John A. Turner and Lorna M. Dailey, 117–44. Washington, D.C.: U.S. Government Printing Office.

Myers, R. 1985. *Social Security,* 3rd ed. Homewood, Ill: Richard D. Irwin.

———. 1991. "Early Retirement, Delayed Retirement Factors in Japanese Social Security System." *Actuary,* 27 (April): 3–5.

National Commission for Employment Policy. 1985. *Older Workers: Prospects, Problems and Policies, 9th Annual Report.* Washington, D.C.: National Commission for Employment Policy.

National Medical Expenditure Survey. 1987. National Center for Health Services Research and Health Care Technology Assessment (NCHSR). Rockville, Md.: Public Health Service.

Newquist, D. 1986. "Toward Assessing Health and Functional Capacity for Policy Development on Work-Life Extension." In *Age, Health, and Employment,* ed. J. E. Birren, P. K. Robinson, and J. E. Livingston, 24–44. Englewood Cliffs, N.J.: Prentice-Hall.

Newquist, D., and Robinson, P. K. 1983. "Health and Extended Worklife." Center on Employment and Retirement. University of Southern California, Andrus Gerontology Center.

Newsham, D. B. 1969. "The Challenge of Change to the Adult Trainee." Reviewed by R. M. Belbin in *Industrial Gerontology* (October): 32–33.

Niles, H. 1820. Editorial. *Niles Register* (September 2): 19.

Noe, R. A. 1986. "Trainees' Attributes and Attitudes: Neglected Influences on Training Effectiveness." *Academy of Management Review,* 11:736–49.

Novick, L. R. 1988. "Analogical Transfer, Problem Similarity, and Expertise." *Journal of Experimental Psychology: Learning, Memory, and Cognition,* 14:510–20.

Nusberg, C. 1990. "Job Training for Older Workers Lags in the Industrialized World." *Ageing International,* (June): 23–30.

Nylander, S., and Carmean, G. 1984. *Medical Standard Project Final Report,* vol. 1. 3rd ed. San Bernardino, Calif.: Office of Personnel Management, Personnel Division.

Ogawa, N., and Clark, R. 1993. *Aging Labor Force and Labor Market Responses in Japan.* Americans over 55 at Work Program, background paper no. 17. New York: Commonwealth Fund.

Ogburn, W. 1964. *On Culture and Social Change: Selected Papers.* Chicago: University of Chicago Press.

Olson, L., Caton, C., and Duffy, M. 1981. *The Elderly and the Future Economy.* Lexington, Mass.: Lexington Books, D.C. Heath and Co.

Opinion Research Corporation. 1992. *Investing in the Older Worker: A Study of Employer-Provided Training.* Survey conducted for the American Association of Retired Persons. Washington, D.C.: American Association of Retired Persons.

O'Rand, A., Henretta, J., and Krecker, M. 1992. "Family Pathways to Retirement." In *Families and Retirement,* ed. M. Szinovacz, D. Ekerdt, and B. Vinick, 81–98. Newbury Park, Calif.: Sage Publications.

O'Reilly, P., and Caro, F. 1992. "Productive Aging: An Overview of the Literature." Working paper. Boston: University of Massachusetts at Boston. Gerontology Institute.

Organization for Economic Cooperation and Development. 1991. *Employment Outlook.* Paris: Organization for Economic Cooperation and Development.

Owsley, C., Ball, K., Sloane, M. E., Roenker, D. L., and Bruni, L. 1991. "Visual/Cognitive Correlates of Vehicle Accidents in Older Drivers." *Psychology and Aging,* 6(3):403–15.

Ozawa, M. 1985. "Non-Whites and the Demographic Imperative in Social Welfare Spending." Paper presented at the 1985 National Association of Social Workers Professional Symposium. Chicago, Illinois, November 8.

Palmore, E., Burchett, B., Fillenbaum, G., George, L., and Wallman, L. 1985. *Retirement: Causes and Consequences.* New York: Springer Publishing Co.

Palmore, E., Fillenbaum, G., and George, L. 1984. "Consequences of Retirement." *Journal of Gerontology,* 39(1):109–16.

Palmore, E., George, L., and Fillenbaum, G. 1982. "Predictors of Retirement." *Journal of Gerontology* 37:733–42.

Parnes, H. 1983. *Policy Issues in Work and Retirement.* Kalamazoo, Mich.: W. E. Upjohn Institute for Employment Research.

Parnes, H., Crowley, J., Harrison, J., Less, L., Morgan, W., Mott, F., and Nestel, G. 1985. *Retirement among American Men.* Lexington, Mass.: Lexington Books, D.C. Heath and Co.

Parnes, H., Gagen, M., and King, R. 1981. "Job Loss among Long-Service Workers." In *Work and Retirement,* ed. Herbert Parnes, 175–208. Cambridge: Massachusetts Institute of Technology Press.

Parnes, H., and Nestle, G. 1975. "Early Retirement." In *The Preretirement Years,* vol. 4, ed. Herbert Parnes. U.S. Department of Labor. Washington, D.C.: U.S. Government Printing Office.

Parsons, D. 1980. "The Decline in Male Labor Force Participation." *Journal of Political Economy,* 88(1):117–34.

———. 1983. "The Industrial Demand for Older Workers." Unpublished manuscript.

Paul, C. 1987. "Work Alternatives for Older Americans: A Management Perspective." In *The Problem Isn't Age: Work and Older Americans,* ed. Steven Sandell. New York: Praeger Publishers.

Peirce, J. L., Gardner, D. G., Cummings, L. L., and Dunham, R. B. 1989. "Organizational-Based Self-Esteem: Construct Definition, Measurement, and Validation." *Academy of Management Journal,* 32:622–48.

Pellechio, A. 1978. "The Effect of Social Security on Retirement." NBER working paper 260. Cambridge, Mass.: National Bureau of Economic Research (NBER).

Pencavel, J. 1986. "Labor Supply of Men: A Survey." In *Handbook of Labor Economics*, vol. 1, ed. Orley C. Ashenfelter and Richard Layard, 3–102. Amsterdam: North-Holland.

Pension Commission of Ontario, Canada. 1993. "Understanding Your Pension Plan: A Guide for Members of Employer Sponsored Plans."

Perachhi, F., and Welch, F. 1994. "Trends in Labor Force Transitions of Older Men and Women." *Journal of Labor Economics*, 12(2):210–42.

Perlmutter, M., Kaplan, M., and Nyquist, L. 1990. "Development of Adaptive Competence in Adulthood." *Human Development*, 33:185–97.

Pesando, J., and Gunderson, M. 1987, September. "Retirement Incentives Contained in Occupational Pension Plans and their Implications for the Mandatory Retirement Debate." University of Pennsylvania, Pension Research Council Working Paper no. 87–1.

Peterson, D., and Wendt, P. 1995. "Training and Education of Older Americans as Workers and Volunteers." In *Older and Active*, ed. Scott Bass. New Haven, Conn.: Yale University Press.

Peterson, D. A. 1986. *Facilitating Education for Older Learners*. San Francisco, Calif.: Jossey-Bass Publishers.

Phelan, C., and Rust, J. 1991, January. "Social Security Policy: A Dynamic Analysis of Incentives and Self-Selection." Unpublished manuscript.

Pienta, A., Burr, J., and Mutchler, J. 1994. "Women's Labor Force Participation in Later Life: The Effects of Early Work and Family Experiences." *Journal of Gerontology*, 49 (September): S231–39.

Pifer, A., and Chisman, F. 1985. *The Report of the Committee of Economic Security, 50th Anniversary Edition*. Washington, D.C.: National Conference on Social Welfare.

Pilcher, D., Ramirez, C., and Swihart, J. 1968. "Some Correlates of Normal Pensionable Age." *International Social Security Review*, 21:387–411.

Plett, P. 1990. *Training of Older Workers in Industrialised Countries*. Geneva, Switzerland: International Labor Office.

Podoff, D. 1986. "Increasing the Social Security Retirement Age: Older Workers in Physically Demanding Occupations." *Social Security Bulletin*, 49(10):5–23.

Pontiff, J., Shleifer, A., and Weisbach, M. 1990. "Reversions of Excess Pension Assets after Takeovers." *Rand Journal of Economics*, 21 (Winter): 600–613.

Poon, L. 1987. "Learning." In *The Encyclopedia of Aging*, ed. George Maddox. New York: Springer.

Porter, M. 1992. "Capital Disadvantage: America's Failing Capital Investment System." *Harvard Business Review* 70 (September–October): 65–82.

Pozzebon, S., and Mitchell, O. 1989. "Married Women's Retirement Behavior." *Journal of Population Economics*, 2:39–53.

Putnam, J. K. 1970. *Old-Age Politics in California*. Stanford, Calif.: Stanford University Press.

Quadagno, J. 1988. *The Transformation of Old Age Security: Class and Politics in the American Welfare State*. Chicago: University of Chicago Press.

Quinn, J. 1977. "Microeconomic Determinants of Early Retirement: A Cross-Sectional

View of White Married Men.'' *Journal of Human Resources*, 12 (Summer): 329–47.

———. 1978. "Job Characteristics and Early Retirement.'' *Industrial Relations*, 17 (October): 315–23.

———. 1993. "Is Early Retirement an Economic Threat?'' *Generations* (Winter): 10–14.

Quinn, J., and Burkhauser, R. 1991. *Retirement Plans and Preferences of Older Workers.* Americans over 55 at Work Program, background paper no. 5. New York: Commonwealth Fund.

———. 1994a. "Public Policy and the Plans and Preferences of Older Americans.'' *Journal of Aging and Social Policy*, 6(3):5–20.

———. 1994b. "Retirement and the Labor Force Behavior of the Elderly.'' In *The Demography of Aging*, eds. L. G. Martin and S. H. Martin, 50–101. Washington, D.C.: National Academy Press.

Quinn, J., Burkhauser, R., and Myers, D. 1990. *Passing the Torch: The Influence of Economic Incentives on Work and Retirement.* Kalamazoo, Mich.: W. E. Upjohn Institute for Employment Research.

Rabbitt, P. 1991. "Management of the Working Population.'' *Ergonomics*, 34(6):775–90.

Ransom, R., and Sutch, R. 1986. "The Labor of Older Americans: Retirement of Men On and Off the Job, 1870–1937.'' *The Journal of Economic History*, 46(1):1–30.

———. 1988. "The Decline of Retirement in the Years Before Social Security.'' In *Issues in Contemporary Retirement*, ed. Rita Ricardo-Campbell and Edward P. Lazaer, 3–37. Stanford, Calif.: Hoover Institution Press.

Ransom, R., Sutch, R., and Williamson, S. 1993. "Inventing Pensions.'' In *Societal Impact on Aging*, ed. K. W. Schaie and W. Achenbaum. New York: Springer Publishing Company.

Reich, R. 1989. "America Pays the Price.'' *New York Times Magazine* (January 29): 32–40.

———. 1993. "Companies Are Cutting Their Hearts Out.'' *New York Times Magazine* (December 19): 54–55.

Reis, M., and Gold, D. 1993. "Retirement, Personality, and Life Satisfaction: A Review and Two Models.'' *Journal of Applied Gerontology*, 12(2):261–82.

Rhine, S. 1984. *Managing Older Workers: Company Policies and Attitudes.* New York: The Conference Board.

Rhine, Shirley H. 1985. *Managing Older Workers: Company Policies and Attitudes.* Research report no. 860. New York: The Conference Board.

Rhodes, S. 1983. "Age-Related Differences in Work Attitudes and Behavior: A Review and Conceptual Analysis.'' *Psychology Review*, 93(2):328–67.

Richter, J. 1992. "Economic Aspects of Aging: Review of the Literature.'' In *Demographic Causes and Economic Consequences of Population Aging*, ed. G. J. Stolnitz, 171–86. Economic Studies no. 3. New York: United Nations, UN Economic Commission for Europe.

Robinson, P. 1986. "Age, Health, and Job Performance.'' In *Age, Health, and Employment*, eds. J. E. Birren, P. K. Robinson, and J. E. Livingston, 63–77. Englewood Cliffs, N.J.: Prentice-Hall.

Rones, P. 1982. "The Aging of the Older Population and the Effect on Its Labor Force Rates.'' *Monthly Labor Review*, 105(9):27–29.

———. 1988. "Employment, Earnings, and Unemployment Characteristics of Older Workers." In *The Older Worker*, ed. M. Borus, H. Parnes, S. Sandell, and B. Seidman, 21–53, Madison, Wisc.: Industrial Relations Research.

Rones, P., and Herz, D. 1989. *Labor Market Problems of Older Workers*. Washington, D.C.: U.S. Department of Labor.

Root, L., and Zarrugh, L. 1987. "Private-Sector Employment Practices for Older Workers." In *The Problem Isn't Age: Work and Older Americans*, ed. Steven Sandell. New York: Praeger Publishers.

Rosen, B., and Jerdee, T. 1976. "The Nature of Job-Related Age Stereotypes." *Journal of Applied Psychology*, 61 (April): 180–83.

———. 1977. "Too Old or Not Too Old." *Harvard Business Review* 55(6):97–106.

Rosen, B., and Jerdee, T. H. 1990. "Middle and Late Career Problems: Causes, Consequences, and Research Needs." *Human Resource Planning*, 13(1):59–70.

Rosen, S. 1985. "Implicit Contracts: A Survey." *Journal of Economic Literature* 23 (September): 1144–75.

Rosenblum, M. 1975. "The Last Push: From Discouraged Worker to Involuntary Retirement." *Industrial Gerontology*, 2(1):14–22.

Rosow, I. 1985. "Status and Role Change through the Life Cycle." In *Aging and the Social Sciences*, ed. R. H. Binstock and E. Shanas, 62–93. New York: Van Nostrand Reinhold Company.

Rossi, A., and Rossi, P. 1990. *Of Human Bonding: Parent–Child Relations Across the Life Course*. New York: A. de Gruyter.

Rothman, D. 1971. *The Discovery of the Asylum*. Boston: Little, Brown.

Rubin, R., and Nieswiadomy, M. 1994. "Expenditure Patterns of Retired and Nonretired Persons." *Monthly Labor Review* (117) 4.

Ruhm, C. 1989. "Why Older Americans Stop Working." *The Gerontologist*, 29(3):294–99.

———. 1990. "Bridge Jobs and Partial Retirement." *Journal of Labor Economics*, 8(4): 482–501.

———. 1991. "Career Employment and Job Stopping." *Industrial Relations*, 30(2):193–208.

———. 1992a. "Do Pensions Increase the Labor Supply of Older Men?" University of North Carolina, Greensboro. Mimeograph.

———. 1992b. "The Effects of Physical and Mental Health on Female Labor Supply." In *Economics and Mental Health*, ed. Richard G. Frank and Willard G. Manning, 152–81. Baltimore, Md.: Johns Hopkins University Press.

———. 1993a. "Gender Differences in Employment Behavior during Late Middle-Age." University of North Carolina, Greensboro. Mimeograph.

———. 1993b. "Secular Changes in the Work and Retirement Patterns of Older Men." University of North Carolina, Greensboro. Mimeograph.

Ruhm, C., and Sum, A. 1989. "Job Stopping: The Changing Employment Patterns of Older Americans." *Proceedings of the Forty-First Annual Industrial Relations Research Association Meetings*, 21–28.

Rupp, K., Bryant, E., Mantovani, R., and Rhoads, M. 1987. "Government Employment and Training Programs, and Older Americans." In *The Problem Isn't Age: Work and Older Americans*, ed. Steven Sandell, 121–42. Westport, Conn.: Praeger.

Russell, L. 1982. *The Baby Boom Generation and the Economy*. Washington, D.C.: Brookings Institution.

Rust, J. 1989. "A Dynamic Programming Model of Retirement Behavior." In *The Economics of Aging*, ed. David Wise, 359–98. Chicago: University of Chicago Press.

———. 1990. "Behavior of Male Workers at the End of the Life Cycle: An Empirical Analysis of States and Controls." In *Issues in the Economics of Aging*, ed. David A. Wise, 317–79. Chicago: University of Chicago Press.

Ruth, J., and Birren, J. E. 1985. "Creativity in Adulthood and Old Age: Relations to Intelligence, Sex, and Mode of Testing." *International Journal of Behavioral Development*, 8:99–109.

Ryscavage, P. 1987. "Income Trends of the Young and the Elderly." *Family Economic Review*, 2:1–8.

Salthouse, T. A. 1984. "Effects of Age and Skill in Typing." *Journal of Gerontology*, 113:345–71.

———. 1985. "Speed of Behavior and its Implications for Cognition." In *Handbook of the Psychology of Aging*, ed. J. E. Birren and K. W. Schaie, 400–426. New York: Van Nostrand Reinhold.

Salthouse, T. A., Kausler, D. H., and Saults, J. S. 1988. "Investigation of Student Status, Background Variables, and Feasibility of Standard Tasks on Cognitive Aging Research." *Psychology and Aging*, 3:29–37.

Saluter, A., "Changes in American Family Life." *Current Population Reports: Special Studies* (Washington, D.C.: U.S. Bureau of the Census), series P-23, no. 163.

Sammartino, F. 1987. "The Effect of Health on Retirement." *Social Security Bulletin*, 50 (February): 31–47.

Samuelson, R. 1988. "The Elderly Aren't Needy. *Generational Journal*, 1(1):52.

Samwick, A. 1993. "The Joint Effect of Social Security and Pensions on the Timing of Retirement: Some New Evidence." Massachusetts Institute of Technology. Mimeograph.

Sandell, S. 1994. *Are Retirement Benefits Too High and Will They Be Too Low? An Examination of Wage Indexation in Social Security*. Research paper. Washington, D.C.: Urban Institute.

Sandell, S., ed. 1987. *The Problem Isn't Age: Work and Older Americans*. New York: Praeger.

Sandell, S., and Baldwin, S. 1990. "Older Workers and Employment Shifts: Policy Responses to Displacement." In *The Aging of the American Work Force*, ed. I. Bluestone, R. Montgomery, and J. Owen, 126–48. Detroit, Mich.: Wayne State University Press.

Sanders, M. S., and McCormick, E. J. 1987. *Human Factors in Engineering and Design*. New York: McGraw-Hill.

Schaie, K. W. 1965. "A General Model for the Study of Developmental Problems." *Psychological Bulletin*, 64:91–107.

———. 1974. "Translation in Gerontology—From Lab to Life: Intellectual Functioning." *American Psychologist*, 29:802–7.

———. 1985. "Intellectual Development in Adulthood." In *Handbook of the Psychology of Aging*, ed. J. E. Birren and K. W. Schaie. New York: Van Nostrand Reinhold.

Schaie, K. W., and Achenbaum, W. 1993. *Societal Impact on Aging: Historical Perspectives*. New York: Springer Publishing Company.

Schieber, S. 1982. *Social Security: Perspectives on Preserving the System*. Washington, D.C.: Employee Benefits Research Institute.

Schneier, C. E., Guthrie, J. P., and Olian, J. D. 1988. "A Practical Approach to Conducting and Using the Training Needs Assessment." *Public Personnel Management*, 17:191–204.

Scholl, K., and Moon, M. 1988. *Dispelling the Myth of the Undeserving Rich*. Washington, D.C.: American Association of Retired Persons, Public Policy Institute.

Schonfield, D. 1982. "Who Is Stereotyping Whom and Why?" *The Gerontologist*, 22(3): 267–72.

Schouler, J. 1870. *A Treatise on the Law of Domestic Relations*. Boston: Little, Brown.

Schulz, J. 1992. *The Economics of Aging*. 5th ed. Dover, Mass.: Auburn House Publishing Company.

Schulz, J., Borowski, A., and Crown, W. 1991. *Economics of Population Aging: The "Graying" of Australia, Japan and the United States*. New York: Auburn House.

Schwab, D. P., and Heneman, H. G., III. 1978. "Age Stereotyping in Performance Appraisal." *Journal of Applied Psychology*, 63:573–78.

Seike, A., and Shimada, H. 1986. "Work and Retirement in Japan." Paper presented at the Conference on National and International Implications of Population Aging, Oiso, Japan.

Serow, W. 1981. "Population and Other Policy Responses to an Era of Sustained Low Fertility." *Social Science Quarterly*, 62:323–32.

Serow, W. J. 1976. "Slow Population Growth and the Size and Productivity of the Male Labor Force." *Atlantic Economic Journal*, 4:61–68.

Serow, W. J., and Espenshade, T. 1978. "The Economics of Declining Population Growth: An Assessment of the Current Literature." In *The Economic Consequences of Slowing Population Growth*, ed. T. J. Espenshade and W. J. Serow 13–40. New York: Academic Press.

Shanas, E., Townsend, P., Wedderburn, D., Friis, H., Milhøj, P., and Stehouwer, J. 1968. *Old People in Three Industrial Societies*. New York: Atherton Press.

Shank, Susan E. 1988. "Women and the Labor Market: The Link Grows Stronger." *Monthly Labor Review* III (March): 3–8.

Shapiro, D., and Sandell, S. 1985. "Age Discrimination in Wages and Displaced Older Men." *Southern Economic Journal*, 52(1):90–102.

———. 1987. "Older Job Losers' Reduced Pay: Age Discrimination and Other Explanations." In *The Problem Isn't Age: Work and Older Americans*, ed. Steven Sandell. New York: Praeger Publishers.

Shaw, L. 1988. "Special Problems of Older Women Workers." In *The Older Worker*, ed. M. Borus, H. Parnes, S. Sandell, and B. Seidman, 55–86. Madison, Wisc.: Industrial Relations Research.

Shearer, R., and Steger, J. 1975. "Manpower Obsolescence: A New Definition and Empirical Investigation of Personal Variables." *Academy of Management Journal*, 18(2):263–75.

Shephard, R. J. 1984. "Technological Change and the Aging of Working Capacity." In *Aging and Technological Advances*, ed. P. K. Robinson, J. Livingston, and J. E. Birren, 195–207. New York: Plenum Press.

Sheppard, H. 1988. "Work Continuity Versus Retirement: Reasons for Continuing Work." In *Retirement Reconsidered*, ed. Robert Morris and Scott Bass. New York: Springer Publishing Company.

Sheppard, H., and Rix, S. 1989. *Training of Older Workers in the United States*. Geneva, Switzerland: International Labor Organization.

Sherman, S. 1985. "Reported Reasons Retired Workers Left Their Last Job: Findings from the New Beneficiary Survey." *Social Security Bulletin*, 48(3):22–30.

Shleifer, A., and Summers, L. 1988. "Breach of Trust in Hostile Takeovers." In *Corporate Takeovers: Causes and Consequences*, ed. A. Auerbach, 33–68. Chicago: University of Chicago Press.

Shover, J. L. 1976. *First Majority—Last Minority*. DeKalb: Northern Illinois University Press.

Sickles, R., and Taubman, P. 1986. "An Analysis of the Health and Retirement Status of the Elderly." *Econometrica*, 54 (November): 1339–56.

Siegel, P. 1989. "Educational Attainment in the United States: March 1982 to 1985." *Current Population Reports* (Washington, D.C.: U.S. Bureau of the Census), series P-20, no. 415.

Siemen, J. 1976. "Programmed Material as a Training Tool for Older Persons." *Industrial Gerontology*, 3(3):183–90.

Silvestri, G. 1993. "Occupational Employment: Wide Variations in Growth." *Monthly Labor Review*, 116(11):58–86.

Simonton, D. K. 1990. "Creativity and Wisdom in Aging." In *Handbook of the Psychology of Aging*, ed. J. E. Birren and K. W. Schaie, 320–29. 3rd ed. New York: Academic Press.

Skocpol, T. 1993. *Mothers and Soldiers*. Cambridge, Mass.: Harvard University Press.

Smith, D. S. 1979. "Life Course, Norms, and the Family System of Older Americans in 1900." *Journal of Family History*, 4(3):285–98.

Smith, K., and Moen, P. 1988. "Passage through Midlife: Women's Changing Family Roles and Economic Well-Being." *Sociological Quarterly*, 29:503–24.

Smolensky, E., Danziger, S., and Gottschalk, P. 1988. "The Declining Significance of Age in the United States: Trends in the Well-Being of Children and the Elderly since 1939." In *The Vulnerable: America's Young and Old in the Industrial World*, ed. J. Palmer, T. Smeeding, and B. Torrey. Washington, D.C.: Urban Institute Press.

Snook, S. 1971. "The Effects of Age and Physique on Continuous-Work Capacity." *Human Factors*, 13(5):467–79.

———. 1978. "The Design of Manual Handling Tasks." *Ergonomics*, 21:963–85.

Snyder, C. J., and Barrett, G. V. 1988. "The Age Discrimination in Employment Act: A Review of Court Decisions." *Experimental Aging Research*, 14:3–55.

Social Security Administration. 1993. *Social Security Handbook*. 11th ed. Washington, D.C.: U.S. Government Printing Office.

Sonnenfeld, J. 1978. "Dealing with an Aging Workforce." *Harvard Business Review*, (November–December): 109–20.

Spencer, L. M., Jr. 1986. *Calculating Human Resource Costs and Benefits: Cutting Costs and Improving Productivity*. New York,: John Wiley and Sons.

Squier, L. W. 1912. *Old Age Dependency in the United States*. New York: Macmillan.

Stagner, Ross. 1985. "Aging in Industry." In *Handbook of the Psychology of Aging*, ed. J. Birren and K. Schaie. 2nd ed. New York: Van Nostrand Reinhold.

Stalson, J. O. 1969. *Marketing Life Insurance*. Homewood, Ill.: Richard D. Irwin.

Standing, G. 1986. "Labour Flexibility and Older Worker Marginalisation." *International Labour Review*, 125(3):329–48.

Stein, B. S. 1989. "Memory and Creativity." In *Handbook of Creativity*, ed. J. A. Glover, R. R. Ronning, and C. R. Reynolds, 163–76. New York: Plenum Press.

Steinmann, G. 1989. "Malthusian crises, Boserupian Escapes and Long Run Economic Progress." In *Demographic Change and Economic Development*, ed. A. Wenig and K. Zimmerman, 3–28. Berlin: Springer-Verlag.

Stern, S. 1989. "Measuring the Effect of Disability on Labor Force Participation." *Journal of Human Resources*, 24(3):361–95.

Sterns, H., and McDaniel, M. 1994, January. "Job Performance and the Older Worker" (draft). Paper prepared for the American Association of Retired Persons. University of Akron, Ohio.

Sterns, H., and Sterns, A. 1994. "Age, Health, and Employment Capability of Older Americans." In *Older and Active*, ed. Scott Bass. New Haven, Conn.: Yale University Press.

———. 1995. "Health and Employment Capability of Older Americans." In *Older and Active: How Americans over 55 Are Contributing to Society*, ed. Scott Bass. New Haven, Conn.: Yale University Press.

Sterns, H. L. 1986. "Training and Retraining Adult and Older Workers." In *Age, Health, and Employment*, ed. J. Birren, P. Robinson, and J. Livingston. Englewood Cliffs, N.J.: Prentice-Hall.

Sterns, H. L., and Alexander, R. A. 1987. "Industrial Gerontology: The Aging Individual and Work." *Annual Review of Gerontology and Geriatrics*, ed. K. W. Schaie, 93–113. New York: Springer.

———. 1988. "Step 6: Use Objective Performance Appraisals." In *Fourteen Steps to Managing an Aging Work Force*, ed. H. Dennis, 171–90. Lexington, Mass.: D.C. Heath.

Sterns, H. L., and Doverspike, D. 1988. "Training and Developing the Older Worker: Implications for Human Resource Management." In *Fourteen Steps in Managing an Aging Work Force*, ed. H. Dennis. Lexington, Mass.: D.C. Heath.

Sterns, H. S., and Barrett, G. V. 1992. "Work (Paid Employment) and Aging." Paper presented at the National Institute of Aging Workshop, "Applied Gerontology Research: Setting A Future Agenda." Department of Health and Human Services, National Institute on Aging, Bethesda, Md., August 12–13.

Stewart, J. S. 1969. "Retraining Older Workers for Upgraded Jobs." *Industrial Gerontology*, (Summer): 26–31.

Stigler, G., and Becker, G. 1977. "De Gustibus Non Est Disputandum." *American Economic Review*, 67(2):76–90.

Stine, E. L., Wingfield, A., and Poon, L. W. 1989. "Speech Comprehension and Memory through Adulthood: The Roles of Time and Strategy." In *Everyday Cognition in Adulthood and Later Years*, ed. L. W. Poon, D. C. Rubin, and B. A. Wilson, 195–221. Cambridge: Cambridge Press.

Stith, R., and Kohlburn, W. 1992. "Early Retirement Incentive Plans After Passage of the Older Workers Benefit Protection Act." *Saint Louis University Public Law Review*, 11(243):263–79.

Stock, J., and Wise, D. 1990a. "The Pension Inducement to Retire: An Option Value Analysis." In *Issues in the Economics of Aging*, ed. David A. Wise, 204–24. Chicago: University of Chicago Press.

———. 1990b. "Pensions, the Option Value of Work, and Retirement." *Econometrica*, 58(5):1151–80.

Stolzfus, E. R., Hasher, L., Zacks, R. T., Ulivi, M. S., and Goldstein, D. 1993. "Investigations of Inhibitions and Interference in Younger and Older Adults.'' *Journal of Gerontology: Psychological Sciences*, 48:179–88.

Straka, J. 1992. *The Demand for Older Workers: The Neglected Side of a Labor Market.* Washington, D.C.: Social Security Administration, Office of Research and Statistics.

Streib, G., and Schneider, C. 1971. *Retirement in American Society: Impact and Process.* Ithaca, N.Y.: Cornell University Press.

Streufert, S., Pogash, R., Piasecki, M., and Post, G. 1991. ''Age and Management Team Performance.'' *Psychology and Aging*, 5:551–59.

Sueyoshi, G. 1989. ''Social Security and the Determinants of Full and Partial Retirement: A Competing Risks Analysis.'' NBER working paper no. 3113. Cambridge, Mass.: National Bureau of Economic Research (NBER).

Sum, A., and Fogg, W. N. 1990a. ''Labor Market and Poverty Problems of Older Workers.'' In *Bridges to Retirement*, ed. Peter B. Doeringer, 64–91. Ithaca, N.Y.: ILR Press.

———. 1990b. ''Profile of the Labor Market for Older Workers.'' In *Bridges to Retirement*, ed. Peter B. Doeringer, 33–63. Ithaca, N.Y.: ILR Press.

Szalai, J. 1991. ''Hungary: Exit from the State Economy.'' In *Time for Retirement: Comparative Studies of Early Exit from the Labor Force*, ed. Martin Kohli, Martin Rein, Anne-Marie Guillemard, and Herman van Gunsteren, 324–61. Cambridge: Cambridge University Press.

Szinovacz, M., Ekerdt, D., and Vinick, B. 1992. ''Families and Retirement: Conceptual and Methodological Issues.'' In *Families and Retirement*, ed. Maximiliane Szinovacz, David Ekerdt, and Barbara Vinick. Newbury Park, Calif.: Sage Publications.

Taylor, R. N. 1975. ''Perception of Problem Constraints.'' *Management Science*, 22:22–29.

Tayyari, F., and Sohrabi, A. 1990. ''Carpal Tunnel Syndrome Update.'' In *Advances in Industrial Ergonomics and Safety II*, ed. B. Das, 201–6. New York: Taylor and Francis.

Terleckyj, N. E. 1990. ''Getting to 2020: The Coming Demographic Changes and the U.S. Economic Uncertainties.'' In *1989 Proceedings of the Social Statistics Section, American Statistical Association*, 64–69. Alexandria, Va.: American Statistical Association.

Thomas, R. seriatim. ''Father Simkins.'' *Farmer's Almanac* (Springfield, Mass.).

Thompson, W., and Whelpton, P. [1933] 1969. *Population Trends in the United States.* New York: Krauss. Reprint.

Thorndike, E. L., and Woodyard, E. 1926. ''The Relation of Earning Power to Age on Professional Workers under Conditions of Nearly Free Competition.'' *Journal of the American Statistical Association*, 21 (September): 293–306.

Thornstam, L. 1992. ''The Quo Vadis of Gerontology: On the Scientific Paradigm of Gerontology.'' *The Gerontologist*, 32(3):318–26.

Thorpe, F. N. 1909. *Federal and State Constitutions. Colonial Charters and Other Organic Laws 1492–1908.* 7 vols. Washington, D.C.: U.S. Government Printing Office.

Tipper, S. P. 1992. ''Section for Action: The Role of Inhibitory Mechanisms.'' *Current Directions in Psychology*, 1:105–9.

Tipper, S. P., Weaver, B., Cameron, S., Brehaut, J. C., and Bastedo, J. 1991. ''Inhibitory

Mechanisms of Attention in Identification and Localization Tasks: Time Course and Disruption." *Journal of Experimental Psychology: Learning, Memory, and Cognition*, 17:681–92.

Torres-Gil, F. 1992. *The New Aging: Politics and Change in America*. Westport, Conn.: Auburn House.

Torrey, B. 1982. "Guns vs. Canes: The Fiscal Implications of an Aging Population." *American Economic Review*, 72(2):309–13.

Treas, J. 1986. "The Historical Decline in Late-Life Labor Force Participation in the United States." In *Age, Health, and Employment*, ed. J. Birren, P. Robinson, and J. Livingstone, 158–75. Englewood Cliffs, N.J.: Prentice-Hall.

Treat, N., Poon, L., and Fozard, J. 1981. "Age, Imagery, and Practice in Paired-Associate Learning." *Experimental Aging Research*, 7(3):337–42.

Trutko, J., Barnow, B., Chasanov, A., and Pande, A. 1993. *Labor Shortage Case Studies*. Research and Evaluation Report Series 93-E. Washington, D.C.: U.S. Department of Labor, Employment and Training Administration.

Turner, J. 1993. *Pension Policy for a Mobile Labor Force*. Kalamazoo, Mich.: W. E. Upjohn Institute for Employment Research.

Turner, J., and Beller, D. 1992. *Trends in Pensions 1992*. Washington, D.C.: U.S. Government Printing Office.

United Nations. Department of Economic and Social Development. 1993. *The Sex and Age Distribution of the World Populations: The 1992 Revision*. New York: United Nations.

United States. (seriatim). *Revised Statutes*.

U.S. Bureau of the Census. 1983. "Money Income of Households, Families, and Persons in the United States: 1981." *Current Population Reports* (Washington, D.C.: U.S. Government Printing Office), series P-60, no. 137.

———. 1989. "The Hispanic Population of the United States: March 1988." *Current Population Reports* (Washington, D.C.: U.S. Government Printing Office), series P-20, no. 438.

———. 1992a. "An Aging World II." *International Population Reports* (Washington, D.C.: U.S. Government Printing Office), P95/92–3.

———. 1992b. "Money Income of Households, Families, and Persons in the United States: 1991." *Current Population Reports* (Washington, D.C.: U.S. Government Printing Office), series P-60, no. 180.

———. 1992c. "Population Projections of the United States by Age, Sex, Race, and Hispanic Origin: 1992 to 2050." *Current Population Reports* (Washington, D.C.: U.S. Government Printing Office), P25–1092.

———. 1992d. "What's It Worth? Educational Background and Economic Status: Spring 1990." *Current Population Reports*. (Washington, D.C.: U.S. Government Printing Office), series P70–62.

———. 1993. "Money Income of Households, Families and Persons in the United States: 1992." *Current Population Reports*. (Washington, D.C.: U.S. Government Printing Office), series P60–184, Table 29, 116–43.

———. 1994. *Statistical Abstract of the United States: 1993*. 113th ed. Washington, D.C.: U.S. Government Printing Office.

U.S. Congress, Joint Economic Committee, subcommittee on Education and Health. 1989. *The Education Deficit*. Washington, D.C.: U.S. Government Printing Office.

U.S. Congressional Budget Office. 1993. *Displaced Workers: Trends in the 1980s and Implications for the Future.* Washington, D.C.: U.S. Congressional Budget Office.

U.S. Congressional Research Service. 1991. *Older Workers in the Labor Market.* Report to the Select Committee on Aging, U.S. House of Representatives. Washington, D.C.: U.S. Government Printing Office.

U.S. Department of Health and Human Services. 1982. *1978 Survey of Disability and Work, Data Book.* Washington, D.C.: U.S. Government Printing Office.

————. 1990. *Healthy People 2000.* DHHS Publication no. (PHS) 91–50213. Washington, D.C.: U.S. Government Printing Office.

————. 1991. *Aging America: Trends and Projections.* DHHS Publication no. 91–28001. Washington D.C.: U.S. Government Printing Office.

————. 1993. *Social Security Handbook, 1993.* 11th Edition. Washington, D.C.: U.S. Government Printing Office.

————. Secretary's Commission on Nursing. 1988, December. "Final Report."

U.S. Department of Labor. 1965a. *The Dictionary of Occupational Titles.* 3rd ed. Washington D.C.: U.S. Government Printing Office.

————. 1965b. *The Older American Worker, Age Discrimination in Employment.* Report of the Secretary of Labor to the Congress under Section 715 of the Civil Rights Act of 1964. Washington, D.C.: U.S. Government Printing Office.

————. 1985. *How Workers Get Their Training.* Washington, D.C.: U.S. Government Printing Office.

————. 1987. "Most Occupational Changes Are Voluntary." *News* (October 22).

————. 1989a. *Handbook of Labor Statistics.* Bulletin 2340. Washington, D.C.: U.S. Government Printing Office.

————. 1989b. *Investing in People: A Strategy to Address America's Workforce Crisis.* Washington, D.C.: Commission on Workforce Quality and Labor Market Efficiency.

————. 1989c. *Older Worker Task Force: Key Policy Issues for the Future.* Report to the Secretary of Labor. Washington, D.C.: U.S. Government Printing Office.

————. 1990a. "Education and Training of American Workers." Paper prepared for the OECD National Experts Group on Training Statistics. U.S. Bureau of Labor Statistics. Mimeograph.

————. 1990b. *Employment and Earnings* (Washington, D.C.: U.S. Government Printing Office), 30(1): (whole issue).

————. 1991. *Employment and Earnings* (Washington, D.C.: U.S. Government Printing Office), 31(1): (whole issue).

————. 1992a *Care of Aged Persons in the United States.* Bulletin 489. Washington, D.C.: U.S. Government Printing Office.

————. 1992b. *Employment and Earnings* (Washington, D.C.: U.S. Government Printing Office), 32(1): (whole issue).

————. 1992c. *How Workers Get Their Training: A 1991 Update.* Washington, D.C.: U.S. Bureau of Labor Statistics.

————. 1992d. *News* (Washington, D.C.: Bureau of Labor Statistics) (June 26).

————. 1992e. *Training and Employment Report of the Secretary of Labor.* Washington, D.C.: U.S. Government Printing Office.

————. 1993a. "Abstract of 1990 Form 5500 Annual Reports." *Private Pension Plan*

Bulletin, 2 (Summer). Washington, D.C.: Pension and Welfare Benefits Administration.

———. 1993b. *Employee Benefits in Medium and Large Private Establishments, 1991.* Washington, D.C.: U.S. Bureau of Labor Statistics.

———. 1993c. *Employment and Earnings* (Washington, D.C.: U.S. Government Printing Office), 33(1): (whole issue).

———. 1993d. *Employment in Perspective: Women in the Labor Force.* Report 860. Washington, D.C.: U.S. Bureau of Labor Statistics.

———. 1993e. *Employment in Perspective: Women in the Labor Force.* Report 848. Washington, D.C.: U.S. Bureau of Labor Statistics.

———. 1993f. *Work and Family: Women in their Forties.* Report 843. Washington, D.C.: U.S. Bureau of Labor Statistics.

———. 1994. *Employment and Earnings* (Washington, D.C.: U.S. Government Printing Office), 34(1): (whole issue).

U.S. Department of Labor, U.S. Social Security Administration, U.S. Small Business Administration, and Pension Benefit Guarantee Corporation. 1994. *Pension and Health Benefits of Older Workers.* Washington, D.C.: U.S. Government Printing Office.

U.S. General Accounting Office. 1990, February. "Age Discrimination: Use of Age-Specific Provisions in Company Exit Incentive Programs." Washington, D.C.

U.S. House of Representatives. Committee on Ways and Means. 1987. *Retirement Income for An Aging Society.* Washington, D.C.: U.S. Government Printing Office, August 25.

———. 1992. *Background Material and Data on Programs within the Jurisdiction of the Committee on Ways and Means.* Washington, D.C.: U.S. Government Printing Office.

———. 1993. *Background Material and Data on Programs within the Jurisdiction of the Committee on Ways and Means.* Washington, D.C.: U.S. Government Printing Office.

U.S. House of Representatives, Committee on Ways and Means. 1994. *1994 Green Book: Background Material and Data on Programs within the Jurisdiction of the Committee on Ways and Means.* Washington, D.C.: U.S. Government Printing Office.

U.S. Senate. 1967. Age Discrimination in Employment: Hearings before the Subcommittee on Labor, Senate Committee on Labor and Public Welfare. 90th Cong., 1st Sess.

———. 1984. *The Costs of Employing Older Workers.* Washington, D.C.: U.S. Government Printing Office.

———. *Developments in Aging: 1992.* Vol. 1: *A Report of the Special Committee on Aging, United States Senate.* Washington, D.C.: U.S. Government Printing Office.

U.S. Social Security Administration. 1993. *Social Security Bulletin: Annual Statistical Supplement.* Washington, D.C.: U.S. Government Printing Office.

Useem, Michael. 1993. "The Restructuring of American Business and the Aging Workforce." Paper prepared for a conference of the National Planning Association/ National Council on the Aging, Joint Project on U.S. Competitiveness and the Aging American Workforce, Washington, D.C.

Verbrugge, L. 1991. In *Proceedings of the Second Conference of the National Academy of Social Insurance.* Washington, D.C.: National Academy of Social Insurance.

Vistnes, J. 1994. "An Empirical Analysis of Married Women's Retirement Decisions." *National Tax Journal*, 47 (March): 135–55.

Vroman, W. 1985. "Some Economic Effects of the Social Security Retirement Test." In *Research in Labor Economics*, ed. Ronald Ehrenberg. Greenwich, Conn: JAI Press, 31–90.

Waldman, D., and Avolio, B. 1986. "A Meta-Analysis of Age Differences in Job Performance." *Journal of Applied Psychology*, 71 (February): 33–38.

Wander, H. 1978. "ZPG Now: The Lesson From Europe." In *The Economic Consequences of Slowing Population Growth*, ed. T. Espenshade and W. Serow. New York: Academic Press.

Warr, P. 1993. "Age and Employment." In *Handbook of Industrial and Organizational Psychology*, vol. 4, ed. M. Dunnette, L. Hough, and H. Triandis. Palo Alto, Calif.: Consulting Psychologists Press.

Wattenberg, B. 1987. *The Birth Dearth: A Graying Economy*. New York: Pharos Books.

Weaver, D. 1994. "The Work and Retirement Decisions of Older Women: A Literature Review." *Social Security Bulletin*, 57 (Spring): 3–24.

Webster, N. (S.V.). *An American Dictionary of the English Language*.

Welford, A. 1958. *Aging and Human Skills*. London: Oxford Press.

———. 1988. "Preventing Adverse Changes of Work with Age." *International Journal of Aging and Human Development*, 27(4):283–91.

Wexley, K. N., and Latham, G. P. 1981. *Developing and Training Human Resources in Organizations*. Glenview, Ill.: Scott, Foresman.

Whaples, R. 1994. "A History of Retirement." In *Encyclopedia of Financial Gerontology*, ed. Lois Vitt and Jurg Sieganthaler. Westport, Conn.: Greenwood Publishing Group, Inc.

Whelpton, P. K. 1926. "Occupational Groups in the United States." *Journal of the American Statistical Association*, 21 (March): 26–47.

Wiber, G., and Adams, M. 1991. "Benefit Plans and the U.S. Economy." Reprint from *Pension World*, (January).

Williams, D. 1991. "RIFs, Early Retirement, and Releases after the OWBPA." *Ali-Aba Course Materials Journal*, 16 (December 1): 87–106.

Willis, S. L., and Dubin, S. S. 1990. "Maintaining Professional Competence: Directions and Possibilities." In *Maintaining Professional Competence*, ed. S. L. Willis and S. S. Dubin, 306–14. San Francisco, Calif: Jossey-Bass.

Wiseman, A. C. 1989. "Projected Long-Term Demographic Trends and Aggregate Personal Savings in the United States." *Journal of Post Keynesian Economics*, 11: 497–508.

Woodbury, R. 1991. "Why Businesses Design Policies that Induce Retirement: An Analysis of the Retirement Policy Motivations at Twenty Large United States Employers." Ph.D. dissertation, Harvard University.

Work in America Institute, Inc. 1980. *The Future of Older Workers in America: New Options for an Extended Working Life*. Scarsdale, N.Y.: Work in America Institute.

Ycas, M. 1986. "Recent Changes in Health near the Age of Retirement." Paper presented at the 1986 Annual Meeting of the Gerontological Society of America, New Orleans.

Zabalza, A. Pissarides, C., and Barton, M. 1980. "Social Security and the Choice Between Full-Time, Part-Time Work, and Retirement." *Journal of Public Economics*, 14 (October): 245–76.

Zedeck, S., Jackson, S. E., and Summers, E. 1983. "Shift Work Schedules and Their Relationship to Health, Adaptation, Satisfaction, and Turnover Intention." *Academy of Management Journal*, 26(2):297–310.

Zoghlin, G. 1989. "Departing Executives, Emerging Entrepreneurs." *Personnel Administrator*, 34 (March): 78–82.

Zweimuller, J. 1991. "Earnings, Social Security Legislation and Retirement Decisions: The Austrian Experience." *Applied Economics*, 23 (May): 851–60.

Index

Absenteeism. *See* Costs of older workers; Labor force participants
Activity theory, 254–56
Actuarial Adjustments. *See* Defined benefit plans; Social security provisions
Age-earnings profile, 381, 383. *See also* Labor force participants
Age Discrimination in Employment Act (ADEA), 173, 182, 191, 194, 276, 282, 394; Court decisions under, 203–5; institutionalized ageism, 270–71; legal background, 198–99; legislative history of, 200–203; unresolved areas of litigation, 206–7
Americans with Disabilities Act (ADA) of 1990, 270, 282–83
Arrow-Capron dynamic shortage model, 353–54. *See also* Labor shortages
Attitudes toward older workers: management, 324–28; societal, 130–32
Average indexed monthly earnings (AIME), 152, 227

Backloading of pension accruals, 171

Benefits of older workers, lower turnover, 343–44
Blank-Stigler model, 352. *See also* Labor shortages
Bona fide occupational qualification (BFOQ) defense, 201
Bridge jobs, 98–100

Capital deepening, 389
Capital formation, effects of population on aging, 383, 386
Charitable supports for the aged, 140–41
Class, and labor market opportunities, 136–37
Committee on Economic Security (CES), 129. *See also* Social security
Computer design, implications for productivity, 300–301
Consolidated Omnibus Budget Reconciliation Act of 1987 (COBRA), 191
Continuity theory, 254–58
Costs of older workers: absenteeism, 336–37; health care, 330–32; pensions, 332–35; training, 338–40; wages and

salaries, 329–30; workplace injury, 336–38
Cultural lag, 272

Defined benefit plans: actuarial adjustments in, 177–80; deferred retirement under, 173–74; early retirement age, 169; early retirement reduction factors, 169–70; integration with social security, 170–71; nonaccrued early retirement benefits, 171; normal retirement age, 168; pension accruals, 171, 175–77; as personnel tools, 167; supplemental early retirement benefits, 170; work incentives and disincentives in, 95–96
Defined contribution plans, 94, 166, 235
Delayed retirement. See Defined benefit plans; Social security provisions
Delayed retirement credit (DRC), 227
Demand for older workers, 240–41. See also Labor markets, reasons for slow adjustment
Demographic forecasts, alternate census bureau projections, 58–67; by age, 59–65, 375–80; by race/Hispanic origin, 59, 66–67, 69–70, 377, 379
Dependency ratios, 68
Disability and older workers, 138–39
Disability benefits, and labor force participation, 91–92
Disability pensions, international comparisons, 125–26
Discouraged workers, 22–25
Disequilibrium in occupational labor markets: decrease in supply of labor, 358–60; increase in demand for labor, 358–59; restrictions on prices, 360–61. See also Labor markets, reasons for slow adjustments; Labor shortages
Dynamic models of older worker labor supply. See Economic studies of retirement
Dynamic programming models of labor supply, 233–35
Dynamic versus static models of retirement, 226

Early retirement age. See Defined benefit plans; Social security (international comparisons); Social security provisions
Early retirement incentive programs (ERIPs), 172–73, 182–93, 324; characteristics of organizations, 184–85; characteristics of plans, 183–84; cost to employers, 189–90; eligibility for, 186–87; employee/employer reactions to, 190; frequency offered 184; reasons for offering, 185–86; timing of, 189; variation in benefits, 187–88
Earnings as a proxy for productivity, 381
Earnings of older workers, 195–97. See also Age-earnings profile; Costs of older workers
Economic growth and productivity, 380–81, 383
Economic studies of retirement, 220–38
Educational attainment and productivity, 383
Education levels, 70–71, 383, 385
Eligibility. See Defined benefit plans; Early retirement incentive plans (ERIPs); Social security provisions
Employee Retirement Income Security Act (ERISA), 169; reduction factors for early leavers, 172; suspension of pension payments under, 171–72; work restrictions on retirees, 393–94
Employer responses to labor shortages. See Labor shortages
Employment opportunities: by class, 136–37; by ethnicity, 135; by race, 135
Employment programs: private employer, 396–97; Senior Community Service Employment Program, 312, 394–95
Endogeneity of pension contracts, 167. See also Private pensions
Equal Employment Opportunity Commission (EEOC), 194
Equity considerations, policy implications of, 402–3
Ethnicity and labor market opportunities. See also Labor force participation trends
Exchange theory, 257

Family composition, changes in, 71–72; implications for caregiving, 72; implications for labor force participation, 72

Family retirement models, 241–242

Family support for the elderly, 139

Female workers: characteristics of, 105–6; labor market problems of, 106–7; life course perspective of, 107–8; obstacles facing, 134–35; retirement transitions, 108–9; trends in labor force participation of, 75, 82–85, 104–5. *See also* Labor force participation trends; Retirement

Financial Standards Accounting Board (FASB) Statement, 88–91

Functional capacity, changes with age, 281–82

Functional capacity assessment (FCA), 281

General Motors (GM), 173

Golden handshakes, 172

Hazard rates of retirement, 86–87, 92

Health benefits, affects on labor force participation, 92–93

Health care costs of older workers. *See* Costs of older workers

Health status of older persons: affects on retirement, 222–23, 230–31, 240; changes with age, 285–87; and labor force participation, 88–90; relationships between life expectancy, morbidity, and disability, 77–79. *See also* Costs of older workers; Job performance

Inadequate social demand, 351–52. *See also* Labor shortages

Intergenerational conflict, 271–72

Job analysis, 278–79. *See also* Job performance; Productivity, difficulties in measuring

Job characteristics, affects on retirement, 222–23

Job performance: affects of age on, 281–82; body dimensions, 284–85; cognitive changes, 287–91; creativity, 292–94; expertise, problem solving, and decision making, 291–92; health status, 285–87; hearing, 296; motor speed and reaction time, 297–98; perceptual speed, 296–97; physical mobility, 284; strength, 283; vision, 294–96. *See also* Job analysis; Productivity, difficulties in measuring

Job Training and Partnership Act (JTPA), 312, 394–95

Labor force age composition, affects of aging on population, 375, 377

Labor force participants: absenteeism, 34, 42–45; comparison with non-working population, 40–44, 50–56; earnings, 32–33, 39–40; employment type, 28–29, 32; occupations, 29–38; reasons for working, 2, 25–26; training desired, 36, 48; training received, 36, 47; unionization, 33, 41; work schedules, 35, 46, 84, 87–89; work status, 27–28, 29–31. *See also* Older workers, defined

Labor force participation trends: by age, 15–20; by country, 6, 110–13; implications of, 77; by race, 17, 75–76, 83; by sex, 16–19, 73–76, 82–84

Labor force, projected growth in, 69, 73, 326

Labor markets, reasons for slow adjustment, 367–70. *See also* Disequilibrium in occupational labor markets

Labor shortages: alternative theories of, 351–55; characteristics of, 357; concern about, 349; consequences of, 370; description of, 350–51; employer responses to, 361–67; implications for older workers, 371–72; policy implications of, 398–400. *See also* Disequilibrium in occupational labor markets

Life-cycle models of labor supply, 217–19, 228–32

Lorillard v. *Pons*, 204

Mandatory retirement: by country, 124; emergence of, 134

Marriage bars, 104, 134

Massachusetts Board of Retirement v.
    Murgia, 203
Monopsonistic labor market model, 354–
    55. *See also* Labor shortages

Needs analysis, 279–80
Normal retirement age. *See* Defined bene-
    fit plans; Social security (international
    comparisons); Social security
    provisions

Occupation. *See* Labor force participants
Occupational labor shortages. *See* Labor
    shortages
Older workers, defined: by chronological
    age, 276–77; by functional age, 277;
    by life-span, 277; by organizational
    roles, 277. *See also* Benefits of older
    workers, lower turnover; Costs of older
    workers; Demand for older workers;
    Labor force participants
Older Workers Benefit Protection Act
    (OWPBA), 189, 191–92, 202; and
    Public Employees Retirement System v.
    Betts, 202
Omnibus Budget Reconciliation Act of
    1986, 182, 201
Option value of postponing retirement,
    177, 236–37
Oscar Mayer & Co. v. *Evans*, 204

Partial retirement, 98, 232–33
Pension accruals. *See* Defined benefit
    plans
Pension and health care financing, policy
    implications, 400–402
Pension costs of older workers. *See* Costs
    of older workers
Physical abilities analysis, 280
Physical changes with age. *See* Job per-
    formance
Population aging, 4, 57, 59, 81, 375, 377;
    by country, 110–11. *See also* Demo-
    graphic forecasts, alternate census bu-
    reau projections; Dependency ratios;
    Social security
Primary Insurance Amount (PIA). *See*
    Social security

Private pensions: benefits, 37–39, 49; de-
    fined benefit plans, 166–74, 177–80,
    235–36; defined contribution plans,
    165, 235; early plans, 141–42; over-
    view of, 165–66. *See also* Costs of
    older workers; Defined benefit plans
Private pensions (international compari-
    sons): adjustment of benefits for post-
    poned retirement, 123–24; coverage,
    121; eligibility provisions, 121–23; role
    in encouraging retirement, 121–23
Private pension wealth, 174–75
Productive aging: Commonwealth Fund
    Productive Aging Survey, 264–65; con-
    ceptual framework for, 268–70; defini-
    tion of, 262–63; recent research, 273–
    74
Productivity, difficulties in measuring,
    340–43, 381. *See also* Job analysis;
    Job performance
Public pensions, early development of,
    142–43

Race, and labor market opportunities,
    135. *See also* Labor force participation
    trends
Rate of return model, 354. *See also* La-
    bor shortages
Rate of time preference, 217
Retirement: affects of demand-side fac-
    tors on, 97; affects of health and disa-
    bility benefits on, 88–93; affects of
    pension and non-pension wealth on,
    93–96, 174–75; affects of spousal re-
    tirement on, 96–97; social
    gerontological models of, 253–58
Retirement transitions, 97–100
Retirement windows, 237. *See also* Early
    retirement incentive programs
Roosevelt, Franklin Delano (FDR), 128–
    29

Senior Community Service Employment
    Program (SCSEP), 312
Shifting resources model, 259–60
Social demand model, 351–52. *See also*
    Labor shortages
Social security: early history of, 129–30;

implications of population aging for, 113; theories regarding development of, 251–52

Social security (international comparisons): benefit levels, 113–14; delayed retirement provisions, 117–19; early retirement provisions, 115–16; earnings tests, 119–20; eligibility ages, 114–15; role in reducing unemployment, 116–17

Social security provisions: earnings test, 154–58, 162; effects on social security wealth, 147–51; legislated changes in, 147; payroll tax, 159–60; primary insurance amount, 147, 223, 227; recomputation of benefits, 152–54; taxation of benefits, 158–59; work incentives and disincentives of, 94–96, 145–46, 160–61, 392

Social security wealth, calculation of, 146

Structural versus reduced-form models of retirement, 224–25

Tontine insurance, 140

Training of older workers: ability to learn, 315–19; costs and benefits of, 313–15; definition of, 304; evidence from case studies, 338; evidence from employer and establishment surveys, 308–11; general need for, 304–6; Job Training and Partnership Act, 312, 394–95; receipt of training, 306–8; Senior Community Service Employment Program, 312, 394–95; training in

other countries, 305–6, 311. *See also* Costs of older workers; Labor force participants

Unemployment: by age and sex, 20–25; prior labor force status, 26; by race, 21, 23; retirement by unemployed, 197. *See also* Private pensions (international comparisons); Social security; Social security (international comparisons)

Unionization. *See* Labor force participants

Voluntary separation programs, 183

Wage and salary costs of older workers. *See* Costs of older Workers

Western Air Lines v. *Criswell*, 204

Window plans. *See* Early retirement incentive programs

Women workers. *See* Female workers; Labor force participation trends

Workers. *See* Labor force participants

Work–leisure choice model, overview of, 215–16

Workplace design, implications for productivity, 299

Workplace injury. *See* Costs of older workers

Work schedules. *See* Labor force participants

Workspace design, implications for productivity, 299–300

Work status. *See* Labor force participants

About the Contributors

W. ANDREW ACHENBAUM is a professor of history at the University of Michigan, Ann Arbor, and deputy director of its Institute of Gerontology. He received his B.A. from Amherst College, an M.A. from the University of Pennsylvania, and his Ph.D. from the University of Michigan. His publications include *Old Age in the New Land* (1978) and *Social Security: Visions and Revisions* (1986). He recently completed work on *Crossing Frontiers: Gerontology Emerges as a Science* (1995) and with Daniel M. Albert, *Profiles in Gerontology: A Biographical Dictionary* (1995).

BURT S. BARNOW is Principal Research Scientist at the Institute for Policy Studies, Johns Hopkins University, where he teaches a course in labor economics and program evaluation. He has a B.S. degree in economics from the Massachusetts Institute of Technology and M.S. and Ph.D. degrees in economics from the University of Wisconsin at Madison. His current research interests include employment and training policies for disadvantaged and dislocated workers and evaluating programs for improving parenting skills.

MICHAEL C. BARTH is Executive Vice President of ICF Kaiser International Consulting Group. Dr. Barth received a B.A. from Harpur College of the State University of New York at Binghamton, an M.A. from the University of Illinois, and a Ph.D. in economics from the City University of New York. Prior to joining ICF, Dr. Barth was Deputy Assistant Secretary for Income Security Policy, U.S.

Department of Health and Human Services. He has taught labor economics, human resources economics, economic theory, principles of economics, and statistics at the University of Wisconsin and the City College of New York. Listed in Who's Who in America and Who's Who in Finance and Industry, Dr. Barth is the author of more than a score of publications in professional journals and books.

SCOTT A. BASS is a professor at the University of Massachusetts, Boston and director of the University's Gerontological Institute. He is the editor of *Older and Active: How Americans over 55 Are Contributing to Society* and his research interests center around productive aging. Dr. Bass is also a co-editor of *Achieving a Productive Aging Society, Diversity in Aging*, and *Retirement Reconsidered*, and co-editor and co-founder of the *Journal of Aging and Social Policy*. He holds a joint Ph.D. in psychology and education for the University of Michigan.

FRANCIS G. CARO is a professor at the University of Massachusetts, Boston and director of the Research Division of its Gerontology Institute and of its Ph.D. program in gerontology. He was formerly director of research for the Community Service Society of New York and has taught at a number of universities. His major research interests are long-term care and productive aging. He is editor of *Readings in Evaluation Research* and a co-editor of *Achieving a Productive Aging Society*. He earned the Ph.D. degree in sociology from the University of Minnesota.

YUNG-PING CHEN holds the Frank J. Manning Eminent Scholar's Chair in Gerontology at the University of Massachusetts, Boston. A delegate to the 1995 White House Conference on Aging (as well as a consultant and a delegate to both the 1971 and 1981 White House Conferences on Aging), Dr. Chen also served on the Panel of Actuaries and Economists of the 1979 Advisory Council of Social Security. A fellow in the Gerontological Society of America, he is a founding member of the National Academy of Social Insurance (and its visiting scholar in 1989). He is a frequent contributor to scholarly journals and congressional hearings. Books he has written or edited include *Income: Background and Issues, Unlocking Home Equity for the Elderly, Social Security in a Changing Society, Checks and Balances in Social Security, Choices and Constraints: Economic Decisionmaking*, and *Achieving a Productive Aging Society*.

WILLIAM H. CROWN is a Senior Project Manager at The MEDSTAT Group. Dr. Crown's research focuses on the economics of aging, health policy, and regional economics. He has published extensively in gerontological and regional science journals on the economic implications of population aging and interregional migration. He is co-author (with James H. Schulz and Allan Borowski) of *Economics of Population Aging: The "Graying" of Australia, Japan, and the United States*, and co-author (with Leonard Wheat) of *State Per-Capita Income Change Since 1950: Sharecropping's Collapse and Other Causes of Convergence*. He received his Ph.D. in urban and regional planning from the Massachusetts Institute of Technology in 1982.

TABITHA DOESCHER is a public policy economist and consultant. Her clients include federal and state government agencies and professional associations with interests in non-partisan policy analysis. Much of her work has been in the area of private pensions, social security, and retirement. She is a co-author of *Advising Clients on Retirement Plans*, a contributing author to *Pension Policy for a Mobile Labor Force*, and has published articles appearing in the *American Economic Review*, the *Journal of Marketing*, and the *Journal of Public Policy and Marketing*. She received her B.A. from Vanderbilt University, her M.P.A. from Syracuse University, and her Ph.D. from the University of North Carolina at Chapel Hill.

STUART DORSEY is professor of economics at Baker University. Since completing his graduate work at Washington University, he has held appointments at Western Illinois University, the U.S. Department of Labor, West Virginia University, and was staff economist for the U.S. Senate Committee on Finance. His primary research interests are private pensions in labor markets and pension policy.

BARRY L. FRIEDMAN is an economist in the Florence Heller Graduate School, Brandeis University. He has studied welfare and social security systems in the United States and other countries (especially the pension system of China). His work has encompassed the analysis of both public and employer-provided benefits.

LISA A. HOLLIS is currently a graduate student at the University of Akron. Ms. Hollis is a doctoral candidate in the Industrial/Gerontological Psychology program. Her research interests include human factors engineering interventions in the workplace to improve older worker productivity, legal issues regarding employment rights of older workers, retirement and post-retirement employment issues, elder caregiving and possible workforce participation constraints on middle-aged and older female caregivers, and training studies involving enhancement of functional capabilities of older workers.

ERIC R. KINGSON is an associate professor of social policy at the Boston College Graduate School of Social Work. A member of the board of directors of the National Academy of Social Insurance, he served as an advisor to the 1982–1983 National Commission on Social Security Reform and to the 1994 Bipartisan Commission on Entitlement and Tax Reform, and directed the Emerging Issues Program of the Gerontological Society of America (1984–1985). He has authored or co-authored numerous articles addressing social security policy, the generational equity debate, and the aging of the baby boom cohort. He is primary author of *Ties that Bind: The Interdependence of Generations* and of *Social Security and Medicare: A Policy Primer*. Along with James H. Schulz, he is co-editor of a volume *Social Security Bridging the Centuries: Issues, Answers and Challenges* (forthcoming) which examines contemporary policy questions in the social security program.

THOMAS LEAVITT was educated at Dartmouth College and Northwestern University. He is managing partner of Analytic Resources in Needham, Massachusetts, a policy analysis firm specializing in issues related to the elderly. Before starting Analytic Resources in 1989, he was an associate of the Policy Center on Aging at the Heller School of Brandeis University.

MICHAEL V. LEONESIO is an economist in the Division of Economic Research in the Office of Research and Statistics at the Social Security Administration. His research interests concern the relationship between social security programs and labor market activity. He received his Ph.D. in economics from Cornell University. His recent publications include studies of the effects of social security on the timing of retirement and the effects of the social security earnings test on older workers' labor supply.

CHARLES F. LONGINO, JR. currently holds the title of Wake Forest Professor of Sociology and Public Health Sciences at Wake Forest University and the Bowman Gray School of Medicine. He earned his Ph.D. from the University of North Carolina at Chapel Hill in 1967. His interests are the demography of aging, health policy and ideology, and long-term care. His recent books include *Retirement Migration in America*, and, with John Murphy, *The Old Age Challenge to the Biomedical Model*.

RICHARD W. McCONAGHY is a doctoral candidate in gerontology at the University of Massachusetts, Boston. He has a Master of Government Administration degree from the Fels Center, University of Pennsylvania. Before entering graduate school, he spent nineteen years as an associate and partner in a Philadelphia law firm.

WILLIAM McNAUGHT is currently an assistant director at the U.S. General Accounting Office. The research reported upon in Chapter 17 was performed while he served first as a grantee and then Director of Research of the Commonwealth Fund. He received his Ph.D. in economics from Harvard University in 1978.

PHYLLIS H. MUTSCHLER is Director of Education at the Policy Center on Aging and an Associate Research Professor at Brandeis University's Heller

School. In 1992, she was named a Brookdale National Fellow, an award by the Brookdale Foundation to persons who show the most promise for leadership in gerontology. Dr. Mutschler is an authority on the economic status of older women, issues related to caregiving, and the "early retirement trend." She currently is conducting a study of older women to identify factors that critically affect their well-being at older ages and, at the National Bureau of Economic Research, is investigating the impact of private pension plan provisions and special early retirement incentive plans on employees' retirement decisions. She continues to study the effects of caregiving responsibilities on "working caregivers" and has collaborated with the Washington Business Group on Health and business coalitions across the nation to help support workers having family caregiving responsibilities.

REGINA O'GRADY-LeSHANE is Director of the Part-Time Program in the Graduate School of Social Work at Boston College. She received her doctoral degree from the Heller School at Brandeis University. Her research has focused on the economic well-being of older women with special concern for the effect of caregiving on retirement income. Most recently she was a member of the Congressional Study Group on Women and Retirement that was convened in 1992 for the purpose of discussing and recommending policy options to address problems in retirement income policies.

SARA E. RIX is a senior analyst with the economics team of the Public Policy Institute of the American Association of Retired Persons (AARP), where she specializes in issues associated with an aging labor force. Her current research and policy interests focus on employment and retirement policy, older worker employment problems, and worker training and retraining. Prior to coming to AARP, she was director of research for the Women's Research and Education Institute and editor of *The American Woman*.

PHILIP RIZZI is a Project Manager with the ICF Kaiser International Consulting Group. He holds a B.A. degree in political science from Brown University and a Master of Public Policy degree from the John F. Kennedy School of Government at Harvard University. Since joining ICF Kaiser in 1988, Mr. Rizzi has worked extensively on economic issues related to labor markets and government regulation. Mr. Rizzi served as the principal analyst for the final three years of the Commonwealth Fund's *Americans over 55 at Work Program*, directed by his colleague, Dr. Michael C. Barth. More recently, Mr. Rizzi completed case studies of the actual and perceived costs and benefits of older workers in ten companies. Mr. Rizzi has co-authored chapters in two other books on the subject of employment opportunities for older people.

MARC ROSENBLUM holds a Ph.D. from the University of Minnesota and a J.D. from the Georgetown University Law Center, where he is an adjunct professor of law specializing in employment discrimination. A career federal employee, Rosenblum has been with the Equal Employment Opportunity Commission since 1979. He was the 1992–1993 Judicial Fellow at the Administrative Office of the United States Courts, and has written primarily on employment law issues.

CHRISTOPHER J. RUHM is a professor of economics at the University of North Carolina Greensboro and a research associate at the National Bureau of Economic Research. He received his Ph.D. in economics from the University of California at Berkeley in 1984. Dr. Ruhm has conducted extensive research examining the retirement patterns of older Americans, the causes and effects of labor displacement in the United States, the economic consequences of alcohol and illegal drug policies, and the impacts of mandated employment benefits such as advance notice and parental leave. He is co-author of the book *Turbulence in the American Workplace* and has published more than thirty articles in professional journals such as the *American Economic Review, Review of Economics and Statistics, Journal of Labor Economics*, and the *Journal of Health Economics*.

STEVEN H. SANDELL is head of the Evaluation Unit at the Office of Research and Statistics of the Social Security Administration. He has published widely in the areas of labor economics, gerontology, and public policy. He is the editor of *The Problem Isn't Age: Work and Older Americans* and a co-editor of *The Older Worker*. Dr. Sandell earned a BBA degree from the Baruch School of the College of the City of New York, and a Ph.D. in economics from the University of Minnesota.

WILLIAM J. SEROW is Director of the Center for the Study of Population and Professor of Economics at the Florida State University in Tallahassee. His undergraduate degree is from Boston College; his masters and doctoral work in economics and demography was completed at Duke University. His research interests include the economic and demographic aspects of population aging, human migration, and small area demography. Among his recent books are: *Introduction to Applied Demography* (with N. W. Rives), *Population Aging in the United States* (with D. Sly and J. Wrigley), *The Impact of Immigration on the United States* (with B. Weller and D. Sly), *International Handbook of Internal Migration* (edited by C. Nam and D. Sly), *Handbook of International Migration* (edited by C. Nam, D. Sly, and R. Weller), and *Nurses in the Workplace* (edited with M. Cowart).

ANTHONY A. STERNS received his B.S. in engineering from the University of Michigan, Ann Arbor and is a doctoral candidate in Industrial and Organizational Psychology at The University of Akron. Mr. Sterns is the Director of

Data Management for LIFESPAN Associates, a market research firm in Akron, Ohio.

HARVEY L. STERNS is professor of psychology and the Director of the Institute for Life-Span Development and Gerontology at The University of Akron. He is also a research professor of gerontology at the Northeastern Universities College of Medicine in Rootstown, Ohio. He received the 1994 Clark Tibbits Award for outstanding contributions to the advancement of gerontology in higher education, which includes authoring more than seventy-five articles and chapters and giving over 200 presentations.

JOHN A. TURNER is Deputy Director of the Office of Research and Economic Analysis, Pension and Welfare Benefits Administration, U.S. Department of Labor and adjunct lecturer of economics at George Washington University, where he teaches the economics of aging. He formerly worked in the research office of the Social Security Administration. He received a Fulbright Senior Scholar Award to do pension research at the Institut de Recherches Economiques et Sociales in Paris in 1994. He has written or edited seven books on pensions, one of which has been translated into Japanese, and has published more than forty-five articles on pension and social security policy. He has a Ph.D. in economics from the University of Chicago.

ROBERT M. WHAPLES is an assistant professor of economics at Wake Forest University. He earned a Ph.D. in economics from the University of Pennsylvania in 1990. His primary research interests are in the history of the American labor market, with an emphasis on retirement and the length of the workweek. With Dianne Betts, he is editor of *Historical Perspectives on the American Economy*.